I0820632

Orthodoxia

2016–2017

Please order at:
Institute for Ecumenical Studies
University of Fribourg Switzerland
Av. de l'Europe 20, CH-1700 Fribourg
iso@unifr.ch
tel + 41 300 74 10
fax + 41 300 97 83
www.unifr.ch/iso
www.oki-regensburg.de

ORTHODOXIA
2016–2017

In the tradition of the *Ostkirchliches Institut* Regensburg
edited by the Institute for Ecumenical Studies
at the University of Fribourg Switzerland

Münster
2016

Compiler:
Nikolaus Wyrwoll
Easter 2016

Editions up to now:

1	1982	13	2002
2	1984	14	2003
3	1986–1987	15	2004
4	1988–1989	16	2005
5	1990–991	17	2006
6	1992–1993	18	2007
7	1994–1995	19	2008
8	1995	20	2009–2010
9	1996	21	2011
10	1997–1998	22	2012–2013
11	1999–2000	23	2014–2015
12	2001	24	2016–2017

Veröffentlicht mit Unterstützung des Hochschulrates
der Universität Freiburg Schweiz

Printed in Germany
Gedruckt auf säurefreiem, alterungsbeständigem Papier ♾

ISBN 978-3-402-13191-6

Preface

The Second Vatican Council created within the Western Churches a new attention for the Eastern Churches. The political changes opened the way to renewed encounter and exchange in a dialogue of love and a dialogue of truth. In order to contribute to a better knowledge of the Orthodox partners, the *Ostkirchliches Institut Regensburg* has published since 1982 a catalogue of the Eastern Orthodox and the Oriental Orthodox Churches. Thus, ORTHODOXIA has become a useful instrument of communication for the Orthodox Churches as well.

The 24th edition is published by the Institute for Ecumenical Studies of the University of Fribourg Switzerland. The Institute also established an online-version of ORTHODOXIA that will be regularly updated:

www.orthodoxia.ch

The new printed edition is accessible in time for the Holy and Great Synod of the Orthodox Church, convoked for June 2016 on Crete. ORTHODOXIA nourishes the hope that the Spirit of God will bring together to a common Synod the larger community of Eastern Churches, presented in this book, and even the communion of all Christians, at the *kairos* that God the Father knows and will reveal – so that we give witness together to the one, holy, catholic and apostolic Church of Jesus Christ.

In format and colour the book corresponds to the *Annuario Pontificio,* the worldwide directory of catholic churches and institutions, in order to remind us that the Orthodox Churches are Sister Churches to the Catholic Churches.

Fribourg, Easter 2016

Barbara Hallensleben
barbara.hallensleben@unifr.ch

How to use this book

This book lists the names of bishops who belong to one of the Eastern Orthodox or the Oriental Orthodox Churches. They are presented with their titles and addresses, in so far as we know them through correspondence or from the yearbooks and websites of these Churches. The book is not meant as an ecclesiological manual and does not decide about the canonical status of the mentionned Churches. ORTHODOXIA contains three indexes:

In the primary *Index of Churches* the Orthodox Churches are listed in alphabetical order (see the Table of contents on the next page) along with their respective bishops who themselves are presented with their first name, followed by their baptismal name and surname. On the right side of the first line, the name of the respective eparchy (diocese) is indicated. For vicar and auxiliary bishops, the reference to the eparchy is given within the title (second line).

The second line of each entry starts with T: followed by the title or the ministry of the bishop and his postal address, starting with ✉. The address gives street, town, country and postal zip code. The telephone number includes in brackets the prefix for calling the country.

The following lines, printed in slightly smaller and more condensed characters, normally start with the bishop's birthday, ordination to the diaconate (diak), mon(astic) vows, elevation to the honour of archim(andrite), ⊖ ordination to the priesthood and ⊕ episcopal consecration, adding some elements of the vita of the bishop, listed in chronological order.

Autonomous ecclesial structures within a Church are included in the presentation of the Mother Church as a proper subsection.

Retired bishops are either listed at the end of the presentation of a Church, or they are mentioned at the place of their former ministry.

In the *Index of Names* all bishops are listed in alphabetical order, with reference to the primary index. You can search for the first name (bishop's name) or the family name. Since only a few of the listed churches use latin characters, transcriptions for the same name can be quite different (e.g. Petrus or Boutros, Gregorian or Krikorian etc.).

In the *Index of Places* you can look for a town (taken from the addresses), an eparchy (*E), a Metropolia (*M) or Episcopia (*Ep) and Metropolitan Regions (*MR) or for a country (presented in capitals). The eparchies are partially presented in alphabetical order, and partially they follow the honorific order and the length of service of the titular bishop.

Table of Contents

Explanation of the Abbreviations and Symbols

Most of the abbreviations used in the book explain themselves.

*	date of birth, followed by the place of birth (if known)
*E	Name of Eparchy
*Ep	Name of Episcopal Region
*M	Name of Metropolia
*MR	Name of Metropolitan Region
⊖	Date of ordination to the priesthood
⊕	Date of episcopal consecration
(I)	degree of a decoration: first (I), second (II), third (III) class
A	Archbishop of ...
archim	elevated to the honor of archimandrite
B	Bishop of ...
BA	Bachelor of Arts
BCom	Bachelor of Commerce
BDiv	Bachelor of Divinity
BSc	Bachelor of Science
BTh	Bachelor of Theology
CCCC	Comité catholique pour la collaboration culturelle avec les Églises orthodoxes et les Églises orthodoxes orientales
CEC	Conference of European Churches
DEA	Diplôme d'études approfondies
diak	Date of ordination to the diaconate
Dz.	Dzairaguin – high degree of Vardapet (Ecclesial Teacher)
Fac	Faculty of ...
Kon/pel	Konstantinopel
Lic	Licentiate
M	Metropolitan of ...
M tit	titular Metropolitan
MA	Master of Arts
MDiv	Master of Divinity
Metr.	Metropolia of ...
MTh	Master of Theology
mon	Date of monastic vows
N	Nameday (N? = Saint Patron unknown)
p	private telephone number
PhD	Philosophical Doctor
STM	Sacrae Theologiae Magister (MTh)
T	Title for addressing the hierarch
WCC	World Council of Churches

ORTHODOX CHURCH OF ALBANIA

His Beatitude **Anastasios**
Archbishop of Tiranë, Durrës and All Albania

Anastasios Anastasios Yannulatos *Tiranë*
T: M Tiranë+Durrës+Elbasan ▪ ✉ Kisha Orthodhokse Autoqefale e Shqiperise Rruga Kavaja 151, ALBANIA-Tiranë • [355] 4 234117, 235095, fax 232109 • orthchal@orthodoxalbania.org • albaniaorth@gmail.com • www.orthodoxalbania.org
*4.11.1929 Piraeus, N22.1.1952 dipl theol Athens. diak1.8.1960 ⊖1964 archim1964. 1965-1969 stud Hamburg Marburg Tübingen. 1970 Dr. theol Athens. 1971-1990 General Director Apostoliki Diakonia Church of Greece. 1972-1992 Prof Religions Athens ⊕19.11.1972 B Androusa. Director Theol Seminary Nairobi. 1983-1996 Dean Theol Fac Athens. 1983-1986 Acting Archbishop Archdiocese East Africa (Patr Alexandria). 1984-1991 President Commission "Mission et Evangélisation" WCC Geneva. 1989 DD Orth Theol Seminary Brookline USA. 8.1.1991 Exarque Patriarcal (Konst) d'Albanie. 20.8.1991 M Androusa. 24.6.1992 A Tiranë. 2.8.1992 Inthronisation. 1993-2005 Corresponding Member Ethics Politics, Dr.hc.: 1995 Theol Uni Thessaloniki, Phil Uni Ioannina, 1996 Phil Agric Uni Athens, 1998 Phil Political Sc Uni Athens, Phil Fac Uni Athens, 2001 Phil International and European Studies Uni Piraeus. 2002 Phil Uni Creta. Phil Physics Medicine Engineering Uni Patras. 2004 Human Letters Uni Boston USA. 2005 Phil Medicine Fac Agric Uni Thessalia. 2010 University Cyprus. 1998 Hon Member Theol Acad Moskva. 2003 DD St. Vladimir's USA, Fr Staniloae dipl Bucureşti. 2003 Vice President CEC. 2005 Honorary Member Athens Acad Sciences. 2006 president WCC Geneva. 22.-28.1.2016 Synaxis of the primates of the Local Orthodox Churches Chambésy Switzerland.

Andon Merdani *Elbasan*
T: M Elbasan ▪ ✉ Rruga Kavaja 151, ALBANIA-Tiranë • [355] 4 234117, 235095, fax 232109 • albaniaorth@gmail.com
*1969, N17.1., stud theol Athens. teacher Seminary Durrës ⊕21.11.2006 B Kruja. vicar Tiranë. 2016 M Elbasan.

Nikolla Hyka *Apolonia*
T: B Apolonia+Fieri ▪ ✉ Rruga Kavaja 151, ALBANIA-Tiranë • [355] 4 234117, 235095, fax 232109 • albaniaorth@gmail.com
*26.1.1972 Albania, N6.12.1993 Valta Peloponnes Greece. 11.3.1995 baptized Valta. mon11.3.1995 diak2000 ⊖2001 stud theol Academy "Resurrection of Christ" in St. Vlash of Durrës. 2006 dipl theol Athens ⊕19.11.2006 B Apolonia assistant Director Theol Academy "Ngjallja e Krishtit" Shën Vlash. 2016 M Apolonia+Fieri.

Nathanael Konstantinos Stergiou
T: M Amantia, vicar Tiranë ▪ ✉ Rruga Kavaja 151, ALBANIA-Tiranë • [355] 4 234117, 235095, fax 232109 • albaniaorth@gmail.com
*1957 Taxiarches Trikala, N22.4. 1976-1978 stud theol Athos. 1978-1982 stud theol Thessaloniki. mon1979 diak1982 ⊖1987 archim1990. 1998-2004 hierokēryx Argyrokastron, teacher religion ⊕21.1.2012 B Amantia, vicar Tiranë, supervision of Monastery Properties, 2016 M.

Asti Christos Bakallbashi
T: B Bylis, vicar Tiranë ▪ ✉ Rruga Kavaja 151, ALBANIA-Tiranë • [355] 4 234117, 235095, fax 232109 • albaniaorth@gmail.com
*1974 in Durrës. N6.7. 1993-1997 stud theol Academy Durrës. 1998-2003 stud theol Thessaloniki. diak2003. 2004 hierokēryx teacher Academy Durrës ⊖2009. 2010-2012 MTh Thessaloniki ⊕22.1.2012 B Bylis, vicar Tiranë, Apostolic Diakonia.

Ignatios Triantis ***Berat***
T: M Berat+Avlon+Kanin ▪ ✉ Lagja 22 Tetori, ALBANIA-Berat • [355] 32 238120, fax 233532 • mitropoliaberat@yahoo.com
*1934 in Prodromos Thebai, N20.7. 1960 dipl theol. mon1967 diak1967 ⊖1967. 1968 igoumenos, arhieratikos epitropos. archim1974. 1974 hierokēryx Thebai. 22.6.1992 nominated M Berat ⊕27.7.1996 İstanbul Phanar M Berat. 18.7.1998 entered in Albania.

Demetrios Ntigkbasanis ***Argyrokastro***
T: B Gjirokastra ▪ ✉ Lagja 11 Janari ALBANIA-Gjirokastër • [355] 84 264266, 268951, fax 263773 • albaniaorth@gmail.com
*20.9.1940, N26.10. 1968 dipl theol Thessaloniki. 1969-1974 teacher Theol High School. 1974-1975 teacher Ampetios School Kairo. 1975-2006 Monastery St. Catherine Sinai. 1977-1990 director Library St. Catherine Sinai. mon1978 Monastery St. Catherine Sinai "Dimitrios". diak14.1.1988 ⊖20.1.1988. 1990-2006 Ekonom Metochion of St. Ekaterini Ioannina and Representative of Sinai Monastery in Epirus. 1993-2006 protosingel Gjirokastra ⊕26.11.2006 B Gjirokastra. 22.-28.1. 2016 Synaxis of the primates of the Local Orthodox Churches Chambésy Switzerland.

Joan Fatmir Pellushi ***Korça***
T: B Korça ▪ ✉ Rruga Stefan Luarasi, ALBANIA-Korça • [355] 82 42876, fax 46100 • albaniaorth@gmail.com
*1.1.1956, N7.1. 1975 orth. 1979 baptized. 1994 MDiv Holy Cross Greek Orthodox School USA. mon1994 diak27.2.1994 ⊖4.12.1994 archim4.12.1994 ⊕20.7.1998 B Korça. 1999 Commission Orthodox Collaboration WCC Geneva. 16.12.2015 Athens Interorthodox committee preparation Panorthodox Synod. 22.-28.1.2016 Synaxis of the primates of the Local Orthodox Churches Chambésy Switzerland.

Greek Orthodox Patriarchate of Alexandria and All Africa

His Divine Beatitude **Theodoros II**
Pope and Patriarch of Alexandria and All Africa

Theodoros Nikolaos Horeftakis ***Alexandria***
T: His Divine Beatitude, Patriarch of Alexandria ▪ ✉ B.P. 2006, Egypt-Alexandria • [20] 3 4822890, 4868595, 4844876, 4875839, 4861744, fax 4875684 • Kairo [20] 2 510-0013, -3516 • patriarxeo.alexandreia@gmail.com • patriarchate@greekorthodox-alexandria.org • goptalex@tecmina.com • www.patriarchateofalexandria.com
*25.11.1954 Koukounarià Chanià Kreta, N17.2. mon1972, dipl theol Thessaloniki. stud history, literature, philosophy Odessa. diak1975. 1975-1985 chancellor Lambis Kreta ⊖23.4.1978 archim1985. 1985-1990 Exarch in Soviet Union Odessa ⊕1990 B Kyrene. 1990-1997 Exarch Athens. 1997 patriarchal councillor. 1997-2002 M Kamerun. 2002-2004 M Zimbabwe. 2004 Patriarch 22.-28.1.2016 Synaxis of the primates of the Local Orthodox Churches Chambésy Switzerland.

Petros Georgios Jakumelos ***Aksum***
T: M Aksum ▪ ✉ P.O.Box 571, Ethiopia-Addis Ababa • [251] 11 1226459 +fax, [30] 210 6745511 • alex@otenet.gr
*1932 Zakynthos Greece. N29.6. dipl theol Athens. diak1955 Mon. Pendeli ⊖1956 Athens. 1956-1965 protosynkellos Elasson. 1966-1968 Institut Catholique Paris. 1968 Bossey. 1968-1970 priest Bristol, Liverpool. 1970 Asmara. 1970-1972 Djibuti. 1972 Grand protosynkellos Cairo ⊕30.11.1972 B Babylon. 1974-1978 patriarchal vicar Cairo. 30.11.1979 M Aksum. 1996-1997 Patriarchal Exarch Kenya Irinupolis. 2004-2010 Representative Athens.

Kallinikos Pippas ***Pelusion***
T: M Pelusion, Patriarchal Vicar ▪ ✉ P.O.Box 251, Egypt-Port Said • [20] 66 3224534
*1936 Megara Attika. N29.7. dipl theol Chalki. diak1964 ⊖1964. 1964-1979 hierokēryx Grevenà, 1978-1999 hierokēryx Peristeri ⊕11.12.1999 B Mareotis, Patr Vicar. 2001-2006 M Khartum. 2006 A Pelusion. 2009 Cross St. Savvas with star, Elder M.

Makarios Andreas Tillyridis ***Kenya***
T: M Nairobi, Exarch Kenya ▪ ✉ P.O.Box 46119, Kenya-Nairobi • [254] 2560750, 2564995, [254] 733 617292 • makarios_africa@yahoo.com

*18.4.1945 Limassol Cyprus. N19.1. 1967-1972 stud theol Institut St-Serge Paris, stud hist byz Sorbonne. 1972-1976 Dr. phil Oxford. 1977-1997 Prof, 1992-1997 Dean Seminary "Archbishop Makarios III" Nairobi. 1978-1981 stud Church History Louvain-la-Neuve. diak19.7.1992 (Riruta, M Accra Petros) ⊖20.7.1992 ⊕25.7.1992 Church "Archbishop Makarios III" Nairobi. 1997-1998 Director patriarchal Library, Alexandria, B Riruta. 1998-2001 M Zimbabwe. 1999 Commission Orthodox Collaboration WCC Geneva. 2001 M Kenya. 2004 Mondo Migliore. 2015 M Nairobi, Exarch Kenya.

Jonah Luanga ***Kampala***
T: M Uganda ▪ ✉ P.O.Box 3970, UGANDA-Kampala • [256] 41 542461, 533771 • uochurch@swiftuganda.com • uochurch@africaonline.co.ug
*18.7.1945 Odegeya. N26.2. 1952-1964 Primary and Secondary education Uganda. 1965-1968 Seminary Kreta. 1968-1973 dipl phil Athens. 1973-1978 dipl theol Athens. 1979-1981 secretary Orth Mission Uganda. diak1.5.1981 ⊖1982. 1982-1991 Deputy Director "Archbishop Makarios III" Nairobi ⊕26.7.1992. 1992-1997 B Bukoba, for the mission in Tanzania. 1992-1995 SYNDESMOS South of Sahara Africa Representative. 1997 M Uganda.

Damaskinos Papandreou ***Johannesburg***
T: M Johannesburg, Pretoria ▪ ✉ P.O. Box 1096, Houghton 2041, SOUTH AFRICA-2000 Johannesburg • [27] 11 880205-0, -7, 8805680, fax 8809630, [27] 731538933 • archbishop@orthodoxjhb.co.za •
stmark@ mweb.com.za
*1957 Ermioni Argolidos. N4.12. diak1987 ⊖1987 parish priest Durban, Kwa Zulu Natal ⊕30.10.2004 B Ghana. 2009 M Accra. 2010 M Johannesburg.

Alexandros Georgios Gianniris ***Nigeria***
T: M Nigeria, Exarch of the Gulf of Guinea ▪ ✉ Orthodox Diocese of Nigeria, P.O.Box 75550, Victoria Island, NIGERIA-Lagos • [234] 1 7741447, 7915880, fax 2631659, [234] 8033016788 •
archbishop@orthodoxnigeria.org • www.orthodoxnigeria.org
*15.5.1960 Athens. N30.8. 1978-1983 Fac Agriculture Athens. diak1.10.1988 ⊖2.10.1988 1990-1994 dipl theol Thessaloniki. 1997 secretary to the Patriarchal office ⊕4.11.1997 Alexandria B, 2004 M Nigeria

Theophilaktos Konstantin Tsoumerkas ***Libya***
T: M Tripolis, Exarch of Libya ▪ ✉ P.O. Box 2451, LIBYA-Tripoli •
[218] 21 3402340, 4448045, 3348045 • [20] 10 1089639
*1945 Exochi Nea Pieria "Konstantin". N8.3. mon Vatopediou, stud Athonite Eccl School. Librarian Vatopediou. dipl theol Athens. diak1966 ⊖1969 parishes Veria,

Larisa, Rhodos, 1991 Carthage Tripolis ⊕26.11.1999 B Babylon, Inspector Monastery St. George Cairo. 2004 M Tripolis. 2009 Cross of the Order St. Savvas with a star.

Sergios Kykkotis ***Cape Town***

T: M Good Hope (Kalis Elpidos) ▪ ✉ P.O.Box 387, Rondebosch 7701, SOUTH AFRICA-8000 Cape Town • [27] 21 6897639, 6851797, [27] 83 5902110 • kykkotis@iafrica.com

*1967 Kaminaria Myrianthouse Cyprus N7.10. mon1986 Kykkos diak1986 Kykkos. 1988-1992 dipl theol Athens. 1992-1997 Archiepiskopi Athens ⊖1996 Kykkos archim1996 Kykkos. 1997-1999 Dean Port Elizabeth ⊕27.11.1999 M Good Hope. 2009 Cross of the Order St. Savvas with a star.

Athanasios Kykkotis ***Kyrene***

T: M Kyrene, Exarch Libya, Patriarchal Representative ▪ ✉ hram Vsjeh Svjatyh v Kuličah, Slavjanskaja Ploščad 2, ROSSIJA-109240 Moskva • [7] 495 923-7566, -4468, 7248629, fax [7] 495 6234757 • church.kulishki@gmail.com

*1958 Morphou Cyprus. N18.1. scholarship Mon Kykkos stud Athens theol and byz Music, Paris Sorbonne Histoire du monde byzantin. diak15.8.1976 ⊖18.3.1984 archim18.3.1984 Ephoros Kykkos. 1997 Patriarchal Representative Moskva ⊕28.11. 1999. 2003 Orden Sergij Radonež. 2009 M Kyrene. 2009 Cross St. Savvas with star.

Alexios Panagiotis Leontaritis ***Carthage***

T: M Carthage ▪ ✉ rue de Rome 5, TUNESIA-Tunis • [216] 71 247958, residence 331775, fax [216] 70 939335 • Casablanca [212] 276892 • gopcair@hotmail.com • mealca64@hotmail.com • bialui@hotmail.com

*10.6.1964 Athens. N17.3. dipl Greek Literature Athens, dipl theol Thessaloniki. diak13.12.1987. 1987-1990 secretary Trikkis ⊖2.12.1990 archim2.12.1990. 1990-1999 protosynkellos Trikkis. 1995-1996 Chambésy Genève ⊕29.11.1999 B Nitria, Patr Vicar for Cairo. 2004 M Carthage. 2009 Cross of the Order St. Savvas with a star.

Narkissos Samer Gammoh ***Accra***

T: M Accra, Ghana ▪ ✉ Greek Orthodox Bishopric, P.O.Box LG 274, Legon, GHANA-Accra • [233] 21 400977, fax 413737, [233] 24 255713, Côte d'Ivoire [225] 07 0510077 • Greece [30] 210 884291-4, -5, fax 8230490, [30] 29307 430045, 22430 23028 • grathinon@patalex.gr • orthodoxghana@internetghana.com • orthodoxghana@hotmail.com

*1968 Amann Jordania. N? 1988-1994 dipl theol Athens. mon14.2.1994 (Jakovos Ginis, Nikaia) diak15.2.1994 ⊖11.6.1994 archim11.6.1994 ⊕1.12.2013 M Nubia. 2015 M Accra, Ghana.

Emmanuel Xenophon Kagias ***Ptolemais***

T: M Ptolemais ▪ ✉ P.O. Box 47, SUDAN-Khartum • [249] 11 772973, [249] 183 772973, 771748 • gr_orth_archbishopric_khartoum@yahoo.com

*1956 Athens. N26.12. dipl theol Athens. Deacon in Cairo ⊕14.11.2004. 2004-2006 B Babylon, igumen St. George Cairo. 2006-2013 M Khartum. 2013 M Kavasos. 2014 M Ptolemais.

Serafim Georgios Iakóvou ***Zimbabwe***

T: M Zimbabwe ▪ ✉ 77 Churchill Avenue East, Gunhill, P.O.Box 2832, ZIMBABWE-Harare • [263] 4 7449-91, fax -28, [263] 91 2261258, [263] 77 2611258 • stmark@mweb.co.za • greekorthodox@zol.co.zw • zimbabwe@greekorthodox-zimbabwe.org • www.greekorthodox-zimbabwe.org

*2.2.1961 Paphos Cyprus. N2.1. Serafim of Sarov. 1973 Kykkos Monastery Cyprus. diak8.9.1983. 1983-1987 dipl theol Athens. 1988-1991 stud Christ Church Canterbury, Uni Durham ⊖15.8.1991 archim1991. Missionary Section British Council of Churches, missions to African states. 1995-1997 SYNDESMOS Southern Europe Representative. 1997 Vicar General Kenya and Tanzania ⊕28.9.1997. 1997-2001 M Kenya, Dean Seminary "Archbishop Makarios III" 2001-2010 M Johannesburg. 2010 M Zimbabwe, representative WCC, AACC, EU, United Nations.

Nikolaos Antoniou ***Hermoupolis***

T: M Hermoupolis ▪ ✉ Abou Sombol 12, Heliopolis, EGYPT-Cairo • [20] 2 25881795, [20] 12 4445001 • Tanta [20] 40 335163, 669202 • EGYPT-11351 Alexandria [20] 3 4868595

*20.3.1944 Cairo. N6.12. 1974 dipl mechanical engineering Helouan University Cairo. diak1980 ⊖1983. 1988 dipl theol Balamand. archim1992 ⊕11.3.2002 M Hermoupolis.

Dimitrios Themistokles Zacharengas ***Irenoupolis***

T: M Irenoupolis, Exarch of Eastern Tanzania and Seychelles Islands ▪ ✉ P.O.Box 1090, TANZANIA-Dar es salaam • [255] 744376161, 713466266, fax 222600151, [255] 51 11-8814, fax -6700, 483584 • orthodoxtanzania@yahoo.com • www.orthodoxtanzania.com

*28.2.1965 Sohos Thessaloniki. N26.10. Eccl school and Fac theol Thessaloniki. mon1989 (A Michail Rhodos). 1994-1999 missions Madagascar, India, Hongkong, Philippines. diak2.2.1999 Hongkong (M Nikita) ⊖7.2.1999 Hongkong (M Nikita). archim5.9.1999. 1999-2002 parish Alexandria, director Publication Department ⊕16.10.2002. 2002-2004 M Kamerun. 2004 M Irenoupolis.

Nikiphoros Georgios Konstantinou ***Central Africa***
T: M Central Africa, Exarch of all Equator ▪ ✉ Boulevard du 30 juin, P.O.Box 11097, CONGO-Kinshasa • [243] 81 7004204, 88 40178
*1949 Thessaloniki. N8.2. 1967-1969 Eccl School, 1969-1975 Fac theol Thessaloniki. mon1971 Agia Trias Tzankarolon "Agianannitis". missions Madagascar, India, Hongkong, Philippines. diak22.8.1971. 1977 Agion Oros Athos Skit Mikras Agias Annis "Mikragiannanitis". 1977-1997 teacher Theol school Athos ⊖1978 archim. 1997-2006 Organization Theol school Albania. 1999 Dr. theol Thessaloniki. 2006 Prof University Congo ⊕24.10.2010 M Central Africa.

Gregorios Georgios Stergiou ***Kamerun***
T: M Kamerun ▪ ✉ B.P. 949, KAMERUN-Yaounde • [237] 22201514, fax 22210576, [237] 9716879 • gregoriosfr@yahoo.gr • archevech@camnet.cm
*1961 Megara Attika. N25.1. mon1984 Megara Salom. diak1984 ⊖1988 archim, dipl theol Athens. 2001-2003 director personal office patr. 2003-2004 stud Belle arti Gregoriana Roma ⊕25.11.2004 M Kamerun.

Ieronymos Mouzey ***Mwanza***
T: M Mwanza ▪ ✉ Greek Orthodox Archbishopric, P.O.Box 1704, TANZANIA-Bukoba • [255] 28 2561161, 6620967, 282220967 • orthodoxtz@bukobaonline.com
*18.3.1963 Bulopa Busoga Uganda. N15.6. 1986-1996 dipl theol and post-graduate studies Athens. diak1995 ⊖1996 vicar General Kampala ⊕23.11.1997. 1997 B vicar general Bukoba, 2007 M Mwanza. 2009 Cross of the Order St. Savvas with a star.

Ioakim Konstantinos Kontovas
T: M ▪ Jerusalem, ISRAEL-Jerusalem • ioakim@zamtel.zm
*1966 Volos. N9.9. dipl theol Athens. diak1986 ⊖1993 (M Chrysostomos Peristeri). 1996-1997 parish St. Frumentios Addis Ababa. 1997-2002 secretary of the patriarchate ⊕23.3.2003 (Alexandria). 2009-2015 M Zambia. 2015 Prof Jerusalem School Hl. Sion.

Savvas Basilios Heimonettos ***Nubia***
T: M Khartoum, Sudan, Nubia ▪ ✉ P.O.Box 47, SUDAN-Khartum • [249] 11 772973, [249] 183 772973, 771748 • gr_orth_archbishopric_khartoum@yahoo.com
*1971 Rhodos. N5.12. stud Patmos, Fac social theol Athens, stud English, Arabic. mon1990 St.Michael Tharris Rhodos. diak1991 ⊖1993 archim1993 parishes Rhodos. 1999 St. Savvas Alexandria, Press Office patriarchate. 2001 patriarchal vicar Finances Alexandria. 2005 Dean Academy "Megas Athanasios" ⊕11.10.2009. 2009-2012 B Burundi+Rwanda. 2012 M Akkra, 2015 M Khartoum, Sudan, Nubia.

Ignatios Paulos Sennís *Madagascar*
T: M Madagascar ▪ ✉ Orthodox Diocese P.O.Box 456-101, MADAGASCAR-Antananarivo • [261] 20226-3205 +fax, -2523 -0899, 202224000 • orthodoxia@freedsl.mg • kellis@simicro.mgsimicro.mg • orthodoxmadagascar@hotmail.com
*1951 Korinthos. N20.12. foreman mechanic. dipl theol Athens. mon1972 diak1976 ⊖1976. 1980-1985 Monastery Stavronikitas Hagion Oros. 1985-1991 Orthodox Mission Korea. 1991-2004 India – expelled for missionary activities ⊕14.11.2004, 2012 M Madagascar.

Joannis Tsaphtaridis *Zambia*
T: M Zambia ▪ ✉ Greek Orthodox Bishopric, P.O.Box 51333, ZAMBIA-Lusaka • [260] 97 7740011, fax [260] 211 291473 • grorthzm@zamnet.zm
*1969 Ankeryko Zakynthos. N7.1. stud Ekkl. Scholi Athens, Fac theol Athens, Fac theol Sofia, 2001 dipl. diak21.11.1993 ⊖17.12.1993 archim. 1998 parish priest Germi. 2010 M.phil Johannesburg ⊕17.10.2010 B Mozambique. 2015 M Zambia.

Meletios Meletios Grigoriatis *Katanga*
T: M Katanga ▪ ✉ Orthodox Church, P.O.Box 108, CONGO-Kolwezi • [243] 814826813, 814040100 • ierapkol_athos@yahoo.gr
*1948 Larisa. N12.2. stud Lamia, Fac theol Athens. diak1972 mon1974 Grigoriou Mount Athos ⊖1976. 1989 Kolwezi ⊕25.11.2006 B, 2014 M Katanga.

Innokentios Biakatonta *Burundi*
T: B Burundi+Rwanda ▪ ✉ P.O.Box 3569, BURUNDI-Bujumbura • [257] 222 75335, 222 57800, [257] 791 50762 • frsavvas@hotmail.com
⊕7.12.2012. 2012 B Burundi+Rwanda.

Panteleimon Arathymos *Brazzaville*
T: B Brazzaville+Gabon ▪ ✉ P.O.Box 183, Av. Stephane Tchitchelle 24, CONGO-Brazzaville • [242] 06884936444457626 • p.arathymos@gmail.com • theologos.congo@gmail.com
*1974 Tinos. N27.7. dipl theol Athens, French Institute Athens. diak2000 (M Syros Steka) ⊖2001 archim2001 Syros. 2006 Archigrammateus Holy Synod Alexandria, delegate King Abdullah International Centre for Interreligious and Intercultural Dialogue ⊕2.12.2012.

Georgios Georgios Vladimirou *Guinea*
T: M Guinea, Patriarchal Representative Athens ▪ GUINEA-Konakry • Sierra Leone [232] 76 245111 • rev.t@pk4a.com • grathinon@patalex.gr

*27.3.1966 Zakaki Limassol Cyprus. N23.4. 1974 school Athens. dipl iur Thessaloniki, dipl Business Administration Thames Valley University London. Teacher Camberwell Green, 1993-1997 Madagaskar and India. 1993-1997 dipl theol Athens. 1998 Cyprus Bank Athens. diak30.6.1998 ⊖5.7.1998. 1998-1999 protosynkellos Hong Kong, redactor "The Censer". archim18.10.1998. 1999 secretary Alexandria ⊕4.3.2001 B Nilopolis, Epitropos Alexandria. 2004 M Zimbabwe. 2010 M Accra, Patriarchal Representative Athens. 2012 M Guinea Patriarchal Representative Athens. 16.12.2015 Athens Interorthodox committee preparation Panorthodox Synod. 22.-28.1.2016 Synaxis of the primates of the Local Orthodox Churches Chambésy Switzerland.

Gabriel Raftopulos ***Leontopolis***

T: M Leontopolis ▪ ✉ B.P. 2006, EGYPT-Alexandria • [20] 3 4861744, 4875-839, fax -684, [20] 12 5316840

*1957 Athens. N8.11. dipl theol Athens. N? diak1981 Athens ⊖1984 Serres, Ecumenical Department Holy Synod. archim1990 Alexandria, protosynkellos Zimbabwe, Exarchos Odessa. 2005 Epitropos Alexandria ⊕4.11.2006 Patr Theodor St. Savva Church Alexandria. 2006-2012 B Mareotis, Epitropos Alexandria. 2012 M Leontopolis. 22.-28.1.2016 Synaxis of the primates of the Local Orthodox Churches Chambésy Switzerland.

Nikodemos Athansios Priangellos

T: M Memphis ▪ ✉ P.O.Box 40, Hamzawi, EGYPT-Cairo • [20] 2 5103516, [20] 10 8080900 • gopcair@hotmail.com

*1967 Volos. N17.6. dipl theol Athens. diak19.6.1996 (Damaskinos Diaoulias) ⊖2.2.1997 Helioupolis. 2003 Zimbabwe. 2005 Kairo ⊕12.11.2006 B Nitria, Epitropos Cairo. 23.11.2013 M Memphis.

Niphon Nikitas ***Pelusion***

T: M Pelusion ▪ ✉ P.O.Box 251, EGYPT-Port Said • [20] 66 32124534

*1959 Nikaia Attikis. N11.8. Sivitanidion College Engineering, Seminary Athos, Teacher Academy Heraklion Kreta. dipl theol Athens. mon1982 Angarathos Kreta ⊖1984 Bali Rethymis. 1984-2004 parish Peristeri. archim2004. 2005 igumen St. Georges Old Cairo ⊕18.10.2009 B Babylonos, vicar. 2014 M Pelusion.

Vasilios Vasilios Varvelis ***Botswana***

T: B Botswana ▪ ✉ P.O.Box 00217 Plot 18694, Masokwe St, BOTSWANA-Gaborome • [267] 393810-6, fax -7, [267] 76 106066

*1969 Peristerion Attika, N? 1978 stud theol Athens. diak6.7.1997. 1998-2014 parishes Johannesburg, Kairo, patriarchal representative Athens ⊖25.3.1998 ⊕26.11. 2014 B Botswana.

Meletios Konstantinos Koumani ***Alexandria***
T: B Alexandria ▪ ✉ P.O.Box 2006, EGYPT-Alexandria • [20] 3 4822890
*1970 Kalamata Messinia, N? 1980-1996 stud Patras, Anotera E. Athens, Fac theol Athens, Catechesis school Apostoliki Diakonia, English, Russian, Arabic. diak1996 mon1998. 2000 parish Kalamata ⊖2000 archim2005. 2007-2008 Messinia. 2008 parish Alexandria. 2009 skevophylax Patr Alexandria. 25.11.2010 igoumenos St. Savva, teacher Teletourgika patr school Alexandria ⊕26.11.2014 B Navkratos, auxiliary. 5.12.2014 B Alexandria.

Chrysostomos Georgios Karagunis ***Mozambique***
T: B Mozambique ▪ ✉ P.O.Box 01010 Polana Cimento B, MOZAMBIQUE-Maputo • [258] 821 490481 • naosgr@gmail.com
*1960 Tithorea Phthiotis. 1975-1983 stud Hieratiki school Lamia, Anotera E. Athens, Fac theol Athens. diak1983. 1986-2005 hierokēryx Phthiotis, Peristerion ⊖1986. 2005-2008 protosynkellos Tripolis. 2008-2013 Cathedral Kairo. 2013 protosynkellos Tripolis ⊕7.12.2014 B Bereniki, auxiliary Tripolis.

Neophytos Kongai ***Noéri***
T: B Noéri ▪ ✉ P.O.Box 2006, EGYPT-Alexandria • [20] 3 4822890
*1970 in Kesengai Nandi Kenya. 1990 stud Seminary Makarios Nairobi. diak13.9. 1997 ⊖27.9.1998. 1999-2005 stud Holy Cross Boston USA. archim27.2.2005. 2007 Dr. theol Thessaloniki (Pastoral theol). mon15.8.2007 ⊕21.12.2014 B Nitria, auxiliary to the patriarch. 28.11.2015 B Noéri.

Athanasios Amos Akunda ***Kenya***
T: B Kisumu+West-Kenya ▪ ✉ P.O.Box 46119, KENYA-Nairobi • [254] 2560750, 2564995, fax 202025449, mobile 733617292
*1971 Kenya, 1979 orth.,N? Makarios III Sem. Kenya, dipl.theol., Holy Cross School of Theol. Dr. theol. diak1998 Kenya (A Seraphim) ⊖2002 (A Seraphim). Parishes in Soshanguve and Johannesburg. Dean and lecturer at Petros VII Sem. 2003-2008 Director of missions, until 2010 vicar in charge of missions, patriarchal representative of Alexandria at the WCC and All African Conf. of Churches. 2009-2015 parish St. Nicholas of Japan. archim2010 (A Damaskinos) ⊕6.12.2015 St. Nicholas Cathedral Kairo B Kisumu+West-Kenya (Patr Theodoros II).

Nikodemos Boulaxis ***Nitria***
T: B Nitria ▪ ✉ No. 625th Street, Corner Glenhove Road Melrose, SOUTH AFRICA-Johannesburg • 082-564-7939 • nitrias@gmail.com • nboulaxis@gmail.com • http://www.pantanassa.co.za/contact-us
⊕27.3.2016 B Nitria.

Retired Hierarchs :

Panteleimon Georgios Lampadarios

T: M Antinoes ▪ ✉ St. Theodore, 7101 Capriano Rd, USA-Lanham, MD20706 • [1] 443 5353643 • metropolianantiones@gmail.com • www.orthodox-mitropolianantiones-panteleimoncom

*14.5.1955 Kalymnos. N27.7. emigration USA. St. Panteleimon Kalymnos. dipl theol Athens. diak1980 ⊖1983. 1987-1992 Vicar General Johannesburg+Pretoria. 1992 MA Classics (Greek) Univ RAU South Africa. Specialist in Byzantine Art and Restoration of ancient icons. Hierokēryx: 1992 Cape Town, 1993-1995 Kalymnos, 1995-1996 Kos. 1996-1997 Vicar General Good Hope. 1997-1999 patriarchal vicar Alexandria ⊕30.11.1999 B Ghana. 27.10.2004 M Pelousion. 10.1.2005 founder Center Learning Greek Language Culture of the Holy metropolis of Peluse in Port Said and Damietta. 2006 M Antinoes, General Patriarchal Vicar. 2010 Hierarchal Rector Lanham.

Ignatios Mandelidis

T: M Pentapolis ▪ ✉ Archevêché d'Afrique Central, B.P. 11097, CONGO-Kinshasha • [243] 12 25211 • Iliados 24, GREECE-116 33 Athens

*1930 Edessa. N20.12. 1950 dipl theol. 1950-1968 Lay preacher. diak1968. 1968 preacher Larissa ⊖1969 missionary Kananga Congo ⊕14.3.2003. 2003-2010 M Central Africa. 2010 spiritual ministry School St. Athanase created by him.

Joakim Tsakiris

T: M Tamiathis ▪

*1934 Port Said, N9.9.diak1953 ⊕19.5.1988. 1990-1998 patriarchal vicar. 1998 M Tamiathis.

Porphyrios Konstantinos Skikos

T: M Thivais ▪

*1940 Inakos Argolidos Greece. N26.2. diak1966 ⊖1969 archim1970. 1985 igumen St. Georges Old Cairo ⊕17.6.1990 B Babylon. 1990-1997 patriarchal vicar. 1997-1999 B Bukoba. 2003 B Siinis. 2004 M Thivais.

Hierotheos Petrakis

T: B Elefsis ▪ ✉ Paparrigopoulou 3, GREECE-184 52 Nikaia

*1930 N4.10. ⊕6.2.1977 B Elefsis, patr vicar Alexandria. 1982 assistant of Piraeus.

Theodoros Antonios Dimitriou

T: M Heliopolis ▪ ✉ 01010 Polana Cimento B, MOZAMBIQUE-Maputo • [258] 821 490481

⊕27.11.2006, 2006-2009 B Mozambique.

Gennadios Stylianos Stantzios
T: B Botswana ▪ ✉ B.P. 00217 Plot 18694, Masokwe St., BOTSWANA-Gaborome • [267] 393810-6, fax -7, [267] 76 106066 • bishop@orthodoxbotswana.org • secretary@orthodoxbotswana.org • genadgreece@yahoo.com
*1969 Esslingen Germany. N17.11. stud theol Thessaloniki. mon1986 (Spyridon Langada) diak1990 ⊖1990 archim1990 (Prokopios Philipp). 1990-2002 eparchy Philippi. 2002 archigrammateus Alexandria. 2002-2004 stud Missiology Urbania Roma Vatican scholarship ⊕26.11.2006 B Niloupolis, archigrammateus Patriarchiou. 2010 B Niloupolis in Botswana. 2.6.2012 B Botswana. 26.11.2014 retired.

Proterios Stylianos Pavlopulos
T: former M Ptolemais, Exarch of Upper Egypt ▪ ✉ Eptanisou 11, GREECE-13231 Petroupolis Attika
*28.7.1946 Naxos. N28.2. dipl theol Athens. stud Durham England. diak12.12.1972 ⊖13.12.1972 ⊕3.3.2001. 2001-2004 M Dar es Salaam. 2004-2014 M Ptolemais. 26.11.2014 retired.

Orthodox Church of America (OCA)

His Beatitude **Tikhon**
Metropolitan of All America and Canada

Tikhon Marc Mollard ***Washington***
T: A Washington, M All America and Canada ▪ ✉ Route 25 A, Oyster Bay Cove, P.O.Box 675, USA-Syosset, NY11791-0675 • [1] 516 9220550, fax 9220954 • rector@st-catherine.ru • Mettikhon@oca.org
*15.7.1966 Boston MA episcopalian. N? 1984 graduated Wyomissing High school. 1988 BA French and Sociology Lancaster PA. 1989 orth, stud St. Tikhon Seminary. 1993 MDiv teacher St. Tikhon's. mon1995 diak1995 ⊖1995. 1998 igumen. archim2000 ⊕14.2.2004 B South Canaan. 2005 B Philadelphia. 2012 A Washington, M All America and Canada. 20.3.2016 concelebration Phanar Istanbul.

Michael Dahulich ***New York***
T: A New York, New Jersey ▪ ✉ 33 Hewitt Ave, USA-Bronxville, NY10708 • [1] 914 779658-0, fax -1 • bishopmichael@nynjoca.org
*29.8.1950 Johnson City NY. N? 1969 BA Binghamton. 1969-1972 Seminary Johnstown PA. 1.1.1973 married Deborah Sandak (killed in a car accident 28.2.1973). diak3.2.1973 ⊖18.2.1973. MA Phil St. Vincent College Latrobe, PhD Theology Duquesne University Pittsburgh. Dean Carpatho-Russian diocese. 1993-2009 teacher NT AT St. Tikhon's Seminary South Canaan PA. 2001 OCA. mon30.3.2009 archim31.3.2009 ⊕8.5.2010 B New York, New Jersey, 2013 secretary Holy Synod of Bishops. 2015 A New York, New Jersey.

Mark Maymon ***Philadelphia***
T: A Philadelphia and Eastern Pennsylvania ▪ ✉ 144 St. Tikhon's Road, USA-Waymart, PA 18472 • [1] 570 937 9331 • vladyka.mark@gmail.com • http://oca.org/holy-synod/bishops/the-most-reverend-mark
*22.6.1958 New Albay Indiana roman-catholic. N25.4. MA Biblical Literature Oral Roberts University Tulsa. 1989 Holy Chrisam Orthodox Church (Antiochia). 1991 MDiv. St. Vladimir's. diak17.8.1997 ⊖7.9.1997. 1997-2000 pastor Beaver Falls ⊕5.12.2004 Damascus (Patr Ignatios). 2004-2010 B Toledo (Antiochia). 2011 received in OCA. B Baltimore, admin Dallas 10.5.2014 B, 2015 A Philadelphia and Eastern Pennsylvania.

Nathaniel William George Popp ***Detroit***
T: A Detroit and the Romanians ▪ ✉ P.O. Box 309, USA-Grass Lake, MI 49240-0309 • [1] 517 522-4800, -3598, -3656, fax -5907 • nathaniel@roea.org chancery@roea.org

*12.6.1940 "Romanian Greek Catholic Church" Aurora IL. N22.4. stud OSB Lisle IL, Gregoriana Roma, Greek College. diak17.6.1966 (B Cristea "Romanian Greek Catholic Church") Colle di Tora ⊖23.1.1967 (B Cristea). 15.2.1968 orth Vatra Grass Lake. rector Hermitage PA ⊕25.11.1980 B Dearborn Auxiliary Detroit. 1984 B Detroit.

Irineu Duvlea

T: B Dearborn Heights, vicar Detroit and the Romanians ▪ ✉ P.O.Box 309, USA-Grass Lake, MI 49240-0309 • [1] 517 5224800, [1] 517 5225907 • irineu@roea.org bishopirineu@aol.com

*19.4.1962 Alba Iulia. N23.8. 1981-1987 Seminary Cluj. mon24.5.1983 Brâncoveanu Sâmbata de Sus. diak3.5.1984 (A Ioann Helsinki) ⊖17.11.1984 Sibiu (A Antonie Plamadeala). 1987-1991 Fac theol Sibiu. 15.8.1988 protosingel. 1.1.1993 igumen, Exarch. archim15.8.1993. 2001 Detroit Holy Ascension monastery ⊕2.11.2002 B Dearborn.

Paul Apostolos Gassios ***Chicago***

T: B Chicago and the Midwest ▪ ✉ 927-933 N. La Salle Dr., USA-Chicago, IL 60610-3204 • [1] 312 202042-0, fax -7 • bishoppaul@domoca.org

*6.4.1953 Detroit, N6.11. 1971-1976 Wayne State University. 1973 moved to Detroit. 1980 Master of Social Work Wayne State University. 1991-1994 MDiv St. Vladimir's Seminary. diak1.1.1991. 1994-2005 parish Kokomo IN ⊖25.6.1994. 2006 monastery Hayesville OH. 2007-2014 Dean St. George Cathedral Rossford OH. mon20.10.2014 archim ⊕27.12.2014 B Chicago.

Irénée Rochon ***Canada***

T: A Ottawa, administrator Canada ▪ ✉ 15 Le Breton St. N., CANADA-Ottawa, ON C1R7H1 • [1] 613 223 7780, fax -1931 • bishopirenee@archdiocese.ca

*25.12.1948 Montreal, in large French Canadian Roman Cath family. 20.1.1967 orth Montreal (A Vitaly ROCOR). 1971 BA Slavic Studies Ottawa. 1971-1975 stud theol Holy Trinity Jordanville. mon1975 diak19.5.1978 ROCOR Brussels ⊖20.8.1978 ROCOR Geneva. 1978-1982 ROCOR parish Lyon. 1982 ROCOR French mission Montréal Canada. 1986 from ROCOR to OCA. 1992 igumen. 1993-1996 parish Montreal. 1996-2007 Russian Cemetery Rawdon QC. archim2.4.2009 ⊕1.10.2009 B Quebec vicar Canada. 2010 administrator Canada. 2015 A Ottawa, administrator Canada.

Nikon Nicholas Liolin ***Albanians***

T: A Albanian Archdiocese Boston ▪ ✉ P.O. Box 149, USA-Southbridge, MA 01550 • [1] 508 7643222 • bpnikon@aol.com

*9.10.1945 New York. N23.3. stud St. Vladimir Crestwood, Iona College, New School for Social Research. 1967 married Sarah, Arthur †25.7.2000. reader (Fan Noli). diak5.7.1969 (Stephen Lasko) ⊖6.7.1969 rector (Albanian Archdiocese) Southbridge Massachusetts, Farmington Hills Michigan. Editor "The Vine", coordinator "The Voice of Orthodoxy". 2002 St. Tikhon Seminary South Canaan ⊕25.5.2002 B Baltimore, auxiliary to His Beatitude for the Albanians OCA. 22.10.2003 B Boston 2005 Admin. New England. 16.12.2005 B Boston, New England and the Albanian Diocese. 2011-2015 also Locum tenens Diocese of the South. 9.5.2012 A.

Benjamin Vincent Peterson ***San Francisco***

T: A San Francisco and the West ▪ ✉ 1520 Green St, USA-San Francisco, CA 94123 • [1] 415 567-west (9378), [1] 702 2771857 • vikenty@msn.com

*1.6.1954 Pasadena CA. 27.4.1972 baptized Virgin Mary Los Angeles. N31.7. 1978 MDiv St. Vladimir's, choirmaster Detroit, chairman OCA Liturgical Music Department. diak15.11.1987-1997 deacon Pasadena. mon1988 St.Tikhon's. 1991 archdeacon ⊖19.7.1997. 1999 St. Innocent Alaska. archim2002. 2004 chancellor diocese of the West ⊕1.5.2004 B Berkeley, auxiliary to His Beatitude. 2008 B San Francisco. 9.3.2012 A San Francisco and the West.

Daniel Brum

T: B Santa Rosa, assistant San Francisco ▪ ✉ 1203 W Campbell Ave., USA-Phoenix, AZ 85013 • [1] 415 567 9378, [1] 702 2771 857

*16.11.1954 Fresno CA, roman catholic, Portuguese area USA. 1973 absolv high school Riverdale CA. 1977 BA Humanities Roman Catholic St. Patrick's College Mountain View CA. 1981-1992 diocesan director of vocation, director diocesan newspaper ⊖29.6.1981. 1981 MDiv St. Patrick's Seminary Menlo Park CA. 1992-1995 degree in canon law Catholic University Washington DC. 1995-1997 Diocesan Tribunal. 1997 vested as an Orthodox priest by B Tikhon San Francisco. 1998-2000 Mission Flemington NJ. 2000-2005 secretary to the Metropolitan. 2005-2015 rector Phoenix AZ. 2014 elected B Santa Rosa CA, auxiliary San Francisco ⊕24.1.2015 B Santa Rosa, assistant San Francisco.

Alejo Antonio Pacheco Vera ***Mexico***

T: A Mexico City ▪ ✉ Rio Consulado e Irapuato 53, Col. Peñón de los Baños, MEXICO-15520 Ciudad de México • [52] 55 57845198 • obispoalejo@yahoo.com.mx www.oca.org

*6.9.1954 Mexico. N17.3. 1.8.1972 Orthodox. stud Mexiko M Antonius Chedraoui. mon8.7.1978 diak14.1.1979 Ascension Cathedral Mexico ⊖1.3.1981. 2001 igumen. archim2003 ⊕28.5.2005 B Mexico. 16.10.2008 B Mexico City and the Exarchate of Mexico. 9.5.2012 A Mexico.

Melchisedek Thomas Pleska ***Pittsburgh***

T: A Pittsburgh+Western Pennsylvania ▪ ✉ P.O.Box 1769, USA-Cranberry Township, PA16066-1769 • [1] 724 7765555 +fax • melchisedek999@yahoo.com www.ocadwpa.org

*20.8.1942 Dayton OH USA. N? Father born Brest Litowsk, 1925 USA. University Music school Michigan, BA Philosophy Oxford OH, stock brokerage, real estate. 1980 MDiv St. Vladimir's (John Meyendorff). diak21.11.1985 ⊖25.3.1986. 1986-1989 instructor Dogmatic St. Tikhon's Seminary. 1989-1998 rector Meriden CT. 1998-2003 Holy Cross monastery Theben Greece, 2003-2009 Monastery Dormition Patras. mon2004 archim1.1.2004 ⊕27.6.2009 Pittsburgh and the Diocese of West Pennsylvania. 21.3.2014 A Pittsburgh+Western Pennsylvania.

Alexander Golitzin ***Toledo***

T: B Toledo, B of the Bulgarians ▪ ✉ 519 Brynhaven Drive, USA-Oregon, Ohio 43616, [1] 419 693 -9540, fax -9541 • alexander@bdoca.org • www.oca.org

*1948 Burbank, CA,N30.8. 1973-1980 doctoral studies Oxford (M Kallistos Ware), one year Simonos Petras Mount Athos. 1980 PhD. diak1.1982 USA ⊖1984 mon1986 archim1987. 1989-2012 teacher theology Milwaukee Marquette Uni ⊕5.5.2012 B Toledo.

David Sterry Mahaffey ***Sitka***

T: B Sitka+Alaska ▪ ✉ 7031 Howard Ave., USA-Anchorage, AK 99504-1899 • [1] 907-538-9318, fax 907-677-0646 • otyetz@hotmail.com • www.dioceseofalaska.org

*1952 Altoona PA.1.3. 1973 married with Karen Meterko†, four children. 1975 orthodox. MDiv St. Tikhon South Canaan PA. diak1981 diocese of Pittsburgh USA ⊖1993. 1993-2006 rector Old Forge PA. 2003 BA, 2005 MA theol and phil University of Scranton, 2006-2009 rector Pottstown PA, 2009 Bethlehem. teacher theology St. Tikhon's and Alvernia University Philadelphia ⊕21.2.2014 Sitka+Alaska.

Retired Hierarchs:

Herman Joseph Swaiko

T: former A Washington, M All America and Canada ▪ ✉ Route 25 A, Oyster Bay Cove, P.O.Box 675, USA-Syosset, NY 11791-0675 •
[1] 516 9220550

*1.2.1932 Briarford, PA. N9.8. stud Pittsburgh business administration. 1959 discharge from US Army Labrador. 1959-1963 St. Tikhon Theol Seminary. diak1.3.1964 ⊖7.4.1964 parishes Dundaff, Uniondale. mon4.12.1970 (St. Herman

of Alaska). 17.10.1971 igumen ⊕10.2.1973 B Wilkes-Barre, auxiliary Philadelphia. 1981-1994 B, 1994-2001 A Philadelphia. 1994 Dr. theol h.c. Nashotah, Dr.h.c. business Robert Morris College, Order of St. Innocent Silver Class. 2002-2008 M.

Theodosius Lazor
T: former A Washington, M All America and Canada ▪
✉ 156 Rifgon Dr., USA-Canonsburg, PA 15317
*27.10.1933 Canonsburg, Pennsylvania. N9.9. mon10.10.1961 diak14.10.1961 ⊖22.10.1961 ⊕6.5.1967 B Washington. 1.6.1967 B Alaska. 30.5.1972 B Pittsburgh. 1977 M USA and Canada, A New York, 1980-2002 A Washington.

Lazar Lev Puhalo
T: former A Ottawa ▪ ✉ 37323 Hawkins Road, CANADA-Lax KW'Alaams, V0M 1H0 BC • [1] 604 8269336, fax 8209758 •
synaxis@orthodoxcanada.org
*12.1.1941 Lady Lake SK, Ron Haler. N16.6. diak1972 ROCOR, 1980 defrocked as heretic ⊖1981 (New Gračanica, later Patriarchat Kiev, later Milan Synod) 15 years director Anti-Drogue Institute. Abbot All Saints Monastery ⊕28.9.1990 B Ottawa. 2003 OCA as "retired B" New Ostrog Monastery. April 2004 Alba Iulia.

Seraphim Storheim
T: former A Ottawa+Canada ▪ ✉ Box 179, CANADA-Spencerville, Ontariao C0E 1X0, [1] 613 925-5226, fax -1521
*25.1.1946 Edmonton luth "Kenneth-William". N4.12. 1971 Vancouver School of Theology, 1972 Anglican priest. 1978 orth. diak28.10.1979 (A Sylvester) ⊖21.11. 1979 (M Theodosius) ⊕13.6.1987 B Edmonton. 1987-1990 Auxiliary to the M. 10.5.1990 B, 2007-2010 A Canada.

Tikhon Stephen Fitzgerald
T: former B San Francisco ▪ ✉ 649 Robinson St., USA-Los Angeles, CA 90026 • [1] 323 9133615, [1] 800 3236921
*14.11.1932 Detroit. 18.12.1932 baptized Lutheran. N13.8. 1952-1954 St. Olaf College. 1954-1971 U.S. Air Forces. Converted to Orth 9.1960. 1958 graduated Wayne State University Detroit. 1965-1966 St. Vladimir's Theological Seminary. diak1971. 1972-1978 Protodeacon Los Angeles ⊖9.7.1978. 1984-1986 Diocesan Chancellor. mon24.3.1987 ⊕30.5.1987. 1987-2003 B San Francisco, retired.

Varlaam Vasili Novakshonoff
T: former B Vancouver ▪ ✉ 37323 Hawkins Pickle Road, CANADA-Lax KW'Alaams, V0M 1H0 BC • [1] 604 8269336, fax 8209758
N6.11.mon1981, ⊕1.4.1994 B "Holy Synod of Milan". 2003 OCA.

Mark Forsberg

T: former B Boston ▪ ✉ 9511 Sun Pointe Drive, USA-Boynton Beach, FL 3343 • [1] 561 3690247

*2.4.1934 Dearborn Mich. N19.1. ⊖26.7.1964 ⊕10.11.1979 B Boston. 1983 B Bethesda. 1985 B Fort Lauderdale, Flor. 3.5.1991 former B Bethesda.

Nikolaj Soraich

T: former B Sitka and Alaska ▪ ✉ 5170 Evaline St., USA-Las Vegas, NV 89120-1002 • [1] 907 279002-5, -6, fax 2799748 • www.dioceseofalaska.org

*9.4.1949 Butte MDiv Serbian parents. N6./19.12. 1967 Christ the Saviour. Seminary Johnstown PA. mon8.8.1970 diak 9.8.1970 ⊖4.6.1972 Serbian Orth Cath Alhambra. 1972-1978 Serbian parish Billings MT. 1978-1979 stud theol Beograd. 1979-1988 Serbian parish Las Vegas NV. 1988 OCA. 1994 Chancellor of B Tikhon. archim13.5.1995 ⊕22.4.2001 B Baltimore, auxiliary to M. 2002-2008 B Sitka.

Seraphim Josif Sigrist

T: former B Sendai ▪ ✉ 329 S Broadway, Unit P 7, USA-Tarrytown, NY 10591

*13.12.1941 New York,1967 (Presbyterian, Orth) N? stud Nyack College NY. 1967 absolvent St. Vladimir's Seminary. 1967 teacher Japan. diak14.9.1969 mon18.10.1969 ⊖26.10.1969 ⊕12.12.1971 B Sendai (by B Nagashima in Japan). 1971-1987 B Sendai East Japan. 1987 USA teacher religion Drew University. 2009 received in OCA.

Matthias Moriak

T: former B Midwest ▪ ✉ 1414 Roosevelt St., USA-Morgantown, WV 26505-5234 • monkmatthias@hotmail.com

*4.4.1949 "David Lawrence" Cleveland OH. N9.8. John Moriak had emigrated 1913 to Cleveland from Horowa Galicia Austria. 1967 graduated Parma OH High school. 1967-1972 stud Christ the Saviour Seminary Johnstown PA. 1972 married Pani Jeannette († 1997), two children (Matthew priest). diak1972 ⊖18.6.1972. 1975-1982 mission parish Freehold NY. 1982-2004 Saint Claire PA. mon14.10.2003 Iveron Athos. 2004-2006 prefect Christ the Saviour Seminary. archim18.10.2010 ⊕30.4.2011. 2011-2013 B Chicago and the Midwest, retired.

Greek Orthodox Patriarchate of Antioch and All the East

His Beatitude **Youhanna**
Rum-Orthodox Patriarch of Antioch and All the East

Youhanna Yazigi ***Damascus***
T: Patriarch of Antioch and All the East ▪ ✉ B.P. 9, SYRIA-Damas, [963] 11 542440-0, -1, -2, -3, fax -4, 543140-0, -1 • Balamand [961] 6 931 257, 6 933 257 • info@antiochpat.org • secretary@antiochpatriarchate.org • www.antiochpatriarchate.org • parish Antiochia Turkey Fr Dimitri Dogum +90 326 213 6496, +90 532 524 2735 • ddogum@mynet.com
*1955 Mor Marita Syria, N7.1. 1978 Tishreen University degree Civil Engineering. dipl Fac theol Balamand. 1978-1982 dipl Liturgy Byzantine Music Thessaloniki, Dr. theol Thessaloniki. diak1979 Lattakia (M Youhanna Mansour). 1981 Prof Liturgics Balamand ⊖1983 Lattakia (M Youhanna Mansour). 1989-1992 Dean Fac theol Balamand. 1993 Abbot St. George Al-Humayrah ⊕24.1.1995 B Al-Hosn. 1995-2008 B Al-Hosn, auxiliaire Akkar, spiritual father Our Lady of Blemmana Convent Lattakya. 2001-2005 Dean Fac theol Balamand. Abbot Balamand. 2008-2013 M West and Central Europe.19.8.2010 title changed "M Europe". 10.2.2013 Patriarch at Damascus. 17.2.2013 Patriarch at Beirut with B Gerhard Magdeburg, Dr. Oeldemann. 2015 Dr.h.c. St. Vladimir's New York.

Moises Moussa El Khoury
T: B Darayia, auxiliaire patriarcal ▪ ✉ B.P. 9, SYRIA-Damas • [963] 944 261 954
*1953 Syria. N4.9. 1971-1974 stud Balamand ⊕24.1.1995.

Lukas El Khoury
T: B Seidnaya, auxiliaire patriarcal ▪ ✉ B.P. 9, SYRIA-Damas • [963] 944 270 100
*1965 N18.10 ⊕5.10.1999.

Nikolaos Baalbakee
T: B Bludan, auxiliaire patriarcal, President Spiritual court ▪ ✉ B.P. 9, SYRIA-Damas • [963] 933 359 697 • nicholasbaalbakee@outlook.com
⊕12.7.2011 Damascus. Daten von Diakon Romanos OKI.

Markos Khoury
T: B, auxiliaire ▪ ✉ B.P. 9, SYRIA-Damas • [963] 11 5431400
⊕6.11.2011 Damascus.

Kostas Kaial
T: B, auxiliaire ▪ ✉ B.P. 9, SYRIA-Damas • [963] 11 5431400
⊕24.7.2011 Damascus.

Grigorios Abdullah Khoury
T: B United Arab Emirates, auxiliaire patriarcal ▪ ✉
B.P. 9, SYRIA-Damas • [963] 11 5431400.
2010 stud theol Athens ⊕16.11.2014.

Sadiq Qais
T: B Darayia, auxiliaire patriarcal ▪ ✉
B.P. 9, SYRIA-Damas • [963] 11 5431400.
1970 founder and president Orthodox Youth Fellowship Jordan. 1972-1982 Dr. theol Institut Theol de Grad Universitar Bucureşti. 1977-1979 dipl juridical Science University Bucureşti, Academy Ştefan Gheorghiu Bucureşti. 1982-1990 Prof canon law University Balamand. 1990-1995 Ecclesiastical Court of Appeal Damascus, Chief Department of Foreign and Ecumenical Affairs Damascus. 1996 founder and president Ecumenical Study Center. 2004-2013 Regional Coordinator Arab States Religion for Children. 2011 Senior Felow World Engagement Institute ⊕23.11.2014 B Erzurum, Adrun Darayia auxiliary to patriarch.

Ephraim Elias Malouli
T: B Seleukia, auxiliaire patriarcal, secetary Holy Synod ▪ ✉ B.P. 9, SYRIA-Damas • [963] 932 730 000 • efraimmonk@gmail.com • bp.efraim@antiochpatriarchate.org
*1.3.1978 Jdaidet Artouz Damascus. N? 1997-2000 stud Electro-Ingenieur University Damascus. 2000 novice. mon2001 St. George Al-Humayrah Homs. 2001-2002 Language course Modern Greek Athens. 2002-2005 Language course Ancient Greek Athens. 2002-2006 BTh Athens. 2005 English Course Dublin. 2006-2009 Master Byzantine Literatur Athens "Historical comments on the life of St. Stephan Sabbait". 2006-2010 MTh Athens "Islam in the writings of Joh. Damask. and his contribution to the Ecumenical Dialogue". diak11.11.2007 al-Hosn (Johannes Yazigi) ⊖12.12.2007. 2009 English course, 2009-2010 "61st Graduate School" Ecumenical Institute Bossey Geneva. 2009 Dr. theol Byzantine Literature Athens "The monastic life in Palestine during 8th and 9th centuries". 2009 Master Greek Literature Athens. 2010 Master Patristics Athens ⊕28.8.2011. 2011 auxiliaire Europe Köln. 1.5.-20.7.2012 language course Regensburg. 2015 secetary Holy Synod.

Athanasios Saliba

T: B Yabroud, Igumen ▪ ✉ P.O.Box 238 Shrine Matan, LEBANON-5567 Bikfaiya • [961] 4 271 120

*26.2.1920 Abou Mizan Lebanon, N17.1. BDiv Institut St-Serge Paris. BA ML MAT CAGS, USA. diak1946 ⊖1957 ⊕10.2.1980. 1980-1982 Patriarchal assistant. 1983-1991 igumen Balamand. 1992-1999 Patriarchal assistant.

Nifon Saikali

T: M Philippopolis ▪ ✉ Patriarchal Metochion, Arhangelskij Pereulok 15, ROSSIJA-109052 Moskva • [7] 495 6250417, fax 6246774 • Zahle [961] 8 820527, [961] 3 347065 • antioch@list.ru

*4.12.1941 Zahle, N5.1. Evangelical College Beirut. Fac Mathematics University Beirut 1959-1963 Kandidat Academy Moskva. mon27.9.1958 diak27.9.1959. 1963-1977 Vicar General Zahle Lebanon, teacher Mathematics English Rayak ⊖20.8.1964. 1977 Representative of the Patriarch of Antioch to to Moscow Patriarchate. 1983 Cross St. Vladimir. Decoration of Glory and honour from St. Andrew's fund ⊕13.11.1988 Al Shahba Lebanon B Philippopolis (Patr Ignatius, M Filaret Minsk head Department External Church Relations Moskva). 1988 Cross Kyrill Method Cecoslov. 1997 Cross St. Daniel (Patr Moskva). 1999 Cross St. Kliment (Patr Bulgaria). 2001 Decoration St. Innokentij (Patr Moskva). 2002-2008 assistant Western Europe. 2002 Honorary Member dipl Academy Moskva. 2002 Decoration of the Kosaks. 2003 First badge of honour Republic Lebanon. 2006 Decoration St. Serafim Moskva. 2008 Orden Družby (Putin). 2009 A, 2014 M. Decoration of St. Innokentij (I). 18.10.2009 Golden Jubilee Zahle – with Dutch ambassadors Dirkse Daphne (Slowakia) and Jan-Paul (Turkey) Dirkse, M Spyridon (Zahle), M Elia (Tyr), M Antonius Chedraui. 29.6.2015 visit to Ecumenical Patriarch Bartholomaios İstanbul. 13.12.2015 International Andrey Pervozvanny premium "For belief and faith" Kreml palace (M of the City of Omsk).

Paul Yazigi ***Aleppo***

T: M Aleppo (Berrhoea), Alexandretta and Dependencies ▪ ✉ P.O.Box 6976, 6976 Al-Villat, Patriarch Elias Moawad Street, SYRIA-Aleppo • [963] 21 4660680, 466067-0, fax -1, [963] 94476211 •
arch@alepporthodox.org • secretary@alepporthodox.org •
www.alepporthodox.net.sy • www.alepporthodox.org

*1.1.1959 Lattakya Syria. N29.6. stud Civil Engineering Tishreen. diak1985. 1989 dipl theol Thessaloniki. 1992 Dr. phil Thessaloniki "Eschatology and Ethics" ⊖1992. 1992-2000 teacher Patristic, Ethics, 1994-2000 Dean Fac theol Balamand ⊕2.10.2000 M Aleppo. 2013 kidnapped together with Syrian A of Aleppo.

Saba Esber ***Bosra***
T: M Bosra ▪ ✉ Archevêché Grec Orthodoxe, P.O.Box 18, SYRIA-Soueida • [963] 16 318459, fax 16 319520 • bp.saba@yahoo.com • www.orthodoxhauran.net
*1959 Lattaqia, N? 1987 BA Civil Engineering University Tishreen Lattakia, BTh Balamand ⊖1988-1998 parish of the Archangels Lattakia ⊕20.12.1997 B Seidnaya, 1997-1999 auxiliaire Lattaquié, vicaire Damas. 1999 M Bosra.

Youhanna Mansour ***Lattaquié***
T: M Laodikea ▪ ✉ Archevêché Grec Orthodoxe, P.O.Box 27, SYRIA-Lattaquié • [963] 41 468342, 24534-1, -2, fax -0
*1927 Lattaquié. N7.1. 1961-1964 stud Balamand ⊖1962. Abbot Bkeftine Monastery Tripoli. Patriarchal Vicar in Lattakia. Abbot Balamand ⊕21.10.1979.

Elia Saliba ***Hama***
T: M Hama ▪ ✉ Archevêché Grec Orthodoxe, Almadena, SYRIA-Hama • [963] 33 511991, 33 252 5216, fax 33 251 1991 • metro.h@mail.sy • metro.h@scs-net.org
*1924. Kfarsaroun, Lebanon N20.7. ⊖1950 member Spiritual Court, general director Assia Schools Damascus. 1951 dipl jur University Damascus, dipl theol Chalki İstanbul ⊕1966 B Salamia, auxiliaire patriarcal Couvent St. Georges. 1986 M Hama.

Georges Abu Zacham ***Homs***
T: M Homs ▪ ✉ Archevêché Grec Orthodoxe, P.O.Box 386, SYRIA-Homs • [963] 31 221139, 31 2484858, fax 31 2488550 • metropolitan.george@hotmail.com
*1953 Hina Syria N23.4. 1971-1974 stud Balamand, dipl theol Thessaloniki ⊖1980. Dean Institute Balamand ⊕26.10.1988. 1988-1998 B Belmond. 1990-1995 igumen, Doyen Institut Théol Couvent Notre Dame Balamand. 1995 secrétaire Saint Synode, 1995-1998 auxiliaire patriarcal. 1998 B Qara, secrétaire Synode, auxiliaire Soueida. 1998 M Homs.

Georges Khodre ***Jbail***
T: M Byblos, Botrys, Mont Liban ▪ ✉ Archevêché Grec Orth, Al Matri, LEBANON-Broummana • [961] 4 86241-8, -9, 961647, 961209 • arch@ortmtlb.org.lb • www.ortmtlb.org.lb
*6.7.1923 Tripoli Liban. N23.4. 16.3.1942 together with fifteen students faculties of Law and Medicine, he founded the Orthodox Youth Movement. 11.11.1943 pacifist demonstration against the French colonial government. 1943 Dr. iur Université St. Joseph Beyrouth. 1944-1952 dipl theol Institut St-Serge Paris. diak12.12.1953

⊖14.12.1953. 1955-1970 parish Tripoli. 1968 Dr.h.c. Institut St-Serge Paris, 1988 Dr.h.c. St. Vladimir's New York ⊕10.2.1970. 2004 Mondo Migliore.

Elia Awde ***Beirut***

T: M Beirut ▪ ✉ Archevêché Grec Orth P.O.Box 126, LEBANON-Beirut • [961] 1 20061-2, -3, fax -1 • metbey@quartos.org.lb • www.quartos.org.lb

*1941 Amfeh Alkoura Tripoli. N20.7. BA Philosophy Lebanese University, BTh St. Vladimir's New York ⊖1969 Yonkers, New York. Vice Dean St. John of Damascus Institute of Theology in Balamand ⊕18.11.1979 Vicar to Patr. 6.2.1980 M Beirut.

Basilius Mansour ***Arkadia***

T: M Akkar ▪ ✉ Archevêché Grec Orthodoxe, Cheikh Taba, Halba, LEBANON-Akkar • [961] 6 690012, 6 69319-6, fax -4 • tartousorthodox@hotmail.com • www.akkarorthodox.com

*1962 Mzairaa Syria. N1.1. stud Athens. 1984 BTh Balamand, PhD Thessaloniki ⊖1985-1995 parish St. Andrews Lattakia ⊕24.1.1995 B Tartus, Safita auxiliaire Akkar. 2008 M Akkar. 16.12.2015 Athens Interorthodox committee preparation Panorthodox Synod 2016.

Athanasios Fahd

T: B Tartus, auxiliaire Arkadia ▪ ✉ Greek Orthodox Archdiocese, P.O.Box 46, SYRIA-Tartus • [963] 43 319635, fax 43 319603 • tartousorthodox@hotmail.com

*1961, N18.1 ⊕18.7.2011.

Elias Tome

T: B Arthoussa, auxiliaire Arkadia ▪
✉ St. John square, Marmarita, Talkalakh, SYRIA-Homs •
[963] 31 7732184, fax [963] 30 7731184 • wadi.episcopal@gmail.com

⊕18.7.2011 B Arthoussa, vicaire Arkadia.

Demetri Athanasios Sharbak

T: B Banias, auxiliaire Arkadia ▪ ✉ Greek Orthodox Archdiocese, P.O.Box 23, SYRIA-Safita • [963] 43 530643, 43 525803, fax 43 522744 • demetrios.charbak@yahoo.com

⊕18.7.2011.

Elias Kfoury ***Tyr***

T: M Tyr et Saida ▪ ✉ Archevêché Grec Orthodoxe, P.O.Box 4, LEBANON-Marjayoun Tyr • [961] 7 830004 • Sidon 7 720881 • Tyre 7 740182 • Rashaya Aleadi 8 595012, fax 7 733889 • greekorthodox.arch@yahoo.com

*1948 Chrine Metn Beirut. N20.7. 1954-1975 dipl theol Balamand ⊖1978 ⊕17.2.1986. 1986-1995 B Seidnaya, auxiliaire Patriarcal Damas, secrétaire du Saint Synode. 1995 Tyr et Saida. 18.10.2009 jubilee A Nifon Zahle with M Spyridon (Zahle), M Antonius Chedraui.

Efrem Kyriakos ***Tripoli***

T: M Tripoli ▪ ✉ Archevêché Grec Orthodoxe, P.O.Box 345, LEBANON-Tripoli • [961] 6 33446-4, -5, 6 44226-4, -5, fax -7 • [961] 3 291132 • archorthotripoli@yahoo.com • info@archtripoli.org • www.archtripoli.org

*1943 in Beirut, N28.1. BA Electrical Engineering St. Joseph University Beirut. BTh Balamand. mon1983 St. Paul's Monastery, Mount Athos ⊖1987. Dean Balamand. Abbot Archangels Monastery Bekaata Lebanon ⊕18.10.2009.

Younan Antoni Alsouri ***Zahle***

T: M Helioupolis ▪ ✉ Archevêché Grec Orthodoxe, St. Nicolas, LEBANON-Zahle • [961] 8 820527, 806772, [961] 3 806882

*20.7.1970 Mina, Tripoli. National Orthodox School Mar Elias in Mina. 1994 dipl Fac of Engineering Lebanese University. 24.6.2001 subdeacon Monastery of St. John the Baptist in Douma (M Georges Khodr). diak20.3.2005 (M Elias Kurban) ⊖24.7.2005 Mina "priest for the youth" vice-president SYNDESMOS. 2006 dipl theol Institut St-Serge Paris. archim7.9.2008 Tripoli ⊕14.11.2015 M Zahle Damascus (Patr John).

Silvan Moussa ***Buenos Aires***

T: M Buenos Aires ▪ ✉ Av. Raúl Scalabrini Ortiz 1261, ARGENTINA-Buenos Aires, C1414 DNM • [54] 11 4776 2283, 11 4777 1360, 11 4776 0208 • arzobispado@acoantioquena.com • www.acoantioquena.com

*1967 Maracay Venezuela, N? 1973-1985 College des Frères de la Salle in Tripoli, Lebanon. 1990 BA Electrical Engineering University St. Joseph Beirut. 1990-1994 Beirut Paris analyst and chief project in developing software for Banks and Financial Institutions in the Middle East and Europe. 1994-1995 Institut St-Serge Paris. 1995-2001 MTh Thessaloniki. diak 1996 (M Youhanna of Lattakia) ⊖2000 archim (M Paul of Aleppo). 2000-2006 Aleppo Metropolitan's Vicar ⊕1.10.2006 M Buenos Aires (Patr Ignatius IV).

Damaskinos Mansour ***São Paulo***

T: M São Paulo ▪ ✉ Rua Vergueiro 1515, Paraiso, BRAZIL-São Paulo 04101 • [55] 11 5579-0019, -3835, fax 5572 0017 • catedralortodoxa@uol.com.br • catedralortodoxa.conselho@uol.com.br • contato@catedralortodoxa.com.br • secretaria@catedralortodoxa.com.br • www.catedralortodoxa.com.br

*1948 Damascus Syria, N4.12. 1961-1970 stud Balamand 1970-1974 dipl theol Balamand, dipl Philology Arab University Libanese Beirut. diak8.12.1974 (Patr Elias IV) ⊖1975 Thessaloniki (M Panteleimon Rodopoulos). 1976-1980 MTh Thessaloniki, Lic Liturgia, Arte Bizantina, Biblioteconomia. Prof Fac theol Balamand in Thessaloniki. 1980-1986 Damascus. archim1984 (Patr Ignatios IV). 1987-1991 vicaire Akkra for Syria ⊕18.8.1992. 1992-1997 B Edessa Vicar São Paulo. 1997 M São Paolo. 2006-2013 Central Committee WCC.

Romanos Dawd

T: B Edessa, auxiliaire Brasilia ▪ ✉ av. Gomes Freire 559, BRAZIL-Rio de Janeiro, 20231 • [55] 21 2241332, fax 5089999 • bp.romanosdaoud@hotmail.com • bp.romanosdaoud@catedralortodoxa.com.br

⊕6.11.2011 Damascus.

Antonius Chedraoui ***Mexico***

T: M Mexico ▪ ✉ Pirules 110 C.P. 01900, Jardinas del Pedregal, MEXICO-Ciudad de México • [52] 55 56527772, 55682292, fax 56525433 • ortodoxia@prodigy.net.mx • www.iglesiaortodoxa.org.mx

*17.1.1932 Tripoli. N17.1. diak20.7.1952. 1957 dipl theol Athens. 1957-1966 President Spiritual court Tripoli and Mount Lebanon. Abbot Bkeftine Monastery. Tripoli. vicar Houran's ⊖29.8.1958 ⊕5.6.1966. 1966-1996 B Caesarea, Vicaire Patr, Exarch Mexico. 4.10.1994 Nacionalidad Mexicana. 12.6.1996 M Mexico. 18.10.2009 jubilee A Nifon in Zahle with M Spyridon (Zahle). M Elia (Tyr).

Ignacio Isaak Samaan

T: B, auxiliaire Mexiko ▪ ✉ Av. "E", Quinta San Antonio Abad, El Pinar, El Paraíso, VENEZUELA-1010 Caracas • [58] 212 461 16 67, 424 460 55 90, fax 212 462 92 86 • Mexiko [52] 155 51 04 51 31 • mons.ignacio@iglesiaortodoxa.org.mx • www.venezuela.iglesiaortodoxa.org.mx

⊕12.7.2011 Damascus Daten von Diakon Romanos OKI.

Sergio Abad ***Chile***

T: M Chile ▪ ✉ c/o Ortodoxo Av. Pedro de Valdivia 92, Casilla 54-Corréo 4, CHILE-Santiago de Chile • [56] 2 7374697, 2 2211 5649, fax 2 2951 5208 • s-abad@mi.cl • www.chileortodoxo.cl • www.iglesiaortodoxa.cl

*4.11.1930 Antiochia, N7.10. 1956 dipl theol Chalki. diak1956 Aleppo (M Elias Mahouad) ⊖10.10.1956. 1956-1961 rector Seminary Balamand. 1962-1967 paroisses Kuwait. archim1967 Tripoli (M Theodosios Aburejaile). 1968-1975 paroisses Brazil. 1975-1988 paroisses Venezuela ⊕4.12.1988 B Salamia, vicaire patriarcal, Exarch Chile. 1996 M Chile.

Ignatius Rafiq alHoshi ***Western Europe***
T: M Western Europe ■ ✉ 22 avenue Kléber, FRANCE-75116 Paris • [33] 1 47048064, 1 45002749 • bp.ignatius@antiocheurope.org • secretary@antiocheurope.org • info@antiocheurope.org • www.antiocheurope.org
*1970 Damascus. N? 1988-1994 stud electrotechnics University Damascus. mon1995. 2001-2003 dipl Byzantine Music Athens. 2001-2006 Fac theol Athens. diak2007 (Johannes Yazigi). 2008-2010 stud patristics Chambésy ⊖2010 Penteli Athens (Johannes Sakilarion) ⊕24.7.2011 B Lorissa, auxiliaire Paris. 2013 M Western Europe Paris.

Isaak Barakat ***Germany***
T: M Germany and Central Europe ■ ✉ Geranien Weg 27-29, GERMANY-50769 Köln • [49] 221 3795688 • info@rum-orthodox.de • isaac.barakat@hotmail.com • www.rum-orthodox.de
*1966 Damascus. N? stud Jura Damascus. 1987-1990 military service. 1990 stud theol Thessaloniki. 1998-1999 stud New Testament Erlangen. diak2000 Dr. theol "The childhood Jesus according to the protoevangelium of Jacobus" ⊖2000 Orthodox Youth Movement. 2005 abbot Balamand. 2005 WCC Geneva. archim2007-2008 teacher Fac theol Maronite Kaslik. 2009 Paphos Orth Cath Joint Commission ⊕12.7.2011 Damascus B Apameia. 2011-2013 auxiliaire patriarcal. 2013 MGermany and Central Europe. 22.-28.1.2016 Synaxis of the primates of the Local Orthodox Churches Chambésy Switzerland with p. Porfirio George.

Johannes Haikal
T: B Palmyra, auxiliaire Central Europe ■ ✉ Ludwigsfelderstr. 30, GERMANY-14165 Berlin • [49] 3 8049982-1, fax -0 • hh@rum-orthodox.de • pr.haikal@t-online.de • www.rum-orthodox.de
*7.6.1967 Jouret Arsoun Lebanon. N? 1986 Bachelor Abitur Balamand. 1989-1993 dipl theol Thessaloniki. diak1.12.1995 Lebanon (George Khodr). 1995-1999 Dr. theol Thessaloniki ⊖1.11.1997 Lebanon. 1999 parish priest Berlin Germany ⊕6.8.2011.

Paul Badih Saliba ***Sydney***
T: B Sydney, Exarch Australia and New Zealand ■ ✉ 2 Bampton Ave, AUSTRALIA-Illawong, NSW 2034 • [61] 2 9543-6939, fax -9354 • archbishop@antiochian.org.au • archbishopppaul@bigpond.com • www.antiochian.org.au
*10.7.1939 Bsarma El-Koura Lebanon. N29.6. Orthodox School Amyoun. 1952-1957 Seminary College Balamand. mon1957 Patmos. 1957-1958 Patmos. diak1958. 1958-1961 stud theol Athens, 1962-1963 Thessalonica. 1963-1965 secretary Diocesan Board Tripolis, teacher. 1965-1968 teacher Balamand. archim1966 ⊖1968-1970 St.

Ilyan Bransville Pennsylvania. 1970 BA World Civilisation University Pittsburgh. 1970-1979 rector New Kensington. 1972 BA Education Uni Pittsburgh. 1979-1999 rector Washington, special care Alcohol and Drug Addicts ⊕10.10.1999 Damas B Sydney.

Archdiocese of North America

Joseph Zehlawi ***New York***

T: M New York and All North America ▪ ✉ 358 Mountain Road P.O.Box 5238, USA-Englewood, NJ 07631-5238 • [1] 201 8711355 • archdiocese@antiochian.org • metjoseph@antiochian.org • www.antiochian.org

*2.11.1950 Damascus,N2nd Sunday after Pascha (Joseph of Arimathea). 1970-1974 stud Balamand, diak4.12.1976 Thessaloniki (M Panteleimon Rodopoulos) mon25.12.1980 ⊖1980 Damascus (Patr Ignatius IV) 1980-1991 dean Cathedral Damascus, 1980 MTh Thessaloniki (languages, music). 1983-1986 London, 1986-1991 Cyprus ⊕30.6.1991 Damascus B Katana. 1991-1995 patriarchal assistant, secretary Holy Synod. 1995-2004 auxiliary North America. 2004 B, 11.12.2011 A Los Angeles. 2010 Dr.h.c. St. Tikhon Seminary South Canaan Pennsylvania. 2014 M of All North America.

Nicholas Ozone

T: B vicar Brooklyn, resident Assistant to the Metropolitan ▪ ✉ Mountain Road 358, Post Office Box 5238, USA-Englewood, NJ 07631-5238 • [1] 201 871135-5, -6, fax 8717954 • bpnicholas@antiochian.org • www.antiochian.org

*1.1.1963 Damascus, N6.12. French Lycée Laïque, Omia High School. 1.2.1981 emigrated to USA. Northeastern University Master Science Electrical Engineering, Object-Oriented Design, Architecture, Coding. 2002-2005 MDiv Holy Cross Greek Orthodox School of Theology Brookline, Massachusetts. diak23.4.2004 (M Philip) ⊖9.1.2005 (B Antoun). 2005-2011 parish Fort Lauderdale, Florida. archim14.2.2010 (M Philip) ⊕11.12.2011 B Brookline, Auxiliary North America Monastery of Our Lady Balamand Lebanon. 2016 Doctor of Ministry program at Pittsburgh Theological Seminary.

John Abdullah

T: B Worcester, New England, Auxiliary North America ▪
✉ 2 Lydias Path, USA-Westborough, MA 01581-1841 •
[1] 201 871135-5, -6, fax 8717954 •
archdiocese@antiochian.org • Frjpa@aol.com • www.antiochian.org

*1954 Boston Massachusetts. N? MDiv St. Vladimir's Theological Seminary. BSc Business Administration Suffolk University Boston ⊖1978. 1978-2008 married with Joanne Josephs (†25.5.2008, three children Gregory, Joseph, Maria). 1978-1994 parish New Kensington, 1994-2010 Cathedral Pittsburgh. archim2008 ⊕11.12.2011 Monastery of Our Lady Balamand Lebanon.

Anthony Richard Michaels
T: B Toledo, vicar ▪ ✉ 2635 Manchester Boulevard, USA-Toledo, OH 43606 • [1] 260 615 8777 • bpanthonymichaels@gmail.com • www.antiochian.org
*17.1.1956 Ironwood Michigan Lebanese father, Serbian mother. N? University Michigan, MDiv St. Vladimir's Theological Seminary. diak18.9.2004 ⊖19.9.2004 (B Antoun). 2004-2011 parish Fort Wayne Indiana. archim19.9.2010 ⊕11.12.2011 Monastery of Our Lady Balamand Lebanon.

Thomas Joseph
T: B Charleston, Oakland+Mid-Atlantic, Auxiliary North America ▪ ✉ 4407 Kanawha Ave., S.E., USA-Charleston, WV 25304 • [1] +1 724 787 -9832, [1] 304 346 0146 Cathedral • bpthomasjoseph@gmail.com
*1953 Peterson New Jersey. N6.10. 1974 Department Community Improvements City of Peterson. diak1.7.1988 ⊖28.8.1994. 1994-1996 pastor Houston, 1996-2004 Pinellas Park Florida. 2004 MA Balamand ⊕5.12.2004 Damas B Pittsburgh (Patr Ignatios) 2015 B Charleston.

Alexander Mufarij ***Ottawa***
T: B Ottawa ▪ ✉ 10820 Rue Laverdure, CANADA-Montreal, Quebec H3L2L9 • [1] 514 388 - 4344, fax 514 388 - 4051 • themutran@yahoo.com • www.antiochian.org
*1956 Lebanon. N30.8. stud Boy's school Tripoli, American University Beirut, 1976 biology, M.Business University of North Texas. 1981-1985 Beirut. 1985 manager hospital Washington DC. 1997 St. Vladimir's. diak 9.1.2000 ⊖9.4.2000 pastor Maryland. archim4.7.2004 ⊕5.12.2004 Damas B Ottawa (Patr Ignatios).

Antoun Yssa Khoury ***Miami***
T: B Miami ▪ ✉ 1012 N Ocean Blvd. Apt. 1502, USA-Pompano Beach, FL 33062-4060 • [1] 954 942 2361, Mobile [1] 201 463 9111 • bpantoun@antiochian.org • www.antiochian.org
*17.1.1931 Damascus. N17.1. diak28.10.1951. 1957 dipl theol Balamand. 1957 Brasilia, 1959-1962 MDiv. St. Vladimir's Theological Seminary USA ⊖29.5.1960 Boston, stud St. Vladimir's Theological Seminary. 1962 parish. archim3.8.1969.

1978 Vicar General ⊕4.11.1982 (St. Nicholas Brooklyn NY) B Selevkias, Auxiliary to Metr of North America. 1983-2004 B Englewood. 2004 B Miami.

Basil Essey ***Wichita***
T: B Wichita, Auxiliary to Archdiocese of North America ▪ ✉ 1559 North Woodlawn, USA-Wichita, KS 67208-2429 • [1] 316 6873-169, fax -327 • bpbasil@aol.com • www.antiochian.org
*26.11.1948 Monessen, PA USA. N1.1. 1973 MDiv St. Vladimir's New York. 1975 director department youth. diak30.9.1979 ⊖27.1.1980 Bergenfield NJ. Dean Wichita ⊕31.5.1992 (St. Georges Wichita) B Enfeh al-Koura, Auxiliary to Archdiocese of North America. 2004 B Wichita.

Retired Hierarchs:

Spyridon Khoury
T: M former Helioúpolis (=Zahle) ▪ ✉ Archevêché Grec Orthodoxe, St. Nicolas, LEBANON-Zahle • [961] 8 820527, 806772, [961] 3 806882
*1926 Uberlandia Brazil. N12.12., moved to Beaino Akkar Lebanon. 1955 dipl theol Balamand and Institut St-Serge Paris ⊖1956 -1966 parish of the Dormition in Alexandria, Egypt ⊕26.9.1966 M Zahle. 18.10.2009 jubilee A Nifon. Moskva/Zahle with Dutch ambassadors Daphne (Slowakia) and Jan-Paul (Turkey) Dirkse, M Elia (Tyr), M Antonius Chedraui. 26.6.2015 retired.

Konstantin Papastefanou
T: former M Baghdad+Kuwait ▪ ✉ Archevêché Grec Orthodoxe, LEBANON-Choueifat
*1924 Syria N21.5. stud Athens ⊕17.10.1969-2014 M Baghdad. 2014 moved to Lebanon, retired.

Demetri Khoury
T: B Jableh, retired ▪ ✉ 11241 SW 145 Ave., USA-Miami, FL 33186 • [1] 305 382-2101, 305 505-1314, fax 305 503-6751 • bpdmk5@gmail.com • www.almoutran.com
*20.9.1948 Ramallah. N26.10. stud Balamand, 1974 BA Hellenic College. diak6.9.1975 ⊖7.9.1975. 1975-1983 parishes Boston Massachusetts, Cambridge Massachusetts, Allentown Pennsylvania. 1978 MDiv Holy Cross Brookline. 1978-1988 teacher Practical Theology St. Vladimir's New York. archim1981 (M Philip). 1983-1987 St. Nicholas Cathedral, Brooklyn, New York, the Mother Church of the Archdiocese. 1987-1995 Dean and Pastor Cathedral Coral Gables, Florida ⊕12.3. 1995 Damascus B Jableh (Patr Ignatios IV). 1995-2004 auxiliary North America.

ARMENIAN APOSTOLIC CHURCH

Catholicos of All Armenians **Karekin II.**
Supreme Patriarch and head of the Armenian Apostolic Church
Dzayraguyn Badriark yev Gatoğigos Amenayn Hayotz

Karekin Ktrich Nersissian ***Ararat***
T: A Patriarch Catholicos, Episkoposapet, Supreme Patriarch, A Ararat
▪ ✉ Catholicossate of All Armenians, ARMENIA-1101 Etchmiadzin •
[374] 10 517-100, -133, -122, fax -301, -700 •
holysee@etchmiadzin.am • frvahram@etchmiadzin.am •
www.armenianchurch.org • http://armenianchurch.ca
*21.8.1951 Voskehat Armenia. NVartanans Thursday before Lent. 1965-1971 stud Seminary Etchmiadzin. diak1970. 1971-1972 teacher Seminary Etchmiadzin. mon1972 ⊖1972 Etchmiadzin. 1972-1976 stud Vienna. 1975-1979 pastor Deutschland, stud Bonn. 1979-1980 Academy Moskva. 1980-1983 vicar General Ararat Yerevan. archim1982 Vardapet ⊕23.10.1983 Etchmiadzin. 1989 established in the former Communist Pioneer Palaces the Vaskenian Seminary at Lake Sevan to educate young men in religious studies, completing a five-year course prior to the entrance to the Theological Academy at Holy Etchmiadzin, where they would study for one additional year. 1992 A. 1998-1999 Patriarchal Vicar General, patriarchal Vicar Diocese Ararat (Araradian). 1998 dipl theol Erivan "Hans Küng's Ecumenical Theology". 1999 (132.) Patriarch Catholicos. 2000 "The Star of Romania". 2006 Summit Religious leaders Moskva.

Aršak Samuel Khatchatrian
T: B vicar, Chancellor of the Mother See, Member Supreme Spiritual Council ▪ ✉ Catholicossate of All Armenians, ARMENIA-1101 Etchmiadzin • [374] 10 517-119, office -118, [374] 91 204808 •
divanatun@etchmiadzin.am
*5.8.1973 Voskehat Armavir. N? 1980-1990 school Voskehat. 1990-1996 Gevorkian Theol Seminary Etchmiadzin. diak19.5.1996. 1996-1997 secretariat Divan. 1997 graduated "The Indo-Armenian Colony" ⊖14.12.1997 "Aršak". 1998-1999 administration, 1999 Acting Editor in Chief "Etchmiadzin". 2001 Chancellor. archim22.2.2001Vardapet. 2004 Dzairaguin Vardapet "Episcopal power in the Armenian Church" ⊕26.9.2004 Etchmiadzin (Patr Karekin).

Ararat Hagob Kaltakčian
T: B ▪ ✉ Catholicossate of All Armenians, ARMENIA-1101 Etchmiadzin
• araratsrpazan@gmail.com

*11.12.1962 Hatchn Beirut. NVartanans Thursday before Lent. 1977-1978 Seminary Antelias. 1979-1985 Seminary Etchmiadzin, dipl "Published texts of Armenian ancient bibliography" diak1985 Damascus ⊖20.4.1986 Damascus. archim1988 (A Nerses Bozabalian) Vardapet. 1990 parish Toronto, 1993 Montréal, stud St. Nerses Theol Seminary New York, St. Vladimir's. 1999 Dzairaguin Vardapet. 2006 Armenia ⊕19.11.2006 Etchmiadzin. 2006-2011 Grand Sacristan, Dean Monasteries Mother See.

Navasart Samuel Kjojan

T: A vicar General Araratian Diocese Erivan, Member Supreme Spiritual Council ▪ ✉ Israelian St. No. 21, ARMENIA-0010 Erivan • [374] 10 587-505, -506, -368, 584722, fax 374-10-151040 • press@araratian-tem.am • www.araratian-tem.am • www.mypriest.araratian-tem.am

*18.9.1957 Erivan. NVartanans Thursday before Lent. 1981-1985 Seminary Etchmiadzin. diak1984 ⊖7.6.1987. 1989 Vardapet. parish Oshakan. Honorary citizen 1991 Oshakan, 1995 Albertville France. 1996-1999 Primate Aragadzodn ⊕15.6.1997 Etchmiadzin, 1999 Vicar General Araratian. 2000 Russian Academy Natural Sciences. Member Supreme Council. 2001 International Economical Academy Italia, Golden Hercules Malta. 2002 Dr.h.c. National Academy Armenia, Scientist Association Hannover Germany. 2003 Prof Erivan. 2006 A vicar General Araratian Diocese Erivan, Member Supreme Spiritual Council.

Hovakim Vardkes Manukian ***London***

T: Primate Great Britain ▪ ✉ St. Sarkis Iverna Gardens Kensington, GREAT BRITAIN-London, W8 6TP • [44] 20 7937-0152, fax -9049 • bphovakim@gmail.com • artikitem@gmail.com • prmoff@armeniandiocese.org

*19.10.1976 Voskehat Armenia. 1983-1989 school Voskehat. 1994-1999 Vaskenian Academy Lake Sevan. 1998 Ecumenical School Bossey. 1999-2000 Gevorkian Theol Seminary Etchmiadzin. diak16.7.2000 (A Mesrop Grigorian). 2000-2015 Inter Church Relations Office. 2005-2015 Director. teacher Church History Gevorkian Seminary and Vaskenian Academy ⊖22.11.2001 (A Voskan Galpakian) thesis "Extracts from the History of the Coptic Orthodox Church". 2001 Diaconal School Aarhus. 2002-2004 stud Academy Moskva. 2004-2009 Church and Society commission CEC. archim23.4.2006 Vardapet (A Yeznik Petrosian) "Ecumenism in the 20th Century and the Armenian Church". 2008-2009 stud Yerevan University School of Political Studies. 2009 Central Committee CEC ⊕18.4.2010 Etchmiadzin. scholarship fr. Andreas Hayk. 2012-2015 Primate Artik. 2015 Primate Great Britain A London.

Artak Gegham Tigranian
T: B Dean Monasteries ▪ ✉ Catholicossate of All Armenians, ARMENIA-1101 Etchmiadzin • [374] 10 517321, [374] 231 46458 • 58755sb.vanorayq@gmail.com
*12.4.1971 Dimitrov Artashat Armenia. NVartanans Thursday before Lent. 1988-1994 Theol Seminary Etchmiadzin, dipl "Exaltation of the Holy Cross". diak28.12. 1993. 1994-1995 director Manoogian Museum ⊖23.7.1995-1999 secretary to Karekin I. archim10.10.1999 Vardapet "Catholicos Karekin I." 1999-2000 Paris. 2001-2005 Grand Sacristan. 2006-2008 Primate Gugarq. 2009 Dean of Monasteries ⊕18.4.2010 Etchmiadzin.

Vertanes Kamo Abrahamian
T: B Chaplain General of the Armed Forces Republic Armenia ▪ ✉ St. Bagrevandi 5, ARMENIA-0010 Erivan • [374] 10 294438, [374] 98 788 887 • srbvrtanes@mail.ru • armchaplain@mail.ru
*21.3.1962 Nagorno Karabach. N son of Gregor the Enlightener. 1980-1987 Theol Seminary Etchmiadzin. 1981-1983 Soviet Army. 1987 Museum Etchmiadzin. diak25.12.1987. 1988 dipl "The Brief History of the Aghvank Church in the IV-XVII centuries" ⊖22.5.1988 Pentecost. 1988-1994 abbot Artsakh Nagorno Karabach. 1994-1996 vicar diocese Artsakh. 1996-2001 abbot St. Hripsime Armenia. 1997-1999 Chaplain Armed Forces. 2001-2006 pastor Gougark Tavuš. 2006-2007 vicar New Nakhičevan in Rostov. 2007 Chaplain General Armed Forces ⊕24.8.2008 Etchmiadzin.

Mkrtich Hayk Prošian ***Aragatsotn***
T: B Primate of Aragatsotn ▪ ✉ Catholicossate of All Armenians, ARMENIA-1101 Etchmiadzin • [374] 32 36150 • aragacotnitem@mail.ru
*13.8.1975 Vagharšabat Armenia. N St. John Baptist. 1993-1998 Vaskenian Academy Lake Sevan. 1998-2000 Seminary Etchmiadzin. diak23.5.1999 ⊖14.1.2001. 2001-2004 MA Leeds and Cardiff "Classical Redemption and Feminist Theology". 2005-2008 Dean Lake Sevan. archim2006 Vardapet. 2008-2009 Philadelphia USA ⊕18.4.2010 Locum tenens Aragatsotn.

Mikayel Kevork Adžabahyan ***Shirak***
T: B, Primate of Shirak ▪ ✉ St. Mary's Church, ARMENIA-3101 Gyumri • [374] 312 31621, 23777, fax 22511 • shirakdiocese@gmail.com
*27.12.1963 Leninakan Gyumri. N? 1981-1987 Theol Seminary Etchmiadzin. diak25.12.1986. 1988 graduation thesis ⊖22.5.1988 vicesacristan Etchmiadzin. 1989 Abbot Holy Cross Yeghegnadzor, Abbot Ganzasar Monastery Artsakh. 1989 doctoral thesis, hegumen, archimVartaped. 1994 Dz. Vartaped. 1995-1997 stud

Istituto Orientale Roma, 1997-1999 secretary Interchurch Relations. 2000-2001 Locum tenens Shirak ⊕30.9.2001 B Shirak.

Narek Arshavir Shakarian ***Gyumri***
T: B Gyumri ▪ ✉ St. Mary's Church, ARMENIA-3101Gyumri • [374] 312 31621, 23777, fax 22511 • shirakdiocese@gmail.com
*2.8.1932 Damascus NSt. Mesrob. 1957 Etchmiadzin ⊖25.10.1962 Mother See. 1967-1972 spiritual Mon Gegard, director Museum. 1971 vicar General Shirak ⊕30.9.1973 Etchmiadzin. 1973-1991 Primate Shirak, Primate Diocese Russia and New Nakhichevan. 1993-1996 Vicar Paris. 1996-2013 Nice. 2013 Gyumri.

Abraham Mgrdičian ***Vajos Dsor***
T: B Primate of Vayk ▪ ✉ St. Gregory the Illuminator Church, Grigor Tatevatzi, ARMENIA-377830 Goris • [374] 931 408518 • abm72@mail.ru
*1960 N? ⊖1987 ⊕15.6.1997. 2000 member Supreme Spiritual Council of the Armenian Apostolic Orthodox Church. 2011 B Vayk.

Georg Arman Saroyan
T: B, Dean Fac theol St. Georges Etchmiadzin ▪ ✉ Catholicossate of All Armenians, ARMENIA-1101 Etchmiadzin • [374] 10 517-100, -133, -122, fax -301, -700 • holysee@etchmiadzin.am • frkevork@yahoo.com
*1977 Masis Armenia Nsaturday before last Sunday in September. diak1999 ⊖2001. 2002-2003 stud Psychology Philosophy Concordia College New York. 2003-2004 BTh theol pastoral, 2005-2006 MTh Oxford. 2008-2010 rector Theol school Vasken Armenia. 2010 Vardapet, Dean Fac theol St. Georges. Etchmiadzin ⊕6.11.2011 Etchmiadzin.

Armen Nelson Museg Babajan
T: B, Director Administration Etchmiadzin ▪ ✉ Catholicossate of All Armenians, ARMENIA-1101 Etchmiadzin • [374] 10 517-100, -133, -122, fax -301, -700 • holysee@etchmiadzin.am • varchatntesakan1@etchmiadzin.am
*1978 Datev Armenia. NVartanans Thursday before Lent. diak2000. 2000 master of ceremonies Katholikos ⊖2002. 2002-2006 stud Moskva. 2006-2007 stud Pont Università Salesiana Roma. 2007-2008 director finances Etchmiadzin. 2009 director administration Etchmiadzin ⊕6.11.2011 Etchmiadzin.

Hovnan Arthur Hakobian
T: B, Grand Sacristan Etchmiadzin ▪ ✉ Catholicossate of All Armenians, ARMENIA-1101 Etchmiadzin • [374] 10 517-100, -133, -122, fax -301, -700 • holysee@etchmiadzin.am • hovnanhakobyan@gmail.com

*1978 Gyumri Armenia. N? diak2002 ⊖2003. 2006-2011 private secretary to the Katholikos. 2008 master of ceremonies, 2011 Grand Sacristan Etchmiadzin ⊕6.11.2011 Etchmiadzin.

Mesrop Barsamian ***Geneva***

T: vicar of Switzerland ▪ ✉ 2 Chemin Lullin, Troinex, SUISSE-1256 Genève • [41]22 -431370, fax 3004418 • www.armenianchurch.org

*1952 Aleppo Syria. N? ⊖1973. stud King's College London, St. Andrews Scotland, Columbia University New York. Vice Chancellor of the Mother See of Holy Etchmiadzin. 1995-2000 Dean Seminary Etchmiadzin. 2000-2011 parishes England, USA, citizen USA. 26.3.2011 St. Mesrop Mashtots Church in Oshakan Vardapet (B Anushavan Zhamkochian) "Being God – the three phases of the divinization of a man according to the doctrine of St. Nerses the Graceful". 1.4.2011 Patriarchal Delegate Switzerland. Vice Chancellor of the Mother See of Holy Etchmiadzin.

Karekin Dikran Bekdjiyan ***Köln***

T: A Köln, Primate of Germany ▪ ✉ Allensteiner Str. 5, GERMANY-50735 Köln • [49] 221 71262-23, fax -67 • info@armenische-kirche.de * www.armenische-kirche.de

*12.12.1942 İstanbul. NVartanans Thursday before Lent. 1959 Mittlere Reife Wiener Mechitarist in İstanbul. 1962 Abitur Surp Khatch Tıbrevank Üsküdar Holy Cross Seminary Armenian Patriarchate of Constantinople. 1962-1965 stud Uni İstanbul Sociology, History, and Holy Cross Seminary. diak1963 ⊖25.7.1965 (Patr Shnork Kalustian – "Karekin" Hatchedurian Patr İstanbul 1950-1961, founder Holy Cross Seminary). 1965-1972 stud Bonn Bochum Pädagogik, Psychologie. archim1970 Vardapet. 1973-1991 Marseille paroisse Surp Gerabet, Sırpotz Tarkman čatz. 1991 Primate ⊕27.9.1992 Etchmiadzin. 1992 B, 1998 A Deutschland.

Silouan Oner ***British Isles***

T: M British Isles and Ireland ▪ ✉ St. George's Cathedral, 1A Redhill St/Albany St, GREAT BRITAIN-London, NW1 4BG • [44] 207 383 0403, [44] 01507 358487 • orthodox@btinternet.com • fr.s.gholam@antiochianorth.co.uk • www.almanarah.net/wp

*21.8.1970. 1989-1994 Mechanical Engineering Tishreen University, Lattakia. 1995-2000 MTh St. John Damascus Institute, Balamand, Lebanon. 2000-2015 parishes Lattakia ⊖2000 archim. 2001-2003 director orthodox Youth Movement Lattakia. 2005-2010 Dr. theol Ethics University Thessaloniki. 2010-2015 councillor Metropolitan John Mansour, abbot St. George ⊕30.8.2015 B British Isles and Ireland. 22.-28.1.2016 Synaxis of the primates of the Local Orthodox Churches Chambésy Switzerland.

Khajak Sarkis Barsamian ***New York***
T: A, Primate of Armenian Church of Eastern USA ▪ ✉ 630 Second Ave, USA-New York, NY 10016-4806 • [1] 212 686071-0, -1, fax 4476674, 7793558 • primoff@armeniandiocese.org • primate@armeniandiocese.org • www.armenianchurch.net
*4.7.1951 Arapkir Turkey NVartanans Thursday before Lent. mon1972 Jerusalem ⊖1972 Jerusalem. stud Patrology St. John's University Collegeville Minnesota. 1983-1986 stud Liturgy Istituto Orientale Roma ⊕7.10.1990 Etchmiadzin. 1990 Dr. theol Erivan. 1993 A New York. 2000 Supreme Spiritual Council. 2002 Dr.h.c. Seton Hall Catholic University East Orange. 2011 International Joint Commission Theol Dialogue between Catholic and Oriental Orthodox Churches.

Vicken Aykazian ***Washington***
T: A, Director Ecumenical Relations Armenians USA, Diocesan Legate in Washington ▪ ✉ 122 C St. NW, Suite 360, USA-Washington, DC 2001 • [1] 703 671-9200, fax -8400 • avicken@aol.com
*1951 Siirt Turkey. NVartanans Thursday before Lent. school Üsküdar İstanbul, Seminary Jerusalem. diak1968 ⊖1971. 1971 Jerusalem. 1972-1974 teacher Seminary translator Jerusalem. 1974-1975 assistant to Patriarch Shnork İstanbul. 1975-1980 King's College London. 1976 Vardapet Jerusalem. 1980-1992 Geneva delegate to WCC, stud theol Fac theol Fribourg. 1985-1991 Central Committee WCC. 1990 Dzairaguin Vardapet Jerusalem ⊕27.9.1992 Etchmiadzin. 1992-1996 B Geneva. MTh King's College London. 1996-1999 Fund Armenian Relief USA Etchmiadzin. 2000 Director Ecumenical Relations Armenians USA, Diocesan Legate. 2006 A, Summit Religious leaders Moskva.

Hovnan Vahram Derderian ***California***
T: A, Primate of Armenian Church of Western Diocese USA. Member Supreme Spiritual Council ▪ ✉ 3325 North Glenoaks Blvd., USA-Burbank, CA 91504 • [1] 213 4665265, fax 4667612, [1] 818 558-7474, fax -6333, -8333 • mgizlechyan@armenianchwd.com • armenianchwd@earthlink.net • www.armenianchwd.com
*1.12.1957 Beirut. Jonas Seminary: 1970-1975 Antelias, 1975 Etchmiadzin ⊖1980. 1980 Oxford BA, 1983 lecturer history Etchmiadzin. 1984-1990 Vardapet, parish Toronto. 1987 MTh Theology. 1987 Dzairaguin Vardapet ⊕7.10.1990 Etchmiadzin B Montreal. 1993 A Montreal Primate of the Canadian Diocese. 2003 eighth A Western diocese since 1927.

Nathan Samvel Hovhannisianan
T: A ▪ ✉ Catholicossate of All Armenians, ARMENIA-1101 Etchmiadzin • [374] 10 517-100, -133, -122, fax -301, -700 • divanatun@etchmiadzin.am • hbishopnathan@aol.com
*9.5.1955 Erivan. NBartholomaios 12 Apostels. 1980 graduated Komitas State Conservatory Jerevan. 1984-1987 Gevorkian Seminary Etchmiadzin. diak1988 ⊖7.6.1988.1989 Vardapet "Shepherd of Hermas", teacher Patristics Gevorkian Seminary, vice-dean. 1991-2000 Locum tenens and Primate Ukraina. 1994 Dzairaguin Vardapet "Petros Qutur and his Anthology of Theology". 1995 Medal "Prince Daniel of Moscou" ⊕15.6.1997 Etchmiadzin. 1997-2000 member Supreme Spiritual Council. 2000-2010 Primate Great Britain. 2001-2006 President Commission Oriental Orthodox Churches. 2001 Order of Merit Ukraina. 2006-2010 Co-President Council of Churches England. 2006 honorary citizen Bethlehem. 2006 A. 2010-2013 Director Publishing Center Etchmiadzin. 2013 fourth Primate Canada. 2014 director External relations and protocol department Etchmiadzin.

Epiphani Ghattas Hazim ***Baghdad***
T: M Baghdad+Kuwait ▪ ✉ Archevêché Grec Orthodoxe, P.O.Box 35218, IRAQ-Baghdad • [964] 1 66228 • KUWAIT-Salmya, [965] 2 561 7367, fax 2 563 1538 • Ave Roosevelt 103, IRAN-Teheran, [98] 21 826764 • Dubai [971] 4464578, Abu Dhabi • b.ghattas@antiochpat.com • arch@gulforthodoxchurch.org • www.gulforthodoxchurch.org
*1963 Mhardeh Syria, N6.1. nephew of patriarch Ignatiıs Hazim. stud Balamand. diak1988 ⊖1.11.1989 archim1.11.1989. 1990 vicar Hama 1995 Abbot St. George Mhardeh, head Christian Education Department Hama ⊕26.10.1999 B Qara vicar patriarcal. Dean Institute Balamand. 2000 hegoumenos Balamand. 2014 M Baghdad, Kuwait.

Kissak Manug Mouradian ***Buenos Aires***
T: A Buenos Aires, Primate of Argentina ▪ ✉ Armenia Acevedo 1369, ARGENTINA-1414 Buenos Aires • [54] 11 4772-3558, -2261, -2326, fax 47762810 • kissagm@yahoo.com
*1951 Aleppo NVartanans Thursday before Lent ⊖1971 Abbot St. Saviour's Monastery Jerusalem ⊕7.10.1990 Etchmiadzin. 1993 A Buenos Aires. 2000 member Supreme Spiritual Council of the Armenian Apostolic Orthodox Church.

Narek Vasken Berberian ***Brazil***
T: B Primate Brazil ▪ ✉ Avenida Santos Dumont 55, BRAZIL-0110-1000 São Paulo • [55] 11 228-5239, -8597, fax 227-0896 • holysee@etchmiadzin.am • vberberian@hotmail.com www.armenianchurch.org

*28.10.1967 Beirut. 1981 graduated Vahan Tekeyan School Beirut. diak1986. 1987 graduated Gevorkian Seminary "The study of Job, by St. Gregory of Tatev". 1990 MDiv St. Vladimir's New York, St. Nersess Armenian Seminary. 1991-1992 grand sacristan St. Vartan New York. 1992 MTh General Theol Seminary New York. 1992-1993 parish Houston ⊖26.7.1992. 1994-2000 parish Richmond, Dr. theol Union Theological Seminary. 1994 archim. 2000-2002 parish Hartford CT. 2003-2013 parish Bica Raton. 2013-2014 vicar general Brazil ⊕16.11.2014 Primate Brazil.

Hakob Hakob Kelendjian ***Montevideo***
T: A Montevideo ▪ ✉ Av. Agraciada 2842, URUGUAY-11800 Montevideo • [598] 2 2090165, p 2081247, fax 2037900, [598] 99 616288 • kessab@adinet.com.uy • diocesisarmenia@adinet.com.uy
*17.12.1955 Kessab Syria Krichilian. NSt. Jakob of Nisibis. 1968-1972 Theol Seminary Catholicossate Cilicia. 1973-1975 stud theol Etchmiadzin. diak1974 ⊖14.11.1976. 1976-1978 Etchmiadzin. 1978-1983, 1992 Jubilee, August 1999, September 2006 Ostkirchliches Institut Regensburg. archim1980 Vardapet, 1985 Dzairaguin Vardapet. 1983-1984 Etchmiadzin. 1984 Locum tenens Armenian Diocese Uruguay and General Director Nersissian School ⊕7.10.1990 Etchmiadzin. 2001 A Montevideo, Primate Uruguay.

Haigazun Vrej Najarian ***Sydney***
T: A Sydney, Primate of Australia+New Zealand ▪ ✉ P.O.Box 694, Chatswood, AUSTRALIA-Sydney, NSW 2067 • [61] 2 9938 4816 prelacy, 9419-8056 office, -6394 assistant, fax 94131709 • primate@armenian.com.au • teravetis@yahoo.com
*1952 in Aleppo Syria NVartanans Thursday before Lent. 1967 dipl school Vahan Tekeyan and Hovakimian-Manoukian Beirut. 1967-1973 Gevorkian Theol Seminary Etchmiadzin "Mkhitar Gosh Interpretation of the Prophet Yeremia". diak1973 Etchmiadzin (A Husik Santurian). 1973-1974 Chancellery Etchmiadzin. 1974-1979 stud Kings College London, St. Andrews Scotland ⊖1975 St. Sarkis London, A Nerses Pozapalian. 1979-1981 parish London. 1981-1986 teacher NT and Church History, Dean Seminary Etchmiadzin. archim1986 Vardapet "The Origin of the monastic movement in Armenia", Dz. Vardapet "The rules of St. Barsegh Kesaratsi". 1986-1988 vicar general Eastern USA. 1988-1991 parish New Jersey. 1991-1995 vicar general Eastern USA. 1993 MA History Columbia University New York. 1995-1999 teacher NT and Church History, Dean Seminary Etchmiadzin. 2000-2010 parishes England, citizen USA, 2000-2002 parish St. Sargis Dallas USA. 2001-2010 vicar general Eastern USA. 2002-2007 parish St. Sahak-St. Mesrop Philadelphia USA. 2010-2012 Patriarchal Delegate Austria Czechia Denmark Finland Hungary Norway Slovakia Sweden ⊕6.11.2011 Etchmiadzin. 2013 Primate Australia.

Bagrat Vazgen Galsdanian ***Tavush***
T: A Tavush ▪ ✉ Catholicossate of All Armenians, ARMENIA-1101 Etchmiadzin • [374] 10 517-321, office -214 • dprevank@gmail.com
*20.5.1971 Gyumri Armenia. NVartanans Thursday before Lent. 1988-1991 Seminary Etchmiadzin. 1991-1995 Fac theol Erivan. diak1994 ⊖23.7.1995 (Karekin I.) 1995-1998 editor Journal Etchmiadzin. 1998-2000 stud Leeds England, pastor Manchester. 2000-2002 dean Seminary Sevan. 2002-2003 primate Aragadzodn ⊕22.6.2003 (Etchmiadzin). 2003-2013 third primate Canada. 2013 Etchmiadzin. 2015 A Tavush.

Abgar Samvel Hovakimya ***Canada***
T: B ▪ ✉ 615 Stuart Ave, CANADA-Outremont, H2V 3H2 • [1] 514 2769479 • canarmdiocese@gmail.com
*23.7.1972 Batumi Georgia Kaukasus. 1979-1989 Stepan Shahumyan Armenian School Batumi. 1989-1995 Gevorkian Seminary Etchmiadzin "Reflections of the Armenian Doctrinal Concept in the interpretation of Matthew" diak1995 ⊖2.6.1996. 1996-2001 parish Ajaria Georgia. 2001-2006 MTh Salzburg Austria "Armenian-Latin ecclesiastical relations". 2004-2005 vicar general Georgia. 2005-2010 vicar general Syunik. archim1.5.2006. 2006 Dr. theol "Dionysios Areopagita in Armenian Bibliography". 2010-2011 stud Canada. 2011-2014 Locum tenens Bulgaria ⊕16.11.2014 Fifth primate Canada.

Vardan Aristakes Navasardyan
T: B ▪ ✉ Catholicossate of All Armenians, ARMENIA-1101 Etchmiadzin • frvardan@yahoo.com
*4.8.1979 Yerevan. 1986-1996 Russian school Yerevan. 1996-1997 Spiritual Academy Shirak. 1997-2002 Gevorkian Theol Seminary Etchmiadzin. diak25.12. 2001 Mother Cathedral of Holy Etchmiadzin (B Michael Ajapahyan). 2002-2005 assistant Grand Sacristan Etchmiadzin ⊖27.2.2003 (A Parkev Martirosyan). 2005-2008 Sydney. 2009 director Christian Education Center, coordinator Armenian Academy Kolkata West Bengal, dean Eurnekian public school Etchmiadzin, Kindergarten Armavir. archim1.2.2013.Dr. theol "Christian Education in the Third Republic", Gold Metal of the Ministry of Culture Armenia ⊕10.11.2014. 2014 Movses Khorenatsi medal Republic Armenia President Serzh Sarkisian.

Vahan Hovhannisyan ***France***
T: A France ▪ ✉ 15, rue Jean-Goujon, FRANCE-75008 Paris • [33] 143596703 • primate@armenianchurch.co.uk
*1.1.1963 Baghdad Iraq. 1969-1979 school Baghdad. 1979-1985 stud Electric Engeneering University Baghdad. 1985-1990 dipl theol St. Nersses Seminary, St.

Vladimir's Seminary New York "The Council of Shahapivan". diak1987 (A Khajag Barsamian) ⊖1990.1990-1991 parishes Baghdad and Mossul. 1992-1999 parishes New York. archim1994. 1998 Dr. theol Fordham University "Third Corinthians". 1999-2014 visiting prof Biblical Studies. 2006 Dzajragujn Vardapet "Coptic reading – New Testament Apokrypha". 2009-2015 Primate Great Britain ⊕6.11.2011. 2015 Primate France.

Arakel Elbek Karamian ***Kotaik***

T: B Kotaik ▪ ✉ Episkoposat Tsaghkadzor, ARMENIA-2301 Kotaik • [374] 223 60629, 22113, 22891, [374] 93 408130 • kecharis1@hrazdan.am

*20.7.1963 Jeranos Martuni, N12 Apostle. 1979-1985 stud pedagogics. 1980-1989 dipl Gevorkian Theol Seminary Etchmiadzin "Interpretation of John the prophet according to Catholicos Asetsi Ajapahian 1809-1831". 1982-1984 Soviet Army. diak12.5.1988 (Husik Santurian) ⊖15.7.1989. 1989-1993 parishes Sisian Kotaik, vicar Siunik diocese Goris. 1993-1996 rector Seminary Sevan, vicar Araratian diocese. archim1994 Vardapet "All the Evil is torturous according to Arakel of Siunik". 1995 Ostkirchliches Institut Regensburg.1996 Primate Kotaik ⊕15.6.1997 B Kotaik.

Sebuh Haik Tshuldzhian ***Kukark***

T: A Kukark ▪ ✉ Surp Astvatzazin, ARMENIA-2001 Vanadzor • [374] 322 20386, 53507 • gugaracterm@rambler.ru

*24.3.1959 Malatya Turkey, N Vartanans Thursday before Lent. 1969 Gyumri. 1979-1981 Soviet Army. 1980-1985 Theol Seminary Etchmiadzin. diak1985. 1985-1986 secretary to the Catholicos Patriarch ⊖7.6.1987. 1987-1988 teacher Seminary. 1989-1990 Geneva. 1990-1996 vicar general Gyumri. archim1996 administrator, Dzaraguin Vardapet ⊕15.6.1997 Kukark.

Sion Robert Adamian ***Armavir***

T: B Armavir ▪ ✉ Surp Grigor Lusavoric 22 Har-Dos 1, ARMENIA-0901 Armavir • [374] 31 48016, [374] 91 401402 • armavir_tem@yahoo.com

*20.9.1963 Abadan Iran, N Vartanans Thursday before Lent. 1970 Etchmiadzin. 1978-1980 Soviet Army. 1980-1985 Theol Seminary Etchmiadzin ⊖1987 (Nerses Bozabalian). 1987-1998 pastor Varna Bulgaria. archim1992 Vardapet. 1998-2000 Ararat diocese. 2000 vicar general Kegharkunik ⊕29.9.2001 B Armavir.

Markos Hovhannissian ***Ukraina***

T: B Ukraina ▪ ✉ vul. Armenian 27/4, UKRAINA-79008 Lviv • [380] 322 742956 • gavartem@yahoo.com • ukrhaytem@ukr.net

*1973 Bardzrashen Ararat, N4 Evangelists. 1977 secondary school Vagharshabad Etchmiadzin. 1990-1996 Seminary Etchmiadzin. diak1996 (B Anania Arabadjian).

1996-1998 Alex and Marie Manoogian Treasury House Etchmiadzin. 1998-2000 spiritual councillor army chaplaincy program ⊖29.2.2000 (A Shahe Ajemian). 2000-2001 assistant to the primate of Russia. 2001-2005 pastor Rīga, stud St. Tikhon University Moskva. archim2005 Vardapet "Inscriptions from the viewpoint of ecclesiastical studies". Locum tenens Kegharkunik ⊕19.11.2006 Etchmiadzin B Kegharkunik. 2015 Primate Ukraina.

Anushavan Andranik Jamkotchian

T: B Dean Theol Fac State University ▪ ✉ 52 Abovian St, ARMENIA-0001 Erivan • [374] 1 522458, 583159 • ysufth@arminco.com • a.a.zhamkochyan@gmail.com

*1971 Vagharshapat Etchmiadzin, NVartanans Thursday before Lent. 1976 Vahan Rshtuni school Vagharshapat. 1989-1994 dipl theol Seminary Etchmiadzin "Movses Jughayetsi's Collection of Philology". diak1993. 1994-1998 Komitas state conservatory Jerevan, teacher liturgical music Seminary Etchmiadzin ⊖1995. 1998-2000 Protestant College Halle Germany. 2000 Martin Luther Universität Halle-Wittenberg Germany. archim2001 Vardapet "Komitas and the Armenian Church". 2002-2004 Dr. theol Universität Bonn Germany. 2003 Kanonistisches Institut Münster Germany "Grundzüge des armenischen Kirchenrechts 4. bis 20. Jahrhundert". 2004 dean Cathedral Jerevan ⊕19.11.2006 Etchmiadzin (Patr Karekin II.) Dean Theol Fac Jerevan State University.

Pargev Gourgen Martirossian ***Karabagh***

T: A Artsakh Karabagh ▪ ✉ 11 Kazanchetsots St., ARMENIA-9750 Shushi • [374] 1 58 12 32, [374] 1 28 69 17 • arran123@mail.ru

*20.3.1954 Sumgait Azerbeidjan, NVartanants Thursday before Lent. 1971-1972 Erevan Karl Marx Politechnikum. 1972-1976 V. Briusov Institute Russian Studies. 1976-1979 teacher Oktembrian. 1980-1985 stud theol Etchmiadzin ⊖8.9.1985. 1985-1986 stud theol Leningrad. 1986-1987 teacher Seminary Etchmiadzin. archim4.4.1987 Vardapet Etchmiadzin.1987-1988 igumen St. Hripsime Monastir ⊕13.11.1988. 1989 B, 1999 A Nagorny Karabagh. 1993 Supreme Spiritual Council Armenian Church. 2006 Summit Religious leaders Moskva. 20.11.2011 Burbank.

Avak Vazgen Asadurian ***Baghdad***

T: A Baghdad ▪ ✉ Younis El-Sabawi Sq., P.O.Box 2280 Jadrıya, IRAQ-Baghdad • [964] 1 815185-3, -6, fax -7 • iraqitem@yahoo.com

*26.2.1942 Baghdad, NVartanans Thursday before Lent. 1970 BA Philosophy Illinois Benedictine College Lisle. 1972 MA Philosophy Tulane University New Orleans. diak1974. 1976 MDiv St. Vladimir's Seminary ⊖29.5.1977 archim1978 ⊕14.2.1982 Etchmiadzin B, 1993 A Baghdad. 1995-1998 Dr. phil Università S. Croce Roma "Al Ghazali +1111".

Vozgan Jirair Kalpakian
T: A ▪ ✉ Catholicossate of All Armenians, ARMENIA-1101 Etchmiadzin • [374] 10 517-0 • vosskan@gmail.com • archvosskan@onebox.com
*12.10.1942 Beirut. 1947-1957 Forty Martyrs. Armenian National School and Eshreli National Secondary College. 1957-1960 chemists apprentice apothecary. 1960-1964 Gevorkian Theol Seminary Etchmiadzin. diak1963 (A Haigazun Abrahamyan) ⊖10.1.1965 (A Asoghik Ghazaryan) visiting priest Melbourne Australia. archim1967. 1968-1972 vicar general Australia, Vardapet. 1970 Dzajraguin Vardapet (A Haigazun Abrahamyan). 1973-1994 Primate Damascus. 1977 Armenian Church becomes member CEC: delegate ⊕14.2.1982 B Etchmiadzin (Patr Vazken I.). 1994-2010 Primate Greece. 1997 European Ecumenical Assembly Graz. 2006 Summit Religious Leaders Moskva.

Datev Hratch Hagopian ***Romania***
T: B Romania ▪ ✉ str. Armeneasca 9, ROMANIA-021042 Bucureşti • [40] 21 6140208, 6121083 • arhiepiscopie@armeni.ro • bishopdatev@armeni.ro
*7.7.1966 Mossul,NVartanans Thursday before Lent. 1972-1979 school Baghdad. 1979-1986 stud theol Etchmiadzin. diak15.2.1986 (Husik Santurian). 1986-1987 deacon Iraq. 1988-1990 stud Geneva "Eusebios of Caesarea in old armenian literature". 1990-1993 Netherlands ⊖18.2.1993 Baghdad (Aak Asadurian). 1993-1996 teacher Baghdad. 1996-1997 redactor İstanbul and Etchmiadzin. 1997-2004 parishes France. 1999 Dr. theol Vardapet Lyon. 2004-2010 parishes Netherlands. 2010 Primate Bucuresti ⊕6.11.2011.

Vazgen Edward Mirzakhanian ***Georgia***
T: B Georgia ▪ ✉ Somchuri Eklesia Samgebros 5, GEORGIA-0105 Tbilisi • [995] 32 754111, [995] 99 413474 • armenian_diocese@yahoo.com • www.armenia.ge
*21.7.1965 Artimed Atarbekian Vagharshapat Etchmiadzin, NVartanans Thursday before Lent. 1971-1982 school Artimed. 1982-1990 Gevorkian Theol Seminary Etchmiadzin "The life and literary heritage of Archmandrite Grigor Skearatsi". 1984-1986 Soviet Army. 7.5.1989 diak (A Husik Santurian) ⊖21.7.1991 (A Nerses Bozabalian). 1991-1993 lecturer Gevorkian Seminary. 1993-1999 director center for Christian Education. archim20.6.1996 Vardapet (Karekin I.) Dr. theol "The Quotation sources of the books Hartsmants ... by St. Gregory of Datev". 1999 director WCC Ecumenical Information Center Yerevan. 1999-2001 vicar ot the diocese Aragatsotn. 4.9.2002 Primate of Georgia ⊕23.7.2003 Etchmiadzin (Patr Karekin II.) B Georgia.

Ashot Mnatsakanian ***Egypt***

T: B Egypt and All Afrika ▪ ✉ Ramses Ave. 179 P.B. 48 Faggada, EGYPT-Cairo • [20] 2 2590-1385, -4219, fax -6671 • armpatrcai@yahoo.com

*4.11.1972 Tatev Siunik, N Vatamams Thursday before Lent. 1989-1995 BA Gevorkian Theol Seminary Etchmiadzin. diak1.10.1995. 1995-1996 director Manuscript Treasury Etchmiadzin ⊖1.6.1996. 1996-2001 director "1700 Anniversary Proclamation of Christianity as the State Religion of Armenia". archim2002 Vardapet. 2002-2004 vicar general Cairo. 2004 Primate Egypt ⊕15.1.2006 Primate Egypt.

Movses Kamo Movsisian ***South Russia***

T: B South Russia ▪ ✉ Turgenjeva 165, ROSSIJA-350002 Krasnodar • [7] 612 442957, 263217 • eparhiya@ctf-kuban.ru

*13.9.1964 Goght Abovian Armenia. 1970-1981 school Goght. 1982-1989 Theol Seminary Etchmiadzin. 1983-1985 Soviet Army. diak7.5.1989 (Hussik Santurian) ⊖28.7.1991 (Nerses Bozabalian). 1991 Kandidat Akad Moskva. 1991-1999 parish St. Harotyoun Moskva. archim23.6.1996 Vardapet. 1999-2001 vicar general South Russia ⊕30.9.2001 B South Russia.

Armash Hagop Nalbandian ***Damascus***

T: B Damascus ▪ ✉ St. Sarkis Bab Sharki P.O.Box 2059, SYRIA-Damas • [963] 11 5447969 • armdiocesedamas@web.de

*29.1.1973 Aleppo Syria, N Vartanans Thursday before Lent. 1979-1987 school Kilikian Aleppo. 1987-1993 Seminary Etchmiadzin. diak1993-1994 German language course Köln Germany. 1995-2000 stud luth theology Erlangen Germany ⊖28.11.1998 Köln (A Karekin Bekdjian) "Armaş". 2000-2003 parish Göppingen Germany. 2003 Vardapet Etchmiadzin (A Nerses Bozabalian). 5.7.2004 Ostkirchliches Institut Regensburg Germany ⊕15.1.2006 Etchmiadzin B Damas. 2009 Catholic Academy Berlin Germany.

Yezras Mkrtich Nersissian ***Nor-Nahichevan***

T: B Nor-Nahichevan-Russia ▪ ✉ Sergeja Makejeva 10, ROSSIJA-123022 Moskva • [7] 499 2555019 • eparxia.aa@mail.ru

*3.10.1959 Voskehat, NVartanans Thursday before Lent. 1978-1980 Soviet Army. 1980-1984 Theol Seminary Etchmiadzin. diak25.12.1983. 1984-1986 teacher New Testament Etchmiadzin, stud theol Sankt-Peterburg ⊖8.9.1985 (A Nerses Bozabailian). 1986-1988 stud theol Academy Leningrad. 1988-2000 rector St. Catherine's Leningrad Sankt-Peterburg, Representative Armenian Church to the patriarchate Moskva. archim22.2.2001 Vardapet ⊕30.9.2001 B Nor-Nahichevan.

Narek Avagyan ***Artik***
T: Primate Artik ▪ ✉ Mother of God Cathedral, ARMENIA-3007 Artik • artikitem@gmail.com
*11.8.1979 Oshakan Aragatsotn. 1986-1996 school Mesrob Mashtots Oshagan. 1996-2002 Gevorkian Theological Seminary Etchmiadzin. diak25.12.2001 the Feast of St. Stephen the Protodeacon, (B Mikael Ajapahyan, Shirak) St. Gregory the Illuminator Mother Cathedral of Yerevan ⊖31.8.2003 (A Shahan Svajyan), Feast of the Discovery of the Belt of Holy Mother of God, 2005-2006 Abkhasia. 2007-2013 abbot of the Khor Virap Monastery. 2013-2014 Iraq. 5.10.2013 Doctoral Thesis "Burial Sevice according to the scripture and printed Mashtots (Liturgical book) in the XVI-XVII centuries and national traditions". archim9.10.2013 Vardapet St. Mesrop Mashtots church of Oshakan village (B Mikael Ajapahyan, Shirak). 2015 primate Artik.

Kjud Nakkashian
T: A ▪ ✉ 15, rue Jean -Goujon, FRANCE-75008 Paris • [33] 143596703, fax 142564608 • kude1@hotmail.com
*28.11.1933 Aleppo. N? stud Antelias Seminary ⊖20.11.1955 Jerusalem. priest in Lebanon. 1960 France. 1968 Vicar General ⊕29.9.1973 Etchmiadzin. 1984-2007 prelate Paris, Dél. Patriarcal Europe Occidentale. 1988-2007 A Paris. 2000-2007 member Supreme Spiritual Council of the Armenian Apostolic Orthodox Church.

Retired Hierarchs:

Yeznik Samuel Petrossian
T: former A ▪ ✉ Catholicossate of All Armenians, ARMENIA-1101 Etchmiadzin • [374] 10 585509, [374] 10 542039, [374] 91 401776 • ypetrosyan@biblesociety.am • tavushitem@gmail.com
*19.1.1955 Tbilisi Georgia. 1958 moved to Erevan. mon1972 diak1.1.1973 ⊖1973 absolvent Theol Seminary Etchmiadzin. 1973-1975 secretary Journal Etchmiadzin. archim1975 Vardapet. 1976-1981 stud University Athens. 1981-1990 Dean Seminary Etchmiadzin. 1987 Dr. theol Athens. 1991-1996 vicar North Caucasus. 13.1.1997 Dz. Vardapet, Prelat Krasnodar ⊕15.6.1997 B South Russia North Caucasus. 1999-2010 chairman Department Interchurch Relations. Delegate CEC 2006 A Summit Religious leaders Moskva. 2010 General Secretary Bible Society of Armenia. 2011-2012 International Joint Commission Theol Dialogue between Catholic and Oriental Orthodox Churches. 2011-2015 A Primate Tavuš, he is proofreading the translation of the Bible into modern Armenian and making the critical Interlinear of the Septuagint (Greek Bible) and the Old Armenian Bible. He is also preparing a "Synaxary" the ritual collection of the Armenian Church for publication.

Norvan Armen Zakarian

T: A ▪ ✉ 15, rue Jean -Goujon, FRANCE-75008 Paris • [33] 143596703, fax 142564608 • eglise.apostolique.armenienne@wanadoo.fr

*3.4.1940 Beirut. NVartanans Thursday before Lent. Seminary Antelias. 1958-1959 stud Jerusalem. 1959-1967 Comptabilité Lebanon. diak24.12.1967 Paris ⊖27.10.1968 Paris (Manukian). 1968-1975 Institut Catholique Paris. 1975-1980 curé Paris. 1980-2007 prélat Lyon ⊕14.2.1982 Etchmiadzin (Vasken). 2004 Mondo Migliore. 2007-2013 A France, retired.

Mesrob Georg Krikorian

T: A, retired ▪ ✉ Kolonitzgasse 11/11, AUSTRIA-1030 Wien • [43] 1 7122506 • terandreas@yahoo.com

*25.10.1932 Aleppo Syria. N? Volksschule Haykazian, evangelische Mittelschule Bethel Aleppo. 1947-1953 stud Seminary Beirut ⊖1953 Antelias (B Derenik Poladian), celib. Mesrob. 1953-1956 Prof Seminary Antelias Old Armenian, History. 1956 Vardapet "Armenische Handschriften Antelias". 1956-1957 rector Seminary Antelias. 1956-1958 teacher Hovagimian Manugian gymnasium Antelias. 1959-1961 stud Durham. 1961 Wien. 1964 Dr. theol, Dz. Vardapet "Armenians in the Service of the Ottoman Empire 1860-1908". 1964-1975 Repr Etchmiadzin to WCC Geneva. 1972-1974 Vorsitzender Ökum. Rat Österreich. 1980 Exarch Mitteleuropa, Schweden. 1981 Lektor ⊕21.9.1986 Etchmiadzin B Wien. 1987 Prof Armenian Univ Wien. 1992-2013 A Wien, Patriarchal-Delegat für Österreich, Zentraleuropa und Schweden, Ungarn, Tschechien, Member Supreme Spiritual Council.

Vatché Hovsep Hovsepian

T: former A Primate Western Diocese USA ▪ ✉ 3325 North Glenoaks Blvd., USA-Burbank, CA 91594 • armenianchwd@earthlink.net

*11.6.1930 Beirut. N? 1944-1951 Seminary Antelias. diak1948 ⊖24.6.1951 Antelias. 1953-1956 stud Edinburgh. 1956-1967 Parish USA ⊕1967 Etchmiadzin. 1967-1971 Diocesan Legate Canada. 1971-2003 seventh primate Western diocese since 1927. 1976 A. 1986 member Supreme Spiritual Council. Organization National Ecclesiastical Assembly for the election of Karekin I. 2003 retired.

Daron Jirair Djeredjian

T: B, retired ▪ ✉ chemin de la Poste 5, FRANCE-06650 Opio • [33] 491 778 470, fax 491 778 928 • gibertetiemble@sfr.fr

*11.7.1937 Beirut. N? 1952 Seminary Antelias. diak1957. 1960-1963 stud England ⊖8.8.1963. 1963 paroisse Valence France. archim23.4.1965 Vardapet ⊕27.9.1992 Etchmiadzin.1992-2007 B Marseille.

Paren Avedikian
T: B, former vicar, former Director of Administrative Organizational Matters of the Mother See ▪ ✉ Catholicossate of All Armenians, 1101 ARMENIA-Etchmiadzin • [374] 10 517-321, office -214
*1939 Beirut Lebanon. N? stud Antelias, Beit Mary, Seminary Jerusalem ⊖1960. 1963 stud USA, parishes Washington D.C., Detroit, Michigan, Chicago. 1967 Vardapet. 1970-1997 collection Manoogian Historical and Art Museum. 1975 Dz. Vardapet. 1997-1999 vicar Locum tenens Shirak. 1999 Executive Museums Etchmiadzin ⊕17.9.2000.

Special situation:

Anania Avedik Arapadjian
T: 2007 lay person, former A Keğarkounik ▪
*27.1.1951 Erevan N? ⊖1973 ⊕1983 Etchmiadzin. 1983-1990 B Baku Azerbeičan. 1990 -2000 A Keğarkounik. 2000-2007 New York. 2007 lay person.

Assoğik Smpad Aristakessian
T: 2007 lay person ▪
*13.9.1959 Etchmiadzin N? 1977-1982 stud theol Etchmiadzin. mon1978 diak25.12.1980 Etchmiadzin ⊖16.10.1983. 1985 staff-bearer to the Catholicos. 1985 pastor Paris. Vardapet1987 ⊕13.11.1988 Etchmiadzin. 1988-1993 B Siunik, igumen Datev Monastir. 1988-1997 member Supreme Spiritual Council Armenian Church. 1993-1998 Redacteur journal "Etchmiadzin". 1996 B Armavir. 2007 lay person.

Catholicossate of Cilicia

Aram Pedros Kiskisian Keshishian
T: Catholicos, Episkoposapet, Sis ▪ ✉ Armenien Catholicossate P.O.Box 70317, LEBANON-Antelias • [961] 4 41000-1, -3, fax -2, 419724, p [961] 1 416170, Summer [961] 4 980060, 98363-4, -5, p 983532, 523-461 • catholicos@armenianorthodoxchurch.org •
chancellor@armenianorthodoxchurch.org •
info@armenianorthodoxchurch.org •
www.armenianorthodoxchurch.org • http://westernprelacy.org
*8.5.1947 Beirut ⊖1968 archim1970 Vardapet ⊕22.8.1980 Antelias. 1980-1995 B Beirut. 1991-2007 Moderator Central Committee WCC Geneva. 1991 Executive Committee. 1995 Catholicos. 2007 president Middle East Council of Churches. MDiv, STM, PhD 2007 in charge of Ecumenical Relations Armenian Coptic Syrian Middle East Patriarchates.

Datev Khajak Sarkissian
T: A Catholicossate of Cilicia, lecturer Seminary ▪ ✉ Catholicossate of All Armenians, ARMENIA-1101 Etchmiadzin • [374] 231 271420 • bedod40@yahoo.com
*1941 Aleppo "Khajak" N? ⊖1960 ⊕1974 Antelias. 1974-1984 Antelias. 1984-1994 Los Angeles, Western Prelacy. 1996 Etchmiadzin.

Gomidas Parseg Ohanian ***Venezuela***
T: A Venezuela Catholicossate of Cilicia ▪ ✉ Avenida Los Mangos esq. Calle Armenia (antes Pomogas) La Florida, VENEZUELA-1050 Caracas • serpagomidas@cantv.net
*1942 Damas Syria "Parseg". N? ⊖1963. 1969-1973 stud Thessaloniki BA theol. 1989-1996 vicar Jezireh ⊕1994. 1996 B Caracas, San Gregorio el Iluminador. 2000 A Venezuela. 2006-2014 Antelias.

Oshagan Manoog Choloyan ***New York***
T: A, Eastern Prelacy of North America Catholicossate of Cilicia ▪ ✉ 138 East 39th Street, USA-New York • [1] 212 6897-810, fax -168 • prelateny@aol.com
*1947 Aleppo Syria "Manoog". N? Haikazian School Aleppo. 1960 Seminary Antelias diak1964 ⊖1967 (Karekin Sarkissian) 1968-1970 stud hist American University Beirut. 1974-1978 MA Education Princeton Theological Seminary. 1979-1998 Middle East Council of Churches. 1980-1998 pontifical legate Kuwait, teacher Antelias, Mardigian Beirut, Karen Jeppe and Sahagian Aleppo ⊕1994 (Karekin Sarkissian). 1994-1998 B Kuwait. 1998 B North America. 2011 International Joint Commission Theol Dialogue between Catholic and Oriental Orthodox Churches.

Dirayr Panos Panossian
T: A Catholicossate of Cilicia ▪ ✉ Armenien Catholicossate, P.O.Box 70317, LEBANON-Antelias • [961] 4 41000-1, -3, fax -2, 419724, [961] 9 540867
*1937 Panos Aleppo "Panos" N? ⊖1965 ⊕22.6.1997 Antelias. 1997-2002 chairman Printing Office, 1997-2002 Responsable Tertchnots Bujn, Nest of birds Djubeil Biblos. 2002 Director Library. 2010 A.

Sebouh Ohan Sarkissian ***Teheran***
T: A Teheran Catholicossate of Cilicia ▪ ✉ Avenue Ostad Nejatollahi 311, Karmikhan Zand St, IRAN-Teheran • [98] 21 889798-0, -1, 890163-4, -5, -6, 892323, fax 8892617 • temakan@hyenet.ir

*1946 Qamishly Syria "Ohan". N? Armenian school Qamishly. 1961 Seminary Antelias. diak1965 ⊖1968. 1968-1970 stud Arab Lit and Islam Philosophy St. Joseph University Beirut. 1978 Middle East Council of Churches. 1978-1998 Director General Sunday schools. 1979-1981 MA Christian Muslim relations Birmingham ⊕1992-1998 B Kuwait and the Gulf, Patriarchal vicar. 1999 A Tehrān.

Magar Ashkarian

T: B vice-prelate of Teheran Catholicossate of Cilicia ▪ ✉ Avenue Ostad Nejatollahi 311, Karmikhan Zand St, IRAN-Teheran • [98] 936 7735234, [98] 21 889798-0, -1, 890163-4, -5, -6, 892323, fax 8892617 • iasseyblonnd@yahoo.com

*24.3.1972 Antelias. diak1996 ⊖2001 Antelias. 2001-2007 vice dean Theol Seminary Antelias. 2007-2014 parish priest Thessaloniki. 2013 Dzairaguin Vardapet ⊕26.4.2014 B vice-prelate of Teheran Catholicossate of Cilicia (Aram I, Antelias).

Krikor Chiftjian ***Tabriz***

T: B Prelate of Tabriz Catholicossate of Cilicia ▪ ✉ Avenue Khomeini, Ave. Shanaz Eglise Arménienne, IRAN-4455 Tabriz • [98] 411 5553059 • arajnordaran.tavriz@gmail.com • www.armenianorthodoxchurch.org/

*1969 Beirut Lebanon. Khanamirian School. Theol Seminary of the Catholicossate of Cilicia. diak1986 ⊖1990 (A Zareh Aznavorian). hypodiakon Catholicos, redacteur journal "Hask". 1995 Vardapet "St. Nerses of Lampron and his explication of the Twelve Prophets" (Karekin II.) Prof Seminary Cilicia and University Etchmiadzin. Assistant to the prelate of North America. 2000-2011 Communications Officer Catholicossate of Cilicia. 2012 vicar Atrpatakan Tabriz Azerbeidzhan Iran, Catholicossate of Cilicia ⊕26.4.2014 B Tabriz (Aram I, Antelias).

Papken Hagob Charian ***Isfahan***

T: A New Djulfa Catholicossate of Cilicia ▪ ✉ Armenian Cathedral, P.O.Box 81735-115, IRAN-New Julfa Isfahan • [98] 313 624347-1, -2, fax 6270999, p 62448888, [98] 913 3136944 • b_tcharian@yahoo.com • sourbv@yahoo.com • www.newjulfa.org

*9.4.1965 Beirut "Hagop". N? parents from Urfa and Akshehir. 1981 diak Antelias Catholicossate of Cilicia Lebanon ⊖1984 (A Datev Sarkissian). 1984-1986 teacher Theol Seminary Bikhfaya. 1986-1993 private secretary to Catholicos Karekin Catholicossate of Cilicia. 1993-1996 first permanent parish priest United Arab Emirates. 1996-2002 parish priest San Francisco USA. 1998 Dz. Vardapet San Francisco "The great loss of the Armenian clergy during the genocide – 1300 priests bishops archbishops". 2002-2004 vice-prelate Kamishly Syria. 2004 prelate Isfahan ⊕4.6.2006 Antelias. 2014 A Djulfa.

Mushegh Mardirossian ***Los Angeles***
T: A Western Prelacy of North America Catholicossate of Cilicia ▪ ✉ 6252 Honolulu Ave, USA-La Crescenta, CA 91214, [1] 818 248773-7, -8, fax 2487745 • prelacy@aol.com • info@westernprelacy.org • www.westernprelacy.org
*1957 Beirut "Sarkis" N? ⊖1976 Administrator Los Angeles ⊕22.6.1997 Antelias. 1997-2004 Antelias. 2004 Western Prelacy.

Nareg Manoug Alemezian ***Cyprus***
T: A prelate Cyprus Catholicossate of Cilicia ▪ ✉ Armenian Orthodox Bishopric, P.O.Box 21987, CYPRUS-1515 Nikosia • [357] 224935-60, -80, fax 492750 • armprel@spidernet.com.cy • ecumcil@armenianorthodoxchurch.org
*10.5.1962 Beirut ⊖1981. absolvent Theol Seminary Antelias. 1981-1984 dean Theol Seminary Antelias. 1985-1986 secretary to Karekin II. 1986-1991 stud theol Vancouver. 1991-1997 rector Sts. Vartanantz New Jersey USA ⊕12.5.2002 B Antelias. Ecumenical officer of the Great House of Cilicia. parat lauream Vancouver. 2004 Mondo Migliore. 2010 A. 2011 International Joint Dialogue Commission between Catholic and Oriental Orthodox Churches. 2014 prelate Cyprus Catholicossate of Cilicia.

Khoren Doghramajian ***Greece***
T: B Greece Catholicossate of Cilicia ▪ ✉ Odos Kriezi 10, GREECE-105 53 Athens • [30] 210 3252-067, fax -149 • prelacy@otenet.gr • www.armenianprelacy.gr
*1965 Jebeil N? ⊖1984. 1995 prelate Athens ⊕1.8.2006 Antelias B Greece.

Shahan Sarkissian ***Syria***
T: A Aleppo Syria Catholicossate of Cilicia ▪ ✉ B.P. 133, Salibah, SYRIA-Aleppo • [963] 21 362-4858, -4859, -2310, fax -6608, p [963] 21 2284288 • periotem@scs-net.org • www.periotem.com
*1963 Aleppo. N? 1976-1984 Seminary Antelias ⊖1985. 1987-1990 stud Louvain. 1990-2002 prelate Isfahan ⊕2005 B, 2014 A Aleppo Syria.

Anushavan Tanielian
T: B Catholicossate of Cilicia ▪ ✉ 138 East 39th Street, USA-New York, NY 10016-0985, [1] 212 6897-810, fax -168 vicar@armenianprelacy.org www.armenianprelacy.org
*1951 Beirut "Torkom". N? ⊖1972. 1998 Ecumenical Officer North America, Vicar General Eastern Prelacy, Ecumenical Officer Eastern and Western Prelacies ⊕4.6.2006.

Norayr Ashekian
T: B Cilician Brotherhood, Director Publishing House Catholicossate of Cilicia ▪ ✉ B.P. 11-0409, LEBANON-Beirut • [961] 1 9807-30, -60, fax -61
*1956 Kessab Syria "Movses". N? 1969-1975 Seminary Antelias, 1973 Acolyte ⊖1976 Kamishly. 1976-1979 teacher Armenology Antelias. 1979-1991 vicar Djezire Kamishli. archim1986 Dzairaguin Vardapet. 1992-1993 vicar Aleppo. 1994-1997 Greece. 1997-2001 vicar Aleppo ⊕20.4.2008 (Antelias). 2008 Director Publishing House.

Shahe Kevork Panossian ***Lebanon***
T: B Lebanon Catholicossate of Cilicia, Dean Seminary ▪ ✉ P.O.Box 11-0409, LEBANON-Beirut • [961] 1 9807-30, -60, fax -61 • info@armprelacylb.org • azkayin@inco.com.lb • www.armprelacylb.org
*1958 Kessab Syria. 1971-1978 Seminary Antelias. 1976-1982 teacher Armenology Antelias. diak1976 ⊖1980. 1982-1986 pastor Thessaloniki Greece. 1987-1989 pastor South Florida USA. 1990-1994 pastor Chicago. archim1993 Dz. Vardapet. 1995-2002 pastor Toronto. 2003 director orphanage Beirut. 2004-2006 pastor New Jersey ⊕20.4.2008 (Antelias) Dean Seminary. 2014 prelate Lebanon.

Retired Hierarchs:

Suren Abraham Kataroyan
T: former A vicar Canada Catholicossate of Cilicia ▪ ✉ 3401 Olivar-Asselin, CANADA-Montreal, Quebec H4J 1L5 • [1] 514 8561-200, fax -805 • prelacy@armenianprelacy.ca • www.armenianprelacy.ca
*1939 Aleppo Syria ⊖1962 ⊕22.6.1977 Antelias. 1977-2004 A Syria. 2004-2014 vicar Canada.

Varujan Bogos Hergelian
T: former A Prelate Cyprus Catholicossate of Cilicia ▪ LEBANON-1515 Beirut
*1946 Ainjar Lebanon ⊖1967 ⊕22.6.1997 Antelias. 1997-2014 prelate Cyprus Catholicossate of Cilicia. 20.4.2014 retired.

Khajag Sarkis Hagopian
T: former A prelate Canada Catholicossate of Cilicia ▪ ✉ 3401 Olivar-Asselin, CANADA-Montreal, Quebec H4J 1L5 • [1] 514 8561-200, fax -805 • prelacy@armenianprelacy.ca • www.armenianprelacy.ca
*20.6.1946 Arab Punar Qamishly Syria "Sarkis". 1961 Antelias Lebanon. diak1965 (Karekin Sarkissian) ⊖1968. 1971 Vardapet. 1971 Northern Syria and Gulf. 1979

stud Middle East Theol Inst Lebanon. 1981 assistant prelate New York. 1983-1994 Toronto. 1985 Dzairaguin Vardapet (A Ashjian). 1994 Encino. 1995-2002 New York ⊕22.6.1997 Antelias. 2002-2014 Prelate Canada. 25.4.2014 retired.

Yeprem Tabagian

T: former A Catholicossate of Cilicia ▪ ✉ 6252 Honolulu Ave, USA-La Crescenta, CA 91214 • [1] 818 248773-7, -8, fax 2487745 • prelacy@aol.com info@westwernprelacy.org

*24.10.1941 Beirut "Garabed" N? ⊖1963 ⊕22.8.1980 Antelias. 1980-1998 B Los Angeles. 1998-2004 Director Museum Antelias. 2004-2014 Western Prelacy.

Kegham Khatcherian

T: A Catholicossate of Cilicia, retired ▪ ✉ B.P. 11-409, LEBANON-Beirut • [961] 1 98076 -0, fax -1 • B.P. 80810 LEBANON-Bourdj Hammoud-Metn • [961] 1 25830-0, -4, fax -5 • azkayin@inco.com.lb • info@armprelacylb.org • www.armprelacylb.org

*1962 Beirut ⊖1981. 1997-1999 Administrator Lebanon Dz. Vardapet. archim1997 ⊕20.2.2000 Antelias. 2014 A Lebanon.

Meghrig Parikian

T: former B Prelate of Canada Catholicossate of Cilicia ▪ ✉ 3401 Olivar-Asselin, CANADA-Montreal, H4J 1L5[1] 514 8561-200, fax -805 • www.armenianprelacy.ca

*3.1.1968 Beirut Lebanon. diak6.5.1985 (A Datev Sarkissian). 1982-1988 Zarehian Seminary of the Armenian Catholicossate of Cilicia ⊖28.5.1988 (B Zareh Aznavourian). 1988-1995 regent choir "Shenorhali" Zarehian Seminary. archim1.7.1994. 1994 Vardapet "Letters of Catholicos Nerses" (Ardag Manoukian). 1996-1998 stud Bossey. 1997-1999 stud piano The New School for Music Mannes College New York. 1999-2002 director "Birds Nest" Jbeil. 2002-2014 parish Toronto. 2013 vicar general Canada ⊕27.4.2014. 2014-2016 Prelate of Canada Catholicossate of Cilicia (Aram I, Antelias).

Armenian Patriarchate of Jerusalem
Israel, Jordan, Palestinian territories

Nurhan Boghos Manoogian ***Jerusalem***
T: His Beatitude, Patriarch of the Apostolic Throne of St. James. A Jerusalem. Vice-President of the Holy Synod of Armenian Orthodox Bishops ▪ ✉ St. James Monastery, P.O.Box 14001, ISRAEL-91141 Jerusalem • [972] 2 626-2331, -4866, 628 -6895, -2331, fax 6264861, 6264862 • arminf@netvision.net.il • patriarchateofjerusalem@yahoo.com • armpatriarchate@yahoo.com • www.armenian-patriarchate.org
*1948 Aleppo Syria, N Vartanans Thursday before Lent. stud Antelias. 1966 Seminary Jerusalem. diak27.7.1968 ⊖19.12.1977 (Yegishe Derderian) pastor Amsterdam, Geneva, Philadelphia, Springfield, Houston Texas. 1998-2013 Grand Sacristain du Thrône Apostolique ⊕19.12.1999 Etchmiadzin (4th Sunday Advent, Karekin Nersissian). 2009-2013 Patriarchal Vicar. 24.1.2013 97th Armenian Patriarch of Jerusalem.

Aris Armenag Shirvanjan
T: A, Coordinator of External Relations ▪ ✉ St. James Monastery, P.O.Box 14001, ISRAEL-91141 Jerusalem • [972] 2 6282331, fax 6264861 • patriarchateofjerusalem@yahoo.com • armpatriarchate@yahoo.com • arminf@netvision.net.il
*23.7.1934 Haifa "Aris" son of Gregor the Enlightener. 1952 Theol Seminary Jerusalem. diak1954. 1957 grad., member Brotherhood St. James Jerusalem ⊖1957 Jerusalem. 1958 parish Amman/Jordan, teacher primary school. 1964 BA theol Durham/England. archim1964 ⊕1974 Etchmiadzin. 1984 Ostkirchliches Institut Regensburg. 1984-1998 Diocesan legate San Francisco. 1998 Jerusalem. 1998-1999 vice Grand Sacristain du Thrône Apostolique. 2006 A. 2009 delegation German bishops.

Sevan Hovhannes Ğaribian
T: A Director Finance Department ▪ ✉ St. James Monastery, P.O.Box 14235 and 14001, ISRAEL-91141 Jerusalem • [972] 2 6282331 • armpatriarchate@yahoo.com
*1940 Beirut. NVartanans Thursday before Lent. 1961 Seminary Jerusalem. mon1965 ⊖1968 Jerusalem. 1972 Vardapet ⊕13.11.1988 Etchmiadzin. 1988-1996 Rector Archangels Church Jerusalem. 1988-1993 Chief Dragoman. 1990 Dzairaguin Vardapet Jerusalem. 1996 Director Finance Department. 2006 A.

Vahan Topalian ***Amman***
T: A Amman ■ ✉ Armenian Convent, P.O.Box 186, JORDAN-11118 Amman • [962] 6 45775261, 45740550 • armpatriarchate@yahoo.com
*1940 Beirut. NVartanans Thursday before Lent. 1960 mon Jerusalem. diak1961 ⊖21.7.1963 Vardapet Jerusalem. archim1966. 1968-1988 Administrator Amman ⊕13.11.1988. 1998 A Amman.

Armenian Patriarchate of Constantinople

Mesrob Mutafyan ***İstanbul***
T: His Beatitude Ermenileri Patriği, A İstanbul, Turkey ■ ✉ Ermeni Patrikliği, TURKEY-34130 Kumkapı İstanbul • [90] 212 5170970, 5170971, 4580658, fax 5164833 • mesrobII@post.com • patriarchate@post.com • haybad@superonline.com • office@haybad.org
*16.6.1956 İstanbul "Minas-Vartan". N? 1973-1974 American High School Stuttgart. 1974-1979 Memphis University USA. diak1977 İstanbul ⊖13.5.1979 İstanbul. 1979-1981 Patriarchal Seminary, Hebrew Univ., American Institute of Holy Land Studies Jerusalem, Jerusalem University College. 1982-1986 parish Kınalı. 1982-1987 Chancellor of the Patriarchate. 1982-1990 Coordinator of Ecum Relations. 1983 Vardapet İstanbul, 1984-1988 Patriarchal Advisory Council. 1986 Dz. Vardapet ⊕21.9.1986 Etchmiadzin. 1988-1989 Roma Pont. Univ. San Tommaso (Angelicum) Department Ecumenism. 1990 Chairman Spiritual Council, Patriarchal Vicar Ecumenical Affairs. 1991 Patriarchal Advisory Council. 1993 A. 1997-1998 Patriarchal Vicar General. 1998 Patriarch. 2000-2004 Co-Chairman Supreme Spiritual Council of the Armenian Apostolic Orthodox Church, Vice-President of the Holy Synod of Armenian Orthodox Bishops. 2003 Dr.h.c. Baltimore St. Mary's Catholic University. 2008 Silver Rose St. Nicholas of Fribourg. 2010 Surp Pirgic Hastanesi.

Aram Ateşian
T: A General Patriarchal Vicar, Grand Sacristan ■ ✉ Ermeni Patrikliği, TURKEY-34130 Kumkapı İstanbul • [90] 212 2407397 • vartaram2000@yahoo.com
*1.1.1954 Diyarbakır. NVartanans. 1963-1973 Armenian Seminary Jerusalem. diak1973 Jerusalem. 1976 Jerusalem ⊖22.8.1976 İstanbul. 1976-1998 Pastor St. Stephen Haliçoğlu. archim1987 (Vardapet) İstanbul. 1998-2008 Chairman Spiritual Council. 1999 Dzairaguin Vardapet İstanbul ⊕19.12.1999 Etchmiadzin (4th Sunday Advent, Karekin Nersissian). 2000 Grand Sacristain Arm enian Patriarchate of İstanbul. Co-chairman Supreme Spiritual Council.

Sahag Vahan Mashalian
T: B ▪ ✉ Ermeni Patrikliği, TURKEY-34130 Kumkapı İstanbul •
[90] 532 5946667 • mashalian@yahoo.co.uk
*17.3.1962 İstanbul N? 198 3-1987 stud Phil and Religious Education İstanbul University, Fac of Philosophy, services in the patriarchate. diak1986 İstanbul (Patr Shnork Kalustian). 1987-1994 stud theol London Allan Hall College ⊖1992 İstanbul (Patr Karekin Kazanjian). 1994-1997 Dean Holy Translators Seminary Jerusalem. 1997-1999 Master in Spirituality Milltown Institute SJ Dublin. 1999-2007 Director Interchurch relations İstanbul. 2006 Vardapet Etchmiadzin (A Şahan). 2007-2011 Dean Gevorkian Seminary Etchmiadzin ⊕24.8.2008 Etchmiadzin (Katholikos Karekin II.). 2011 İstanbul Chairman Interfaith and Interchurch Dialogues. 23.-30.11.2015 34th Ecumenical Meeting for Bishops, İstanbul.

Holy Apostolic Catholic Assyrian Church of the East

His Holiness Mar **Gewargis III.**
Catholicos Patriarch of the Assyrian Church of the East

Gewargis III. Sliwa *Seleucia-Ktesiphon*
T: A Catholicos Patriarch of the Holy Apostolic Catholic Assyrian Church of the East ▪ ✉ Cathedral St. John, Iraq-Erbil • [964] 1 7176233, 7198574, fax 7184608, [964] 770532877 • qashadr@hotmail.com • www.news.assyrianchurch.org
*23.11.1941 Habbaniya Ramadi Iraq, N? 1960 stud Baghdad, stud USA. diak13.4.1980 Chicago ⊖8.6.1980 Rector Seminary ⊕7.7.1981 Chicago M Baghdad (Mar Dinkha) Baghdad, Basra, Kirkuk, Mosul, Erbil with the title Metropolitan of Iraq, Jordan and Russia. 2010 Synod Near East Rom. 18.9.2015 121st Patriarch of the Assyrian Church of the East, the See of the Assyrian Church of the East is now returned to Iraq, in Erbil.

Aprem George Mooken *India*
T: M Thrissur and All India ▪ ✉ Metropolitan's Palace, High Road, India-680 001 Thrissur Kerala • [91] 487 2420978, fax 2442166, 2428993 • maraprem@sancharnet.in • aprem@vsnl.com • hgmaraprem@gmail.com • www.churchoftheeastindia.org
*13.6.1940, N? diak25.6.1961 ⊖13.6.1965 ⊕21.9.1968 (Mar Thoma Darmu). 1970 Metropolit. BDiv, MTh, STM, Dr theol, PhD 1994 Pro Oriente Wien. 17.11.1995 union with Mar Dinkha.

Awgen Kyriakose
T: B assistant Thrissur ▪ ✉ Bishop's Palace, Anjanadi, India-680 001 Thrissur Kerala • [91] 487 2424599 • marawgin@gmail.com • www.churchoftheeastindia.org
*21.5.1974 Shaju Poulose Pachamparambil N? diak21.5.1996 (Mar Aprem) ⊖11.4.1999 (Mar Aprem) archim14.1.2010 (Mar Aprem), Dr. theol New Zealand ⊕17.1.2010 Thrissur (Mar Dinkha) BA, BDiv, MTh, PhD Biblical Theology.

Yohannan Joseph
T: B assistant Thrissur ▪ ✉ Bishop's Palace, Anjanadi, India-680 001 Thrissur Kerala • [91] 487 2424599 • maryohannan@gmail.com
*14.11.1966 Joju Antony Chirakkekkaran. N? diak16.4.1989 (Mar Poulose) ⊖11.4.1999 (Mar Aprem). archim14.1.2010 (Mar Aprem) ⊕17.1.2010 Thrissur (Mar Dinkha) B.Com, BDiv, MA, PhD Syriac Language and Literature Kottayam (Mar Theophilos syr).

Gewargis Narsai Benyamin ***Iran***

T: B Iran ▪ ✉ P.O.Box, Bagh-e-Shah Sarbaz St., IRAN-Teheran

*1980 Urmia Azerbeidzhan Iran. activist Youth Committee St. Mary Urmia. 2000 University graduate. diak2000 (Mar Dinkha). 2006-2009 stud theol Nohadra Iraq (Fr. Youkhana Hormuz) ⊖10.5.2009 St. Mary Urmia (M Gewargis Sliwa) archim15.5.2009 corepiscopa St. George Teheran (M Gewargis Sliwa) ⊕13.9.2010 B Iran by Mar Dinkha in Teheran with Mar Gewargis Sliwa, Mar Aprim, Mar Awa, Mar Yohannan, Mar Eshaq.

Awa David Royel ***California***

T: B Modesto, Secretary Holy Synod ▪ ✉ Saint Mara Zaia Cathedral, P.O.Box 577500, USA-Modesto, CA 95367-7500 • [1] 209 41640-70, fax -97 • qashadr@hotmail.com • marawaroyel@gmail.com

*4.7.1975 Chicago IL. N? diak19.1.1992 ⊖23.5.1999 ⊕30.11.2008. Secretary of the Holy Synod, Chairman CIRED.

Aprim Khamis ***Arizona***

T: B Western USA ▪ ✉ 18221 N. 59th Dr., USA-Glendale, AZ 85308 • [1] 602 5880267, fax 8964212

*7.1.1943 Hassake, Syria. diak2.3.1973 ⊖2.3.1973 ⊕2.3.1973 B Basrah. 1976 B USA+Canada. 1984 B East USA+Canada. 1990 B East USA. 1994 B West USA. 1999 B Western USA.

Meelis Zaia ***Australia***

T: M Australia+New Zealand ▪ ✉ 25 Edinburgh Circle, AUSTRALIA-Cecil Hill, NSW • [61] 2 9822 113-4, fax -2 • zaiaj@betscape.net • www.assyrianchurch.com.au

*5.8.1956 Baghdad, N? diak1973 ⊖28.3.1982 San Jose (Mar Dinkha) ⊕21.10.1984 B Australia by Mar Dinkha in Chicago. BA History Sydney.1994-2008 secretary Holy Synod. 1994 Delegation Rome. 1995 Trichur full communion two calendars. 1997 "Understanding Eucharist. Theodor of Mopsuestia". 2007 Order of Australia. 2008 M, administrator Lebanon.

Emmanuel Emmanuel Joseph ***Canada***

T: B Toronto and All Canada ▪ ✉ P.O. Box 334, Stn. B, CANADA-Toronto, M9W 5L3 • [1] 416 7449311, fax 7440358, [1] 408 2867377, fax 2861236 • ibem@rogers.com

*24.11.1958 Baghdad, N? diak1.3.1981 Chicago ⊖11.11.1984 Chicago, 27.5.1990 Chorepiscopa and Archdeacon Toronto ⊕3.6.1990 Chicago B Canada (Mar Dinkha) 2015 PhD Toronto.

Odisho Adam Oraham **_Europe_**
T: B Europe ▪ ✉ P.O.Box 3020, SWEDEN-145 03 Norsborg • [46] 853188407, fax 853177979
*12.7.1961 Baghdad Iraq. N? diak1983 Sydney. stud Trinity College Bristol, BA Theology ⊖1986 Syndey ⊕24.7.1994 Sydney (Mar Dinkha) 1994 B Europa.

Aprim Athniel **_Syria_**
T: B Syria ▪ ✉ P.O.Box 137, SYRIA-Hassake • [963] 52 314925 +fax
*8.12.1963 Hassake, Syria N? diak18.10.1992 ⊖8.11.1992 ⊕3.10.1999 B Syria Hassake (Mar Dinkha).

Isaac Hermiz Joseph **_Duhok_**
T: B Nohadra and Armenia, Patriarchal Vicar in Iraq ▪ ✉ Assyrian Church, IRAQ-Duhok • [44] 162 84888499, [964] 62 7773806
*31.5.1959 Barwar Iraq. N? diak25.11.1979 Baghdad ⊖14.9.1990 for Nineveh Church ⊕24.10.1999 Baghdad, B North Iraq, Russia, Armenia, Georgia (Mar Dinkha).

Paulus Benyamin Korosh **_Eastern USA_**
T: B Eastern USA ▪ ✉ 7201 North Ashland Blvd, USA-Chicago, IL 60659 • [1] 773 4654777, [1] 847 9660012, fax [1] 773 4690099 • benjamin968@yahoo.com • qasha@juno.com
*24.6.1968 Qala Urmia Iran. N? diak24.6.1984 Tehrān (Mar Dinkha) 1993 BA Social Communications University Tehrān. 1993-1995 military service. 1995-2001 stud theol Gregoriana Roma. 1999 stud Aramaic, 2002 stud French Besançon. 2007 USA. 2008 assistant vicar Mar Gewargis Cathedral Chicago. archim20.3.2011 cor-episcopa. 17.5.2012 archdeacon ⊖27.5.2012 Chicago B Eastern USA (Mar Dinkha).

Retired Hierarchs:

Sargis Yousif Nesan
T: B former Baghdad ▪ ✉ 1108 Sonoma Avenue, USA-Modesto, CA 95355 • [1] 209 526-2860, fax -9615
*10.4.1950 Kirkuk N? ⊕19.2.1967. B Baghdad by Mar Yosip Khnanisho in Baghdad. 1967-2004 B Baghdad. 2004-2012 B California. 28.5.2012 retired.

Ancient Apostolic and Catholic Church of the East

Addai Shleemon Gheevargese
T: Addai II. Catholicos Patriarch, Ancient Apostolic and Catholic Church of the East Church of the East ▪ ✉ P.O.Box 2363, IRAQ-Baghdad • [964] 1 7198362, fax 7183919
*1.8.1950, N? diak15.9.1968 ⊕22.9.1968 M Baghdad. 20.2.1972 Patriarch, elected by five bishops.

Yacob Daniel Hormuz-Paulose
T: A Australia, Ancient Apostolic and Catholic Church of the East ▪ ✉ Saint Zaia Cathedral, 145-155c Mc Iver Ave, AUSTRALIA-West Hoxton, NSW 2171 • [61] 2 9826 985-3, fax -4 • www.stzaiacathedral.org.au
*28.4.1964 N? Karanjok Mossul Iraq. diak6.10.1983 Karanjok (Mar Addai). Preparatory Education Certificate Iraq ⊖15.11.1987 (Mar Thoma Eramia). 1987 parish St. Joseph Tel Kefe Northern Iraq ⊕5.7.1992 in Baghdad (Mar Addai) B Syria+Lebanon. 2005 A Australia.

Daniel Fakoo Yaqub ***Modesto***
T: B West USA, Ancient Apostolic and Catholic Church of the East ▪ ✉ 225 McLure, USA-Modesto, CA 95735 • [1] 209 5443065
*13.7.1952, N? diak29.4.1970 Baghdad ⊖21.3.1971 Baghdad ⊕23.2.1972 Baghdad, with Mar Dinkha until 1987.

Narsai Thomas Soro ***Kerkouk***
T: M Kerkouk, Ancient Apostolic and Catholic Church of the East ▪ ✉ Assyrian Metropolitan, P.O.Box 37, IRAQ-Kerkouk • [964] 50 216626
*1930 N? ⊖26.9.1968 Baghdad by Mar Aprem of Thrissur ⊕1969. 1970 M Kerkouk. 1993-1994 Haddad Beirut Lebanon. 2010 funeral Mar Narsai Chicago.

Thomas Eramia Silwa Gheevargese ***Ninive***
T: M Ninive, Ancient Apostolic and Catholic Church of the East ▪ ✉ P.O.Box 4006, Hai Al-Noor, Ninive, IRAQ-Mossul • [964] 60 612738
*10.2.1938 Mossul. N? diak1957 ⊖15.9.1968. 1968-1969 USA ⊕9.2.1969. 1969-1972 B Baghdad. 1972 M Ninive.

Zaia Khoshaba ***Toronto***
T: A USA+Canada, Ancient Apostolic and Catholic Church of the East ▪ USA-Chicago
⊕24.4.2009 B Baghdad (Mar Addai). 2015 A USA+Canada Ancient Apostolic and Catholic Church of the East.

Afram Daweed *Duhok*
T: B Duhok, Ancient Apostolic and Catholic Church of the East ▪
✉ P.O.Box 2363, IRAQ-Baghdad • [964] 1 7198362, fax 7183919
⊕11.6.2010 (Mar Addai).

Timotheos Shalita Odisho
T: M Ancient Apostolic and Catholic Church of the East ▪
✉ Im Sampel 13, Kastel, GERMANY-55252 Mainz • Postfach 74, 55247 GERMANY-Mainz-Kastel • [49] 6134 4410
*14.7.1936 Doure Dokuk Iraq. N? diak1.9.1953 ⊖22.5.1957 ⊕1958 (syr, Mar Ignatius Yacoub III, Damascus). 1975 with Mar Addai in YU.

Gewargis Younan *Chicago*
T: B Chicago, Ancient Apostolic and Catholic Church of the East USA-Chicago • bishopgewargisyounan@gmail.com
2015 secretary Holy Synod.

Mari Emmanuel *Australia*
T: B Australia and New Zealand, Ancient Apostolic and Catholic Church of the East ▪
⊕15.8.2011 B Australia and New Zealand (Mar Yacoub Daniel and Mar Zaia Khoshaba).

Emmanuel Haaron Elia
T: B ▪ ✉ 14737 Vintage St, USA-Mission Hills, CA 91345 •
[1] 818 3220737, fax 4913676 • heilya@yahoo.com
*1967 Baghdad. N? diak 4.5.1992 ⊖1992 ⊕11.6.1993 (Mar Addai). 1993-2009 B Baghdad Ancient Apostolic and Catholic Church of the East. 1995 stud theol Jesuit Seminary San Francisco, 1999 stud Chicago. 2009-2015 B USA+Canada Ancient Apostolic and Catholic Church of the East. 2015 left the Ancient Apostolic and Catholic Church of the East.

Bulgarian Orthodox Church

His Holiness **Neofit**
Patriarch of the Orthodox Church of Bulgaria

Neofit Simeon Nikolov Dimitrov ***Sofia***
T: M Sofia, Patriarch Bulgaria ▪ ✉ Oborište 4, BULGARIA-1090 Sofia • [359] 2 9875611, 9882340, 9872-683, -681, -682 • secr 9867127 • Sv. Sinod [359] 9870289, 888 950986 • synod@aster.net • seminaria@aster.net • www.bg-patriarshia.bg
*15.10.1945 Sofia. N21.1. Seminary Sofia, redécouverte du chant liturgique bulgare traditionel. 1971 dipl theol Academy Sofia. 1973 Kandidat Moskva. 1973-1989 Lektor Musica Eccl. Theol Academy Sofia, "Ioan Kukuzel". mon3.8.1975 diak15.8.1975 ⊖25.3.1976 archim21.11.1977. 1981-1985 protosingel Sofia ⊕8.12.1985 B Levka vicar Sofia. 1989-1992 rector Theol Academy St. Kliment Ohrid. 1991-1992 Dekan Fac theol St. Kliment Ohrid. 1992-1994 General Secretary Holy Synod. 1994 M "Dorostol-Červen", 2002 new name "Ruse". 24.2.2013 Patriarch. 22.-28.1.2016 Synaxis of the primates of the Local Orthodox Churches Chambésy Switzerland.

Naum Andonov Dimitrov ***Ruse***
T: M Ruse, Secretary Holy Synod ▪ ✉ Metropolia pl. Sveta Troica 9, BULGARIA-7000 Ruse • [359] 82820956, [359] 888 950983
*19.10.1968 Varna. mon22.12.1990. 1992-1994 teacher Seminary Plovdiv. 1994 absolvent Fac theol Sofia. 1997 stud Greece. ⊖1997 parishes Preslav. 2004 secretary Holy Synod ⊕17.3.2007 B Stobi. 2013 candidate for M Central Europe. 2014 M Ruse.

Tihon Hristo Georgiev Ivanov
T: B Tiberiopol ▪ ✉ Oborište 4, BULGARIA-1090 Sofia • [359] 2 9875611, 9882340, 9872-683, -681, -682 • secr tichonivanov@aol.com
*26.5.1945 Stuttgart, N13.8. 1952-1959 school Sofia. 1959-1965 Seminary Sofia. 1965-1967 military service. 1967-1971 Academy Sofia, hypodiakon Aleksandr Nevskij. dipl Edinstvo Cerkvi. 1973-1975 redaktor Cerkovni Vestnik. 1977-2003 secretary Mittel- und Westeuropa Stuttgart. 1978-2000 married. mon10.11.2000 diak11.11.2000 ⊖12.11.2000 archim8.7.2001 ⊕6.7.2003 B Tiberiopol, vicar West- und Mitteleuropa. 2009 administrator West- und Mitteleuropa. 2010-2015 Dekan St. Alexandr Nevskij Sofia. 2013 candidate for M Central Europe. 11.6.2014 Patriarchal vicar.

Grigorij Krassimir Tsvetkov
T: B Branitsa, vicar Sv. Sinod ▪ ✉ Oborishte 4, BULGARIA-1090 Sofia • [359] 2 9875611, fax 9897600

*19.9.1970 Botevgrad Vratsa Vračeš. 1993-1995 Seminary Sofia. mon17.11.1996 Hadjidimovo. 1996-1997 stud theol Athens. 1997-2010 protosingel Sofia ⊕29.10.2010 B Branitsa, vicar Sofia. 2011-2014 abbot igumen Mon Trojan. 2013 candidate for M Central Europe. 2014 candidate for M Nevrokop. 2014 vicar Sofia.

Amvrosij Alexandar Paraškevov ***Dorostol***
T: M Dorostol ▪ ✉ Mitropolia, BULGARIA-7500 Silistra • [359] 86 22027 • dormit@abv.bg
*9.6.1942 Svištov. N7.12. stud chimikotechnologičen Institut Sofia. 1983-1987 stud theol Sofia. mon13.8.1983 Klisur. diak19.10.1983. 1983-1984 diakon Vidin ⊖15.8.1984. 1984-1988 teacher Klisur. 1988-1994 igumen Lopušan. archim 29.6.1989 ⊕3.4.1994 (schismatic M Pimen Nevrokop). 1998 (All-Orthodox Synod Sofia) B Branitsa, vicar Vidin. 2004 vicar Vratsa. 2010 M Dorostol.

Gavriil Cvetan Metodiev Dinev ***Loveč***
T: M Loveč ▪ ✉ Mitropolia Čerkovna 12, BULGARIA-5500 Loveč • [359] 68 22079, 22815
*16.7.1950 Sofia. N26.3. 1957-1966 Czechoslovakia. 1966-1969 gymnasium Sofia. 1969 stud architect Sofia. 1973 Monastery St. Petka Klisura. mon28.12.1979 diak1.6.1980 (Vosnesenija) ⊖10.6.1980. 1980 igumen St. Petka. 1980 stud Akad theol Sofia, 1984 Moskva (Prosfirin, M Pitirim). 1986 Kandidat Moskva "Harakternite čerti na podviga na ruskite ... XIX vek". 1986-1991 predstavitel Moskva. archim24.5.1986. 1991-1998 protosingel Metropol Sofia, 1994-1998 also igumen St. Petka ⊕19.10.1998 (Rila). 1998-2001 B Makariopol, vicar Holy Synod. 2001 M Loveč.

Serafim Dinko Željajkov Dinkov ***Nevrokop***
T: M Nevrokop ▪ ✉ P.O. Box 63, Nevrokopska Mitropolia, BULGARIA-2900 Gotse Delčev • [359] 751 24003, 22421, 22161
*4.7.1974 Zorniza Sredez Burgas. N? Woodtechnical University Sofia. 1997 poslužnik Mon St. George Hadžidimovo. 1999 military service. mon18.11.2000 Nevrokop (M Nathaniel) diak19.11.2000 ⊖20.12.2000 archim1.7.2006. 2007-2011 Fac theol Sofia. 2008 igumen Rožen ⊕18.12.2011 Cathedral St. Aleksandr Nevskij Sofia. 2011-2013 B Melnik, vicar Nevrokop. 2013 candidate for M Central Europe. 2014 M Nevrokop. 16.12.2015 Athens Interorthodox committee preparation Panorthodox Synod. 22.-28.1.2016 Synaxis of the primates of the Local Orthodox Churches Chambésy Switzerland.

Nikolaj Metodiev Sevastianov ***Plovdiv***
T: M Plovdiv ▪ ✉ Mitropolia, ul. Stanislav Dospevski 20, BULGARIA-4000 Plovdiv • [359] 32 6223261, 6223263, 6223260

*19.7.1969 Sofia. N? 1987 absolvent gymnasium. 1987-1989 military service. 1987-1990 Seminary Ivan of Rila. 1990-1994 Fac theol Sofia. mon6.12.1990 diak1992 ⊖17.5.1993 efimerij paraklis Fac theol. 1994-1996 Kandidat Moskva. archim29.6.1996. 1996-2001 protosingel Sofia ⊕7.7.2001. 2001-2007 B Snepole, vicar Sofia. 2007 M Plovdiv.

Arsenij Atanas Lazarov
T: B Snepole, vicar Plovdiv ▪ ✉ ul. Stanislav Dospevski 20, BULGARIA-4000 Plovdiv • [359] 32 6223261
*18.11.1986 2001-2006 Seminary theol Sofia. 2006-2009 stud Fac theol Sofia, Fac theol Plovdiv. mon11.8.2007 Monastery St. Kosmas and Damian Kuklen (M Nikolaj, Plovdiv). diak, ⊖2008. 2008-2010 rector parish Borets Plovdiv. archim6.12.2009. 2010 director Orthodox television Plovdiv ⊕6.7.2014 B Znepole, vicar Plovdiv.

Joanikij Ivan Georgiev Nedelčev ***Sliven***
T: M Sliven ▪ ✉ Mitropolia pl. Hadji Dimiter, BULGARIA-8800 Sliven • [359] 44 22325, 26621
*2.3.1939 Pet Mogili, Sliven. N4.11. mon1.4.1961 diak28.8.1961 ⊖17.3.1963 archim 24.11.1968 ⊕20.4.1975 B Velitsa assistant Sliven. 13.4.1980 M Sliven. 1992-1994 President Vrhovni Crkovni Zavet. 1992 Member Permanent Synod.

Jerotej Ivajlo Kosakov Stanislavov
T: B Agatopol, vicar Sliven ▪ ✉ Mitropolia pl. Hadji Dimiter, BULGARIA-8800 Sliven • [359] 44 22325, 26621
*1.2.1977 Veliko Trnovo. mon 22.12.2003. 2003 absolvent Seminary Sofia. 2004 efimerij Pomorije. diak11.5.2004 ⊖16.5.2004. 2005 igumen Pomorije. archim16.5.2008. 2010 MTh Universitet Shumen ⊕1.10.2014 B Agatopol, vicar Sliven.

Ignatij Kolev Karagozov
T: B Provat ▪
*11.7.1972 Sliven. N20.12. 1991 dipl architekt, Technikum Sliven. 1991-1998 stud theol Veliko Tărnovo. mon22.9.1998 Sveta Bogoroditsa Kabila Jambo l (M Gelasij Chief Secr Holy Synod, M Ioannikij Sliven). diak21.11.1998 Sliven (M Ioannikij) ⊖20.12.1998 Sliven (M Ioannikij) 1999-2003 protosingel Sliven. archim8.9.2001. 2004-2011 predstavitel Moskva ⊕6.4.2008 Sliven B Provat. 2011-2014 vicar Sliven. 2013 candidate for M Central Europe. 2014-2015 Cyprus.

Galaktion Tabakov ***Stara Zagora***
T: M Stara Zagora ▪ ✉ Mitropolia Sv. Apostol Karp 4, BULGARIA-6004 Stara Zagora • [359] 42 626110 • Synod [359] 2 9875611 • eparhysz@abv.bg • www.eparhysz.hit.bg

*26.2.1949 Vetren "Georgi Ljubenov". N5.11. 1963-1969 Seminary Gara Čerepiš. mon12.7.1969 Magliš diak27.7.1969 ⊖28.9.1970 Rila. 1970-1976 rector Magliš. 1972-1976 Fac theol Sofia. 1976 dipl theol. 1.7.1976 protosingel Vratsa. archim25.12.1976. 1978-1980 Kandidat Moskva "Social doctrine St. Nil of Sora". 1981-1982 Ostkirchliches Institut Regensburg. 1982-1985 igumen Rila. 1985-1986 igumen Bačkovo ⊕6.7.19 86 B Veličko. 1986-1987 vicar Vidin. 1987 vicar Vratsa. 1988-1993 vicar Stara Zagora. 1993-1995 Deputy Parliament. 1995-2000 Dekan St. Alexandr Nevskij Sofia. 2000 M Stara Zagora. 2002 visit Edirne. 30.8.-6.9.2003 OKI Regensburg, RENOVABIS, Aachen Sant'Egidio, mit Stefan Stefanov. 2005 Administrator Berlin.

Joan Ivo Mihov Ivanov ***Varna***
T: M Varna -Preslav ▪ ✉ Mitropolia, BULGARIA-9000 Varna • [359] 52 61294-4, fax -2, [359] 878 223431
*13.2.1969 Jambol. N? music school (flute). 1989-1991 military service. 1991-1993 Seminary Sofia. 1993-1998 Fac theol Sofia. 1998-2001 Kandidat Moskva "Theology of penitence in St. Tikhon Zadon" mon6.11.1998 manastir Kokaljan (B Gabriel Mariopol). diak24.4.1999 ⊖26.4.1999 archim28.4.2002 (Patr Maxim). 2002-2007 protosingel Sofia ⊕18.3.2007 B Znepole, vicar Sofia. 2013 candidate for M Central Europe. 2013 M Varna. 16.12.2015 Athens Interorthodox committee preparation Panorthodox Synod. 22.-28.1.2016 Synaxis of the primates of the Local Orthodox Churches Chambésy Switzerland.

Grigorij Jorgo Ivanov Stefanov ***Veliko Tarnovo***
T: M Veliko Tarnovo ▪ ✉ Mitropolia Ivan Vazov 25, BULGARIA-5000 Veliko Tarnovo • [359] 62 620005, 625770, 625670, 620-197, -152, [359] 888 939866, [359] 896687444 • mitropolia@abv.bg
*10.10.1950 Kozarevets VelTarnovo. N25.1. 1969 novice Transfiguration Monastery VelTarnovo. 1971-1973 military service. mon, diak1974. 1979 dipl theol Academy Sofia ⊖1980. 1980 protosingel Stara Zagora. archim6.12.1981. 1982-1983 stud Neuchâtel, 1983-1984 Bossey. 1984 Fribourg. 1984-1985 Selly Oak Colleges Birmingham ⊕22.12.1985 B Konstantia. 1985-1987 vicar Stara Zagora. 1987-1990 vicar Veliko Tarnovo. 1990 rector Seminary Plovdiv, 1990-1994 Seminary Sofia. 1992-1994 Administrator Vratsa. 6.3.1994 M Veliko Tarnovo. 1994-1995 Administrator Stara Zagora.

Dometian Topuzliev ***Vidin***
T: M Vidin ▪ ✉ Mitropolia ul. Baba Vida 11, BULGARIA-3700 Vidin • [359] 94 60188-0, -2, [359] 88 8241747

*11.11.1932 Hasovitsa, Smoljan "Dimitar Valčev". N10.1. mon14.1.1959 diak22.3. 1959 ⊖18.7.1962 archim4.12.1963 ⊕15.12.1974 B Znepole. 1974 secretary Holy Synod. 10.8.1979 Adm Akron, 1983-1987 vicar Metr Sofia. 1987 M Vidin. 1992-1996 Chef Department Ecumenical Relations, closed 1996. 1992-1996 Member Central Committee CEC. 2002 honorary citizen Vidin.

Polikarp Petr Petrov
T: B Belogradchik, vicar Vidin ▪ ✉ ul. Baba Vida 11, BULGARIA-3700 Vidin • [359] 94 601880
*21.9.1978 Kjustendil. 1993 school Dubnitsa. 1994-1999 Theol Seminary Sofia (B Sionij). 1995 Monastery Joan Rilski (B Ioan, Dragovitsa). mon23.11.1996 (M Gelasij, M Dometian, M Ignatij). diak2.3.1997 Seminary Sofia (M Gelasij). 1998-1999 gymnasium Kilkis Greece ⊖27.7.1999 Vidin (M Dometian). 1999-2000 stud Academy Moskva. 2000-2006 stud Fac theol Thessaloniki. 2006-2008 igumen monastery Ruen (birthplace St. Joan Rilski), starting Orthodox Radio. archim21.11.2008. 2008 rector Vidin, "Orthodox view" and "Orthodox calendar" television ⊕27.7.2014 Monastery Lopushan B Belogradchik, vicar Vidin.

Sionij Stefan Radev
T: B Velitsa, igumen Trojan ▪ ✉ Manastir Uspenie Bogorodichno Trojan, BULGARIA-5629 Oreshak • [359] 878 979858 • eksoldier.vd@gmail.com
*18.11.1969 Sofia. N22.1. hl. Sion of Edirne Adrianoupolis. 1990 absolvent Seminary Sofia Gara Čerepiš. mon8.6.1991 Kyrill-Method Klisura (Dometian Vidin). diak22.6.1991 ⊖23.6.1991. 1992-1995 igumen Klisura. 1994 absolvent Fac theol Sofia. 1995-1996 stud Erlangen. 1996-2009 rector Seminary "St. Ivan of Rila". archim29.6.1998 ⊕24.3.2007 B Velitsa. 2009-2013 vicar Vidin. 2013 candidate for M Central Europe, abbot Trojan.

Ignatij Ivan Radionov Dimov ***Pleven***
T: M Pleven ▪ ✉ ul. Sv. Paraskeva 15, BULGARIA-5800 Pleven • [359] 64 22147
*10.5.1938 Kirilovo Haskovo. N8.10. 1961-1967 dipl theol Sofia. 1967-1971 Roždestvo Hristovo Šipka. 1971-1976 protosingel Stara Zagora. 1974-1976 Kandidat Moskva. mon13.9.1976 diak20.10.1976 ⊖1.11.1976 archim7.12.1977. 1977-1980 protosingel Stara Zagora. 1980-1981 Ostkirchliches Institut Regensburg. 1981-1988 protosingel Ohio ⊕19.6.1988 B Znepole. 1988-1990 rector Seminary Sofia Gara Čerepiš. 1990-1991 vicar Vratsa. 1992-1994 vicar Plovdiv. 1994 rector Seminary Sofia. 1994-1998 M Vratsa. 1998 M Pleven, 1998 M divided.

Kalinik Dimitar Raičev Alexandrov ***Vratsa***
T: M Vratsa ▪ ✉ Mitropolia, ul. G. Dimitrov 6, BULGARIA-3000 Vratsa • [359] 92 22445 • Kabinet 20213, 27844, 24564
*11.3.1931 Magliš, Stara Zagora. N29.7. 1956 dipl theol Academy Sofia. mon6.6. 1960 diak10.7.1960 ⊖7.7.1962 ⊕6.12.1971 B Velitsa.1974 M Vratsa.

Kiprian Ognjan Dobrinov
T: B Trajanopol, vicar Vratsa ▪ ✉ Mitropolia ul. G. Dimitrov 6, BULGARIA-3000 Vratsa • [359] 92 22445 • Kabinet 20213, 27844, 24564
*8.3.1976 Kazanlăk, Roma N? 1995 music school. mon1.9.1996 Rila (B Ioan Drago vitsa, M Pakratij Stara Zagora) diak8.9.1996 Pavel Banja ⊖14.9.1996 St. Nikolaj Stara Zagora. 1996-1998 efimerij St. Bogoroditsa Kazanlăk, stud theol Sofia. 1998 igumen St. Pror. Ilija Turžiš Vratsa, violin master, dirigent choir "St. Sofronij" Vratsa, 2000 protosingel Vratsa, stud jur Sofia. archim31.8.2003 i gumen Čerepiš, igumen Tržiš, 2006-2007 protosingel USA. nagrada festival Białystok ⊕3.3.2008 Vratsa B Trajanopol, vicar Vratsa, igumen Čerepiš, dirigent chor "St. Sofronij" Vratsa. 2013 candidate for M Central Europe.

Daniel Atanas Triantafil Nikolov
T: B Dragovitsa ▪ ✉ 550 West 50th Street, USA-New York, NY 10019 • [1] 212 2464608 • ep.daniil@dir.bg
*2.3.1972 Smoljan. 1994-1996 military service. 1996-1997 stud English Philology Sofia. 1997 poslužnik Monastery St. Georgij Hadjidimovo. 1997-2002 (correspondence course) Fac theol Sofia. diak8.8.1999 mon21.7.2004 ⊖27.11.2004 archim 1.6.2006. 2008-2010 Monastery St. Georgij Hadjidimovo ⊕20.1.2008. 2011 B Dragovitsa vicar America. 2013 candidate for M Central Europe.

Antonij Zhivko Kirov Mihalev ***Europe***
T: M West and Central Europe ▪ ✉ Krausen-Str. 73, GERMANY-10117 Berlin • [49] 30 2086146 +fax, [359] 888 876376
*17.1.1978 Antonovden Stara Zagora "Živko Mihailov Kirov". N17.1. Seminary Plovdov. mon2000 Klisur M Vidin. diak20.10.2002 ⊖17.1.2003 archim17.11.2006 M Neofit Rusen. Efimeri seminaria Plovdiv. 2007 protosingel Plovdiv ⊕23.3.2008 B Konstantia. 2008-2010 vicar Plovdiv in Smoljan. 2010 vicar, 2013 M West and Central Europe.

Evlogij Božidar Stoyanov Stamboldžiev
T: B Adrianopol ▪ ✉ Igumen Rila, BULGARIA-2643 Rila • [359] 701 25035
*16.6.1954 in Sofia "Božidar Stojanov", N13.2. 1972-1974 military service. 1972 absolvent Technikum Arts Sofia. 1975-1979 Academy theol Sofia. mon14.4.1979 Rila (B Ioan Dragovitsa) diak19.4.1979 Rila (Gelasij Krupnik) 1980-1982 Theol Academy

Moskva, 1982 Kandidat "Bulgarian Orth Church in the Russian Press 19th century" ⊖1.4.1982 Pascha Moskva (Vladimir Dmitr.) 1982-1986 protosingel Sliven. archim27.3.1983. 1986 vice-rector Seminary Ivan of Rila Sofia, igumen Čerepiš. 1986-1987 protosingel Dorostol, 1987-1989 protosingel Sliven, 1989-1990 protosingel Sofia. 1990-2005 teacher and rector Seminary Plovdiv ⊕18.10.1998-2005 B Adrianopel, vicar Plovdiv. 2005 igumen Rila. 21.3.2007 visited by B Gerhard Ludwig Müller with prelates Rauch, Wyrwoll. 2013 candidate for M Central Europe.

Ioan Stojan Kostadinov Stojkov
T: B Glavinitsa ▪ ✉ Oboriste 4, BULGARIA-1090 Sofia
*29.11.1949 Sofia. 1969 absolvent Seminaria Čerepiš. mon11.1.1969 Bačkovo. 1969-1973 Academy Sofia. diak1973. 1976-1976 protosingel Stara Zagora. 1976-1978 Kandidat Moskva. 1978-1982 protosingel Vidin. 1982-1987 teacher, rector Čerepiš. 1988-1992 chairman liturgical commission Hl. Synod. 1991-2006 stud and pastor Germany Weilheim. 2007-2010 Cathedral Aleksandr Nevskij Sofia ⊕30.11.2010 stud theol Erfurt Halle. 2013 B Glavinitsa in Bačkovo. 2014 B Glavinitsa in Sofia. 10.9.2014 Diss Kliment Hristov.

Retired Hierarchs:

Konstantin Koycho Vasilev Petrov
T: B Markianopol, vicar Sofia ▪ ✉ Oborište 4, BULGARIA-1090 Sofia
*18.5.1941 Zlatosel Plovdiv. 1956 stud Seminary Academy Sofia, married, diak ⊖10.3.1968 Sofia. 1997 divorced. mon, archim25.3.1997 (schismatic M Pimen Nevrokop) ⊕27.8.1998 B Markianopol (schismatic M Pimen Nevrokop). Inspector Sofia, vicar Holy Synod. 1998 (All-Orthodox Synod Sofia) rector Prophet Elia Knjaževo Sofia. 2015 retired.

Iakov Ilia Velikov Tasev
T: former B Messemvria ▪ BULGARIA-4230 Manastir Bačkovo • [359] 331 41060
*25.8.1956 Koprivlen Nevrokop. 1978-1982 Academy Sofia. married. diak11.12. 1981 ⊖1.4.1984 widower Samokov. mon, archim14.8.1997 (schismatic M Pimen Nevrokop) ⊕19.10.1997 B (schismatic M Pimen Nevrokop). 1998 (All-Orthodox Synod Sofia) B Messemvria, Monastery Bačkovo. 1999-2013 vicar Ruse 1.12.2012 retired. 2013 candidate for M Central Europe. 2013 Bačkovo.

Inokentij Ivan Stojanov
T: B Krupnik
*1978 Jambol, stud Seminary Academy Sofia. diak ⊖1990-1992 Kandidat Academy Moskva. archim1992 Alternative Synod ⊕19.5.1994 (schismatic M Pimen Nevrokop)

B Krupnik, vicar Sofia Alternative Synod. 1994-2012 M Sofia Alternative Synod (not used title Patriarch). 2012-2015 B Krupnik, vicar Stara Zagora. 2013 candidate for M Central Europe. 12.2.2015 retired.

Boris Vasil Ivanov Dobrev
T: B Agatoniki ▪ ✉ BULGARIA-2643 Rila • [359] 701 25035
*10.3.1953 Ruse. 1983 dipl theol Seminary Academy Sofia with Kiril later M Varna. 1983-1988 teacher Seminary Sofia. mon30.10.1989 Zlatar Šumen (B Gerasim Branitsa, former rector) diak9.11.1989 Preslav (M Kiril) ⊖24.12.1989 Varna. 1991-2001 Podvorie Moskva. archim18.8.1994 Trojan. 2001-2004 secretary Holy Synod Sofia. 15.1.2004 igumen Bačkovo ⊕22.3.2008 B Agatoniki. Bachkovo Monastery. 2013 candidate for M Central Europe. 2014 Rila Monastery, retired.

Josif Ivan Blagoev Bossakov
T: former M USA+Canada+Australia ▪ ✉ 550 West 50th Street, USA-New York, NY 10019 • [1] 212 2464608 • metropolitanjoseph@juno.com • metropolitan.joseph@gmail.com
*6.12.1942 Slavovitsa. mon12.4.1970 Trojan diak3.5.1970 diakon Loveč ⊖27.12. 1970. 1971-1973 Kandidat Moskva. archim21.7.1973. 1973-1980 protosingel Sofia ⊕7.12.1980 B Velitsa igumen Trojan. 1980 vicar Sofia. 1.4.1983 Administrator Akron. 1986-1989 B, M Akron. 1989 M America. 1992-2012 M USA+Canada+ Australia New York.

Simeon Kostadinov
T: former M Mittel- und Westeuropa ▪ ✉ Oborište 4, BULGARIA-1090 Sofia • [49] 177 997319205
*17.9.1926 Varna "Hristo Dimitrov". N1.9. absolvent Sofia, mon6.12.1954 diak12.2.1955. 1957 Kandidat Moskva ⊖8.10.1958 Moskva (Patr Aleksij) 1959 Prof Seminary Sofia. archim1.11.1961. 22.1.1966 protosingel New York ⊕14.1.1973. 1973-1980 B Glavinitsa, vicar New York, Administr Akron. 1980-1986 vicar patriarchal West Europe. 1986-2013 M West and Central Europe Budapest, 1994-2013 M West and Central Europa Berlin. 2013 Hisar Bulgaria.

Pavel Ivanov Petrov
T: B Levka, vicar Sofia ▪
*12.7.1957 Levski, N30.6. 1973-1979 Seminary Gara Čerepiš. 1983-1987 Academy Sofia. mon22.2.1986 Čerepiš diak11.3.1986 ⊖21.5.1986. 1987-1989 protosingel Vratsa. archim11.3.1989. 1989-1992 stud Academy Moskva ⊕20.12.1992 B Levka. 1992 teacher Liturgik. 1998-2000 B Levka, vicar Varna. 2000-2005 Dekan St. Alexandr Nevskij Sofia. 2005 retired.

Teodosij Theodor Minčev Kalinov
T: B Devol, vicar Sv. Sinod ▪
*9.11.1934 Dragiževo N? mon4.12.1955 diak2.2.1956 ⊖21.9.1962 ⊕1.10.1996. 1996-2011 B Devol. 20.2.2011 retired.

Coptic Orthodox Church

His Holiness **Tawadros**
Pope of Alexandria and Patriarch of the See of St. Mark

Tawadros Theodor ***Alexandria***
T: Pope of Alexandria and Patriarch of the See of St. Mark ▪ ✉ Anba Rueiss Building Ramses Street Abbassyea, P.O.Box 9035, Nasr City, Egypt-Cairo • [20] 2 24882606, 68253-57, -58, -74, -75, -76, 26857889, 26821274, fax 6836691, 24871901 • Alexandria [20] 3 48355-22, -33, fax 4841566, [20] 12 3919434, 3110260 •
coptpope@copticpope.org • cop@idsc.gov.eg •
anba_tawadros@hotmail.com • www.copticpope.org
*4.11.1952 Mansura. Pharmacist. N? 1986 El Anba Bishoi, mon31.7.1988 ⊖23.12.1989 ⊕15.6.1997 (Pope Shenouda) B assistant Damanhur member Holy Synod. 4.11.2012 Pope and Patriarch. 31.3.2015 Dr.h.c. Egyptian State University Beni Suef Cairo.

Rueiss Mathias El Suriani
T: B ▪ ✉ Anba Rueiss Building Ramses Street, Abbassyea P.O.Box 9035, Nasr City, Egypt-Cairo • [20] 2 268253-74, -76, fax 6836691 •
anbarewiss@holysynod.copticpope.org
mon13.10.1963 ⊖2.1.1966 ⊕29.5.1977 (Pope Shenouda).

Moussa Angelos El Baramoussy
T: B for the Youth ▪ ✉ P.O.Box 136 Al Abasya, P.O.Box 15 Al Zaher, Egypt-Cairo • [20] 2 64855093, 2 24855093, fax 246825405, [20] 12 2172377, 12 22164519 • anbamoussa@holysynod.copticpope.org •
mossa@intouch.com • www.youthbishopric.com
*30.11.1938 N? mon24.4.1976 ⊖4.6.1976 Chori-Episcopus. 18.6.1978 vicar Beni Suef ⊕25.5.1980 B for the Youth (Pope Shenouda).

Raphael Yustos
T: B Secretary Holy Synod ▪ ✉ Bab el Khalk, P.O.Box 31 b, Egypt-Cairo • [20] 2 2589777, 12 2208220, fax 25884999 • bpraphaeil@yahoo.com •
anbaraphael@copticholysynod.org • www.cairod-church.org
*6.5.1958 Ain Shams. 1987 University Physician. mon28.2.1990 in El Baramoussy ⊖18.5.1995 assistant to bishop Moussa (Youth) ⊕25.6.1997 B General for Old city of Cairo. candidate election pope (Pope Shenouda). 2012 General Secretary Holy Synod.

Dioskoros Bishoi El Antuny
T: B Director Patriarchal Printing Press, Anba Rueiss Building Ramses Street, Abbassyea ▪ ✉ P.O. Box 9035, Nasr City, EGYPT-Cairo • [20] 2 24882612, fax 24832217 • anbadiscorus@holysynod.copticpope.org • discoros@hotmail.com
*11.4.1946 mon15.5.1977 Bishoi Al Antony ⊖15.5.1977. 10.6.1979 Chori-Episcopus ⊕25.5.1980 (Pope Shenouda).

Botros Bishoi El Anba Boula
T: B ▪ ✉ Taymour Street, St. Fatema, P.O.Box 11361, EGYPT-Cairo • [20] 2 26348672, 26373800, fax 22417991 • anbabotros@holysynod.copticpope.org • bishopbotros@hotmail.com
*25.2.1949 Sharqiya Zagazig. N? 1971 B.Sc. Agriculture Cairo University. mon17.10. 1975 ⊖24.11.1977, 10.6.1979 Chori-Episcopus ⊕2.6.1985 (Pope Shenouda). 1985-1998 Auxiliary Ismailia, founder Coptic Television Station AGHAPY. personal secretary Pope Shenouda. 2012 candidate election pope. 29.6.2013 Höxter inthronisation B Damian.

Yohanna Moisses El Anba Bishoi
T: B ▪ ✉ Anba Rueiss Building Ramses Street, Abbassyea, P.O.Box 9035, Nasr City, EGYPT-Cairo • [20] 2 2488260-3, -4, fax 26836691, [20] 12 2114557 • bishopyohanna@aol.com
* mon24.4.1976 Makarios ⊕26.5.1991 (Pope Shenouda). 1991-1999 B Old Cairo. 1999-2008 General B USA.

Yostos Shenouda El Antuny
T: B ▪ ✉ 26 El Kinisa El Markosia St., Klot Bek, Ramses, EGYPT-Cairo • [20] 2 2590-6025, -1500, 12 22114612, fax -8918 • anbayostos@holysynod.copticpope.org • yostosbishop@gmail.com
*14.7.1958 mon12.3.1982 ⊖17.12.1986 ⊕17.11.1991.

Youannes El Anba Boula ***Assiut***
T: B Assiut ▪ ✉ Archangelos Mikhail Kathedrale, Nmis Street, EGYPT-Assiut • [20] 2 24882237, 2 26822215, 12 22108693, fax 26825983 • bishopricbless@yahoo.com • diocese.of.assuit@gmail.com • www.blessegypt.org
*23.11.1960. 1985 Dr. med Assiut. mon17.12.1987 Theofilos Al Anba Bola ⊖27.5. 1991 ⊕6.6.1993 (Pope Shenouda) Evêque Général. 1995-2011 secretary to Pope Shenouda. 2012 candidate election pope. 2015 B Assiut.

Maximos ***Salam City***
T: B Salam City, Al Herfeieen ▪ ✉ St. Mary Church, Garden City, EGYPT-Cairo • [20] 2 22814924, 27951553
*9.9.1947 mon30.1.1976 ⊖7.1976 ⊕30.5.1999 (Pope Shenouda) Coptic Diakonia.

Selwanes Rueiss
T: B ▪ ✉ El Moalaka Church, Masaken Scheraton 1180, No.17, EGYPT-Cairo • [20] 2 25322133, fax 25319162, [20] 12 3321633
*24.9.1953 mon22.3.1978 ⊖30.3.1980 ⊕30.5.1999 (Pope Shenouda). 1999-2001 General B. 2001 B Old Cairo.

Martyros El Suriani
T: B Sekka Hadid, Cairo ▪ ✉ St. Mary's Church, 3838 Mahmasha St, Sharabeya, EGYPT-Cairo • [20] 2 22318881, [20]06676062 • anbamartyros@yahoo.com
*14.1.1964 mon27.10.1990 ⊖30.1.1997 ⊕3.6.2001 (Pope Shenouda).

Daniel El Antuni
T: B ▪ ✉ Deir Anba Rueiss, 222 Ramses Street, EGYPT-Cairo • [20] 2 24882237, fax 26825983
*10.10.1952 mon8.4.1979 ⊖13.5.1979 ⊖7.6.2009 (Pope Shenouda) Monastery St. Anton Australia.

Makary Mataos El Baramoussy
T: B General ▪ ✉ Coptic Orthodox Metropolitan, Ahmad Al Mensiesy, EGYPT-Fakous-Al Scharkya • [20] 2 24882237, 553972817, fax 26825983 • baramosym@gmail.com
*11.11.1961 mon16.11.1996 ⊖18.11.2001 ⊕10.3.2013 (Pope Tawadros).

Yousab Antonios El Shayeb
T: B General ▪ EGYPT-Cairo • [20] 2 24882237, fax 26825983 • bishopyousab@yahoo.com • bishopyousab@gmail.com
*1.3.1955 mon17.11.1998 ⊖26.3.2004 ⊕15.6.2013 (Pope Tawadros).

Abnoub El Antony
T: B General ▪ ✉ St.Samaan Al Kharaz Monastery, EGYPT-El Mokattam • [20] 2 24882237, 122 2734467, fax 26825983
*2.2.1957 mon17.4.1994 ⊖23.1.2005 ⊕15.6.2013 (Pope Tawadros).

Armeya Jeremias Ava Mina
T: B ▪ ✉ Coptic Orthodox Culture Center, 222 Ramses Street, Abbassyea, EGYPT-Cairo • [20] 2 26857889, 24882604, fax 26836691 • fr@tecmina.com • anbaermia@gmail.com • www.anbaermia.com

*15.11.1959 mon2.4.1988 ⊖14.11.1996 ⊕30.5.2004 (Pope Shenouda) Evêque Général, secretary Pope Shenouda.

Takla Deshna El Pachomi
T: former B Deshna, Anba Rueiss Building Ramses Street, Abbassyea ▪ ✉ P.O.Box 9035, Nasr City, EGYPT-Cairo • [20] 2 228253-57, -58, 228253-74, -75, -76, 2821274 • avvatakla@yahoo.com
*1.7.1960 mon15.12.1985 ⊖26.1.1987 ⊕26.5.1991 B (Pope Shenouda). 1991-2005 B Deshna.

Daniel El Anba Boula
T: B Abbot Anba Boula, First Monastery of the Earth, East Egypt, Anba Rueiss Building Ramses Street, Abbassyea ▪ ✉ P.O.Box 9035, Nasr City, EGYPT-Cairo
*17.3.1959 mon12.7.1983 ⊖16.12.1985 ⊕11.6.2006 (Pope Shenouda).

Yulius Ava Mina
T: B General ▪ ✉ P.O.Box 9035, Nasr City, EGYPT-Cairo • [20] 12 8220338 • bishop.yolios@gmail.com
*17.12.1963 mon7.4.1990 ⊖26.9.2001 ⊕10.3.2013 B General Cairo (Pope Tawadros).

Theodosios Anba Mina ***Central Gizeh***
T: B El Ghiza ▪ ✉ Coptic Bishopric, 23 Morad St., EGYPT-El Gizeh • [20] 2 5722656, 5724301, fax 5731307
*1.1.1956 mon 2.4.1988 ⊖23.5.1989 ⊕7.6.2009 B assistant El Ghiza, the old Memphis (Pope Shenouda). 2013 B Central Ghiza.

Yuhanna El Suriani ***North Gizeh***
T: B North Gizeh ▪ ✉ Bahr Al Ghazal St. 9, Ahmad Orabi, EGYPT-El Mohandeseen • [20] 2 5722656, 5724301, fax 5731307, [20] 12 7006500 • anbayouhanna@gmail.com
*10.5.1959 mon22.1.1989 ⊖5.3.1996 ⊕10.3.2013 B North Gizeh (Pope Tawadros).

Zosima El Antuni ***Etfeeh***
T: B Etfeeh, El Saff ▪ ✉ Coptic Bishopric, 23 Morad St., EGYPT-El Gizeh • [20] 2 5722656, 5724301, 238 415489, fax 5731307, [20] 12 7006500 • zosimary@yahoo.com
*24.10.1970 mon20.12.2000 ⊖14.2.2009 ⊕10.3.2013 B Etfeeh El Saff Aphroditopolis from Gizeh (Pope Tawadros).

Domadios El Suriani ***Uossim***
T: B 6 Octobercity and Uossim ▪ ✉ Coptic Bishopric, 23 Morad St., EGYPT-El Gizeh • [20] 2 5722656, 5724301, fax 5731307, [20] 12 7006500
*20.1.1961 mon10.7.1987 ⊖27.11.1993 ⊕10.3.2013 (Pope Tawadros) chose the name of the late B of Gizeh Domadios, B 6 Octobercity and Uossim, from Gizeh.

Samwel El Samueli ***Tamouhm***
T: B Tamu+Badrasheia+Hawamdiya ▪ ✉ Coptic Bishopric, 23 Morad St., EGYPT-El Gizeh • [20] 2 5722656, 5724301, fax 5731307, [20] 12 7006500 • felopateer156@gmail.com
*15.6.1951 mon9.1983 ⊖12.1987 ⊕10.3.2013 B Tamu+Badrasheia+Hawamdiya, all south of Gizeh (Pope Tawadros).

Bakhomios Antonios El Suriani ***Beheira***
T: M la Beheira, Matroukh et des cinq villes de l'Ouest, Nord d'Afrique ▪ ✉ Coptic Bishopric P.O.Box 55, EGYPT-Damanhur • [20] 45 3342876, 3344655, fax 3343482, p [20]12 23219371, [20]12 27481800 • metropolitanpakhom@yahoo.com
*17.12.1935 Shebeen El Kom. N? 1956 Bac Commerce Ein Sham University. mon11.11.1962 Antonios Al-Souriany diak2.1.1966 ⊖28.7.1968 ⊕12.12.1971 (Pope Shenouda). 2.9.1990 M Beheira, Matrouh, Pentapolis, Damanhour.

Bishoi Thoma El Suriani ***Damiette***
T: M Damiette, Barari, Kafr El Sheikh ▪ ✉ Metropoliet-Sorour Place, EGYPT-Damiette • p [20] 1222108199, 1223994504, fax 502880008, [20] 47 223338, [20] 50 2880-007, -034, -763, -679, -218, fax -008, [20] 12 3994504, [20] 12 2108199 • demiana@demiana.org • anbabishoy@holysynod.copticpope.org • www.metropolit-bishoy.org
*19.7.1942 Mansura. N? 1963 Mech. Eng. 28.5.1968 M.Sc. Alexandria. mon16.2. 1969 ⊖12.5.1970 ⊕24.9.1972 (Pope Shenouda). 1.6.1985 General Secretary Holy Synod. 2.9.1990 M. 1999 Commission Orthodox Collaboration WCC Geneva. 2004 Mondo Migliore. 2011 International Joint Commission Theol Dialogue between Catholic and Oriental Orthodox Churches. 2012 candidate election pope.

Sarapamoun Sarapamoun El Suriani
T: B, Prieur Anba Bishoi ▪ ✉ 22 Morkossia St, Klot Beh, EGYPT-Cairo • [20] 2 2591-4448, -7971, fax 25932295, 0459165055 • Alexandria [20] 3 5460511 • anbasarabamoun@holysynod.copticpope.org • afraymcopty@gmail.com

*21.2.1937 Armant Luxor. N? mon8.12.1959 ⊖24.2.1963 Wadi El Natrun, 17.6.1973 Prieur ⊕29.5.1977 (Pope Shenouda).

Hedra Georgios El Suriani ***Assuan***
T: M Assuan, Kom Ombo, Edfou ▪ ✉ Coptic Bishopric P.O.Box 173, EGYPT-Assuan • [20] 97 313995, 302508, fax 264546 • anbahedra@holysynod.copticpope.org • anba.hedra@gmail.com
*13.7.1940 Tanta. N? 1963 Bac Agriculture Uni Alexandria. mon4.4.1971 Georgios ⊖20.12.1974 ⊕22.6.1975 B, 19.3.2006 M Assuan, Kom Ombo, Edfo (Pope Shenouda).

Wissa Makarios El Anba Bishoi ***Baliana***
T: M Baliana, Bardis, Awlad Tokh Shark ▪ ✉ Coptic Bishopric, Motraneyet, EGYPT-Baliana Sohag • [20] 93 800816, fax 801312, p [20] 2 5907476 • hgwissa12@hotmail.com • metropolitwissa@hotmail.com • anbawissa@holysynod.copticpope.org • www.anbawisa.org
*16.7.1939 Tanta. N? 1962 Bac Agriculture. Mon10.3.1972 Anthimos Al Anba Bishoi ⊖3.7.1973 Makarios ⊕22.6.1975 (Pope Shenouda). 2006 M Baliana, Bardees, Awla Touk Schark.

Kyrillos Ava Min ***Mina***
T: B for the Monastery St. Mina ▪ ✉ Bourg El Arab P.O.Box 9, Der Mar Mina Gedidah, EGYPT-Mariout • [20] 3 4595000, 4593401-3, fax 4596565 • stmina@stmina.info • Anbakyrelos@yahoo.com
*13.8.1953 mon29.9.1975 ⊖20.1.1996 ⊕15.6.2003 (Pope Shenouda).

Arsanios Daniel El Baramoussy ***Menya***
T: M Minia, Abou Korkas ▪ ✉ Coptic Bishopric P.O.Box 49, Eltegara St., EGYPT-Menya • [20] 86 2362019, 2341721, 2343733, spec. 2341331, fax 2361320, [20] 2 6825170 • anbaarsanious@holysynod.copticpope.org • bishoparsanios@hotmail.com
*21.8.1928 Cairo. N? 1951 Bac Engineering. mon1958 ⊖1974 ⊕13.6.1976 (Pope Shenouda). 14.11.2004 M Elmenia, Abo Korkas.

Makarios Kyrillos El Baramoussy
T: B assistant Menya ▪ ✉ El Menya, al Tegara Street St. Georg Church, Hammat Al Koba, EGYPT-Cairo • [20] 86 2361-212, -121, [20] 2 5882225, 1004471092 • fr_kyrillos@yahoo.com • macarius.bishop@yahoo.com
*10.6.1958 mon5.12.1978 ⊖30.6.1988 ⊕30.5.2004 Cairo (Pope Shenouda).

Pafnutios Antonios El Suriani ***Samalout***
T: M Samalout, Toha El Aameda ▪ ✉ Coptic Bishopric, Al Ahd Al Gadeed street, EGYPT-Samalout • [20] 86 771171-1, -2, -3, -4, -5, -6, fax 1221729610, [20] 12 73339-40, -50, -60 • anbapafnatious@holysynod.copticpope.org • samdiocese@yahoo.com
*12.11.1948 Cairo. N? 1971 Bac Medicine. mon13.3.1972 Antonios Al Souriany ⊖30.3.1975 ⊕13.6.1976 B, 2016 M Samalout (Pope Shenouda). B Samalout, Taha. 2012 candidate election pope member Holy Synod.

Benjamin Tadros El Baramoussy ***Manufeya***
T: M Menoufeya ▪ ✉ Coptic Bishopric, EGYPT-Chebine al Kom • [20] 48 221836, 224010, 227927, fax 221836, 325577, 482325577, [20]12 23737733, 23763300 • anbabenyamin@holysynod.copticpope.org • anbabenyamin@hotmail.com
*26.6.1947 El Batanon Menufeya. N? 1970 Bac Engineering. mon 24.6.1973 ⊖16.9.1973 ⊕13.6.1976. B, 2016 M El Menoufeya (Pope Shenouda).

Angaelos Philippos El Suriani ***Fakkous***
T: B Charkeiya+10th of Ramadan ▪ ✉ Coptic Bishopric P.O.Box 16, EGYPT-Sharkeiya • [20] 55 3972817, 972517 • anbaangelos@holysynod.copticpope.org
mon1.10.1972 ⊖3.6.1973 ⊕14.11.1976 (Pope Shenouda).

Tadros Arsenios El Anba Bishoi ***Port Said***
T: M Port Said ▪ ✉ P.O.Box 948, Coptic Bishopric, Abd El Salam Aref Street 30, EGYPT-Port Said • [20] 66 239212, 336199, fax 66 3238668 • anbatadros@holysynod.copticpope.org • bishoptadros@yahoo.com
*1.2.1943 mon5.5.1974 Arsanios Al Anba Bishoi ⊖18.4.1975 ⊕14.11.1976 B, 2016 M Port Said (Pope Shenouda). 29.6.2013 Höxter inthronisation B Damian.

Timotheos Emmanuel El Moharraky ***Zagazig***
T: B Zagazig, Minia Al Kamh ▪ ✉ Coptic Bishopric, P.O.Box 66, EGYPT-Zagazig • [20] 55 323607, 329333, 23620011, fax 361944, [20] 12 7666120, [20] 12 3610019 • anba@temotheos.com
*25.12.1960 mon15.5.1995 ⊖25.5.1999 ⊕30.5.1999 (Pope Shenouda). 7.6.2009 B Zagazig.

Kyrillos Antonios El Anba Boula ***Nag Hamadi***
T: B Nag Hamadi+Abu Tescht ▪ ✉ Coptic Bishopric, EGYPT-Nag Hamadi • [20] 96 580672, 1222111997, fax 581211 • anbakyrilos@holysynod.copticpope.org

*29.4.1947 mon3.10.1975 Antonios Al Anba Bola ⊖26.12.1976 ⊕29.5.1977 (Pope Shenouda).

Poula Thoma El Baramoussy ***Tanta***
T: B la Gharbeya+Tanta, President Family Affairs ▪ ✉ Coptic Orthodox Metropolit, El Waleed Street, P.O.Box 296, EGYPT-Tanta • [20] 40 2582221, 331-4735, fax -2833, [20]12 26600088, [20]12 80013001, [20] 2 5902661 • anbapaula@holysynod.copticpope.org • anbapaula@hotmail.com • bishoppaul1@gmail.com
*23.8.1951 N? mon24.4.1976 ⊖4.6.1976, 29.5.1977 Chori-Episcopus ⊕25.5.1980 (Pope Shenouda). 1980-1989 auxiliaire Damiette. 18.6.1989 B Gharbeya.

Mattaos Pafnutios El Suriani
T: B Abbot ▪ ✉ Monastère Deir Es Sourian, P.O.Box 1 Wadi Natrun, EGYPT-Kuwisna • [20] 82 322025, 329025 • Cairo [20] 2 5905161, 01281644355, fax 5922000 • anbamtaeos@holysynod.copticpope.org • egbmataeous@st-mary-alsorian.com
*1939 mon7.2.1965 ⊖4.4.1969 Chori-Episcopus. 18.6.1978 Vicar Beni Suef ⊕25.5.1980 (Pope Shenouda). 1980-1993 B General Old Cairo. 1993 Deir Es Sourian.

Epiphanios El Makarii
T: B, Abbot ▪ ✉ Monastère Deir Es Sourian, P.O.Box 1 Wadi Natrun, EGYPT-Kuwisna • [20] 82 322025, 329025 • Cairo [20] 2 5905161, fax 5922000
*27.6.1954 mon18.2.1984 ⊖17.10.2002 ⊕10.3.2013 (Pope Tawadros) B Abbot monastery El Makary (after spiritual guide Fr Matthew the poor).

Besada Abraham El Anba Bishoi ***Akhmim***
T: B Akhmim+Sakolta ▪ ✉ Coptic Bishopric, Naser Al Zeray street, Akhmem, Sohag, EGYPT-Akhmim • [20] 93 2585807, 2587803, fax 2580380, 01002588480, 0932587803, [20]12 22385238 • anbabisada@holysynod.copticpope.org • bishop.bessada@yahoo.com
*20.10.1945 N? mon7.7.1974 Abraam Al Anba Bishoi ⊖27.9.1975 ⊕25.5.1980 (Pope Shenouda).

Andraos Angelos El Anba Bishoi ***Abu Tieg***
T: B Abu Tieg, Sedffa, El Ghanayem ▪ ✉ Coptic Orthodox Metropoliet, EGYPT-Akhmim • [20] 88 480-867, -314, fax 481511 • Cairo [20] 2 5929658, [20]12 27905279 • anbaandrawes@holysynod.copticpope.org
*23.5.1946 mon24.3.1977 ⊖21.5.1978 ⊕25.5.1980 (Pope Shenouda).

Isheia Anania El Anba Bishoi ***Tahta***
T: M Tahta+Gehenna ▪ ✉ Coptic Orthodox Bishopric, P.O.Box 16, EGYPT-Sahel Tahta, Upper Egypt • [20] 934 770447, 770070, fax 771597 • keriakos3@hotmail.com
*16.5.1940 mon19.3.1977 Angelos Al Anba Bishoi ⊖13.6.1978 ⊕25.5.1980 (Pope Shenouda). 2008 M.

Faam Mina El Anba Bishoi ***Tema***
T: B Tema ▪ ✉ Coptic Bishopric, EGYPT-Tema • [20] 93 2790-538, -107, [20]12 27331175 • anbafam@holysynod.copticpope.org • bishoppham@yahoo.com
*1.2.1957 mon15.12.1977 Mina Al Anba Bishoi ⊖17.7.1979 ⊕25.5.1980 (Pope Shenouda).

Sawiros Bishoi El Moharraky
T: B abbot Monastery El Moharraky Mountain of Coscam ▪ ✉ Deir Al Moharraky El Kousseya, EGYPT-Assiut • [20] 88 591406, 590585, [20] 2 6832055 • anbasawires@holysynod.copticpope.org
* mon11.8.1974 ⊖22.8.1975. 29.5.1977 Chori-Episcopus ⊕2.6.1985 (Pope Shenouda).

Marcos Antonios El Anba Bishoi ***Kaliubeya***
T: B Kaliubeya, Shoubra El Khema, Kanater El Khayria ▪ ✉ P.O.Box 64, St. George Church, EGYPT-Shoubra El Khema • [20] 2 444-8194, -8042, -1335, -7111, -7000 fax -7888, -7698, [20] 12 2114761 • anbamarkos@holysynod.copticpope.org • bmarcos@alanbamarcos.com • bmarcos442@gmail.com • www.alanbamarcos.com
*2.1.1944 N? mon6.10.1976 Antonios Al Anba Bishoi ⊖9.1.1978, 18.6.1978 Chori-Episcopus ⊕2.6.1985 (Pope Shenouda). 14.6.1992 B Kaliubeya Shoubra El Khema Balad.

Abram Timotheos El Anba Bishoi ***Fayoum***
T: B Fayoum, Responsable Publications, Secretary Holy Synod ▪ ✉ Coptic Bishopric P.O.Box 58, EGYPT-Fayoum • [20] 84 333222, 335227, 335247, 334780, [20]12 22113524, fax 338893 • anbaabraam@holysynod.copticpope.org • abraam@link.net
*11.2.1950 mon23.3.1977 Timotheos Al Anba Bishoi ⊖31.1.1978 ⊕2.6.1985 (Pope Shenouda).

Bisinthis El Anba Bishoi ***Heluan***
T: B Heluan+Maassara+Tebin+15thMayCity ▪ ✉ Coptic Bishopric, Deir Al Anba Barsoum Al Erian, EGYPT-Heluan • [20] 2 5554280, 369-0256, fax -5861 • anbapesantee@holysynod.copticpope.org • st.barsoum@link.net • gtimport@hotmail.com
*8.6.1941 Geeza Cairo, N? diak19.1.1962 mon25.8.1971 ⊖12.11.1972 ⊕22.6.1986 (Pope Shenouda). 1986-1988 evêque Général Anba Rueiss Building. 29.5.1988 B Heluan.

Barsum El Suriani ***Sanabu***
T: B Sanabu+Deirout ▪ ✉ Coptic Bishopric, EGYPT-Deirout • [20] 88 770-403, fax -397, [20] 2 5927424 • anbabarsoum@holysynod.copticpope.org • anba.barsom@gmail.com
*25.11.1946 mon9.4.1977 Dioskoros Al Souriany ⊖3.1.1981 ⊕22.6.1986 (Pope Shenouda).

Bakhum El Rizeiqa ***Sohag***
T: B Sohag ▪ ✉ El Taheer Street, Coptic Orthodox Metropolitan, EGYPT-Sohag • [20] 93 322100, 317773, [20]12 23000440, fax 327444 • anbapakhowm@holysynod.copticpope.org • anba.bakhoum@hotmail.com
*24.2.1953 N? mon20.8.1978 ⊖18.7.1979 ⊕22.6.1986 (Pope Shenouda).

Lukas Arsanios El Anba Bishoi ***Abnoub***
T: B Abnoub ▪ ✉ P.O.B 71717 Coptic Bishopric, EGYPT-Abnoub • [20] 88 500-105, fax -644, [20] 2 5912201, 2676349 • Bishoploukas@gmail.com • copticabnoub@yahoo.com
*5.11.1949 mon23.3.1977 Arsanios Al Anba Bishoi ⊖21.5.1978 ⊕22.6.1986 (Pope Shenouda).

Demetrios Archillidis Ava Mina ***Mallawi***
T: B Mallawi, Antinoepolis (Ansena), Hermopolis (Achmunein) ▪ ✉ P.O.Box 13, Coptic Bishopric, EGYPT-Mallawi • [20] 86 2632073, 2652073, fax 2644199, [20] 12 3129270 • mallawi@mallawi-demet.org • demet86@yahoo.com • www.mallawi-demet.com
*23.2.1948 mon24.6.1978 Arscheledes Ava Mina ⊖19.6.1986 ⊕22.6.1986 B Mallawi (Pope Shenouda). 2004 abbot St. Veni Abu Fana monastery.

Antonios Yehnes El Suriani ***Manfalout***
T: B Manfalout ▪ ✉ Coptic Orthodox Metropolitan, EGYPT-Manfalout • [20] 88 4707625, -4711030, [20]12 80197730 • anbaantonious@@holysynod.copticpope.org

*31.5.1951 mon12.1980 ⊖20.6.1986 ⊕22.6.1986 B (Pope Shenouda).

Aghapios Wissa El Anba Bishoi ***Deir Mouas***
T: B Deir Mouas+Dalga ▪ ✉ Coptic Bishopric Deir Mouas, P.O.Box 61737, EGYPT-Elmenea • [20] 86 2010365, fax 2011449, [20] 2 2371113, [20] 12 3191341 • anbaaghaious@holysynod.copticpope.org • anbaaghabios@yahoo.com
*2.4.1944 Zagazig. N? mon15.12.1977 Anba Bishoi Monastery Abuna Wesa Anba Bishoi ⊖17.7.1979 ⊕13.11.1988.

Thomas Matteos El Pachomi
T: B Qousseya+Mair, Director Spiritual Center ANAPHORA Wadi Natrun ▪ ✉ Coptic Orthodox Metropolitan, Gad Elrab Street, Al Kousya, EGYPT-Assiut • [20] 88 753304 751-177, [20]12 22219030, fax 751-799 • anbathomas@holysynod.copticpope.org • thomas@link.net.eg • bishopthomas@anaforaegypt.com • www.anaforaegypt.com
*8.11.1957 Le Caire. N? 1981 Fac méd vétérinaire Cairo. St. Bakhoum, monastère Pafnutios El Bakhoumy. mon31.3.1985 Pafnutios El Bakhoumy ⊖19.11.1987 ⊕13.11.1988 (Pope Shenouda).

Matthias El Pachomi ***Mahala***
T: B Mahala El Kobra Rueiss ▪ ✉ Coptic Orthodox Bishopric, P.O.Box 178, EGYPT-Mahala • [20] 40 21232-50, -60, fax 2227655

Basilios El Anba Samuil
T: B for the Monastery El Anba Samuil ▪ ✉ 26 El Kinisa El Markosia St., Klot Bek, Ramses, EGYPT-Cairo • [20] 2 593-9050, -3766, fax 5894708, [20] 86 530088 • anbabassilious@holysynod.copticpope.org • anbabasilios@yahoo.com
*26.7.1947 mon24.8.1976 ⊖17.12.1978. 11.12.1983 hegoumenos ⊕26.5.1991.

Daniel El Suriani ***Maadi***
T: B Maadi+Kotsika ▪ ✉ Al Souk Al Tugari, P.O.Box 33, EGYPT-Maadi • [20] 2 7003-730, fax -886, [20] 12 3119185 • anbadaniel@holysynod.copticpope.org • bishopdanielmaad@yahoo.com
*6.7.1948 mon31.10.1982 ⊖2.2.1986 ⊕26.5.1991. 1991-1993 assistant Gherghe. 1993 General B Maadi+Kotsika, 2013 B Maadi+Kotsika.

Cherubim Sharobeam ***Kena***
T: B Kena+Red Sea ▪ ✉ Coptic Bishopric, P.O.Box 13, EGYPT-Kena • [20] 96 335101, 330512, 324656, [20]12 81311114, fax 338003 •

anbasharobeam@holysynod.copticpope.org • hgb.sharoubeem@yahoo.com
*17.8.1946 mon24.4.1976 ⊖14.7.1984 ⊕26.5.1991 (18 Bašans by Pope Shenouda).

Biemen El Moharraky ***Kous***
T: B Kous+Nakada ▪ ✉ Coptic Bishopric, P.O.Box 83628, EGYPT-Naqadah • [20] 96 6844998, 660082-0, fax -1, 6841015, [20] 10 1981982 • anbabeemen@holysynod.copticpope.org • bishop_biemen@naqus.com • Bishop_Biemen@hotmail.com • www.naqus.com
*19.12.1959 N? mon15.10.1986 ⊖19.5.1991 ⊕26.5.1991.

Isidoros El Baramoussy ***Baramous***
T: B, Abbot Baramous ▪ ✉ Al Baramous or 25 Al Kanysa Almorkosya Street, Klot Bek, Al Azbakya, EGYPT-Wadi El Natrun • [20] 2 5922775, 12 22161559, fax 5882225 • anbaisidors@holysynod.copticpope.org
*15.9.1939 mon22.6.1977 ⊖12.2.1979 ⊕14.6.1992 (Pope Shenouda). 29.6.2013 Höxter inthronisation B Damian.

Theophilos Ignatios El Suriani ***Hurgada***
T: B Hurgada et la Mer Rouge ▪ ✉ Bishopric, P.O.Box 91, EGYPT-Hurgada • [20] 65 546-430, fax -973, [20] 2 2750108 • anbatheophilus@holysynod.copticpope.org • ava.thaofilos@yahoo.com
*6.4.1939 mon4.10.1975 ⊖1.3.1978 ⊕14.6.1992 (Pope Shenouda).

Maximos El Anba Bishoi ***Banha***
T: B Banha+Quesna ▪ ✉ Saad Zaghlol Street, P.O.Box 38, EGYPT-Banha Galiopeia • [20] 13 25525-7, [20]12 29006970, fax -6, [20] 48 579911 • anbamaximuosbanha@copticholysynod.org
*8.3.1954 N? Kardiolog mon17.7.1986 ⊖8.6.1992 ⊕14.6.1992 (Pope Shenouda).

Ghabreal Rueiss ***Beni Suef***
T: B Beni Suef+El Bahnesa ▪ ✉ Coptic Bishopric, P.O.Box 30, EGYPT-Beni Suef • [20] 82 322025, 329025, 2354730, [20]12 22101595, fax 323420 • bgbsd@yahoo.com
*31.12.1963 Mallawi Egypt, brother of Anba Yoannes El Anba Boula. N? Fac of Engineering Assiut University, construction El Moharraky monastery. 1990 El Moharraky monastery. mon17.1.1992 ⊖10.6.1997 ⊕15.6.1997 (Pope Shenouda). 1997-2001 B General especially for Beni Suef. 2001 B Beni Suef.

Gregorios Boutros El Anba Bishoi ***Matai***
T: B Matai ▪ ✉ Matai P.O.Box 1, EGYPT-Menya • [20] 86 921-823, -515, -580, fax 924333 • anbagregorios@holysynod.copticpope.org • anbageorgeos@yahoo.com
*24.9.1953 mon23.3.1978 ⊖30.3.1980 ⊕30.5.1999 (Pope Shenouda). 1999-2001 B General Cairo. 2001 B Matai.

Estaphanos Moussa El Moharrak ***Beba***
T: B Beba ▪ ✉ El Kenisa Street, EGYPT-Beba • [20] 82 4400459, 440459-2, fax -4, [20] 10 1023100 • anba.stephanos@gmail.com
*1.1.1968 mon11.10.1992 ⊖25.5.1999 ⊕30.5.1999 (Pope Shenouda).B General for Beni Suef. 2001 B Beba.

Serafim El Baramoussy ***Ismailia***
T: B Ismailia ▪ ✉ Bishoy Church, El Sheik Zayed, EGYPT-Ismailia • [20] 64 329294, fax 311990, 919444, [20] 12 2384848, [20] 2 2448672, 4181050 • hg_bishop_saraphim@hotmail.com • ocrs@eic.egnet.net • dawod.fr@gmail.com
*30.1.1955 mon27.1.1981 ⊖6.10.1982 ⊕3.6.2001 (Pope Shenouda). 2001 M Ismailia.

Athanasios ***Beni Mazar***
T: B Beni Mazar ▪ ✉ El Reedy Street, Beni Mazar, EGYPT-Menya • [20] 86 830-503, 7830503 fax -033 • bishop.athanasius2001@gmail.com
*27.4.1948 mon1975 ⊖3.1.1975 ⊕9.9.2001 Cairo.

Aghathon Ezra El Anba Bishoi ***Maghagha***
T: B Maghagha, El Adwa ▪ ✉ P.O.Box 7, EGYPT-Maghagha • [20] 86 7554447, 7550048, [20] 12 730501-20, -30, -40, fax 7559547, [20] 2 3041288 • anba-aghathon@maghagha.com • anba.aghaton@yahoo.com • www.maghagha.com
*5.2.1959 mon22.4.1989 ⊖12.2.1992 ⊕9.9.2001 Cairo.

Kosman Ava Mina ***North Sinai***
T: B North Sinai ▪ ✉ P.O.Box 7, EGYPT-45111 El Areesh • [20] 68 3320-828, fax -507, [20] 12 398 7077 • bishopcosman@hotmail.com • bishopcosman@yahoo.com
*19.12.1948 mon28.11.1982 ⊖24.11.1997 ⊕9.9.2001 Cairo.

Apollo El Baramoussy ***South Sinai***
T: B South Sinai ▪ ✉ Coptic Orthodox Bishopric, P.O.Box 123, EGYPT-Sharm el Sheik • [20] 69 661097, 3663948, fax 3663946 •

anbaapollo@yahoo.com • anbaapollo@gmail.com
*9.12.1961 mon26.1.1996 ⊕3.6.2001 (Pope Shenouda).

Dawoud Moussa El Baramoussy *El-Mansura*
T: B El-Mansura ■ ✉ 3 El Sekka El Gedida, EGYPT-El-Mansura • [20] 50 2242550, fax 2256740, [20] 2 6223744, [20] 12 3151823 • bishopdawoud@gmail.com
*25.1.1957 mon3.7.1989 ⊖29.6.1998 ⊕14.6.2002 (Pope Shenouda).

Mina Athanasios Anba Bishoi *Mar Girgis*
T: B Deir Mar Girgis El Hatatba ■ ✉ 15 Menouf Kileopatra St, EGYPT-Cairo • [20] 2 22912552, fax 250215956, [20] 12 5100440, [20] 12 1900266
*26.6.1951 mon23.3.1977 ⊖1978 ⊕11.6.2006 (Pope Shenouda).

Salib *Mit Ghamr*
T: B Mit Ghamr ■ ✉ Deir Anba Rueiss, 222 Ramses Street, EGYPT-Cairo • [20] 2 24882237, fax 26825983
*30.9.1960 mon11.10.1992 ⊖8.10.1993 ⊖7.6.2009 (Pope Shenouda) B Debre Mitram Delta. 15.6.2013 B Mit Ghamr.

Ologios El Amba Shenouda *Shenouda*
T: B St. Shenouda the Archimandrites Monastery ■ ✉ Anba Schenouda Monastry, Souhag, EGYPT-Cairo • [20] 2 24882237, fax 26825983
*16.12.1959 mon2.4.1987 ⊖2.4.1989 ⊕15.6.2013 (Pope Tawadros).

Potros Anba Mina *Khanka*
T: B El Kanater, Abo Zaabal ■ ✉ Masaken Abo Zaabal, EGYPT-13756 El Werasch • [20] 2 24882237, 244620551, fax 26825983 • anbabtros2001@yahoo.com
*14.8.1947 mon24.6.1978 ⊖3.1.2003 ⊕7.6.2009 (Pope Shenouda).

Sarabamon Ibrahim El Suriani *Omdurman*
T: B Atbarra, Omdurman, North Sudan ■ ✉ Coptic Orthodox Bishopric, P.O.Box 628, SUDAN-Omdurman • [249] 875504-12, -23, 87551671, fax 87556973, [249] 912304334 • anbasarabamon@hotmail.com
*30.3.1954 mon15.12.1985 ⊖8.1.1989 ⊕14.11.1993 B Atbarra (Pope Shenouda).

Elia El Antuny *Khartum*
T: B Khartum, South Sudan ■ ✉ Coptic Archbishopric P.O.Box 4, SUDAN-Khartum • [249] 11 77-0646, -5274, fax 785646, [249] 912306644, 912301921 • bishoyalantony@hotmail.com
*24.12.1951 mon12.3.1982 igumen ⊖7.1982 ⊕3.6.2001 Khartum (Pope Shenouda).

Antonios Theodore El Antuny ***Jerusalem***
T: M Jerusalem+Near East ▪ ✉ Ninth Station Via Dolorosa, Old City, P.O.Box 14006, ISRAEL-91141 Jerusalem • [972] 2 6284405 • copticmet7@yahoo.com • anbaabraham@holysynod.copticpope.org • www.copticjerusalem.com/
*1969 Southern Egypt, father priest, stud agricultura, medicin, pharmacy. mon2008 ⊖2012 ⊕28.2.2016 (Pope Tawadros II).

Pavlos Bola El Anba Bishoi ***Greece***
T: B Greece, Cyprus ▪ ✉ Yalras 9D Akharnes Menidi, GREECE-136 71 Athens • [30]69 40013040, 36008211, 48162820 • pavlos.anba@gmail.com
*3.3.1949 mon194.1978 ⊖18.6.1981 ⊕15.6.2013 (Pope Tawadros II). 29.6.2013 Höxter inthronisation B Damian.

Kirillos El Baramoussy ***Milano***
T: A Milano ▪ ✉ Cinisello Balsamo, via Perbresso 4, ITALIA-20084 Milano • [39] 0266010507, fax 029007169 • Bimen Kamel via Osteno 2, 0248702186 • Cairo [20] 2 5882225
*1952 Sohag. N? ⊕22.6.1986 (Pope Shenouda). 1986-1996 assistant Minia, Abou Korkas, Monastery El Baramoussy.1996 B Milano. 2012. candidate election pope. 29.6.2013 Höxter inthronisation B Damian. 28.2.2016 A Milano.

Barnaba ***Torino***
T: B Torino ▪ ✉ via Laurentina 1571, ITALIA-00143 Roma • [39] 06 713 -6491, -2900, [39] 338 1341131 • anba.barnaba@libero.it • mons.barnaba@hotmail.com • www.coptiortodossiroma.it
*12.1.1959 Dandara Qena. N? stud Archeology Cairo. mon14.10.1984 El Suriani al Soryan ⊖25.5.1988. 1988-1989 priest Paris. 1990-1995 Roma Firenze Torino Bologna. igumen3.12.1994 ⊕10.6.1995 Cairo B Général (Pope Shenouda). 1996 B Torino. 2004 Mondo Migliore.

Athanasios Bernard Canepa ***France***
T: A France ▪ ✉ Ermitage Saint Marc, Chemin de la Chapelle Copte, Fontanieu, FRANCE-83200 Le Revest-les-Eaux • [33] 494 989 560, 12 75547679 • abba.athanasios@eglise-copte-orthodoxe-de-france.fr • www.eglise-copte-orthodoxe-de-france.fr
*7.5.1933 Jullouville Normandie, catholic. N? 1951-1955 stud humanities University Caen. 1955-1970 Journalist Press. 1970-1971 visits to monasteries Greece, Russia. 1971 meets Amba Aghabios Venice, relics of St. Markus. 1971-1974 stud theol Kairo, B Shenouda. 1974 starts emigration. mon4.5.1973 diak5.5.1973 ⊖6.5.1973

archim2.6.1974 Kairo Chori-Episcopus (Pope Shenouda) ⊕18.6.1994 Kairo (Pope Shenouda) évêque général pour la France. 29.6.2013 Höxter inthronisation B Damian. 13.7.2013 Le Revest-les-Eaux inthronisation B France (Pope Tawadros II) 23.-30.11.2015 34th Ecumenical Meeting for Bishops, İstanbul 28.2.2016 A France.

Luka El Baramoussy
T: B France Sud, Suisse Romande ▪ ✉ Meyrin, SUISSE-1217 Genève • [41] 799120470 • plbcopte@yahoo.fr
*14.9.1956. diak1983 mon 26.1.1985 ⊖3.1986 ⊕15.6.2013 (Pope Tawadros).

Arsany El Baramoussy ***Netherlands***
T: B Netherlands ▪ ✉ Mosstraat 2, NETHERLANDS-7585 PK Amsterdam • [31] 65136820
*10.10.1951 diak20.9.1978 ⊖30.5.1979. 2.7.1981 hegoumenos ⊕15.6.2013 (Pope Tawadros). 29.6.2013 Höxter inthronisation B Damian.

Antony Axios El Anba Bishoi ***Ireland***
T: B Ireland, Scotland, North East England ▪ ✉ 40 Kingston Drive, GREAT BRITAIN-Whitley Bay NE26 1JJ • [44] 191 2894047, 2972155, fax 2535558, [44] 191 789975788, 2535558 • bantony2000@blueyonder.co.uk • bishop_antony2000@yahoo.com • www.bishopantony.org
*15.1.1954 N? Civil engineer. diak29.3.1981 ⊖9.9.1984. 1985-1990 priest Switzerland, Einsiedeln ⊕11.6.1995 Cairo (Pope Shenouda). 29.6.2013 Höxter inthronisation B Damian.

Angelos El Anba Bishoi ***Great Britain***
T: B Great Britain ▪ ✉ Shephalbury Manor, Broadhall Way, Hertfordshire, GREAT BRITAIN-Stevenage SG2 8NP • [44] 1438 748-473, -534, 7971032244, 2079939001, office 745232, fax 313879, [44] 70 50288456, pager 336736537 • Cairo [20] 2 5172068 • angaelos@copticcentre.com • www.copticcentre.com
*19.8.1967 mon31.10.1990 ⊖8.6.1993 ⊕11.11.1999 (Pope Shenouda).

Misael Misael El Suriani
T: B Birmingham ▪ ✉ Hill Park House, Lapworth Street, GREAT BRITAIN-Solihull B94 5QS • [44] 156 4783926, 4821352, fax 4784236 • anbamissael@holysynod.copticpope.org
* mon11.11.1962 ⊖1.11.1967 ⊕25.5.1980 B Général (Pope Shenouda). 1991 B Birmingham.

Abakeer Gebran El Anba Bishoi ***Skandinavia***
T: B ▪ ✉ c/o Copt-Orth, Nyköpingsvägen 24, SWEDEN-151 32 Södertälje • [46] 700-363812, -298529 • anbaabakirbishop@yahoo.com • www.copt.se
*4.5.1962 mon22.1.1995 ⊖7.6.1999 ⊕30.5.2004 Evêque Général (Pope Shenouda). 7.6.2009 B Skandinavia. 29.6.2013 Höxter inthronisation B Damian.

Damian Refat Fahmi ***Deutschland***
T: B Deutschland ▪ ✉ Brenkhausen, Propsteistr. 1 A, GERMANY-37671 Höxter • [49] 5271 18905, 36854, 36805, fax 36742, [49] 172 5643647 • bischof@koptisches-kloster-hoexter.de • kopt.kloster.hx@t-online.de • www.koptisches-kloster-hoexter.de
*15.3.1955 Cairo. N? Damian Refat Fahmi El Anba Bishoi. 1979 Dr.med University Ain-Shams Cairo. 1980-1991 Dr. Radiology Ludwigsburg. 1990 assistant at consecration church in Kröffelbach. 1991 restauration Kloster St. Mary and St. Mauritius Brenkhausen (former Zisterzienserinnen St. Johannes Baptist). mon6.11.1992 El Anba Bishoi ⊖1993 priest Stuttgart, München, Trier, Hannover ⊕10.6.1995 Cairo (Pope Shenouda) for Germany. 1997-2007 stellv. Vorsitzender Ökumenischer Rat Berlin Brandenburg. 29.6.2013 inthronisation Brenkhausen.

Michael Samy Salama El Baramoussy ***Kröffelbach***
T: B Kröffelbach und Süddeutschland ▪ ✉ Kröffelbach, Koptisches St. Antonioskloster, GERMANY-35647 Waldsolms • [49] 6085 2319, 2317, 157 39469846, fax 2666 • antonius.1@hotmail.de • www.kroeffelbach.kopten.de
*6.8.1942 Kalubeya. 1961-1978 Central Bank of Kairo. 1967 BC Administration Fac Economics Kairo. 1974 stud theol Kairo. mon16.7.1978 Mikhael El Baramoussy ⊖11.1979 diak1980 stud German language Ostkirchliches Institut Regensburg and Kröffelbach.1983 hegoumenos ⊕15.6.2013 (Pope Tawadros). 29.6.2013 Höxter inthronisation B Damian. 30.6.2013 Kröffelbach.

Gabriel Ghobrial El Anba Bishoi ***Wien***
T: B Österreich ▪ ✉ Quadenstr. 4, AUSTRIA-1220 Wien • [43] 1 2827443, fax 2836424, [43] 650 9009017, [43] 699 19197070 • coptgabriel@hotmail.com • www.kopten.at
*23.4.1959 Minya Upper Egypt. N? 1982 Dr. med. Assiut University. 1983-1991 surgery Minya. 1991-1995 monastery Anba Bishoi. mon11.6.1992 ⊖18.7.1995. 1995-2000 parish Hannover, 1998-2000 also Zürich and Basel. 16.6.2000 igumen Cairo (Pope Shenouda) ⊕18.6.2000 Cairo (Pope Shenouda) 10th bishop for Europe: Austria Helvetia. 5.6.2004 B Österreich. 29.6.2013 Höxter (B Damian).

Paulus [Boulos] ***Nairobi***
T: B Nairobi ▪ ✉ P.O.Box 19697, KENIA-Nairobi • [254] 202 727279, fax 725771 • bishoppaul@hotmail.com • bishoppaul@copticmission.org • www.copticmission.org
*18.6.1949 N? 1993 deacon Youth Movement Assiut. 1993-1994 Youth Office Cairo ⊖1994 El Anba Bishoi. 1994-1995 Johannesburg South Africa ⊕11.6.1995 Cairo General B Evangelisation Mission, assistant Nairobi (Pope Shenouda).

Mina Anba Mina ***Mississauga***
T: B Mississauga Canada ▪ ✉ 1245 Eglinton Ave.W., CANADA-Mississauga, LV 2M4 • [1] 477722233 • anbamina762009@gmail.com
*30.9.1952 mon21.3.1984 Pafnotios Ava Mina ⊖3.1.2003 ⊕7.6.2009 B England (Pope Shenouda). 2010 B General Old City Cairo. 2013 B Canada Mississauga.

David Pavlos El Anba Bishoi ***Northern USA***
T: B Northern USA ▪ ✉ 1 swim club Rd. Stony Point, N.Y. P.O.Box 33, 9 Lynn Dr, USA-Chestnut Ridge, NY 10966 • [1] 973 857-5095, -0078, fax -1315, [1] 20 18520744, 2013441912 • bishopdavid@email.com • anba_david@yahoo.com • www.nacopts.com
*7.8.1967 ⊖21.10.1995 mon22.1.1995 ⊕14.11.1999 B Northern USA (Pope Shenouda).

Michael El Baramoussy ***Washington***
T: B Washington ▪ ✉ 2311 pimmit coptic church, USA-Virginia • [1] 703 38630601, 2084218, 5732362
*3.1.1950 mon22.6.1976 ⊖26.7.1976 ⊕7.6.2009 (Pope Shenouda).

Serapion Serapion El Anba Bishoi ***Los Angeles***
T: A Los Angeles ▪ ✉ P.O.Box 4960, USA-Diamond Bar, CA 91765 • [1] 909 865-8378, -6318, -6306, fax -8348, 2347063, 23470630 • bpserapion@earthlink.net • bishopserapion@lacopts.org • www.lacopts.org
*10.11.1951 N? mon6.8.1979 Abiona ⊖18.7.1981. 1983-1985 first coptic priest in Switzerland, Einsiedeln ⊕2.6.1985 (Pope Shenouda). 1985-1995 Evêque des Services Généraux et Sociaux. 1991-1997 Member Central Committee WCC, Joint Working Group Catholic Church and WCC. 14.11.1995 B, 28.2.2016 A Los Angeles.

Youssef El Suriani ***Dallas***
T: B Southern USA ▪ ✉ Coptic Orthodox Diocese, P.O.Box 1005, USA-Colleyville, TX 75034 1005 • [1] 817 4169526, 7042389, 5213260, 3816080, fax 8871444, [1] 817 4012860 • hgby@suscopts.org •

office@suscopts.org www.suscopts.org
*1.2.1959 mon12.4.1987 ⊖3.7.1988 ⊕14.6.1992 B General Texas (Pope Shenouda). 14.11.1995 B Southern USA.

Suriel Suriel ***Melbourne***
T: B Melbourne ▪ ✉ P.O.Box 1150, AUSTRALIA-Mitcham, North Vic 3132 • [61] 3 9874-8206, 411 344 333, fax -5962 • bishop@melbcopts.org.au • anbasuriel@nacopticchurch.org • www.melbcopts.org.au
*9.5.1963 Port Said. N? 1967 Australia New South Wales. dipl Math. University Sydney. mon6.7.1991 (El Anba Bishoi) ⊖8.6.1993. 1995-1997 parish Honolulu, redactor El Kerasa ⊕15.6.1997 B General for outside Egypt (Pope Shenouda). 1997-1999 USA. 4.12.1999 B Melbourne first Coptic B Australia: Canberra, Adelaide, Perth, New Zealand.

Daniel Metawos El Antuny ***Sydney***
T: B Sydney ▪ ✉ 14 Arthur, AUSTRALIA-Bexly, NSW, 2207 • [61] 291508422, 410454733, fax 291508-499, -577, [61] 405505735 • hg.bishop.daniel@gmail.com • bishop.daniel@coptic.org.au • bishopanbadaniel@gmail.com
*7.3.1959 Sudan. N? mechanic engineer. MA Administration. mon5.8.1984 (El Antuny) ⊕17.12.1985. 1999-2002 secretary B Antony Ireland. 23.6.2002 B Sydney (Pope Shenouda). 2011 International Joint Commission Theol Dialogue between Catholic and Oriental Orthodox Churches.

Youssef Anba Boula ***Bolivia***
T: B Bolivia ▪ ✉ Casilla 9630, BOLIVIA-Santa Cruz • [591] 33 44 2928, 72195804, fax 33442928, [591] 72195804 • coptaortodoxa@scbbs.net • bishop.youssef@gmail.com
*7.3.1976 mon23.8.1995 ⊖3.10.2000 ⊕11.6.2006 (Pope Shenouda).

Aghason (Aghathon) Anba Boula ***Brazil***
T: B Brazil ▪ ✉ Rua São Bor JA201, cid. vargas Jabaquara, BRAZIL-04320 São Paulo • [55] 11 71921571, 55883672, fax 50215956, [55] 012808723 • padreaghason@terra.com.br • www.igrejacopta.org
*12.11.1955 mon10.4.1992 ⊖8.6.1993 ⊕11.6.2006 (Pope Shenouda).

Antonios Markos El Baramoussy ***Johannesburg***
T: B African Affairs ▪ ✉ P.O.Box 72191, 11 Selkirk Rd, Parkview, SOUTH AFRICA-2122 Johannesburg • [27] 11 486354-4, fax -5 • copticafrica@icon.co.za • anbaantoniusmarkos@holysynod.copticpope.org • copticafrica@icon.co.za

*4.9.1936 N? ⊖15.11.1975 mon12.7.1975 Antonios Al Baramousy ⊕13.6.1976 General B of South Africa (Pope Shenouda).

Karas El Anba Bishoi
T: B General Cairo ▪ ✉ Anba Rueiss Building Ramses Street Abbassyea P.O.Box 9035, Nasr City, EGYPT-Cairo • [20] 2 24882606, 68253-57, -58, -74, -75, -76, 26857889, 26821274, fax 6836691, 24871901 • Alexandria [20] 3 48355-22, -33, fax 4841566, [20] 12 3919434, 3110260 • www.copticpope.org
*18.11.1965 mon 8.6.1993 ⊖7.6.1999 ⊕1.6.2014.

Isaac Alkhoury
T: B General ▪ ✉ Metropolitan of Bohyra-Damanhour-Makarios Monastery, EGYPT-Moderiat el Tahreer • [20] 45 3342876, 3344655, fax 3343482 • metropolitianpakhom@yahoo.com
*21.10.1937 mon1963 Al Surian Monastery ⊖2.1.1964. 18.6.1978 Chori-Episcopus ⊕1.6.2014 B assistant to B Bakhomis.

Bemwa Arsanius Alabnobi ***Suez***
T: B Suez ▪ ✉ Coptic Orthodox Metropolitan P.O.Box 137b, EGYPT-Suez • anbabemwa2014@yahoo.com
*6.6.1970. 1993 BA. mon29.9.1999 ⊖22.11.2000 ⊕1.6.2014 B Suez.

Isaac El Anba Bishoi ***Fayoum***
T: B General Bishop ▪ ✉ Coptic Bishopric P.O.Box 85, EGYPT-Fayoum • [20] 84 333222, 335227, 335247, 334780, fax 338893 • bishop.esehak@yahoo.com
*22.10.1955. 1992 BScience. mon4.4.1998 ⊖18.7.2004 ⊕1.6.2014 B Fayoum.

Angelos Sharobim Albaramos ***North Schobra***
T: B General ▪ ✉ Anba Rueiss Building Ramses Street Abbassyea, P.O.Box 9035, Nasr City, EGYPT-Cairo • [20] 2 24882606 • fr.cherubim.2007@gmail.com • www.copticpope.org
*4.9.1966. 1990 degree in medicine. mon13.11.1995 ⊖9.4.2000 ⊕1.6.2014.

Markos Mark Ava Mina
T: B General Cairo ▪ ✉ Anba Rueiss Building Ramses Street Abbassyea P.O.Box 9035, Nasr City, EGYPT-Cairo • [20] 2 24882606 • frmark11307@hotmail.com • www.copticpope.org
*8.5.1966. 1993 Bachelor of commerce. mon20.1.1997 ⊖11.3.2007 ⊕1.6.2014.

Pavle Bola Al Sinaey
T: B General Cairo ▪ ✉ Anba Rueiss Building Ramses Street Abbassyea P.O.Box 9035, Nasr City, EGYPT-Cairo • [20] 2 24882606 • paulasharm@hotmail.com • www.copticpope.org
*22.2.1967. 1991 degree in engineering. mon31.7.1992 first monk to enter Monastery of St. Moses ⊖1999 ⊕1.6.2014.

Rewes
T: B ▪ ✉ Anba Rueiss Building Ramses Street, Abbassyea P.O.Box 9035, Nasr City, EGYPT-Cairo • [20] 2 26836691
*15.10.1939 mon1963 ⊖1963 ⊕1977.

Markorios El Baramoussy ***Gerga***
T: B Gerga ▪ ✉ Coptic Orthodox Metropolitan, EGYPT-Gerga • [20] 934662757, 934660990, 1227373075 • anbamerkorus@gmail.com
*2.10.1958 mon28.2.1990 ⊖28.6.1997 ⊕7.6.2009.

Boktor Bischoi Al Moharaky ***Al Wady***
T: B Al Wady Al Gadeed and Al Wahaat ▪ ✉ St. Mary Church, Al Kharga, Alwady Al Gadeed-Street 15, EGYPT-Ard El • [20] 92 7923623, 122 9094587 • stmaryelkharga@yahoo.com • www.stmaryelkharga.com
*19.3.1953 mon8.5.1980 ⊖19.3.1983 ⊖24.5.2015.

Jouakeem ***Esna and Armant***
T: B ▪ ✉ St. Mary Church, EGYPT-Esna • [20] 2 24882606, 68253-57, -58, -74, -75, -76, 26857889, 26821274, fax 6836691
*24.2.1955 mon8.4.1983 ⊖9.2.1990 ⊕24.5.2015.

Klimandos [Eklemandos] Ava Mina
T: General Bishop ▪ ✉ Church of Virgin Mary 1245 Eglinton Ave. West, CANADA-Mississauga, L5V 2M4 • [1] 905 567-4032
*6.1.1963 mon23.3.1992 ⊖26.9.2001 ⊕24.5.2015.

Mark Abollo El Anba Bischoi
T: B ▪ FRANCE-Paris • anbamarc@hotmail.com
*28.9.1970 mon31.12.2001 ⊖20.4.2008 ⊕24.5.2015.

Hermina ***En Schams***
T: B En Schams and Al Matareya ▪ ✉ St. Georg Church, EGYPT-Een Schams • [20] 1283581035 • mkhermina@gmail.com
*13.11.1972 mon3.8.2002 ⊖7.3.2009 ⊕24.5.2015.

Special situation:

Metias Toma El Suriani
T: former B Mahala ▪ ✉ Anba Rueiss Building Ramses Street Abbassyea P.O.Box 9035, Nasr City, EGYPT-Cairo
*1965 N? ⊕12.6.1989 (Pope Shenouda). 2005 USA, isolated from the province of Mahala.

Ammonius Angelos El Anba Bishoi
T: former B Luxor ▪ ✉ Monastère Anba Bishoi, EGYPT-Cairo • [20] 2 2914448, 2917971
*22.1.1942 El Batach Maragha Sohag. N? Bac Veterinary. mon24.6.1973 ⊖7.7.1974 ⊕13.6.1976 (Pope Shenouda). 1976-2000 B Luxor, Esna, Armant. 2014 suspended.

CHURCH OF CYPRUS

His Beatitude **Chrysostomos**
Archbishop of Nea Justiniana and All Cyprus

Chrysostomos Herodotos Dimitriou ***Nikosia***
T: A Nea Justiniana and All Cyprus ▪ ✉ P.O.Box 21130, CYPRUS-1502 Nikosia • [357] 22 554600, fax 432470
*10.4.1941 Statos Tala Paphos. N13.11. diak3.11.1963.1972 dipl theol Athens ⊖12.11.1972 hegoumenos of St. Neophytos Monastery ⊕26.2.1978. 1978-2006 M Paphos. 5.11.2006 A Cyprus. 22.-28.1.2016 Synaxis of the primates of the Local Orthodox Churches Chambésy Switzerland.

Christophóros Tsiakkas
T: B Karpasia, assistant Bishop ▪ ✉ Iera Archiepiskopi Kyprou, P.O.Box 21130, CYPRUS-1502 Nikosia • [357] 22 554600, [357] 22 432327
*4.5.1964 Pelendri. N9.5. 1982-1984 military service. 1984-1988 dipl theol Athens. diak1990 ⊖1991 archim1991 Troodítissa. 1992-1995 MA Durham. 1995 secretary Holy Synod ⊕3.6.2007 assistant B. 22.-28.1.2016 Synaxis of the primates of the Local Orthodox Churches Chambésy Switzerland.

Epiphanios Machairiotis
T: B Ledra, assistant B ▪ ✉ Iera Archiepiskopi Kyprou, P.O.Box 25272, CYPRUS-1308 Nikosia • [357] 22 35933-4, fax -3
*1971 Levkosia. N12.5. 1988-1991 stud pedagogics Levkosia. 1989-1993 stud Byzantine music Levkosia. 1995 Machaira. diak1999 ⊖2000. 2004 hegoumenos Machaira ⊕23.6.2007 assistant B.

Georgios Papachrysostomou ***Paphos***
T: M Paphos ▪ ✉ Iera Mitropolis P.O.Box 60054, CYPRUS-8100 Paphos • [357] 26 932092, fax 943130
*25.5.1949 Athiaínou. N23.4. 1967 absolvent Pankiprion gymnasion. 1968-1972 stud chemistry Athens. 1980 dipl theol Athens. 1980-1984 stud chemistry, theol England. diak23.12.1984 ⊖17.3.1985 archim1985, hierokēryx. 1985-1996 teacher chemistry. 1994 secretary Holy Synod ⊕26.5.1996. 1996-2006 B Arsinoë. assistant Paphos. 2006 M Paphos. 16.12.2015 Athens Interorthodox committee preparation Panorthodox Synod 2016.

Nektarios Spyrou
T: B Arsinoë, assistant Paphos ▪ ✉ Iera Mitropolis P.O.Box 60054, CYPRUS-8100 Paphos • [357] 26 932092, fax 943130

*15.1.1969 Larnaka. N9.11. stud Thessaloniki, SOAS College London. diak1996 (A Georgíou Kontou) ⊖1998 Ag. Georgíou Mavrovouníou. archim2005. 2005-2007 proistámenos London. 2008 protosynkellos Kition ⊕14.9.2008 B Arsinoë, assistant Paphos.

Leontios Englistriotis
T: B Chytroi, assistant B ▪ ✉ Mon Agios Neophytos, CYPRUS-8100 Paphos • [357] 26 652-481, fax -507
*7.8.1946 Agios Ermolaos Kyreneia. N18.6. 1958 Mon Agios Neophytos. 1961-1967 gymnasion Paphos. diak1967. 1967-1972 Ephoros Mon Agios Neophytos. 1972-1976 dipl theol Athens ⊖1976. archim1978 hegoumenos Mon Agios Neophytos ⊕24.6.2007 assistant B.

Chrysostomos Machairiotis ***Kition***
T: M Kition ▪ ✉ Iera Mitropolis P.O.Box 40036, CYPRUS-6300 Larnaka • [357] 24 652269, fax 655588
*4.6.1938 Paliometochon, N27.1. 1951 Monastery Machairá. diak1956, 1966 dipl jur Athens. 1970 dipl theol Athens ⊖7.6.1970 Archimandrit Machairá ⊕26.10.1973 M Kition. Representative of the Patriarch of Alexandria in Cyprus.

Chrysostomos Constantinos Kykkotis ***Kyrenia***
T: M Kyrenia ▪ ✉ P.O.Box 20258, Achilleos 3 Aglanzia, CYPRUS-2150 Lefkosia • [357] 22 444-242, fax -330 • chrysostomos1@me.com
*14.12.1970 Kyrenia, Papathomas Nfirst Sunday before 14th Sept. school Lefkosia 1989-1993 MTh Thessaloniki 1993-2001 stud theol England France Helvetia Austria. mon7.4.2001 diak8.4.2001 Palmsunday (A Chrysostomos) ⊖8.9.2007 Vienna Austria. archim8.9.2007 (M Kykkos). 2007-2011 Cultural Center Monastery Archangel Michael Metochion Kykkos ⊕10.12.2011 Panagia Evangelistria Pallouriotissa, M Kyrenia (A Chrysostomos II). 25.-27.10.2015 Loppiano Dr.h.c. Patr Bartholomaios 23.-30.11.2015 34th Ecumenical Meeting for Bishops, İstanbul.

Athanasios Nikolaou ***Limassol***
T: M Lemesos ▪ ✉ P.O.Box 56091, odos Agiou Andreou 306, CYPRUS-3304 Limassol • [357] 25 864300, fax 371548 • Spiritual Center Enosis st. 347776, 364016, 347372, fax 341384
*8.2.1959 Limassol. N18.1. 1973-1976 gymnasion Paphos. diak18.4.1976 (A Chrysostomos) 1976-1980 dipl theol Thessaloniki. 1980 Mount Athos. 1982 Mega Schema ⊖29.5.1982 (M Nikodimos Ierissos). 1983 Pnevmatikos Nea Skiti, 1987 Vatopediou. 1991-1992 Protepistates Mount Athos. 1993-1999 igumen Moni Machera Cyprus ⊕14.2.1999 M Limassol.

Nikolaos Timiadis

T: B Amathoús, assistant Lemesos ▪ ✉ P.O. Box 56091, odos Agiou Andreou 306, CYPRUS-3304 Limassol • [357] 25 864300, fax 371548

*1969 Augoros Ammochosto. N6.12. 1987 apofitos gymnasion Larnaka. 1987-1992 dipl theol Thessaloniki. 1991-1992 Mount Athos. 1992 Monastery St. Nicholas Paphos. mon1992. 1993 Monastery Machaira, 1994 Mega Schema. diak1996 (B Basilios Amathoús) ⊖1999 (M Athanasios Lemessos). 2003 Pnevmatikos. archim2003 igoumenos Timíou Prodrómou Mésa Potamou ⊕10.6.2007.

Porphyrios Machairiotis

T: B Neapolis, assistant Lemesos ▪ ✉ P.O. Box 56091, odos Agiou Andreou 306, CYPRUS-3304 Limassol • [357] 25 864300, fax 371548

*16.4.1966 Pera Oreinís Levkosia. N26.2. school Strovolon. 1984-1986 military service. 1986-1990 stud Archeology Athens. 1990-1994 stud theol Athens. 1993 Mitropolis Lemesos. 1995 Machaira, diak1998 ⊖1999 archim2000 ⊕27.10.2007.

Grigorios Hadziouraniou

T: B Mesaoria, Interchurch Relations and European Affairs Office ▪ ✉ Archbishopric, P.O.Box 21130, CYPRUS-1502 Nikosia • [357] 225546 -00, -11, fax 22346254, 22431796 • office@churchofcyprus.org.cy • www.churchofcyprus.org.cy

*25.2.1968 Levkosia. N25.1. 1990 dipl theol Athens. 1992-2000 assistant Patristics Athens. 1992-2008 hierokēryx Nikosia, 1996 Master University Birmingham, Selly Oak College. 2001-2008 teacher gymnasion. diak6.5.2001 ⊖24.3.2002 archim 20.7.2004 ⊕30.3.2008. 2008 postgraduate studies Athens.

Neophitos Omiros Masuras ***Morphou***

T: M Morphou ▪ ✉ Mitropolis Morphou, CYPRUS-2831 Evrychou • [357] 22 932401, 932414, fax 933092

*21.1.1962 Ano Zodia Morphou. N18.9. 1980-1987 Fac theol Athens, Fac jur Athens. diak27.12.1987. 1987-1996 Mitropolis Kition ⊖19.12.1993 archim19.12.1993. 1996-1998 Mon Ag. Georgiou Mavrovouniou ⊕13.9.1998 M Morphou.

Basilios Karayiannis ***Konstantia***

T: M Konstantia+Ammochostos ▪ ✉ Ag. Georgiou 12, P.O.Box 34034, CYPRUS-5309 Paralimni • [357] 23 8124-44, fax -50 • trimith@logos.cy • metropolitan-v@imconstantias.org.cy • www.imconstantias.org.cy

*1.3.1948 Mandres Famagusta. N1.1. 1960-1974 Monastery Apostolos Barnabas, 1967-1970 Ieratiki Scholi Apostolos Barnabas. 1970 Apostolos Barnabas. diak15.8. 1970 Apostolos Barnabas. 1970-1974 gymnasion Ammochosto. 1974-1978 stud theol Athens, stud Byzantine Music Athens. 1978-1980 Stipendiat Catholica Unio,

Sociologie Fribourg, diacre Chambésy Genève ⊖11.4.1981Cyprus archim1981. 1981-1991 paroisse Genève, 1982-1991 protosynkellos Helvetias. 1991 Dr. theol (Prof. Schönborn OP) Université de Fribourg "Maxime le Confesseur, Essence et Énergies de Dieu". 1991 Directeur Bureau Contacts inter-ecclesiastiques Nikosia, prof School Apóstolos Barnábas. 1996 redacteur "Célébration des mariages interconfessionels protestants-orthodoxes en Suisse" Evangelisch/Orthodoxe Gesprächskommission ⊕28.4.1996. 1996-2007 B Trimythoús Amathoús Tremetousiá, assistant Nikosia. Greek French English. 1997 Central Committee CEC. 1999 Commission Orthodox Collaboration WCC Geneva, Commission Faith and Order. 2007 M Konstantia.

Nikiphoros Kykkotis ***Kykkos***

T: M Kykkos+Tylliria ▪ ✉ Igumen Kykkos, P.O.Box 24850, CYPRUS-1304 Lefkosia • [357] 22 390000, [357] 22 351852

*2.5.1947 Kritou Marottou Paphos. N2.6. Lykeion Levkosia. mon1969 diak6.4.1969 Kykkos. 1969-1974 stud jur Thessaloniki. 1974-1978 stud theol Athens ⊖8.9.1979 archim1979. 1979-1985 teacher Apostolos Barnabas, 1979-1982 secretary Holy Synod. 1979-1984 Proedros Ekklesiastikon Dikasterion. 1983 igumen Kykkos ⊕3.3.2002. 2007 M Kykkos.

Isaïas Kykkotis ***Tamassos***

T: M Tamasos+Oreini ▪ ✉ P.O.Box 12123, CYPRUS-2341 Lakatamia • [357] 22 465465, [357] 22 624600, 661462, [357] 99 991999 • isaiask@cytanet.com.cy • imtamasou.org.cy

*1971 Strovolos. N10.9. 1990 military service 1990 Ieratiki scholi Apostolos Barnabas Kykkos. 1992-1997 Academy Moskva. diak1993 Kykkos. 1998 Kandidat Moskva "Life and work of St. Neophytos". 1998-2000 stud Archeology Thessaloniki ⊖2000. 2001-2007 secretary Kykkos, 2003 Dr. theol Moskva "History and Theology ... Ag. Oros Athos". 2005 European Aids Holy Synod ⊕11.6.2007.14.10.2010 Theol Academy 325 years Moskva.

Barnabas Stavrovouniotis ***Trimythoús***

T: M Trimythoús ▪ ✉ P.O.Box 11001, CYPRUS-2550 Idalion • [357] 22 527000, fax 526363

*1958 Limassol "Charalambos Proussiotis". N11.6. 1976-1980 dipl theol Thessaloniki. 1981 Stavrovounion. diak1983 ⊖1985 ⊕21.7.2007.

Retired Hierarchs:

Barnabas Solomou
T: former B Salamis, assistant B ▪ ✉ Iera Archiepiskopi Kyprou, P.O.Box 21130, CYPRUS-1502 Nikosia • [357] 22 554600, [357] 22 474180
*8.7.1931 Levkara, N11.6. 1955 dipl theol Athens. 1955-1969 Katechet. diak26.10. 1969 ⊖4.10.1970 ⊕12.8.1973. 1973-2011 assistant B, retired.

ORTHODOX CHURCH OF THE CZECH LANDS AND SLOVAKIA
PRAVOSLAVNA CIRKEV V CESKYCH ZEMICH A NA SLOVENSKU
PRAVOSLAVNA CIRKEV V CESKYCH KRAJINACH A NA SLOVENSKU

His Beatitude **Rastislav**
Metropolitan of the Czech Lands and Slovakia

Rastislav Andrej Gont *Prešov*
T: Metropolitan of the Czech Lands and Slovakia, A Prešov, Arcibiskup prešovský ▪ ✉ Bayerova 8, SLOVAKIA-08001 Prešov • [421] 51 746026-4, -9, fax -0, -5 • sekretariat@ppepoer.sk • arciep.rastislav@gmail.com • arcibiskup@ppepoer.sk • www.orthodox.sk
*25.1.1978 Snina Slovakia. N? 2002 dipl Fac theol orth Prešov. 2002 stud theol Thessaloniki. rector Medzilaborc. 1.12.2012 igumen ⊕18.11.2012 A Prešov. 2013 mjestobljustitel M. 2014 M. 22.-28.1.2016 Synaxis of the primates of the Local Orthodox Churches Chambésy Switzerland.

Juraj Stránský *Michalovce*
T: A Michalovce+Košice ▪ ✉ Duklianská 16, SLOVAKIA-07101 Michalovce • [421] 566 424 156, fax 566 431 500, [421] 905 316134 • biskup@juraj@yahoo.gr • www.mkpe.sk
*19.10.1979 Jesenik. N23.4. diak14.3.2004 (A Simeon Olomouc) mon2.10.2004 Hesychastérion Kyrill Methodios Thessaloniki ⊖2.1.2005 (M Anthimos Thessaloniki). archim18.4.2007 schema Kykkos Monastery Cyprus ⊕30.9.2007 B Michalovce. 2007 MA Theol Academy Užgorod Ukraina. 2009 MA English, American Studies, Turkology University Prague. 2009 A Michalovce+Košice. 2015 Preparatory Commission Great and Holy Synod 2016 Chambésy. 16.12.2015 Athens Interorthodox committee preparation Panorthodox Synod. 22.-28.1.2016 Synaxis of the primates of the Local Orthodox Churches Chambésy Switzerland.

Simeon Radivoj Jakovljević *Olomouc*
T: A Olomouc+Brno ▪ ✉ Pravoslavná Církev, Tř. Masarykova 17, CZECHIA-77200 Olomouc • [420] 585 222 475, fax 585 224 883, [420] 723 312356 • arcibiskup.simeon@seznam.cz • www.eparchie-ob.cz
*12.2.1926 Prag. N13.2. gymnasium Prag. 1949-1953 Theol Academy Leningrad. 1954-1959 assistant Prof AT Fac theol Prešov. 7.9.1958 marriage. diak1.11.1958 Prag ⊖25.12.1958. 1959-1998 parish Mariánské Lázně Marienbad. 1982 Dr. theol Prešov "Izajášcuv Ebed Jahve a smysl jeho utrpení". 1996 widower. 1998 parish Mariánské Lázne Marienbad. mon1.6.1998 ⊕21.6.1998.1998-2000 B Mariánské Lázně, vicar Prag. 2000 B, 2006 A Olomouc+Brno.

Izajash Igor Slaninka

T: B Shumberk, vicar Olomouc ▪ ✉ Tr. Masarykova 17, CZECHIA-77200 Olomouc • [420] 585 222 475 • arcibiskup.simeon@seznam.cz • www.eparchie-ob.cz

* ⊖30.11.2010 archim2010. 2010 Dr. theol ⊕22.2.2015 B Shumperk vicar Olomouc.

Tihon Tibor Hollósy

T: B Komárno, former vicar Prešov ▪ GREECE-71201 Herakleion, Kreta • biskup-tihon@orthodox.sk

*9.1.1948 Budapest. N? 1971 Economic University Budapest. 1993 Jableczna Poland. diak1993 ⊖1993 (B Abel Lublin). 1998 MA theol Fac theol Prešov. igumen 1999 Mother of God Komárno ⊕8.4.2006. 2006-2012 B Komárno vicar Prešov. 2012 Kreta.

Michal Michael Dandár ***Prague***

T: A Prague and Czech Lands ▪ ✉ Sharecká 1065/36, CZECHIA-16000 Praha • [420] 224 315015, [420] 602 378 644 • arcibiskup.michal@post.cz • www.pravoslavnacirkev.cz

*9.1.1947 Zemplinske Hradishte Trebishov Slovakia. 1963-1965 Fac theol Prešov. 1965-1969 Akad Theol Leningrad, 1969 Kandidat Theol. 1971-1980 parish Dresden (Patr Moskva). diak21.5.1971 Leningrad (M Nikodim) ⊖22.5.1971 Leningrad (M Nikodim). 1974 stud German language Inst. Herder in Radebeul/ Dresden. 1980-1999 parishes Preshov, Prague, Dean Prague and Central Region 1980 protoierej, 1989-1990 stud German language and Bibliographie Martin Luther Bund Erlangen. 1990-1996 Lektor Director Theol school St. Kyrill and Method Prague. 1992 Mitra (M Dorotej). 1997-2000 teacher Orthodox Liturgics Jan Hus Fac University Prague. 1997 Protopresbyter (M Dorotej). Lic theol Jan Hus Fac Prague. 1998 Dr. phil University Preshov. 2000-2004 Exarch to Moscow Patriarchate. 2004-2007 dean Bratislava. mon15.7.2004 Podvorije of Mount Athos in Moskva (igumen Nikon). 2007-2014 parish Schweinfurt Germany Moscow Patriarchate (A Theophan). 24.5.2010 igumen (A Theophan Berlin). 2014-2015 parishes Prague. archim1.3.2015 (A Jáchym Prague) ⊕14.3.2015 A Prague in Prague (A Jiří, A Jáchym, B Damián Kiev, A Antonij Moravický). 22.-28.1.2016 Synaxis of the primates of the Local Orthodox Churches Chambésy Switzerland.

Retired Hierarchs:

Kryštof Radim Pulec

T: former M de toutes les terres Tchèques et de la Slovaquie ▪ ✉ Monastir Milikov Téšov 37, CZECHIA-35002 Cheb • [420] 723 841073 • metropolita.cz@hotmail.cz

*29.6.1953 (Christophoros the Roman from Palestina VI century) father Old-Cath. bishop in Union with orth Church. 1963 gymnasium Praha. 1974 dipl theol Fac Hus Praha. 1974-1982 parish Hořovičky, stud orth theol Prešov, (correspondence course) Academy Moskva. 1982-1987 Dr. theol Athens History Orth Church ČSSR. 7.9.1985 Sergiev Posad. 1987-1988 Proistamenos Cathedral St. Kyrill Method Praha ⊕17.4.1988 Sunday St. Thomas. 1988-2000 B Olomouc+Brno. 1999 Commission Orthodox Collaboration WCC Geneva. 2000 A Praha. 19.5.2003 OKI Regensburg. 2006-2013 M. 2013 Monastir Tessov, Prof Christian Social Teaching Prešov. Retired.

Jáchym Roman Hrdý

T: former A Prague et toutes les terres Tchèques ▪ ✉ Šárecká 36/1065, CZECHIA-16000 Praha • [420] 224 315 015, 233 324065, fax 224 313 137, [420] 723 841073, [420] 777 260556 • joakim@seznam.cz • www.pravoslavnacirkev.cz

*8.3.1973, N9.9. 1995 MA Mathematics Biology. mon1997 Troice-Sergieva Lavra Rossija. diak1997 Troice-Sergieva Lavra Rossija ⊖1999 Olomouc (B Kryštof). 2003 igumen St. Gorazd Monastery Hrubá Vrbka. archim2007 ⊕14.2.2009. 2009-2014 B Hodonín vicar Olomouc. 22.11.2014 retired.

ERITREAN ORTHODOX TEWAHEDO CHURCH

His Holiness Abuna **Dioskoros**
Patriarch of the Eritrean Orthodox Church

Antonios Gebremedin Debretsion ***Eritrea***
T: former Patriarch Eritrea ▪ ✉ P.O.Box 728, ERITREA-Asmara • [291] 1 184547, 182-098, fax -119
*5.7.1927. N? 1932 shrine Abuna Endrias ⊕19.5.1994 (Pentecost, by Pope Shenouda in St. Mark's Cathedral Cairo) 1994-2004 B Hamasiye central region. from 25.4.2004 to 19.4.2007 3rd patriarch of Eritrea (Pope Shenouda in Asmara Cathedral).

Makarios Kyrillos Menghistu
T: ▪ ✉ P.O.Box 373, 5 Woodstone Drive, USA-Cedar Grove, NJ 07009 • [1] 973 857-0078, fax -1315
*5.5.1931 ⊖1956. 1974 Khartoum ⊕26.5.1991 (Pope Shenouda). 1991-2004 Ethiopian B for the Eritrean diaspora.

Markos Petros ***Massawa***
T: B Massawa ▪ ✉ P.O.Box 728, ERITREA-Asmara • [291] 11 84547, 82098, fax 82195
1974 Pro Oriente Wien. 1980-1992 USA ⊕26.5.1991 (Pope Shenouda) Ethiopian B for the Eritrean diaspora. 1997 secretary synod Eritrea. 1999 London. 2004 B Massawa.

Kyrillos Tesfasilassie ***South East***
T: A South Zone East ▪ ✉ Monastery Abune Bitsu Amlak, P.O.Box 728, ERITREA-Asmara
*1928 N? ⊕19.5.1994 (Pope Shenouda). 1994-2004 B Akele-Gusai.

Salama Tesfagaber
T: B ▪ ✉ P.O.Box 728, ERITREA-Asmara • [291] 1 113015
*1927 N? Monastery Debresina St. Mary ⊕19.5.1994 (Pope Shenouda). 1994-2004 B Semharn+Dankalen.

Yoannes ***Anseba***
T: A Anseba ▪ ✉ Eritrean Orth Archbishopric, ERITREA-Assab
⊕19.5.1994 (Pentecost, by Pope Shenouda). 1994-2004 Assab.

Markos Tesfai ***North Red Sea***
T: A North Red Sea ▪ ✉ Eritrean Orth Archbishopric, ERITREA-Assab
*1931 N? Monastery Abune Bitsu Amlak ⊕19.5.1994 (Pope Shenouda). 2004 North Red Sea.

Mattewos Semereab ***Dibarwa***

T: B Dibarwa ▪ ✉ P.O.Box 728, ERITREA-Asmara • [291] 1 113015

*1932. N? 1953 Debre Qusquam St. Mary Monastery. Abba Abraham abbot Dibarwa monastery ⊕30.4.2004 (Patr Antonios).

Lukas Gebrehiwet ***Gash-Barka***

T: B Gash-Barka, Lowlands ▪ ✉ P.O.Box 728, ERITREA-Asmara • [291] 1 113015

*1936. N? 1952 Abune Libanos Monastery. Abba Tsige Southern Eritrea ⊕30.4.2004 (Patr Antonios).

Petros Asfehe ***South Red Sea***

T: B South Red Sea ▪ ✉ P.O.Box 728, ERITREA-Asmara • [291] 1 113015

*1940 N? 1967 Abba Araia abbot Sina St. Mary monastery ⊕30.4.2004 (Patr Antonios).

Shenouda Zeamanuel ***USA***

T: B USA ▪ ✉ P.O.Box 373, 5 Woodstone Drive, USA-Cedar Grove, NJ 07009 • [1] 973 857-0078, fax -1315

*1960 N? Monastery Bizen Abune Filipos, rector St. Michael Roma ⊕30.4.2004 (Patr Antonios). 2004-2005 B Europe without having been in London. 2005 USA.

Orthodox Church of Estonia

His Beatitude **Stefanos**
Metropolitan of Tallinn and All Estonia

Stefanus Christakis Charalambides
T: M Tallinn+Estonia, Eesti Apostlik-Õigeusu Kiriku metropolit ▪ ✉ Wismari 32, Estonia-10136 Tallinn • [372] 6600780 • stefanus@eoc.ee • www.orthodoxa.org
*29.4.1940 Bukavu Rép. Dém. Congo. N27.12. stud Institut St-Serge Paris. diak1963 ⊖1968. 1971-1987 protosynkellos Paris. 1983 Recteur Nice ⊕25.3.1987. 1987-1999 B Nazianz, assistant France (Konst). 1999 M Tallinn+Estonia.

Elijah Ojaperv *Tartu*
T: B Tartu ▪ ✉ Magasini 1-1, Estonia-50304 Tartu • eelija@eaok.ee
*11.5.1977 N? ⊕10.1.2009. chairman Worship book redaction committee.

Aleksander Hopjorski *Parnu*
T: B Pärnu+Saaremaa ▪ ✉ Aia 5, Estonia-80011 Pärnu • [372] 5141215 alexander@eaok.ee
*23.8.1964 N? ⊕12.1.2009.

Makarios Konstantinos Griniezakis
T: B Christoupolis, vicar Estonia ▪ ✉ Wismari 32, Estonia-1036 Tallinn • [372] 6600780 • www.eoc.ee
*15.3.1970 Hierakleion Kreta. diak18.10.1993 mon18.10.1993. 1994-1997 deacon Herakleion. stud Fac theol Athens, MTh Boston, MA Harvard, Master Bioethics Monash. Dr. med Medicin Fac University Kreta "Cloning..." ⊖25.6.1997. 1997-2002 parishpriest Southbridge USA. archim23.4.1998. 2002-2010 director Radio Church of Kreta. 2002-2015 hierokēryx Kreta. 2008 Archimandritis of the Ecumenical Throne. 2011-2015 director typography of the Archbishop ⊕16.5.2015 B consecrated in Heraklion Kreta.

ETHIOPIAN ORTHODOX CHURCH

His Holiness Abuna **Matias**
Patriarch of the Ethiopian Orthodox Church

Matias Teklemariam Asrat
T: Patriarch of Ethiopia, A Axum, Itchege of the See of Tekle Haimanot ▪ ✉ EOC Patriarchate, P.O.Box 1283, ETHIOPIA-Addis Ababa • [251] 11 1550577, 1552216, 1551822, 1111989, 1116507, fax 1551455, 1552211
*1934 "Teklemariam" Sebuha Tigrai. N? stud Monastery Tenben (Eritrea). 1946 Holy Trinity Cathedral Addis Ababa, secr of the Patr. diak1954 ⊖1958 (eth 1951). 1962 Chohay Monastery Tigrai ⊕21.1.1979. 1979-1982 A Jerusalem. 1982-1992 USA. 1984 Bonn, Köln, Heidelberg. 1992-2006 A America and the Western Hemisphere. 2006-2012 A Jerusalem. 2009 delegation German bishops. 28.2.2013 Patriarch.

Elssa Heruy Woldesenbet ***Gondar North***
T: A North Gondar ▪ ✉ P.O.Box 1283, ETHIOPIA-Addis Ababa • [251] 11 1116780 • Debre Tabor [251] 58 441031-4, -5
*1930 Gondar, N? teacher of Religion Monastery Debre Zige Mariam ⊕21.1.1979. 1979-1989 B Jimma Illubabor. 1989-1995 secretary Holy Synod. 1999 chairman Church's Court, 1999-2009 A Debre Tabor. 2009 North Gondar.

Gabriel Petros Iyasu ***Sidamo***
T: A Sidamo, Awassa, Geto Burji ▪ ✉ EOC Patriarchate, P.O.Box 1283, ETHIOPIA-Addis Ababa
*1940 Wagg Zata Wollo. N? Teacher of qené. 1959-1963 stud Addis Ababa St. Paul's Theol Seminary, 1963-1969 stud Holy Trinity Seminary. 1969-1973 and 1974-1979 Dr. theol Leningrad. 1973-1974 USA MTh Princeton. ⊕13.1.1980 B Western Hararge, 1981-1986 A Eritrea. 1986 A Diredawa, 1986 Chief Protocol. 1991-1992 A Southern Shoa. 1992-1993 A Southern Wollo. 1994-1998 A Western Shoa, chairman Department External Relations. 1998-2001 A Jerusalem. 2001 outside Ethiopia, 2004-2007 USA. 2007-2011 Dean St. Paul's Theol Seminary. 2011 A Sidamo.

Timotheos Habteselassie Tesfa
T: A, Dean "St. Trinity Theological College" ▪ ✉ P.O.Box 503, 30477, ETHIOPIA-Addis Ababa • [251] 11 1560146, 1552783
*1938 Tigray. N? "Habteselassie" diak1950 ⊖1958. 1973 Dr. theol Leningrad ⊕13.1.1983 B Kaffa. 1988 Pro Oriente Wien, A Jimma, Assab. 1991-1993 general secretary Holy Synod. 1993 Commissioner for Development and Inter Church Aid. Commission. 1993 Delegation Wien in charge of Western Europe. 1999 Dean "St. Trinity Theological College" Likesiltanat (= rector Holy Trinity Addis Ababa).

Ephraim Tsedalu ***Debre Berhan***
T: ADebre Brhan, North Shoa ▪ ✉ EOC Patriarchate, P.O.Box 1283, ETHIOPIA-Addis Ababa • [251] 22 8811843, 8811877, 8811127
*1930 (eth 1923) Shoa. N? ⊕13.1.1980 B Arssi.1984-1991 A Tigrai.1991 A Debrebrhan, North Shoa.

Gerima Woldekirkos
T: A ▪ ✉ EOC Patriarchate, P.O.Box 1283, ETHIOPIA-Addis Ababa
*18.12.1934 (eth1927) N?"Girma". diak1953. 1965-1974 București, 1974 Dr. theol București.1978 Consultation Wien. 1978-1989 Standing Committee Pro Oriente. mon1982 ⊖3.1.1982 ⊕19.7.1982 B Nubia Khartum. 1982-1991 A Illubabor. 1991-1992 Dean St. Paul's Theol Seminary. 1992-1993 A Gojam. 1993-1999 Chief Administrator of the Church's General Office, secretary to the Holy Synod. 1999-2005 A Diredawa, chairman Department External Relations. 2005-2006 A Jerusalem. 2006 back to Ethiopia. 2007 chairman Department External Relations.

Mathias Teklemariam Nigussie ***Canada***
T: A Canada ▪ ✉ 140-142 West 176th, USA-Bronx, NY 10453
*1927 Wollo. N? "Teklemariam" ⊕21.1.1979, 1983 A Wollo. 1985 A Illubabor. 1991-1993 A Kaffa. 1996 A Canada.

Atnathewos Johannes Kahali ***Dessie***
T: A Dessie, South Wollo ▪ ✉ P.O. Box 1283, ETHOPIA-Addis Ababa • [251] 33 3111205
*1938 (eth 1931) Wollo. N? ⊕24.11.1984 (Patr Tekle Haimanot). 1984-1992 B Jerusalem.1992 A Dessie South Wollo.

Kerlos Merhatsidk Gebrehiwot ***Wollo***
T: A Northern Wollo, Woldya ▪ ✉ EOC Patriarchate, P.O.Box 1283, ETHIOPIA-Addis Ababa • [251] 11 1550099, 1556507 • Wollo [251] 33 1111205
*1945 (eth 1937) Wollo. N? "Gebrehiwot" ⊕15.6.1987 (Patr Teklehaimanot) Ass Wollo. 1988 A Wollo, 1991-1993 A Northern Wollo. 1993 A Eastern Shoa. 1994 A North Wollo. 1999-2002 Chief Administrator of the Headquarters Ethiopian Orthodox Church. 2002 A NorthernWolloWoldya.

Kewstos Zekarias Habtemariam ***Selallie***
T: A Addis Ababa, Selallie ▪ ✉ EOC Patriarchate, P.O.Box 1283, ETHIOPIA-Addis Ababa
*1930 "Habtemariam" N? ⊕15.6.1987 B Wolayta+Dawro. 1992-1994 A Wollega and Assosa. 1994-1997 A North and South Omo. 1997-1999 A Gamogofa. 1999-2001 A

dioceses Eastern Harar, Western Harar, Diredawa. 2001-2004 A Jerusalem. 2005 A Addis Abeba, Selallie.

Tomas Mezemr Tegegne ***Finot Selam***

T: A West Gojjam, Finot Selam Hawi Metekel Pawe ▪ ✉ P.O.Box 503, 30477 ETHIOPIA-Addis Ababa • [251] 11 1560146, office 1552783

*24.3.1941 Gojam. N? ⊖15.6.1987 ⊕1989-1992 A Wollega. 1992-1993 A Western Harrar. 1993 A Selale. 1993-1996 Dean St. Paul's Theological College, 1996-1999 chairman Department Church Catechesis, A Selale. 1999-2000 A North Omo. 2000 instructor Holy Trinity Theological College. 2001 A West Gojam Finot Selam Hawi Metekel Pawe.

Thadewos WoldeGabriel WoldeSelassie ***Trinidad***

T: A Caribbean+Latin America ▪ ✉ Old Golden Grove Road, TRINITAD AND TOBAGO-Arouca • [1] 868 642 42 30

*18.5.1942 "WoldeSelassie" Wollo. N? ⊖3.2.1958 ⊕7.2.1993 (Patr Paulos).1998 A Caribbean+Latin America.

Gorgorios Tetmke Gebre Teklehaymanot ***Nazreth***

T: A East Shoa Nazreth, Shoa (Zewi) ▪ ✉, ETHIOPIA-Nazreth • [251] 22 1112657

*1956 (eth 1949) Tigrai. N? "Gebre Teklehaymanot" ⊕13.11.1994 B Nazreth East Shoa. 2004 Mondo Migliore.

Epifaniyos Asayehgn Amehayesus ***Ambo***

T: A Ambo, Western Shoa ▪ ✉ P.O. Box 503, 30477, ETHIOPIA-Addis Ababa • [251] 11 1560146, office 1552783

*1959 (eth 1952) "Asayehgn" N? ⊕12.7.1999. 1999-2000 B Mizan Teferi, Kaffa. 2000 Addis Ababa. 2001 Western Shoa Ambo.

Isayas Tesfaye ***Mekele***

T: A Mekele ▪ ✉ Ethiopian Orthodox Archbishopric, ETHIOPIA-Mekele • [251] 34 7710185, 44003932

⊕12.7.1999. 1999-2000 A London. 2000-2005 A Axum Tigrai. 2005 A Diredawa, 2005-2007 chairman External Relations. 2007-2011 A Diredawa. 2011 Mekele.

Yonas Serekebrhan ***Afar***

T: B Afar and Ogaden ▪ ✉ Ethiopian Orth Bishopric P.O.Box 8159, ETHIOPIA-Afar • [251] 25 5510155 • Ogaden 7752981

*1953 N? ⊕12.7.1999 B Afar. 2003 West Harrar and Ogaden. 2005 Afar.

Estifanos Gebremichael Beyene ***Jimma***
T: A Jimma ▪ ✉ EOC Patriarchate, P.O.Box 1283, ETHIOPIA-Addis Ababa • [251] 11 1550099, 1556507, [251] 23 1111205
*1959 (eth 1952) N? ⊕12.7.1999.1999-2000 A Ogaden. 2000 A Mizanteferi. 2001-2004 Chief Administrator for the patriarchate head office. MelakeSelam (= rector St. Stephan Addis Ababa). 2004 A Jimma. 2013 Assistant Patriarch.

Elias Tomas Bekele ***Arba Minch***
T: A North Omo Arbaminch ▪ ✉ P.O. Box 1283, ETHIOPIA-Addis Ababa • [251] 47 6611021
*1961 East Shoa N? ⊕12.7.1999 B Wollega, 2002 Omo Arbaminch.

Endryas Gohatsibah Tirune ***Gondar South***
T: A South Gondar, Debre Tabor ▪ ✉ P.O.Box 1283, ETHIOPIA-Addis Ababa • [251] 11 1550923
⊕12.7.1999. 1999-2000 B North Gondar. 2000-2003 chairman St. Paul's Theological Seminary. 2004-2009 A North Gondar. 2009 South Gondar.

Mussie Mussie ***Italia***
T: A Italia ▪ ✉ SS.Gioacchino e Anna ai Monti, via Monte Polacco 5, ITALIA-00184 Roma
*1959 (eth 1952) N? ⊕12.7.1999. 1999 A Dubai. 2000-2003 A West Tigrai. 2004 outside Ethiopia. 2008 A Wolliso, Western Shoa. 2011 Roma Italia.

Simon Fisiha ***East Wellega***
T: A East Wellega, Horogudru ▪ ✉ P.O.Box 1283, ETHIOPIA-Addis Ababa
*1941 "WeldeTsadik" N? ⊕12.7.1999 B Assosa. 2005 A Gambella. 2007 Metekel. 2009 Bahtalemariam Membere Mengest St. Gabriel Nunnery. 2013 East Wellega.

Yosef Hailegiorgis ***Bale Gobba***
T: A Bale Goba ▪ ✉ EOC Patriarchate, P.O.Box 1283, ETHIOPIA-Addis Ababa • [251] 46 661002-1, -7
*1954 (eth 1946) Selallie. N? 1959-1960 Zema School church singing, 1961-1963 school Geez, 1962-1969 teacher elementary Meskerem. mon1964. 1964-1966 Theological Teacher Training School, 1964-1971 teacher Holy Gospel Menagesha. 1970-1974 gymnasium Misrak. 1971-1977 rector Menelik II Memorial Office. European. 1984-1985 Ostkirchliches Institut Regensburg with Emahoy Fikirte. 1994 DebreLibanos.⊕12.7.1999. B Harar. 2000 B Selallie. 2004 A Italia. 2011 A Bale.

Hizkiel Habtemarian Mekonen ***Keffa-Bonga***
T: B Keffa, Benchimaji zone ▪ ✉ EOC Patriarchate, P.O.Box 1283, ETHIOPIA-Addis Ababa • [251] 47 3310045

*1.5.1953 "Habtemarian" South Wollo. N? stud theol Amhara Saynt Merto Lemariam, Debre Libanos, Holy Trinity Theol College. Melake Mihret ⊕26.8.2005. 2011 secretary to the Holy Synod.

Diyoskoros Brhaneselasie GebreTsion ***Maychew***
T: B Maychew ▪ ✉ EOC Patriarchate, P.O.Box 1283, ETHIOPIA-Addis Ababa

*1963 Raya "Gebre Tsion". N? stud Raya Zeway Clergy training center, Holy Trinity Theol College ⊕26.8.2005.

Samuel Welde Samuel Tekeste Brhan
T: B President Comission Development ▪ ✉ EOC Patriarchate, P.O.Box 1283, ETHIOPIA-Addis Ababa • [251] 11 1550099, 1556507 • addiosee@telecom.net

*1962 "Welde Samuel" Tigrai Region, Shere. N? stud Debre Abbey, Waldba Mon, BA theol Buluha College. Dicab College dipl computer programming Administration Georgia USA. stud phil Kennesaw State University. 2005-2011 Memher=teacher ⊕26.8.2005 B Addis Ababa. 2005 Central Committee WCC. 2011-2013 Interchurch Aid, 2013 Development Commission Addis Ababa.

Daniel Fikremariam Tadesse ***West Harargie***
T: B West Harargie ▪ ✉ P.O.Box, ETHIOPIA-Addis Ababa

*1944 (eth 1937) Shoa Fiche. N? stud Debre Libanos, Gondar, dipl theol St. Thomas University USA. teacher liturgy ⊕26.8.2005 B Assosa. 2006 B Sudan. 2011 B Harargie, Asbe Teferi. 2013 Jerusalem.

Abraham ***West Gojjam***
T: B West Gojjam ▪ ✉ P.O.Box 1283, ETHIOPIA-Addis Ababa

⊕2010 B East Harar. 2015 B West Gojjam.

Yared Akaleweled
T: B ▪ ✉ Ethiopian Orthodox Bishopric, P.O.Box 1283, ETHIOPIA-Addis Ababa

*1963 North Shoa N? ⊕26.8.2005 B Eastern Welega, 2011 St. Paul's Seminary, priest college. 2013 Somalia, Holy Trinity College.

Henok Gebreyesus Bultosa ***Gimbi***
T: B Western Welega, ETHIOPIA-Assosa

*1966 "Bultosa" West Welega. N? stud West Welega, East Gojam ⊕26.8.2005 B Western Welega, Assosa.

Kelementos Kife Yohanes ***Hosanna***

T: A Hadiya Silty, Gurage ▪ ✉ EOC Patriarchate, P.O.Box 1283, ETHIOPIA-Addis Ababa

*1961 North Shoa. N? stud North Shoa, Debre Libanos, Gojam, dipl theol St. Paul's College. Tsebate (= abbot Debre Libanos) ⊕26.8.2005. 2005-2011 B Harargue, 2011 A Hadiya Silty, Gurage, Kambata.

Enbakom Tekelehawariat ***Jerusalem***

T: B Jerusalem ▪ ✉ P.O.Box 19025, ISRAEL-91190 Jerusalem, [972] 2 6282848, 6280326 • Debre Genet 6286871 • Bethany 2796936 • Bethlehem 2344204 • Jericho 2322944, fax 6264189

*1957 N? stud Zena Markos, Seka Medhanie Alem, Debre Libanos, Gojam. Tsebate (= abbot Debre Libanos) ⊕26.8.2005 B South Omo, Jinka. 2013 B Diredawa, West Hararguie. 2015 A Jerusalem.

Mekariyos Gebrewahd Girmay ***Addigrat***

T: B Addigrat Shire ▪ ✉ EOC Patriarchate, P.O.Box 1283, ETHIOPIA-Adigrat • [251] 34 4452448, 4452209

*1941 "Gebrewahd" Tigrai Adwa. N? stud Adwa, Nibureid (= abbot Debre Benkko Monastery Axum) ⊕26.8.2005 B Addigrat Shire.

Matthewos Afework Getaneh ***Wollayta Diwaro***

T: B Wollayta Diwaro, General Secretary Holy Synod ▪ ✉ EOC Patriarchate, P.O.Box 1283, ETHIOPIA-Addis Ababa • [251] 11 1550099, 1556507

*1962 "Getaneh" North Shoa. N? stud Menjar, Nazret, Menagsha, Asebot, Ziway, St. Paul's Theol College, Theol school Netherlands. Melakehayl (=rector) St. Raguel ⊕26.8.2005 B Wag Himra, 2007 B Wag Himra, General Secretary Holy Synod. 2011 B Wollayta Diwaro. 2013 General Manager Patriarchate. 2014 General Secretary Holy Synod.

Selama Gebre Silassie Hargewein ***East Harar***

T: A East Harar ▪ ✉ P.O.Box 1283, ETHIOPIA-Addis Ababa

*1941 "Gebre Silassie" Tigrai. N? stud Tigrai, Gondar, Gojjam. Likesiltanat (= rector Holy Trinity Addis Ababa) ⊕26.8.2005 B Axum Tigrai. 2013 Taka Negest Lemariam, Menwere Menghist St. Gabriel. 2015 A East Harar.

Sawiros Moges ***Shoa West***

T: B Western Shoa, Wolliso ▪ ✉ P.O.Box 1283, ETHIOPIA-Addis Ababa

*1964 "Akaleweld". N? stud West Shoa, Adaberga Debre, Meskayehizunan Medhane Alem School ⊕26.8.2005 B Negele-Borena. 2011 B Western Shoa.

Markos Tafara ***Gojjam East***

T: B Eastern Gojjam, Hawi Debre Markos, chairman Comm. Catechesis ▪ ✉ EOC Patriarchate, P.O.Box 1283, ETHIOPIA-Addis Ababa • [251] 11 1550099, 1556507 • P.O.Box 176, Debre Markos • [251] 58 7711140

*16.8.1952 (eth 1944) Gojjam. N? diak12.11.1966 stud Debre Tsege, Zeway. teacher Zeway. preacher Shashemeny. 1992 USA teacher preacher Houston Texas, New York. Meleka Sebat. 2006 Addis Ababa ⊕9.7.2006 B California. 2009 B Hararge. 2011 B Eastern Gojjam Debre Markos. 2015 Chairman Synodal Commission Catechesis.

Entonios GhebreSelassie Hailu ***Western Europe***

T: B Western Europa ▪ ✉ Flat C 16 Princes Crescent, Finsbury Park, GREAT BRITAIN-London • [44] 79 56 281 124 • lttmariam2@aol.com

*12.1.1955 (eth 1948) "Ghebre Selassie Hailu" Tigrai. N? stud Waldba, St. Paul's Seminary Addis Ababa. diak1963 ⊖1969 teacher Liturgy Debre abbey. Meleka Tsahay. 1973 teacher econom Seminary Illubabor. 1995 rector Debre Sion Maryam Roma Italia. Administrator Gambela ⊕26.3.2008 B Western Europa.

Fanuel Melaku Getaneh ***California***

T: B Sewaswo berhan, Sidamo, California ▪ ✉ P.O.Box 1283, ETHIOPIA-Addis Ababa

*1962 (eth 1955) Diredawa. N? stud Diredawa, gymnasium Addis Ababa. diak1979 mon1981 ⊖1982. 1986 Seminary Zeway. archim1991. 1992 preacher Trinidad Tobago ⊕9.7.2006. 2006-2008 B Washington. 2008-2011 B Sidamo. 2011 St. Paulos priest college, Sewaswo berhan, Sidamo, California.

Yakob Woldemikael Gabriel ***East Africa***

T: A East Africa ▪ ✉ P.O.Box 1283, ETHIOPIA-Addis Ababa

*11.1.1963 (eth 1956) "Woldemikael" North Wollo. N? stud North Wollo. diak1989 ⊖1989. 1989 Seminary Zeway. BA Holy Trinity Theol College Addis Ababa. teacher Aba Selama Seminary Mekala ⊕9.7.2006. 2006-2013 B South and West Africa. 2013-2015 B Lebanon. 2015 A East Africa.

Dimetrios Ghebre Mikael ***United Arab Emirates***

T: B Emirates ▪ ✉ P.O.Box 1283, ETHIOPIA-Addis Ababa

*12.11.1966 (eth 1959) North Gondar "Hailemariam". N? stud liturgy music North Gondar. diak1982 stud Seminary Zeway. mon1994 ⊖1994. 1994 econom Seminary Zeway. preacher Middle East ⊕9.7.2006.

Lukas Yigizaw Hayleselassie ***Setithumera***

T: B Setithumera, Secretary Holy Synod ▪ ✉ EOC Patriarchate, P.O.Box 1283, ETHIOPIA-Addis Ababa • [251] 11 1550099, 1556507

*1949 "Hayleselassie" Tigray. N? stud Waghimra, Gondar, Zeway. with Sirgiw Gelaw Awassa Theol Seminary. dipl Academy Leningrad, Kandidat Moskva ⊕26.8.2005. 2013 General Secretary Holy Synod.

Petros Beza ***Bahr dar***
T: B Bahr dar ▪ ✉ EOC Patriarchate, P.O.Box 1283, ETHIOPIA-Addis Ababa
⊕12.7.1999 B South Africa, Australia. 2009 B Debre Markos. 2011 B Bahrdar, Awina Metekel.

Ewostateos Weldegiorgis Gebrekristos ***Borrena***
T: B Borrena ▪ ✉ P.O.Box 1283, ETHIOPIA-Addis Ababa •
[251] 25 5510004, 5510155 • Borrena [251] 46 4450375, 4451168
*1961 West Shoa. N? stud Debre Tsimona, Debre Libanos. BA Holy Trinity Theol College ⊕26.8.2005 Western Harargie, 2009 B California. 2011 B Borrena.

Zacharias Beyene Sbhatleab ***New York***
T: A New York ▪ ✉ EOC Patriarchate, P.O.Box 1283, ETHIOPIA-Addis Ababa
*1938 (eth 1931) Gojam N? "Sbhatleab" ⊕21.1.1979 B North+South Omo. 1994 B Debre Markos, Gojam East. 2008 Washington New York.

Bertolomiwos Fisha Getahun
T: A chairman Ethiopian Faith Congress ▪ ✉ Ethiop Orth Archbishopric, ETHIOPIA-Awasa • [251] 46 2200-448, -121
*1931 (eth 1924) N? ⊕12.7.1999 A Sidamo, Sidamo Gedio Burjie. 2009-2011 Eastern Wollega.

Elias Tsegaye Gebreigziabeher
T: former B Djibouti, East and South Africa, "Archbishop in Europe and East Africa" ▪ ✉ Gillerbacken 26 1tr, SWEDEN-124 64 Bandhagen •
[46] 8 7492928
*19.5.1938 "Gebreigziabeher" Gondar. N? ⊖1964. Secretary to the Patr. 1979 dipl theol Athens, stud Germany ⊕9.7.1981 B Djibouti, Respons for Africa and Europe. Outside Ethiopia since 1992 Stockholm. 11.1993 consecrated church München, with Yohannes.

Gorgorios Hayle Iyesus Kebede
T: B London ▪ ✉ 253 B Ladbroke Grove, GREAT BRITAIN-London, W10 6HF • [44] 20 8960 3848
*1942 "Hayle Iyesus Kebede" Gondar. N? stud Jerusalem. stud Dublin Holy Ghost College. 1988-1992 secretary to the Patriarch ⊕28.10.1990. Outside Ethiopia since 1992.

ORTHODOX CHURCH OF FINLAND

His Beatitude **Leo**
Archbishop of Karelia and All Finland
Suomen Ortodoksinen Arkkipiispakunta

Leo Makkonen ***Karelia***
T: A Karelia+All Finland ▪ ✉ Karjalankatu 1, FINLAND-70110 Kuopio • [358] 17 287223-0, fax -1 • karjalan.hiippakunta@ort.fi • arkkipiispa.leo@ort.fi www.ort.fi
*4.6.1948 Pielavesi, N18.2. 1972 dipl theol Seminary Kuopio. diak 20.7.1973 ⊖22.7.1973. 1978 dipl Pedag Uni Turku ⊕25.2.1979. 1979-1980 B Joensuu. 1979-1993 chairman Fellowship St.Sergius and Herman. 1980-1996 M Oulu. 1995 MTh University Joensuu. 1996-2001 M Helsinki. 2001 A Karelia.

Arseni Jorma Heikkinen
T: B Joensuu, assistant Karelia ▪ ✉ Karjalankatu 1, FINLAND-70110 Kuopio • [358] 206 100236 • kirkollishallitus@ort.fi • piispa.arseni@ort.fi
*14.7.1957 Lapinlahti, N12.6. 1983 dipl theol Seminary Kuopio. diak1986 mon1986 ⊖1989. 1989 Magister theol Leningrad. 1989-2004 deputy chief New Valaamo ⊕23.1.2005 B Joensuu.

Ambrosius R.T. Jääskeläinen ***Helsinki***
T: M Helsinki, Helsingin metropoliitta, Ortodoksinen Hiippakunta ▪ ✉ Kallvikinniementie 35, FINLAND-00980 Helsinki • [358] 206 10024-3, -0, fax [358] 10 2779 770 • metropoliitta.ambrosius@ort.fi • helsingin.hiippakunta@ort.fi • www.ort.fi
*10.8.1945 Tohmajärvi, Luth. N7.12. 1968 MTh University Helsinki. Cambridge University. 1972 Master of Political Sciences Univ Helsinki. 1976 orth. diak1979 ⊖1979 archim1986 ⊕20.11.1988 B Joensuu. 1991-2006 Central Committee WCC Geneva. 1996-2002 M Oulu. 1999-2001 Commission Orthodox Collaboration WCC Geneva. 2002 M Helsinki. 2011 Dr. theol University Helsinki. 29.1.2011 Cholargos Manoussakis. 2011 Dr.h.c. of Divinity University Helsinki.

Elia Matti Wallgrén ***Oulu***
T: M Oulu ▪ ✉ Nummikatu 30 B 16, FINLAND-90100 Oulu • [358] 206 100 258 • metropoliitta.elia@ort.fi
*8.12.1961 Kajaani, N20.7. 1981 Abitur in Kajaani. 1981-2001 stud Chec language. Teacher languages University Helsinki, Tour operator Czechoslovakia. 1994 converted to Orthodoxy. stud theol University Joensuu. 2001-2003 MDiv St. Vladimir's. diak22.5.2003 ⊖1.9.2003 mon5.12.2014 "Elia", archim ⊕11.1.2015 M Oulu.

Retired Hierarchs:

Pantelimon Petri Sarho
T: former M Oulu ▪ ✉ Ajurinkatu 28 B 43, FINLAND-70110 Kuopio • [358] 50 341 8697 • metropoliitta.pantelimon@ort.fi
*17.5.1949 Vieremä, Luth. N27.7. 1970 orth. 1972 Theol Seminary Kuopio. 1977 Kandidat Academy Leningrad. mon1977 New Valaam diak1977 ⊖1977 archim 1986. 1987-1997 igumen New Valaamo ⊕16.3.1997-2002 B Joensuu. 2002-2014 M Oulu. 2014 retired.

Georgian Apostolic Orthodox Church

His Holiness and Beatitude **Ilia II.**
Catholicos Patriarch of all Georgia and Abchasia
Sakartvelos Eklesiis Sapatriarko Patriarhia Georgiei

Ilia Erekle Gudušauri Šiolašvili *Tbilisi*

T: Catholicos Patriarch of All Georgia ▪ ✉ Erekle II. Moedani 1, Georgia-0105 Tbilisi • [995] 32 989528, fax 987114, Secretary 982709, Šorena Tetruašvili 990378, Chancellor 98954-0, Press-Center 989541, Publishing 982634, Youth 987300, Charitable Centre 222367, 738937, Agriculture 989526 • www.patriarchate.ge

*4.1.1933 Ordžonikidze, N2.8. mon16.4.1957 diak18.4.1957 ⊖10.5.1959. 1960 Kandidat Theol Akademy Moskva ⊕25.8.1963 B Batum-Šemokmedi, patriarchal vicar. 1.9.1967 B, 1969 M Ts'khum-Apkhazeti. 25.12.1977 Cath Patr. 1996 visit London, 1997 visit Germany. 22.-28.1.2016 Synaxis of the primates of the Local Orthodox Churches Chambésy Switzerland.

Grigol Katsia *Agarak-Tsalka*

T: B Agarak-Tsalka ▪ ✉ Tsminda Vakhtang Gorgasali Monasteri, Tsminda Ninos kuča, Georgia-3700 Rustavi • [995] 335 149370

⊕16.10.2013 B Martkop+Gardaban. 2014 B Agarak-Tsalka (changing with B Ioann Shomahia).

Ioane Guram Georg Gamrekeli *Rustavi*

T: M Rustavi ▪ ✉ Nutsubidze kuča 193, Georgia-0186 Tbilisi • [995] 5999 45 227, [995] 335 149370 • center@venakhi.ge • eparchy@rustaveli.ge

*28.10.1946 Tbilisi. N? mother German: Katarina Kerbs. school Tbilisi. stud Geology Politechnikum: 1964-1867 Tbilisi, 1967-1970 Novočerkassk. 1970-1985 Institute Geology Tbilisi. 1985-1988 stud theol Mtskheta. diak19.8.1987 ⊖24.4.1988. 1988-1989 Anchischati church Tbilisi, 1989-2008 protopresbyter Cathedral Sioni. 1989-1993 rector Seminary and Academy. 1993 chairman Education Committee patriarchate. 1995 member Academy Sciences Gelati. mon11.9.2008 ⊕14.9.2008 B Tsurtavi. 2010 A Rustavi+Marneuli, 2011 M Rustavi.

Georgij Džandelian *Marneul*

T: B Marneul+Hudžav ▪ ✉ Tsminda Vakhtang Gorgasali Monasteri, Tsminda Ninos kuča, Georgia-3700 Rustavi • [995] 335 149370

⊕16.10.2013 B Marneul+Hudžav.

Kalistrate Shota Margalitašvili *Kutaisi*
T: M Kutaisi+Gaenati ▪ ✉ Džavakhišvili II per 2, GEORGIA-4600 Kutaisi • [995] 231 70105, 60105, 58863, [995] 33 101028, [995] 32 923454, 250313
*1938 Vardisubani Telavi N? ⊖7.4.1982 ⊕1983 B Kutais-Gaenati, 8.2.1989 A Kutais-Gaenati. 1991 rector Seminary Academy Gelati. 1993 M Kutasi-Gaenati.

Anania Tengiz Džaparidze *Manglisi*
T: M Manglisi+Tetritskaroj ▪ ✉ Sakatedro Tadzari, Cathedral, GEORGIA-2309 Manglisi • [995] 363 32473, [995] 32 342150, [995] 99 181097
*20.8.1949 Tkibuli N? 1974 Politechnikum Tbilisi. mon14.2.1979 diak9.5.1979 ⊖27.9.1979. 1980 dipl Seminary Mts'cheta. archim7.3.1981 ⊕15.3.1981 B Nikortsminda, 29.6.1981 B Mes'chet-Džavakheti, 1983-1992 B Akhaltsikhe Mes'chet-Džavakheti. 1988-1992 chairman of Financial Department. 1992-1996 Manglisi. 1996 A. 1999 Kandidat History Academy Science. 2002 M Manglisi+Tsalka, 2013 M Manglisi+Tsalka+Tetritskaroj.

Ioann Šomahia *Martkofi*
T: B Martkofi+Gardabani ▪ ✉ Tsminda Vakhtang Gorgasali Monasteri, Tsminda Ninos kuča, GEORGIA-3700 Rustavi • [995] 335 149370
⊕16.10.2013 B Agarak-Tsalka. 2015 B Martkofi+Gardabani (changing with B Grigol Katsia).

Giorgi Guri Šalamberidze *Tkibuli*
T: M Tkibuli, Teržola ▪ ✉ Čkondidis Monasteri, GEORGIA-3100 Martvili • [995] 32 303338, [995] 313 21338, 22308, [995] 99 143330
*25.2.1940 Persati Maiakovski (1991 =Bağdati), N? 1963-1971 Seminary Academy Leningrad, Kandidat PhD presviter Cathedral Sioni ⊕14.10.1988 B Čkondidi. 1989 Chor Basilika Köln. 1994 A. 2000 M Čkondidi. 2007 M Tkibuli.

Jobi Elgudža Akiašvili *Urbnisi*
T: M Mrovi+Urbnisi Mrovel Urbneli ▪ ✉ Leselidze 8, GEORGIA-5706 Khašuri • [995] 268 23052 • Tbilisi [995] 32 982708, [995] 99 577839
*29.5.1960 Sno Kazbegi, N? 1983 dipl Agrar Inst. mon3.1.1988 diak19.1.1988 ⊖29.3.1988. 1989 dipl Seminary Mts'cheta. 21.9.1989 igumen. archim28.8.1990 ⊕17.5.1992 Manglisi Batum-Shemokmedi. 1995 B Batum. 1996 A Batum+Šemokmedi. 1996-2003 Locum tenens Patriarch. 2000 M Urbnisi+Ruissi. 2003 chairman Department examination liturgical books. 2014 M Mrovel Urbneli.

Simon Tsakašvili *Suram*
T: M Suram+Chašura ▪ ✉ Leselidze 8, GEORGIA-5706 Khašuri • [995] 268 23052 • Tbilisi [995] 32 982708, [995] 99 577839
⊕11.10.2013 M Suram+Chašura.

Danieli David Datuašvili *Čiatura*
T: M Sačkhere Čiatura ▪ ✉ Leselidze 75, GEORGIA-4005 Ivantsminda • [995] 122 22616, 22971, [995] 99 532000 • Tbilisi [995] 32 982710
*1955 Tbilisi N? diak1983 ⊖1985 mon1991 ⊕1992 B Bodbe. 1992 A, 1997-2002 chairman Department Mission Evangelization. 2000-2002 M Ts'khum-Apkhazeti. 2002 Admin, 2010 M Čiatura.

Daviti Irakli Makharadze *Alaverdi*
T: M Alaverdi ▪ ✉ Vazha Pshavela 8, GEORGIA-2200 Telavi • [995] 350 33193 • Architectural Centre [995] 32 986554, [995] 99 956030
*1960 Tbilisi N? diak23.11.1987 ⊖1988 mon1990 ⊕24.5.1992 B Nikortsminda, 1992-1993 chairman Department External Relations. 1993 Bodbe, 1.9.1993 Alaverdi. 1996 A, Chairman Architectural Centre. 2000 M. 2007 chairman Centre Church Music. 2009 chairman Centre Agricultural Development.

Sergi Zurab Čekurišvili *Nekresi*
T: M Nekresi ▪ ✉ Cathedral, GEORGIA-2700 Lagodekhi • [995] 32 232268, [995] 99 558950
*13.4.1959 Rustavi. N? mon13.4.1988 diak1988. 1989 dipl Seminary Moskva ⊖1989 archim1990 ⊕27.12.1992. 1992-1997 B Akhaltsikhe+Mes'chet-Džavakheti. 1997 A, 2000 M Nekresi.

Melqisedek Khatčidze *Margveti*
T: B Margveti+Ubisa ▪ ✉ Sakatedro Tadzari, Cathedral, GEORGIA-2000 Zestaphoni • [995] 71 262527, [995] 32 736023, 982708 • melkhisedek75@yahoo.gr
*25.4.1975 Khašuri. N? 1981-1992 gymnasium Kutaisi. 1992-1995 Seminary, 1995-1998 Academy Tbilissi. 1998-2003 dipl theol Athens. 2003 preparing doctoral thesis Athens. diak3.4.2004 Athens ⊖12.4.2004 Athens mon31.8.2005 Tbilissi. 11.9.2005 igumen. 2008 Arnedo Spain ⊕3.5.2009 B Hereti in Azerbeidzhan separated from Nekresi. 20.3.2011 consecration Elpidoforos İstanbul. 2014 B Margveti+Ubisa (changing with B Dimitri Kapanadze).

Mikael Gabričidze *Tušeti*
T: B Pšav-Chevsureti+Tianeti ▪
✉ Sakatedro Tadzari, GEORGIA-200500 Tianeti
⊕11.10.2013 Pšav-Chevsureti+Tianeti.

Dimitrij Kapanadze *Dedoplistskaro*
T: B Dedoplistskaro+Hereti ▪ ✉,Sakatedro Tadzari Cathedral, GEORGIA-1600 Dedoflistskaro • [995] 99 180753
⊕11.10.2013 B Margveti+Ubisa. 2015 B Dedoplistskaro+Hereti (changing with B Melqisedek Khatchidze).

Zosime Šota Šiošvili *Tsilkani*
T: M Tsilkani, Dušeti ▪ ✉ Saepiskoposo sakhli, GEORGIA-3309 Tsilkani • [995] 32 314777, 710711
*1951 Tbilisi. N? 1972 dipl Politechnikum. diak1976. 1977 Seminary Mts'cheta ⊖27.7.1977 mon1981 ⊕11.10.1983 B Čkondidi. 1984-1989 rector Seminary Mts'cheta. 1984-1994 chairman Publishing Department. 1996 A, 2009 M Tsilkani.

Iosebi Givi Kikvadze *Šemokmedi*
T: M Šemokmedi ▪ ✉ Sakatedro Tadzari, Cathedral Tšra Aprili kuča 18, GEORGIA-3500 Ozurgeti • [995] 99 576472, 531966, 157767
*17.9.1959 Čohatauri. N? dipl Academy Art Painting Tbilisi, absolvent Seminary Tbilisi mon16.5.1991 diak23.5.1991 ⊖3.11.1991. 1992-1995 igumen Cvetitskhoveli. archim1993 ⊕7.4.1995 B, 2000 A, 2007 M Šemokmedi.

Issaia Zurab Tčanturia *Nikozi*
T: M Nikozi+Tskhinvali ▪ ✉ Sakatedro Tadzari, Cathedral, GEORGIA-1417 Nikozi • [995] 99 412745
*1961 Zugdidi. N? dipl Theatral University Tbilisi. mon12.1993 ⊖1994 igumen Monastery Martkopi ⊕7.4.1995. 1995-1996 chairman Financial Dep. 2000 A, 2006 M.

Serapime Tamaz Džodžua *Bordžomi*
T: M Bordžomi+Bakuriani ▪ ✉ Saakadze 40, GEORGIA-1200 Bordžomi • [995] 262 22306, [995] 267 24880, [995] 99 500487
*15.2.1961 Sokhumi. N? 1990 dipl Academy Art Painting Tbilisi, mon28.8.1992 diak2.10.1992 ⊖26.11.1992. 1.5.1994 igumen Monastery Foka ⊕20.4.1995, 2000 A Bordžomi+Akhalkalaki, 2002 Bordžomi+Bakuriani, 2009 M.

Grigori Gurami Berbičašvili *Poti*
T: M Poti+Khobi ▪ ✉ Guriis kuča 1, GEORGIA-4400 Poti •
[995] 393 21456, fax 21000
*18.7.1956 Tbilisi. N? diak14.10.1989. 1990 dipl Seminary Mts'cheta Tbilisi ⊖27.3.1990. 1994 dipl Fac Tbilisi. parish Čemokmedi. Editor Tscharo Fountain. 2.2.1994 protoierej. mon20.3.1996 archim23.3.1996 ⊕24.3.1996 B Poti, Chairman Department Interaction Armed Forces. 1996-1999 chairman Department Law Enforcement Institutions. 2003 A, 2007 M Poti Khobi.

Nikolosi Paata Pačuašvili *Akhalkalaki*
T: M Akhalkalaki+Kumurdo, South America ▪ ✉ Darbiniani 23, GEORGIA-0700 Akhalkalaki • [995] 32 98911-5, -6, fax 987114, 923688
*10.2.1961 Tbilisi. N? 1985 dipl State University Moskva. diak30.9.1990 ⊖1991. 1991-1996 Dekan Metechi. protoierej. 1992 dipl Academy Tbilisi. 4.1.1993 protoierej. mon25.3.1996 archim29.3.1996 ⊕24.3.1996 A Tsageri-Svaneti. 1997 Akhaltsikhe. 1998 B Bodbe. 2002 A, 2006 M Akhalkalaki.

Teodore Dimitri Tčuadse *Akhaltsikhe*
T: M Akhaltsikhe+Taoklardžeti Lazeti ▪ ✉ Gogebašvili 16, GEORGIA-0800 Akhaltsikhe • [995] 32 9827-08, -10, [995] 99557373, [995] 99982708 • teodore@mail.com
*11.4.1967 Siğnaği. N? 1983-1990 Politechnikum Tbilisi. 1990 dipl University Tbilisi. 1990-1993 Seminary Akhaltsikhe. mon12.2.1991 diak2.6.1991 ⊖8.9.1991. 12.7.1993 igumen. archim 25.10.1996 ⊕26.10.1996 B Bodbe. 2003 A. 2003 chairman Financial-Economical Department. 2004 rector Academy Tbilisi. 2005 vicar katolikos. 2006 M Akhaltsikhe, rector Seminary. 2006 Orth-Cath Joint Commission Beograd.

Saba Zaza Gigiberia *Khoni*
T: M Khoni+Samtredi ▪ ✉ Sakatedro Tadzari, Cathedral Solomon kuča, GEORGIA-5900 Khoni • [995] 295 22272, [995] 99 580605 • bishop@khonichurch.org.ge • www.khonichurch.org.ge
*28.8.1966 Senaki. N? 1984-1989 Politechnikum Tbilisi. 1990-1992 Seminary Akhaltsikhe. mon14.6.1991 diak12.1.1992 ⊖4.10.1992. 1994 igumen. archim26.10. 1996 ⊕3.11.1996. 1996-1997 chairman Finance Economy Department. 2003 A. 2007 chairman Pilgrim Department. 2008 M Khoni.

Antoni Markos Buluhia *Vani*
T: M Vani+Bağdati ▪ ✉ Sakatedro Tadzari, Cathedral, GEORGIA-1000 Vani
*7.5.1956 Očchamuri Kobuleti. N? 1976-1982 Agricultural Institute Moskva. 1980-1982 Juridical Institute Moskva. 1987-1990 Seminary Mts'cheta. diak16.3.1989 ⊖26.4.1989. 1995 Dekanos. mon25.10.1996 archim26.10.1996 ⊕11.11.1996. 1999 Law Enforcement Institutions. 2004 A. 2010 M Vani.

Dimitri Nodar David Šiolašvili *Batumi*
T: M Batumi, Lazeti ▪ ✉ Parnavas Mepis kuča 91, GEORGIA-6000 Batumi • [995] 222 76717, 34935, fax 76218 • www.eparchy.batumi.net
*16.2.1961 Mts'cheta. 1979-1982 Seminary Mts'cheta, 1982-1986 Academy Moskva. Dr. theol Kandidat Moskva. diak28.7.1985 ⊖12.1.1986. 1987-1988 Alaverdi Monastir. 1988-1989 Ankhiskati. 13.5.1989 Dekanos Batumi St. Virgin Church. 14.10.1991 Rector gymnasium "Ap. Andreas" Batumi, 14.9.1993 also Rector St. John

Theol Seminary Batumi. mon25.10.1996 archim26.10.1996 ⊕8.11.1996 B, 2003 A Batumi-Skhalta. 2007 M Batumi Kobuleti USA Canada. 2014 M Batumi Lazeti.

Gerasime Šarašenidze ***Zugdidi***
T: M Zugdidi+Tsaiši ▪ ✉ Džortsheli, GEORGIA-2100 Zugdidi • [995] 99 573111
*20.5.1958 Tbilisi. N? 1985 Politechnikum Tbilisi. mon28.6.1997 diak20.7.1997 ⊖10.8.1997. 29.3.1998 igumen ⊕11.10.1998. 2002 chairman Department External Relations. 2006 A, 2007 M Zugdidi-Tsaish. 16.12.2015 Athens Interorthodox committee preparation Panorthodox Synod. 22.-28.1.2016 Synaxis of the primates of the Local Orthodox Churches Chambésy Switzerland.

Iakobi Konstantine Iakobašvili ***Bodbe***
T: A Bodbe ▪ ✉ Tsminda Ninos Monasteri Bodbe, GEORGIA-4200 Siğnaği • [995] 255 32056, 32752, [995] 32 982710, [995] 99 706555
*1.3.1962 Tbilisi. N5.11. mon15.3.2003 ⊕9.5.2010. 2010-2013 B Tsurtavi, Marneuli, Martkofi. 2013 A Bodbe.

David Tikaradze ***Adish***
T: A Adiš ▪ ✉ Erekle II. Moedani 1, GEORGIA-0105 Tbilisi
*1.5.1963 Lančkhuti. N? 1989 dipl Politechnikum. mon18.12.1995 diak19.1.1996 ⊖6.5.1996. 17.5.1997 igumen ⊕14.10.1998 B Tsageri-Svaneti. 2006 A Bodbe, 2013 A Adiš.

Andrea Amiran Gvazava ***Gori***
T: M Gori+Ateni ▪ ✉ Sakatedro Tadzari, Cathedral, GEORGIA-1400 Gori • [995] 32 300151, 221199, [995] 99531014
*24.4.1968 Sokhumi. 1988 Subtropical Institute. mon1995 diak17.9.1996 ⊖13.12. 1996. 1997-1998 superior St. Davit-Garedželi monastery. igumen1997 ⊕1998 B, 2002 A Sagaredžo. 2010 M Samtavisi-Gori, 2013 M Samtavisi-Kasp. 2014 M Gori+ Ateni. 16.12.2015 Athens Interorthodox committee preparation Panorthodox Synod. 22.-28.1.2016 Synaxis of the primates of the Local Orthodox Churches Chambésy Switzerland, with Georgi Zviadadze.

Damiane Hupenia ***Samtavisi***
T: B Samtavisi+Kaspi ▪ ✉ Tsminda Vakhtang Gorgasali Monasteri, Tsminda Ninos kuča, GEORGIA-3700 Rustavi • [995] 335 149370
⊕16.10.2013 B Gorij+Aten. 2014 B Samtavisi+Kaspi.

Petre Paata Tsava ***Čkondidi***
T: M Čkondidi ▪ ✉ Čkondidis Monasteri, Terjola zakatedro Tadzari, GEORGIA-3100 Martvili • [995] 32 303338, [995] 313 21338, 22308

*7.4.1970 Samegrelo. N? 1990-1997 stud Economics Uni Tbilisi. 1997-2000 Seminary Tbilisi. 2000 chairman center Spirituality Culture Sno Kazbeki. mon27.8.2000 diak28.8.2000 ⊖3.11.2000. 16.7.2002 igumen ⊕27.10.2002 B Stepansminda. 2003 A Stepansminda. 2010 M Čkondidi.

Jegudiel Tabatadze ***Stepansminda***

T: A Stepansminda+Khevi ▪ ✉ Saepiskoposo sakhli, GEORGIA-4704 Sno Kazbeki

*30.1.1964 Čiatura. N? Politechnikum. mon1995 diak1995 ⊖1995. 17.6.2000 igumen ⊕18.8.2003 B, 2009 A Stepansminda+Khevi.

Stefane Kalaidžišvili ***Tsageri***

T: A Tsageri+Lentechi ▪ ✉ Sakatedro Tadzari, Rustavelis Šesaxvevi 1, GEORGIA-5100 Tsageri • [995] 206 2144, [995] 99 517747

*9.2.1959 Akhaltsikhe. N? 1981 Technical University Tbilisi, Seminary Akhaltsikhe. diak1984 mon1986 ⊖1986. 1987 igumen. 1995 History State University ⊕27.10.2002 B, 2010 A Tsageri Lentechi.

Ilarioni Kitiašvili ***Mestia***

T: B Mestia+Svaneti ▪ ✉ Sakatedro, Tetnuldi 2, GEORGIA-3200 Mestia • [995] 99 282922

*22.11.1957 Kašuri. N? stud Technical University Tbilisi. diak4.11.1998 ⊖15.2.1999 mon4.12.2000. 4.12.2001 igumen ⊕3.11.2002 B Mestia+Svaneti.

Ekvtime Ležava ***Gurdžani***

T: B Gurdžani+Velistsiche ▪ ✉ Sakatedro Tadzari, Rustaveli Šesachvevi 1, GEORGIA-5100 Gurdžani • [995] 206 2144, [995] 99 194303

*1953 Tbilisi. N? dipl Academy Art Painting Tbilisi. mon1990 ⊖1991 ⊕18.8.2003 B Gurdžani+Velistsiche.

Luka Lomidze ***Sagaredžo***

T: B Sagaredžo+Ninotsminda ▪ ✉ Sakatedro Tadzari, GEORGIA-3800 Sagaredžo • [995] 206 2144, [995] 99 223461

*14.9.1966. N? 1992 Politechnikum Tbilisi. 1995 novice. mon1997. 1998-2003 superior St. Davit-Garedželi monastery. diak1999 ⊖1999 igumen. archim2000 ⊕27.8.2003.

Zenon Imeda Iaradžuli ***Dmanisi***

T: A Dmanisi, Agarak-Tashira, Great Britain ▪ ✉ Sakatedro Tadzari, GEORGIA-1700 Dmanisi • [995] 99 221818 • g.orthodox@yahoo.co.uk

*17.5.1972 Tbilisi. N? 1992 Theol Seminary. mon14.8.1993 diak19.8.1993 ⊖25.10. 1993. 10.11.1994 igumen. rector Theol school Siğnaği. 1995-1996 vice-rector Tbilisi

Seminary Academy. 1996-1997 Istituto Orientale Roma. 1998 secretary Patriarch. 1998-2002 chairman Financial Department. 2000-2002 rector St. Davit-Garedželi Tbilisi. archim16.6.2001. 2002-2003 rector Svetitskhoveli ⊕18.8.2003 B Dmanisi, 2006 also Agarak-Tashira, 2010 also Great Britain. 2011 A Dmanisi.

Šio Elizbar Mudžirij ***Senaki***

T: M Senaki+Tškhorotskhu, Australia ▪ ✉ Sakatedro Tadzari, GEORGIA-4100 Senaki • [995] 99 151589

*1969 Tbilisi. N? Conservatory Tbilisi. Theol Seminary Batumi. Academy Moskva. St. Tikhon Theol Institute Moskva. mon1993 diak1995 ⊖1996. 1998 igumen ⊕18.8.2003 B, 2010 M Senaki.

Spiridon Abuladze ***Skhalta***

T: B Skhalta ▪ ✉ D. Agmašenebeli kuča 9, GEORGIA-8000 Xulo Adjaria

*14.6.1950 Zestafoni. N? 1967-1972 Dr. cybernetics Uni Batumi. 1976-1987 teacher Politechnicum. 1987 librarian patriarchate. 1990 monastery Skhalta, diak21.9.1990 ⊖4.12.1990. 1991 pastor Bodbe. 1994 mitroforni Zestafoni. mon22.12.2006 ⊕24.12.2006 B Skhalta.

Eprem Gamrekelidze ***Bolnisi***

T: B Bolnisi ▪ ✉ Sakatedro Tadzari, Cathedral, GEORGIA-1100 Bolnisi • [995] 32 350407, 342186, 352186

*24.10.1975 Batumi. N? 1991-1996 stud Economics Batumi. 1994 hypodiakon. mon8.4.1996 diak6.5.1996 Batum ⊖7.4.1997 Ruis-Urbnisi. 1998-2004 rector Kareli. 2000 igumen. 2004-2006 abbot Qozipha ⊕31.12.2006 B Bolnisi.

Vakhtangi Badri Akhvlediani ***Tsurtaveli***

T: B Tsurtaveli, respons. Sweden ▪

*1953 Latsoria Tsageri ⊖1977 ⊕1982 B Agarak Tsalka, 1984 B Čkondidi, 1988 B, 1994 A Urbnisi. 1995 A Samtavisi. 2002 A, M Margveti. 2013 M Tsurtaveli, respons. Sweden.

Vakhtang Giorgi Liparteliani ***Nikortsminda***

T: B Nikortsminda ▪ ✉ Sakatedro Tadzari, Nikortsminda Cathedral, vGEORGIA-0408 Ambrolauri • [995] 99 581826

*25.10.1965. 1985 stud pedagogics University Tbilisi. mon13.12.2008. 2009 Holy Synod Russia and Holy Synod Georgia decided Russian priest Roman Pukin to serve Russian faithful in St. John Ev. Tbilisi. diak8.3.2009 ⊖24.9.2009 archim 2010-2015 Moskva, Georgian parish St. George, Bolshaja Gruzinskaja ulitsa ⊕1.6.2015 B Nikortsminda.

Lazar Samarbegisvili ***Germany***
T: B Germany ▪ ✉ Erekle II. Moedani 1, GEORGIA-0105 Tbilisi
⊕11.6.2014.

Abraham Amiran Garmelia ***West Europe***
T: M West Europa ▪ ✉ 6 Impasse Boieldieu, FRANCE-94190 Villeneuve-Saint-Georges • [33] 620 951 562, [372] 59223929, [995] 77 405970
*15.11.1948 Sukhumi, N? 1971 dipl Pedagogical University. 1988 dipl Seminary Mzcheta. mon3.1.1988 diak3.4.1988 ⊖29.5.1988 ⊕25.12.1992 B Nikortsminda. 1993-2003 Rector Tbilisi Theological Academy and Seminary. 1995-2002 chairman Department External Relations, 1996 B, 1998 A Sagaredžo+Gurdžaani. 2000 M Čiatura. 2002 M West Europa. 2003-2004 Ostkirchliches Institut Regensburg Germany. 20.3.2011 consecration Elpidoforos İstanbul.

Dosipe Bogveradze ***Benelux***
T: B Benelux ▪ ✉ Erekle II. Moedani 1, GEORGIA-0105 Tbilisi
⊕15.6.2014.

Sava Intskirveli ***America***
T: B America ▪ ✉ 59 Charles St, USA-Ashley, PA18706 •
gaocna.meupesaba@gmail.com • gaocna.secretary@gmail.com
⊕22.6.2014.

Greek Orthodox Church

His Beatitude **Hieronymos**
Archbishop of Athens and All Greece

Hieronymos Ioannis Liapis ***Athens***
T: A Makariótatos Archbishop of Athens and all Greece ▪ ✉ Ag. Philotheis 21, GREECE-105 56 Athens • [30] 210 3352300, 3238413, 3248-731, -732, -733, -734, p 3234253, fax 3224673 • gpapanicolaou76@yahoo.gr

*30.3.1938 Oinófyta. N15.6. 1967 dipl theol Athens. diak3.12.1967 ⊖10.12.1967. 1977-1978 Ostkirchliches Institut Regensburg. 1978-1981 Chief Secretary Holy Synod ⊕4.10.1981 M Thebae. 16.2.2008 A Athens and All Greece. 6.7.2010 Dr.h.c. Social Theol Athens. 16.4.2016 visit to the island of Lesbos together with Patriarch Bartholomaios and Pope Francis.

Klimis Dimitrios Kotsomytis
T: B Methoni, Archigrammateus Holy Synod ▪ ✉ Ag. Philotheis 21, GREECE-105 56 Athens • [30] 210 3238413

*1954 Aipeia Kalamata. 1973-1978 dipl theol and phil (Byzantine studies) Fac theol Athens. 1978-1982 stud Byzantine philology München Germany. 1982-1998 hierokēryx Theben, redactor monthly "Ekklesiastiki Martyria". mon15.8.1982 diak23.8.1982 ⊖1.5.1985 archim (M Theben Levadia Hieronymos). 1999-2014 grammateus, 2014 Archigrammateus Holy Synod ⊕13.10.2014.

Polykarpos Chrysikos
T: B Tanagra ▪ ✉ Ag. Philotheis 21, GREECE-105 56 Athens

*1933 Avlida Euboia. N23.2. diak21.11.1959 ⊖23.11.1959 ⊕22.5.2010.

Basilios Panagiotakopulos
T: M Euripos ▪ ✉ Ag. Philotheis 21, GREECE-105 56 Athens

*1929 Agrinion. N1.1. 1951 dipl theol Athens. diak21.11.1958 ⊖23.11.1958 ⊕18.12. 1968. 2000 M tit Euripos.

Euthýmios Stylios
T: M Achelóos, assistant Athens ▪ ✉ Joanninon 9, P. Psychikón, GREECE-154 52 Athens • [30] 2106711196, 2103237654

*1929 Agrinion, N20.1. 1952. dipl theol Athens. 1955-1964 General Secretary Syndesmos. mon1962 diak1962 ⊖1963 ⊕22.12.1968. 1968-2000 assistant Athens. 1980 Dr. theol Athens. 2000 M tit Achelóos.

Alexandros Kalpakidis
T: M Stavropegion ▪ ✉ Kon. Karamanli 16, GREECE-567 27 Thessaloniki • [30] 2310 510976, fax 706777
*1938 Thessaloniki, N30.8. diak1961. 1965 dipl theol Thessaloniki ⊖1967 archim 1967. 1974 protosynkellos Neapolis. 1992 nominated M Argyrokastro Gjirokastro Kisha Ortodokse Autoqefale e Shqipërisë ⊕26.7.1996 İstanbul, not entered into Albania. 1998 resigned. 1999 M Kampania. 2000 M tit Stavropegion.

Christodoulos Mustakis
T: former M Avlonos ▪ ✉ Ag. Philotheis 21, GREECE-105 56 Athens • [30] 210 3352300
*1951 Hagia Paraskevi, Trikala. N21.10. 1974 dipl theol Athens. diak1982 ⊖1982 archim hierokēryx Trikke. 1992 nominated M Korçë Kisha Ortodokse Autoqefale e Shqipërisë ⊕28.7.1996 İstanbul, not entered into Albania. 1999-2002 M Nea Chalkidon+Kouphalia. Meliton Oakes. 2000 M tit Avlonos.

Athanasios Chatzopulos
T: M Achaïa ▪ ✉ Bld Saint-Michel 50, BELGIUM-1040 Bruxelles • [32] 2 2800-639, fax -299 • ecclesiagr@skynet.be • info@regue.org • www.regue.org
*17.10.1950 Athens. 1968-1972 Lettres, Byzantinistics Athens. 1972-1976 dipl theol Athen, Greek Army. 1976-1978 Lic Orientale Rom Russicum. 1977 Ostkirchliches Institut Regensburg German language and Ecumenical Information. 1978-1979 Sorbonne Paris. 1979-1984 Dr. phil Oxford. 1983-1994 conservator manuscripts National Library Athens. 30.3.-8.4.1986 Rom Centro Mariapoli 20 years Ostk. Institut Regensburg. 1987 British Museum Library. 1988-1990 Istituto Orientale Rom. diak1991 ⊖5.10.1991. 1991-1994 teacher Seminary Tiranë. 1994-1997 Professeur Institut Œcuménique de Bossey, 1997-2000 Prof Institut Chambésy ⊕15.10.2000. 2004 Mondo Migliore. 2006 Papal visit Regensburg. Joint International Commission for the Theological Dialogue between the Catholic Church and the Orthodox Churches (as a whole). 2007-2015 Directeur Représentation de l'Église de Grèce auprès de l'Union Européenne. 2007 M Achaïa, auxiliaire Athènes.

Ioannis Sakellariou
T: M Thermopylai, Igumen ▪ ✉ Monasterion Pentelis, GREECE-152 36 Penteli • [30] 210 8042212, [30] 29440 278903
*8.11.1940 Athens. N7.1. diak22.2.1970 dipl theol Athens ⊖3.5.1970. 1970 Penteli, teacher Anotera Theol school English, Theology. mon1970. 1981 Dr. theol Strasbourg. 1994 igumen Penteli ⊕14.10.2000 auxiliaire de l'archevêque d'Athènes, igumen. 3.11.2011 M tit.

Pavlos Athanatos

T: B Neochorion, assistant Athens ■ ✉ Ag. Philotheis 21, GREECE-105 56 Athens • [30] 2103237654, 2106394141

*1941 Karditsa. N29.6. 1969 dipl theol Thessaloniki. diak1970 ⊖1970. 1970-1995 Sweden ⊕28.1.1995.

Meliton Kavatsiklis

T: M Marathon, assistant Athens ■ ✉ Ag. Philotheis 21, GREECE-105 56 Athens • [30] 210 3238413, fax 3224673, 5137788

*16.2.1946 Athens, N9.3. 1962-1986 Jerusalem. 1964 Jerusalem, diak1.11.1964 ⊖1967 private office of A Seraphim Athens. stud Sorbonne, Institut St-Serge Paris. 1981-1986 igumen Gaza. 1986 offices A Athens ⊕29.1.1995 B Marathon, assistant Athens. 27.1.2000 COMECE Athens. 11.10.2012 M tit.

Damaskinos Ioannis Kazanakis

T: M Velestinon, assistant Athens ■ ✉ Ag. Philotheis 21, GREECE-105 56 Athens • [30] 210 3238413, fax 3224673

*23.1.1934 Mallais Lasithiou Kreta. N4.12. 1955-1960 dipl theol Athens. mon1.7. 1960 diak24.7.1960 ⊖30.7.1960 archim6.8.1960. 1961-1968 hierokēryx Dimitrias. 1968-1974 stud Freie Universität Berlin. 1974-1986 protosynkellos Dimitrias. 1976-1977 scholarchis Volos. 1986-1994 protosynkellos Hierapytna. 1994-2003 protosynkellos Dimitrias ⊕12.1.2003 B, 2010 M Velestinos assistant Athens.

Agathangelos Vasilios Charamantidis

T: B Fanarion, assistant Athens ■ ✉ Ioannou Gennadiou 14, GREECE-115 21 Athens • [30] 210 72723-00, -01, fax -10

*1961 Chalkis. N23.1. mon1983 Hosios Lukas. diak1983. 1983-1988 diakonos Levadeia. 1986-1987 stud Deutschland (EKD) ⊖1988 (M Hieronymos Levadeia). dipl theol Athens. MTh Thessaloniki. 1988-2003 parish St. Georges Levadeia. 1991-1994 redactor Dípt. Ecum. Patriarchate. 1994 stud Deutschland (EKD), 1995-1996 stud Geneva. 1995 Grammat. Holy Synod. 1999-2001 Synodal Committee Public Rel. 2001 General Director of Apostolic Diakonia of the Church of Greece ⊕13.1.2003 B Fanarion assistant Athens. 27.2.2006 Rome with students.

Panteleimon Kathreptidis

T: M Koroneia, assistant Athens ■ ✉ Attaleias 128, GREECE-184 53 Nikaia • [30] 210 3238413, fax 3224673

*1937 Nikaia. N27.7. 1959 dipl theol Athens. diak1962. 1962-1967 hierokēryx Trikke ⊖1963. 1967-1969 stud Deutschland. 1970-1974 director pastoral care airports. 1974-2003 hierokēryx Athens ⊕14.1.2003 B, 2010 M Koroneia assistant Athens.

Antonios Avramiotis
T: B Salona, assistant Athens ▪ ✉ Ioannou Gennadiou 14, GREECE-11521 Athens • [30] 210 72723-00, -01, fax -10
⊕10.3.2012 B Salona, assistant Athens.

Iakovos Bizaourtis
T: B Thaumakos, assistant Athens ▪ ✉ Ioannou Gennadiou 14, GREECE-115 21 Athens • [30] 210 72723-00, -01, fax -10
2000 Director personal office A Hieronymos. igumen Moni Petraki. participant Bose ⊕11.3.2012 B Thaumakos, assistant Athens.

Kosmas Papachristos ***Aitolia***
T: M Aitolia+Akarnania ▪ ✉ Mitropolis, GREECE-30200 Mesolongi • [30] 26310 22322, 28232, fax 28701 • www.imaa@otenet.gr
*1945 Skoutesiadi Agrinion. N24.8. diak1974 ⊖1974. 1974-2005 hierokēryx Aitolia. 1976 dipl theol Thessaloniki ⊕8.10.2005.

Nektarios Antonopoulos ***Argolis***
T: M Argolis ▪ ✉ Mitropolis, GREECE-211 00 Navplion • [30] 27520 28645, 27328, fax 28361
*1954 Naroussi N?. diak1976 ⊖1983 (M Hieronymos Theben). hierokēryx Theben. 1991-2013 abbot Sagmata ⊕20.10.2013 M Argolis.

Kallinikos Korobokis ***Epidauros***
T: B Epidauros ▪ ✉ Mitropolis, GREECE-211 00 Navplion • [30] 27520 28645, 27328, fax 28361
*1967 Argos N29.7. diak1991 ⊖1996 ⊕26.10.2009 Epidauros, assistant Argolis.

Ignatios Alexiou ***Arta***
T: M Arta ▪ ✉ Mitropolis, GREECE-471 00 Arta • [30] 26810, 28842, 28090, 71835, fax 78419, 28610 • info@imartis.gr • www.imartis.gr
*1945 Kastanià Arta. N20.12. 1969 dipl theol Athens. diak2.5.1971 ⊖1.12.1974 ⊕21.11.1988 M Arta.

Athenagoras Georgios Dikaiakos ***Ilion***
T: M Ilion, Petroupolis, Acharnon ▪ ✉ Ag. Georgiou 5, GREECE-134 51 Kamateró • [30] 210 2388398, fax 210 2325437 • contact@imiliou.gr • www.imiliou.gr
*1951 Athens. N24.7. 1974 dipl phil, dipl theol. diak1977 ⊖1979. 1979 hierokēryx Thebai. 2006 hierokēryx personal secretary to archbishop Hieronymos Athens. Antiproedros Hidryma Poimantiki Epimorphosis. 2010 Didaktor Athens ⊕13.5.2010 M Ilion.

Kyrill Konstantinos Misiakoulis *Kifissia*
T: M Kifissia, Amarousion, Oropos ▪ ✉ Grigoriou Lampraki 32, GREECE-145 10 Kifissia • [30] 210 808884, fax 8085888 • imkifissias@otenet.gr • www.imkifissias.gr
*27.9.1963 Athens. N9.6. stud iur and theol Athens. 1990-1993 Juridical Department Greek Church. mon3.10.1991 diak4.10.1991. 1993-2010 parishes Ilision ⊖28.11.1993 Athens, 2003-2010 Archigrammateus Holy Synod ⊕14.5.2010 M Kifissia.

Pavlos Evstratios Tsaousoglou *Glyphas*
T: M Glyphas ▪ ✉ Vasileos Paulou 2, GREECE-166 73 Voula • [30] 210 9658838, fax 9610773 • imgl@otenet.gr • www.imglyfadas.gr
*1943 Hermopolis Syros. N29.6. dipl theol Athens ⊖1960 hierokēryx: 1966-1970 Preveza, 1970-1976 Tinos, 1976-1988 Nikaia, 1988-2001 Athens. 1988-1999 missions Africa. 1999-2002 igumen Moni Petraki Athens ⊕14.10.2002 M Glyphada.

Ieremias Fountas *Gortyna*
T: M Gortyna+Megalopolis ▪ ✉ Mitropolis, GREECE-222 00 Megalopolis • [30] 27910 25026, 22618, fax 21160 • iakovoskanakis@yahoo.com • www.imgortmeg.gr
*1941 Nafpaktos. N1.5. dipl theol Athens. diak1969 ⊖1972 served in Attika, Phokis, Piraeus, Megara. 2000 Synodic Youth Committee Athens. 2000 Dr. theol Athens. 2003 Epikouros Prof Biblical Studies Athens ⊕14.10.2006 M Gortyna.

Chrysostomos Dimitrios Korakitis *Mani*
T: M Mani ▪ ✉ Mitropolis, GREECE-232 00 Gýtheion • [30] 27330 22080, 22214, fax 23396
*1933 Athens. N13.11. 1957 dipl theol Athens. 1959 secretary Commission Monachism Holy Synod, teacher Piraeus. mon1.10.1960 diak2.10.1960. 1963-1996 parish Ag. Irene Athens ⊖1966 ⊕6.10.1996. 1996-2010 M Gýtheion+Oítylon: 2010 new name eparchy M Mani.

Ignatios Panayotis Georgakopoulos *Dimitrias*
T: M Dimitrias+Almyros ▪ ✉ K. Kartali 227, GREECE-382 21 Volos • [30] 24210 9350-0, -6, -8, 9, fax 67903, [30] 694 6764175 • idiaitero@imd.gr • www.imd.gr
*25.4.1956 Agios Dimitrios Attikis. N20.12. dipl theol Athens. mon17.7.1975 Chrysopeghi diak24.10.1976 ⊖3.4.1983. 1984 Chancellor Diocese Piraeus ⊕10.10.1998 M. 1999 President Bible Society Greece. 2004 vice-president World Bible Society. Vice-president Syndesmos. 2005 chairman External Relations. 16.12.2015 Athens Interorthodox committee preparation Panorthodox Synod 2016.

Dionysios Dimitrios Siphnaios ***Zakynthos***
T: M Zákynthos ▪ ✉ Mitropolis, GREECE-291 00 Zakynthos • [30] 49109, 22233, 42552, fax 22348 • imzante@yahoo.gr • www.imzante.gr
*1954 Athens. N17.12. mon14.8.1977 diak15.8.1977 Ampelokipon. 1983 dipl theol Thessaloniki. 1983-1984 hierokēryx Langada ⊖17.12.1983. 1984-2010 hierokēryx Kaisariani ⊕13.5.2010 B Photiki, (same day not same ceremony as M Ilion Athenagoras) assistant Athens. 2011 M Zákynthos.

Chrysostomos Dimitrios Synetos ***Dodonis***
T: M Dodonis ▪ ✉ Mitropolis, GREECE-291 00 Zakynthos •
[30] 26950 22552, 42552, 42619, 22348
*1939 Zakynthos. N13.11. mon1961 Sinai diak1961 ⊖1962 igumen Metochion Sinai Zakynthos. 1972 dipl theol Athens. 1974-1994 igumen Moni Penteli ⊕16.8.1976 B Dodónis, 1991 M Dodónis. 1994-2011 M Zakynthos. 2011 M Dodonis.

Chariton Christos Toubas ***Elasson***
T: M Elasson ▪ ✉ Mitropolis, GREECE-402 00 Elassona •
[30] 24930 22245, fax 25146 • imelasson@gmail.com
*1953 Kozani, N28.9. 1975 dipl theol Athens. diak1996. 1996-2000 hierokēryx Langadas ⊖1998. 2000-2014 hierokēryx protosynkellos Elassona ⊕29.6.2014.

Germanos Ioannis Paraskevopulos ***Elias***
T: M Ilias ▪ ✉ Mitropolis, GREECE-271 00 Pyrgos •
[30] 26210 22069, 31533, 22527, fax 30592 • contact@imilias.gr
*1932 Kardamas. N12.5. dipl theol Athens. 1958 dipl theol Athens. 1960-1969 hierokēryx. diak20.11.1960 ⊖6.12.1960. 1974-1975 stud France. 1979-1981 Archigrammateus Holy Synod ⊕3.10.1981 M Elias. 16.12.2015 Athens Interorthodox committee preparation Panorthodox Synod. 22.-28.1.2016 Synaxis of the primates of the Local Orthodox Churches Chambésy Switzerland.

Athanasios Bachos
T: B Olena, assistant Ilias ▪ ✉ Mitropolis, GREECE-271 00 Pyrgos •
[30] 26210 22069, 2621031533, 26210 22527
*1954 Ilia N18.1. diak1976 ⊖1982 ⊕1.11.2009 B Olena, assistant Ilias.

Georgios Mantzouranis ***Thebae***
T: M Thebae+Levadeia ▪ ✉ Aghiou Dimitriou 1, GREECE-321 00 Levadeia • [30] 22610 29222, 28079, 28330
*1952 Naxos. N23.4. stud theol Korinthos, Tinos, Athens. 1973-1975 military service. diak1976. 1976-1982 pastoral care hospital. 1981 absolvent Fac theol Athens ⊖1982 (Hieronymos Thebai). 1982-2008 hierokēryx Thebai. mon1986. 1987-2008

igoumenos Hosios Loukas. 2002 Synodiki Epitropi Christianikôn Mnimeíon ⊕28.6.2008.

Timotheos Nikolaos Anthis ***Thessaliotis***

T: M Thessaliotis+Phanariophersala ▪ ✉ Mitropolis Iezekiel 30, GREECE-431 00 Karditsa • [30] 24410 22968, fax 21550 • mitropolitis@imthf.gr

*1964 Kontokali Kerkyra. 1982 St. Mary's Monastery Palaiokastra Kerkyra. 1985 dipl Logistik. mon8.5.1986 diak12.7.1986 ⊖15.8.1992. 1992-1999 hierokēryx Kerkyra. 1993 dipl theol Athens. 2003 MTh Thessaloniki. 2010-2014 secretary Holy Synod, head commission editions ⊕30.6.2014.

Theokletos Theodoros Koumaniaros

T: M Vrestheni ▪ ✉ Ag. Philotheis 21, GREECE-105 56 Athens

*27.11.1953 Volos. N26.2. stud Ekkl. Scholi Thessaloniki, diak13.4.1978. 1981 dipl theol Athens ⊖26.12.1981. 1981-1985 Radio Volos, protosynkellos. 1985-1998 protosynkellos Dimitrias, Volos. 1998-1999 spokesman of A Christodoulos ⊕16.10.1999. 1999-2005 M Thessaliotis+Phanariophersala. 2006 M tit Vrestheni.

Epiphanios Michael Artemis ***Thera***

T: M Thera, Amorgos, Anaphea+Islands ▪ ✉ Mitropolis, GREECE-847 00 Phyrrà Theras • [30] 22860 22260, 25920, fax 22362 • imthiras@mail.gr

*1934 Vroutsi Amorgou. N12.5. 1958 military service. diak1958-1959 deacon Theras. 1959-1964 dipl theol Athens ⊖1964 archim. 1965-2002 hierokēryx Thera, igumen Chozoviotissa ⊕11.1.2003.

Daniel Dionysios Pourtsouklis ***Kaisariani***

T: M Kaisariani, Vyron+Hymettos ▪ ✉ Formionos 83, GREECE-161 21 Kaisariani • [30] 210 7237133, 7224123, fax 7223584 • info@imkby.gr • www.imkby.gr

*19.9.1952 Nea Manolada Elias, N17.12. 1971-1973 Anotera Hieratiki Scholi Chalandrion Attikis. mon19.5.1973. 1973-1977 dipl theol Athens. diak29.12.1974. 1978-1998 hierokēryx Dimitrias ⊖11.3.1979 archim1979. 1986-1998 president Youth movements. 1998-2000 hierokēryx Athens, Chief Secretary Holy Synod ⊕22.1.2000 B, 2000 M Kaisariani.

Ambrosios Athanasios Lenís ***Kalávryta***

T: M Kalavryta+Aigialeia ▪ ✉ Romanioli 43, P.O.Box 83, GREECE-251 00 Aigion • [30] 26910 6125-1, -2, fax 21634, 21776 • Kalávryta 26920 22235 • imka@otenet.gr • imkaigial@gmail.com • mkka@otenet.gr • www.im-ka.gr

*22.7.1938 Athens. N7.12. mon25.4.1961 diak31.5.1961. 1963 dipl theol Athens. ⊖17.7.1963. 1963-1974 Police Chaplaincy. 1974-1978 Chief Secretary Holy Synod

⊕17.8.1976 M tit Talantion, 12.10.1978 M Kalavryta. 1998-2005 Chairman Committee External Church Relations. 2000 Member Commission EU.

Georgios Rempelos ***Karpenision***
T: M Karpenision ▪ ✉ Mitropolis, GREECE-361 00 Karpenision • [30] 2370 22993, 22191, fax 23993 • imkarpenisiou@jmc.gr
* 1963 Castella, Evia. 1985 dipl pedagogics Academy Lamia. 1993 dipl theol Athens. 1985-1987 military service air force. 1988 work in primary school in Chalkida. 1995 teacher. diak 9/1994 ⊖9/1994 (M Hieronymos, now archbishop of Athens) ⊕12.3.2016.

Nikólaos Drosos
T: former M Karpenision ▪ ✉ Mitropolis, GREECE-361 00 Karpenision • [30] 22370 22993, 22191, fax 23993 • Athens 2109752299, 2109752229 imkarpenisiou@jmc.gr
*1929 Thera. N6.12. 1956 dipl theol Athens. diak16.11.1958 ⊖1.1.1959 ⊕28.1.1979 M. 2016 retired.

Seraphim Sokrates Roris ***Karystia***
T: M Karystia+Skyros ▪ ✉ Mitropolis, GREECE-340 03 Kymi • [30] 22220 22230, 22237, 24040, fax 23440 • imkarystias@windowslive.com
*1929 Kosmas Kynouria. N8.11. 1955 dipl theol Athens. mon1962 Elona diak1962 ⊖1962 ⊕24.11.1968 M Karystia.

Dimitrios Spyridon Argyros ***Kefallinia***
T: M Kefallinia ▪ ✉ Mitropolis, GREECE-281 00 Argostolion • [30] 26710 28011, 22231, fax 25177, [30] 6944 542617
*1958 Fterno Levkadia. mon23.12.1980 Vella diak25.12.1980 Ioannina (M Theoklitos). 1982-1986 stud Fac theol Athens. 1986-1991 stud Roma Pontificio Istituto di Archeologia Cristiana. Pontificio Istituto Orientale and University Ioannina dipl Church History ⊖26.2.1987 Ioannina (M Theoklitos). 1993-2007 hierokēryx Ioannina. 2007-2015 director Academy Vella ⊕9.10.2015 M Kefallinia.

Nektarios Demetrios Dovas ***Kerkyra***
T: M Kerkyra+Paxos, Overseas Islands ▪ ✉ Mitropolis Arseniou 1, GREECE-491 00 Kerkyra • [30] 26610, 39912, 39409, fax 41740 • info@imcorfu.gr • bishopnektarios@imcorfu.gr • www.imcorfu.gr
*1953 Volos. N9.11. mon1973 Ano Xenia. 1975-1986 hierokēryx Dimitrias. diak1.1.1975. 1979 dipl theol Athens ⊖4.3.1979. 1986-2002 igumen Ano Xenia ⊕13.10.2002 M Kerkyra.

Dionysios Mantalos *Kórinthos*
T: M Korinthos, Sikyon, Zemenon, Tarsos, Polyphengos ▪ ✉ Pylarinou 76, GREECE-201 00 Korinthos • [30] 27410 22549, 22547, fax 20340 • mitropoli@imkorinthou.org • www.imkorinthou.org
*1952 Athens. N? dipl theol Athens, postgraduate Thessaloniki. diak1974 ⊖1979. 1990 protosynkellos Chalkidos ⊕15.10.2006 M Korinthos.

Seraphim Lambros Stergiulis *Kythera*
T: M Kythera ▪ ✉ Mitropolis, GREECE-801 00 Chora Kythiron • [30] 27360 31281, fax 31202 • Athens 2108225396 • www.imkythiron
*27.12.1950 Vrangiana Karditsis. N4.12. 1970 graduate Rizareios Ekkl Scholi. diak1970. 1976 dipl theol Thessaloniki. 1979 hierokēryx Hydra ⊖1981 archim1981 protosynkellos Hydra ⊕2.7.2005 M Kythera.

Ignatios Iakovos Lappas *Larissa*
T: M Larissa+Tyrnavos ▪ ✉ Ioanninon 3, GREECE-413 34 Larissa • [30] 2410 61768-5, fax -4
*1946 Salamis. N20.12. dipl theol, dipl Nomos Athens. diak1976 ⊖1976. 1984-1994 secretary Holy Synod ⊕28.5.1994. 5.3.1998 Fanar.

Theofilos Konstantinos Manolatos *Levkás*
T: M Levkás+Ithaka ▪ ✉ Mitropolis, GREECE-311 00 Levkás • [30] 26450, 22645, 22415, fax 25354, [30] 6946 76275 • www.imli.gr
*1963 Levkáda. N8.7. absolvent Fac theol Athens. diak1991 ⊖1992 (Sergios Grevenón). 1992-2008 proistamenos Moschato. 1993 Archeiophylax ⊕27.6.2008.

Alexandros Papadopulos *Mantineia*
T: M Mantineia+Kynouria ▪ ✉ Grigoriou V 13, GREECE-221 00 Tripolis • [30] 2710 22244-5, -6, fax 226926 • alieys@yahoo.com
*28.10.1936 Papari Mantineia Arkadia. N30.8. diak29.12.1968 ⊖27.4.1969. 1969 dipl theol Athens ⊕5.5.1984 M Navpaktos. 1995 M Mantineia+Kynouria.

Konstantinos Jakoumakis *Mégara*
T: M Mégara+Salamis ▪ ✉ Mitropolis Odos Kourkouri, GREECE-191 00 Mégara • [30] 22960 2779-5, -4, fax 25972 • Athens 210 7 2273 75
*1960 Kreta, N21.5. mon1970 Piraeus (Archim Christophoros Papadopulos) 1975 Rizareion E.S. Athens, Anot. E.S. Athens, Fac theol Athens 1983-2014 hierokēryx, efimerios, pneumatikos Athens. diak1983 ⊖2.1.1986. 1995-2014 grammateus Holy Synod, bibliothekarios, kodigographos, personal office A Athens ⊕11.10.2014.

Dorotheos Mourtzoukos
T: B Eleusis, assistant Mégara+Salamis ▪ ✉ Mitropolis Odos Kourkouri, GREECE-191 00 Mégara • [30] 2296027795, 2296027794, fax 25972 • Athens 210 7227 375
*1947 Megara N5.6. diak1972 ⊖1973 ⊕7.11.2009 B Eleousina, assistant Mégara.

Nikolaos Hatzinikolaou ***Mesogaia***
T: M Mesogaia+Laureotiki ▪ ✉ Thoukydidou 6, GREECE-190 04 Spata Attikis • [30] 210 6632687, 6632276, fax 6025101
*13.4.1954 Thessaloniki. N6.12. 1972 dipl Physic Thessaloniki. MA Astrophysics Harvard. Massachusetts Institute of Technology MIT. Deaconess Hospital New England. mon18.3.1989 diak19.3.1989 ⊖10.9.1989. 1990-2004 efimerios Metochi Simonos Petras Athens. 1990 teacher Fac Medicin Kreta. MTh Boston. teacher bioethics University Thessaloniki. archim1992. 2003 Dr. theol Thessaloniki, Director Hellenic Center Biomedical Ethics ⊕30.4.2004 M Mesogaia.

Chrysostomos Savvatos ***Messinia***
T: M Messinia, Methoni, Koroni+Androusa ▪ ✉ Mitropolitou Meletiou 13, GREECE-241 00 Kalamata • [30] 27210 24165, 22455, fax 22994 • Athens 2106710327 • mitropolis_messinias@yahoo.gr • fatherdim@yahoo.com
*1961 Peristéri Attikis. N22.8. 1983-1987 dipl theol Athens. diak10.7.1988. 1988-1991 Lic Roma with scholarship CCCC, Gregoriana, Scuola di Paleografia, Ist. Orientale. 1988-1995 hierokēryx Peristerion, ⊖8.11.1991. 1991-1992 Dr. theol Strasbourg CCCC. 1993-1999 Dr. theol Athens, secretary Holy Synod. 1995-2007 Athens. 1999 Lektor Dogmatik, 2001 Prof. Ass. Athens. 2007 Prof Fac theol Bari. 2007 member official Commission Orth-Cath Dialogue ⊕18.3.2007. 22.-28.1.2016 Synaxis of the primates of the Local Orthodox Churches Chambésy Switzerland.

Eustathios Konstantinos Spiliotis ***Monembasia***
T: M Monembasia+Sparta ▪ ✉ Mitropolis Lyssandrou 5, GREECE-231 00 Sparti • [30] 27310 26481, 26580, 26581, fax 26581 • immspar@otenet.gr • www.immspartis.gr
*1940 Messinia. N20.9. mon1964 Voulkano Messinia. diak13.8.1964. 1964 dipl theol Athens ⊖6.12.1966 ⊕31.8.1980 M Monembasia.

Hierotheos Vlachos ***Navpaktos***
T: M Navpaktos+Ag. Blasios ▪ ✉ Georgiou Athana 1, GREECE-303 00 Navpaktos • [30] 26340 22980, 27207, fax 27665
*1945 Ioannina. N4.10. 1968 dipl theol Thessaloniki. diak1971 ⊖1972 Director Apostoliki Diakonia ⊕20.7.1995 M Navpaktos+Ag. Blasios.

Gabriel Georgios Papanikolao ***Nea Ionia***
T: M Nea Ionia+Philadelphia ▪ ✉ Leoforos Irakleiou 340, GREECE-142 31 Nea Ionia • [30] 210 275-2422, fax -3800 • imni_f@on.gr • www.ecclesia.gr
*1976 Athens. diak18.2.1996 (Damaskinos, Diavlia-Didymoteichon). 1999 dipl theol Athens. 2001 dipl theol Chambésy Fribourg Switzerland ⊖30.5.2002 Parish St. Marina Theseios (A Christodoulos). 2009 protosynkellos Athens ⊕9.10.2012 B Diavlia, assistant Athens. 1.11.2014 M Nea Ionia.

Konstantinos Pharantatos
T: M former Nea Ionia+Philadelphia ▪ ✉ Mitropolis Leoforos Irakleiou 340, GREECE-142 31 Nea Ionia • [30] 2102752422, 2102753400, fax 2753800
*1930 Kephallinia. 1956 dipl theol Athens, dipl philology Athens. 1957-1966 Apostoliki Diakonia. 1966-1974 protosynkellos Maroneia. 1974-1994 protosynkellos Nea Ionia ⊕29.5.1994. 1994-2014 M Nea Ionia. 2.9.2014 retired.

Symeon Periklis Koutsas ***Nea Smyrna***
T: M Nea Smyrna ▪ ✉ Mitropolis Nea Smyrna, Plastira 70, GREECE-171 21 Nea Smyrni • [30] 2109346788, 2109344693, fax 9321743 • imns@otenet.gr • www.imns.gr
*1945 Pterounda Lesbos. N12.10. 1963-1968 dipl theol Athens. diak1973 hierokēryx: 1973-1974 Attika, 1974-1979 Hydra, 1979-2002 Nea Smyrna ⊖1975. 1981-1984 stud Paris Strasbourg. 1984 Dr. theol Strasbourg (Patrologia) ⊕12.10. 2002 M Nea Smyrna.

Alexios Vryonis ***Nikaia***
T: M Nikaia ▪ ✉ Odos Kyprou kai Ionias, GREECE-184 50 Nikaia • [30] 210 4903969, 4917598 • imnikaia@otenent.gr
*1944 Piraeus, N17.3. dipl theol Athens, diak1967 ⊖1972. 1989-1995 protosynkellos Athens ⊕29.1.1995 M Nikaia.

Prokopios Petridis
T: B Christianoupolis, assistant Nikaia ▪ ✉ Mitropolis Plateia Osias Xenis, GREECE-184 50 Nikaia • [30] 2104903969, 2104917598, fax 2104903968
*1960 Rhodos. N8.7. diak1984 ⊖1989 ⊕18.10.2009 B Kernitsa, assistant Kalavrita. 2010 Nikaia.

Kallinikos Nikolaos Demenopoulos ***Paronaxia***
T: M Paros+Naxos ▪ ✉ Mitropolis, GREECE-843 00 Naxos • [30] 22850 24644, 22400, 22233, fax 24600 • Paros [30] 22840 21761, fax 21761 • paronaxias@otenet.gr • www.i-m-paronaxia.gr

*1959 Athens. N29.7. stud theol jur Athens. military service, teacher religion. diak25.10.1986 ⊖29.10.1989 archim1989 hierokēryx, secretary Holy Synod ⊕30.6.2008.

Chrysostomos Christos Skliphas ***Patras***

T: M Patras ▪ ✉ Votsi 34, GREECE-261 10 Patras • [30] 2610 320602, 277535, 272604, fax 339391 • Athens 2109563769 • i-m.patron@otenet.gr • www.i-m.patron.gr

*1958 Louka Tripoleos son of priest. N27.1. stud Fac theol Athens. mon1981 Agios Nikolaos Barson. diak1981 (Theoklitos Filippaios) ⊖1983 (Theoklitos Filippaios). hierokēryx Mantineia. 1986-2003 igumen Ag. Nikolaos Barson. 1993 secretariat Holy Synod, 2000 Second, 2003-2005 Chief Secr Holy Synod ⊕20.2.2005 M Patras.

Chrysanthos Gerasimos Stellatos

T: B Kernitsa, auxiliary Patras ▪ ✉ Votsi 34, GREECE-261 10 Patras • [30] 2610 320602, 277535, 272604, fax 339391 www.i-m.patron.gr

*1952 Kampitsata Kephalinia. mon1975 diak1975. 1982 director oikothrophion Patras, teacher theology ⊖1982 archim1982. 2000 Orden St. Sava Serbian Patriarchate ⊕13.10.2014 B Kernitsa, auxiliary Patras.

Seraphim Mentzelopoulos ***Piraeus***

T: M Piraeus ▪ ✉ Mitropolis Akti Themistokleous 198, GREECE-185 39 Piraeus • [30] 210 4514930, 4514833 • info@imp.gr www.imns.gr

*29.12.1956 Athens. N4.12. 1978 dipl jur Athens. 1978-1980 military service. mon1980 Lawyer, Penteli. diak1980 ⊖1981. 1981-2000 rector parishes Athens, secretary Ecclesiastical Spiritual Courts. archim1981. 1984 dipl theol Athens. 2000-2001 rector St. Anthony Prospect South Australia ⊕21.1.2001 Adelaide. 2001-2002 assistant Australia. 2003 attached to Archdiocese of Athens but seconded to Piraeus. 2005-2006 Chief Secretary Holy Synod. 2006 M Piraeus.

Kallinikos Karusos

T: former M Piraeus ▪ ✉ Mitropolis Akti Themistokleous 198, GREECE-185 39 Piraeus

*1926 Elis. N29.7. diak1956 ⊖1959. 1967 dipl theol Athens ⊕25.10.1975 M tit Rogon, Director Ekklesiastike Aletheia. 1978-2006 M Piraeus. Igoúmenos Chrysopigi. 30.6.2008 retired.

Chrysostomos Gerásimos Zaphiris ***Peristérion***

T: M Peristérion ▪ ✉ Chalkokondyli kai Ethnikis Antistaseos 92, GREECE-121 35Peristérion • [30] 210 5719777, fax 5748713

*1935 Arta. N13.11. diak20.7.1960. 1960 dipl theol Chalki. 1960-1971 stud Münster, Strasbourg ⊖1.5.1970 Wuppertal Germany (M Iakovos). 1971 Dr. theol, 1971. Prof.

Holy Cross Boston. 1972-1974 vice-rector Tantur. 1974-1976 Theol Eparchial Bonn ⊕22.2.1976 M tit Gardikion. 1976-1978 Director Interorthodox Centre. 12.10.1978 M Peristérion. 1992-2003 Central Committee CEC. 1999 Commission Orthodox Collaboration WCC Geneva. 16.12.2015 Athens Interorthodox committee preparation Panorthodox Synod. 22.-28.1.2016 Synaxis of the primates of the Local Orthodox Churches Chambésy Switzerland.

Seraphim Vyron Stephanou ***Stagai***
T: M Stagai+Metéora ▪ ✉ Mitropolis, GREECE-422 00 Kalambaka • [30] 24320 23000, 22752, 22753
*1932 Fanarion Karditsa. N4.12. 1955 dipl theol Athens. diak11.1965 ⊖4.12.1966 ⊕31.5.1970 M Trikke. 1970-1974 Stagai. 1974-1991 M tit Oreos. 1991 M Stagai+ Metéora.

Dorotheos Polykandriotis ***Syros***
T: M Syros, Tinos, Andros, Kea+Melos ▪ ✉ Mitropolis, GREECE-841 00 Ermoupolis Syros • [30] 22810 82603, 82582, 82583, fax 83013 • iera.mitropoli.syrou@gmail.com • www.im-syrou.gr
*1953 Mykonos. N5.6. dipl iur Athens. dipl theol Athens. diak1977. 1977-2001 hierokēryx Syros ⊖4.12.1978. 1988-2001 secretary Holy Synod, redactor Hemerológion ⊕15.12.2001.

Chrystomos Georgios Nasis ***Trikke***
T: M Trikke ▪ ✉ Mitropolis Apollonos 19, GREECE-421 00 Trikala • [30] 24310 27365, 27282, fax 26352 • www.imts.gr
*30.1.1975 Patras. school Preveza. dipl theol Thessaloniki. mon18.10.1999 St. Theodora Thessaloniki (M Ioannes, then igoumenos) diak20.10.1999 Thessaloniki (M Panteieimon Chrysophakis) ⊖5.10.2000 archim Thessaloniki (M Panteieimon Chrysophakis). 2000-2014 oikonomos Thessaloniki. 2014-2015 protosynkellos Trikke ⊕9.10.2015 M Trikke.

Alexios Theódoros Michalopulos
T: M former Trikke ▪ ✉ Mitropolis Apollonos 19, GREECE-421 00 Trikala
*10.10.1932 Piraeus. N17.3. mon19.2.1954 Penteli diak7.3.1954. 1960 dipl theol Athens ⊖3.9.1961 ⊕22.8.1976 B Diauleia, assistant Athens. 1981-1991 M Trikke+ Stagai. 1991 M Trikke. 22.9.2015 retired.

Chrysostomos Alexandros Stavropoulos ***Triphylia***
T: M Triphylia+Olympia ▪ ✉ Mitropolis, GREECE-245 00 Kyparissía • [30] 2761022218, fax 2761022217 • Athens 2108223370 • mhtropol@hol.gr • imtko@otenet.gr

*1959 N13.11. Vlachiotin Lakonias. stud Athos, stud Athens. mon1982 Tesserakonta Athos. diak20.9.1982 Archidiakon (A Serafim) ⊖7.7.1987 protosynkellos Monemvasia ⊕17.3.2007.

Efraim Evangelos Stenakis ***Hydra***
T: M Hydra, Spetsai, Aigina ▪ ✉ Mitropolis, GREECE-180 40 Hydra • [30] 22980, 52204, 52207, fax 52887
*1948 Kypseli Aigina. N28.1. 1972 dipl theol Athens. diak1973 ⊖1979. 1983-2001 Chancellor Hydra, 1985-2001 igumen Life-Giving Font ⊕14.1.2001 M Hydra.

Nikolaos Protopapás ***Phthiotis***
T: M Phthiotis ▪ ✉ Mitropolis, GREECE-351 00 Lamía • [30] 22310 50551, 50552, fax 5055-3, -4 • imfth@otenet.gr
*1948 Plateia Tinos. N6.12. Rizareio Ekkl Scholi. 1972 dipl theol Athens. mon3.12. 1972 St. David the Elder Euboea; 1973-1975 archdeacon Mitropolis Chalkis. diak26.7.1973. 1975-1984 Prof Ekkl Lykeion Tinos ⊖23.2.1975. 1984-1996 parish Ag. Eleftherios Gkyzi, Radio Station Greek Church ⊕6.10.1996 M Phthiotis.

Theoktistos Kloukinas ***Phokis***
T: M Phokis ▪ ✉ Mitropolis, GREECE-331 00 Amphissa • [30] 22650 28624, 28224, fax 29146 • www.imfok.gr
*1950 Sparta,N3.9. diak1973 ⊖1977 ⊕25.10.2009 Androusa, assistant Sparta. 2014 M Phokis.

Chrysostomos Konstantinos Triantafyllou ***Chalkis***
T: M Chalkis, Istiaia, Sporades ▪ ✉ Mitropolis Vaki 21, GREECE-341 00 Chalkis • [30] 22210 6040-4, -5, -6, -7, 22502, 27925, fax 61505 • imchalkidos@yahoo.gr • www.imchalkidos.gr
*1957 Vassiliko Chalkidos. N13.11. diak1983 ⊖1983 Epitropos Chalkis. 1998 dipl theol Athens, Dr. theol Thessaloniki ⊕17.12.2001 M Chalkis.

Anthimos Christos Koukouridis ***Alexandroupolis***
T: M Alexandroupolis ▪ ✉ Mitropolis, GREECE-681 00 Alexandroupolis • [30] 25510 27853, 25510, 26359, fax 25510 21657 • Athens 2105247212 • imalex@imalex.gr • www.imalex.gr
*2.1.1962 Alexandroupolis. N3.9. 1981 absolvent Theol Scholi Xanthi. 1983 absolvent Pedagogical Academy Alexandroupolis. diak1985. 1987 dipl theol Thessaloniki ⊖1989 ephimerios Alexandroupolis "Thraki Hellada mou" english turkish ⊕9.10.2004.

Panteleimon Ioannis Kalpakidis *Berroia*
T: M Berroia+Naoussa, Kampania ▪ ✉ Mitropoleos 30, GREECE-591 00 Berroia • [30] 2331072622, 2331022510, 22270 • imveria@compullink.gr • imverias@gmail.com • gerbekes@yahoo.gr • www.imverias.gr
*15.10.1945 Thessaloniki. N27.7. Theol school Athos. diak1969 London with name Theophilos. mon1975 Skit Mikra Agia Anna Mount Athos. 1975 dipl theol Thessaloniki ⊖1976 Thessaloniki. 1976-1978 stud theol Oxford. 1978-1994 protosynkellos Thessaloniki ⊕29.5.1994.

Dimitrios Bekiaris-Mavrogonatos *Gouménissa*
T: M Gouménissa+Axioúpolis+Polýkastron ▪ ✉ Moni Panagias, GREECE-613 00 Gouménissa • [30] 2343043363, 2343043333 +fax, 41222 • gimgap@gmail.com • www.imgap.gr
*1948 Loutraki Korinthos. N26.10. 1972 dipl theol Athens. mon6.9.1975 diak 8.9.1975 ⊖14.1.1976 hierokēryx Philippi+Larissa. 1984-1989 protosynkellos Athens igumen Petraki ⊕15.10.1989 M Larissa, election annulled 18.2.1990 Court decision 3804/90. 20.8.1991 M tit Gardikion. 10.9.1991 M Gouménissa+Axioúpolis+Palaeokastron.

David Konstantinos Tzioumakas *Grevena*
T: M Grevena ▪ ✉ Mitropolis, GREECE-511 00 Grevena • [30] 24620 22404, fax 28919 • www.imd.gr
*1958 Litochoro Piera, N7.10. 1979 dipl Pedagogical University. 1980-1983 director personal office M Panteleimon Chrysophakis. mon1980 diak6.8.1980. 1983 dipl Fac theol Thessaloniki. 1983-2014 proistamenos St. John Thessaloniki ⊖23.1.1983 archim29.1.1983 ⊕12.10.2014.

Damaskinos Minas Karpathakis *Didymoteichon*
T: M Didymoteichon+Orestias+Souphlion ▪ ✉ Mitropolis, GREECE-683 00 Didymoteichon • [30] 2553022900, 2553022700, fax 22901 • Orestias, Odos 40 Ekklesion 6 • 2552022532 • imdos@otenet.gr • www.imdos.gr
*10.5.1959 Athens N4.12. dipl iur Athens. dipl theol Athens. mon1.2.1985 Monastir Petraki Athens. diak23.3.1985 ⊖14.9.1987. 1990-1998 Chief Secretary Synod ⊕27.1.1995 Diavlia, assistant Athens. 2009 M Didymoteichon.

Paulos Alexandros Apostolidis *Drama*
T: M Drama ▪ ✉ Mitropolis, Venizelou 168, GREECE-661 00 Drama • [30] 25210 32362, fax 2521033014 • imdramas@otenet.gr • www.imdramas.gr

*1963 Veroea. N29.6. diak1983 ⊖archim1988 (Paulos, Berroia). 1988 dipl theol Thessaloniki. 1988-1991 rector Agios Antonios Berroia. 1991-2005 igumen Panagia Soumelá. 1995 completion of doctoral studies. 2002 Dr. theol Thessaloniki ⊕9.10.2005 M Drama.

Andreas Trebelas ***Dryinoupolis***
T: M Dryinoupolis+Pogonion+Konitsa ▪ ✉ Mitropolis, GREECE-440 02 Delvinakion • [30] 26570 22203, fax 22344 • Konitsa 26550, 22273 • imdpk@imdpk.eu • www.imdpk.gr

*1939 Patras. N30.11. 1963 dipl theol Athens. 1967-1995 hierokēryx Dryinoupolis diak1968 ⊖1969 ⊕28.1.1995 M Dryinoupolis+Pogonion+Konitsa.

Ioil Panagiotis Frangakos ***Edessa***
T: M Edessa, Pella+Almopia ▪ ✉ Mitropolis, GREECE-582 00 Edessa • [30] 23810 23300, 23500, fax 29945

*1949 Nikaia. Piraeus. N19.10. 1967-1972 dipl theol Athens. 1972-1974 military service. 1974-1975 laikos hierokēryx Edessa. diak1.9.1975. 1976-2002 hierokēryx Edessa ⊖1.6.1979 ⊕15.10.2002 M Edessa.

Chrysostomos Ioannis Avagianós ***Eleutheroupolis***
T: M Eleutheroupolis ▪ ✉ Mitropolis, GREECE-641 00 Eleutheroupolis • [30] 25920 23464, 22246, fax 22486, 22186 • imelef@otenet.gr • www.imelef.gr

*1947 Mesagrós Lésbos. N13.11. dipl theol Athens. assistant to Prof. Konidaris. 1970-1973 military service. diak1973 ⊖1977. 1977-2004 hierokēryx Phlorina, Mytilene, Athens ⊕28.4.2004 M Eleutheroupolis.

Hierotheos Dimitrios Tsoliakos ***Zichna***
T: M Zichna+Nevrokopion ▪ ✉ Mitropolis, GREECE-620 42 Nea Zichni • [30] 23240 22243, 22203 • Nevrokopion • imzixnon@otenet.gr

*1945 Megara. N4.10. diak1969. 1974-1989 parishes Megara ⊖1974 dipl theol Athens. 1989-2003 secretary Holy Synod ⊕17.5.2003 M Zichna.

Anthimos Dionysios Roussas ***Thessaloniki***
T: M Thessaloniki ▪ ✉ Vogatsikou 7, GREECE-546 22 Thessaloniki • [30] 2310 228823, 227677, fax 230722, 227677 • gr_imth@yahoo.com • protimth@yahoo.com

*1934 Salmoni Pyrgos. N3.9. 1957 dipl phil Athens. 1963 dipl theol Athens. diak1964 ⊖1965. 1965-1972 syntáktes "Phoni Kyríou" ⊕14.7.1974 M Alexandroupolis. 2004 M Thessaloniki.

Theóklitos Panagiotis Athanasópulos *Ierissos*
T: M Ierissos, Agion Oros Athos+Ardamerion ▪ ✉ Mitropolis, GREECE-630 74 Arnaia • [30] 2372022641, 2372022207, fax 23070 • im-ierissoy@hotmail.com • www.im-ierissou.gr
*13.11.1955 Tritolis Arkadia. N26.2. stud theol Athens. mon6.12.1978 diak10.12. 1978 ⊖26.10.1980 archim26.10.1980 ierokēryx, 1992 protosynkellos Mantineia ⊕7.10.2012 Ierissos, Agion Oros Athos+Ardamerion.

Maximos Vasilios Papayiannis *Ioannina*
T: M Ioannina ▪ ✉ Ioakeim III 10, GREECE-452 21 Ioannina • [30] 2651026397, 2651026379, fax 34500
*1968 Leverkusen, Germany. 1988 dipl theol Athens. priest in Stuttgart. 1992 parish Bietigheim-Bissingen, stud church history Strasbourg and Tübingen. 2008-2014 hierokēryx Athens, protosynkellos. 2009 rector St. Panteleimon Acharnon Athens ⊕25.6.2014.

Nikodimos Konstantinos Korakis *Kassandreia*
T: M Kassandreia ▪ ✉ Mitropolis, GREECE-631 00 Polygyros • [30] 2180 -0,-1,-2,-3,-4, fax 21810 • mitrkass@otenet.gr • www.imkassandreias.gr
*1942 Siphnos. N14.7. diak1965. 1967 dipl theol Athens ⊖1969. 1974-2001 Chancellor Nea Krini ⊕13.1.2001 M Kassandreia.

Seraphim Ioannis Papakóstas *Kastoria*
T: M Kastoria ▪ ✉ Plat. Pavlou Melá 1, GREECE-521 00 Kastoria • [30] 24670 27783, fax 22334 • info@imkastorias.gr • www.imkastorias.gr
*21.1.1959 Agnantero Karditsa. N4.12. 1983 dipl Anotéra Ekkl Scholi Athens. diak16.10.1983. 1986 dipl theol Athens ⊖4.1.1987. 1990-1996 secretary Holy Synod, parish Ag. Nikolaos Kato Patisia ⊕5.10.1996 M Kastoria.

Georgios Georgios Chrysostomou *Kitros*
T: M Kitros+Katerini+Platamon ▪ ✉ Mitropolis, GREECE-601 00 Katerini • [30] 23510 23512, 23542 • info@imkitrous.gr
*3.8.1964 Thessaloniki. N3.11. 1986-1990 dipl theol Thessaloniki. diak1989 Thessaloniki ⊖1990 Thessaloniki. 1994 Dr. phil Byzantinology "The Monk Gerasimos Mikragiannanitis as Hymnograph". stud France, Italy. 1995-2014 teacher, Prof. Thessaloniki. 2011-2013 Prof. Congo and Ukraina Kiev ⊕1.3.2014 M Kitros+ Katerini+Platamon.

Agathonikos Georgios Phatouros
T: M former Kitros ▪ ✉ Mitropolis, GREECE-601 00 Katerini • [30] 23510 23512, 23542

*1937 Aigion, N1.12. diak1960 dipl theol Athens. mon1963 Varlaam Metéora ⊖1964. 1964-1968 hierokēryx Gortyna. 1968-1974 teacher Tinos. 1974-1985 hierokēryx Athens ⊕24.11.1985. 2014 retired.

Johannis Tassias ***Langadas***
T: M Langadas ▪ ✉ Mitropolis, 27 Oktovriou 1, GREECE-572 00 Langadas • [30] 2394022998, 23940, 22234 • imlagada@otnet.gr • www.imlagada.gr
*1958 Thessaloniki. N7.1. 1979 dipl pedagogics, 1982 dipl theol Thessaloniki. diak1982 director Youth Department ⊖1983 Prof Theol Užgorod. 1983-1994 rector Kyrill and Method Thessaloniki. 1994-2010 protosynkellos Thessaloniki ⊕16.5.2010 M Langada.

Hierotheos Garýfallos ***Limnos***
T: M Limnos+Agios Eustratios ▪ ✉ Mitropolis, GREECE-814 00 Mýrina Limnou • [30] 22540 24630, 22474, fax 24042 imlimnou@gmail.com
*1934 Athens. N4.10. mon16.10.1954 Penteli diak13.11.1954 ⊖1.3.1959. 1959 dipl theol Athens ⊕22.11.1988 M Limnos.

Panteleimon Stavros Moutafis ***Maroneia***
T: M Maroneia+Komotini ▪ ✉ Mitropolis, Plateia Autokratoros Theodosiou 7, GREECE-691 00 Komotiní • [30] 25310 22569, 25310, 22642 • immkom@otenet.gr • www.immaroniaskomotinis.gr
*14.6.1970 Kavala (Petro, Thomai). N27.7. 1988 absolvent Lykeion Kavala. 1988-1991 Anotera Ekklesiastiki scholi Athens, 1991-1994 dipl theol Thessaloniki. 1995-1996 military service Thrakia. mon16.10.1995 Penteli diak8.9.1996 ⊖29.9.1996. 1996-2013 protosynkellos Xanthi. 2006 postgraduate theol Athens ⊕24.2.2013 M Maroneia+Komotini.

Chrysostomos Kyriákos Kalamatianós ***Methymna***
T: M Methymna ▪ ✉ Mitropolis, GREECE-811 07 Kalloni Lesbou • [30] 22530 22335, 22337
*1930 Chalkis. N13.11. diak3.10.1954. 1954-1984 hierokēryx spiritual director Attika ⊖23.7.1967. 1971 dipl theol Athens ⊕6.5.1984 M Methymna.

Iakovos Frantsis ***Mytilini***
T: M Mytilini, Eresson+Plomarion ▪ ✉ Mitropolis, GREECE-811 00 Mytilini • [30] 2251028687, 2251028514, 22654, 24437 • immit@otenet.gr • www.immyt.gr
*1942 Agiassos Lesbos. N23.10. diak6.6.1965 ⊖19.9.1965. 1966 dipl theol Chalki. 1966-1976 hierokēryx, 1976-1988 protosynkellos Mytilini ⊕20.11.1988 M Mytilini.

Iustinos Bardakas *Nea Krini*

T: M Nea Krini+Kalamaria ▪ ✉ odos M Chrysanthou 1, GREECE-551 32 Kalamarià • [2310] 426812

*1.1.1969 Meliti Florina. 1991 postgraduate studies Athens, Neapolis Cyprus. mon1993 diak1993 ⊖1996 archim Florina (M Augustinos Kantiotis). 1997-2000 hierokēryx Holy Synod and Florina. 2000 protosynkellos Florina. 2013 director television 4E ⊕1.6.2015.

Varnavas Markos Tyris *Neapolis*

T: M Neapolis+Stavropolis ▪ ✉ Mitropoleos 11, GREECE-567 28 Neapoli • [30] 2310 611128, 611129.

*1958 Diavatá Thessalonikis N11.6. 1984 dipl theol Thessaloniki. diak1984 ⊖1984 archim1984. 1984-2004 protosynkellos Neapolis. 1989-2004 Oikonomikon Grafeion Thessaloniki ⊕10.10.2004 M Neapolis.

Chrysostomos Georgios Tsirigas *Nikopolis*

T: M Nikopolis+Preveza ▪ ✉ Mitropolis Ethnikis Antistaseos 101, GREECE-481 00 Preveza • [30] 26820 28715, 26734, fax 27953 • imprevez@otenet.gr • www.imprevezis.gr

*1957 Athens. N13.11. mon1993 Asomaton Petrakis diak1.12.1993 ⊖28.5.1995. 1995-2012 secretary Holy Synod. 1996-2012 St. Nicholas Kato Patissia. 2011 Fac theol Athens ⊕6.10.2012 Nikopolis+Preveza.

Panteleimon Michail Kalaphatis *Xanthi*

T: M Xanthi+Peritheorion ▪ ✉ Mitropolis, GREECE-671 00 Xanthi • [30] 25410 28305, 22505, fax 25581 • ieramxp@otenet.gr

*1943 Petrokerassa Chalkidikis. N27.7. 1967 dipl jur Thessaloniki. diak1970 ⊖1970 hierokēryx Monembasia. 1973 dipl theol Thessaloniki. mon 40 Martyrs Sparta. ⊕29.1.1995 M Xanthi+Peritheorion.

Titos Sotirios Papanakos *Paramythía*

T: M Paramythía, Philiates+Geromerion, Parga ▪ ✉ Mitropolis, GREECE-462 00 Paramythia • [30] 26660 22092, 22260 • imparam@otenet.gr • www.imparamythias.gr

*1931 Piraeus. N25.8. 1964. dipl theol Athens. diak1966 ⊖1966. 1966-1974 hierokēryx Kefallinia ⊕17.7.1974 M Paramythia.

Emmanouel Sigálas *Polyane*

T: M Polyane+Kilkis, Exarchos Makedonia ▪ ✉ El. Venizelou 2, GREECE-611 00 Kilkis • [30] 23410, 22508, 22248, fax 28625 • info@impk.gr • www.impk.gr

*1953 Ermoupolis Syros, N25.12. 1973 stud theol Thessaloniki. Gymnasiarchis. diak1980 ⊖1980. 1980-1983 hierokēryx Thera Amorgos, 1983-2009 hierokēryx Thebai ⊕12.10.2009 M Polyane.

Evsébios Evangelos Pistolís ***Samos***
T: M Samos+Ikaria ▪ ✉ Mitropolis 28 Oktovriou, GREECE-831 00 Samos • [30] 22730 8764-1, -2, fax -6 •info@imsamou.gr • www.imsamou.gr
*1949 Palaio Karlóvasi Samos. N22.6. dipl theol Athens. mon Chrysopeghi diak1972 ⊖1976. Director Pastoral Assistence Police ⊕22.7.1995 M Samos.

Pavlos Panagiotis Papalexiou ***Servia***
T: M Servia+Kozani ▪ ✉ Mitropolis Char. Megdani 6, GREECE-501 00 Kozani • [30] 2461, 0 34949, 26136, 36050 • info@imsk.gr • www.imsk.gr
*27.5.1942 Rodia Aegialias. N29.6. dipl Ius Athens. dipl theol Athens. monPenteli diak24.10.1971 Athens (A Hieronymos). 1971-1975 Oikonomos Penteli, Director Catechisis School Penteli ⊖13.5.1973 Penteli (A Dimitrios Amerika). archim19.2. 1978. 1979-1989 hierokēryx protosynkellos Kalavryta. 1990 hierokēryx Athens. 1991 parish Astoria USA. 2001 hierokēryx Athens, secretary Holy Synod ⊕29.4.2004 Servia+Kozani.

Theologos Ioannis Apostolides ***Serrai***
T: M Serrai+Nigrita ▪ ✉ Mitropolis Kyprou 10, GREECE-621 22 Serres • [30] 23210 68100, fax -68119 • mitropoli@imsn.gr • www.imsn.gr
*27.3.1967 Volos. N8.5. 1988 dipl theol Athens. 1988-1992 stud Athens. diak1992 ⊖1994 archidiak Dimitrias. 1999 secretary Holy Synod. 2000-2003 Chief Secretary Holy Synod, assistant Athens ⊕14.10.2001 B Salona. 2003 M Serrai.

Makarios Sotirios Philotheou ***Siderókastron***
T: M Siderókastron ▪ ✉ Mitropolis, GREECE-623 00 Siderókastron • [30] 23230, 22142, 22340, fax 24349
*1952 Nikosia Cyprus. N19.1. 1972 Theol Scholi. 1976 dipl theol Athens. diak1977. 1980 dipl phil Athens ⊖1981 archim (M Anthimos, Alexandroupolis) 1981 hierokēryx Alexandroupolis. 1983 postgraduate Durham (Patrologia). 1991 director Youth Movement, Radiostation ⊕16.12.2001.

Pavlos Ioannou ***Sisanion***
T: M Sisanion+Siátista ▪ ✉ Mitropolis, GREECE-503 00 Siatista • [30] 24650, 21365, 21257, fax 21204
*1947 Chalkis. N29.6. 1971 dipl theol Athens. diak1973 (M Nikolaos, Chalkis) ⊖1974 Chalkis (M Chrysostomos) igumen St. Georges Arma. Synodal Commission Family ⊕4.3.2006 M Sisanion.

Prokopios Mihail Tsakumakas ***Philippi***
T: M Philippi, Neapolis+Thasos ▪ ✉ Mitropoleos 1, GREECE-654 03 Kavala • [30] 2510 223141, fax 2510 223283, 2510 223222 • Athens 210 6827024 • imphnth@otenet.gr • www.im-philippon.gr
*2.6.1939 Chios, N8.7. diak9.4.1960-1970 hierokēryx, 1963 dipl theol Athens ⊖29.8.1965. 1971-1974 teacher ecclesiastical school Korinth ⊕25.5.1974 M Philippi. 1974-1982 President Juridical Comm Holy Synod. 2000 President Commission EU.

Theóklitos Thomas Passalís ***Phlorina***
T: M Phlorina, Prespa, Eordaia ▪ ✉ Mitropolis, GREECE-531 00 Phlorina • [30] 23850, 28860, 23300, fax 28869 • Athens 210 3626100 • imflorin@otenet.gr • www.imflorinas.gr
*1932 Kyparission Grevena. N26.2. 1957 dipl theol Thessaloniki. mon20.10.1967 Dormition Kladorrachi Phlorina. diak22.10.1967 (M Augustinos) ⊖7.4.1968 archim (M Augustinos) ⊕23.1.2000 M Phlorina.

Markos Vasilakis ***Chios***
T: M Chios, Psara+Oinousai ▪ ✉ Mitropolis, GREECE-821 00 Chios • [30] 22710 4404-4, office -5, fax -6 • mhtr34@otenet.gr • mhtr97@otenet.gr • www.imchiou.gr
*26.4.1965 Chios. N? dipl phil Athens Classical Philology, teacher Byzantine Philology University Athens. dipl theol Athens. mon1994 diak22.10.1994 hierokēryx Chios ⊖7.4.2000 ⊕7.10.2011 M Chios.

Indian Orthodox Church
Malankara Orthodox Syrian Church

His Holiness Baselius Mar **Thoma Paulose II.**
Catholicos of the East and Malankara Metropolitan

Paulose Thoma

T: Eighth Catholicos of the East, 21st Malankara Metropolitan, 91th Successor of the Throne of St. Thomas the Apostle ▪ ✉ Catholicate Palace Devalokam, INDIA-686 038 Kottayam Kerala • [91] 481 2578234, 2578499, 2578392, [91] 4885 224001, T 223001 • Theol Seminary INDIA-686 001 Kottayam • [91] 481 2566526, fax 2568500 and 2302571 • frjohnmat@rediffmail.com • catholikos@mosc.in • www.orthodoxsyrianchurch.com

*30.8.1946 Pazhangi Kunnamkulam, N? diak31.5.1973 ⊖2.6.1973 mon14.5.1985 ⊕15.5.1985 M Kunnamkulam, President Youth Movement. 2006 Successor to the Catholicos. 2010 Catholicos.

Nicholovos Zachariah

T: B assistant North East America ▪ ✉ Indian Orthodox Church Center, 80-34 Commonwealth Bd, USA-Bellrose, NY 11426 • [1] 718 4709844

*13.8.1959 Mepral Kerala. N? 1974-1980 stud Malabar Christian College Kozhikode Kalikut; BA 1975-1981 St. Joseph's College Kozhikode. 1981-1985 United Theol College Bangalore BDiv. diak 4.1.1986. 1987-1989 MTh; 1990 research Bangalore (Cath Fac) ⊖16.5.1990 ⊕15.8.1993 in Damascus M Antiochian (Syr) Malankara Diocese USA Canada. 1999 from "Syr" to "India". 2002 B assistant North East America, 26.2.2011 M.

Thomas Athanasios ***Chengannur***

T: M Chengannur ▪ ✉ Bishop House Cathedral Rd, INDIA-686 661 Muvattupuzha Kerala • [91] 479 452731, 453310, [91] 944 7083340 • thomasmarathanasius@gmail.com

*3.4.1938 Puthencave Chengannur. N? diak 7.5.1970 ⊖26.5.1970 mon14.5.1983 ⊕15.5.1985 M Chengannur.

Geevargese Ivanios ***Kottayam***

T: M Kottayam ▪ ✉ Kuriakose Mar Gregorios Centre P.B. 686, INDIA-686 001 Kottayam Kerala • [91] 481 2564329 • kmgcentre@gmail.com

*14.11.1940 Othara Thiruvalla. N? diak1963. 1965-1973 stud theol Oxford ⊖1.12. 1973. 1973-1985 Prof. Greek Syriac Hebrew Seminary Kottayam. mon1979. 1981 Ostkirchliches Institut Regensburg Sommerkurs ⊕15.5.1985. 1991 M Kottayam.

Athanasius Thomas Puttanil ***Kandanadu East***
T: M Kandanadu East ▪ ✉ Bishop's House, INDIA-686 661 Muvattupuzha Kerala • [91] 485 2832401, p 2833401, [91] 944 7083340 • mbparamana@gmail.com
*28.6.1952 Arikuzha Kerala, N? 1969-1972 English Uni Kerala, 1973-1975 Uni St. John's Agra (Taj Mahal, Delhi), 1975-1979 stud theol Ev Fac Uni Serampore, 1980-1983 Ostkirchliches Institut Regensburg, 1989 Dr. theol München. diak21.12.1989 ⊖23.2.1990 mon31.3.1990 ⊕3.5.1990. 1990-1998 M Kandanadu. MA BDiv. 1992-1998 President Kerala Committee of Churches. 1999/2001 from "Syr" to "India". 2002 M Kandanadu East.

Meletius Yuhanon Murimakil ***Thrissur***
T: M Thrissur ▪ ✉ Gethsemani Seminary, Mannuthy, INDIA-680 651 Thrissur Kerala • [91] 487 2371039, fax 2371748
*4.7.1954 Ezhakaranadu Vettithara Kerala. N? 1984 MTh Bangalore. 1984-1985 stud Syriac, teacher English Damascus. 1985-1989 teacher Malankara Syrian Orthodox Theol Seminary Puthencruz ⊖23.5.1986. 1989-1990 Lutheran School of Theol Chicago, MTh ⊕23.12.1990 Damascus BA, BDiv, MTh. 1991 stud Pontifical Institute Dharmaram Bangalore. mon8.11.1995. 10.-16.11.1996 Ostkirchliches Institut Regensburg. 16.-21.11. 1996 Ecumenical Bishop's Congress London. 1997 stud theol Chicago. 1999/2001 from "Syr" to "India".

Kuriakose Clemis ***Thumpamon***
T: M Thumpamon ▪ ✉ Mar Basil Aramana, INDIA-689 645 Pathanamthitta Kerala • [91] 468 2222243, [91] 944 7942243
*1936 Taluk. stud Kerala University. teacher Botanik Catholicate College. stud Orth Theol Seminary ⊖1964⊕1991 B Sultan Battery. 19.2.2009 M Thumpamon.

Zachariah Antonios ***Kollam***
T: M Kollam ▪ ✉ Bishop's House, Cross Junction, INDIA-691 001 Kollam Kerala • [91] 474 274-3535, -6900 • kollamdiocese.gmail.com
*19.7.1946 Valakkode Punalur Kerala N? ⊖1974 mon31.3.1990 ⊕30.4.1999 M Kochi. 2009 M Kollam.

Mathews Severios Mattathil ***Kandanadu West***
T: M Kandanadu West ▪ ✉ Prasadam Centre, Kolencherry, INDIA-682 311 Ernakolam Kerala • [91] 484 2760286 • mpcsociety.gmail.com
*12.2.1949 Vazoor Kottayam. N? diak 1976 ⊖30.6.1978. 1981 Dr. theol Istituto Orientale Roma. Ostkirchliches Institut Regensburg Sprachkurs. mon31.3.1990 ⊕30.4.1991 assistant Kottayam Central, Kandanadu. 1993 M Kandanadu. 2002 M Kandanadu West.

Youhanon Demetrios ***New Delhi***
T: M Delhi ▪ ✉ Orthodox Centre, House 70, Godawari Ap. Gate 3, Alaknada, INDIA-110 019 New Delhi • [91] 11 416 50135, 26986417, 26984975, 26449203, 26974971, p 6413527, fax 26474975, 26436417, [91] 9810891894 • mar.demetrios@gmail.com
*1953 John Mathews N? Dr ⊕13.5.2010. 2011 International Joint Commission Theol Dialogue between Catholic and Oriental Orthodox Churches.

Geevargese Koorilos ***Mumbai***
T: M Bombay ▪ ✉ Juhu Nagar, Sector 10A Vashi, INDIA-400 703 New Mumbay • [91] 22 27801427, 27669850 • bombayaramana@gmail.com
*7.10.1949 Kollad Kottayam. N? 1967-1973 Orthodox Theol Seminary Kottayam. 1971-1976 University Andra Pradesh diak26.12.1974 ⊖21.12.1975. 1986-1988 Vicar, stud London, Sheffield. mon31.3.1990 ⊕30.4.1991. 1991-1998 assistant. 1998 M Bombay/Mumbai.

Paulus Pachomios ***Mavelikkara***
T: M Mavelikkara ▪ ✉ Theo Bhavan, Thazhakkara, INDIA-690 102 Mavelikkara Kerala • [91] 479 2309900 • marpachomios@gmail.com
*26.1.1946 Kurichi Kottayam. N? diak1973 ⊖8.1.1974 mon18.12.1992 ⊕16.8.1993 assistant Ankamaly. 1994 M Idukki. 2002 M Ankamaly. 2009 M Mavelikkara.

Jacob Iranios ***Kochi***
T: M Kochi ▪ ✉ Zion Seminary Koratty, INDIA-680 308 Chalakudy Kerala • [91] 480 2732023, 2734818 • sionseminary@gmail.com
*15.8.1949 Kallupara Thiruvalla, N? diak25.5.1975 ⊖8.2.1975 mon18.12.1992 ⊕16.8.1993. 1993 USA Dr. theol. 1994-1998 assistant Malabar. 1997 M Madras President Youth Movement. 2009 M Kochi.

Gabriel Gregorios ***Thiruvananthapuram***
T: M Thiruvananthapuram ▪ ✉ Orthodox Church Centre, Ulloor Medical College P.O., INDIA-695 011Thiruvananthapuram Kerala • [91] 475 2273493, 442509, [91] 944 7166857 • gabrielmargregorios@gmail.com • www.tvmdiocese.org
*10.2.1948 N? ⊕5.3.2005 Parumala. 2009 M Thiruvananthapuram. 2010/2011 International Joint Commission Theol Dialogue between Catholic and Oriental Orthodox Churches.

Zacharia Theophilos ***Malabar***
T: M Malabar ▪ ✉ Mount Hermon, Chathamangalam NITC P.O., INDIA-673 601 Kozhikode Kerala • [91]495 228 7278, 228 8278 •

hermonaramana@gmail.com
*17.8.1952 Kallupara, N? stud theol Kottayam and Serampore University, St. George College Jerusalem. Dr. theol St. Vladimir's Seminary New Jersey USA "Strengthening Prayer Life in Parishes". diak1977 ⊖15.5.1991 ⊕5.3.2005 Parumala.

Yuhanon Chrisostum ***Niranam***
T: M Niranam ▪ ✉ Bethany Aramana, R.E. College P.O., INDIA-689 101 Thiruvalla Kerala • [91] 469 2701 357, 260 3357 • marchrystostomos@ yahoo.co.in • dioceseofniranam@gmail.com • www.dioceseofniranam.org
*7.1.1955 Thiruvalla, N? Dr. phil San Fransisco Theol Seminary. diak19.4.1982 ⊖5.6.1982 ⊕5.3.2005 Parumala. Dialogue between Catholic and Oriental Orthodox Churches.

Yuhanon Polykarpos ***Ankamaly***
T: M Ankamaly ▪ ✉ Thrikunnathu Seminary, P O Box 61, INDIA-683 101 Aluva Kerala • [91] 486 962248, [91] 484 2624339, [91] 944 7475544 • thrikunnathuseminary@gmail.com • marpolycarpos @yahoo.com
*30.5.1955 Palakkad, N? Master Sociology. 1973-1974 Syriac Language 1979 BDiv Theol Seminary. diak8.12.1979 ⊖7.1.1980 ⊕2009 M Ankamaly.

Mathew Theodosios ***Idukki***
T: M Idukki ▪ ✉ Gethsemon Aramana, Chakkupallom Kumali, INDIA-686509 Idukki Kerala • [91] 4868 282-248, -504 [91] 949 5112665 • idukkidiocese@yahoo.co.in • mathewsmartheodosius@gmail.com
*16.9.1955 Alapuzha, N? 1982 BDiv Theol Seminary Kottayam ⊖1982. MA History University Kerala. 1987-1996 Principal Bethany. 1996-2009 Superior Bethany Ashram ⊕19.2.2009.

Dionysius Joseph ***Kolkotta***
T: M Calcutta ▪ ✉ P.O.B.24 St. Thomas Asram, Kaialash Nagar, INDIA-490 001 Bhilai Durg Madhya Pradesh • [91] 788 228 5309, 356309, [91] 944 6181314 • josephdionysius@gmail.com • calcuttadiocese@gmail.com • www. calcuttadiocese.org
*15.6.1956 Valanjavattom, N? mon15.7.1971 Mount Tabor Ashram. 1980 MPhil, Dr. phil University Serampore. diak1.7.1980 ⊖4.12.1085. 2005 dipl Christian leadership Haggai Institute Singapore. 2000-2009 director research department Zoology. 2003 man of the year American Biographical Institute. 2008 best University teacher St. Berchmans ⊕19.2.2009.

Abraham Epiphanios ***Sultan's Battery***
T: M Sultan's Battery ▪ ✉ Nirmalagiri Poomala, INDIA-673 592 Sultan's Battery Kerala • [91] 4936 220969 • [91] 944 7908814 • marepiphanios@gmail.com • nirmalagiribathery@hotmail.com
*7.9.1960 Malaysia, N? MTh Serapore University. diak1986 ⊖1987. 31.3.2002 title "ramban". 1990-1996 Ashram Parumala. 1996-2002 St. Thomas Cathedral. 2003-2006 Manager Parumana Seminary ⊕19.2.2009 M Sultan's Battery.

Mathews Timotheos ***Europe***
T: M UK, Europe, Africa ▪ ✉ St. Gregorios Indian Church, Cranfield Rd Brockley, GREAT BRITAIN-London, SE4 1UF • [44] 20 869 19456 • Oic.ukeuropeafrica@gmail.com • themotheosmathews@gmail.com
*3.5.1963 Mavelikkara, N? MTh Sermpore Univerity, Lic Pontifical Institute Rome, Pontifical Bible Institute Jerusalem ⊕19.2.2009.

Alexios Eusebios ***West America***
T: M West America ▪ ✉ 3101 Hopkins Rd, USA-Beasley, TX 77417 • [1] 281 4030670, 4590814 • mareusebius@gmail.com • dswadiocesanoffice@gmail.com • www.ds-wa.org
*Puthoor. stud theol Erlangen Germany. 1994 Dr theol St. Peter's Pontifical Institute Bangalore. 2005 Lutheran Institute Germany ⊕19.2.2009.

Dioskorus Yuhanon ***Chennai***
T: M Chennai ▪ ✉ 4/51 Rajeswari St, Mehta Nagar, INDIA-600 029 Chennai • [91] 44 64543128, 2374-2462, -6010,-6011, [91] 944 7464090, 979 1020730 • mardiascoros@yahoo.com • madrasorthodoxdiocese@gmail.com
*28.5.1964 Kundara, N? 1988 BDiv Serampore University. 1991 MTh and 1995 Dr. theol Pontificio Istituto Orientale Roma. 1997 dipl Pastoral Counselling Glasgow University Scotland. diak15.5.1989 ⊖3.6.1989. 1994-1997 teacher Holy Trinity College Addis Ababa. 1997-2006 Radio Sophia Kottayam ⊕19.2.2009 B Chennai (Chennai=Madras).

John Panicker
T: B ▪ ✉ Theol Seminary, INDIA-686 001 Kottayam Kerala • [91] 481 2566526
*28.5.1964, N? 1984 B.Sc. Kerala University. 1988 B.D. Serampore University. diak15.5.1989 ⊖3.6.1989. 1995 Dr. theol Pontificio Istituto Orientale Roma. 1995-1997 teacher Addis Abeba. 1997 Pastoral Counselling Glasgow University Scotland. 2006 Dean of Studies Seminary Kottayam. 4.12.2008 title "ramban" ⊕19.2.2009.

Abraham Seraphim ***Bangalore***
T: M Bangalore ▪ ✉Bishop House 1 Malankara, Doddagubi, INDIA-560 077 Bangalore • [91] 961 1353977, [91] 961 1353977 • moc.bangalorediocese@ gmail.com • marseraphim@gmail.com • www.bangaloreorthodoxdiocese.org
*28.12.1969 Thumpamon, N? BDiv Mahatma Gandhi University, Theol Seminary Kottayam, MTh Bangalore, Dr. theol Chicago USA ⊕13.5.2010.

Geevarghese Julius ***Ahmedabad***
T: M Ahmedabad ▪ ✉ St. Mary's Church, Naroda, INDIA-382 330 Ahmedabad Gujarat • [91] 469 229 80253 • [91] 944 7383931 • hgyulios@gmail.com • ahmedabaddiocese@gmail.com • www.moscad.in
*17.5.1967 George Pulikkottil. N? BSc Calicut University. BDiv Seminary Kottayam. MTh Gurukul University Chennai. Dr. theol Erlangen ⊕12.5.2010.

Yakob Elias ***Behrampura***
T: M Brahmawar ▪ ✉ Mount Horeb Bishop House 3E9-746/3, Vivekananda Nanthoor, INDIA-575 005 Mangalore • [91] 824 2210018, [91] 948 3530018 • metropolitanelias@yahoo.co.uk • www.moscdob.com
*24.2.1953 Budhanoor. MTh Kerala University, Seminary Kottayam ⊕13.5.2010.

Youhanon Theodoros ***Kottarakkara***
T: M Kottarakkara ▪ ✉ Kottapuram Seminary, Pulamon, INDIA-686 038 Kottarakkara Kerala • [91]474 2652755, [91]944 6664270 • kottapuramseminary@gmail.com
*10.2.1953 Mavelikkara, N? Dr. Serampore University ⊕13.5.2010 Kottarakkara Punalur.

Zechariah Aprem ***Adoor***
T: M Adoor Kadampanadu ▪ ✉ Sreyas Aramana, Kannamcode Pathanamthitta, INDIA-691 523 Adoor Kerala • [91] 4734 227117, 227271, [91] 944 7184303 • drzachariasmaraprem@gmail.com • akdiocese@gmail.com • 2010aprem@gmail.com
* Chungathara. MTh Bangalore, Dr. theol Sathri Bangalore ⊕13.5.2010.

Joshua Nikodemos ***Nilackal***
T: M Nilackal ▪ ✉St. Thomas Aramana Pathavangadi, Ranni, INDIA-689 673 Pathanamthitta Kerala • [91] 4735 224477 • nilackaldiocese@gmail.com
*8.10.1962 Pandalam. 1978 Ashram Ranni. diak27.4.1986 ⊖1.11.1986. 1987-2003 USA. 2007 MTh Spiritual Theol ⊕13.5.2010.

Orthodox Church in Japan

His Eminence **Daniel**
Archbishop of Tokyo, Metropolitan of All Japan

Daniel Iuda Ikuo Nashiro ***Tokyo***
T: M Tokyo ▪ ✉ 1-3 Nikolai-Do 1-3 4 Chome, Surugadai Kanda, Chiyoda -ku, Japan-Tokyo • [81] 33 2911885, 2912583
*5.9.1938 Tojochaši Japan. N12.9. 1956 orth. 1965 absolvent theol Seminary Tokyo. 1968 absolvent St. Vladimir's New York. diak1.1.1969 ⊖1.1.1971. 1971-1973 parish Nagoja. 1973-1999 parish Tojochaši. mon22.8.1999 Holy Trinity Monastery Sergiev Posad (St. Daniel of Moskva). 6.9.1999 igumen Uspenskij Moskva ⊕14.11.1999 B Kyoto, assistant Tokyo. 2000 A Tokyo.

Seraphim Noboru Andrey Tsudzie ***Sendai***
T: B Sendai ▪ ✉ 4-20 Chuo 3 Chome, Aobaku, Surugadai Kanda Chiyoda -ku, Japan-Sendai • [81] 22 2252744, fax 2243080
*23.3.1951 Akita Japan. N15.1. 1969-1973 photo school Tokyo. 1973-1987 advertising company. 1987 orth (Andrey). 1987-1990 Seminary Tokyo. diak5.11.1989. 1989-1991 deacon Tokyo ⊖18.8.1991. 1991-1993 inspector Seminary Tokyo. 1993-1999 St. Nicholas parish Tokyo. mon20.8.1999 Holy Trinity Monastery Sergiev Posad (St. Serafim Sarov). 6.9.1999 igumen Uspenskij Moskva. archim9.1. 2000 Uspenskij Moskva ⊕22.1.2000 Moskva B Sendai, (Patr Aleksij).

Greek Orthodox Patriarchate of Jerusalem

His Beatitude **Theophilos III.**
Greek Orthodox Patriarch of Jerusalem

Theophilos Ilias Giannopulos ***Jerusalem***
T: Greek Orthodox Patriarch of Jerusalem ■ ✉ Greek Orthodox Patriarchate P.O. Box 14518, ISRAEL-91145 Jerusalem • [972] 2 627-1657, fax -1511 • www.jerusalem-patriarchate.info
*1952 Gargalianoi Messini. N9./22.3. 1964 Holy Land. 1964-1970 patriarchal school Jerusalem. mon28.6.1970 (Patr Benediktos 1957-1980) diak1.7.1970 (A Vassilios Jordan) ⊖1.6.1975 (A Diodoros Hierapol). 1975 stud theol Athens. archim1978. 1981 redactor Néa Sión. 1981-1986 stud England. 1986-1988 Press+Information office. 1988-1991 WCC Geneva. 1991-1996 parish Cana Galilaea. 1997-2003 exarch Moskva. 2003-2004 Qatar. 2004 Sacristan ⊕27.2.2005 A Tabor. 22.8.2005 elected 97. Patriarch of Jerusalem (95. Diodoros 1981-2000, 96. Irenaios 2001-2005). 2009 delegation German bishops. 22.-28.1.2016 Synaxis of the primates of the Local Orthodox Churches Chambésy Switzerland.

Irinaios Emmanuél Skopelitis
T: former Patriarch of Jerusalem ■
*17.4.1939 Chora Samos, N23.8. /6.9. 1953 Jerusalem. School Mount Zion. mon1958 diak19.12.1959. 1959-1965 Senior Deacon ⊖17.6.1965 archim1966. 1966 stud theol Athens. Chief editor Néa Sión. 1979-2001 Exarch Holy Sepulchre in Greece ⊕29.3.1981 A Hierapolis. 1994 M. 13.8.2001-24.5.2005 96. Patriarch of Jerusalem. 17.6.2005 monk.

Kornelios Emmanuél Rodoussakis
T: M Petra ■ ✉ Greek Orth Patr P.O.Box 19632, ISRAEL-91190 Jerusalem • [972] 2 6271961
*1936 Kreta, N13./26.9. 1951 Jerusalem. School Mount Zion. 1958-1963 stud theol Chalki. mon20.5.1958 diak30.6.1959 ⊖29.6.1964 archim1965. 1972 member Holy Synod. 1976 Bossey ⊕6.11.1976 A Sebasteia. 1978 Patriarchal Vicar Bethlehem. 1981 chairman School Commission. 1991 M Sebasteia, President Eccl Court. 1998 senior M Petra Vicar General, Epitropos.

Kyriakos Andreas Georgopetris ***Nazareth***
T: M Nazareth ■ ✉ Greek Orthodox Convent, P.O.Box 15, ISRAEL-Nazareth • [972] 4 6574-566, fax -277
*1945 Kerkyra, N29.9./12.10. 1958 Jerusalem. mon1964 diak1964 ⊖1966 archim1966. 1966-1972 superior Mount Tabor. 1972-1976 deputy sacristan, 1976-

1981 Superior St. George's Beit-Jala. 1981 sacristan Holy Sepulchre. 1983-1987 stud Athens. 1984 Epitropos Ptolemais Akkra. dipl Hebrew University ⊕14.9.1989 B Anthidon auxiliary Nazareth. 1991 M Nazareth.

Ambrosios Nikolaos Antonopulos
T: M Neapolis ▪ ✉ Greek Orth Patr P.O.Box 19632, ISRAEL-91190 Jerusalem • [972] 2 6276531, 6287762
*1934 Piraeus, N7./20.11. 1953 Jerusalem. mon1957 diak1957⊖1962. 1963 stud theol Athens. enthronement Patr Maximos Bulgaria. 1971 Superior Gethsemani. 1979 Epitropos Ptolemais ⊕22.3.1981 A. 1999 M Neapolis. 2001 Patr Vicar Bethlehem, Archigrammateuon.

Hesychios Elias Kontoyannis
T: M Kapitolias ▪ ✉ P.O.Box 14518, ISRAEL-91190 Jerusalem • [972] 2 6260493, 6276492
*1944 Acharnai Attikis, N2./15.3. 1958 Jerusalem. mon1961 diak1961. 1962 absolvent school Mount Zion ⊖1964. 1964-1967 superior Karaq. archim 1967. 1967-1975 stud iur Athens. 1978 President Eccl Court Jaffa. 1981 Epitropos Ptolemais ⊕26.3.1984 B Abila. 1984-1991 Patriarchal Vicar Irbed Jordan. 1991 A, 1994 M Kapitolias. 2005 Legal Advisor Patriarchate.

Timotheos Theodoros Margaritis
T: M Bostra ▪ ✉ Greek Orth Patr, P.O.Box 19632, ISRAEL-91190 Jerusalem • [972] 2 6274941 fax, 6282048 +fax
*31.8.1951 Patras, N22.1. /4.2. 1967 Jerusalem. mon1970 diak1970 ⊖1975. 1975-1980 Kandidat Leningrad. archim1978 (M Nikodim). 1981 Archigrammateuon, 1983-2001 Archigrammateus, 1985-2001 Member Holy Synod ⊕21.2.1988 B Porphyroupolis. 1991 A, 1994 M Lydda, 12.2.1998 senior M Bostra. 18.10.2005 responsible for reorganization of Exarchate in Cyprus.

Christodoulos Christos Saridakis
T: M Eleutheroupolis, Geron Dragumanos ▪ ✉ P.O.Box 19632, ISRAEL-91190 Jerusalem • [972] 2 6280862
*1943 Kreta, N21.10. /3.11. 1957 Jerusalem. mon1962 diak1962 ⊖1964 archim1967. dipl Hebrew University, stud theol Athens. 1985 Chief Dragoman ⊕6.3.1988 B Areopolis. 1991 A, 1994 M Eleutheroupolis.

Benediktos Georgios Tsekouras ***Philadelphia***
T: M Philadelphia ▪ ✉ Greek Orth Metropolia, P.O.Box 310933, JORDAN-11191 Amman • [962] 6 5921-146, fax -928, fax -146

*1957 Kalavryta Greece. N14/.27.3. School Aigeon. 1976 Kalavryta. 1982 Jerusalem. diak1983 ⊖1986 archim1986. 1986 Treasurer of the Brotherhood. 1994 member Holy Synod ⊕23.2.1998 A Gaza. 2001 M Philadelphia.

Nikiphoros Nikolaos Baltatsis
T: A Askalon ■ ✉ Greek Orth Patr, P.O.Box 19632, ISRAEL-91190 Jerusalem
*1944 Mytilini. N? 1961 Jerusalem ⊖1964. 1970-1981 stud Florida USA ⊕13.3.1988 B Konstantini. 1990 resigned. 1994-2006 defrocked. 2006 A Askalon.

Theophanis Theodosios Chasapakis
T: A Gerasa, Exarch of the Holy Sepulchre ■ ✉ Greek Orth Convent, P.O.Box 19632, ISRAEL-91190 Jerusalem •
[972] 8 2863419, fax 2844417, 2818013
*18.1.1948 Mytilini. N6./19.1. 1961 Jerusalem. mon1966 diak1.7.1966. 1970-1974 stud theol Athens ⊖1.9.1970 archim1974. 1983-1986 stud Durham University MDiv London. 1986-1993 Epitropos Konstantinopel ⊕19.3.1988 B Iamnia. 15.3.1992 A Gerasa. 1993-1997 Epitropos Bethlehem. 2005-2009 Exarch Holy Sepulchre in Greece. 2009 Epitropos Accra/Acre. Joint International Commission for the Theological Dialogue between the Catholic Church and the Orthodox Churches.

Alexios Alexios Moschonas
T: A Tiberias ■ ✉ Greek Orth Convent, P.O.Box 19632, ISRAEL-91190 Jerusalem • [972] 8 2863419, fax 2844417, 2818013
*1954 Lechaia Elias Greece, N17./30.3. 1967 Jerusalem. mon1972 diak1972. 1975-1978 stud Athens ⊖1975 archim1978. 1978 secretary, 1979 liaison officer, director Museum ⊕10.11.1991. 1991-1996 B Porphyroupolis. 1996 A Tiberias, President Comm Education. 2001 patriarchal councillor Gaza.

Aristarchos Antonios Peristeris
T: A Konstantina, Geron Archigrammateus ■
✉ Greek Orth Patr, P.O.Box 14234, ISRAEL-91190 Jerusalem •
[972] 2 6274204, d 6274938, fax 6282601
*22.8.1948 Kreta. N27.9./0.10. 1962 Jerusalem. 1962-1966 School Mount Zion. mon 1966. 1966-1970 secretary financial dep., stud English, stud Ulpan, stud Arabic. diak1969 ⊖1970. 1970-1974 stud phil Athens. archim1973. 1975-1988 principal Mount Zion. 1975-1981 BA theol Athens. 1984 stud Ostkirchliches Institut Regensburg. 1988 Chief editor Néa Sión. 1990 Director personal office Patriarch Diodoros. 1991 member Holy Synod. 1992 director library Holy Synod ⊕19.10.1998. 1999 Commission Orthodox Collaboration WCC Geneva. 2000 A Konstantina. 2001 Archigrammateuon, 2005 Archigrammateus. 16.12.2015 Athens Interorthodox

committee preparation Panorthodox Synod. 22.-28.1.2016 Synaxis of the primates of the Local Orthodox Churches Chambésy Switzerland.

Dorotheos Dimitrios Leovaris
T: A Abila ▪ ✉ P.O.Box 19632, ISRAEL-91190 Jerusalem • [972] 2 627 6492
*22.8.1948 Chios. N5./18.6. 1963 Jerusalem. diak1969 ⊖1973. dipl theol Athens. archim1975. 1991 member Holy Synod. 1991-1998 Epitropos St. Jean d'Acre ⊕12.10.1998. 1998 Epitropos Irbed. 2000 A Abila. 2000 patriarchal vicar Bethlehem. 2001 patriarchal councillor Madaba. 2005 Chairman Land Commission.

Damaskinos Anastasios Gaganiaris
T: A Joppe ▪ ✉ Greek Orth Patr, P.O.Box 19632, ISRAEL-91190 Jerusalem • [972] 2 6271196, fax 6282601
*1.1.1952 Aghia Larisis. N4./17.12. 1967 Jerusalem. mon1968 diak1970 ⊖1977 archim1980. 1986 Dr. theol Thessaloniki. 1996 member Holy Synod ⊕18.10.1998, 2000 A Joppe. 2001 Exarch Greece. 2005 patriarchal councillor America.

Theophylaktos Theodosios Georgiadis
T: A Iordanes ▪ ✉ Greek Orth Patr, P.O.Box 19632, ISRAEL-91190 Jerusalem • [972] 2 6271196, fax 6282601
*1951 Charaugi Kozani. N8./21.3. 1972 Jerusalem. mon16.2.1973 diak19.2.1973 ⊖19.9.1977 archim1981. 1989-2001 patriarcal councillor Moscow. 2001 member Holy Synod ⊕17.12.2005 (Anastasis).

Methodios Nikolaos Liberis
T: A Tabor ▪ ✉ Greek Orth Patr, P.O.Box 19632, ISRAEL-91190 Jerusalem • [972] 2 6271196, fax 6282601
*1935 Biros Kerkyra. N14./27.6. 1953 Jerusalem. mon4.12.1957 diak9.12.1957 ⊖9.11.1959 archim1963 ⊕11.12.2005 A Tabor (Anastasis).

Theodosios Attallah Nzar Hanna
T: A Sebastia ▪ ✉ Greek Orth Patr, P.O.Box 19632, ISRAEL-91190 Jerusalem • [972] 2 6271196, fax 6282601
*1965 Rameh Upper Galilea. N11./24.1. 1984-1990 stud theol Thessaloniki mon11.10.1991 diak14.10.1991 ⊖2.2.1992 archim23.2.1992 spokesman patriarchate ⊕24.12.2005 A Sebastia (Anastasis).

Dimitrios Nikolaos Vasiliadis
T: A Lydda ▪ ✉ Greek Orth Patr, P.O.Box 19632, ISRAEL-91190 Jerusalem • [972] 2 6271196, fax 6282601

*1958 Thessaloniki. stud theol Thessaloniki. mon1981 Ag. Anna Athos. 1987 Jerusalem. diak1987 ⊖1989 archim1990. 1991 secretary Holy Synod ⊕24.2.2013 Anastasis, A Lydda.

Philoumenos Souchel Machamre

T: A Pella ▪ ✉ Greek Orth Patr, P.O.Box 19632, ISRAEL-91190 Jerusalem • [972] 2 6271196, fax 6282601

*1970 Safrut Jordania. 1988-1994 Military Service Jordania. 1997-2004 stud theol Thessaloniki. mon2006 Ag Gregorios Athos. 2007 Jerusalem. diak2008 ⊖2010 archim, member Holy Synod ⊕4.3.2013Anastasis A Pella.

Makarios Georgios Mavrojannakis

T: A Katar ▪ ✉ Greek Orth Patr, P.O.Box 19632, ISRAEL-91190 Jerusalem • [972] 2 6271196, fax 6282601

*1968 Heraklion Kreta. 1980 Jerusalem. mon1986 diak1987. 1990 stud Theol school Jerusalem ⊖1992 archim1993. 1995-2011 Dr. theol Fac theol Beograd. 2004 Doha Katar ⊕25.2.2013 Anastasis, A Katar.

Isidoros Elias Facitsas

T: A Hierapolis ▪ ✉ Greek Orth Patr, P.O.Box 19632, ISRAEL-91190 Jerusalem • [972] 2 6271196, fax 6282601

*1973 Trikala. 1986 Jerusalem. diak1991 ⊖1996 archim. 2005-2013 stud theol Athens. 17.9.2008 Skevophylax Jerusalem ⊕16.3.2013 Anastasis, A Hierapolis.

Nektarios Konstantinos Selalmadzidis

T: A Anthidonos ▪ ✉ Oruc Reis Sok. 24/7, TURKEY-34973 Heybeliada İstanbul • [90] 216 3518541 • [90] 539 9172792

*1962 Drama N? Lyceum Xanthe, Academy Rhodos, Fac theol Thessaloniki. mon1983 diak1983 ⊖1984 archim. 1985-2001 teacher Greek, Spanish, Psychatry Argentina and Brazil 2001 South America. 2003 Apokrisiar Konstantinopel ⊕4.3. 2013 Phanar Konstantinopel A Anthidonos (Patr Bartholomaios) 22.-28.1.2016 Synaxis of the primates of the Local Orthodox Churches Chambésy Switzerland.

Damianós Samartsis ***Sinai***

T: A Sinai+Pharan+Raitho, Igumen, Autonomous Holy Monastery and Archdiocese ▪ ✉ St. Katharina, Midan El -Daher 18, EGYPT-Cairo • [20] 69 3470-8, fax -9 • www.sinaimonastery.com

*4.4.1935 Athens. N1./14.11. mon1961 Sinai diak1962 ⊖1965 ⊕23.12.1973 A Autonomous Holy Monastery and Archdiocese of Sinai.

PATRIARCHATE OF KONSTANTINOPEL

His All-Holiness **Bartholomaios**
Archbishop of Constantinople Nea Roma
Ecumenical Patriarch

for canonical ranking of hierarchs
see • www.orthodoxia.be/Hierarchen/Hierarchen00.html.

Bartholomaios Dimitrios Archondonis ***Konstantinopolis***
T: A Konstantinopel, Ecumenical Patriarch ▪ ✉ Fatih, Sadrazan Ali Paşa Cad. 35, TURKEY-34220 İstanbul • [90] 212 531967-0, -1, -9, fax 5316533 • patriarchate@ec-patr.org • bartholomaios@superonline.com • www.patriarchate.org • www.ec-patr.org • www.orthodoxia.be
*29.2.1940 (Pass: 12.3.) Agioi Theodoroi Imbros. Todestag Mutter 12. Oktober 1961. dipl theol Chalki. diak13.8.1961 Imbros (M Meliton). 1961-1963 Turkish Army. 1963-1968 stud Roma Murnau München, Bossey. 1968 Dr. canon law Gregoriana Roma. 1968-1972 Professor Chalki ⊖19.10.1969 archim1969. 1972-1990 Director personal office Patriarch Dimitrios ⊕25.12.1973 M Philadelphia. 1974 Holy Synod. 1990 M Chalcedon. 22.10.1991 Patriarch. Dr.hc.: 1990 theol Athens, Boston. 1994 theol City University London. 1994 Université de la mer Egée "Protection de l'environnement". 1995 Faculté de droit Université d'Aix Marseille. 1996 Louvain, Edinburgh. 1997 iur Wien, Thessaloniki, Iaşi. 1998 Yale USA, St. Andrew Winnipeg, Preshov Slovakia. 1999 Athens. 2001 Budapest. 2003 Batumi. 2004 theol Wien, iur Graz. 2005 psych Panteion. 2008 Trieste. 2010 Lublin.2015 Sociology Izmir/Smyrne, Philosophy University Cyprus, Sophia University Movimento dei Focolari Loppiano/ Florence. St. Mary's University Twickenham London. 2001 Great Cross Ungarn. 2002 Sophia Prize Environment Norway, Binding-Preis Umweltschutz Liechtenstein. 2004 Großes Goldenes Ehrenzeichen Österreich. 2007 Kardinal-König-Preis. 2008 Bischof-Klaus-Hemmerle-Preis. 2012 Roosevelt Award. 6.8.2015 Steward of Creation Award by the National Religious Coalition on Creation Care (Prinkipo/ Büyükada). 16.4.2016 visit to the island of Lesbos together with Pope Francis and Archbishop Hieronymos of Athens and All Greece.

Joakím Elias Nerantzulis
T: M Geron Nikomedia ▪ ✉ Koç Universite Hastane Maltepe Mahalle, Topkapi Cad, Litras Yolu, TURKEY-34220 İstanbul
*29.2.1940 N9.9. gymnasion Zografou. 1966 dipl theol Chalki. diak1966. 1971 2. Diakonos Patr ⊖20.9.1973 ⊕23.9.1973 B Melitene. 1974-1992 patr protosynkellos. 1977 M Melitene. 1991-2008 M Geron Chalkedon, 2008 M Geron Nikomedia.

Athanasios Papas ***Chalkedon***

T: M Geron Chalkedon ▪ ✉ Bahariye, Şair Lâtifi Sok 15/5, Kadıköy, TURKEY-34710 İstanbul • [90] 216 3360401, 3381286, fax 3370513, 3382499, [90] 532 2964393 • mitropolishalkidonos@yahoo.gr

*22.3.1936 Kadiköy. N18.1. diak26.4.1959. 1959 dipl theol Chalki. 1965 Dr. phil München, Prof. Chalki. 1972-1990 assistant Chalcedon ⊖17.9.1972 ⊕24.9.1972 B Helenopolis. 1976-1990 M Helenoupolis. 1985 Holy Synod. 1990 M Helioúpolis+ Theira. 1999 Commission Orthodox Collaboration WCC Geneva. 2002 Responsible for Chalkedon, 2008 M Geron Chalkedon.

Apostolos Daniilidis ***Derkoi***

T: M Geron Derkoi ▪ ✉ Akarsu Cad. Coşkun Sok. Saray apt. No. 6/4, TURKEY-34433 İstanbul • [90] 212 245-3465, fax -4012, [90] 212 571 6013, [90] 533 5568725 • apostol@ttmail.com

*1952 Galata. Astiki school Galata. gymnasion Zografeiou, lykeion Chalki. diak30.12.1973. 1975 dipl theol Thessaloniki. 1976 Diakonos Grammateus Fanar. 1982 stud italiano Bari Perugia. 1984 secretary Holy Synod. 1986 stud English Birmingham ⊖21.11.1995 ⊕26.11.1995. 1995-2000 M Agathonikeia. 1996-2011 igumen Holy Trinity Chalki. 2000-2011 M Moschonesia. 2010 member Holy and Sacred Synod. 2011 M Geron Derkoi.

Kyrillos Dragunis ***Imbros***

T: M Imbros+Tenedos ▪ ✉ Çınarlı Merkez P.K. 42, Gökçeada, TURKEY-17760 Çanakkale • [90] 286 8873042, fax 8873535

*1942 Agridia Imbros. N18.1. 1967 dipl theol Chalki. diak1967 Megas Archidiakonos. ⊕27.10.1985 M tit Seleukia. 1994-2002 M Seleukia, Epoptes Hypsomatheia. 2002 M Imbros.

Konstantinos Charisiadis ***Nikaia***

T: M Geron Nikaia ▪ ✉ Karanfil sokak 12/4, Yeşilköy, TURKEY-34149 İstanbul • [90] 212 66388-22, fax -21

*23.7.1929 Kadıköy, N21.5. diak17.12.1950. 1950 dipl theol Chalki. 1950-1956 Archidiakonos Derkoi ⊖22.4.1956 secretary Fac theol Chalki. 1962 stud theol Paris. 1966-1971 Prof Chalki ⊕16.1.1972 B Apollonias, protosynkellos Patriarcheion. 1974 M Prinkiponisi. 1977 M Derkoi. 2011-2012 member Holy Synod Phanar. 2011 M Geron Nikaia.

Germanos Yiannaki Athanasyadis ***Theodoroupolis***

T: M Theodoroupolis ▪ ✉ Yeni Yuva Sokak 40/2, Beyoğlu, TURKEY-34420 İstanbul • [90] 212 2933012

*17.9.1930 Bakırköy İstanbul, N12.5. mon10.10.1953 diak11.10.1953. 1954 dipl Chalki ⊖15.8.1966 ⊕6.2.1972 B Arianzos vicar Derkoi. 1987 M Theodoroupolis. (1987-1990 M tit). 1991-1996 igumen Monastery of the Holy Trinity Chalki Aya Triada Rum Ortodoks Manastir. 1996 Confessor Kon/pel.

Evangelos Galanis ***Perge***
T: M Perge ▪ ✉ Gümüşsuyu İnönü cad. Hayırlı Apt No 31/3, TURKEY-34437 İstanbul • [90] 212 2410533
*1928 Therapeia Bosporos. 1949 gymnasion Zografion. 1953 dipl theol Chalki. diak1953 Patriarcheion: 1957-1958 Kodikografos, 1965 Megas Archidiakonos, publishing "Orthodoxia, Apostolos Andreas", "Ek Phanariou". 1983 "Perge Pamphilias" ⊖1970 ⊕30.11.1970. 1983 Dr. theol Thessaloniki. President Musicophilôn Kon/pel.

Maximos Vgenopoulos ***Silivria***
T: M Silivria ▪ ✉ Fatih, Dr. Sadık Ahmed cad. 19, TURKEY-34220 İstanbul • [90] 212 5319670, [90] 5372479000 • maksimosvge@gmail.com
*1968 Patras, N21.1. 1978 school Patras, school Athens, stud Fac theol Beograd. diak 26.12.1993 (M Ioakim Chalkedon). 1995-2005 Kodikographos Phanar. 1997-2002 Dr. theol London "Primacy in the Church – From Vatican I to Vatican II: An Orthodox Perspective". 2005 Megas Archidiakonos ⊕27.7.2014 M Silivria Phanar (Patr Bartholomaios).

Spyridon Georgios Papageorgiou
T: former M Chaldia ▪
*24.9.1944 Warren Ohio USA. N12.12. 1962-1966 dipl theol Chalki. 1966-1967 WCC Geneva. 1967-1968 stud Switzerland. diak30.11.1968. 1969-1973 stud Germany. 1973-1975 Chambésy ⊖1.2.1976. 1976-1985 parroco via Sardegna Roma. 1984 secretary Orthodox Catholic dialogue ⊕24.11.1985 B Apamia assistant Austria (via Sardegna Roma). 1991-1996 M Italia (Venezia). 1992 Inter-Orth Commission for the dialogue with the Lutheran World Federation. 1996-1999 A America, Exarch of the Ecum Patr in America to preside at meetings of the canonical hierarchs in America. 1999-2000 M Chaldia.

Iakovos Sophroniadis ***Prinkiponisi***
T: M Prinkiponisi ▪ ✉ Cihangir Cad. 30-32/11, Beyoğlu, TURKEY-34420 İstanbul • [90] 212 2444905, [90] 532 2124733, [90] 212 2441577
*14.3.1947 Feriköy N23.10. diak14.9.1969. 1970 dipl theol Chalki, patriarchate: kodikographos, 1974 subsecretary, ⊖1984 Archigrammateus St. Synode ⊕25.12.1987 M tit Laodikeia. 1994 M ord Laodikeia. 2002 M Prinkiponisi. 2011-2012 member Holy Synod Phanar.

Ioseph Emmanuel Harkiolakis ***Proikonnisos***
T: M Proikonnisos ▪ ✉ 150 Kallikratida, GREECE-18546 Piraeus • [30] 21140 66991, [30] 6948464725 • jharkiolakis@gmail.com
*1955 Siteia Kreta. N22.1. 1973-1974 Preparatory school Catechizers. 1977-1979 director Christian Youth Federation Paleo Faliro. 1978 BTh (Honours) Athens. mon2.6.1979 Joseph diak3.6.1979 hierokēryx Levkás ⊖27.12.1981. 1981-1987 protosynkellos Hierapetra Siteia Kreta. 1987-1989 rector parish and Lecturer Sydney ⊕3.12.1989. 1989-2003 B Arianzós, assistant Australia. 1989-2001 Adelaide. 2001 Melbourne. 2003-2005 M New Zealand. 2005 hierokēryx Piraeus. 2008 M Proikonnisos. 2009-2010 member Holy Synod.

Meliton Karás ***Philadelphia***
T: M Philadelphia ▪ ✉ İstanbul Rum Patrikliği, Haliç-Fener, TURKEY-34220 İstanbul • [90] 212 6639231 melito@superonline.com
*1951 Agridia Imbros. N9.3. Chalki. 1974 dipl theol Thessaloniki. diak4.8.1974. 1984 subsecretary Holy Synod. 1986 Dr. theol Thessaloniki. 1987-2005 Archigrammateus Holy Synod ⊕28.10.1990. 2011-2012 member Holy Synod Phanar.

Dimitrios Kommatás ***Sebasteia***
T: M Sebasteia ▪ ✉ İstanbul Rum Patrikliği, Haliç-Fener, TURKEY-34220 İstanbul • [90] 212 5254982, 2472271, 5823081 • dimitrios.kommatas@ttmail.com
*26.10.1952 Tatavla=Kurtuluş. Megali tou genous scholi. 1971 Chalki. 1975 dipl theol Thessaloniki. 1975-1977 Tritevon, 1977-1985 Devterevon. 1980-1981 Anglican Theol College Oak Hill London. 1985-1990 Megas Archidiakonos. diak14.7.1990 ⊖14.10.1990 ⊕04.11.1990 M tit Sebasteia. 1990-1992 igumen Zoodochos Pigi Baloukli. 1991-2008 Director Personal Office Patriarch. 1994 M Sebasteia, Exarchos Paphlagonia. 2003-2006 the problems with the Nea Chora "The Patriarchal and Synodical Praxis of 1928". 24.5.2005 Panorthodox Synod Kon/pel "Jerusalem". 17.5.2006 Synod Geneva "Cyprus". 2011-2012 member Holy Synod Phanar.

Germanos Kaviaropulos ***Tranoupolis***
T: M Tranoupolis ▪ ✉ Harbiye Cumhuriyet Cad., King Apt 275/7, TURKEY-34220 İstanbul • [90] 212 2470176
*1.1.1931 İstanbul, N12.5. mon1954 Patriarchate, dipl theol Chalki. diak21.1.1967. 1970 Holy Synod ⊖12.1.1973 ⊕14.1.1973 B Tralles. 1987 M Tranoupolis.

Irinaios Ioannidis ***Myriophyton***
T: M Myriophyton+Peristasis ▪ ✉ Satış Meydanı 22, Arnavutköy, TURKEY-34220 İstanbul • [90] 212 2635744, 2125144, 2570556 • miriofitoueirinaios@yahoo.com

*19.12.1951 Stavrodromion İstanbul. N23.8. Zografion gymnasion, Fac theol Chalki. diak1972 tis seiras etc. 1975 dipl theol Thessaloniki. 1978-1979 Turkish Army. 1981-1982 stud theol Paris. 1991 Megas protosynkellos ⊖21.11.1995. 1995-2000 M tit Evdokias. 1997 proistamenos Bosforos. 2000 M Myriophyton+Peristasis. 1.3.-31.8.2010 member Holy and Sacred Synod.

Chrysostomos Kalaïtsís ***Myra***
T: M Myra ▪ ✉ Kurtuluş Cad. 156/3, TURKEY-34375 İstanbul • [90] 212 2916466, fax 2301074, [90] 532 2923518, [90] 536 5783505 • chrysostome@mynet.com • myralykias@gmail.com • www.metropolitanofmyra.com
*1946 Agridia Imbros, N13.11. 1956 gymnasion Imbros, Lykeion Chalki. 1972 dipl theol Chalki. mon1.4.1972 diak2.4.1972. 1974 dipl theol Thessaloniki. 1974-1979 stud theol Regensburg München Paris. 1979-1995 Rum Patrikhanesi İstanbul: patriarchikos diakonos – Megas Archidiakonos. 1989 Dr. theol Thessaloniki ⊖18.11. 1995 (Chrysostomos Ephesos, proin Myra) ⊕25.11.1995 M tit Myra (Patr Bartholomaios). 2000 en energeia M Myra. 13.12.2014 repres. Moni Vatopedi Skit St. Andreas Karaköy, Fr. Panaretos.

Nikitas Loulias ***Dardanelles***
T: M Dardanelles, Director Patriarch Athenagoras Orthodox Institute ▪ ✉ 2311 Hearst Ave, USA-Berkeley, CA 94709-1319 • [1] 510 649 3450, fax 510 8416605 • mnikitas@ses.gtu.edu
*22.6.1955 Tampa Tarpon Springs Florida. N15.9. 1976 BA Florida University. 1980 MDiv Holy Cross Boston. 1980-1982 stud Thessaloniki. diak1985 (A Iakovos) ⊖1985 pastor Merriville Indiana. 1987-1995 chancellor Chicago. archim1988. 1988-1991 lecturer Loyola University Chicago. 1992-1993 stud Sankt-Peterburg ⊕14.12.1996 Fanar İstanbul. 1996-2007 M Hongkong. 2007 M Dardanelles.

Dionysios Charalambos Sakatis ***Synada***
T: M Synada ▪ ✉ İstanbul Rum Patrikliği, Haliç-Fener, TURKEY-34220 İstanbul • [90] 212 53196706, fax 5349037
*4.9.1946 Prinkipos N3.10. 1971 dipl theol Chalki. 1971-1989 hierokēryx Princes Islands ⊖21.12.1989 Megas Archimandritis ⊕15.9.1996 B Synada (Fanar, M Konstantin Derkoi). 2015 M new erected metropolis Synada (today Şuhut Afyonkarahisar).

Gennadios Nikolaos Limouris ***Sasima***
T: M Sasima ▪ ✉ İstanbul Rum Patrikliği, Haliç-Fener, TURKEY-34220 İstanbul • [90] 212 531967-9, -1, [90] 532 2173767 • neosalkyon@gmail.com • gennad@attglobal.net

*27.7.1951Thessaloniki, N17.11. 1957-1967 American College Neapoli Italia. 1967-1973 stud Harvard, Princeton. 1967-1969 military service NATO Anatolia. 1973-1978 Institut St-Serge Paris, stud jur Paris. mon26.9.1974 diak27.9.1974. 1978-1983 Strasbourg Dr d'état. USA PhD ⊖18.1.1981 Dortmund Germany. 1983-1993 WCC Geneva. "Faith and Order". archim1989 (Patr Dimitrios). 1993 Phanar. 1994 igumen Baloukli. 1995 Megas Synkellos (Patr Bartholomaios) ⊕1.6.1997 M Sasima (Fanar), Third B Sasima after St. Gregory and M Ieremias of France/Switzerland. 1998 member, 1999 Head Standing Committee Commission Faith and Order. 2002-2007 Central Committee WCC Geheva. 2007 en energeia M of the Throne.

Theoliptos Iakovos Fenerlis ***Ikonium***

T: M Ikonium ▪ ✉ Tarabya Sitesi 11, Blok D.1., TURKEY-34100 İstanbul • [90] 212 2621892, fax 2236883 • ikoniou@hotmail.com

*17.4.1957 Therapia Bosporus. N1.11. Gymn Zografion. 1975-1980 dipl theol Thessaloniki. diak27.4.1977 Phanar "Theoliptos" (M Bartholomaios, Philadelphia). 1995-1997 Megas Archidiakonos. 1997-2007 Great Chancellor ⊖21.11.1997 archim Feast Entry of the Theotokos (Patr Bartholomaios) ⊕10.9.2000 M Ikonium. 19.12.2015 consecration A Lorenzo Piretto İzmir.

Elpidophoros Ioannis Lambriniadis ***Bursa***

T: M Proussa, Igumen Holy Trinity Chalki ▪ ✉ Rum Ortodoks Aya Triada Manastiri Heybeliada, TURKEY-34973 İstanbul • [90] 216 351-8563, fax -9278, [90] 532 2970258 • elpidof@attglobal.net

*1967 İstanbul, N2.11. dipl theol (Pastoral) Thessaloniki. 1992-1994 MPhil Bonn Byzantinische Geschichte "Brothers Nikolaos and Johannes Mesarites". diak1994 St. George Phanar. 1995 secretary Holy Synod Sofia, secretary International Dialogue Lutheran World Federation, Member Faith and Order. 1996-1997 stud Arabic Balamand. 2001 Dr. theol Thessaloniki (Severus of Alexandria). 2005-2011 Chief secretary of the Holy Synod, secretary Ecumenical Commission ⊖20.3.2005 Sunday Orthodoxy. 2009 Prof Thessaloniki ⊕20.3.2011 M Proussa. igumen Holy Trinity Chalki. 2011-2012 member Holy Synod Phanar.

Stephanos Dinidis ***Kallioupolis***

T: M Kallioupolis+Madyta ▪ ✉ İstanbul Rum Patrikliği, Haliç-Fener, TURKEY-34220 İstanbul • [90] 212 5252117, fax 5319014

*1968 İstanbul, N27.12. 1974-1986 Zographeion Lykeion İstanbul. 1986-1990 stud History State University İstanbul. 1990-1995 stud theol, stud History Thessaloniki. diak1996 (M Germanos, Theodoroupolis). 2005 Megalos Archidiakonos ⊖30.11.2007 (Patr Bartholomaios) megalos protosynkellos ⊕13.3.2011 Sunday Orthodoxy M Kallioupolis.(Patr Bartholomaios). 2011-2012 member Holy Synod Phanar. 28.7.2013 Chorostasia Phanar.

Athenagoras Konstantinos Chrysanis ***Kydonies***
T: M Kydonies ▪ ✉ Rum Patrikliği, Haliç-Fener, TURKEY-34220 İstanbul • [90] 212 5319670, [90] 535 6410620
*Boiotikos Orchomenou, N24.7. diak ⊖ (M Hieronymos, Levadeia Theben, since 2008 A Athens) 2000-2012 Phanar İstanbul Grand Archimandrite ⊕18.11.2012 M Kydonies (Ayvalık opposite Lesbos, last titular Agathangelos †) 18.1.2016 nameday M Athanasios Chalkedon.

Amphilochios Stergios ***Edirne***
T: M Adrianoupolis, Patriarchal Representative Athens ▪ ✉ Neophytou Douka 9, GREECE-10674 Athens •
[30] 210 7257 86-2, -4, 6913769, fax 7252540 • oikpat@otenet.gr
*1961 Megara Greece. 1966-1979 school Megara (with Grigorij now M Kamerun). 1979-1983 Fac theol Athens. diak1984 mon Megara (M Bartholomaios). 1984-2014 parish St. Apostels Elevsini, ⊖1986 archim. 1987 priest Megara (M Bartholomaios) confessor, hierokēryx eparchy Megara. 2000 new monastery St. Paraskevi Mazion. 15.6.2014 proposed by Patriarch Bartholomaios to be M Ioannina (Neai Chorai) ⊕18.10.2014 B İstanbul M Adrianoupolis Patriarchal Representative Athens (Patr Bartholomaios, M Milet, M Hierapitna, M Ikonium, M Kamerun, M Didymoteichon, M Nilopolis, M Bursa, B Irinej Bachka).

Adrianos Nikolaos Sergakis ***Bodrum***
T: B Halikarnassos, vicar patr Phanar ▪ ✉ İstanbul Rum Patrikliği Haliç Fener, TURKEY-34220 İstanbul
1994-1997 diakonos Kon/pel.1997-2015 parishes USA, Australia, England. archim 2015 Imbros Tenedos, proistamenos Phanar Keratiou Kolpou ⊕26.7.2015 Bodrum, Imbros B Halikarnassos (Patr Bartholomaios, M Kyrillos, B Nikiphoros Amoriou).

Irinaios Athanassiadis ***Kreta***
T: A Kreta, M Herakleion ▪ ✉ Mitropolis Agiou Mina 25, GREECE-71201 Herakleion, Kreta • [30] 2810 282632, 282209, fax 335863 • iak@iak.gr • www.iak.gr
*1933 Rethymnon Kreta. N23.8. dipl theol Chalki, stud St. Boniface Warminster England, parish Bristol. protosynkellos Kisamos ⊕23.2.1975 M Kydonia. 2006 A Kreta.

Evgenios Evangelos Antonopoulos ***Rethymne***
T: M Rethymne+Aulopotamos ▪ ✉ P. O.Box 64 Mitropolis, GREECE-74100 Rethymnon, Kreta • [30] 28310 36162 • eugenios_mra@imra.gr
*14.2.1968 Herakleion. N13.12. 1990 dipl theol Athens, mon1991 Ag. Georgios Selinari. diak24.2.1991 ⊖03.3.1991. 1991-1994 hierokēryx Petra. archim24.12.1991.

1992 History Thessaloniki. 1994-1997 efimerios Neapolis. 1997-2001 rector Ag. Nikolaos. 2001 subsecretary Holy Synod Kreta. 2004 redaktor Apostolos Titos ⊕28.5.2005 B Knossos. 2010 B Rhethymne. 2011-2012 member Holy Synod Phanar.

Makarios Dimitrios Dulufakis ***Gortyna***
T: M Gortyna+Arkadia ▪ ✉ Mitropoleos 9, GREECE-70400 Moĩrai, Kreta • [30] 28920 22824, 22208, fax 28920 23483
*1961 Dafni Herakleion. N19.1. dipl theol Beograd, dipl theol Thessaloniki, stud Sorbonne Paris. mon1985 Ankarados diak1985 Ankarados (A Evgenios) ⊖1987 Ankarados (A Evgenios). 1990 protosynkellos Kreta. 1992 Archim Oikumenikos Thronos. 8.10.2000 B B Knossos, assistant Kreta. 2005 M Gortyna.

Damaskinos Papagiannakis ***Kydonia***
T: M Kydonia+Apokoronas ▪ ✉ Mitropolis plateia Patr. Athenagorou, GREECE-73132 Chaniá, Kreta • [30] 28210 2780-7, -8, fax [30] 6947946035 • imka@imka.gr • www.imka.gr
*1958 Chania. N4.12. mon1976. 1976 stud Ekklesiastiki scholi Kreta, Fac theol Thessaloniki. diak1981 ⊖1982. 2001 protosynkellos Kydonia ⊕18.11.2006 Kydonia+ Apokoronas.

Irinaios Nikólaos Mesarchakis ***Lampis***
T: M Lampis+Syvritos+Sphakia ▪ ✉ Mitropolis, GREECE-74053 Spili, Kreta • [30] 28320 22133, 22301 • imlssspili@yahoo.gr
*1944 Spiliá Kissamou Kreta. N23.8. 1963 dipl Ekklesiastiki scholi Kreta. mon1964 Gonia diak1964 ⊖1970 dipl Athens. 1970-1980 protosynkellos Kisamos, teacher religion gymnasia. 1987-1990 igumen Gonia ⊕14.2.1990 M Lampis+Syvritos+ Sphakia.

Eugenios Mihail Politis ***Hierapytna***
T: M Hierapetra+Siteia ▪ ✉ Mitropolis, GREECE-72200 Hierapetra, Kreta • [30] 28420 61210, 22251, fax 22786 • imis@imis.gr • www.imis.gr
*1952 Herakleion. N13.12. 1973 dipl Ierodidaskalos Thessloniki. 1977 dipl theol Thessaloniki. 1978-1980 docent canon law Thessaloniki. mon1980 Ag. Geórgios Epanosifi. diak1980 Monastery Ag. Geórgios Epanosifi ⊖1982 archim hierokēryx Herakleion. 1984-1994 igumenos Ag. Geórgios Gorgolaini ⊕26.6.1994 M Hierapetra+Siteia.

Nektarios Papadakis ***Petra***
T: M Petra+Cherronisos ▪ ✉ Mitropolis, GREECE-72400 Neaopolis, Kreta • [30] 28410 32236, 31345, 32020 • info@impeh.gr • www.impeh.gr

*1951 Katalagari Pediados Herakleion. N9.11. 1969-1975 dipl theol Athens. mon1970 Ag. Geórgios Epanosifi. diak1971 ⊖1972 Epitropos protosynkellos Kreta ⊕6.10.1990 M Petra, 2001 Petra+Cherronisos.

Amphilochios Andronikakis ***Kisamos***

T: M Kisamos+Selinon ▪ ✉ Mitropolis, GREECE-73400 Kastelli Kissamos, Kreta • [30] 28220 22018, 22128 • Orthodox Academy of Creta GREECE-73006 Kolymbari • [30] 28240 22250, 22245, fax 22060 • info@imks.gr • www.imks.gr

*1964 Chania. N23.11. 1982 absolvent Ekkl. gymnasion Kreta, dipl theol Thessaloniki. Georgios. mon 990 Gonia. Kolymvarios (M Irenaios. Lampis) diak1990 (M Irenaios. Lampis) ⊖1992 (M Irenaios. Lampis) archim18.11.1992 Ecumenical Throne. 1993-1998 pastor Wales, MTh pastoral theol Cardiff. 1998 protosynkellos Platánou (M Irenaios, Kissamos). 2003-2005 scholarchis Ekkl. gymnasion Kreta ⊕8.10.2005 M Kisamos+Selinon.

Andreas Nanakis ***Arkalochori***

T: M Arkalochori, Kastelli, Viannos ▪ ✉ Mitropolis, GREECE-70300 Arkalochori, Kreta • [30] 28910 22041, 24610 • imarkal1@otenet.gr • www.imakb.gr

*1957 Heraklion. N4.7. (St. Andreas Kreta) dipl pedagogics Heraklion, dipl theol Thessaloniki. Prof history Fac theol Thessaloniki. mon1991 Agarathou (M Timotheos). diak1991 (M Timotheos) ⊖1991 (M Timotheos). 1992-1994 scholarchis theol Kreta ⊕3.11.2001 M Arkalochori. Doktorvater Archim Simeon Hannover. 2010 member Holy and Sacred Synod.

Kyrillos Kogerakis ***Rhodos***

T: M Rhodos ▪ ✉ Plateia Eleutherias, GREECE-85100 Rhodos • [30] 22410 22314, 44550, fax 44199

*1964 Koumasa Monofatsiou Heraklion. N18.1. mon17.2.1991 Agarathos diak23.2. 1991, dipl theol Athens, dipl theol Graz Austria. 1991-1995 archdiacon M Austria ⊖16.8.1995 (M Timotheos), hierokēryx Kreta. 2000 chancellor archdiocese Kreta ⊕25.4.2004 M Rhodos Balukli İstanbul (Patr Bartholomaios).

Nathanael Diakopanagiotis ***Kos***

T: M Kos+Nisyros ▪ ✉ Plateia Mitropoleos 1, GREECE-85300 Kõs • [30] 22420 222 30, fax [30] 22420 26530 • imkosnis@gmail.com

*3.9.1960 Kos,N22.4. 1980 stud Journalism Athens. diak1985 ⊖1986. 1986 dipl Anotera Ekklesiastiki Scholi Athens, 1986 hierokēryx Karpathos+Kos. 1995 protosynkellos Karpathos+Kos. 1998 dipl theol Athens. 2000 igumen. 2003 igumen St. George Basson Karpathos ⊕7.3.2009 İstanbul Phanar M Kos+Nisyros (Patr

Bartholomaios). 1.3.-31.8.2010 member Holy and Sacred Synod. 2013-2014 member Holy and Sacred Synod. 2013 Epitropos Patmos.

Ambrosios Lavriotis Panagiotidis ***Karpathos***
T: M Karpathos+Kasos ▪ ✉ Mitropolis, GREECE-85700 Apereion Karpathou • [30] 22450 31222, fax 31000 • imkk@otenet.gr
*1939 Xanthi. N7.12. diak1961. dipl theol Chalki. mon1962 ⊖1965. 1965-1977 Archigrammateus Megisti Lavra Athos. 1967-1983 protosynkellos Kos ⊕24.5.1983 M Karpathos.

Païsios Panagiotis Aravantinos ***Leros***
T: M Leros, Kalymnos+Astypalea ▪ ✉ Mitropolis, GREECE-85200 Kalymnos • [30] 22430 23000, 28854 • Leros [30] 22470 22211, fax 22470 22339 • imkalymnoy2011@yahoo.gr
*1944 Lexouri Kefallinia. N19.6. 1966 stud theol Thessaloniki. mon9.2.1967 Ixia Rhodos. diak10.2.1967. 1977-1988 Prof Pedagogics Academy Rhodos. 1977-2005 protosynkellos Rhodos ⊖28.6.1981 (M Spyridon). 1982-2005 igumen Ixia ⊕21.5.2005 M Leros.

Chrysostomos Ioannis Dimitriadis ***Symi***
T: M Symi ▪ ✉ Iera Mitropolis, GREECE-85600 Symi • [30] 22460 72261, fax 72273
*26.10.1944 Agridioi Imbros. N13.11. Lykeion Chalki, dipl theol Thessaloniki mon1968 diak13.6.1968 ⊖6.8.1968 parish Hannover, 1974 St. Anargyroi New York, 1978-2004 Hannover ⊕8.11.1980 B Pamphilon, assistant Germania in Hannover. 2004 M Symi.

Chrysostomos Panayotis Anagnostopoulos
T: B Rodostolos ▪ ✉ Megisti Lavra, GREECE-63086 Karyes Agion Oros • [30] 23770 23220, 23221, 23315, 23224
*1933 Serrai, N13/26.11. 1950 Agion Oros. 1956-1958 secretary community Agion Oros. 1958-1962 stud Chalki. diak1960 Megisti Lavra (M Nathanael, Miletupolis, Kos). mon1962 Chalki. 1963-1988 Prof, 1968 Scholarchis Academy Athos ⊖1965 Megisti Lavra (M Nathanael, Miletupolis, Kos) ⊕22.4.1978 Patriarchion Kon/pel B Rodostolos assistant Patr, monk Megisti Lavra.

Apostolos Voulgaris
T: M Milet, Igumen ▪ ✉ Moni Ag. Anastasias Pharmakolytrias, GREECE-57006 Basilika Chalkidikis • [30] 23960 22440, 22661, 22662
*14.7.1948 Volos. N30.6. stud theol Louvain, Chalki. mon4.8.1973 Agias Anastasias. diak5.8.1973 ⊖8.9.1974 dipl theol Thessaloniki. archim1977 ⊕3.11.1985. 1990 M Milet.

Theodoretos Tsirigotis
T: B Elaia ▪ ✉ Alpheiou 2, Vrilissia, GREECE-15235 Athens • [30] 210 8031713
⊖1983. igumen Vlatadon ⊕25.3.1984 B Elaia.

Panteleimon Sklavos
T: B Theoupolis ▪ ✉ Tsavella 41, GREECE-54249 Thessaloniki • [30] 2310 306949, [30] 23510 29552, 22679
*24.8.1936 Thessaloniki. N27.7 ⊖6.7.1961 ⊕1.1.1971 B Theoupoleos Ass Australia. 1985 Ekklesiastiki Scholi Katerini.

Panteleimon Evangelos Rodopulos
T: M Tyroloi+Serention, Prof Fac theol ▪ ✉ Moni Vlatadon, Eptapyrgiou 64, GREECE-54634 Thessaloniki • [30] 2310 209913, 991438 • Xenonos 247492 • bookshop 246357, fax 246349
*1929 Athens, N27.7. diak1952, dipl theol Athens ⊖1954, stud theol London Oxford, 1957-1958 Frankfurt. B Literature Oxford. 1958-1963 protosynkellos Thessaloniki. 1958 Dr. theol Thessaloniki. 1960 Lecturer University Thessaloniki. 1963-1966 Director Holy Cross Boston. 1968 Prof canon law Thessaloniki. 1972-1979 Dean St. Johannes Damascenus Fac theol Balamand ⊕9.6.1974 M Tyana. 1977-1978 Dean Thessaloniki, 1977 M Tyroloi+Serention. 1981-1982 vice-rector, 1982-1983 Rector Univ Thessaloniki. 1982-1983 igumen Moni Vlatadon. 1982. Dr. theol h.c. Boston. 2010 member Holy and Sacred Synod.

Nikiphoros Psychloudis
T: B Amorion ▪ ✉ Moni Vlatadon, Eptapyrgiou 64, GREECE-54634 Thessaloniki • [30] 2310 209913, 991438 • Xenonos 247492 • bookshop 246357, fax 246349
diak1970 Neapolis (M Dionysios) four years deacon Neapolis ⊖1974 Vlatadon (M Panteleimon). 1.9.2013 Phanar. 14.10.2013 Ukraina Feast Pokrov ⊕2.2.2014 Phanar İstanbul B Amorion, abbot Vlatadon.

Dimitrios Michail Grollios
T: B Thermai ▪ ✉ Olympiados 95, GREECE-54634 Thessaloniki • [30] 2310 219222, [30] 6942422653, 6942422553
*3.3.1939 Ossa, N26.10. 1965 dipl theol Thessaloniki ⊖16.7.1970 ⊕9.11.1980. 1980-2001 assistant M Germania OKI Regensburg. 1989 p. Navrotsidis.

Ioannis Ioannis Zizioulas
T: M Geron Pergamon ▪ ✉ Neophitou Louka 9, GREECE-10674 Athens • [30] 210 7257862 • oik@otenet.gr

*10.1.1931 Kataphygion Kozanis. N8.5. 1952 dipl theol Athens. 1955 STM Harvard University. 1965 Dr. theol Athens, Prof. Edinbourgh, Prof Thessaloniki and London. Dr.h.c.: 1965 Institut Cath Paris, 1991 Beograd, 2008 St-Serge Paris, Cluj-Napoca, 2010 Münster in Westfalen Germany. mon1986 Chalki. diak14.6.1986 ⊖15.6.1986 ⊕22.6.1986 B, M Pergamon. 1993 member, 2002 president Academy Athens. 2000-2014 Director Ecum Patriarchal Representation Athens. 2004 Mondo Migliore. 2011-2012 member Holy Synod Phanar. 2014 Geron M Pergamon. 16.12.2015 Athens Interorthodox committee preparation Panorthodox Synod 2016.

Kyrillos Katerelos
T: B Abydos, Prof Athens ▪ ✉ Karaoli Dimitriou 15, GREECE-16231 Byron Attikis • [30] 210 7643749, [30] 694 5430190

*21.11.1956 Lamia Greece, N21.11. Dr. theol Thessaloniki, DEA Strasbourg, Dr. theol Freiburg i.Br. Germany ⊖1983 (M Nikopolis Meletios). 1985 Baden Württemberg Germany. 1998 Prof Athens ⊕24.2.2008.

Gennadios Tsambikos Zervos ***Italia***
T: M Italia, Esarca dell'Europa meridionale ▪ ✉ San Giorgio, Castello 3419, ITALIA-30122 Venezia • [39] 0415225446, 0415239569,
fax 0415227016, [39] 3292922124 • arcidiocesiortodossa@gmail.com •
www.ortodossia.it

*8.7.1937 Kremasti Rhodos. N17.11. diak1960 (M Spyridon, Rhodos) dipl theol Chalki ⊖28.4.1963 Napoli Italia. archim1967 Napoli. 1970 Dr. theol Bari Italia "Proposals of the Ecumenical Patriarchate for the unity of the Christians" ⊕17.1.1971 B Krateia. 1971-1991 assistant Austria in Napoli, prof Patrology Bari. 1991-1996 assistant Italia in Napoli. 1996 M Italia. 1999 Dr. theol Thessaloniki. 2005 M Italia+Malta.

Arsenios Kardamakis ***Austria***
T: M Austria, Exarch Ungarn ▪ ✉ Griech. Orientalische Metropolie, Fleischmarkt 13, AUSTRIA-1010 Wien • [43] 1 533-2965, -3889 •
kirche@metropolisvonaustria.at • www.metropolisaustria.at

*31.10.1973 Herakleion Kreta. N10.11. 1991 absolvent Risarion Athens. 1991-1997 MTh Athens. mon25.6.1998 Gortyna (M Kyrillos) diak9.8.1998 Agios Georgios (A Timotheos). 1999 DEA theol Strasbourg. 1999-2002 deacon Germany. 2000 dipl theol Thessaloniki. 2002 Mag iur Strasbourg ⊖17.1.2002 archim (B Makarios, Knossos). 2002-2004 parish Karlsruhe Germany. 2004-2011 vicar general chancellor Paris. 2004 Conference European Churches CEC. 2005-2011 secretary National Council of Churches France. 2009 Central Committee CEC. 2011 Dr. theol Strasbourg ⊕30.11.2011 M Austria.

Jeremias Paraschos Kaligiorgis ***Helvetia***
T: M Helvetia ▪ ✉ Centre Orth du Patr Œcum, 37, Chemin de Chambésy, SUISSE-1292 Chambésy • [41] 22 758986-0, Institut théol -4, fax Centre -1 • mitropolis@dioceseorthodoxe.org • www.dioceseorthodoxe.org
*17.1.1935 Kos. N1.5. 1948-1952 Theol school Patmos. 1952-1959 dipl theol Chalki. diak 9.8.1959. 1959-1964 peritus sacrae liturgiae Institut liturgique Paris, stud Paleographie Sorbonne ⊖26.7.1964. 1964-1971 protosynkellos Paris ⊕31.1.1971 B Sasima, first B Sasima after St. Gregory. 1988-2003 M France. 1992-2002 Central Committee Conference European Churches CEC, 1997-2002 President CEC. 2000 Interorth Seminary Cooperation Churches İstanbul. 2002 Knight of the Legion of Honour France. 2003 M Helvetia.

Job Igor Getcha
T: A Telmissos ▪ ✉ Centre Orthodoxe du Patriarcat Œcuménique, Chemin de Chambésy 37, SUISSE-1292 Chambésy • [41] 22 7916348 • archeveque.job@gmail.com
*31.1.1974 Montréal Canada dans une famille orthodoxe originaire de Galicie Ukraina, N6.5. 27.4.1979 baptised Ukrainian Cathedral Montréal. études secondaires collège français Montréal. 1992-1996 stud theol St. Andrew's College Winnipeg, stud Greek University of Manitoba. mon28.9.1996 diak29.9.1996. 1996-2003 Dr. theol orth, 1998-2003 Dr. theol Institut catholique Paris "La réforme liturgique du métropolite Cyprien de Kiev". 2001-2008 Prof Liturgics Institut St-Serge Paris, ⊖20.6.2003 St. Serge (A Gabriel Komana). archim2004. 2004-2005 chargé de cours Fribourg Suisse. 2004 membre groupe St-Irénée. 2005-2008 dekan Institut St-Serge. 2009 Prof Centre Orthodoxe Chambésy Genève. 2012 HDR Université de Lorraine Metz. 2013 co-président groupe St-Irénée ⊕30.11.2013 Phanar, 2013-2015 A Telmissos Archdiocèse Russe Orth d'Europe Paris. 28.11.2015 Representant of the Ecumenical Patriarchate at WCC Geneva. 22.-28.1.2016 Synaxis of the primates of the Local Orthodox Churches Chambésy Switzerland.

Makarios Pavlos Pavlidis
T: B Lampsakos, Vicar Helvetia ▪ ✉ Centre Orth du Patr Œcum, 37, Chemin de Chambésy, SUISSE-1292 Chambésy • [41] 22 7581629
*24.9.1937 Yannitsa Pellis. N19.1. diak 6.2.1961 mon1963, dipl theol Chalki ⊖19.5.1963. 1964-1969 London. 1969 Melbourne. 6.12.1969-1985 Bonn ⊕3.11.1985 B Lampsakos vicar Helvetia.

Augustinos Georgios Labardakis ***Germania***
T: M Germania, Exarch Zentraleuropa ▪ ✉ Beuel, Dietrich Bonhoeffer Str. 2, GERMANY-53227 Bonn • [49] 228 973784-0, fax -24 • metropolit@orthodoxie.net • www.orthodoxie.net
*7.2.1938 Vukoliés Chania Kreta. N15.6. diak1960. 1960 dipl theol Chalki. 1960-1963 stud Salzburg, 1963 Münster, Berlin ⊖1964 Agios Nikolaos Berlin ⊕26.3.1972 B Elaia, assistant Germania in Berlin. 1980 M Germania. 2005-2006 member Holy Synod K/polis. 2006 Dr.h.c. Bonn.

Vassilios Tsiopanas
T: B Aristi, assistant Germania ▪ ✉ Obere Paulusstr. 82-i, GERMANY-70197 Stuttgart • [49] 711 6572134, fax 93319950
*4.5.1939 Mesolongi. N1.1. 1963. dipl theol Chalki. diak17.6.1963. 1963-1966 stud Tübingen Kirchengeschichte (Prof. Fink) ⊖23.10.1966. 1966-1975 via Sardegna Roma ⊕1.2.1976 B Aristi, assistant Germania.

Evmenios Georgios Tamiolakis
T: B Levka, assistant Germania ▪ ✉ Jesuitenstr. 6, GERMANY-52062 Aachen • [49] 241 28572, fax 406896, [49] 174 2431000 • gog-ac@online.de
*26.11.1945 Ag. Charalambios Kreta. N18.9. mon1.11.1959. 1959-1964 St. Mary's Monastery Kroustallenia Kreta. diak23.12.1964. 1964-1969 Monastery Selinari. 1969-1970 deacon M Chania. 1970-1976 deacon A Athens. 1972-1976 Fac theol Athens ⊖3.4.1977 (Palm Sunday). 1977 Archimandrit Aachen ⊕15.1.1994 Düsseldorf B Levka assistant Germany (M Augustinos). 1995 Aachen Bundesverdienstkreuz 1. Klasse. 23.-30.11.2015 34th Ecumenical Meeting for Bishops, İstanbul (participated since 1982).

Bartholomaios Ioannis Kessidis
T: B Arianzós, assistant Germania ▪ ✉ Beuel, Dietrich Bonhoeffer Str. 2, GERMANY-53227 Bonn • [49] 228 973784-15, fax -24 • bischof.bartholomaios@orthodoxie.net
*12.8.1968 Kastoria Makedonia Greece. N11.6. 1986 stud Chemie Univ Bonn. 1995 dipl theol Thessaloniki. diak4.3.1995 (M Augustinos) ⊖8.9.1996 archim. 1996-2004 Pfarrer Prophet Elias Frankfurt am Main, Kommission Publikationen, Redaktion ⊕10.6.2004.

Gregorios Theocharous Hadjifotis ***Thyateira***
T: A Thyateira+Great Britain ▪ ✉ Thyateira House, 5 Craven Hill, GREAT BRITAIN-London, W2 3EN • [44] 20 7723 4787, fax 7224 9301 • mail@thyateira.org.uk • www.thyateira.org.uk

*28.10.1928 Marathovounos Cyprus. (2.1.1929 passport) N25.1. 1938 gymnasion Levkosia. mon1951 Stavrovouni. diak24.5.1953. 1958 dipl theol Athens ⊖19.4.1959 London. 1964 protosynkellos Thyateira. 1969-1970 stud theol Cambridge ⊕12.12.1970 B Tropaion North London. 16.4.1988 A Thyateira. 1999 Dr.h.c. Univ North London. 2011-2012 member Holy Synod Phanar.

Kallistos Timothy Ware

T: M Diokleia, assistant GB ▪ ✉ 19b Northmoor Road, GREAT BRITAIN-Oxford, OX2 6UW • [44] 1865 554023 +fax • diokleia@gmail.com

*11.9.1934 Bath Great Britain, N22.11. 1956 BA Oxford. 1958 orthodox. 1965 Dr. phil Oxford. diak10.3.1965. 1966-2001 Lecturer Eastern Orthodox Studies University Oxford ⊖8.5.1966 mon18.8.1966 Patmos. 1970 Fellow Pembroke College Oxford ⊕6.6.1982. 2007 M Diokleia, assistant GB. Dr.h.c.: 1998 Cluj România. 1999 Lawrence University Wisconsin USA. 1999 Russian Academy of Sciences Moskva. 2000 American College Athens. 2002 Fac theol Belgrade. 2006 Institut St-Serge Paris. 2007 Fac phil Athens. 2014 Aspirantura Moskva. 2007 Orthodox chair of Orthodox-Anglican dialogue. 2008 corresponding member Athens Academy. 6.-8.2.2015 Symposion Canterbury "80 years".

Chrysostomos Georgios Mavrojannopulos

T: B Kyanea, assistant GB ▪ ✉ Greek Cathedral St. Andrew, 112 Kentish Town Road, GREAT BRITAIN-London, NW1 9QA • [44] 20 7485-6385, -0198, fax -9972

*8.4.1927 Naxos. N13.11. 1952 dipl theol Athens. diak18.1.1952 ⊖14.12.1954. 1961 London ⊕19.12.1970.

Athanasios Theocharous

T: B Tropaion, assistant GB ▪ ✉ Greek Cathedral of St. Mary, Trinity Road, GREAT BRITAIN-London, N22 8LB • [44] 20 8888 2295 • [44] 20 8889 1122, fax [44] 20 8881 4455, [44] 78 02 287544

*20.11.1943 Marathovounos Cyprus. diak 6.8.1969 dipl theol Athens ⊖10.8.1969 archim Chancellor ⊕12.4.1997 B Tropaion assistant GB.

Theodoritos Polizogopulos

T: B Nazianzos ▪ ✉ c/o Agías Philothéis 21, GREECE-105 56 Athens

*1948 Athens. N3.3. dipl phil Athens, dipl theol Athens. Dr. phil Manchester. diak9.9.1972 ⊖17.9.1972 ⊕18.3.2000 B Nazianzos. 2000-2009 assistant GB. 2009 Athens.

Athenagoras Yves Peckstadt ***Belgium***

T: M Belgium, Exarch Netherlands+Luxemburg ▪ ✉ 71 Avenue Charbo, BELGIUM-1030 Bruxelles • [32] 2 7365278, fax 7353264, [32] 475 351301 • metropolitanathenagoras@gmail.com • athpeck@gmail.com • belgiou@orthodoxia.be • www.orthodoxia.be

*24.3.1962 Gent. N24.7. stud Fac of Law Univ Gent. dipl theol Thessaloniki, Bossey Suisse. diak12.11.1989 Brussels (M Bartholomaios Archondonis). Archidiakon M Belgium, Orthodox Radio and Television. 1994-2003 Office Ecumenical Patriarchate to the European Union. Chaplain airport Bruxelles ⊖17.3.1996 Bruges (M Panteleimon of Belgium) archim30.9.1996 vicaire episcopal Belgium ⊕22.6.2003 Bruxelles B Sinope assistant Belgium. 2013 M Belgium, Exarch Netherlands+Luxemburg.

Petros Bozinis

T: B Troas, assistant Belgium ▪ ✉ Avenue de Stalingrad 26, BELGIUM-1000 Bruxelles • [32] 474 832768 ppetrosm@yahoo.gr • www.orthodoxia.be

*1971 Patras, N29.6. (ancestres from Panormos Anatolia). diak1997 Patras (M Nikodimos Vallindra). 1998-2002 Archdeacon Patras. 1998 dipl Physics Patras ⊖2002 archim2003 Patras (M Nikodimos). dipl theol Athens. 2004-2013 parish Freiburg Germany. 2005 DEA theol Strasbourg. 2013 Dr. theol Strasbourg "Baptism Liturgy" (Prof. Marcel Metzger, Jean Luc Hiebel). 2013-2015 University chapel Patras. 2015 Postdoc Philosophy Patras ⊕8.11.2015 Bruxelles B Troas assistant Belgium.

Ivan Derewianka

T: B Parnassos ▪ ✉ Azalealaan 2 (bus 10), BELGIUM-3600 Genk • [32] 89 382695

*6.7.1937 Zinkiv Ukraina. N7.1. 1937-1947 Deutschland. 1947 Belgium, school Zwartberg, Genk. 1959-1961 stud mathematics Leuven. 1966-1989 married to Vira Bačynska, widower. diak20.7.1980 ⊖19.9.1982 Genk (A Anatolij) mon26.9.1989 South Bound Brook USA. archim27.9.1989 ⊕27.10.1991 London (M Mstyslav). 1991-1995 B London UAOC in USA and Diaspora. 1995 B "Konst". 1999 A. 2006 retired. 2012 B Parnassos.

Panteleimon Nikolaos Kontogiannis

T: former M Belgium, Exarch Netherlands+Luxemburg ▪ ✉ Odos Efesou 12, GREECE-821 00 Chios • [30] 2271023696

*7.2.1935 Chios. N27.7. diak28.11.1954 ⊖18.10.1957. 1957 dipl theol Chalki. priest in Mons, Charleroi. 1969-1974 protosynkellos M Belgium ⊕8.8.1974 B Apollonias assistant Belgium. 1982-2013 M Belgium, Exarch Netherlands+Luxemburg. 2013 Chios.

Emmanuel Adamakis ***France***

T: M France ▪ ✉ 7, rue Georges Bizet, FRANCE-75116 Paris • [33] 147208-235, -315, 147021822, fax 146 830 568 • oeu@compuserve.com • eglise.orthodoxe.grecque@wanadoo.fr • www.metropolegrecque.fr

*19.12.1958 Agios Nikolaos Kreta. N25.12. 1981 stud German language Ostkirchliches Institut Regensburg. Paris: DEA sciences des religions Sorbonne, stud Institut Catholique, Institut St-Serge Paris. diak1985 ⊖1985. 1987-1995 vicaire général Bruxelles. 1987 stud Holy Cross Boston, Dr. theol, 1994-2014 Directeur Bureau de l'Eglise auprès de l'Union Européenne, archim1995 ⊕11.11.1996 Bruxelles B Rhigion, auxiliaire Belgium. 2000 Interorth Seminary Cooperation Churches İstanbul. 20.1.2003 M France. 2003 President CEC, president Dialog Oriental Orthodox Churches. 16.12.2015 Athens Interorthodox committee preparation Panorthodox Synod. 22.-28.1.2016 Synaxis of the primates of the Local Orthodox Churches Chambésy Switzerland with Archim. Bartholomaios Samaras.

Irénée Avramidis

T: B Righion, assistant France ▪ ✉ 7, rue Georges Bizet, FRANCE-75116 Paris • [33] 147208-235, -315, 147021822, fax 146 830 568

1997-2004 teacher Religion Serra, hierokēryx Kastoria. 2004-2015 parishes Paris, dean Northern France, teacher Religion Greek schools. 2008 MTh Thessaloniki "The poimantike of the Saints of our age" ⊕8.2.2015 Paris Cathedral St. Etienne B Rhighion – today Küçükçekmece western part of İstanbul.

Jean Renneteau

T: B Charioupolis, Archdiocèse Russe Orthodoxe d'Europe ▪ ✉ 12, rue Daru, FRANCE-75008 Paris • [33] 1 46226761 • administration.diocesaine@exarchat.eu • www.exarchat.eu

*13.11.1942 Bordeaux. 1967-1974 stud theol Institut St-Serge Paris (Père Sophrony Sakharov) ⊖1974 (A Georges Tarassov). Responsable de l'émission "Orthodoxie" France 2. 1976-2015 Genéve paroisse orthodoxe francophone Ste-Trinité–Ste Cathérine. 1995-2015 co-président de la Commission mixte orth-cath en Suisse (co-présidente catholique Prof. Barbara Hallensleben). 4.3.2010 secrétaire de l'Assemblée des évêques orthodoxes en Suisse ⊕15.3.2015 Geneva B Charioupolis vicar Archdiocese of the Russian Orthodox Churches in Western Europe (M Jeremias, B Job Getcha, B Makarios Lampsakos). 28.11.2015 Locum tenens Russian Orthodox Archdiocese of Western Europe. 28.3.2016 elected candidate for the canonical election of the Archbishop of the Archdiocese of the Russian Orthodox Churches in Western Europe. 22.4.2016 election confirmed by the Holy Synod of the Ecumenical Patriarchate.

Paul Pierre Alderson
T: B Tracheia ▪ ✉ Monastère Saint-Antoine-le-Grand, Font-de-Laval, FRANCE-61900 Saint-Laurent-en-Royans
*3.11.1942 Hollesley England, anglican. N29.6. 1963 orthodox. 1963-1968 stud Institut St-Serge Paris. 1967 married ⊖1967. 1967-1975 aumônier foyer d'enfants Montgeron. 1975-1991 Eglise de la Dormition-de-la-Mère-de-Dieu Ste Geneviève des Bois (Essone) widower, mon1988 ⊕2.6.1991. 1991-2001 assistant Archdiocese of the Russian Orthodox Churches in Western Europe. 2001 retired.

Michel Storojenko
T: B Klaudiopolis ▪ ✉ St. Serge, 93, rue de Crimée, FRANCE-75019 Paris • [33] 142 081 293 • 4, rue de la Pyramide, 28250 Senonches
*1929 Kharkiv Ukraina. N8.11. 1943 France. 1948-1953 stud Institut St-Serge Paris. diak12.1957. 1965 Protodiakon cathédrale St-Alexandre rue Daru, electrician, widower, two children ⊖25.5.1995 mon1995 ⊕8.10.1995 B Claudiopolis, assistant Archdiocese of the Russian Orthodox Churches in Western Europe.

Polykarpos Panagiotis Stavropulos ***España***
T: M España+Portugal, Esarca Mar Mediterraneo ▪ ✉ Calle Nicaragua 12, SPAIN-28016 Madrid • [34] 913454085, 913503705, fax 913509374, 913506493 • metropoliespo@yahoo.es • www.iglesiaortodoxa.net
*15.10.1963 Nafpaktos (Lepanto). N23.2. 1986 dipl theol Athens. 1986-1988 Greek Army. 1988-1990 stud Church history Pontificio Istituto Orientale Roma. mon13.1.1990 Phanar diak15.1.1990 (M Bartholomaios) ⊖16.1.1990 archim Phanar (M Alexandros Nafpaktos). 1990-2007 rector San Giorgio dei Greci Venezia. 1992-2007 General vicar Italia. 1998 Archimandrite of the Ecumenical Throne ⊕6.5.2007 Phanar M España+Portugal (Patr Bartholomaios). 2010 member Holy and Sacred Synod. 23.-30.11.2015 34th Ecumenical Meeting for Bishops, İstanbul.

Kleopas Panagiotis Strongylis ***Skandinavia***
T: M Sweden and All Skandinavia ▪ ✉ Grekisk Orth Metropolit Birger Jarlsgatan 92, SWEDEN-11420 Stockholm • [46] 8 6462421 • metropolitancleopas@gmail.com • metropolisofsweden@gmail.com • https://ortodoxakyrkan.org
*20.8.1966 Nea Smirni Athens. 1984 absolv Fac theol Athens. diak1989 Thessaloniki (M Kleopas). 1992 MTh Durham England ⊖1992 Thessaloniki (M Kleopas). 1994 MTh Holy Cross Boston, teacher Holy Cross, Master Harvard. 1996 Dr. theol Thessaloniki, Prof. Queens College Massachusetts ⊕21.5.2014 Phanar İstanbul, M Sweden and All Skandinavia (Patr Bartholomaios).

Pavlos Menevissoglou

T: M Amasia ▪ ✉ Hägersten Selmedalsvägen 72/3, SWEDEN-12937 Stockholm • [46] 8 6462421, fax 973212

*27.11.1935 Makrochorion Bakırköy İstanbul. N29.6. diak1.4.1956. 1958 dipl theol Chalki "Monastic life according to M. Basilios". 1958-1974 Patriarcheion Phanar ⊖30.11.1970. 1970 Archigrammateus. 1973 Dr. theol Thessaloniki "Holy Myron in the Eastern Orth Church", dipl jur Thessaloniki ⊕12.5.1974 M Sweden and all Skandinavia. 2014 M Amasia.

Demetrios Trakatellis ***New York***

T: A Greek Orth Archdiocese of America ▪ ✉ 10 East 79th Street, USA-New York, NY10075-0106 • [1] 212 6282500, 570-3500, fax 8618060, 5704005 • communications@goarch.org • archdiocese@goarch.org • alice@goarch.org • www.goarch.org

*1.2.1928 Thessaloniki. N26.10. 1946-1950 dipl theol Athens 1950-1963 Brotherhood Zoë. diak1960 ⊖1964. 1965-1972 PhD Harvard "Justin Martyr", 1965 USA ⊕17.9.1967 B Vresthena assistant Athens. 1968 elected M Attika (did not accept). 1977 Dr. theol Athens. 1983-1993 Prof Biblical Studies and Christian Origins, Holy Cross Boston USA. 1984-1985 visiting Prof NT Harvard, 1988-1989 visiting Prof NT Harvard. 1991-1999 M Vresthena attached to Archdiocese Athens. 1999 A America. 1999 Dr.h.c. Hum. Letters New Jersey. 2002 member Academy of Athens.

Apostolos Evangelos Koufallakis

T: B Medeia, auxiliary to Archbishop of Amerika ▪ ✉ 10 East 79th Street, USA-New York, NY 10021 • [1] 212 6282500 • archdiocese@goarch.org • www.goarch.org

*1969 Rhodos. mon1993 diak1993. 1993-1996 stud theol Patmos ⊖1996 (M Apostolos Rhodos). 1997-2002 stud theol Thessaloniki. 2002-2004 MTh Boston University. 2004 Cathedral New York. 28.11.2014 confession to Holy Synod Phanar ⊕20.12.2014 B (M Demetrios).

Ilia Katre

T: B Philomelion, Albanian Diocese of America ▪ ✉ 6455 Silver Dawn Lane, USA-Las Vegas, NV 89118 • [355] 575 223-80, -97, -98 • akademia-teol-ngjallja-krishtit@yahoo.com • bishop.ilias@yahoo.com

*1937 Sault Ste. Marie, Michigan. N20.7. 1972 BA Hellenic College. 1973 MDiv Holy Cross. 1983-1988 director of student affairs Holy Cross ⊖1988. 1988-2002 pastor Las Vegas NV, Vicar General of the Albanian Orth Diocese. widower, two married children and two grandchildren ⊕12.5.2002 Phanar B Philomelion. 2003 Dean Theol Academy Durrës.

Philotheos Markos Karamitsos
T: M Meloa ▪ ✉ 10 East 79th St, USA-New York, NY 10021 • [1] 212 5703500, 6282500
*1.9.1924 İstanbul, N29.1. diak30.6.1950. 1950 dipl theol Athens. 1960 USA ⊖6.1961 ⊕6.6.1971 B Meloa, vicar New York. 1998 retired. 2015 M Meloa, Metropolis of the Throne.

Dimitrios Koutsogeorghas Couchell
T: B Xanthos ▪ ✉ 10 East 79th St, USA-New York, NY10021 • [1] 212 5703500, 6282500
*1938 Greenville Spartanburg South Carolina, N26.10. 1957 stud Northwestern University. 1963 dipl theol Holy Cross. 1964 campus ministry program Greek Orth Archdiocese. 1981 St. Photios Foundation. 1983 Orth Christian Mission Center OCMC ⊕31.5.1998 St. George Philadelphia (A Spyridon) assistant New York, liaison Orth Christian Charities IOCC, OCMC, Ecumenical Affairs, SCOBA. 2008 retired.

Sebastianos Skordallos
T: B Zela, assistant New York ▪ ✉ 10 East 79th St, USA-New York, NY 10075 • [1] 212 5703500, 6282500 • archdiocese@goarch.org • bishopsevastianos@goarch.org
*1955 Ano Zodia Cyprus, N18.12. 1973 absolvent Gymnasion Morphou. 1973-1978 stud theol Athens. diak17.1.1974 Morphou ⊖4.3.1978 London (A Gregorios), parishes England. 1979-1982 MTh Columbia Theol Seminary (scholarship WCC). archim (A Athenagoras London) 1980 Caraway Methodist Medical Center, 1982 Vanderbilt University Nashville Tennessee. 1984-2006 parishes USA. 2006 archigrammateus Holy Synod New York ⊕17.12.2011 Phanar.

Antonios Allen Paropulos
T: B Phasiane, assistant New York ▪ ✉ 10 East 79th St, USA-New York, NY 10075 • [1] 212 5703500, 6282500 • bishopandonios@goarch.org
*15.1.1953 Jersey Pontus immigrants. N17.1. BA Accounting St. Peter's College. 1976-1979 MDiv Holy Cross Brookline. 1980-1984 Hellenic College. 1984 Director LOGOS. diak18.8.1985. 1985-1989 deacon to A Iakovos ⊖3.12.1989 archim24.2.1991. 1991 sabbatical Greece. 1992-1995 rector Bronx. 1996 director Department Philanthropy ⊕23.2.2002 B Phasiane, assistant New York. 2007 Benevolence Fond retired clergy. 2009 Chancellor Archdiocese.

Savvas Zebillas ***Pittsburgh***
T: M Pittsburgh ▪ ✉ 5201 Ellsworth Avenue, USA-Pittsburgh, PA 15232, [1] 412 621-5529, fax -1522 • info@pittsburgh.goarch.org • metropolitansavas@goarch.org • www.pittsburgh.goarch.org

*11.6.1957 Gary Indiana, N5.12. 1979 BPhil Waterville Maine. 1979 coffee company. 1981 Athos, Patmos. 1982 stud theol Holy Cross. 1985 St. Nicholas Cincinnati Ohio. 1987-1994 stud Oxford. diak21.11.1992 ⊖8.1.1995. 1995 proistamenos Kalamazoo Michigan. 1997 Merrick, Long Island. 1999 Chancellor of the Archdiocese ⊕2.2.2002 B Troas, assistant New York, Chancellor. 3.11.2011 M Pittsburgh.

Maximos Agiorgousis
T: former M Pittsburgh ▪ ✉ 5201 Ellsworth Avenue, USA-Pittsburgh, PA 15232 • [1] 412 621-5529, fax -1522
*5.3.1935 Chios. N21.1. 1957 dipl theol Chalki. diak28.4.1957 ⊖26.7.1959. 1966 USA. 1966-1979 Prof Theol Holy Cross ⊕18.6.1978 B Diokleia. 1979 B Pittsburgh. 1997 M Ainos, presiding hierarch Pittsburgh, 2002 M Pittsburgh. 2011 retired.

Alexios Anthimos Panajotopulos ***Atlanta***
T: M Atlanta ▪ ✉ 2480 Clairmont Rd, N.E., USA-Atlanta, GA 30329 • [1] 404 634-9345, fax -2471 • info@atlmetropolis.org • alexios@atlmetropolis.org • www.atlmetropolis.org
*25.12.1943 Ano Sudeneika Patras. N17.3. 1959 stud Academy Athos. mon6.4.1963 Saturday Lazaros Vatopedi. 1964 dipl Academy Athos. diak1.11.1965. 1965-1967 Archidiakon Patras. 1967-1971 diakonos Athens ⊖27.8.1972. 1972-1974 igumen Patras. 1973 dipl theol Athens. 1977 Doctor of Ministry Boston. 1977-1978 igumen Patras. 1978 Brooklyn, 1979 Astoria ⊕17.5.1987. 1987-1997 B Troas assistant New York. 1997-1999 B Troas, vicar for Atlanta. 1999 B Atlanta. 2002 M Atlanta.

Evangelos Kurunis ***New Jersey***
T: M New Jersey ▪ ✉ 215 East Grove Street, USA-Westfield, NJ 07090-1656 • [1] 908 301-0500, fax 1397 • metropolis@nj.goarch.org • dnphilotheos@nj.goarch.org • www.nj.goarch.org
*20.9.1961 New York. N25.3. 1968 Bossey Geneva. 1983 dipl Hellenic College. 1983-1986 MDiv Holy Cross. diak1.2.1987. 1987 Deacon Orth Center Chambésy. 1988 assistant Director Archives of A Iakovos ⊖30.6.1989. 1989 Cathedral Astoria NY. archim30.3.1991. 1993-1999 chancellor New Jersey. 1996-2001 Director of the Registry of the Archdiocese. 1996 President Spiritual Court. 2001-2003 dean Astoria NY ⊕10.5.2003 M New Jersey.

Iakovos Garmatis ***Chicago***
T: M Chicago ▪ ✉ 40 East Burton Place, USA-Chicago, IL 60610-1697, [1] 312 3374130, fax 3379391 • metropolis@chicago.goarch.org • diosectary@aol.com • www.chicago.goarch.org

*4.4.1928 Athens. N23.10. dipl theol Athens. diak16.3.1952 Athens ⊖14.2.1954. 1954-1966 stud Boston, Harvard USA, parishes Boston. 1966-1968 director Ecumenical Relations Athens ⊕25.12.1969. 1969-1979 B Apameia, 1979 B Chicago. 1997 M Krini, presiding hierarch Chicago, 2002 M Chicago.

Demetrios Kantzavelos

T: B Mokissos, assistant Chicago ▪ ✉ 40 East Burton Place, USA-Chicago, IL 60610-1697 • [1] 312 3374130, fax 3379391 • bishopdemetrios@aol.com

1987 dipl Holy Cross School Brookline. diak1.10.1989 ⊖1992 archim1995 Chancellor Chicago ⊕19.12.2006 B Mokissos, assistant Chicago.

Nicholas Pissaris ***Detroit***

T: M Detroit ▪ ✉ 2560 Crooks Rd, USA-Troy, MI 48084 • [1] 248 823240-0, fax -1, [1] 313 8645-433, fax -543 • office@detroit.goarch.org • www.detroit.goarch.org

*1953 Glens Falls N.Y. N6.12. 1971-1975 Colgate University War Memorial Scholarship. BA French Philology. 1975-1978 Theol school Brookline, MDiv stud theol Athens. 1980-1990 social worker Hospital St. Antony Denver CO. diak6.7.1991 McKeesport PA (Maximos of Pittsburgh) ⊖13.7.1991 Denver CO. archim13.7.1991. 1991protosynkellos Pittsburgh. 1995 protosynkellos Detroit. 1997 Stewardship Commission, Dean Holy Cross New York ⊕3.4.1999 Saturday Lazarus, Brooklyn. 2002 M Detroit. 2010 member Holy and Sacred Synod.

Methodios Georgios Turnãs ***Boston***

T: M Boston ▪ ✉ 162 Goddard Ave., USA-Brookline, MA 02445 • [1] 617 277-4742, -2082, 7313500, fax 7399229 • metropolis@boston.goarch.org • bostonis@yahoo.com • www.boston.goarch.org

*19.11.1946 New York. N14.6. dipl theol Holy Cross Boston. Master of Studies Boston University. diak22.7.1973 ⊖25.12.1979 ⊕18.7.1982 B Skopelos, assistant New York. 13.3.1984 B Boston. 12.5.1985 Dr. theol Boston University, 2001 Dr. theol Holy Cross Boston. 1989-1995 President Hellenic College and Holy Cross School of Theology. 1997 M Anea, presiding hierarch Boston. 2002 M Boston.

Gerasimos Michaleas ***San Francisco***

T: M San Francisco ▪ ✉ 245 Valencia Street, USA-San Francisco, CA 94103 • [1] 415 753-1165, -3075 • metropolis@sanfran.goarch.org • metgerasimos@sanfran.goarch.org • www.sanfran.goarch.org

*2.8.1945 Kalamata Greece. N20.10. 1969-1973 BA Hellenic College Brookline. 1973-1976 MDiv Holy Cross Brookline. 1976 registrar. diak16.12.1979. 1979-1996 archdeacon to A Iakovos. 1980-1998 Dean of students Brookline. 1988-2000 Director of admissions and records. 1993 PhD School and Counseling Psychology

Boston College. Senior Lecturer Northeastern University. 2000 assistant president Holy Cross ⊖2.2.2002 ⊕9.2.2002 B Krateia, assistant New York, Chief Secretary Holy Eparchial Synod. 2005 M San Francisco. 2011-2012 member Holy Synod Phanar.

Isaias Chronopoulos ***Denver***

T: M Denver ▪ ✉ 4550 East Alamada Avenue, USA-Denver, CO 80246-1208 • [1] 303 333779-4, fax -6, 3415007 • metropolis@denver.goarch.org • chancellor@denver.goarch.org • www.denver.goarch.org

*1931 Portsmouth New Hampshire USA. N9.5. dipl theol Holy Cross, stud theol Chalki, diak1962 ⊖1962 parishes Salt Lake Utah, Youngstown Ohio. mon30.11.1969 archim, dipl theol Thessaloniki, parishes Portsmouth. 1979 protosynkellos Chigaco ⊕25.5.1986 B Aspendos assistant New York. 1986-1992 protosynkellos Archiepiskopia. 1992-1997 B Denver, 1997 President Hellenic College, Holy Cross Greek Orthodox School of Theology. 1997 M Proekonissos, presiding hierarch Denver, 2002 M Denver.

Sotirios Athanasoulas ***Toronto***

T: M Toronto ▪ ✉ 86 Overlea Blvd. 1 Patr Bartholomew Way, CANADA-Toronto, Ont M4H 1C6 • [1] 416 429-5757, fax -4588 • metropolis@gometropolis.org • www.gometropolis.org

*19.2.1936 Lepiana Arta Greece. N6.8. 1961. dipl theol Athens, Magister theol Montreal. diak17.7.1962 Montreal ⊖18.7.1962 Montreal parishes Canada. 1968-1996 archepiscopal councillor North and South America ⊕27.1.1974 Montreal B Constantia. 1979 B, 1996 M Toronto.

Christophoros Rakintzakis

T: B Andida ▪ ✉ Eptanison 15, GREECE-153 41 Agia Paraskevi

*1.5.1931 Athens. N9.5. 1953 dipl theol Athens. 1970 dipl phil (History Archeology) Athens. 1975 Master's Byzantine History Birmingham. diak11.7.1986 ⊖12.7.1986 ⊕26.9.1999 B Andidae, 1999-2011 assistant Toronto.

Athenagoras Georgios Anastasiadis ***Mexico***

T: M Mexico ▪ ✉ Agua Caliente Esq. Saratoga, Colonia Lomas Hipodromo Naucalpan, MEXICO-53900 Mexico • [52] 55 5294-4460, fax -2678 • metropolimexco@yahoo.com.mx

*17.9.1941 Chicago. N24.7. dipl theol Chalki. 1965 dipl theol Athens. dipl theol Holy Cross Boston. diak19.12.1965 ⊖21.7.1967 archim14.8.1973 ⊕22.8.1982. 1982-1996 B Dorylaion, assistant New York. 1996 founder M Hongkong, received Patr Bartholomaios in Hongkong. 1996 M Panama, 2005 M Mexico.

Pankratios Petro Dubas

T: B Skopelos, vicar Mexico ▪ ✉ Agua Caliente Esq. Saratoga, Colonia Lomas Hipodromo Naucalpan, MEXICO-53900 Mexico • [52] 55 5294-4460, fax -2678 • pankratij@gmail.com

*12.7.1955 Holohory Zolochiv Lviv Ukraina. N9.7. 1973-1975 Soviet Army. 1975-1983 singer Holohory. 1983 Leningrad Theol Seminary and Academy. 1991 instructor Volyn Seminary (Moscow Patriarchate). 1993 USA by invitation of B Vsevolod, Skopelos Ecumenical Patriarchate. mon5.8.1993 (M Athenagoras, Ecumenical Patriarchate). diak12.12.1993 Bridgeport Connecticut (B Vsevolod) ⊖19.12.1993 All Saints Ukrainian Orth Church New York (B Vsevolod). 2.10.1994 igumen Winnipeg Canadan (B Vsevolod). 1995-1997 teacher Pastoral Theology St. Sophia Seminary New Jersey. archim28.7.1996 Allentown Pennsylvania. 1997-2012 parish-priest St. Volodymyr Ukrainian Orthodox Cathedral Chicago ⊕9.9.2012 Mexiko City (B Skopelos Synod Konstantinopel).

Tarasios Peter Anton ***Buenos Aires***

T: M Buenos Aires ▪ ✉ Avenida Figueroa Alcorta 3187, Cap. Fed., ARGENTINA-1425 Buenos Aires • [54] 11 48051451, 4508540-2, -3, fax -4 • buenosaires@ortodoxia.org • www.ortodoxia.org

*16.3.1956 Gary, Indiana USA. N25.2. 1970 reader, San Antonio Texas. 1978 Hellenic College, BA 1980 MDiv Theol school Boston. 1983 MTh University of Notre Dame. 1983-1987 Pont Istituto Orientale Roma, Scuola di Paleografica ed Archivista Vaticano. diak30.12.1990 (M Bartholomaios of Chalcedon). 1990 patriarchikos diakonos, 1993 Tritevon, 1995 Devterevon, 1999 Megas Archidiakonos ⊖27.5.2001 Prokonion Cappadocia (Patr Bartholomaios) ⊕3.6.2001 Phanar (Patr Bartholomaios). 14.7.2001 M Buenos Aires. 2010 member Holy and Sacred Synod.

Iosif Leandro Bosch

T: B Patara, vicar Buenos Aires ▪ ✉ Avenida Figueroa Alcorta 3187, ARGENTINA-1425 Buenos Aires • [54] 11 4802-3204, fax 4801-0127

*1.1.1976 Cordoba Argentina N25.2. 1982-1994 Orthodox College St. Georges Cordoba. 1995 Syria St. Georges Monastery. 1995stud theol Balamand Lebanon, 1997-2002 Thessaloniki (scholarship Ecumenical Patriarchate) diak1997 (M Gennadios Sasimon) ⊖2000 Cordoba (M Gennadios Buenos Aires). 2000 proistamenos St. John Freiburg Germany. 2002-2005 stud theol Angelicum Roma. 2006-2007 stud theol Thessaloniki. archim2007 Santiago de Chile. 2008 Cordoba, 2010 protosynkellos Buenos Aires. 2011 Dr. theol Angelicum Roma "Influence of Johannes Damaskinos in St.Thomas Aquin". 2012 Dr. theol Thessaloniki "The Areopag in the First Part of the Summa St.Thomas Aquin" ⊕19.8.2012 Buenos Aires (Patr Bartholomaios).

Gennadios Chrysoulakis
T: M former Buenos Aires ▪ ✉ Posidonos 31, Kalamaki, GREECE-142 50 Athens • [30] 210 981 7714, fax 988 5688
*1924 Perivolakia Siteias Kreta. N17.11. 1944 Toplou Siteias, dipl theol Thessaloniki. diak1944 ⊖1946 ⊕8.4.1979 B,1996 M Buenos Aires. 2001 retired.

Grigorios George Tatsis
T: B Nyssa, presiding hierarch Karpatho Orthodox ▪ ✉ 312 Garfield St, USA-Johnstown, PA 15906 • [1] 814 5399143, fax 5364699 • bishopgregoryofnyssa@gmail.com • www.acrod.org
*7.12.1958 Charlotte NC USA. NGregor Palamas. 1981 BA, 1983-2003 Cardovascular Research Carolina Medical Center. 1989 MSc Biology University of North Carolina. 2003-2006 MDiv Holy Cross Brookline. diak4.11.2006 Charlotte (M Alexios Atlanta) ⊖28.1.2007 Atlanta archim hierokēryx Atlanta. mon17.7.2007 Kalavrita Greece "St. Gregory Palamas" ⊕28.9.2012 B Nyssa, presiding hierarch Karpatho Orthodox.

Yurij George Kalistchuk ***Winnipeg***
T: A Winnipeg, M Canada ▪ ✉ St. John's Avenue, CANADA-Winnipeg, MB R2W 1G8 • [1] 204 6693654, 5863093, fax 5825241, mobil 7810572 • metuocc@mymts.net • metropolitan@uocc.ca • www.uocc.ca
*26.5.1951 Lachine Quebec. N23.4. 1965 school Hamilton Ontario. 1987 BTh College St. Andrews Winnipeg, BMusics University McMaster Hamilton, BPedagogics Toronto. diak1988 ⊖17.7.1988. 1988-1991 Prof Church Music St. Andrews. mon24.9.1989 archim ⊕22.10.1989 B Saskatoon Ukrainian Orthodox Church of Canada. 1990 B Saskatoon Ukrainian Greek Orthodox Church of Canada. 1992 B Saskatoon, Auxiliary Central Canada. 2010 A Winnipeg, M Canada.

Antonij Scharba ***Hierapolis***
T: M Hierapolis of the Ukrainian Orthodox Church of the USA ▪ ✉ P.O.Box 495, von Steuben Lane 4, USA-South Bound Brook, NJ08880 • [1] 732 356 0090, [1] 908 356-0090, fax -9437, [1] 201 4697248 • uocofusa@worldnet.att.net • consistory@uocofusa.org
*30.1.1947 Sharon PA, USA. N17.1 ⊖26.11.1972 mon29.5.1985 ⊕6.10.1985 A New York, UAOC in USA and Diaspora. 12.3.1995 A Hierapolis "Konst". 2012 M of the Ukrainian Orthodox Church of the USA.

Ilarion Roman Rudnyk ***Edmonton***
T: B Edmonton and the Western eparchy ▪ ✉ 11404-112 Ave, CANADA-Edmonton, Alta T5G 0H6 • [1] 780 45-51938, -45287 • admin@uocc-we.ca • rudnyk1@telus.net • www.uocc-we.ca
*14.1.1972 Lviv Ukraina. N21.10./3.11. Seminary Kiev. 1997 dipl theol Thessaloniki "Die kanonischen Beziehungen Kiev Kon/pel bis 1240". mon 5.12.1997 diak21.12. 1997 (Panteleimon Tyroloïs) ⊖2000 (Vsevolod Scopelos). 2002 rector S. Panteleimon Porto Portugal ⊕29.1.2005 B Telmissos, assistant Spain in Portugal. 2008 B Edmonton and the Western eparchy Ukrainian Orthodox Church.

Ivan Stinka
T: former M Canada ▪ ✉ 11404-112th Ave, CANADA-Edmonton, Alta T5G 0H6 • [1] 403 4551938, fax 4545287
*14.1.1935 Buchanan, Sask. Canada N7.1 ⊖1974 mon ⊕27.11.1983 B Saskatoon Ukrainian Orthodox Church of Canada, 1985-2005 B Edmonton. 1990 Ukrainian Greek Orthodox Church of Canada. 2005-2010 head of the Ukrainian parishes in Canada belonging to the Ecumenial Patriarchate. A Winnipeg, M.

Andrij Bogdan Peško
T: B Krateia ▪ ✉ 3281 Cindy Crescent, USA-Mississauga, ON L4Y 3J7 • [1] 905 206937-2, fax -3, mobil [1] 647 9911610 • uocceast@rogers.com • bishopandriy@yahoo.com
*27.4.1972 Ukraina. N30.11./13.12. 1989-1993 Seminary Sankt-Peterburg. 1994-1995 stud Johnstown Pennsylvania USA Carpatho-Russian Diocese "Konst". 1995-1999 Kandidat Kiev "Hist-Lit Research of the Rites of Installations and Ordinations". diak8.4.2001 Chicago, A Vsevolod Maidanski. mon21.9.2005 ⊖25.9.2005 Chicago, A Vsevolod. archim25.9.2005 ⊕13.12.2005 Chicago B Krateia, assistant to M Konstantin. 2008 B Saskatoon assistant Central eparchy of the UOCC. 1.2.2011B of the Eastern eparchy.

Daniel Volodymyr Zelinskyy
T: B Pamphilos ▪ ✉ 135 Davidson Ave., USA-Somerset, NJ 08873 • [1] 773 8570780 • St. Volodymyr Cathedral, West Cortez St. 2230-50, USA-Chicago IL 60622 • [1] 773 8570780 • ladykadaniel@aol.com
*28.9.1972 Buchach Ternopil. N? 1993-1996 Seminary Ivano-Frankivsk. 1996-2000 Catholic University Washington USA. diak17.11.1998. 2000 UOC. 2000-2002 St. Sophia Ukrainian Orth Theol Seminary South Bound Brook NJ ⊖12.5.2001. 2002 MTh Antiochian House of Studies USA. mon22.5.2002. 2002 Editor-in-Chief Ukrainian Orthodox Word. 2007 Dr. theol Pittsburgh Theol Seminary.

archim3.10.2007 ⊕10.5.2008 B Pamphilos, assistant Western eparchy. 2009 presiding hierarch Western eparchy. 2014 St. Volodymyr Cathedral.

Jeremias Ferens

T: A Aspendos ▪ ✉ Caixa Postal 9073, Ave. Candido Hartmann 1278, Bigorilho, BRAZIL-80730 Curitiba • [55] 41 3355142

*29.12.1962 Papanduva, Santa Catarina, Brazil, N1.5. mon25.10.1988 diak30.11.1988 ⊖29.1.1989 ⊕19.9.1993 UAOC in USA and Diaspora (M Konstantin Buggan, A Antonij, B Paisij). 1993-1995 B Curitiba+South America Igreja Ortodoxa Ucrainiana na América do Sul. 12.3.1995 B, 2010 A Aspendos "Konst".

Vikentios Basilios Malametenios

T: former B Apameia ▪ bishopvikentios@StIrene.org

*1954 Athens. N11.11. stud Jerusalem Old Calendar Church. mon1971 New York. 1977 dipl theol USA. 1998 "Konst". diak4.4.1998 ⊖5.4.1998 ⊕11.4.1998. 1998-2010 assistant to Patriarch Bartholomaios, Deputy igumen Patriarchal Stavropegic Monastery St. Irene Chrysovalantou. 17.12.2010 suspended from every clerical function. 28.3.2012 defrocked.

Iakovos Pililis

T: B Katania ▪ ✉ 2650 Pearce Drive, Apt 103, USA-Clearwater, FL 33764

*10.8.1927 Megara. N23.10 ⊕21.5.1967. 1978 10th District Archdiocese America, Buenos Aires.

Stylianos Harkianakis ***Australia***

T: A Australia ▪ ✉ 242 Cleveland St, Redfern, AUSTRALIA-Sydney, NSW 2016 • [61] 2 96906100, 96985066, fax 96985368 • www.greekorthodox.org.au

*29.12.1935 Rethymnon Kreta. N26.11. diak1957 ⊖28.8.1958. dipl theol Chalki. 1958-1066 stud Bonn, 1965 Dr. theol Athens. 1966-1975 igumen Moni Vlatadon. 1969-1975 Prof Thessaloniki ⊕6.12.1970 M Miletupolis, 1975 A Australia.

Iezekiel Kefalas

T: B Derbe, assistant Australia ▪ ✉ Greek Orth Archdiocese, 221 Dorcas Str South, AUSTRALIA-Melbourne, Vic 3205 • [61] 3 9696-2488, fax -3583

*25.12.1938 Akritas Kilkis Greece. N23.7. 1962. dipl theol Chalki. diak1.7.1962 Chalki ⊖24.9.1962 Sydney. 1962 rector Dubbo NSW Australia. 1963-1977 rector Belmore Sydney ⊕20.3.1977 B Derbe. 1977-1980 Perth, 1980-1984 Adelaide, 1984 Melbourne.

Seraphim Ghinis

T: B Apollonias, assistant Australia ▪ ✉ 242 Cleveland St, Redfern, AUSTRALIA-Sydney, NSW 2016 • [61] 2 6985066, fax 6985368

*12.12.1949 Athens. N4.12. stud Chalandri Attika, dipl theol Thessaloniki. diak31.8. 1975 ⊖28.12.1975. 1975-1980 London. 1980 BTh (Honours) Thessaloniki. 1980 rector parish Kalamarià Thessaloniki. 1986 rector parish Melbourne ⊕31.3.1991 Sydney B Apollonias. protosynkellos.

Nikandros Nikolaos Palyvos

T: B Dorylaion, assistant Australia ▪ ✉ Greek Orth Archdiocese, 533 Anzac Highway, Glenelg, AUSTRALIA-Adelaide, SA 5045 •
[61] 8 8295-3866, fax -4373. stbasils@iinet.net.au

*1947 Styra Karystia Greece. N4.11. diak1.1.1969 ⊖1.1.1970. 1970-1989 rector mitropolis Karystia, protosynkellos. 1974 dipl theol Athens. 1989-2000 rector Paleo Faliro, 2000-2001 rector Carlton Melbourne ⊕25.2.2002 Perth B Dorilaion, assistant Australia.

Iakovos Tsigunis

T: B Miletoupolis, assistant Australia ▪ ✉ Greek Orth Archdiocese, 221 Dorcas Str South, AUSTRALIA-Melbourne, Vic 3205 •
[61] 3 9245 9000, 9696-2488, fax -3583

*1966 Sydney, N23.10. 1993 dipl theol St. Andrew's Greek Orth Theol College Sydney. 1993-1999 protodiakonos archdiocese, teacher Greek Orth Theol College ⊖2002 parish priest Melbourne ⊕11.1.2011 Melitoupolis, assistant Australia.

Amphilochios Adamantios Tsoukos ***New Zealand***

T: M New Zealand, Japan ▪ ✉ 365 Broadway, Miramar, NEW ZEALAND-6022 Wellington • [64] 4 881194, 881914, fax 3881486, 4991164 •
info@ecp-metnz.org.nz • imnz@xtra.co.nz • www.ecp-metnz.org.nz •
www.orthodoxarchdiocese.org.nz

*1938 Lardo Rhodos. N23.11. school Patmos. 1959-1963 stud Chalki. mon8.12.1962 Chalki diak9.12.1962 Chalki (Maximos Repanellis) ⊖9.7.1963 Chalki (Maximos Repanellis). 1964-1968 Patmos. 1969-1972 teacher Patmos Church School. archim1972 (Patr Nikolaos Alexandria) missionary Kenya Tanzania Zaire. 1978-1989 teacher Patmos Church School. 1990-2005 igumen Archangel Michael Tharri Rhodos ⊕9.7.2005 B Erythra, assistant Rhodos (M Kyrill Rhodos). 13.10.2005 M New Zealand.

Ambrosios Aristotelis Zographos ***Korea***

T: M Korea ▪ ✉ 43 Mapo-dacro 18-gil, KOREA-Seoul • [822] 3647005, 3626371, fax 3652698 • orthodox@orthodox.or.kr • azographos@yahoo.com • www.orthodox.or.kr

*15.3.1960 Aegina GR. N7.12. 1983 dipl theol Athens. diak1985. 1988-1989 Library Monastery St. Catherine Sinai ⊖1991. 1994 ThM Holy Cross Greek Orth School. 1996 MTh Princeton Theol Seminary. 1998 Dr. phil Athens "Gabriel of Thessalonike". 1998-2005 Dean St. Nicholas Cath Seoul. 2004 Prof Hankuk University Foreign Studies Seoul ⊕5.2.2006. 2011-2012 member Holy Synod Phanar.

Sotirios Trambas

T: M Pissidia ▪ ✉ Monastery Gyonggi-Do Gapyong Gun Sang Myeon Deok Hyeon-Ri, KOREA-610-3 Seoul • [82] 31 5844376, fax 5852278

*1929 Arta, N6.8. 1951 dipl theol Athens. mon Leimonos Kallonis Lesvos. diak1956 ⊖1960. 1965-1968 military chaplain. 1968-1973 protosynkellos Athens. 1975 Korea Head "Orthodox Eastern Mission". 1982 rector Orth theol Seminary Seoul ⊕21.3.1993B Zela Assistant New Zealand, in Korea. 2004M Korea. 27.5.2008 retired.

Nektarios Tsilis ***Hongkong***

T: M Hongkong ▪ ✉ 704 Universal Trade Center, 3 Arbuthnot Road, CHINA-Hongkong • [852] 2573-8328, fax -8379 • metnektarios@omhksea.org • office@omhksea.org • omhksea@netvigator.com • www.omhksea.org

*1.1.1969 Dodoni Ioannina Greece, N9.11. dipl theol Athens, stud technology European Union. diak1990 Piraeus ⊖1995. 1990 hierokēryx Piraeus, deputy manager "Piraiki Ekklisia". 2001-2007 episcopal vicar Samos ⊕20.1.2008 M Hong Kong.

Konstantinos Tsilis ***Singapore***

T: M Singapore ▪ ✉ 856 Dunearn Road, 04-08, SINGAPORE-589472 Singapore • [65] 31080257 • office@omsgsa.org • www.omsgsa.org

*1973 Piraeus brother of Nektarios Tsilis, N21.5. stud Ecclesiastical Academy Athens, Fac theol Athens. stud Eastern Mennonite University USA. stud traditional practical medicine Thailand. teacher Greek Athens, journalist, 1998 Hong Kong. diak25.1.2003 Hong Kong ⊖26.1.2003 Hong Kong. 2005-2011 chancellor Metropolis Hongkong ⊕21.11.2011 Panagia of Pera İstanbul M Singapore.

Macedonian Orthodox Church
Archbishopric of Ohrid (1767)

His Beatitude **Stefan**
Archbishop of Ohrid and Macedonia

Stefan Stojan Veljanovski ***Skopje***
T: A Ohrid+Makedonia ■ ✉ P.F. 69, Makedonska Arhiepiskopija ul. Partizanski Odredi 12, Macedonia-1000 Skopje • [389] 2 3136631, 3230697, fax 3135550, 3230685 • mpc@mpc.mk • www.mpc.org.mk • www.spe.org.mk
*1.5.1955 Dobruševo Bitola. N9.1. 1969-1974 Seminary Skopje. 1975-1979 Fac theol Beograd. 1980-1982 Bari. 1982 Lic theol Bari/Università Angelicum Roma. 1982-1987 Prof Old Testament, Patrologia Fac theol Skopje. mon2.7.1986 diak3.7.1986 ⊖6.7.1986 ⊕12.7.1986 M Zletovo Strumica. 1987-1989 M USA. 1989 M Bregalnica. 1990 rector Seminary Skopje. 9.10.1999 A Ohrid+Makedonia.

Josif Jovica Todorovski ***Tetovo***
T: M Tetovo+Gostivar ■ ✉ ul. Goce Delčev, hram Sveti Kiril i Metodij, Macedonia-1200 Tetovo • [389] 44 353033 • otecjosif@gmail.com
*21.1.1982 Skopje. N8.1. 1997-2002 Seminary Skopje. mon10.9.2003 Monastery St. Jovan Bigorski. diak2004 ⊖7.7.2006. 2010 dipl theol Skopje "Mother of God – fountain of New Testament". 2012 igumen. archim2012 ⊕7.10.2012 B Velitsa, vicar Skopje. 3.11.2013 M Tetovo+Gostivar.

Josif Goran Pejovski ***Kumanovo***
T: M Kumanovo+Osogovo ■ ✉ ul. Dimitar Vlahov 40, Macedonia-1300 Kumanovo • [389] 31 492999, 3164867
*1977 Prilep. N8.1. 1995-2000 dipl theol "St. Kliment Ohrid" Skopje. MTh "Understanding the personality." 2001-2005 Lic Phil University Ohrid. 2005-2009 Dr. theol "Izihazm kod St. Jovana Lestivča". mon2005 diak2005 ⊖2006. 2009 igumen Kalište. archim2011 ⊕21.10.2012 B Lešok, vicar Polog. 10.11.2013 M Kumanovo.

Petar Jovan Karevski ***Prespa***
T: M Prespa+Pelagonija ■ ✉ Vlatko Milenkovski 55, Macedonia-7000 Bitola • [389] 47 236967, fax 221721 • Australia [61] 431640091• petar@mpc.mk
*29.5.1946 Bogomila Veles. N12.7. 1961-1966 Seminary Prizren. 1966-1970 Fac theol Beograd. 1970-1972 Prof Seminary Skopje. diak 6.2.1972. 1972-1976 sekretar eparchy Polog Kumanovo ⊖29.8.1976. 1976-1978 parish Cathedral Skopje. mon27.6.1979. 1979-1982 Lic theol Uni Gregoriana Roma ⊕14.6.1981. 1981-1995 M Prespa+Bitola.

1981-1987 Administrator Europa. 1982-1985 Prof Hebrew Fac theol Skopje. 1992 President Department Foreign Church Relations, Missionary Work and Charitable Activities, President of Commission for Dialog with the Orthodox Churches. 1995-2006 M Australia, Administrator Prespa+Pelagonija. 2006 M Prespa+Pelagonija, 2006-2012 Administrator Australia.

Kliment Goran Božinovski

T: B Heraklea, 2006 Secretary Holy Synod vicar Prespa ▪ ✉ Preobraženie Manastir Zrze, MACEDONIA-7500 Prilep • [389] 48 459400 • manastirzrze@yahoo.com

*20.2.1972 Skopje. N8.12. 1993 Monastery Grigoriou Mount Athos. mon8.4.1994 Athos diak15.8.1995 România. 1996 monasteries Makedonia ⊖21.4.1996 Strumica archim1996. 1998 igumen Zrze. monastery Holy Transfiguration Sv. Preobraženie. 2000-2005 Fac Literature and Fac theol Skopje ⊕12.7.2005 Bitola B Heraklea. 2005-2009 Lic Fac Phil Skopje Byzantine Culture "Isihastirion of the Monastery of Zrze (XIV-XV)".

Timotej Slave Jovanovski ***Ohrid***

T: M Debar -Kičevo ▪ ✉ Mitropolija, MACEDONIA-6000 Ohrid • [389] 46 230784, 262290, p 266805, fax 263346, [389] 70 211711 • Skopje [389] 2 3230784 • timotej@mt.net.mk

*20.10.1951 N4.2. Mlado Nagoričani Kumanovo. 1967-1968 Seminary St. Ilija Gorni, 1968-1972 Seminary Dračevo Skopje. 1972-1976 Fac theol Beograd. 1977-1979 Roma, 1979 Lic Istituto Orientale Roma. 1980-1984 Prof Liturgik Fac theol, Rector Seminary Dračevo Skopje. mon10.9.1981 diak11.9.1981 ⊖13.9.1981 ⊕20.9.1981 M Australia, Administrator Debar Kičevo Ohrid. 1990 secret Sv. Sinod. 10.1.1993 Assisi. 1995 M Debar-Kičevo, 2002-2006 Admin Povardarie, 2012 Admin Australia.

Naum Zvonimir Ilievski ***Strumica***

T: M Strumica ▪ ✉ Eparhia, MACEDONIA-2400 Strumica • [389] 34 322284, fax 326552 • otecnaum@t-home.mk

*13.12.1961 Skopje. N5.1. 1987 dipl jur. 1987-1995 Mon. Grigoriu Athos. mon1988 diak1993 (B Aleksios) ⊖1.8.1995 (B Calinic România). archim19.8.1995 ⊕27.8.1995 M Strumica. 2001 dipl theol Skopje. 2009 Dr. theol Sofia. 2015 MA Psychology.

Agatangel Atanas Stankovski ***Povardarie***

T: M Povardarie ▪ ✉ Povardarska Eparhija, Gjore Orandziev bb, MACEDONIA-1400 Veles • [389] 43 221231 +fax • info@povardarska-eparhija.org.mk • www.povardarska-eparhija.org.mk

*11.3.1955 Skopje. N5.2. 1976 Seminary. diak7.1.1979 ⊖9.1.1979. 1979-1995 parishes Australia. 1995 Fac theol Skopje. mon5.2.1998 archim3.7.1998 ⊕12.7.1998 B Velitsa. 1999 rector Seminary. 2000-2006 M Bregalnica. 2006 M Povardarie.

Ilarion Ivica Serafimovski ***Bregalnica***

T: M Bregalnica ▪ ✉ Bregalnička Eparhija Tošo Arsov 3, MACEDONIA-2000 Štip • [389] 32 397172, fax 387172 • breg.eparhija@t-home.mk • www.bregalnickaeparhija.org.mk

*13.1.1973 Kumanovo. N3.11. absolvent Seminary 1994. absolvent Seminary. mon9.10.1994 diak10.10.1994 ⊖11.9.1996 archim2004. 2005 absolvent Fac theol ⊕2.6.2006 B Bargala, 19.11.2006 B Bregalnica.

Metodi Metodi Zlatanov ***America***

T: M America Canada ▪ ✉ 5028 Paladin Dr, USA-Shelby TWP MI 48316 • [1] 586 260 1548 • ometodij@yahoo.com

*24.8.1963 Berovo. N24.5. mon1996 diak3.7.1996 ⊖14.7.1996. 11.12.1996 igumen. 1998 absolvent Fac theol Skopje. 2000 vice-rector Seminary, Prof St. Kliment Ohridski Skopje. archim2004. 2005 Lic Lettere Fac phil Skopje ⊕21.6.2005 Skopje. 2005-2006 B Velitsa. 2.9.2006 M America Canada.

Pimen Sotir Ilievski ***Europe***

T: M Europe ▪ ✉ Landmannagatan 8, SWEDEN-21444 Malmö • [46] 40122039, 733578639 • mpc_evropa@yahoo.co.uk • opimen@freemail.com.mk

*3.10.1971 Strumica. N9.9. 1997-2004 Fac theol Skopje. mon25.12.1997 Strumica. diak1997 ⊖1997. 1999 igumen St. Leontij Vodoca Strumica. 2003 secretary eparchy Strumica. archim4.4.2004. 2004-2005 dipl theol Institut St-Serge Paris ⊕2.10.2005 B Poljana Strumica. 2006 M Europa.

Gorazd Bogoljub Dimitrijevski

T: former M Europe ▪ ✉ ul. Partizanski Odredi 12, MACEDONIA-1000 Skopje • [389] 2 3230697, 3775512

*13.9.1936 Strzovci Kumanovo. N9.8. 1956-1960 Seminary Rakovica Beograd. 1960-1964 Fac theol Beograd. 1964-1965 Macedonian Archbishopric Skopje ⊖19.12.1965. 1965-1977 parishes Skopje (Cair, Krivi Dol), mon1977 ⊕26.6.1977 B Tiberiopolis. 1977-1980 Administrator Prespa Bitola. 1986-1987 assistant to Archbishop. 1987-1988 Administrator Zletovo. 1990-1995 M Strumica. 1995-2006 M Europa.

PATRIARCHATE OF MOSCOW AND ALL RUS'

His Holiness **Kirill**
Patriarch of Moscow and All Rus'

[7] 495 2302619 • orthsecr@ mospatr.ru • cs@mospatr.ru • www.patriarchia.ru • Department for External Church Relations: Danilovskij Val 22, 115191 ROSSIJA-Moskva • www.mospat.ru • Department Katechesis: Vysoko-Petrovskij Monastyr, Petrovka 28, 209-1310, fax -6815 • Cathedral Christ the Saviour 2024717, 2033823 • Sofrino factory 2764545, fax 338-6386, -3036, tipografija 1989737 • Zastupitel Ruské pravoslavné církve v českých zemích a slovensku, ul. Petra Velikého 26, CZECHIA-36001 Karlovy Vary • [420] 17 3223238 • Repr WCC Geneva [41] 22 3499454, fax 3484967, office 791-6327, fax -0361 • Mission Jerusalem founded 1847 [972] 2 6252565, fax 6256325, 50234874 • Representative at Patr Antiochia, Damas [963] 11 373-7893 +fax, -5718 • Délégation permanente auprès de l'Union Européenne Bruxelles, rue Léon Lepage 33-35, BELGIUM-1000 Bruxelles • [32] 2 2196286, 5137915 • [32] 47 450 9502

Kirill Vladimir Gundjajev ***Moskva***
T: His Holiness Patriarch ▪ ✉ Čistyj Pereulok 5, ROSSIJA-119034 Moskva • [7] 495 201-2840, 201-3416, fax 201-2504 • Kancelaria 201-2340, fax pers. 6372504 7312888, fax 201-2668, Tel Kabinet 201-2682, Tel pers Peredelkino 4355048 • www.patriarchia.ru • www.mospat.ru
*20.11.1946 Leningrad N24.5. mon3.4.1969 (M Nikodim Rotov) diak7.4.1969 ⊖1.6.1969. 1970 Kandidat Leningrad. 1970-1971 teacher dogmatics inspector Seminary Academy Leningrad, secretary to M Nikodim. 1971-1974 Representative WCC Geneva. 1974-1984 rector Seminary Academy Leningrad ⊕14.3.1976 B. 1977 A Wyborg. 1976-1978 vice exarch Western Europe. 1984-1988 A Smolensk+Vjazma. 1988-1991 A, 1991-2009 M Smolensk+Kaliningrad. 1989-2009 Chairman Department External Church Relations Moskva. 1990 member Biblical Comm. 1994 member Theol Comm. Dr.h.c.: 1987 Budapest, 2002 University Perugia Terni, 2004 Warszawa, 2005 Social University Russia, 2007 Politechnik University Sankt-Peterburg, 2009 Academy Kiev, Presidential Academy Rossija, 2010 University MIFI, University Petrozavodsk, University Jerevan, University Dnjepropetrovsk, Academy Moskva, University Pridnjestr, 2011 University Voronež, Lomonossov University Moskva, 2012 Sofia, 2012 St. Tikhon University Moskva, 2015 Diplomatic Academy of the Russian Ministry of Foreign Affairs, 2015 Doktorantura

Moskva. 2002 co-president Conseil européen dirigeants religieux Oslo. 2002 Orden Star Scientific Work. 2003 Honorary Citizen of Smolensk. 2004 laureat Rossijskij nacionalnyj Olimp. 2004 Orden Sergij Radonež (I). 2005 First laureat Silver Rose St. Nicholas of Fribourg and Regensburg. 2006 Vice-Chairman All-World Russian People Sobor. 2006 Orden St. Alexij Moskau (II). 6.12.2008 Locum tenens. 1.2.2009 patriarch. 2011 Sheik ul Islam Orden Caucasian Muslim Board. 2012 Church Orden: Alexandria, Antiochia, Jerusalem, Russia, Georgia, Serbia, Bulgaria, Greece, Poland, Czechia&Slov, Finland. 2013 Grand Cross of the Order of Honour Greece. 22.-28.1.2016 Synaxis of the primates of the Local Orthodox Churches Chambésy Switzerland. 12.2.2016 Meeting with Pope Francis in Cuba.

Juvenalij Vladimir Pojarkov ***Krutitsi***

T: M Krutitsi+Kolomna ▪ ✉ Novodevičij pr. dom 1, korp. 1, ROSSIJA-119435 Moskva • [7] 499 2460881, fax 2466850 • formail@mepar.ru • www.krutitsy.ru • www.mepar.ru

*22.9.1935 Jaroslavl. N15.7. 1953-1957 Seminary, 1957-1961 Academy Leningrad. mon10.10.1959 diak4.11.1959 ⊖1.1.1960. 1960 Bossey. 1960-1964 referent Department External Church Relations. 1961-1962 teacher New Testament Seminary Moskva. 1961-1983 delegate General Assemblies WCC. 7.7.1962 igumen. 14.7.1962 Palitsa. 1962-1963 rector Berlin Tegel, redaktor "Stimme der Orthodoxie". archim21.2.1963. 1963-1964 head Mission Jerusalem. 1964-1977 vice-chairman Departm External Church Relations ⊕25.12.1965 B Zaraisk, 1969 B, 1971 A, 1972 M Tula, 1976 two panagia. 1977-1981 chairman Department External Church Relations. 1977 M Krutitsi+Kolomna. 1978 head delegation inthron. Pope John Paul II. Roma. 1981-2011 chairman Synodal Commission canonization.

Ioann Georgij Roshchin

T: B Naro-Fominsk, vicar Moskva ▪ ✉ 15 East 97St, USA-New York, NY10029 • [1] 212 289 1915, fax 212 427 5003 • representation@ruschurchusa.org • www.ruschurchusa.org

*22.10.1974 Moskva. 1991-1993 stud Fac jur Moskva. 1993-1994 monastery Pskov. 1994-1997 Seminary Moskva. 1996-1997 commission Editions Patr Moskva. 1997-2009 Department External Relations Patr Moskva. 1999-2000 stud Fac theol St. Vladimir's New York. 2000-2002 stud Fac Phil Catholic University Washington. diak28.8.2007 (M Kirill Smolensk+Kaliningrad) ⊖23.9.2007 (M Kirill Smolensk+Kaliningrad) mon11.3.2014 (B Feognost) ⊕1.8.2014 B Naro-Fominsk, vicar Moskva, administrator Russian parishes USA.

Jevgenij Valerij Rešetnikov

T: A Vereja, rector Theol Academy and Seminary Moskva, vicar Moskva ▪ ✉ Troice-Sergieva Lavra, ROSSIJA-141310 Sergiev Posad • [7] 496 541-5601 • mpda@yandex.ru • www.mpda.ru • www.theolcom.ru

*9.10.1957 Kirov Vjatka. N20.3. school Celinograd Kazahstan. 1977 absolvent Technikum Construction Kirov. 1980-1983 Seminary, 1983-1987 Akad theol Moskva. mon27.7.1986 diak3.8.1986 ⊖28.8.1986. 1987-1991 teacher Moskva. archim1.1.1989. 1989-1991 Administrator. 1990-1991 Inspektor Seminary Moskva. 1991-1994 rector Seminary Stavropol ⊕16.4.1994 B, 2000 A Vereja, vicar Moskva, President Synodal Commission Education. 1994 Vice, 1994 rector Theol Academy and Seminary Moskva. 1999 President Synodal Commission Theology. 16.12.2004 Fribourg. 14.10.2010 Moskva Theol Academy 325 years.

Irinarh Vladimir Kuzmić Grezin

T: A Krasnogorsk, vicar Moskva ▪ ✉ Danilovskij Wall 22, ROSSIJA-115191 Moskva • [7] 495 953919-7, fax -8 • pris.fel@mail.ru • bishop@anastasia-uz.ru • www.bishop-irinarkh.ru

*23.11.1951 Šumerlja Čuvaš. N26.1. 1968-1969 stud Technikum Moskva. 1970-1971 electrician Zagorsk. 1971-1972 Soviet Army, 1971-1973 evening school Šumerlja. 1973-1974 electrician Zagorsk. 1974 Troice-Sergieva Lavra. 1975-1978 Seminary, 1978-1982 Academy Moskva, Kandidat "The Dogmatic system of the Fathers". 1982-1985 Aspirant. 1982 Department External Church Relations. mon3.5.1985 diak13.4.1985 ⊖15.4.1985. 1987 stud Birmingham, 1987-1988 Bossey, 1988-1989 Harvard Cambridge USA, blagočinnyj dean All Saints Moskva ⊕13.3.2002 B, 2003 A Perm+Solikamsk. 2010 A Krasnogorsk, President Synodal Commission Prisons.

Hilarion Grigorij Alfejev

T: M Volokolamsk, Chairman Department for External Church Relations ▪ ✉ Danilovskij Wall 22, ROSSIJA-115191 Moskva • [7] 495 9556767, 9526708, 2302250, [7] 499 131 5809, [7] 495 633 7281 • metropolitan.hilarion@gmail.com • cs@mospat.ru

*24.7.1966 Moskau. N? 1973-1983 music school Moskva. 1983-1986 Konservatorium Moskva (composition). 1984-1986 Soviet Army. mon19.6.1987 Holy Spirit Vilna. diak21.6.1987 (Viktorin of Vilna) ⊖19.8.1987 (Anatolij Kuznetsov). 1987-1989 Seminary (correspondence course) theol Sergiev Posad. 1989-1991 (correspondence course) Kandidat theol Sergiev Posad. 1990-1991 dean Cathedral Kaunas. 1991-1993 teacher dogmatics, New Testament, byzantine Greek, homiletics Seminary and Academy Moskva. 13.1.1991 Order of the State of Lithuania for avoiding civil war. 1992-1993 teacher New Testament St. Tikhon Institute, teacher

patristics Orth University St. John Moskva. 1993-1995 stud theol Oxford. 1994 member redaction Studia Monastica Montserrat. 1995 member redaction Vestnik Paris. 1995 Dr. phil Oxford. 1995-2002 St. Ekatarina na Vspolje Moskva. 1995-1997 teacher patristics seminaries Kaluga and Smolensk. 1996 member commission dialogue Reformed World Alliance. 1997-2002 chairman Interchurch Relations Department External Church Affairs Moskva. 1997 member Synodal Commission Theology, commission dialogue Roman Cath Church, commission dialogue Evangelical Church Germany. 1998-2002 chief editor Cerkov i Vremja. 1998 member commission dialogue Lutheran Church Finland, commission dialogue Church of England, Central Committee CEC. 1998 lecturer St. Vladimir's New York. 1999 lecturer Cambridge. 1999 Dr. theol Institut St-Serge Paris. 1999 member executive committee and member central committee WCC Geneva. 1999 lecturer Volos ⊕14.1.2002 B Kerč, vicar to M Anthony (Blum, Sourož/ London). 2002-2009 Délégation permanente auprès de l'Union Européenne Bruxelles. 2002 B Podolsk, 2003-2009 B Wien. 2003 medal Konstantin Ostrog Białystok. 2005 habilitation +Privatdozent (dogmatics) Fac theol University Fribourg, 2009 A Chairman Department External Relations Moskva. 2010 Titularprofessor Fac theol Fribourg Schweiz. 2010 M. 2011 chairman Synodal Comm Theology after M Filaret. 2010 Dr. theol h.c. RSSU (Moscow), Catalonia (Spain), 2011 Lugano Switzerland, Sankt-Peterburg, Prešov, 2012 Nashotah House Theol Seminary (USA), Villanova (USA), 2013 Minsk, 2014 St. Vladimir (OCA), RSUH (Moscow), Veliko Tarnovo (Bulgaria). 2009 Rector the St. Cyril and Method Institute of Post-Graduate Studies (Aspirantura). 2012 Dean Theology Chair NRNU MEPhI. 2014 Aspirantura first time grants Dr.h.c.: to Prof. Andrea Riccardi Comunità Sant' Egidio, to M Kallistos (Ware). 22.-28.1.2016 Synaxis of the primates of the Local Orthodox Churches Chambésy Switzerland, with Nikolai Balashov. Fellow Academy of Russian Language and Literature. Member Russian Union of Composers.

Feognost Ivan Guzikov

T: A Sergiev Posad, vicar Moskva, namestnik ▪ ✉ Troice-Sergieva Lavra, ROSSIJA-141300 Sergiev Posad • [7] 496 5405334, 5474354 • piligrimus@stsl.ru • www.stsl.ru

*6.10.1960 Selivanovo Vladimir (Igor Cernigov). N27.3. 1979-1981 Soviet Army. 1981-1983 churches Vladimir. mon22.11.1983 "Feognost M Kiev" (A Serapion, Vladimir). 1984 Zagorsk. diak14.1.1984 ⊖19.1.1984. 1985-1987 Seminary. archim 1986. 1987-1991 Academy Moskva, Kandidat "Pastoral work". 1988 namestnik Troice-Sergieva Lavra. 1990 teacher Patrology Akad ⊕31.3.2002 B, 2010 A Sergiev Posad vicar Moskva. 2010 President Synodal Commissions Monasteries.

Arsenij Georgij Epifanov
T: M Istra, vicar eparhia Moskva ▪ ✉ Čistyj Pereulok 5, ROSSIJA-119034 Moskva • [7] 495 637-4759, 2012840, [7] 916 5095474 • mge@patriarchia.ru
*3.3.1955 N? Vostrjakovo Domodedovo Moskovskaja oblast. N25.6. 1976 Seminary Moskva. 1978-1986 sekretar to M Aleksij Leningrad. 1983 Kandidat Moskva. diak1984. 1984-1989 Cathedral Aleksandr Nevskij Leningrad ⊖1986 protoierej ⊕5.10.1989 B Ladoga. 1989-1990 vicar Leningrad. 1990 B, 1997 A, 2014 M Istra, vicar Moskva.

Paramon Feodor Golubka
T: B Bronnitsi, vicar patriarha ▪ ✉ Danilovskij Val 22, ROSSIJA-115191 Moskva • [7] 499 5780358
*26.6.1977 Ugla Zakarpatia. 1984-1994 school Ugla. 1994-1997 Seminary Moskva. 1996 reader (B Jevgenij, Vereja). 1997-2001 Academy Moskva. mon30.3.1998 Troice-Sergieva Lavra. diak23.7.1998 Moskva (B Aleksij, Orekhovo) ⊖14.10.2000 (Patr Aleksij). 2001-2010 rector Cathedral Juzhno-Sakhalinsk. 2003 igumen. 2004 palitsa. 2010-2012 Kliros kanonarkh Troice-Sergieva Lavra. 2011 member Commission Canonization, president Commission Administration. 2012 namestnik Donskoj Monastyr ⊕2.12.2015 Christ the Saviour Moskva, B Bronnitsi, patr vicar (Patr Kirill).

Tikhon Georgij Shevkunov
T: B Jegorjevsk, vicar Moskva ▪ ✉ Danilovskij Val 22, ROSSIJA-115191 Moskva • [7] 499 5780358
*2.7.1958 Moskva. 1982 dipl "literatura kino" Institute of Kinografia Moskva. 1982-1986 Publication Center of the Russian Orthodox Church with M Pitirim Nechajev. mon1991 diak1991 Moskva ⊖1991Moskva. 1995 igumen Monastyr Sretenje Moskva. archim1998. rector Seminary Sretenje. 2010 secretary Patriarcal Council Culture ⊕24.10.2015 B Jegorevsk, vicar Moskva.

Antonij Anton Sevrjuk
T: B Bogorodsk, vicar patriarha ▪ ✉ Danilovskij Val 22, ROSSIJA-115191 Moskva • [7] 499 5780358
*12.10.1984 Tver. 1991-1995 school Tver. 1995-2002 Tverskoj Litsej, altarnik Cathedral Tver. 2002-2007 dipl Seminary Sankt-Peterburg "Eschatology in the World Religions". 2006 Syndesmos. 2007-2010 Academy Sankt-Peterburg, teacher English. 2007 stud University Joensuu Finlandia. 1.10.2007 referent Department of External Church Relations Moskva. 2008 teacher Seminary Smolensk. 2009-2010 personal secretary Patriarch Kirill. mon5.3.2009 diak8.3.2009 Christ the Saviour

Moskva (Patr Kirill) ⊖3.4.2010 Christ the Saviour Moskva (Patr Kirill). 2011 parish Roma Italia. archim18.7.2013 Sergiev Posad (Patr Kirill) ⊕26.10.2015 B Bogorodsk, patr vicar for the parishes in Italy. Chairman Department Church Institutions outside Russia.

Panteleimon Arkadij Šatov

T: B Orehovo-Zujevo, vicar Moskva, chairman Department Humanitarian Aid, Social welfare ▪ ✉ ul Nikolojamskaja 57, st 7, ROSSIJA-109004 Moskva • [7] 499 9210257 • pantaleon177@gmail.com • www.diaconia.ru

*18.9.1950 Moskva, N9.8. 1977 Seminary Moskva. diak26.8.1978 ⊖15.4.1979. 1992 duhovnik medicin school Moskva, protoierej. widower, four daughters, eleven grandchildren. 2010 chairman Department Humanitarian Aid, Social welfare. mon17.7. 2010 archim18.7.2010 ⊕21.8.2010 B Orehovo-Zujevo, vicar Moskva. 2011-2013 B Smolensk+Vjazma, chairman Department Humanitarian Aid, Social welfare 2013 B Orehovo-Zujevo, vicar Moskva, chairman Department Humanitarian Aid, Social welfare.

Feofilakt Nikolaj Moisejev

T: B Dmitrov, Vicar Moskva ▪ ✉ Andrejevskaja nab. dom 2, ROSSIJA-119334 Moskva • [7] 963 7701030 • asmm2013@mail.ru • www.andreevskymonru

*30.4.1949 Smolensk Moisejev. N21.3. 1968-1970 Soviet Army. 1978-1984 Seminary Academy Moskva. diak6.1.1982 mon28.4.1983 ⊖28.8.1983. 4.12.1985 igumen Skit Gethsemane Sergiev Posad. archim28.4.1995 ⊕20.4.2002 B Brjansk+ Sevsk. 2011 B Dmitrov, vicar Moskva.

Pankratij Vladislav Žerdjev

T: B Troitsk, vicar eparhia Moskva ▪ ✉ Valaam Monastery, ROSSIJA-186756 Valaam, (7) 81430 44584. ulTverskaja-Jamskaja 2-JA52, ROSSIJA-125047 Moskva • [7] 499 2510573 • admin@valaam.ru • sekretariat@valaam.ru • www.valaam.ru

*21.7.1955 Perm. N10.9. 1970-1980 stud architecture Perm and Dušanbe. 1980-1986 St. Nikolaj sobor Dušanbe. 1986 Seminary Moskva. mon3.7.1987 diak18.7. 1987 ⊖8.6.1988. 17.7.1988 igumen. ekonom Lavra. archim4.5.1990. 1993 igumen Monastery Transfiguration Valaam. 2004 Orden Sergij Radonež (II). ⊕2.6.2005 B Troitsk,vicar eparchy Moskva. 2011 chairman Synodal Commission canonization.

Grigorij Jurij Čirkov

T: A Možaisk, vicar of M Juvenalij ▪ ✉ Novodevičij pr. dom 1, korp.1, ROSSIJA-119435 Moskva • [7] 495 2460881, 2453003 • i-samojlov@yandex.ru • www.mepar.ru

*1.1.1942 Kozly obl. Kirov. N25.3. 1963 Inspektor Kontrol-Laboratorium. 1966-1969 Soviet Army. 1969 Seminary Leningrad, mon15.3.1973 (M Nikodim Rotov) diak25.3.1973 ⊖4.12.1973. 1975 Kandidat, 1975-1978 Aspirant Moskva Department External Church Relations. 1976 igumen. 1977-1993 Secretary eparchy Moskva. archim1978. 1981 Uspenskij Hram ⊕13.9.1987 B,1997 A Možaisk. 2012 Orden Sergij Radonež.

Iov Viktor Smakouz

T: B Kašira, vicar Moskva ▪ ✉ 10812-108 Street, CANADA-Edmonton, Alberta T5H ZA6 • [1] 780 426 51 63, fax 4209945, [1] 403 4265163 • bishjob@telus.net • www.orthodox-canada.com

*19.2.1964 Počajev Kremenets Ternopol, father priest. N10.9. 1982-1987 Seminary Leningrad. 1984-1986 Soviet Army. 1987-1991 Academy Sankt-Peterburg. Kandidat "History Church Preaching Ukraine 17th-18th century". diak26.8.1991 ⊖27.8.1991. 1991-1997 sekretar, inspektor, Prof Greek Language NT canon law Akademy Kiev. mon17.4.1997 archim13.6.1997 ⊕22.6.1997 Pečerska Lavra Kiev, B Cherson+ Tavričessk, 1999-2005 B Sumy+Ahtyrka. 2005 B Kašira vicar Moskva, Parishes Russian Orth Church Canada, 2009-2010 also USA.

Tihon Nikolaj Nedosekin

T: B Vidnoje, vicar eparhia Moskva ▪ ✉ Novodevičij projezd 1, ROSSIJA-119435 Moskva • [7] 499 2460881 • formil@mepar.ru

*14.2.1956 Jaroslavl. N9.10. 1972-1977 Technikum Moskva. 1977-1979 Soviet Army. 1979-1986 Seminary Academy Moskva. 1981-1987 hypodiakon M Juvenalij. 1987-1990 ekonom eparchy Moskva. 1988 Orden St. Vladimir (III) mon1.1.1990 Novodevičij Monastery. diak7.1.1990 ⊖21.1.1990 rector sobor Vidnoje. 1992 rector Mon. St. Katerina Vidnoje, blagočinnyj dean Vidnoje. 1997 blagočinnyj dean monastyrej oblast Moskva. archim25.6.1999 ⊕10.8.1999 B Vidnoje, vicar eparchy Moskva. 2006 Orden Sergij Radonež (II).

Roman Gennadij Gavrilov

T: B Serpuhov, vicar Moskva ▪ ✉ Novodevičij projezd 1, ROSSIJA-119435 Moskva • [7] 499 2460881

*3.2.1957 Kolčugino Vladimir. N11.8. 1975-1977 Soviet Army. mon4.12.1981 ⊖7.12.1981. 1983 Moscow Seminary. 7.4.1985 igumen. 1987-1991 blagočinnyj dean Moldavia. archim6.1.1988. Orden St. Vladimir, Sergij Radonež. 1991 blagočinnyj dean Dmitrov eparchy Moskva. 1997-2005 rector Cathedral Dmitrov. 2005-2011 igumen Vosnesenskaja Dav. Pustyn, pos. Novyj byt, Čechovskijr-n ⊕10.8.2006 Novodevičij Monastery B Serpuhov. 2011 igumen Vysotskij Monastery Serpuhov. 1.2.2012 pam. Panagia.

Sergij Nikolaj Čašin
T: B Solnečnogorsk, head administr. secretariat, patriarchal vicar ▪ ✉ Danilovskij Val 22, ROSSIJA-115191 Moskva • [7] 499 5780358
*19.6.1974 Komsomolskij Čamzin ASSR Mordova. N8.10. mon16.3.1993 Vladivostok "Sergij Radoneškij". diak7.4.1993 sekretar eparchy Vladivostok. 1995 prorector duhovn. učilišče Vladivostok ⊖17.2.1996. 2000 igumen. archim2005 ⊕15.2.2007 B Ussurijsk, vicar Vladivostok. 2009 B Solnečnogorsk, vicar Moskva.

Savva Aleksandr Micheev
T: B Voskresensk, vicar Moskva ▪ ✉ Krestjanskaja pl. 10, ROSSIJA-115172 Moskva • [7] 495 6769570 • inbox@spasnanovom.ru • m-novospassky@mtu-net.ru • www.spasnanovom.ru • www.novospaskiymon.ru
*10.5.1980. 1997 absolvent Gymnasium Kasimov Rjazan. 1997-2001 Seminary Moskva. 2001 teacher Liturgika Homiletika Rjazan. mon27.11.2001 diak2.12.2001 ⊖4.12.2001. 2003-2005 teacher dogmatics University Rjazan. 15.4.2005 na štat. 15.5.2005 blagočinnyj dean Jaroslavl. 2007 Kandidat Moskva. 2008 prorector Seminary Jaroslavl. 19.4.2009 igumen. 20.3.2011 namestnik Novospasskij Mon Moskva ⊕11.7.2011 Valaam (Patr Kirill) B Voskresensk, vicar Moskva vicariat South-East. 2015 president Commission Church Art, Restauration.

Nikolaj Svjatoslav Pogrebnjak
T: B Balašiha, vicar eparchy Moskva, chairman Departm. Editions ▪ ✉ Novodevičij projezd 1, ROSSIJA-119435 Moskva • [7] 495 637-2517
*15.5.1950 Moskva. N? 1967-1971 stud medicine Moskva. 1971-1973 Galerie Tretjakov. 1972-1978 dipl biblio-science. 1974-1981 Dom knigi Moskva. 1975 redaktor "Žurnal Mosk. Patr." (archim Innokentij Prosvirin) 1976-2009 married, daughter Sophia. 6.11.1979 baptized. 1981-1990 biblioteka Mosk. Patr. diak25.2. 1990 Ljubertsi ⊖27.8.1990 Ljubertsi. 1991-1993 teacher dogmatics, New Testament, byzantine Greek. "Moskovskije eparh. vedomosti". 1992 rector Balašihi. 1997 red. 1998 dipl Seminary Moskva (correspondence course). mon28.9.2011 Novodevičij Monastery. archim9.10.2011 ⊕1.1.2012 Moskva B Balašiha, vicar Moskva.

Konstantin Ilja Ostrovskij ***Zaraisk***
T: B Zaraisk, vicar eparchy Moskva ▪ ✉ Novodevičij projezd 1, ROSSIJA-119435 Moskva • [7] 495 637-2517
*3.8.1977 Moskva, father priest. N2.10. 1994 absolvent Church music school Krasnogorsk. 1995-2003 Seminary Academy Moskva, 1997-2002 hypodiakon to M Juvenaly. mon6.1.2001 diak15.2.2001 ⊖2.12.2002 prorector Seminary Kolomensk. 2009 regent priest-choir Moskva. 2012 Kandidat "Sekta Vissarion". archim29.7.2012 ⊕12.8.2012 B Zaraisk, vicar Moskva.

Ionafan Igor Tsvetkov ***Abakan***
T: A Abakan+Hakasija ■ ✉ ul. Katanova 5, ROSSIJA-655012 Abakan • [7] 3902 242847, 243710, fax 242915 • abakan-eparchy@mail.ru • www.abakan-eparchy.ru
*8.6.1962 Sovietskaja Gavan Khabarovsk. Nnedelja praotec. shipbuilder Khabarovsk, 1979-1982 Psalomščik. 1982-1986 Seminary Moskva. mon25.12.1985 Troice-Sergieva Lavra diak25.2.1986 Monastery St. Daniel Moskva, Academy ⊖20.3.1988. 1990 Kandidat Moskva. 1990-1993 rector St. Ksenia Južno-Sachalinsk, blagočinnyj dean Sachalinsk. 1994-1995 rector Južno-Kurilske, blagočinnyj dean Kurily. 1995-1997 archim rector Cathedral Južno-Sachalinsk ⊕1.8.1997 (Moskva, Patr Aleksij) B Južno-S+Kurily. 1999 B, 2010 A Abakan+Hakasija.

Matfei Konstantin Kopylov ***Anadyr***
T: B Anadyr+Čukotka ■ ✉ ul. Lenina 21, ROSSIJA-689000 Anadyr • [7] 42722 28822 • eparhia87@mail.ru • press@anadyr-eparhia.ru • www.anadyr-eparhia.ru
*5.7.1979 Perm. baptized in adolescence. 1994-1997 stud school Perm. 1997-2002 Chemical Engineering Perm State Technical University "Machines and devices of industrial production and construction materials". 2000 Michael the Archangel monastery Kozihi Novosibirsk. 2002-2007 stud Tomsk Theol Seminary (correspondence course). 2003 regent monastery choir. mon31.3.2006 (abbot Artemije Snigur) diak17.6.2007 (A Tikhon Novosibirsk) 2008-2011 dean podvorje ⊖5.4.2009. 2009-2015 Kandidat Moscow Academy (correspondence course) "The persecution of the church in the town of Kungur and Kungur Perm diocese deanery 1917-1941". 2010 professor church music Novosibirsk Seminary. 2011 eparchy Petropavlovsk secretary diocesan administration. 2012 head Department Architecture and Construction. Member Public Council Kamchatka region. archim25.12.2015 ⊕3.1.2016 Moskva Uspenskij Sabor B Anadyr (Patr Kirill).

Aleksandr Aleksandr Iščein ***Baku***
T: A Baku+Azerbeidzhan ■ ✉ ul. Krasnyj Vostok 126, AZERBEIDZHAN-1065 Baku • [994] 12 539729-1, -2, -4, 440-0442, fax -4352 • baku@eparhia.ru • orthodox@azdata.net • www.baku-eparhia.ru
*13.6.1952 Jaroslavl. N6.12. stud Leningrad Pharmaceutical Institute. 1973-1974 Soviet Army. mon1975 diak1975 ⊖1975. rector Dagestan Kabardino-Balkaria. Seminary Moskva (correspondence course). archim1988. 1995-1999 Baku blagočinnyj dean Azerbeidžan ⊕14.1.1999 B Baku+Prikaspia. 2011 B, 2012 A Baku+Azerbeidžan.

Jefrem Roman Prosjanok ***Birobidzhan***
T: B Birobidzhan+Kuldursk ▪ ✉ ul. Lenina 34, ROSSIJA-679016 Birobidžan • [7] 426222-07-92 • mnich-efrem@yandex.ru • eparhiya_b@mail.kht.ru • www.eparh.ru
*27.6.1977 Gukovo Rostov. N? 1994-1998 stud management Rostov. 1998-1999 vahter administrator Academy Moskva. 1999-2008 Seminary Academy Moskva. mon26.3.2004 diak2.5.2004 ⊖5.3.2006 klirik. 2009 prorector Seminary Khabarovsk. 2009 Easter igumen. archim30.10.2011 ⊕28.1.2012 Moskva B Bikinsk, vicar Khabarovsk (Patr Kirill). 2015 B Birobidzhan+Kuldursk.

Lukian Leonid Kutsenko ***Blagoveščensk***
T: B Blagoveščensk+Tynda ▪ ✉ ul. Kalinina 120, ROSSIJA-675000 Blagoveščensk • [7] 4162 77-11-26, 51-55-39, 424496, 535042, 515538 • goldcup@amur.ru • blaginfo@bk.ru • blag_kancel@mail.ru • www.blaginform.ru
*8.4.1965 Belka Odessa. N? 1978-1984 technik učilišče Odessa. 1984-1986 residencia metropolit Rostov-na-Donu. 1986-1990 Seminary Leningrad. mon26.4.1989 (M Aleksij). diak3.9.1989 (M Aleksij) ⊖24.5.1990 (M Aleksij) 1990-2009 nastojatjel Sankt-Peterburg. 8.4.1998 igumen. archim14.10.2004 namestnik Aleksandr Monastyr Sankt-Peterburg. 2004 Orden Ukrainskoj Prav. Cerkvi Nestor (III). 2005 serebr. medal Sankt-Peterburg. 2006 Orden Serafim Sarov (II), Orden Ukrainskoj Prav. Cerkvi knjaz Vladimir (I), 2008 Orden Družby. 26.7.2010 nominated B Lodejnoje polje, vicar Sankt-Peterburg ⊕16.10.2011 Christ the Saviour Church Moskva (Patr Kirill) B Blagoveščensk+Tynda.

Roman Aleksej Lukin ***Jakutsk***
T: B Jakutsk+Lensk ▪ ✉ ul. Kirova 8, ROSSIJA-677018 Jakutsk • [7] 4112 335152, fax 335258 • prav.yakutia@mail.ru • www.pravyakutia.ru
*11.10.1968. N? mon20.3.1992 Stavropol ⊖9.8.1992 Stavropol. 1993 absolvent Seminary Stavropol, 1999 absolvent Academy Moskva. 2005 rector Cathedral Stavropol, missions Respublika Čečnia, Ingušia. archim6.10.2008 (B Michajlov, vicar Stavropol). 2009-2011 repres. Russian Church in Tbilisi ⊕30.5.2011B Jakutsk+ Lensk.

Ioann Ivan Timofeev ***Joškar-Ola***
T: A Joškar-Ola+Marij El ▪ ✉ ul. Voznesenskaja 27, Respublika Marij El, ROSSIJA-424000 Joškar-Ola • [7] 362 429858, 429190, bookkeeper 428927 • mari@eparhia.ru • www.mari.eparhia.ru
*20.1.1958 Kazan. N21.5. 1973-1978 Monastyr Pečera Pskov. 1978-1981 Theol Seminary Moskva. 1981-1985 Kandidat Moskva. 1985-1987 Kazan. diak1987

mon1989 ⊖1990 archim11.6.1993 ⊕25.7.1993 Joškar-Ola. B, 2004 A Joškar-Ola+ Mari El. 2013 Orden St. Innokentij Moskva.

Tikhon Viktor Dorovskih ***Južnosakhalinsk***
T: A Južnosakhalinsk+Kurily ▪ ✉ ul. Lenina 158, ROSSIJA-693000 Južno-Sachalinsk • [7] 4242 422823, fax 423500 • eparhia_sakh@mail.ru • sakhalin@orthodoxy.ru • www.pravosakh.ru
*1959 Voronež worker's family. N26.8. 1978 absolvent montažnyj Technikum Voronež, 1983 absolvent Politechnikum (elektrik) Voronež. mon10.4.2003 diak13.4. 2003 ⊖20.4.2003 Južno-Sahalinsk. 7.7.2004 igumen. archim21.9.2010 ⊕23.1.2011 B, 2014 A Južnosahalinsk+Kurily.

N.N. ***Kaliningrad***
T: .... ▪ ✉ Tenistaja Alleja 39-6, ROSSIJA-236040 Kaliningrad • [7] 0112 274743, [7] 4012 • hram 274743 • secr 536880 • kdeparh@yandex.ru

Serafim Vladimir Melkonian
T: B Baltijsk, vicar Kaliningrad,▪ ✉ Tenistaja Alleja 39-6, ROSSIJA-236040 Kaliningrad • [7] 0112 274743, [7] 4012 • hram 274743 • secr 536880 • kdeparh@yandex.ru
*29.12.1961 Adler Krasnodar. N15.1. 1979-1980 worker construction. 1980-1982 Soviet Army. 1982-1984 diocesan administration Ufa (B Anatolij). 1984-1988 Seminary Odessa. 1988-1992 Academy Moskva. mon23.12.1990 diak19.1.1991 ⊖1.4.1991. 1992-1999 Mission Jerusalem. 1999-2001 Department External Relations Moskva ⊕19.5.2001 B Baltisk (Pillau). 2001-2009 vicar Smolensk in Kaliningrad, 2009 vicar Kaliningrad.

Ferapont Dmitrij Kašin ***Kostroma***
T: B Kostroma+Galič ▪ ✉ Simanovskogo 26/37, ROSSIJA-156000 Kostroma • [7] 4942 313681, 351496, fax 316473 • dom 548535, 548050 • is-ke@yandex.ru • kobishop@kmtn.ru • www.kostroma-eparhia.ru
*21.4.1969 Moskva. N25.12. 1986-1991 Institute of informatics. 19.11.1989 baptized. 1991-1993 military service. 1993-1995 psalomshchik Moskva. 1995-1999 monastery Pokrov Kostroma. mon25.12.1999 diak26.12.1999 (A Aleksandr Kostroma) ⊖7.4.2000. 2006 igumen. 2008 Kandidat Academy Moskva "The monasteries of Kostroma – points of education" archim25.3.2013 ⊕28.4.2013 Moskva (Patr Kirill) B Makarjev, vicar Kostroma. 2014 B Kostroma.

Feofan Aleksej Kim ***Kyzyl***
T: B Kyzyl+Tyva ▪ ✉ ul. Moskovskaja 7, ROSSIJA-667008 Kyzyl • [7] 39422 567-71, fax -44 • inkyzyl@gmail.com • www.pravtuva.ru

*19.1.1976 Južnosahalinsk. N? 1993-1997 stud commerce filial Južnosahalinsk University Moskva. 1.5.1995 baptized Južnosahalinsk. mon14.8.1997 diak17.8.1997 ⊖19.8.1997. 1998-2000 Seminary Smolensk. 2000-2010 klirik Abakan in the eparchy Korea of Konstantinopel. 6.6.2006 igumen. 2010 absolvent (correspondence course) Academy Moskva ⊕5.10.2011 B Kyzyl+Tyvinsk.

Ioann Akeksandr Pavlihin ***Magadan***

T: B Magadan+Sinegorje ▪ ✉ Gagarina 14, ROSSIJA-685024 Magadan • [7] 4132 622568 • sobor 629111, 631894 • eparhia.magadan@mail.ru • www.magadan-eparchy.ru

*30.8.1974 Moskva 1991-1998 Seminary Academy Moskva. Kandidat "Tradition of Church life in Russia". mon31.3.1995 Troice-Sergieva Lavra (A Filaret Dmitrov) diak18.4.1995 Troice-Sergieva Lavra (B Jevgenij Vereja). 1998-2001 regent Moskva ⊖31.3.2001 Rovno (A Varfolomej). 15.4.2001 igumen Rovno (A Varfolomej). archim11.5.2003 Rovno (A Varfolomej). 2004 klirik Kostroma ⊕12.10.2011 B Magadan+Sinegorsk. 2015-2016 member Holy Synod.

Varlaam Vladimir Ponomarjov ***Mahačkala***

T: B Mahačkala+Grozny ▪ ✉ ul. Ordžonokidze 148, ROSSIJA-367009 Mahačkala • [7] 722 693719, fax 691809 • diocese@goragospodnya.ru • www.goragospodnya.ru

*22.6.1974 Izobilnyj Stavropol, N6.11. 1989-1992 Politechnik Licej Stavropol. 1992-1998 Seminary Stavropol. diak15.9.1996 Stavropol (M Gedeon) ⊖27.9.1996 Stavropol (M Gedeon). 1999-2004 rector Sleptsov Ingušetija. 2004 rector Grozny blagočinnyj dean Ingušetija and Čečenija. 2005 igumen. 2008 absolvent Academy Kiev. 2011 rector Murom eparchy Vladimir. archim2.1.2013 Murom (Evlogij Vladimir) ⊕27.1.2013 Christ the Saviour Moskva (Patr Kirill) B Mahačkala+Grozny. 2015-2016 September-February member Holy Synod.

Tikhon Vladimir Lobkovskij ***Majkop***

T: B Majkop+Adygeja ▪ ✉ ul. Dalnjaja 1, Respublika Adygeja, ROSSIJA-385008 Majkop • [7] 772 555-782, fax -006, 53-7222, -8711, fax 576563 • ortodox3@radnet.ru • adygeya.eparhia@gmail.com • www.adygeya-orthodoxia.ru

*1.12.1968 stanitsa Brjuhovetskaja Krasnodar. N7.4. 1969 baptized. 1985 relegated from Fac of medicine because of worship. 1987-1989 Soviet Army. diak28.8.1989 Krasnodar. 1989-1997 Cathedral and parishes Krasnodar. mon19.12.1989 (A Isidor) ⊖4.6.1990. 1997-2001 Seminary Kiev (correspondence course). 1997-1998 eparchy Syktyvkar namestnik Uljanov Respublik Komi, prorector Theol school. 1998 rector.

2001 igumen. 2004 ključar Cathedral St. Jekaterina Jekaterinodar. archim30.12.2004 ⊕3.4.2005 B Jejsk vicar Jekaterinodar. 2009 B Majkop.

Artemij Aleksandr Snigur ***Petropavlovsk***
T: B Petropavlovsk+Kamčatka ▪ ✉ ul. Vladivostokskaja 18, ROSSIJA-683000 Petropavlovsk-Kamčatskij • [7] 4152 410-677, -597 • pke@list.ru • www.pravkamchatka.ru
*5.9.1962 Dnjeprodzeržinsk. N23.5./6.6. 1984 absolvent vojenno-transportnyj universitet Sankt-Peterburg. 1992-1995 construction church Alma Ata. diak17.12. 1995 Ivanovo ⊖11.2.1996 mon31.3.1996. 1996 Novonikolajevska Novosibirsk chairman architect department. 2000-2004 (correspondence course) Seminary, 2004-2008 (correspondence course) Academy Moskva. Orden Sergij Radonež. archim3.4. 2011 ⊕22.3.2011 B Petropavlovsk+Kamčatka.

Feofilakt Denis Kurjanov ***Pjatigorsk***
T: A Pjatigorsk+Čerkessk ▪ ✉ bulvar Garagina 2 B, ROSSIJA-357500 Pjatigorsk • [7] 793 389090, 31780-2, -3, -4, -5, 332533, fax 330488 • blagokavkaz@gmail.com • www.blago-kavkaz.ru
*27.8.1974 Grozny Čečnia Ingušia, N21.3. 1992-1996 Seminary Stavropol. mon5.4.1994 diak23.4.1994 ⊖5.6.1994. 1996 rector Ryzdvjanyj. 1998 blagočinnyj dean Blagodarnij. 2000-2004 stud psychology Stavropol. 1.4.2001 igumen. 2002 teacher liturgics Seminary Stavropol. 2003-2007 Academy Moskva ⊕24.9.2006. 2006-2008 B Magnitogorsk, vicar Čeljabinsk. 2008-2009 B Bronnitsy, vicar Moskva. 2009 B Smolensk. 2011 B, 2014 A Pjatigorsk.

Nikolaj Sergej Čašin ***Salekhard***
T: B Salekhard+Novyj Urengoj ▪ ✉ ul. Nogo 8, Jamalo Nenetskij avtonomnyj okrug, ROSSIJA-629007 Salekhard • [7] 34922 33582, 41299, 40430 • eparhi@yamalrpc.ru • missioner@yamalrpc.ru • www.yamalrpc.ru
*28.4.1972 Mordovia. N? 1990-1992 military service. mon6.10.1996 Boris Gleb Tutaev Jaroslavl. diak8.12.1996 ⊖15.12.1996. 1997-2010 namestnik Novonikolajevska Novosibirsk. 2000 igumen. 2000-2004 (correspondence course) Seminary, 2004-2008 Academy Moskva. 2010 blagočinnyj dean Vladivostok ⊕17.4.2011 B Zvenigorod vicar Moskva. 30.5.2011 B Salechard+Novyj Urengoj.

Pitirim Pavel Voločkov ***Syktyvkar***
T: A Syktyvkar+Komi-Zyryansk ▪ ✉ ul. Babuškina dom 20, ROSSIJA-167000 Syktyvkar • [7] 212 240407, 441232, 425497, fax 440880, 411302 syktyvkar-ep@mail.ru • kantsler1995@yandex.ru • www.syktyvkar.eparchia.ru

*2.2.1961 Krasnodar. N11.2. 1980-1982 Soviet Army. 1982 eparchy Astrahan. diak23.12.1982. 1982-1984 Aikino Respublika Komi. mon1984. 1984-1988 Seminary Moskva, diakon Syktyvkar ⊖1.5.1987 Arhangelsk. 1987-1988 rector Onega Arhangelsk. 1989 Pečora Komi. 1993 Academy Moskva. 7.4.1994 igumen monastery Troice-Stefanovo Uljanovsk Respublika Komi. archim6.10.1995 ⊕19.12.1995 B Syktyvkar+Vorkuta. 2001 Orden Družba Naroda. 2005 Kandidat Kiev. 2005 Gramota Respublika Komi. 2016 A Syktyvkar+Komi-Zyryansk.

Zosima Vladimir Ostapenko ***Vladikavkas***

T: A Vladikavkas+Alanija ▪ ✉ ul. Barbašova 38, Respublika Severn. Osetija, ROSSIJA-362020 Vladikavkas • [7] 672 253643, 553453, 25-36-43 • diocese@blagos.ru • www.blagos.ru

*12.7.1950 Novočerkasskoje Kazakhstan. N21.8. 1973 absolvent Seminary Moskva. 1976 absolvent Academy Moskva. diak13.12.1981 ⊖27.12.1981. 1985-1995 rector Elista. mon21.8.1987. 1987-1995 blagočinnyj dean Respublika Kalmykija. archim 7.10.1995 ⊕24.12.1995. 2006 A Elista+Kalmykija. 2011 A Vladikavkas+Mahačkala, 2013 Vladikavkas+Alanija.

Metropolia Altaj

Sergij Sergej Ivannikov ***Barnaul***

T: M Barnaul+Altaj, Metr. Altaj ▪ ✉ per. Jadrintseva 66, ROSSIJA-656008 Barnaul • [7] 3852 680381, 634717, 639897, 630588, 636329, fax 633540 • editor 636329 • priembiaeparh@mail.ru • alt.eparhia-press@ya.ru • eparhia@alt.ru • www.altai.eparhia.ru

*29.8.1957 Trotskoe Liven Orlov, baptized youngster. N? 1975-1977 Soviet Army. 1978 chauffeur. 1979-1986 Seminary Academy Moskva, Kandidat homiletika. mon28.2.1980 diak21.11.1985 ⊖23.2.1986. 1986-2003 Estonia, Pjühtitsa, Narva, Tallin, citizenship Estonia. 2003 Department External Church Affairs Moskva. 2004 igumen. 2004-2007 Russian Mission Jerusalem. 2007-2012 Prag. archim8.1.2008 ⊕18.3.2012 Moskva Christ the Saviour B Kamensk+Alapajev. 2013 B, 2015 M Barnaul.

Roman Andrej Kornjev ***Rubtsovsk***

T: B Rubtsovsk+Alejsk, Metr. Altaj ▪ ✉ per. Jadrintseva 66, ROSSIJA-656008 Barnaul • [7] 3852 680381, 634717, 639897, 630588, 636329, fax 633540 • editor 636329 • rubtsovsk-eparhia@mail.ru • http://rubtsovsk-eparhia.ru

*16.12.1972 Belovo Kemerovo. N14.10. school Mamontovo. 1990-1998 Politechnikum Altaj, ingenieur. 1991 baptized Cathedral Barnaul. 1992-1994 military

service. 1999-2002 Theol school Barnaul. mon13.10.1999 (B Antonij Masendić) diak14.10.1999 (B Antonij Masendić) ⊖17.10.1999. 2009 igumen namestnik Mon Kazan Barnaul. archim2012 dipl Seminary Barnaul ⊕29.9.2013 B Rubtsovsk, vicar Barnaul. 2015 B Rubtsovsk+Alejsk, Metr. Altaj.

Kallistrat Kallistrat Romanenko ***Gornoaltaj***

T: B Gornoaltaj+Čemali, Metr. Altaj ▪ ✉ prospekt Kommunisticheskij 146 Respublika Altaj, ROSSIJA-649002 Gorno-Altajsk • [7] 388-22 6-10-09 • alt.eparhia-press@ya.ru • eparhia@alt.ru • eparhia.gornyaltay@gmail.com • http://eparhia-gorniyaltay.ru

*8.8.1974 Technological College Moskva. 1991-1995 Seminary Moskva. 1995-1999 Academy Moskva. mon13.4.1995 Sergiev Posad, regent, ekskursovod. diak2.6.1996 Sergiev Posad (B Arsenij) ⊖17.3.2002 Danilov Monastery Moskva (Patr Kirill). 2002-2003 Solovetskij Mon. 2003-2007 nastojatjel Antarktide. 2007-2013 ieromonah Ust-Koksin Altaj ⊕10.11.2013 Patriarch Kirill, Vladyna Moskva, B Gornoaltaj+Čemali.

Serapion Igor Dunaj ***Bijsk***

T: B Bijsk+Belokuriha, Metr. Altaj ▪✉ ROSSIJA-649336 Bijsk

*2.10.1967 in Kišinjev Moldavia, N29.3. 1974-1984 school Gulboka Kišinjev. 1984-1986 Technikum Kišinjev. 1986-1988 Soviet Army. diak10.11.1988 Cathedral Kišinjev (M Serapion). 1989-1995 Seminary Moskva (correspondence course) ⊖15.2.1989 Cathedral Kišinjev (M Serapion). 1989 moved to eparchy Tula. mon15.5. 1989. 1989 igumen. archim21.11.1989. 1993 Orden St. Daniel Moskva, 1997 St. Vladimir, 2005 St. Sergij Radonež, 2010 St. Innokentij Moskva, 2013 Service Church Kazakhstan. 5.5.2015 Holy Synod created eparchy Bijsk ⊕28.6.2015 B Bijsk+Belokuriha, Metr. Altaj.

Vsevolod Vladimir Ponich ***Slavgorod***

T: B Slavgorod+Kamenski, Metr. Altaj ▪ ✉ ROSSIJA-658820 Slavgorod

*12.11.1961 Zolotoje Lugansk Ukraina N10.12. baptized youngster. 1979-1984 Seminary Leningrad. 1982-1984 Soviet Army. 1989 Rostov-na-Donu. diak22.1.1989 (M Vladimir) ⊖18.6.1989 (B Sergij Azov). 1995 teacher Theol school Rostov-na-Donu. 1997 protoierej. 1999 dipl Academy Sankt-Peterburg "The letter to the Romans 13,1-7". 2001 Orden St. Daniel Moskva, 2003 medal St. Peter 300 years Sankt-Peterburg. mon20.11.2003 Pečerska Lavra Kiev (A Pavle Vishgorod) – St. Vsevolod duke Novgorod. 2005 igumen, 2007 palitsa. archim20.5.2015 ⊕9.7.2015 Moskva (Patr Kirill).

Metropolia Arhangelsk

Daniil Aleksandr Dorovskih ***Arhangelsk***

T: M Arhangelsk+Holmogory, Metr. Arhangelsk ▪ ✉ Iljinskaja 5, Rossija-163002 Arhangelsk • [7] 182 680773, 681775, 643202 • kantsler Učitelskaja 73: 463486 • arh-eparhia@yandex.ru • press@arh-eparhia.ru • www.arh-eparhia.ru

*27.12.1960 Voronež. N12.9. 1978-1979 factory. 1979-1981 Soviet Army. 1981-1984 Seminary Odessa. 1984-1988 Academy Moskva. mon20.6.1985 diak3.7.1985 eparchy Vladimir ⊖28.8.1986. 1988 Kandidat Moskva. 26.3.1988 igumen. 1988 blagočinnyj dean Troice-Sergieva Lavra. archim29.12.1989 ⊕11.11.2001 B Južnosachalinsk+Kurily. 2010 B, 2012 M Arhangelsk+Holmogory, Metr. Arhangelsk.

Jakov Jevgenij Tislenko ***Narjan-Mar***

T: B Narjan-Mar+Mezen, Metr. Arhangelsk ▪ ✉ Ul. Lenina 7, Rossija-166000 Narjan-Mar • [7] 1853 41283 • orthodox-arctica@yandex.ru • www.orthodox-arctica.ru

*19.8.1960 Mineralnye Vody Stavropol. baptized youngster. N? 1965 Vladimir. 1977-1982 Lomonossov University Moskva, Fac Philology English. 1982-1984 Soviet Army. 1985-1988 Seminary Moskva, 1988-1992 Academy Moskva. mon1990 Sergiev Posad. 1990-1994 referent Patr Aleksij. 1994 teacher Seminary Moskva. 1996-2011 kinostudio Lavra, diak8.4.2001 ⊖5.10.2008. 2009-2011 redaktor "Makovets". archim6.1.2012 ⊕25.2.2012 B Narjan-Mar+Mezen, Metr. Arhangelsk.

Vasilij Nikolaj Danilov ***Kotlas***

T: B Kotlas+Velsk, Metr. Arhangelsk ▪ ✉ g. Korjazhma, Kedrovaja 1, Rossija-165300 Kotlas • [7] 818 5039114 • eparhia_kotlas@rambler.ru • www.kotlas-eparhia.ru

*23.9.1956 Gorodišče Brest Belorussia. N? 1977-1978 chauffeur. 1978-1984 Fac Economics University Gomel. 1984-1987 economist Taškent. 1987 Seminary Moskva. mon22.12.1989 diak14.8.1990 ⊖23.3.1991 klirik Nižnij Gorod ⊕18.11.2012 B Kotlas+Velsk, Metr. Arhangelsk.

Metropolia Astrahan

Iona Jurij Karpuhin ***Astrahan***

T: M Astrahan+Kamyzja, Metr. Astrahan ▪ ✉ Pokrovskaja Ploščad 6, Rossija-414056 Astrahan • [7] 51 2257060 dom, 2250980 secretary, fax 2289923 • ast_en_eparxija@mail.ru • www.astreparh.ru

*13.6.1941 Moskva. N28.7. 1959 Seminary Moskva. 21.12.1965 Sergiev Posad. diak6.2.1966. 1967 Kandidat Academy Moskva. 1967 Cerkovno-arheologičeskij

kabinet Seminary Moskva ⊖5.5.1968. 1970-1991 blagočinnyj dean Pokrovskij hram Akad. 1991 blagočinnyj dean Troitskij okrug Moskva ⊕25.10.1992 Astrahan B, 2002 A Astrahan+Jenotajevka. 2012 Orden St. Innokentij (II). 2013 M Astrahan+ Kamyzja, Metr. Astrahan.

Antonij Igor Azizov ***Ahtubinsk***

T: B Ahtubinsk+Jenotajevka, Metr. Astrahan ▪ ✉ ul. Frunze 27, ROSSIJA-416500 Ahtubinsk • [7] 5141 52178 • mail@ahtuba-eparhia.ru • www.ahtuba-eparhia.ru

*18.6.1979 Astrahan. N30.1. 1996-2000 electromechanic college. 2000-2004 Dr.ing Astrahan. 2004-2005 Theol school Volgograd. Seminary Moskva. mon15.8.2005 Astrahan diak27.9.2005 ⊖30.10.2005. 2005-2013 ekonom monastery St. John Astrahan. 2005-2012 University St. Tikhon Moskva (correspondence course). archim17.3.2013 ⊕7.5.2013 Novodevičij Mon. Moskva (Patr Kirill). 2013 B Ahtubinsk+Jenotajevka, Metr. Astrahan.

Metropolia Bashkortostan

Nikon Nikolaj Vasjukov ***Ufa***

T: M Ufa+Sterlitamak, Metr. Bashkortostan ▪ ✉ Sočinskaja 29, ROSSIJA-450103 Ufa • [7] 347 25618-43, secr -39, referent -42, fax -41, 2533100 • kancufa@mail.ru • bishop_nikon@bashnet.ru • www.eparhia-ufa.ru

*1.10.1950 Marjevka Sampur Tambov. N3rd Sunday after Pascha. 1974 absolvent Institute of Medicine Krasnojarsk, Therapeut. diak26.6.1983 (A Ioann Snyčóv Kujbyšev) ⊖21.9.1983 (A Ioann Snyčóv Kujbyšev). 1983-1990 parish Ikona "Neopalimaja Kupina" Uljanovsk, blagočinnyj dean Uljanovsk, mon15.3.1984 (A Ioann Snyčóv Kujbyšev), "Nikon" Radonež. 1986 absolvent Seminary Moskva. 1990 Kandidat Academy Leningrad ⊕26.8.1990 B, 2012 M Ufa+Sterlitamak, Metr. Bashkortostan.

Amvrosij Vitalij Munteanu ***Neftekamsk***

T: B Neftekamsk+Belebejev, Metr. Bashkortostan ▪ ✉ ul. Traktovaja 13A, ROSSIJA-452681 Neftekamsk • [7] 34783 91560, 22317 • kancneftekamsk@mail.ru • www.nefeparhia.ru

*25.10.1973 Taksoben Respublika Moldova. baptized youngster, N23.10. 1990 University and Seminary Kišinjev. mon8.4.1993 Chitsani. 1993-1995 kancelaria Benderu. klirik eparchy Ufa. diak2.5.1994 Benderu. 1994-1999 teacher Seminary Kišinjev. 16.1.1995 second orar ⊖28.11.1996. 1996-1999 Academy Moskva (correspondence course). 28.11.1997 igumen. 1998-2002 rector Edineț. 2000-2004 Academy Kiev (correspondence course). 2011 Doktorantura Fac History ⊕4.3.2012 B Neftekamsk+Belebejev, Metr. Bashkortostan.

Nikolaj Vasilij Subbotin ***Salavat***

T: B Salavat+Kumertau, Metr. Bashkortostan ▪ ✉ Ufimskaja 35, ROSSIJA-453261 Salavat • [7] 3476 35090-1, -2. -3, fax -4 [7] 917 4656915 • kancsalavat@mail.ru • www.eparhia-salavat.ru

*24.6.1973 Bugulme Tatarstan. N? diak1990 (!) Ufa. 1991-1994 Seminary Moskva, 1994-2004 protodiakon Ufa, 2001-2005 (correspondence course) Kandidat Academy Kiev ⊖7.1.2004 Ufa mon22.12.2006. 2006-2009 blagočinnyj dean Kiev. archim2009 Ufa ⊕27.9.2011 B Birsk, vicar Ufa. 15.3.2012 B Salavat+Kumertau, Metr. Bashkortostan.

Metropolia Belgorod

Ioann Sergej Popov ***Belgorod***

T: M Belgorod+Starij Oskol, Metr. Belgorod, chairman Missionary Department ▪ ✉ Svjato-Troitskij bulvar 24, ROSSIJA-308000 Belgorod • [7] 4722 33579-1, -0, fax 311732 • Missionerskij Dep. Mal. Kyselnij pereulok, dom 6, str.1, 103031 Moskva • [7] 495 928-3822, fax -4574 • beleparh@gmail.com • www.belmitropol.ru

*1.9.1960 Irkutsk. N23.6. Irkutsk Fac Historia, teacher. 1984 Psalomščik Irkutsk, Kursk. 1988-1992 Academy Leningrad Sankt-Peterburg. mon1.3.1990 diak3.4.1990 ⊖7.4.1990. 1.6.1990 rector Theol school, Theol Seminary Kursk ⊕4.4.1993 B Belgorod. vicar Kursk+Ryla. 1995 A. 1996 chairman Synodal Missionerskij Otdel. 14.10.2010 Moskva Theol Academy 325 years. 2012 M new eparchy Belgorod+ Starij Oskol, Metr. Belgorod.

Sofronij Vitalij Kitajev ***Gubkin***

T: B Gubin+Grajvoron, Metr. Belgorod ▪ ✉ ul. Skvortsova 13, ROSSIJA-309186 Gubkin • [7] 47241 76527, 76573 • gubeparh@gmail.com • www.gubeparh.ru

*29.11.1978 Verhnij Žirim Resp. Burjatija staroobrjadtsev. N? altarnik Ulan-Ude. 1996-2000 Seminary Belgorod. mon5.4.2001(A Ioannij) diak7.4.2001 ⊖12.4.2001 blagočinny ekonom Seminary Belgorod. 2002-2004 Academy Kiev (correspondence course), 2006 Kandidat "Old rite Zabajkal – ethnocultural potential for Sibiria". 2009 igumen. archim9.7.2012 ⊕22.7.2012 Tušino near Moskva, B Gubin+Grajvoron, Metr. Belgorod (Patr Kirill).

Savva Jevgenij Nikiforov ***Valujki***

T: B Valujki+Aleksejevka, Metr. Belgorod ▪ ROSSIJA-308000 Valujki • [7] 4722 33579-1, -0, fax 311732 • valeparh@gmail.com • http://valeparh.ru

*2.1.1974 Voronež, baptized in childhood. 1985-1993 artistic school Voronež. 1990-1993 restauration periods monastery Zadonsk. 1993-1995 military service. 1995-1999 writing icons monastery Zadonsk. mon1999 Zadonsk (B Nikon) diak2000 Zadonsk (B Nikon). 2000-2004 Seminary Voronež ⊖2001Zadonsk (B Nikon). 2009 igumen. 2010-2011 rector Cathedral Voronež, teacher icon writing class. 2011-2012 stud Fac Arts University Voronež. 2012-2014 MTh Academy Sankt-Peterburg. archim24.10.2015 Voronež (M Sergij) ⊕22.11.2015 Moskva B Valujki+Aleksejevka, Metr. Belgorod (Patr Kirill).

Metropolia Brjansk

Aleksandr Vasilij Agrikov ***Brjansk***

T: M Brjansk+Sevsk, Metr. Brjansk ▪ ✉ ul. Pokrovskaja Gora 5, ROSSIJA-241000 Brjansk • [7] 4832 746181 • kabinet 729918, 740097, fax 741407 • Klimenovsk [7] 495 5465922 • bryansk_orthodox@mail.ru • www.bryansk-eparhia.ru

*13.5.1953 Astrahan. N6.12. Medical College Moskva. diak2.6.1974 ⊖5.6.1974 Seminary Academy Moskva (correspondence course). 1974-1976 Soviet Army. 1977 rector Pushkino, 1978-1983 Losino-Petrovsk. mon6.12.1980. 1983-1986 Šubino, 1986-1991 Obraztsovo. 9.3.1987 igumen. 1991-2001 Mytiši, 1994 blagočinnyj dean. archim21.6.2001 ⊕5.8.2001 B Dmitrov, Vicar Moskva. 2011 B, 2013 M Brjansk+Sevsk, Metr. Brjansk.

Vladimir Vladimir Novikov ***Klintsy***

T: B Klintsy+Trubčevsk, Metr. Brjansk ▪ ✉ per. Bogunskogo polka 13a, 243140 Klintsy • [7] 4832 746181, fax 741407 • eparhia-klintsy@yandex.ru • http://eparhia-klintsy.ru

*2.4.1958 Moskva, father priest N7.2. 1978-1981 Seminary Moskva 1978-1985 hypodiakon M Pitirim, B Sergij, B Iov. 1981-1985 Kandidat Moskva. diak7.6.1985 Lefortova Moskva (B Iov) ⊖27.6.1985 Moskva (M Pitirim). 2013 Orden St. Vladimir, St. Serafim Sarov, St. Sergij Radonež, St. Daniel Moskovskij. 31.10.2013 Christ the Saviour Moskva Patr Gramota. mon21.6.2014 Moskva (B Feofilakt) archim16.7.2015 Danilov Monastir Moskva (M Varsonofij) ⊕1.9.2015 Monastir Moskva, B Klintsy, Metr. Brjansk (Patr Kirill).

Metropolia Burjatija

Savvatij Sergej Antonov ***Ulan-Ude***

T: M Ulan-Ude+Burjatija, Metr. Burjatija ▪ ✉ ul. Proizvodstvennaja 6, ROSSIJA-670031 Ulan-Ude • [7] 3012 455535, 212767, fax 212797 • uud-eparh@mail.ru • www.uud-eparh.ru

*1.9.1968 Čeboksary Respublika Čuvašia, N21.8. 1986-1989 Soviet Army. mon20.8.1989 Cheboksary (A Varnava) diak29.8.1989 Cheboksary (A Varnava) ⊖22.10.1989 Cheboksary (A Varnava) 30.6.1993 igumen. 1993 absolvent Seminary Academy Moskva. 1993 namestnik St. Troitskij Monastyr Čeboksary. archim1996 (Patr Aleksij II) ⊕30.1.2005 B Alatyr' vicar Čeboksary. 2009 B, 2015 M Ulan-Ude+ Burjatija, Metr. Burjatija.

Nikolaj Aleksij Krivenko ***Severobaikalsk***

T: B Severobaikalsk+Sosnovo-Oserskoje, Metr. Burjatija ▪ ROSSIJA-671701 Severobajkalsk • [7] 30130 24141 [7] 924 0159655, 9027645925 • sbk-eparh@mail.ru

*1.1.1971 Chernyshevsk Chitinsk. 1990-1995 stud Fac Mathematics State University Novosibirsk. 1998-2001 monasteries Mordovia and Burjatija. mon1.6.2001 diak2.6.2001 ⊖3.6.2001 (B Evstatij Chitin-Zabajkal). 2001-2009 abbot Kaban. 2009 dipl Theol Seminary Tomsk (correspondence course). 7.4.2010 igumen. 2014 dipl History State University Burjatija. 5.5.2015 eparchy Severobajkalsk created. archim16.5.2015 Monastery Burjatija (A Savvatij Ulan Ude) ⊕12.7.2015 B Severobaikalsk+Sosnovo-Oserskoje Metr. Burjatija.

Metropolia Cheljabinsk

Nikodim Jurij Čibisov ***Cheljabinsk***

T: M Cheljabinsk+Zlatoust, Metr. Cheljabinsk ▪ ✉ Kyshtymskaja ul. 34, ROSSIJA-454087 Čeljabinsk • [7] 351 727-11-07 • eparhiaya@info.ru • eparhia74@mail.ru • http://mitropolia74.ru

*30.12.1969 Pavlovskij Posad. N8.1. gymnasium Pavlovskij Posad. 1988-1990 Soviet Army. 1990 ponomar Pokrovsko-Vasilevskij monastyr. 1992 Seminary Moskva, teacher Seminary Saratov. mon24.12.1997 diak7.1.1998 Saratov ⊖18.1.1998 Saratov. 1999 rector Začatjev Monastery. 2000 Kandidat (correspondence course) Academy Moskva. archim9.3.2008 ⊕23.3.2008 B Šatura, vicar Moskva. 2009-2011 B Anadyr+ Čukotka. 2011-2014 B Jenisejsk+Norilsk, 2014 new name Jenisejsk+Lesosibirsk. 2014 M Metr. Cheljabinsk.

Grigorij Andrej Petrov ***Troitsk***

T: B Troitsk+Južnoural, Metr. Cheljabinsk ▪ ✉ ul. Krasnokvardejskaja 81, ROSSIJA-475100 Troitsk • [7] 35163 2-08-75 • troitsk-eparchy@mail.ru • http://troitsk-eparchy.ru

*26.12.1974 Ljubim Jaroslavl. Baptized youngster. N27.11. St. Gregor Palamas Thessaloniki. 1992-1997 stud Physics University Jaroslavl. 1997-2000 Seminary Moskva. 2000-2004 Kandidat Moskva "St. Paul's letter to Kolossae in the Russian biblical teaching". 2004 teacher Theol school Perm. diak11.7.2004 ⊖12.7.2004

mon3.5.2009 archim2011 Moskva ⊕26.12.2013 BTroitsk+Južnoural, Metr. Cheljabinsk.

Innokentij Ivan Vasetskij ***Magnitogorsk***
T: B Magnitogorsk+Verhneural, Metr. Cheljabinsk ▪ ✉ Voznesenskaja 33, ROSSIJA-455038 Magnitogorsk • [7] 3519 359292, 340518, 348942 +fax • magniteparh@yandex.ru • www.mgn-eparhia.cerkov.ru
*16.4.1977 Pjatigorsk Stavropol. N? 1994-1998 Seminary Stavropol. diak7.1.1998 mon25.1.1998. 1998-2010 teacher Seminary Stavropol ⊖7.4.2001. 2001-2005 (correspondence course) Academy Kiev. 2007 igumen Pasha. 2011 klirik Čeljabinsk. archim26.8.2012 ⊕11.10.2012 B Magnitogorsk+Verhneural, Metr. Cheljabinsk.

Metropolia Chuvashija

Varnava Vladimir Kedrov ***Čeboksary***
T: M Čeboksary+Čuvašija, Metr. Chuvashija ▪ ✉ ul. K. Ivanova 23, ROSSIJA-428018 Čeboksary • [7] 352 584068, 584140 • chuveparhia@cbx.ru • www.cheb-eparhia.ru
*21.4.1931 Vysokoje Rjazan. N24.6. 1953-1955 hypodiakon Cathedral Rjazan. mon10.12.1955 Sergiev Posad diak15.2.1956 1956 riznik Lavra ⊖9.3.1957. 1960 igumen. archim1965. 1971 Orden St. Vladimir, member National Council ⊕30.11. 1976 Lavra Zargorsk. B, 1984 A Čeboksary+Čuvašija. 1983 Athos, 1984 Bulgaria (Patr Pimen). 2001 M Čeboksary, Metr. Chuvashija. 2003 Orden Holy Sepulchre (Patriarchate Jerusalem), 2011Orden početa, početnyj graždanin Čeboksary.

Stefan Sergej Gordejev ***Kanaš***
T: B Kanaš+Jantikovsk, Metr. Chuvashija ▪ ✉ ul. Filatova 2, ROSSIJA-429335 Kanaš • [7] 3533 21644, 21642 • kanash-eparhia@mail.ru • www.kan-eparhia.ru
*5.7.1966 Čeboksary Respublika Čuvašia. N? 1984-1987 Soviet Army. 1987-1995 Seminary Academy Moskva. mon5.4.1996 diak10.4.1996 ⊖19.5.1996. 1996 prorector school Čeboksary. 2000 igumen ⊕5.10.2011 B Alatyr' vicar Čeboksary. 4.10.2012 B Kanaš+Jantikovsk, Metr. Chuvashija.

Fjodor Aleksandr Belkov ***Alatyr***
T: B Alatyr+Poretskoje, Metr. Chuvashija ▪ ✉ ul. Lenina 132, ROSSIJA-429820 Alatyr • [7] 3531 25306, 25320 • alat-eparhia@mail.ru • www.alat-eparhia.ru
*9.5.1960 Dresden Germany. N? 1977-1983 stud Soviet Army Medicine Fac Sankt-Peterburg, 1983-1998 Medical Service Army. 1998-2005 Nevropatologe Ahtubinska Astrahan. 2001-2005 Theol school Volgograd. Academy Moskva. diak19.9.2005

Astrahan ⊖10.12.2006 Astrahan. 2010 klirik Čeboksary (parent's illness). mon8.4. 2012 Čeboksary ⊕2.12.2012 B Alatyr+Poretskoje, Metr. Chuvashija.

Metropolia Don

Merkurij Igor Ivanov ***Rostov***

T: M Rostov+Novočerkassk, Metr. Don, Chairman Department Catechesis ▪ ✉ Stanislavskogo 58, Odesskaja 10, ROSSIJA-344002 Rostov-na-Donu • [7] 63 21017-01, -27, -47 • info.rostov@mail.ru • rostoveparhia@mail.ru • www.rostoveparhia.ru

*21.1.1964 Porhov Pskov, N? 1981-1982 medbrat Pskov. 1982-1989 dipl pediatr Leningrad. mon12.3.1988 diak15.1.1989 (A Smolensk Kirill) ⊖6.8.1989. 1989-1990 Sv. Nikolaj sobor Kaliningrad. 1990-1991 rector Jantarnyj, 1991-1993 Svetogorsk. 17.11.1992 igumen. 1992-1994 Seminary Akad Sankt-Peterburg (correspondence course). 1993-2000 Kaliningrad. archim9.1.2000 ⊕12.2.2000 B Zarajsk. vicar Moskva, 2000-2009 Administrator Patriarchal Parishes of the Russian Orthodox Church USA. 2009 Chairman Department Catechesis. 2011 M Rostov+Novočerkassk, Metr. Don.

Simon Aleksandr Morozov ***Shakhty***

T: B Shakhty+Millerovo, Metr. Don ▪ ✉ pl. Sobornaja 1, ul. Sovietskaja 74, 346500 Shahty • [7] 636 250985, 253682 • shahteparh@mail.com • www.shahteparh.ru

*13.10.1975 Engels Saratov. 1993-1994 Technological Institute Engels. baptized youngster. 1994-1996 podvorja Troice-Sergieva Lavra. 1996-1999 Seminary Saratov. mon22.5.1997 diak1.6.1997 Saratov (A Aleksandr Timofejev) ⊖8.10.1999 Saratov (A Aleksandr Timofejev). 2000-2004 Academy Moskva. 2004-2009 teacher Seminary Saratov Patrology, Modern Greek. 2009-2010 Aspirantura Moskva. 2010 parish Pozdnejev Millerovo Rostov. 2011 klirik Shakhty. archim31.5.2014 Cathedral Shahty (B Ignatij, Vologda) ⊕11.7.2014 B Monastery Valaam, B Shakhty-Millerovo, Metr. Don (Patr Kirill).

Kornilij Vladimir Sinjajev ***Volgodonsk***

T: B Volgodonsk+Salsk, Metr. Don ▪ ✉ ul. K. Marksa 1, ROSSIJA-347383 Volgodonsk • [7] 639 255252, fax 265160 • volgodonsk.eparhia@gmail.com • www.viseparchia.ru

*22.12.1976 Kyjbyšev Samara. N? mon3.7.1993 Pskov diak6.6.1994 Samara ⊖31.7. 1995 rector Orehovka. 1996-1998 Seminary Samara. 2000 igumen. 2003-2007 Jerusalem. 2007 Samara, absolvent Academy Kiev. archim4.4.2010 ⊕11.9.2011 B Volgodonsk+Salsk, Metr. Don.

Metropolia Irkutsk

Vadim Vladimir Lazebnyj ***Irkutsk***

T: M Irkutsk+Angara, Metr. Irkutsk ▪ ✉ ul. Angarskaja 14, ROSSIJA-664001 Irkutsk • [7] 3952 778126, fax 778341 • eparhia_irkutsk@mail.ru • www.iemp.ru

*14.10.1954 Gubkin Belgorod. N22.4. 1977 Seminary Odessa, Kandidat Moskva. diak1978. 1978-1981 Department External Relations Moskva. mon1979 ⊖1980. 1981 Kandidat Moskva. 1981-1984 Kursk, 1984-1985 Staryj Oskol, 1985-1988 Vladivostok, 1988-1990 Dekan Irkutsk ⊕4.2.1990 Moskva B Irkutsk+Čita. 1990-1991 Administrator Khabarovsk, Magadan+Kamčatka. 1994 new name Irkutsk+Angara. 2000 A, 2011 M, Metr. Irkutsk+Angara.

Maksimilian Maksim Kljujev ***Bratsk***

T: B Bratsk+Ust-Ilim, Metr. Irkutsk ▪ ✉ 27 Lesnoj Massiv, ROSSIJA-665727 Bratsk • [7] 3953 470094, 471064, fax 478993 • eparhia_bratsk@mail.ru • www.bratsk-pravoslavny.ru

*16.7.1971 Irkutsk. 1972 baptized, N17.8. 1986-1990 dipl aviatsonnyj Technikum. 1989-1994 married, one daughter. 1995 dipl kybernetik University Irkutsk, manager airport Irkutsk. 1998-2002 (correspondence course) Seminary Tobolsk, Seminary Leningrad. diak6.6.1998 mon18.12.2004 ⊖19.12.2004. 2006 sekretar eparchy Irkutsk. 2008 igumen. archim4.11.2011 ⊕18.12.2011 B Bratsk+Ust-Ilim, Metr. Irkutsk.

Aleksij Aleksandr Muljar ***Sajansk***

T: B Sajansk+Nižneudinsk, Metr. Irkutsk ▪ ✉ P.O.Box 352, ROSSIJA-666304 Sajansk • [7] 39553 51779 • [7] 952 618-30-20 • sayansk-eparchy@mail.ru • www.sayansk-eparchy.ru

*4.11.1967 Lutsk Volyn son of mitrofornij protoierej. N12.9. 1994-1998 Seminary Moskva. 1998-2002 Academy Kiev (correspondence course) dipl "Christian mission Europa Asia Africa I-III century". 2002-2004 hypodiakon Kiev. klirik Magadan. mon2.4.2005 Kostroma diak10.4.2005 ⊖12.4.2005. 2010 igumen. 2011 rector Magadan. archim6.10.2013 Magadan ⊕2.12.2013 B Sajansk+Nižneudinsk, Metr. Irkutsk.

Metropolia Ivanovo

Iosif Nikolaj Makedonov ***Ivanovo***

T: M Ivanovo-Voznesensk+Vičug, Metr. Ivanovo ▪ ✉ ul. Smirnova 76, ROSSIJA-153000 Ivanovo • [7] 4932 327477, 41494-8, fax -7 • diocese@mail.ru • iv-eparhiya@gmail.com • bishopjosef@mail.ryazan.ru • eparchia@hotmail.com • www.iv-eparhya.blogspot.com

*11.9.1964 Rjazan. N? 1979-1983 Elektronik Technikum Rjazan. 1983-1991 Commander school Soviet Army Rjazan. diak28.7.1991 Rjazan mon1.8.1991 Rjazan ⊖28.8.1991 Rjazan. 1992 blagočinnyj dean St. Ioan Bogoslov Rjazan. 23.2.1992 igumen. 1994 blagočinnyj dean Monasteries eparchy Rjazan. 1994 dipl Theol school Rjazan. 1994-1998 Seminary Moskva (correspondence course). archim18.8.1998 Rjazan ⊕8.9.1998 Sretenskij Monastery Moskva B Šatsk, vicar Rjazan. 2006 B, 2012 M Ivanovo+Vičug, Metr. Ivanovo.

Ilarion Jan Kajgorodtsev ***Kinešma***
T: B Kinešma+Paleh, Metr. Ivanovo ▪ ✉ Volžskij bulvar 4, ROSSIJA-155800 Kinešma • [7] 49331 55611, fax [7] 901 4824154 • kin.eparhiya@gmail.com • www.kp-eparhya.blogspot.com
*16.7.1971 Novosibirsk. N? school Kaluga, worker Moskva "Radonež", altarnik Ivanovo. diak9.4.1993 mon (A Amvrosij) ⊖27.6.1993 Ivanono (A Amvrosij). 2003 igumen. 2009 absolvent Seminary Ivanovo (correspondence course), 2011 absolvent Academy Kiev (correspondence course) ⊕8.7.2012 B Kinešma+Paleh, Metr. Ivanovo.

Nikon Nikolaj Fomin ***Šuja***
T: B Šuja+Tejkovo, Metr. Ivanovo ▪ ✉ ul. Štatnaja 19, Nikolo Monastyr Vvedenje, ROSSIJA-155921 Šuja • [7] 49351 24436, fax 36216 • shuyagrad-eparhia@yandex.ru • www.shuya-eparhia.ru
*7.1.1963 Mord-kanadej Nikolajevsk Uljanovsk. N? 1967-1979 Majerovsk Kujbyšev. 1979-1982 kolkhoz-technikum Bedno-Demjanov Penza. 1982-1984 Soviet Army. diak11.9.1985 mon20.10.1985. 1985-1990 Cathedral Ivanovo ⊖18.10.1990. 1990-2012 monastery with school and orphanage. archim26.2.1992. 1998 absolvent Seminary Samara. 1999 dipl "religion" University Šuja ⊕1.7.2012 B Šuja+Tejkovo, Metr. Ivanovo.

Metropolia Jaroslavl

Panteleimon Anatolij Dolganov ***Jaroslavl***
T: M Jaroslavl+Rostov, Metr. Jaroslavl ▪ ✉ Bogojavlenskaja ploshchad 14, ROSSIJA-150000 Jaroslavl • [7] 4852 7317-62, -58, -59, fax -61, 450295, [7] 905 6333991 • kancelyria@yareparhia.ru • alexvin@e-mail.ru • yareparhia@yandex.ru • www.yareparhia.ru
*12.9.1941 Rudnja Volgograd. N9.8. 1959-1961 Technikum. 1961-1964 Soviet Army. 1965-1973 Seminary Academy Moskva, Kandidat "Spiritual character St. Paul in ... St. John Chrysostom". mon26.12.1969 diak14.1.1970. 1971-1976 kellejnik to Patr Pimen ⊖2.4.1972. 1976-1986 Russ Orth Mission Jerusalem. archim22.6.1983 ⊕17.5. 1987 B Arhangelsk. 1995 B, 2008 A Rostov. 2011 M Jaroslavl+Rostov, Metr. Jaroslavl.

Veniamin Nikolaj Lichomanov ***Rybinsk***
T: B Rybinsk+Uglič, Metr. Jaroslavl ▪ ✉ ul. Krestovaja 7, ROSSIJA-152901 Rybinsk • [7] 4855 295434 • rybinskepar@mail.ru • www.rybeparhia.ru
*2.10.1952 Sokol Volograd. N5.10. 1969-1975 stud mechano-mathematics University Lomonossov Moskva. 1975-1976 engineer Alma Ata. 1976-1978 mineral Aleksandrov. 1978-2002 married, his wife Ioanna Lichomanova abbess Stavropol. diak8.10.1978 ⊖14.10.1978 blagočinnij Tutajev. 1984-1999 Seminary Academy Moskva. 1994-2006 commission catechesis Jaroslavl, redaktor gazeta. mon13.3. 2003. 2007 duhovnik Jaroslavl. archim ⊕22.8.2010 B Rybinsk, vicar Jaroslavl. 2012 B Rybinsk+Uglič, Metr. Jaroslavl.

Feodor Nikolaj Kazanov ***Pereslavl***
T: B Pereslavl+Uglič, Metr. Jaroslavl ▪ ✉ ROSSIJA-152020 Pereslavl-Saleski • [7] 48535 450295 • kancelyria@yareparhia.ru • yareparhia@yandex.ru • www.yareparhia.ru
*10.7.1973 Jaroslavl in a family of employees. Baptized in adolescence. 1988 Jaroslavl Railway College in the specialization "Automation – Remote Control". 1992 Jaroslavl Politechnik Institute. 1997 dipl Jaroslavl State Technical University on specialty "Automobiles and automobile economy." 1998-2000 stud Theol school Jaroslavl. mon30.6.2000 diak2.7.2000 (A of Jaroslavl Micah) ⊖16.7.2000 parishes and monasteries. 2006-2010 (correspondence course) of Moscow Theol Seminary. 2007 abbot. 23.10.2007 chairman Department cooperation with medical institutions, 29.4.2009 Dean Nekrasovsky district. 2010 chairman Department charity, social service and interaction with medical institutions. Abbot St. Cyril and Athanasij Monastery. 2014 Moscow Theological Academy (correspondence course).Fac theol Jaroslavl State Pedagogical University (correspondence course). archim25.12.2015 ⊕27.12.2015 Church of the Holy Virgin Jasenevo B Pereslavl+Uglič (Patr Kirill).

Metropolia Jekaterinburg

Kirill Mihail Nakonečnyj ***Jekaterinburg***
T: M Jekaterinburg+Verchoturje, Metr. Jekaterinburg ▪ ✉ ul. Repina 6-a, ROSSIJA-620086 Jekaterinburg • [7] 343 2281525, 2335960, fax 2424662 • ekb_eparhia@bk.ru • baibakov@etel.ru • www.ekaterinburg-eparhia.ru
*15.5.1961 Verhnečusovsk Gorodki Perm, N22.6. 1978-1986 Seminary Moskva (correspondence course). mon25.10.1980 Vladimir diak26.10.1980 Vladimir. 1980-1981 diakon Cathedral Vladimir ⊖6.5.1981 Vladimir. 1981-1982 klirik Aleksandrov. 1982-1984 blagočinnyj dean Kiržač. archim7.4.1984. 1984-1987 blagočinnyj dean Vladimir. 1987-1989 blagočinnyj dean Chişinău. 1989-1995 blagočinnyj dean Tula ⊕15.3.1998 Epiphania Cathedral Moskva B Bogoroditsk vicar Tula. 2000 B Tula+ Belev. 2002 B, 2003 A Jaroslavl. 2011 A, 2011 M Jekaterinburg.

Innokentij Jakov Jakovljev *Nižnij Tagil*
T: B Nižnij Tagil+Serov, Metr. Jekaterinburg ▪ ✉ ul. Pervomajskaja 15, ROSSIJA-622001 Nižnij Tagil • [7] 3435 423269, 42313-2, -0, [7] 982 639 3065 • eparhiyant@gmail.com • www.tagileparhiya.ru
*30.4.1947 Južno-Sahalinsk. N? 1953 baptized Moskva. 1965-1970 stud Arhitektur Novonikolajevska Novosibirsk, ikonopisec. 1970-1992 married. diak28.3.1992 ⊖19.4.1992 Vladimir. mon13.4.1997. 12.4.1998 igumen. 1998 absolvent Seminary Vladimir. archim19.3.2007 ⊕19.8.2011 B Nižnij Tagil+Serov, Metr. Jekaterinburg.

Mefodij Mihail Kondratjev *Kamensk*
T: B Kamensk+Alapajevsk, Metr. Jekaterinburg ▪ ✉ ul. Revoljutsionnaja 45, ROSSIJA-623409 Kamensk Uralskij • [7] 3439 324298, 323737 • admin@kamensk-eparhiya.ru • kancelyria@kamensk-eparhiya • info@kamensk-eparhiya.ru • www.kamensk-eparhiya.ru
*10.11.1857 Ufa, baptized youngster, N17.6. 1975-1982 stud molecular physics Moskva. 1982-1984 teacher physics Ufa. mon6.12.1984 Ivanovo (B Amvrosij) diak11.8.1985 Ivanovo ⊖19.8.1985 Ivanovo. 1992 igumen Pascha. 1999-2004 Seminary Moskva (correspondence course). 2005 medal "Za sodejstvije Gosnarko-kontrolju Rossii". 2008-2012 court eparchy. archim5.1.2014⊕25.1.2014 St. Tatiana Church Moskva B Kamensk+Alapajevsk, Metr. Jekaterinburg (Patr Kirill).

Metropolia Kaluga

Kliment German Kapálin *Kaluga*
T: M Kaluga+Borovsk, Metr. Kaluga, Chairman Department Publications ▪ ✉ Naberežnaja 4, ROSSIJA-248000 Kaluga • [7] 4842 577271, 576500, fax 562700, p 744700 • eparhia@eparhia-kaluga.ru • www.eparhia-kaluga.ru
*7.8.1949 Ramenskoje Moskva worker's family. N8.12. 1967 mašinostroitelnyj technikum Moskva. 1970 Seminary Moskva. 1970-1972 Soviet Army. 1974-1978 Kandidat Moskva. 1977 Syndesmos. mon7.12.1978 diak24.12.1978 ⊖7.4.1979. 1979 teacher Seminary. archim13.7.1982 ⊕8.8.1982 B, 1989 A Serpuhov, vicar Moskva. 1983-1990 New York. 1990 A Kaluga. 1990-2004 First Deputy Chairman Department External Church Relations. 2004 M Kaluga. 2004-2009 Chancellor Moscow Patriarchy. 2009 Chairman Department Publications. 14.10.2010 Moskva Theol Academy 325 years.

Serafim Vladimir Savostjanov
T: B Tarusa, vicar Kaluga, Metr. Kaluga ▪ ✉ Naberežnaja 44, ROSSIJA-248000 Kaluga • [7] 4842 577271, 576500, fax 562700, p 744700 • www.eparhia-kaluga.ru

*15.12.1971 Serove Sverdlovsk, N15.1. 1985 altarnik. 1990-1994 Seminary Moskva. mon3.1.1992 diak2.2.1992 ⊖23.8.1992. 1994 klirik. igumen1998 archim2009. 2011-2015 Academy Kiev Kaluga ⊕4.12.2015 Presentation of Mary Sabor Kreml B Tarusa vicar Kaluga (Patr Kirill).

Maksimilian Aleksandr Lazarenko ***Pesochensk***

T: A Pesochensk+Juhnovsk, Metr. Kaluga ▪ ROSSIJA-610000 Kirov

*9.11.1950 Frunze in the family of an architect, N4.11. 1966-1970 Technikum Kaliningrad Moskva. Konstruktbureau Kaliningrad Moskva. 1970-1972 Soviet Army. 1972-1979 Central Institute of Physical Culture, teacher Forestry Institute. 1978-1982 Seminary Moskva, 1982-1986 Academy Moskva. mon26.10.1984 Troice-Sergieva Lavra. diak2.2.1985 Vladimir (M Serapion) ⊖10.2.1985 Vladimir (M Serapion) archim7.4.1993 Moskva (Patr Aleksij) ⊕10.4.1993 Moskva B, 2004 A Vologda+Velikij Ustjug (Patr Aleksij) 2005 Orden Serafim Sarov. 2014 A Pesochensk +Juhnovsk, Metr. Kaluga.

Nikita Oleg Ananiev ***Kozelsk***

T: B Kozelsk+Ljudinovo, Metr. Kaluga ▪ ✉ Tulskaja 44, ROSSIJA-249722 Kozelsk • [7] 48442 24430 • [7] 800 250 9626 • cantseliaria.eparhia@yandex.ru • www.kozelsk-eparhia.ru

*14.11.1969 Dedtsevo Kaluga. N16.4. 1985-1989 stud agronom Technikum. 1989-1996 Seminary Academy Moskva. mon9.4.1992 diak20.5.1992 ⊖19.8.1992. 1996 inspektor Kaluga. 18.1.1998 igumen. 2000 Orden Sergij Radonež, 2002 Orden St. Innokentij. 2002-2005 blagočinnyj dean. archim2004 ⊕27.5.2012 Moskva B Ljudinovo, vicar Kaluga. 2013 B Kozelsk+Ljudinovo, Metr. Kaluga.

Metropolia Karelia

Konstantin Oleg Gorjanov ***Petrozavodsk***

T: M Petrozavodsk+Karelia, Metr. Karelia ▪ ✉ ul. Pravdy 5, Respublika Karelia, ROSSIJA-185005 Petrozavodsk • [7] 8142 77-27-00, fax 773301 • eparhia@karelia.ru • http://eparhia.karelia.ru

*23.3.1951 Kenessy Sverdlovsk Djambul Kazahstan, N3.6. 1968-1974 Medical Institute Vinnitsa. 1981 Kandidat Medical Institute Smolensk Dr. med. 1983-1985 Seminary Moskva. 1985-1989 Academy Moskva. mon14.4.1986 diak4.5.1986 ⊖12.6.1986. 1989 teacher Moskva. 1990 Kandidat Moskva. 2.3.1990 igumen. 1990-1996 rector Seminary Minsk, archim2.9.1991. 1991 Bethel ⊕16.6.1991 B Novogrudok, vicar Minsk. 1992-1996 B Novogrudok+Lida. 1995 USA. 1996 B, 2003 A Tihvin. 1996-2008 Rector Academy Sankt-Peterburg. 2008 A Kurgan. 2014 head Commission Liturgy Holy Synod. 2015 M Petrozavodsk+Karelia.

Ignatij Aleksij Tarasov ***Kostomukša***

T: B Kostomukša+Kem, Metr. Karelia ▪ ✉ ul. Sovjetskaja 20, ROSSIJA-186931 Kostomukša • [7] 921 4657191, fax [7] 814 5952944 • costa.eparhia@gmail.com • www.costa.cerkov.ru

*26.3.1976 Satka Čeljabinsk, N? 1993-1997 Seminary Tobolsk. 1997-2000 Academy Sankt-Peterburg. mon24.12.1999 diak2.1.2000 ⊖23.4.2000. 2001 Kandidat "Učenije o vere v Boga ... prof. Vvedenskij". 2001-2003 teacher Church History Seminary Sankt-Peterburg. 2003-2006 stud theol Helsinki, scholarship Lutheran Church Finland. 2006 teacher. 2008 igumen Pascha. 2011 prorector Seminary Tobolsk. 2011 eparchy Krasnoslobodsk. archim9.6.2013 Krasnoslobodsk ⊕11.7.2013 Danilov Monastir Moskva B Kostomukša+Kem, Metr. Karelia.

Metropolia Khanty-Mansijsk

Pavel Paulin Fokin ***Khanty-Mansijsk***

T: M Khanty-Mansijsk+Surgut, Metr. Khanty-Mansijsk ▪ ✉ ul. Čekova 2, ROSSIJA-628012 Khanty-Mansijsk • [7] 3467 31837-5, fax -6 • ugra.eparhia@gmail.com • www.ugraeparhia.ru

*9.1.1956 Kučerovka Gluchov Sumy Ukraina, Semenović. N? 1974-1976 Soviet Army. 1976-1985 director children choir Sumy, 1985-1989 Leningrad. 1989-1996 Seminary Academy Leningrad, Kandidat "Order of Malta". diak21.9.1996 (A Aleksandr, Kostroma) ⊖27.9.1996 mon8.10.1996. 1996-2002 namestnik Mon Ipatija Kostrom, teacher Seminary, blagočinnyj dean. 17.10.1997 igumen. archim21.5.1998. 2002-2003 Russian Mission Jerusalem. 2003-2007 nastojatjel San Francisco, 2007-2011 Roma Italia ⊕12.6.2011 Sergiev Posad B, 2015 M Khanty-Mansijsk+Surgut (Patr Kirill).

Fotij Ivan Evtiheev ***Jugorsk***

T: B Jugorsk+Njagansk, Metr. Khanty-Mansijsk ▪ ✉ ul- 40 Letpobedy 19, ROSSIJA-628264 Jugorsk • [7] 34675 72832, 24033 • [7] 982 2189299 • yugorskeparhia@mail.ru • http://yugorsk-eparhia.ru

*31.5.1962 Kirovsk, region Alma Ata. 1965 parents and 9 children moved to Irkutsk 1969-1977 school at Irkutsk. 1980-1982 Soviet Army. 1984-1992 Kandidat Moscow Seminary and Academy. mon21.8.1990 diak28.8.1990 Pokrovskij church Academy Moskva (A Aleksandr, Dmitrov) ⊖9.9.1993. 1993 teacher Seminary Tobolsk, inspektor. 20.4.1994 igumen. 1997-2002 blagochinnyj eparchy of Tobolsk-Tjumen'. 2008 moved to Irkutsk. archim5.4.2011. 7.6.2014 dipl Russian Language and Literature University Nizhnevartov (correspondence course). 18.1.2015 Rite of Nomination in home church of patriarcal residence ⊕15.2.2015Sretenje Monastery Moskva B Jugorsk+Njagansk, Metr. Khanty-Mansijsk (Patr Kirill).

Metropolia Krasnojarsk

Panteleimon Nikolaj Kutovoj ***Krasnojarsk***
T: M Krasnojarsk+Ačinsk, Metr. Krasnojarsk ▪ ✉ P.O.Box 25410, pr. 43, ROSSIJA-660021 Krasnojarsk • [7] 3912 277402, 274615, fax 277991 • kerpc@bk.ru mira43@mail.ru • www.kerpc.ru
*15.12.1955 Mogilev, N9.8. 1970-1975 Agriculture Technikum Kustanai Kazakhstan. 1975-1976 Zootechnik Krasnodar. 1976-1981 stud (correspondence course) Agriculture Institute Kuban. 1981-1985 Theol Seminary Leningrad. diak4.1985 Smolensk ⊖1985. 1985-1986 rector Cathedral Smolensk. 1986 blagočinnyj dean Vjazma. mon4.1986. 1987-1989 Academy Moskva. 1988 igumen. 1989-1991 Vjazma. 1991-1993 rector Cathedral Kaliningrad ⊕2.5.1993 Smolensk. 2000 B Baltijsk (= Pelau, Ostpreußen), vicar Smolensk+Kaliningrad. 2001-2009 A Majkop. 2009-2011 A Orël. 2011 M Krasnojarsk+Ačinsk, Metr. Krasnojarsk.

Nikanor Nikolaj Anfilatov ***Jenisejsk***
T: B Jenisejsk+Lesosibirsk, Metr. Krasnojarsk ▪
✉ ul. Rabotshe-Krestjanskaja 101, ROSSIJA-663180 Jenisejsk •
[7] 391 2141126 • www.eniseyep.ru
*23.2.1970 in Belovo, region of Kemerovo. 1977-1987 school Belovo. 1987 Agriculturale Institute Novosibirsk. 1988-1989 military service. diak7.4.1992. 1992 Izhevsk. mon5.12.1993 ⊖7.12.1993. 1995 Juzhno-Sahalinsk. 2001 eparchy Krasnojarsk. 2003-2008 Moscow Seminary (correspondence course). 2008-2012 Kiev Theol Academy (correspondence course). 2008 Namestnik Spaso-Preobrazhenskij monastery Jenisejsk. archim5.6.2014 ⊕22.6.2014 B Jenisejsk+ Lesosibirsk, Metr. Krasnojarsk.

Filaret Valerij Gusev ***Kansk***
T: B Kansk+Bogučany. Metr. Krasnojarsk ▪ ✉ ul. Moskovskaja 68, ROSSIJA-663600 Kansk • kanskaya.eparhiya@gmail.com •
www.kanskaya-eparhiya.ru
*14.8.1975 Lubenkov Kalinin. N? 1987 (!) ponomar Troitsa Udomli. 1992-1995 Seminary Moskva. 1995 teacher gymnasium Udomli. 1996-1999 MHist University Tver. diak15.4.2002 Tver (A Viktor, Udomli) ⊖1.8.2002 mon7.12.2003. 2005-2008 (correspondence course) Academy Sankt-Peterburg. 2008 president Commission Catechesis Tver. 2009 igumen Pascha. 28.12.2011 elected B Bežetsk+ Vesjegonsk. archim1.1.2012 ⊕24.3.2012 B Kansk+Bogučany, Metr. Krasnojarsk.

Agafangel Andrej Dajneko ***Norilsk***

T: B Norilsk+Tuhuransk, Metr. Krasnojarsk ▪ ✉ ul. Pushkina 11, ROSSIJA-663305 Norilsk • [7] 3919 423269 • norilskeparhia@mail.ru

*30.9.1975 Norilsk. 1992 psalmsinger Norilsk. mon16.7.1995 diak30.7.1995 Norilsk (B Antonij, Krasnojarsk) ⊖18.1.1996. 1997-2014 abbot monastery Turuhansk. 30.5.1999 igumen. 2004-2010 (correspondence course) Academy Moskva and St. Tikhon University Moskva. archim5.6.2014 ⊕6.7.2014 Novodevičij Monastery Moskva, B Norilsk+Turuhansk, Metr. Krasnojarsk, (Patr Kirill).

Metropolia Kuban

Isidor Nikolaj Kiričenko ***Jekaterinodar***

T: M Jekaterinodar+Kuban, Metr. Kuban ▪ ✉ ul. Sobornaja (Lenina) 60, ROSSIJA-350000 Krasnodar • [7] 861 2622081, fax 2620948 • eparchy@mail.kuban.ru • eparhkuban@yandex.ru • www.pravkuban.ru

*25.5.1941 Vejmarn Kingisepp Leningrad, N21.1. mon5.1.1967, 4th year Academy Leningrad (M Nikodim Rotov). diak5.2.1967 Aleksandr Nevskij Leningrad Krasnoje Selo (M Nikodim) ⊖7.4.1967 (M Nikodim). 1973 igumen Pascha. 1975 Prof Liturgics Theol Academy Leningrad. archim12.6.1977. 18.6.1977 narechenje (M Nikodim, M Juvenalij, A Melkisedek, Penza; B Irinej, Serpuhov; B Antonij, Baku; B Kirill, Vyborg; B Valentin, Ufa; B Meliton, Tihvin) ⊕19.6.1977 B Arhangelsk+ Holmogorsk. 1985 B, 1987 A Arhangelsk+Murmansk. 1987-2011 rector Seminary. 2001 M Krasnodar+Kuban. 2008 Head Ecclesiastical court. 2003 Orden M Innokentij, 2012 Orden Sergij Radonež (I). 2013 M Kuban, Metr. Kuban.

German Aleksij Kamalov ***Jejsk***

T: B Jejsk+Timašev, Metr. Kuban ▪ ✉ ul. Sobornaja 60, ROSSIJA-350000 Krasnodar • [7] 861 2622081, fax 2620948

*22.3.1968 "Ališer Muzaffarovič" Samarkand Uzbekistan. N11.7. 1979 Krasnodar. 1986-1988 Soviet Army. 1988-1991 Seminary Leningrad, 1991-1997 Academy Leningrad. Kandidat Kiev "Soteriologičeskoe svidetelstvo Russk. Prav. Cerkvi" mon10.7.1991 diak12.7.1991 ⊖19.8.1991. 1991-2008 rector Seminary Krasnodar. 2006-2008 teacher liturgics Jekaterinodar. 2008 Roma Italia ⊕22.3.2011 B Jejsk vicar Jekaterinodar. 2013 B Jejsk+Timašev, Metr. Kuban.

Feognost Mihail Dmitriev ***Novorossijsk***

T: B Novorossijsk+Gelendžik, Metr. Kuban ▪ ✉ Divnomorskoje, ul. Kirova 13, ROSSIJA-353490 Gelendžik • [7] 8617 611237 • eparhia2013@yandex.ru • www.eparh.info

*9.11.1965 Karaganda Kazakhstan. N? 1984-1986 Soviet Army. 1986-1990 Seminary Moskva. mon3.7.1988 diak18.7.1988. 1990-1994 Kandidat Academy Moskva ⊖1995

(Patr Aleksij). 1995-1997 organization podvorie Gelendžik. 1997 rector podvorie Gelendžik. 2005 igumen. 2012 krest s ukrašijami ⊕14.4.2013 B Novorossijsk +Gelendžik, Metr. Kuban.

Stefan Andrej Kavtarashvili ***Tikhoretsk***
T: B Tikhoretsk+Korenovsk, Metr. Kuban ▪✉ ROSSIJA-Tikhoretsk • [7] 918 394 03 98 • info@tiheparh.ru
*16.5.1971 village Urazovskij, district Valujskij, region Belgorod. 1989-1991 military service. 1991-1994 stud Stavropol Seminary. mon22.4.1994 diak26.4.1994. 1996 pomoshnik inspektora and teacher of liturgics Stavropol Seminary. 1997 archdeacon. 2001 moved to Ekaterinodar eparchy ⊖25.12.2001. 2004 Kiev Theol Academy. archim31.12.2013. 24.1.2014 rite of nomination of archimandrite Stefan (Kavtarashvili) as Bishop at Patriarcal residence in Danilov Monastery Moscow ⊕25.2.2014 B Tikhoretsk+Korenovsk, Metr. Kuban.

Ignatij Konstantin Buzin ***Armavir***
T: B Armavir+Labinsk, Metr. Kuban ▪ ✉ Cathedral ul. Komsomolskaja 121a, ROSSIJA-352947 Armavir • [7] 86137 33498 • www.armeparh.ru
*21.6.1973 Krivoj Rog, region Dnepropetrovsk, Ukraina N23.5. 1980-1988 school in Gelendzhik. 1988-1991 Institute of medicine, Novorossijsk. 1991-1995 Sankt-Peterburg Seminary. mon22.1.1994 diak3.2.1994 ⊖7.4.1994. 1995 blagochinnyj Holy Trinity monastery Primore Sankt-Peterburg. 2002 monk Aleksandr Nevskij Lavra, Sankt-Peterburg. 2005-2008 Sankt-Peterburg Theol Academy. 21.10.2008 superior (nastojatjel) Antonievo-Dymskij monastery. archim21.3.2014 ⊕13.4.2014 B Armavir +Labinsk, Metr. Kuban.

Metropolia Kurgan

Iosif Igor Balabanov ***Kurgan***
T: M Kurgan+Belozersk, Metr. Kurgan ▪ ✉ ul. Volodarskogo 42, ROSSIJA-640000 Kurgan • [7] 3522 42-18-18 kurgan-eparhia@mail.ru • www.kurgan.orthodoxy.ru
*31.1.1954 Kašira Moskva. NPonedjelnik Strastnoj sedmicy. Spiritual guidance: Angelina Travinoj, 1973-1974 Soviet Army. 1975-1978 Seminary Moskva. 1978-1980 Academy Moskva. mon5.3.1979 Novodevičij Monastery Moskva. diak9.3. 1979 Novodevičij Monastery Moskva. 1979 štatnij diakon Novodev. Mon. 1980 patriarchal gramota ⊖23.4.1981 Great Wednesday Novodev. Mon. 1982 Serpuhovskij. 1983 blagočinnyj dean Serpuhovskij. archim7.11.1987. 1990-1993 deputat gorodskij Soviet Serpuhovskij namestnik Vysotskij Serpuhovskij Monastery ⊕31.1.1999. 1999-2002 B Uglič vicar Jaroslavl. 2000 igumen Kostroma. 2002 B, 2013 A Birobidžan. 2015 M Kurgan+Belozersk, Metr. Kurgan.

Vladimir Vasilij Mashtanov ***Shadrinsk***

T: B Shadrinsk+Dalmatovo, Metr. Kurgan ■ ✉ ul. Pionerskaja 42, ROSSIJA-641870 Shadrinsk • shadreparh@mail.ru • www.shadreparh.cerkov.ru

*17.1.1965 in Gaj Orenburg. 1974-1982 school Novocherkassy. 1982-1985 Politechnikum Novocherkassy. 1983-1985 Soviet Army. 1990-1994 Seminary Moskva (correspondence course). diak28.11.1991 Lugansk (B Ioannikij Kobzev) ⊖1.12.1991 Lugansk (B Ioannikij Kobzev). 1991-1993 parish priest Antratsit.1993-2009 parish priest Tatsinsk Rostov. 1998 protoierej. 2007-2011 (correspondence course) Academy Kiev. 2009-2015 dean blagochinnij eparchy Volgodonsk. mon9.5.2015 Volgodonsk Rostov. archim10.5.2015 Morosov Rostov (B Kornilij). 17.6.2015 narechen Danilov Monastery Moskva ⊕11.7.2015 Monastery Varlaam B Shadrinsk (Patr Kirill), Metr. Kurgan.

Metropolia Kursk

German Lev Moralin ***Kursk***

T: M Kursk+Rylsk, Metr. Kursk ■ ✉ ul. Lenina 55, ROSSIJA-305000 Kursk • [7] 4712 512160, 7017-22, -23, fax -19 • ke701719@mail.ru • mitropolit@eparchia.kursk.ru • arhiepiskop@eparchia.kursk.ru • www.kurskaja-eparchia.ru

*24.12.1956 Novo-Jarykovo Arzamas Gorkij, N11.7. 1975 absolvent Medicin School Arzamas. 1975-1977 Soviet Army. 1977-1983 feldšer Arzamas, stud History Philology Gorkij. diak19.8.1983 Vladimir Suzdal. mon8.3.1984 ⊖10.3.1984. 1984-1989 rector Likino. 1989 blagočinnyj dean Jurjev-Polskij ⊕28.3.1993 Moskva B Jakutija+Viljujsk. 1996 new name Jakutija+Lensk. 2000 A Jakutija+Lensk. 2004 A Kursk+Rylsk. 25.2.2007 Orden Sergij Radonež (II). 2012 M Kursk. 2012 Orden St. Innokentij (II).

Veniamin Viktor Korolov ***Železnogorsk***

T: B Železnogorsk+Lgovsk, Metr. Kursk ■ ✉ ul. Gagarina 22, ROSSIJA-307179 Železnogorsk • [7] 47148 31074, 76960, fax 44904, [7] 951 0808000 • Zheleznogorsk.eparhia@gmail.com • Zheleznogorsk.eparhia@gmail.ru • korennaya@yandex.ru • www.zheleznogorsk.cerkov.ru

*26.10.1965 Verhososenie Orël, N? 1984-1986 Soviet Army. 1987-1990 stud and teacher music school Orël. 1990-1995 teacher Art Institute Orël, construction new church. mon23.2.1997 Kursk (Benjamin Pečera) diak15.3.1997 ⊖7.4.1997 Kursk. 1999 rector skit Korenna pustina. 2010 absolvent Seminary Kursk. archim19.8.2012 ⊕1.9.2012 B Železnogorsk+Lgovsk, Metr. Kursk.

Paisij Viktor Jurkov ***Ščigry***
T: B Ščigry+Manturov, Metropolia Kursk ▪ ✉ ul. Lenina 11, ROSSIJA-306530 Ščigry • [7] 471-45 4-27-71, [7] 905 041-88-86 • shigryeparh@mail.ru • http://shigrovskaja-eparchija.ru
*1973 Moskva. baptized youngster. 1989-1991 military service. mon24.4.1992 monastery St. Nikolaj Jekaterinburg. diak29.4.1992 Jekaterinburg (A Melkisedek) ⊖31.5.1992 Jekaterinburg (A Melkisedek). 1993-2014 dean Novospasskij monastery Moskva. 1994-1996 teacher Sunday school, 1997-2011 kelar, 1996-2005 (correspondence course) Seminary Academy Moskva, dipl "Knjaz Sergej Aleksandr Romanov 1882-1905". 29.8.2007 igumen (A Aleksij, Orehovo-Zujev). archim29.7. 2014 Novospasskij Monastery Moskva (B Savva, Voskressensk) ⊕19.8.2014 B Solovets (Patr Kirill) B Shchigry+Manturov, Metr. Kursk.

Metropolia Kuzbass

Aristarh Vadim Smirnov ***Kemerovo***
T: M Kemerovo+Prokoljev, Metr. Kuzbass ▪ ✉ ul. Sobornaja 24, ROSSIJA-650004 Kemerovo • [7] 3842 358255, 350890, 357135, 350938, 319407 • kemup@yandex.ru • www.mitropolit.info • www.kneparhia.ru
*17.1.1959 Kemerovo, N28.4. 1982-1988 Seminary Academy Moskva. 1988 teacher Akad. mon27.3.1998 diak7.4.1998 ⊖19.7.1998 archim21.7.2006 ⊕20.8.2006 B Kemerovo+Novokuznetsk. 14.10.2010 Moskva Theol Academy 325 years. 2012 M Kemerovo+Prokoljev, Metr. Kuzbass.

Innokentij Dmitrij Vetrov ***Mariinsk***
T: B Mariinsk+Jurga, Metr. Kuzbass ▪ ✉ pr. Kuzbasskij 15 a, ROSSIJA-652 062 Jurga • [7] 38451 48383, fax 44554 • me260712@yandex.ru • www.mariinsk-eparhia.ru
*8.9.1973 Tomsk, N6.10. cook Tomsk. 1991-1992 Seminary Tobolsk, 1992-1995 Seminary Kursk. diak7.4.1994 ⊖1.6.1995 blagočinnyj dean Kursk. 1996 klirik Belgorod, missions Jakutia, Kalmykia, Čukotka. mon5.1.1997. 1997-1999 Academy Kiev. 2003 klirik Kemerovo, teacher, 2004-2005 prorector Seminary Novokuznetsk. 2007 Kandidat "Apologetika ... 16th-17th century". archim29.7.2012 ⊕31.7.2012 B Mariinsk +Jurga, Metr. Kuzbass.

Vladimir Vladimir Agibalov ***Novokuznetsk***
T: B Novokuznetsk+Tashtagol, Metr. Kuzbass ▪ ✉ ul. Vodopadnaja 15, ROSSIJA-654034 Novokuznetsk • [7] 3843 367040 • kuzbishop@mail.ru • www.eparhia-nk.ru
*17.7.1966 Tomsk. 1983-1990 State University Kemerovo Fac history. 1984-1986 Soviet Army Kazakhstan. 1986 baptized. 1990-1991 Technol Institute Kemerovo.

diak18.8.1992 (B Antonij Krasnojarsk) ⊖13.7.1994 (B Sofronij Bulko). 2014 Donskoj Monastery Moskva B Novokuznetsk+Tashtagol (Patriarch Kirill). mon27.7.2014 Monastery Bezrukovo Novokuznetsk. archim28.7.2014 Kemerovo ⊕1.9.2014 B Novokuznetsk, Metr. Kuzbass.

Metropolia Lipetsk

Nikon Nikolaj Vasin ***Lipetsk***

T: M Lipetsk+Zadonsk, Metr. Lipetsk ▪ ✉ ul.Lenina 34a, ROSSIJA-398020 Lipetsk • [7] 4742 277724, 274607 • info@le-eparchy.ru • www.le-eparchy.ru • www.mitropolia-lip.ru

*1.1.1942 Panino Lipetsk, N5.4. 1961-1964 Soviet Army. 1973-1976 Seminary Odessa. diak9.9.1976 ⊖10.9.1976. 1976-1990 Pavlovka Lipetsk ⊕31.3.1996. 1996-2003 B Zadonsk, vicar Voronež. 2003 B Lipetsk+Jelets. 2012 Orden Sergij Radonež (I). 2013 M Lipetsk+Zadonsk, Metr. Lipetsk.

Maxim Vasilij Dmitriev ***Jelets***

T: B Jelets+Lebedjan, Metr. Lipetsk ▪ ✉ Krassnaja ploshchad dom 1, ROSSIJA-399770 Jelets • [7] 47467 60738 • el.eparhy@gmail.com • http://el-eparhy.ru

*23.2.1961 Karaganda, N3.2. 1979 absolvent Kultprosvetučilišče Karaganda. 1979-1981 Soviet Army. 1982-1986 Seminary Regent school Zagorsk. 1986 Academy Zagorsk. mon1988 diak19.5.1988 ⊖12.3.1989. 6.10.1989 igumen. 1989 inspector, 1990-1997 rector Seminary Tobolsk. 1997-2002 blagočinnyj dean Išim. archim30.12.2001 ⊕20.1.2002 B Barnaul+Altaj. 2013 B Jelets+Lebedjan, Metr. Lipetsk.

Metropolia Mordovija

Zinovij Anatolij Korzinkin ***Saransk***

T: M Saransk+Mordovija, Metr. Mordovija ▪ ✉ ul. Moskovskaja 2, ROSSIJA-430000 Saransk • [7] 342 471147, 240335 • sarep@yandex.ru • http://sarep.ru

*19.6.1948 Slavjansk Donetsk. N12.11. 1967-1972 music school Donetsk, konservatorium Moskva. 1972-1973 Soviet Army. 1973-1978 teacher music school Zaporože. diak29.4.1978 Rylsk ⊖25.10.1978 Kursk mon22.2.1984. 1987 blagočinnyj dean Šigrovsk. 4.11.1988 igumen. 1998 dekan Fac theol University Kursk. archim1999. 1999 Dr. pedagogics. 2003 teacher religiovedenija ⊕3.4.2011 B Elista+Kalmykija. 2014 M Saransk+Mordovija, Metr. Mordovija.

Kliment Viktor Rodaikin ***Krasnoslobodsk***

T: B Krasnoslobodsk+Temnikov, Metr. Mordovija ▪ ✉ Bolničnyj per. 2, ROSSIJA-431260 Krasnoslobodsk • [7] 963 1477313 • wip-23@yandex.ru • www.krasnoslobodsk-eparhia.ru

*9.2.1971 Staroe Šajgovo Mordovia. N5.2. 1986-1990 Music school Saransk. 1990-1992 hypodiakon Saransk. 1992-1995 Seminary Moskva. 1995-1999 Kandidat Sankt-Peterburg "Simvolika znamenij v Evangelii ot Ioanna". diak11.9.1999 ⊖12.9.1999 rector Penza, Kuznetsk, rector Theol school Penza. mon24.8.2003. 2006 igumen. archim9.8.2009 ⊕2.12.2009 B Ruzaev, vicar Saransk. 2011 B Krasnoslobodsk+Temnikov, Metr. Mordovija.

Venjamin Eduard Kirillov ***Ardatov***

T: B Ardatov+Atjaševo, Metr. Mordovija ▪ ✉ ul. Djučkova 80, ROSSIJA-431860 Ardatov • [7] 3431 32869, 31402 • ardatovnikol@yandex.ru • www.ardatep.ru

*17.9.1979 Murgab Turkmenistan. N? 1981 Dubenki Mordovia. 1984 baptized. 1986-1997 school Dubenki. 1997-1999 Theol school Saransk. mon6.4.1999 diak17.4.1999 ⊖9.6.1999. 1999-2001 Seminary Nižegorod. 2001-2009 Historical Institut Mordovia. 2010 Aspirantura University Mordovia. archim7.10.2011 ⊕14.10. 2011 B Ardatov+Atjaševo, Metr. Mordovija.

Metropolia Murmansk

Simon Valentin Getja ***Murmansk***

T: M Murmansk+Mončegorsk, Metr. Murmansk ▪ ✉ Nikolskij hram ul. Zelenaja 11, ROSSIJA-183010 Murmansk • [7] 8152 251277, fax 255338 • mmeparh.ru@gmail.com • murmansk_eparchy@mail • www.mmeparh.ru

*14.11.1949 Krjukovo Poltava Ukraina, son of a soldier. N7.12. 1967 Kombinat Poltava. 1968-1970 Soviet Army Jüterbog Potsdam Germany. 1971-1977 stud med Akad Medicine Army Poltava and Kujbyšev/Samara. 1977-1979 military doctor Kaliningrad Černiachkovsk. 1979-1980 Therapeut Kujbyšev/Samara. 1980-1983 Seminary Moskva. 1983-1987 Lektor pastoral, canon law Academy Moskva. mon2.12.1983 diak8.1.1984 ⊖15.2.1984. 1987 Kandidat Moskva. 1987 rector Kujbyšev/Samara. 1988 igumen. archim1990 blagočinnyj dean Kujbyšev/Samara. 1990 sekretar to M Ioann St-P. 1991 Lektor Seminary St-P ⊕3.10.1993 (Moskva) B Tihvin. 1993-1995 vicar Sankt-Peterburg+Ladoga. 1995 Regensburg. 1995 B, 2005 A, 2013 M Murmansk+Mončegorsk, Metr. Murmansk.

Mitrofan Vladimir Badanin ***Severomorsk***
T: B Severomorsk+Umba, Metr. Murmansk ▪ ✉ ul. Komsomolskaja 23, Rossija-184600 Severomorsk • [7] 81537 55074, fax 62953 • info@severeparh.ru • www.severeparh.ru
*27.5.1953 Leningrad son of a soldier, baptized youngster, N? 1976 lieutenant Severnaja Flota. 1992 Kapitan Morska Academy. 1998 press-sekretar eparchy Murmansk. 1999-2005 Tikhon University Moskva. mon12.6.2000 diak13.6.2000 ⊖15.6.2000 rector Varzuga. 2005-2009 Kandidat Aspirantura Moskva. 28.3.2007 igumen. archim1.11.2013 Čistyj per. Moskva ⊕24.11.2013 B Severomorsk+Umba, Metr. Murmansk.

Metropolia Nižnij Novgorod

Georgij Vasilij Danilov ***Nižnij Novgorod***
T: M Nižnij Novgorod+Arzamas, Metr. Nižnij Novgorod ▪ ✉ Suzdalskaja 58, Rossija-603058 Nižnij Novgorod • [7] 831 2585698, 2555662, 2580919, fax 2580417 • canc@nne.ru • www.nne.ru
*14.8.1964 Žlobin Gomel. N6.5. 1986-1990 Seminary. mon22.12.1989. 1990-1995 Academy Moskva, Kandidat "Life and patriarcal service St. Tikhon Belavin". diak9.10.1990 ⊖9.4.1991. 1993-2003 ekonom Troice-Sergieva Lavra ⊕2.2.2003 B, 2008 A, 2012 M Nižnij Novgorod+Arzamas, Metr. Nižnij Novgorod. 2016 member Synodal Commission Theology.

Ilia Nikolaj Bykov
T: B Balahninsk, vicar Nižnij Novgorod, Metr. Nižnij Novgorod ▪ ✉ Suzdalskaja 58, Rossija-603058 Nižnij Novgorod • [7] 831 2585698, 2555662, 2580919, fax 2580417 • canc@nne.ru • www.nne.ru
*3.4.1954 Černorečje Kujbyšev. N? 1971-1972 podšipnik zavod Kujbyšev. 1972-1976 Kazan tankovo učilišče. 1976-1980 Borisov, Polotsk. 1980 Psalomščik Ivanovo Brest. diak20.7.1980 Ivanovo (M Filaret) ⊖12.10.1980 (M Filaret) nastojatjel Kossovo Brest. 1982 eparchy Nižegorod. 1991-2005 sekretar eparchy Nižegorod. 2005 blagočinnij Kstovo Nižegorod, widower. mon29.7.2010 ⊕1.8.2010. 2010-2011 B Jakutsk+Lensk. 2011-2013 B Ruzaev, vicar Saransk. 2013 B Balahninsk, vicar Nižnij Novgorod, Metr. Nižnij Novgorod.

Avgustin Anatolij Anisimov ***Gorodets***
T: B Gorodets+Vetluga, Metr. Nižnij Novgorod ▪ ✉ pl. Proletarskaja 34 B, Rossija-606502 Gorodets • [7] 960 1944478, [7] 3161 91471, fax 91662 • gor.eparchia@gmail.com • www.egiv.ru
*14.1.1945 Moskva, baptized youngster. N? Soviet Army. 1977 absolvent Institut Juris Moskva. 1977-1987 jurist Moskva. 1987-1990 ekonom Troice-Sergieva Lavra.

diak22.5.1990 ⊖2.8.1990. 1991-2007 Ivanovo. mon5.9.1993 (B Avgustin Hippo) 1995 igumen. 1997-2001 Seminary Moskva. 2008 eparchy Nižnij Novgorod. archim18.3.2012 ⊕8.4.2012 B Gorodets+Vetluga, Metr. Nižnij Novgorod.

Varnava Roman Baranov ***Vyksa***

T: B Vyksa+Pavlovo, Metr. Nižnij Novgorod ▪ ✉ Spartaka 33, ROSSIJA-607060 Vyksa • [7] 3177 35632, fax 30604 • eparhiya.vyksa@yandex.ru • www.vyksaeparhia.ru

*11.2.1965 Kaluga N? 1983-1985 Soviet Army. 1985-1995 married. 1987-1991 Pedagogical Institut Gorkij. 1990 baptized Žyzdry. 1992 Brotherhood Aleksandr Nevskij. diak24.4.1999 Nižnij Novgorod (M Nikolaj) ⊖1.6.1999 Arsamas (B Ierofej). 1999-2004 parishes, 2000-2004 Seminary Nižnij Novgorod. 2005-2012 Monasteries. archim18.3.2012 ⊕22.4.2012 Moskva, B Vyksa+Pavlovo, Metr. Nižnij Novgorod.

Siluan Aleksandr Glazkin ***Lyskovo***

T: B Lyskovo+Lukojanov, Metr. Nižnij Novgorod ▪ ✉ per. Shaposhnikov 7 A, ROSSIJA-606210 Lyskovo • [7] 83149 5-03-78, 5-03-48 • lyskovskaya-eparhya@yandex.ru • http://lyskovskaya-eparhya.ru

*19.12.1969 Moskva, N12.8. baptized youngster. 1976 Zagorsk/Sergiev Posad. 1987-1992 Seminary Moskva. 1988-1989 military service. 1996 Kandidat Moskva "Life and pastoral service Varnava Gefsiman". mon18.4.1997 diak5.1.1998 Moskva ⊖8.10.1998 Sergiev Posad (M Vladimir Sankt-Peterburg). 2002 igumen Rostov Veliki. archim27.4.2006 ⊕17.11.2013 Kaliningrad Königsberg B Lyskovo+Lukojanov, Metr. Nižnij Novgorod (Patr Kirill).

Metropolia Novgorod

Lev Nikolaj Tserpitskij ***Novgorod***

T: M Novgorod+Staraja Rus, Metr. Novgorod ▪ ✉ Slavnaja 12, ROSSIJA-173000 Velikij Novgorod • [7] 162 49602 (Monastery Hutin), kantsler 635413, dom 636509, fax 633342 • noveparhia@mail.ru • eparhia@novgorod.net.ru • www.vn-eparhia.ru

*13.4.1946 Zalužje Stolbcy Minsk, N3.3. 1966-1969 Soviet Army. 1969-1975 Seminary Academy Leningrad. mon28.3.1971 (M Nikodim) diak7.4.1971 ⊖20.4.1971. 1972-1975 sekretar M Nikodim. 1975 Kandidat "Constitutio Liturgiae Vaticanum II". 1975-1978 stud Gregoriana Roma. archim8.8.1978. 1978-1980 Propst Olonez, teacher Seminary Leningrad. 1980-1983 Rabat, 1981-1983 President Council Christian Churches Marokko. 1983-1987 Cathedral Vyborg ⊕1.11.1987 B Taškent. 1990 B, 1995 A, 2012 M Novgorod+Staraja Rus, Metr. Novgorod. 2012 Orden Sergij Radonež (II).

Jefrem Jefrem Barbinjagr ***Borovoči***

T: B Borovoči+Pestovo, Metr. Novgorod ▪ ✉ Aleksandra Nevskogo 6, ROSSIJA-174401 Borovoči • [7] 921 1928422, fax [7] 1664 42938 • bor-eparhia@yandex.ru • www.boreparhia.ru

*1.5.1941 Gandraburi Odessa, baptized youngster, N? 1956-1969 worker kolkhoz, ponomar Gandraburi. 1969-1972 Seminary Leningrad. diak1.1.1972 Leningrad (M Nikodim) ⊖27.2.1972. 1972-1976 Academy Leningrad. 23.3.1976 -1.2.1977 three different parishes near Odessa. 1977 Novgorod (M Nikodim). rector Borovoči, namestnik monasteries. mon12.2.1980 (M Antonij) archim21.7.1981 (M Antonij) ⊕5.2.2012 B Borovoči+Pestovo, Metr. Novgorod.

Metropolia Novosibirsk

Tihon Leonid Emeljanov ***Novosibirsk***

T: M Novosibirsk+Berdsk, Metr. Novosibirsk ▪ ✉ ul. Žukovskogo 55-57, ROSSIJA-630123 Novosibirsk • [7] 383 2170011, fax 2201310 • mail@nskmi.ru • orthodox-nsk@ngs.ru • www.nskmitropolia.ru • www.nskmi.ru

*2.6.1948 Voronež, N26.8. Technikum, Soviet Army, altarnik Pereslavl-Zalesskij. 1974-1981 Seminary Academy Moskva. 1976-1990 publication sector Moskva. diak4.12.1978 redactor Žurnal Mosk Patr. mon19.3.1981 ⊖1.5.1981 Kandidat. 1984 Aspirantura. archim4.7.1984. 1986 ekonom, 1987 namestnik Danilov Mon ⊕19.8.1990. 1990 B Novosibirsk (1990 +Barnaul, 1994 +Tomsk, 1995 +Berdsk). 1995 chairman Department Editions, 1995 B, 2000 A Bronnitsy. 2001 A, 2012 M Novosibirsk+Berdsk, Metr. Novosibirsk.

Pavel Aleksandr Grigorjev

T: B Kolyvan, vicar Novosibirsk, Metr. Novosibirsk ▪ ✉ ul. Žukovskogo 55-57, ROSSIJA-630123 Novosibirsk • [7] 383 2170011, fax 2201310

*30.6.1974 Enbekshilderskogo Shchors district of Kokchetav region Kazakh SSR. 1980-1990 high school Schorsovsk. 1990-1996 Chelyabinsk State Technical University (CSTU) speciality "Design and technology of radio-electronic means". 1996 grad CSTU, radio engineer-technologist. 1992 baptized. 1998 Provost, Kozihi Novosibirsk. mon10.7.1998 "Pavel" (hieromonk Artemije Snigur) honor of the Holy Apostle Paul. diak12.9.1998 (B Sergius Novosibirsk+Berdsk) ⊖26.12.1998 hieromonk. 1999-2004 stud Tomsk Theol Seminary (correspondence course), 2004-2009 stud Kiev Theol Academy (correspondence course). 2006-2010 Abbot Mochishe Novosibirsk, teacher Theol Institute, teacher Seminary. 4.10.2012 Holy Synod: Abbot Kozihi Novosibirsk. 15.7.2013 rector parish St. Vladimir Novosibirsk. 2014 chairman commission for monasteries eparchy Novosibirsk, Synodal Department

monasteries. 24.12.2015 elected bishop, vicar Novosibirsk. archim25.12.2015 ⊕8.1.2016 Uspenskij sobor Kreml B Kolyvan, vicar Novosibirsk. (Patr Kirill).

Feodosij Sergej Čaščin *Kainsk*
T: B Kainsk+Barabinsk, Metr. Novosibirsk ▪ ✉ ul. Pugačova 2, ROSSIJA-632382 Kujbyšev • [7] 38362 67034 • key-orthodox@ngs.ru • info@kainsk-eparhia.ru • www.kainsk-eparhia.ru
*23.4.1973 Moskva, N? 1996 dipl Aviation Institute Moskva. 1997-1999 Raketnyh vojskah. 2000 Monastery Arhangel Mihail Koziha Novonikolajevska = Novosibirsk. mon29.12.2000 Koziha. diak24.5.2001 Novonikolajevska Novosibirsk (A Tikhon) ⊖17.6.2001. 2001-2005 (correspondence course) Seminary Tomsk. 2005 napersny krest. 2005-2010 (correspondence course) Academy Kiev. 22.3.2011 namestnik Koziha. archim19.1.2012 ⊕17.3.2012 St. Daniel Monastery Moskva B Kainsk+ Barabinsk, Metr. Novosibirsk (Patr. Kyrill).

Filip Igor Novikov *Karasuk*
T: B Karasuk+Ordynskoje, Metr. Novosibirsk ▪ ✉ ul. Oktjabrskaja 31, ROSSIJA-632868 Karasuk • [7] 38355 32085 • [7] 906 9069301 • pravkarasuk@mail.ru • www.pravkarasuk.ru
*17.7.1973 Staraja Kupavna Nogina Moskva, N16.7. 1988-1992 Technikum Kupavna. 1992-1997 (correspondence course) Seminary Moskva. 1993-1994 Military Service Krasnojarsk. mon15.7.1996 diak16.7.1996 ⊖18.7.1996 eparchy Novonikolajevska Novosibirsk. 1998 blagočinnyj dean, 2007-2009 Academy Kiev. archim19.1. 2012 ⊕11.3.2012 B Karasuk+Ordynskoje, Metr. Novosibirsk.

Luka Andrej Volčkov *Iskitim*
T: B Iskitim+Čerepanovo, Metr. Novosibirsk ▪ ✉ ul. Kollektivnaja 1, ROSSIJA-633210 Iskitim • [7] 38343 91257, 68242 • iskitimeparhia@yandex.ru • www.iskitimeparhia.ru
*27.4.1971 Solnečnogorsk Moskva, N? 1988-1989 elektro-mehanik. 1989-1991 Military Service. 1991-1997 ingenieur elektro-mehanik Moskva. mon21.5.1997 Kozyha Ordynsk Novonikolajevska Novosibirsk. diak31.8.1997 ⊖21.12.1997. 1999-2004 Seminary Tomsk (correspondence course). 2004 (correspondence course) Academy Moskva. archim19.1.2012 ⊕10.3.2012 B Iskitim+Čerepanovo, Metr. Novosibirsk.

Metropolia Omsk

Vladimir Vasilij Ikim ***Omsk***

T: M Omsk+Tavričesk, Metr. Omsk ▪ ✉ ul. Internatsionalnaja 25, ROSSIJA-644099 Omsk • [7] 3812 338007, 223700, 253703 • omskeparhia@rambler.ru • www.omsk-eparhiya.ru

*1.2.1940 Novo -Varzarešty Moldavia. N28.7. 1959-1961 Military. 1963. absolvent Seminary Odessa. mon27.7.1965 diak1.8.1965 ⊖4.2.1966. 1967 Kandidat Moskva. 1971 Aspirant Moskva. 1978-1988 Karlovy Vary ⊕30.6.1985 B Podolsk. 1988-1990 Dep Ext Aff. 1990 B, 1991 A, 2002 M Taškent+Srednjaja Asia. 2011 M Omsk+Tara, 2012 M Omsk+Tavričesk, Metr. Omsk. 2016 Rector Omsk Theol Seminary.

Feodosij Sergej Gazhu ***Isilkul***

T: B Isilkul+Russko-Poljansk, Metr. Omsk ▪ ✉ ul. Lenina 40, ROSSIJA-646024 Isilkul • [7] 963 0535872, [7] 962 0558861m fax [7] 38173 23272 • eirp2014@mail.ru

*18.7.1970 Kizhinev Moldavia, N16.5. 1988-1990 Soviet Army. 1991-1998 Seminary Academy Moskva. mon13.4.1995 Sergiev Posad. diak29.4.1995 Pokrov Moskva (Patr Alexij) ⊖13.4.1996 Epiphany Cathedral Moskva. (Patr Alexij). 19.12.2005 igumen Jekaterinburg Mon. Tsarstvennyh stratoterptsev. 2011 absolvent Juristic Academy Ural. 15.3.2011 igumen Jekaterinburg (A Vikentij, Jekaterinburg) archim8.10.2011 Lavra Sergiev Posad (M Vikentij, Tashkent) ⊕4.12.2011 Monastery Donsk Moskva B Biškek+Kyrgyzstan (Patr Kirill). 2014 B Isilkul+Russko-Poljansk.

Pjotr Pjotr Mansurov ***Kalačinsk***

T: B Kalačinsk+Muromtsev, Metr. Omsk ▪ ✉ ul. Semashko 21, ROSSIJA-646900 Kalachinsk • [7] 38155 21157 • kalach.eparhia@rambler.ru • www.kalachinsk-eparhiya.ru

*6.9.1954 Krakovets Lvov Ukraina, N12.7. 1972-1974 Soviet Army. 1975-1981 stud Biology University Moskva. 1978-1988 married, son Grigorij priest. 1981-1990 Kandidat "Virusologija". diak8.11.1995 klirik Omsk ⊖26.11.1995 teacher Dogmatics Theol school Omsk. 2009 dipl Seminary Tobolsk "The creation of the world". 2010 sekretar eparchy. mon4.1.2012 archim17.6.2012 ⊕12.7.2012 B Kalačinsk+ Muromtsev, Metr. Omsk.

Savvatij Sergej Zagrebelnyj ***Tara***

T: B Tara+Tjukalin, Metr. Omsk ▪ ✉ ul. Spasskaja 46, ROSSIJA-646527 Tara • [7] 38171 23420 taraeparhia@rambler.ru • www.tara-eparhiya.ru

*5.8.1967Sosnovskoje Tavričesk Omsk, N10.10. 1974-1984 school Novomoskovka Omsk. 1984-1988 military school Omsk. 1988-1990 lieutenant Murmansk, generalštab. 1990 baptized, married Anastasija. 1993 commander Novosibirsk.

diak4.11.1995 klirik Omsk ⊖5.11.1995 rector Ust-Išim, Vjatka. 1999 divorced. mon2002. 2006 dipl Seminary Tobolsk. 2007 igumen ⊕21.7.2012 Moskva, B Tara+Tjukalin, Metr. Omsk.

Metropolia Orël

Antonij Ivan Čeremisov ***Orël***

T: M Orël+Bolhov, Metr. Orël ▪ ✉ ul. Normandija Neman 27, ROSSIJA-302026 Orël • [7] 4862 432955, 475277 • [7] 962 475 2626 • cerkovorel@yandex.ru • mansteinkurrant@mail.ru • www.orel-eparhia.ru

*6.11.1939 Ternovka Voronež, N27.4. 1946 Vilnius. Musiktechnikum. 1957 Seminary Minsk. 1958-1962 Soviet Army. 1965 Seminary Moskva, mon7.4.1971 diak14.4.1971. 1972 Aspirant Moskva and Secretary President Department External Church Relations ⊖4.11.1972. 1973-1975 Institut de Bossey. 1975-1979 Monastyr Sv. Duh Vilnius. 8.4.1979 igumen. 1979-1982 Kaunas. 1982-1985 Podvorie Tokyo. 1986 Danilov Monastyr Moskva. archim24.3.1987 ⊕22.4.1989 B Vilnius. 25.1.1990 B Tobolsk. 20.7.1990 B, 1999 A Krasnojarsk+Jenisejsk (2011 Krasnojarsk+Ačinsk). 2005 Orden Početa (Pres Putin). 2011 M Orël+Livny (Sergij Bulgakov born in Livny 1871), 2014 Orël+Bolhov, M Metr. Orël.

Nektarij Nikolaj Seleznjev ***Livny***

T: B Livny+Maloarhangelsk, Metr. Orël ▪ ✉ ploshchad Sergij Bulgakov 15, ROSSIJA-303850 Livny • [7] 48677 20055 • livnyeparhia@gmail.com • www.livnyeparhia.ru

*7.5.1974 Tchulman Jakutsk. 1991-1998 Cathedral Holy Trinity Krasnojarsk. diak1.3.1998. 1999 Medal St. Daniel Moskovskij. 2000-2004 (correspondence course) Seminary Moskva. mon26.4.2002 St. Nektarios Optin ⊖21.11.2002. 2006 igumen. 2008 correspondece course Kandidat Kiev. archim2009. 2010 secretary eparchy Krasnojarsk; 2011 secretary eparchy Orël Livny ⊕9.9.2014 Kaluga B Livny +Maloarhangelsk (Patr Kirill), Metr. Orël (Sergij Bulgakov born in Livny 1871).

Metropolia Orenburg

Veniamin Vladimir Zaritskij ***Orenburg***

T: M Orenburg+Saraktaš, Metr. Orenburg ▪ ✉ pereulok Ševčenko 4, ROSSIJA-480000 Orenburg • [7] 3532 779718, [7] 922 547 1476 • kanc_eparh@mail.ru • www.oepress.ru

*12.9.1953 Stodyltsy Vinnitsa, N? 1970-1973 Troice-Sergieva Lavra. 1973-1974 hypodiakon Rjazan. 1974-1975 čtets Ivanovo. diak30.3.1975 ⊖6.4.1975 mon27.5. 1977. 1977-1978 rector Volhov. 1978-1987 dean St. Nicholas Kromy Orël. 1980 Orden St. Vladimir (III). 1981-2002 Seminary Academy Moskva. 3.6.1982 igumen.

archim1987. 1987-1988 sekretar eparchy Orël. 1988 Orden St. Vladimir (II). 1989-1990 ekonom Monastery Rjazan. 1990 igumen. 1990-2010 rector Seminary Ugreškij Monastery St. Nicholas. 2000 Orden Sergij Radonež (II) ⊕24.3.2003. 2003-2010 B Ljubertsi, vicar Moskva. 2010 B Penza, 2012 M Penza+Nižnelomov. 2013 M Rjazan+Mihajlov, Metr. Rjazan. 2015 M Orenburg+Saraktaš, Metr. Orenburg.

Irinej Sergej Tafunja ***Orsk***
T: B Orsk+Gajsk, Metr. Orenburg ■ ✉ ul. Kirova 18, ul. 1 Maja 33, ROSSIJA-462422 Orsk • [7] 987 8586074, [7] 905 8998922, [7] 922 8555730 • evharistia@rambler.ru • orskpress-eparh@mail.ru • orsk.eparh@gmail.com • www.orskeparh.ru
*30.5.1971 Varvarovka Moldavia, N5.9. 1986-1989 Technikum Bălţi Moldavia. 1989-1991 Soviet Army. 1991-1992 poslužnik Monastery Novo-Hjamets. 1992-1999 Seminary Academy Moskva. mon13.4.1995 diak28.5.1995 ⊖10.9.1995. 1998-2004 teacher Seminary Kišinjev. 20.5.2004 igumen. 2005 councillor of the Moldavian ambassador in Moskva. 2009 Kandidat Academy Moskva "M Gabriil Banulescu Bodoni". archim27.10.2011 ⊕22.11.2011 B Orsk+Gajsk, Metr. Orenburg.

Aleksij Leonid Antipov ***Buzuluk***
T: B Buzuluk+Soročinsk, Metr. Orenburg ■ ✉ ul. Sergo 7, ROSSIJA-461040 Buzuluk • [7] 35342 5-51-01, 5-51-28, 5-30-38 • buzulukeparh@yandex.ru • www.buzulukeparh.ru • www.buzulukskaja-eparchia.ru
*13.8.1956 Staro-Boriskino Orenburg, N25.2. 1973-1978 industrialno-pedagogičeskij Technikum Bugulminsk. 1974-1976 Soviet Army. 1978-1981 pedagogics Naberežnye Čelny. 1981-1984 Seminary, 1983 marriage. diak4.12.1983 Academy Moskva (B Aleksandr Dmitrov). 1984-1991 Academy Moskva ⊖25.2.1984 Orenburg. 1988 Kybandyka. 1989 Staro-Boriskino. 1998 blagočinnyj dean Buzuluk, 2000-2009 Orenburg. 2009 rector Seminary Orenburg. mon10.3.2012 (his wife nun "Sofia") ⊕25.3.2012 B Buzuluk+Soročinsk, Metr. Orenburg.

Metropolia Penza

Serafim Sergej Domnin ***Penza***
T: M Penza+Nižnelomov, Metr. Penza ■ ✉ Sobornaja (Sovietskaja) Pl. 1, ROSSIJA-440026 Penza • [7] 412 660815, 660011, fax 560929 • Seminary 690210 • penzeparch@km.ru • ortodoxpenzadu@yandex.ru • penzeparch@yandex.ru • www.penzaeparhia.ru
*25.9.1977 Kamenka Penza, N? 1992-1995 altarnik Kamenka. 1995-2000 Seminary Saratov. diak27.7.1997 Lunin, A Serafim Tihonov ⊖11.9.1997. 1997 Katredal Penza. mon2.4.1999. 2000-2009 inspektor Theol school Penza. 2005-2011 stud St. Tikhon

University. 2006 igumen. archim14.8.2012 ⊕12.9.2012 B Kuznetsk+Nikolsk. 2013 M Penza.

Nestor Andrej Ljuberanskij ***Kuznetsk***

T: B Kuznetsk+Nikolsk, Metr. Penza ▪ ✉ ul. Darvina 23, ROSSIJA-442500 Kuznetsk • [7] 4157 2-48-78 and 3-07-78 kyzneckeparh@gmail.com • http://kuzneparhia.ru

*16.8.1975 Shelkovo, 1982-1990 school Shelkovo, 1992-1997 stud mathematics Moscow Pedagogical State University. 1997-2002 teacher mathematics and informatics Shelkovo, Moscow region. 2002-2007 Seminary Nikolo-Ugreshskij monastery. 2004 work at web sites of Nikolo-Ugreshskij monastery and Seminary. 2006 novice at Nikolo-Ugreshskij monastery. Director of editions of the monastery. 2006-2008 teacher at Seminary. mon17.3.2007 diak5.4.2007 ⊖12.7.2010. 2010 moved to Penza eparchy. archim28.3.2014 ⊕18.5.2014 B Kuznetsk+Nikolsk, Metr. Penza.

Mitrofan Mihail Serjogin ***Serdobsk***

T: B Serdobsk+Spassk, Metr. Penza ▪ ✉ per. Leninskij 26, ROSSIJA-442895 Serdobsk • [7] 4167 23253, [7] 963 1051862 • eparhiya-serdobsk@yandex.ru • http://serdobsk-eparh.cerkov.ru

*7.8.1972 Penza, N? 1987-1990 Technik School Penza. 1990 singer Penza. 1990-1992 military service. diak27.12.1992 ⊖11.4.1993 mon24.8.1993. 1996-1999 Seminary Moskva. 9.7.1998 igumen. archim2012. 2013 dipl Academy Kiev ⊕10.8.2013 B Serdobsk+Spassk, Metr. Penza.

Metropolia Perm

Mefodij Nikolaj Nemtsov ***Perm***

T: M Perm+Kungur, Metr. Perm ▪ ✉ Ordžonikidze Monastirskaja 93, ROSSIJA-614990 Perm • [7] 342 2372471, 2105574, fax 2105574 • peu_kancel@mail.ru • eparhia@permonline.ru • www.pravperm.ru

*16.2.1949 Rovenki, N24.5. railway engineer. 1968-1972 Seminary Odessa, 1972-1976 Akademy Leningrad, mon5.1.1974 diak7.1.1974 ⊖24.4.1974. 1976 Kandidat Leningrad. 1977 Department External Church Relations. 1979 parish Moskva ⊕27.4.1980 B Irkutsk, 1982 B, 1985 A, 1988 M Voronež. 1999 Cross St. Daniel (Patr Moskva). 2003-2010 M Astana. 2005 Orden Sergij Radonež (II). 2010 M Metr. Perm.

Nikon Oleg Mironov ***Kudymkar***

T: B Kudymkar+Vereshchagino, Metr. Perm ▪ ✉ Monastyr Pečera, ROSSIJA-Pskov • [7] 81122 92145

*26.5.1960 Zarečnyj, Altaj, N30.11. 1977-1978 stud accountant Bijsk, Altaj. 1978-1980 Soviet Army. 1981-1982 manufactory candle eparchy Irkutsk. 1981-1985 secretary eparchy Irkutsk. diak24.4.1983 mon19.12.1985 ⊖6.1.1986. 1987 absolvent Theol Seminary Moskva. archim20.6.1989 rector Cathedral Voronež ⊕21.7.1993 (Moskva) B Zadonsk, vicar Voronež. 1994-1999 B Jekaterinburg+Verchoturje. 1999-2013 na pokoj. 2002-2013 honorary rector Vishnjakah Moskva. 29.5.2013 B Dobrjansk, vicar Perm. 19.3.2014 B Kudymkar+Vereshchagino, Metr. Perm.

Metropolia Priamurje

Ignatij Sergej Pologrudov **_Khabarovsk_**
T: M Khabarovsk+Priamurje, Metr. Priamurje ▪ ✉ Leningradskaja 65, ROSSIJA-680021 Khabarovsk • [7] 4212 310102, 301383, 338317, 328317, 391862 • kantsler 380681, 380671, fax 310131 • p 397796 • eparhiya@email.kht.ru • khveparhia@yandex.ru • www.pravostok.ru
*25.3.1956 Irkutsk. N13.5. 1978 dipl University Irkutsk. 1990 Monastery Sv. Duh Vilnius. diak27.9.1990 Vilnius. 1990 kurator internat Vilnius. mon13.4.1992 Vilnius ⊖10.5.1992 Vilnius. 1992 blagočinnyj dean Mon Sv. Duh Vilnius. 1993 dipl Seminary Moskva (correspondence course). 12.11.1997 igumen. archim1.3.1998 Kreml Moskva ⊕29.3.1998 Epiphanias Cathedral Moskva. 1998 B, 2007 A Petropavlovsk+Kamčatka. 2011 M Khabarovsk+Priamurje, Metr. Priamurje.

Aristarh Vladimir Jatsurin
T: B Nikolajev, vicar Khabarovsk, Metr. Priamurje ▪ ✉ Leningradskaja 65, ROSSIJA-682460 Nikolajevsk-na-Amurje
*16.10.1965 Zagorsk Sergiev Posad. N17.1. 1982 absolvent school Noginsk. 1982-1985 stud med, feldšer. 1985-1987 Soviet Army. 1987-1991 Seminary Moskva. mon19.12.1991 diak21.6.1992 ⊖12.9.1993. 1996 klirik Khabarovsk. 25.2.1996 igumen. 2000-2003 rector Birobidžan, 2003-2011 Elban ⊕6.10.2011B Amur+Čegdomynsk, 2012 B Nikolajev, vicar Khabarovsk, Metr. Priamurje.

Nikolaj Denis Ašimov **_Amursk_**
T: B Amursk+Čegdomyn, Metr. Priamurje ▪ ✉ ul. Kopylova 54, ROSSIJA-681018 Komsomolsk-na-Amurje • [7] 4217 242019, 273436, [7] 914 2129264 • amureparhiya@mail.ru • inform_amur_eparhia@mail.ru • www.eparhia-amur.ru
*3.12.1980 Millerovo Rostov. N? 1998-2006 Seminary Academy Moskva, Kandidat (correspondence course) "Antifonarij VI-VII vv". 2004-2006 Khabarovsk. mon24.5. 2005 diak25.5.2005 ⊖28.5.2005. 2006-2011 prorector Academy Moskva. archim 29.12.2011 Moskva ⊕29.1.2012 B Amursk+Čegdomyn, Metr. Priamurje.

Iustinian Viktor Ovčinnikov ***Elista***
T: A Elista+Kalmykija, Metr. Priamurje ▪ ✉ ul. Sergija Radonezhskogo 97, ROSSIJA-358001 Elista • [7] 84722 30669 • e-08@mail.ru • www.blagovest-elista.ru

*28.1.1961 Kosteriova Vladimir Rossija. N27.11. 1983 absolvent Fac History University Ivanovo. 1984-1988 Seminary Moskva. 1985-1986 Soviet Army. 1986-1988 starshij hypodiakon B Aleksandr. 1988-1992 MTh Bucureşti. mon24.3.1988 diak18.4.1988 Pascha ⊖24.6.1988. 1991 referent Department External Church Relations Moskva. 1992-1995 igumen rector Tver ⊕1.9.1995 Don Monastery Moskva B Dubossari, vicar Chişinău. 1996 Orden republici moldoveneşti Transnistria. 2010 Orden Sergij Radonež, 2000 Orden Rozhdjestvo X. Orden St. Stefan cel Mare, 2011 Orden St. Innokentij Moskva.1998-2010 B, A Tiraspol. 2010-2014 A Naro-Fominsk, Administrator Patriarchal Parishes of the Russian Orthodox Church USA. 2012-2013 administrator Argentina. 2012 Honorary citizen Komrat. 25.7.2014 B Elista+Kalmykija, Metr. Priamurje.

Metropolia Primorje

Veniamin Boris Puškar ***Vladivostok***
T: M Vladivostok+Primorje, Metr. Primorje ▪ ✉ ul. Pologaja 65, ROSSIJA-690091 Vladivostok • [7] 423 2402780, 2401501, fax 2400835, 260792 • veu99@mail.ru • veniamin@stl.ru • www.vladivostok.eparhia.ru

*8.11.1938 Chorol Primorskij. N New Russian Martyrs. School Vladivostok. 1959-1963 Seminary Moskva. 1967 Kandidat Fac theol Moskva. 1967-1992 teacher History Bibl Seminary Moskva. diak1988 ⊖1988 mon13.9.1992 archim20.9.1992 ⊕21.9.1992 Moskva B, 2003 A Vladivostok+Primorskij Kraj. 1998 Prof Theol Far East University Vladivostok. 2011 M Primorje.

Innokentij Vitalij Erohin
T: B Ussurijsk, vicar Vladivostok, Metr. Primorje ▪ ✉ ul. Pologaja dom 64, ROSSIJA-690091 Vladivostok • [7] 4232 402780, 401501, fax 400835 • teologia@wl.dvgu.ru

*17.11.1967 Uspenovka Amur. N13.4. 1985-1987 Soviet Army. 1985-1993 dipl journalist University Vladivostok. 1993-1995 redaktor Vladivostok. 1.5.1993 baptism. 1995 redaktor eparhalnaja gazeta, hypodiakon. mon3.4.1997 Innokentij. 1997-2004 stud theol (correspondence course) St. Tikhon Moskva. diak7.6.1998. 1998 medal Sergij Radonež ⊖3.1.1999. 1.7.1999 teacher Bibleistika, Missiologia University Vladivostok. 1999 nabedrennik. 2000 naperskyj krest. 2004 igumen. 2007 member tribunal eparchy. 2010 Kandidat Theol St. Tikhon ⊕7.12.2010 B Ussurijsk, vicar Vladivostok, Metr. Primorje.

Gurij Vladislav Fjodorov ***Arsenjev***
T: B Arsenjev+Dalnegorsk, Metr. Primorje ▪ ✉ ul. Sotsialističeskaja 115, ROSSIJA-692331 Arsenjev • [7] 42361 31392 • www.arseniev-eparhia.ru
*8.11.1960 Kaliningrad Korolev Moskva. N? 1979-1981 KB Chimmaš. 1985 absolvent Architectural Institute Moskva. 2.4.1985 baptized. 1986-1989 altarnik Moskva. 1989 architect Sergiev Posad. mon8.4.1990 diak21.9.1990. 1990-1995 hypodiakon to Patr Aleksij. 1991-1994 married. 1994-2000 in the group of architects of Christ Saviour Cathedral Moskva ⊖8.11.1995 klirik Moskva. 2000-2006 Academy Moskva (correspondence course). archim27.10.2011 ⊕6.11.2011 B Arsenjev+Dalnegorsk, Metr. Primorje.

Nikolaj Nikolaj Dutka ***Nahodka***
T: B Nahodka+Preobražensk, Metr. Primorje ▪ ✉ Nahodkinski prosp. 33, ROSSIJA-692900 Nahodka • [7] 4236 686181, [7] 914 074 4825 • npeu@mail.ru http://rpcne.ru • www.rpcne.ru
*23.5.1966 Chernovtsy Ukraina. N17.2. 1983 hypodiakon to A Varlaam Iljušenko. 1984-1986 Soviet Army. 1987-1990 Seminary, 1990 Academy Kiev (correspondence course). mon3.1.1991 Sergiev Posad. diak7.5.1991 ⊖2002 Vladivostok. 2008 rector Nahodka ⊕1.9.2011 B Nahodka+Preobražensk, Metr. Primorje.

Metropolia Pskov

Evsevij Nikolaj Savvin ***Pskov***
T: M Pskov+Porhov, Metr. Pskov ▪ ✉ ul. Pozemskogo 83-a, ROSSIJA-180006 Pskov • [7] 8112 723890, fax 720622 • pskov-eparhia@rambler.ru • www.pskov-eparhia.ellink.ru • www.pskov-eparhiya.ru
*15.5.1939 Stegalovka Lipetsk. N17.10. diak1964 mon15.10.1964 (Archim. Pimen Hmelevski) ⊖14.11.1965. absolvent Moskva 1982 namestnik Troice -Sergieva Lavra ⊕1.4.1984 B Alma Ata. 1990 B, 1991 A Kujbyšev (=Samara). 1993 A, 2008 M Pskov+ Velikije Luki, 2014 M Pskov+Porhov.

Sergij Vladimir Bulatnikov ***Velikije Luki***
T: B Velikije Luki+Nevel, Metr. Pskov ▪ ✉ ul. K. Libknehta 5, ROSSIJA-182113 Velikije Luki • [7] 1153 36339, [7] 911 3841560 • vluki-eparhia@mail.ru • http://luki-eparhia.ru
*16.4.1950 Omsk. N? staffbearer B Nikolaj Kutjepov. 1965-1969 Medical College Omsk, feldšer. 1970 monastery Pskov,1974 Smolensk. diak14.4.1974 ⊖21.4.1974. 1974-1979 Seminary Moskva. 1978 eparchy Kursk. mon13.11.1979. 1986-1988 Academy Moskva, 1988-1989 Academy Leningrad (correspondence course). 1989 eparchy Leningrad. 1994 eparchy Brjansk ⊕13.6.2013 Ascension, Moskva B Klintsy

+Trubčevsk (Patr Kirill – priest Vladislav Tsypin). 2013 member commission contacts with Old Believers. 25.12.2014 B Velikije Luki+Nevel, Metr. Pskov.

Metropolia Rjazan

Mark Sergej Golovkov ***Rjazan***

T: M Rjazan+Mihajlov, Metr. Rjazan ▪ ✉ pl. Sobornaja 3, ROSSIJA-390000 Rjazan • [7] 4912 28276-0, -1, 776623, 252934, [7] 903 839 1320 • mark@mospatr.ru • ryazeparh@mail.ru • www.ryazeparh.ru

*31.3.1964 Perm. N8.5. schools Perm. 1982-1984 Soviet Army. 1984-1988 Seminary Moskva. 1988-1992 Academy Moskva, Kandidat "Diadoch Fotijskij". mon19.10. 1990 diak21.11.1990 (A Aleksandr) ⊖7.1.1991. 1991-1992 teacher NT Seminary Moskva. 1992-1999 Mission Jerusalem. 1997 igumen Pentecost Jerusalem (P Aleksij). 1999-2009 Deputy Chairman Department for External Church Relations. archim3.5.2000 ⊕14.1.2004 B, 2010 A Jegorevsk, vicar Moskva. 2009-2015 Chairman Department Church Institutions outside Russia, administrator Wien. 2014 chairman Finances Commission. 2015 M Rjazan+Mihajlov, Metr. Rjazan.

Matfej Gennadij Andrejev ***Skopin***

T: B Skopin+Shatsk, Metr. Rjazan ▪ ✉ ul. Oktjabrskaja 26, ROSSIJA-391800 Skopin • skopin.eparhia@gmail.com • http://skopin-eparhia.ru

*18.5.1971 Tambov. 1988-1991 school eparchy Tambov. 1990-1993 dipl English French University Tambov. 1991-1997 (correspondence course) University Manchester. 1993-2009 teacher gymnasium Bokino. 1991-1998 hypodiakon Cathedral Tambov. 1998-2009 parishes Bokino and Tambov. diak1.3.1998 ⊖4.10.1998. 2000-2005 Seminary Moskva (correspondence course). 2005-2009 prorector Seminary Tambov. 18.5.2008 protoierej Tambov. 2008-2015 Academy and Doktorantura Moskva. 2009-2015 parishes Glasgow and Manchester. 2014 klirik Zurozh. archim24.10.2015 Dosnkoj Monastyr Moskva (igumen Paramon). 4.11.2015 narechenje Moskva (Patr Kirill) ⊕15.11.2015 Kaliningrad B Skopin+Shatsk, Metr. Rjazan (Patr Kirill).

Dionisij Pjotr Porubaj ***Kasimov***

T: B Kasimov+Sasov, Metr. Rjazan ▪ ✉ ul. 50 let SSSR dom 29, ROSSIJA-391308 Kasimov • [7] 49131 4468-4, -5, fax 44687, [7] 960 570 9000 • dionisius@rambler.ru • kaseparh@bk.ru • www.kaseparh.ru

*1.10.1975 Rjazan, N? 1992-1997 stud history University Rjazan. 1998-2001 Monastery St. Johann Rjazan, Theol učilišče Rjazan (correspondence course). diak 27.3.1999 mon28.8.2000. 2002-2009 Academy Moskva (correspondence course) ⊖4.11.2006 klirik Rjazan. 25.5.2009 igumen ⊕6.10.2011 B Kasimov+Sasov, Metr. Rjazan.

Metropolia Samara

Sergij Viktor Poljotkin ***Samara***
T: M Samara+Syzran, Metr. Samara ▪ ✉ Vilonovskaja 22, ROSSIJA-443001 Samara • [7] 846 332367-0, -1, 333466, 335368, Dača 638293, fax 330231 • kancelaria-eparxia@yandex.ru • eparhia@inbox.ru • www.samara.orthodoxy.ru
*13.4.1951 Chanino Rjazan. N18.7.1969 Monteur. 1981 Kandidat Moskva, diak26.4.1981 ⊖24.7.1982. 1982-1989 Cathedral Rostov-na-Donu ⊕5.5.1989 B Azov vicar Rostov. 1993 B, 1998 A, 2012 M Samara+Syzran, Metr. Samara.

Serafim Fjodor Glušakov
T: former B Anadyr+Čukotka ▪ ✉ Vilonovskaja 22, ROSSIJA-443001 Samara • [7] 846 332367-0, -1, 333466, 335368 • eparhia@inbox.ru • kancelaria-eparxia@yandex.ru • www.samara.orthodoxy.ru
*19.3.1969 Karaganda (family deported here 1930). N? 1986-1990 Seminary Moskva. 1990-1992 Pedagogical University Kujbyšev. diak16.2.1992 ⊖5.7.1992 mon23.6.1998. 2000 igumen. 2002 Kandidat Moskva. 2003 namestnik. 2004 absolvent Fac iur, teacher Samara ⊕22.5.2011 B Voskresensk vicar Moskva. 30.5.2011 B Anadyr+Čukotka. 24.12.2015 at disposition of M Samara.

Foma Nikolaj Mosolov
T: B Zhigulovsk, vicar Samara, Metr. Samara ▪ ✉ Vilonovskaja 22, ROSSIJA-443001 Samara • [7] 846 332367-0, -1, 333466, 335368, fax 330231 • www.samara.orthodoxy.ru
*30.11.1978 Sekretarka Orenburg. 1985-1995 school Sekretarka. 1995-1999 Seminary Samara. 1999-2004 Academy Moskva (correspondence course) 1999 teacher Church History, inspektor Seminary Samara. mon3.4.1999 Seminary Samara (A Sergij). diak4.4.1999. 2001 ekonom ⊖29.12.2002. 2004 igumen. 27.3.2005 palitsa. 2010 dipl Municipality Administration ⊕22.10.2015 B Zhigulovsk, vicar Samara.

Sofronij Sergej Balandin ***Kinel***
T: B Kinel+Bezenčuk, Metr. Samara ▪ ✉ ul. Demjana Bednogo 43 B, ROSSIJA-446430 Kinel • [7] 84663 64015, [7] 84626 5586-3, -4 • kinelepar@gmail.com
*12.6.1973 Žigulevske Samara, baptized youngster. N? radiotechnikum. diak1992 Samara A Evsevij ⊖1993 Samara A Sergij. mon26.3.1994. 1994-2002 duhovnik Mon Iverija Samara. 1996-2000 Seminary Samara. 2002-2011 rector Togliatti. 2003-2011 MTh Kişinev (correspondence course) "Life and work Metropolit Filaret Drozdov" (Russian, translated into Romanian) ⊕17.6.2012 B Kinel+Bezenčuk, Metr. Samara.

Nikifor Aleksej Hoteev ***Otradnyj***
T: B Otradnyj+Pohvistnevo, Metr. Samara ▪ ✉ ul. Sovjetskaja 22, Rossija-446330 Otradnyj • [7] 84661 21556, 51550 • mail-otrada@mail.ru • http://otradnenskay.cerkov.ru
*14.8.1975 Legnitsa Polonia father military officer. N? school Erevan Armenia. 1990-1992 military school Minsk, lieutenant Russian Army Aviation school Voronež. 1995-1999 Seminary Samara. 2004 Kandidat Academy Sankt-Peterburg "Istoria Samarskoj eparhii 1917-2000". 2004 press-sekretar eparchy Samara. mon21.2.2007 Togliatti (igumen Germogen Kritsin) diak24.2.2007 ⊖4.3.2007 Samara. 2008 rector Tabynska ikona Pohvistnevo. 19.4.2009 igumen. archim18.3. 2012 ⊕1.4.2012 B Otradnij+Pohvistnevo, Metr. Samara.

Metropolia Sankt-Peterburg

Varsonofij Anatolij Sudakov ***Sankt-Peterburg***
T: M Sankt-Peterburg+Ladoga, Metr. Sankt-Peterburg, Upravljajuščij djelam Mosk Patr ▪ ✉ nab. reki Monastyrki 1, Rossija-191167 Sankt-Peterburg • [7] 812 274-1413, -0628, -2633, 2346072, 2345424, fax 23459990 • tserkovspb@gmail.com • www.mitropolia.spb.ru
*3.6.1955 Malinovka Saratov. N24.4. Soviet Army. Psalomščik Serdobsk Penza. 1976-1979 Seminary Moskva. mon30.3.1978 diak27.4.1978 ⊖26.11.1978. 1982 igumen. 1982-1986 Academy Moskva. 1986 Kandidat Moskva. 1986-1991 rector Cathedral Penza. archim1987 Penza ⊕8.2.1991 B, 2001 A, 2010 M Saransk+Mordovia. 25.12.2009 Upravljajuščij djelam Mosk Patr, Moskva Theol Academy 325 years. 2014 M Sankt-Peterburg+Ladoga, Metr. Sankt-Peterburg.

Vladimir Vladimir Kotljarov
T: former M Sankt-Peterburg+Ladoga, Metr. Sankt-Peterburg ▪ ✉ Naberjóžnaja reki Monastyrki 1, Rossija-191167 Sankt-Peterburg • tserkovspb@gmail.com • www.mitropolia-spb.ru
*27.5.1929 Aktjubinsk Kazahstan Assyrian family. N17.10. diak22.5.1953 ⊖24.5.1953. 1958 Kandidat Leningrad. mon1962 Deputy Chief Russian Orthodox Mission Jerusalem, Observer Vatican Council ⊕30.12.1962. 1962-1964 B Zvenigorod Repres to WCC Geneva. 30.3.1964 B Voronež. 1964-1965 B Podolsk Representant to Patr Antiochia. 1966 B Kirov. 1967 A Berlin. 1970 A Rostov. 1973 A Irkutsk. 1975 A Vladimir. 1980 A Krasnodar. 1987 A Pskov+Porchov (=1991 M Pskov+Velikie Luki). 1993 A Rostov na Donu. 1995 M Sankt-Peterburg, 2000 St. Albert award Ecumenical Council Poland. 2003 Orden St. Aleksandr Nevskij. 2004 Orden "Za zaslugi pered Otečestvom". 19.3.2014 retired.

Markell German Vetrov
T: B Carskoje Selo, vicar Sankt-Peterburg, Metr. Sankt-Peterburg ▪ ✉ Naberjóžnaja reki Monastyrki 1, ROSSIJA-191167 Sankt-Peterburg • [7] 812 5774498, fax 4666697
*8.6.1952 Mineralnye Vody. N20.6. 1970-1978 Seminary Academy Leningrad, hypodiakon to M Nikodim Rotov. mon1973 diak1973 ⊖1976. 1976-1977 stud Institut de Bossey. 1978 teacher Seminary. 1995 rector Carskoje Selo ⊕27.9.2006 B Peterhof, vicar Sankt-Peterburg, 30.5.2007 in Hamburg. 2013 B Carskoje Selo, vicar Sankt-Peterburg, Metr. Sankt-Peterburg.

Nazarij Nikolaj Lavrijenko
T: B Kronstadt, vicar Sankt-Peterburg, Metr. Sankt-Peterburg ▪ ✉ Naberjóžnaja reki Monastyrki 1, ROSSIJA-191167 Sankt-Peterburg • [7] 812 2741702, 2775854 • office@lavra.spb.ru • www.lavra.spb.ru
*11.8.1952 Ivkovtsi Ukraina. N27.10. 1974 Agricultural Institute Krym. 1974-1975 Soviet Army Germany. 1978-1982 botanic garden Ukraina. 1982-1988 Seminary Academy Leningrad. mon1985 diak1985 ⊖1985. 1986 Aleksandr Nevskij Lavra. 1987 rector Vyborg. 1988 igumen. 1990 rector Leningrad. archim1.2.1991. 1991 rector Konevo. 1996 blagočinnyj dean monasteries eparchy Sankt-Peterburg. 1997 namestnik Aleksandr Nevskij ⊕28.5.2009 B Vyborg, vicar Sankt-Peterburg. 2013 B Kronstadt, vicar Sankt-Peterburg, Metr. Sankt-Peterburg.

Amvrosij Vitalij Jermakov
T: A Peterhof, vicar Sankt-Peterburg, Metr. Sankt-Peterburg, Rector Theol Seminary Academy ▪ ✉ Obvodnyj Kanal 17, ROSSIJA-191167 Sankt-Peterburg • [7] 812 717-1673, -3351, -8663, bookkeeper -3373, fax 7178607, 7173984, [7] 911 7070228 • rector@spbda.ru • amvrosy@patriarchia.ru • amvrosij@yandex.ru • www.spbda.ru
*15.6.1970 Lužki Železnogorsk Kursk. N23.10. 1982-1986 akolyte Mihailovka Kursk, 1986-1988 Kromy Orël. 1988-1990 Soviet Army. 1991-1995 Seminary Moskva. mon7.4.1994 diak29.5.1994 ⊖8.10.1994. 1994-2000 dirigent chor. 1995-1999 Kandidat Moskva "Soteriology of St. John Chrysostom". 2000-2004 blagočinnyj dean Sretenskij Monastyr Moskva, prorector Seminary. 2003 teacher Russian Presidential Academy "State Church relations". 3.6.2004 igumen. archim28.12.2004 ⊕26.3.2005. 2005-2006 B Prokopjevsk vicar Kemerovo. 2006-2008 B Bronnitsy, vicar Moskva. 2008 B Gačina, vicar Sankt-Peterburg, rector. 14.10.2010 Moskva Theol Academy 325 years. 2011 Orden St. Isidor (Estonia). 2012 Orden Andrej Rubljov. 2013 B, 2014 A Peterhof, vicar Sankt-Peterburg. Metr. Sankt-Peterburg.

Mstislav Mihail Djatšin ***Tikhvin***
T: B Tikhvin+Lodejnoje pole, Metr. Sankt-Peterburg ▪ ✉ pl. Svobody 9, ROSSIJA-187555 Tikhvin • [7] 81367 57557, [7] 921 6366343 • tikhvin.diocese@gmail.com • www.tikhvinskajaeparchija.ru • http://tikhvin-eparhia.ru

*11.11.1967 Ukraina. 1985-1987 Soviet Army, hypodiakon to A Vladimir Kotljarov Pskov. 1988-1996 Seminary Academy Leningrad. mon26.3.1998 diak12.4.1998 ⊖4.12.1998. 2007 sekretar eparchy Sankt-Peterburg. 28.10.2011 igumen; blagočinnyj dean Lodejnopol. archim1.4.2012 ⊕22.5.2012 Lodejnopol, vicar Sankt-Peterburg. 2013 B Tihvin+Lodejnoje pole, Metr. Sankt-Peterburg.

Mitrofan Mihail Osjak ***Gatčina***
T: B Gatčina+Luga, Metr. Sankt-Peterburg ▪ ✉ Krasnaja 1A, ROSSIJA-188300 Gatčina • [7] 921 9450071 • gatchina-eparhia@mail.ru • www. gatchina-eparhia.ru

*19.11.1973 Rostov-na-Donu, father priest. N? 1990 Seminary Minsk. diak21.9.1992 Rostov-na-Donu ⊖6.6.1993. 1993-1995 Seminary Moskva. mon11.4.1994. 3.7.1998 igumen. 2005-2007 Academy Sankt-Peterburg. archim15.3.2013 ⊕23.3.2013 B Gatčina+Luga, Metr. Sankt-Peterburg.

Ignatij Igor Punin ***Vyborg***
T: B Vyborg+Priozersk, Metr. Sankt-Peterburg ▪ ✉ Sobornaja pl. 1, ROSSIJA-188800 Vyborg • [7] 81278 32910, [7] 495 6717723 • info@eparhiya-viborg.ru • http://eparchiya-viborg.ru

*17.4.1973 Brjansk. N11.2. 1980-1990 school N46 Brjansk. 1990-1995 Seminary Smolensk. 1993-1996 Department External Church Relations Moskva with official delegation Greece Lettonia Polska Germania Israel Spain Cuba Canada. mon23.3.1998 diak7.4.1998 (M Kirill Smolensk). 1999-2005 sekretar eparchy, dean St. John Baptist Smolensk ⊖7.4.1999. 1999 pectoral cross. 2003 igumen Pascha. 2004 palitsa. archim2.5.2005 ⊕7.7.2005 Moskva B Vjazma. vicar Smolensk (Patr Aleksij). 2009 B Bronnitsy, vicar Moskva. 2010 chairman Synodal Department Youth Affairs. 2013 B Vyborg+Priozersk, Metr. Sankt-Peterburg. 2013 Berlin o.Viktor Savik.

Metropolia Saratov

Longin Vladimir Korčagin ***Saratov***
T: M Saratov+Volsk, Metr. Saratov ▪ ✉ ul. Volskaja 55, ROSSIJA-410056 Saratov • [7] 452 734319, fax 737072 • info@eparhia-saratov.ru • panagia@yandex.ru • www.eparhia-saratov.ru

*31.7.1961 Sukhumi Avkhaz. N29.10. 1977-1979 stud philology University Sukhumi. 1979-1981 exkursovod. 1981-1983 teacher Russian language secondary school

Sukhumi. 1983-1985 Soviet Army. 1985-1988 Seminary Moskva. mon1986 Troice-Sergieva Lavra (St. Longin of Sotin). diak1986 ⊖7.6.1988. 1988 Academy Moskva. 1988-1992 Fac theol Sofia Bulgaria. 1992-2003 Head representation of Troice-Sergieva Lavra in Moscow. 1994 igumen. archim2000 ⊕19.8.2003B, 2011 M Saratov.

Pahomij Dmitrij Bruskov ***Pokrovsk***

T: B Pokrovsk+Nikolajevsk, Metr. Saratov ▪ ✉ ploščad Svobody 5, ROSSIJA- 413100 Engels • [7] 8453 568680, fax 568825 • eparhia@pravpokrov.ru • www.pravpokrov.ru

*5.7.1976 Moskva. N28.5. 1989-1993 techn. licej Moskva. 1993-1997 stud techn. University Moskva. 1998-2002 (correspondence course) Seminary Moskva. mon1.4.1999 diak23.7.2000 ⊖28.8.2003 klirik Saratov. 8.4.2007 igumen, teacher Seminary Saratov ⊕19.12.2011 B Pokrovsk+Nikolajevsk, Metr. Saratov.

Tarasij Sergej Vladimirov ***Balašov***

T: B Balašov+Rtiščev, Metr. Saratov ▪ ✉ Sovjetskaja 168, ROSSIJA-412309 Balašov • [7] 4545 63388, 40747, 43003, [7] 917 315 6171, 917 205 7803 • kanc.bal@yandex.ru • www.balashovblag.ru

*18.6.1974 Telešovka Tambov. N? 1989-1993 veterinar. 1993-1995 Military service. 1995-1998 učilišče Tambov. 1998-2002 Seminary Saratov. mon26.8.2001 diak12.9.2001 ⊖7.2.2002 klirik Saratov. 2004-2007 Academy Sankt-Peterburg. 19.4.2009 igumen. archim14.10.2011 ⊕17.12.2011 B Balašov+Rtiščev, Metr. Saratov.

Metropolia Simbirsk

Anastasij Aleksandr Metkin ***Simbirsk***

T: M Simbirsk ▪ ✉ ul. Uljanovskaja 2, ROSSIJA-432017 Uljanovsk • [7] 422 370582, 370399, 370985 • simbirsk-eparhia@mail.ru • www.simbeparhia.ru

*27.8.1944 Stolbovo Kaliningrad, N11.10. 1963 absolvent construction school. 1963 construction Kimry. 1967 čtets Kazan. diak6.5.1968. 1971-1983 Seminary Academy Moskva ⊖7.2.1972 mon5.9.1976 igumen. 1976 rector Kazan, sekretar eparchy Kazan. archim1985 ⊕11.12.1988 B Kazan+ASSR Mari. 11.6.1993 name eparchy Kazan+Tatarstan, 1996 A, 2012 M Kazan+Tatarstan. 1998 rector Seminary Kazan. 2015 M Simbirsk.

Filaret Vjačeslav Konkov ***Baryš***

T: B Baryš+Inza, Metr. Simbirsk ▪ ✉ per. Pushkina 26, ROSSIJA-433750 Baryš • [7] 4253 22626 • upravlenie@barysh-eparhia.ru • www.barysh-eparhia.ru

*6.12.1963 Donbarovskij Orenburg. N? 1971-1981 school Artjuškino Uljanovsk. 1982-1984 Soviet Army. 1985-1991 stud Kybernetics Moskva. 1991-1996 ingenieur Troitski Moskva. mon30.11.1996 Vidnoje. diak7.12.1996. 1998 klirik Simbirsk ⊖22.3.1998. 2004 absolvent Seminary Saratov (correspondence course). 2009 blagočinnyj dean Simbirsk. archim12.8.2012 ⊕28.10.2012 B Baryš+Inza, Metr. Simbirsk.

Diodor Dmitrij Isajev ***Melekess***
T: B Melekess+Čerdaklinsk, Metr. Simbirsk ▪ ✉ Čapajeva 14, ROSSIJA-433508 Dimitrovgrad • [7] 422 461693 • melekess-eparhia@mail.ru • www.melekess-eparhia.ru • http://meleparhia.ru

*7.5.1976 Jazykov Uljanovsk. N12.5. 1989-1993 altarnik Tavolžanka. 1993-1997 Seminary Moskva. diak28.7.1997 klirik Uljanovsk. 2000-2013 sekretar eparchy Simbirsk. mon23.3.2001. 2001 second orar. 2007 dipl Technikum Inza. 2009 archidiakon ⊖13.11.2011. 2012 blagočinnyj Uljanovsk, sekretar eparchy Melekess. archim17.3.2013 ⊕19.5.2013 Melekess+Čerdaklinsk, Metr. Simbirsk.

Metropolia Smolensk

Isidor Roman Tupikin ***Smolensk***
T: M Smolensk+Roslavlj, Metr. Smolensk ▪ ✉ Soborny Dvor 17, ROSSIJA-214000 Smolensk • [7] 4812 380197, fax 381928 • eparxysmolensk@mail.ru • www.smoleparh.ru

*27.5.1974 Krasnojarsk, N27.5. 1992-1995 Technical University Krasnojarsk. 1995-2003 Seminary Academy Moskva. 2003-2007 assistant prorector. mon31.3.2006 Lavra Sergiev Posad diak16.4.2006 (B Jevgenij rector Akad Moskva) ⊖19.12.2006. 2007-2009 rector Seminary Jaroslavl. 16.4.2009 igumen. 19.4.2009 klirik Moskva, vice-chairman Youth department. archim14.3.2013 (Patr Kirill) ⊕17.3.2013 B Smolensk+Vjazma, 2015 M Smolensk+Roslavlj (eparchy Vjazma created 2015), Metr. Smolensk. 2015-2016 member Holy Synod.

Sergij Sergej Zjatkov ***Vjazma***
T: B Vjazma+Gagarin, Metr. Smolensk ▪ ✉ per. Nagornyj 1, ROSSIJA-215110 Vjazma • [7] 4813 41773 • vyazma.eparh@mail.ru • www.vyazmaeparh.ru

*15.2.1967 Drosdovo Roslavlj Smolensk. 1982-1984 stud Technikum Moskva. 1984-1985 hypodiakon Cathedral Smolensk. 1985-1987 Soviet Army. diak28.8.1988 (A Kirill) ⊖14.10.1988 (A Kirill) mon23.4.1992 (A Kirill). 1.9.1995 absolvent Seminary Moskva (correspondence course). 17.4.1996 igumen. 1999-2001 rector St. Zinaida Rio de Janeiro. 2001 director Roslavlja Smolensk. archim9.1. 2007 (A Kirill). 2013 Jurist Institute Moskva Governmental Administration ⊕21.5.2015 Uljanovsk B Vjazem+Gagarin (Patr Kirill), Metr. Smolensk.

Metropolia Stavropol

Kirill Leonid Pokrovskij **_Stavropol_**

T: M Stavropol+Nevinnomyssk, Metr. Stavropol ▪ ✉ ul. Dzeržinskogo 157, ROSSIJA-355017 Stavropol • [7] 652 35516-3, -5, 355233, fax 355042 • krest@mail.stv.ru • www.stavropol-eparhia.ru

*5.8.1963 Miasse Čeljabinsk. N24.5. Matura 1981 Zagorsk. 1981-1983 Soviet Army. 1984-1988 Seminary Moskva. 1988-1990 Seminary Sofia Bulgaria. mon1989 diak1989 ⊖1989. 1993 rector Theol school, 1994 igumen. 1995-2004 Seminary Nižnij Novgorod. archim2000. 2001 Kandidat theol. 2005 professor Slavjanska Academy. 2006 rector Theol school Vyksunsk. 2009 namestnik Monastir Don Moskva ⊕29.11.2009 B Pavlov-Posad. 2010 President Synodal Komitet Kosaks. 2011 B, 2012 M Stavropol+Nevinnomyssk, Metr. Stavropol.

Gedeon Vasilij Gubka **_Georgijevsk_**

T: B Georgijevsk+Praskovejsk, Metr. Stavropol ▪ ✉ ul. Stroitelej 2, ROSSIJA-357831 Georgijevsk • [7] 7951 62203 • georg-eparhia@mail.ru • www.georg-eparhia.ru

*9.12.1962 Vaslovivtsi Chernovtsy. N9.10. Technical University Chernovtsy. 1980 Moldavia. 1981-1983 Soviet Army. 1983-1984 teacher Chernovtsy. 1984-1988 Seminary, 1988-1992 Academy Moskva. mon29.2.1988. 1993-1999 regent Music school Lavra Sergiev Posad. 1999-2006 director Orth Gymnasium. 2003 Orden kn. Vladimir, 2005 patriarchal Gramota, 2007-2012 naselnik administrator Sergiev Posad. 2012 medal oblast Moskva. archim9.10.2012 Stavropol (Patr Kirill) ⊕13.12.2012 Georgijevsk+Praskovejsk, Metr. Stavropol (Patr Kirill).

Metropolia Tambov

Feodosij Sergej Vaznjev **_Tambov_**

T: M Tambov+Rasskazovo, Metr. Tambov ▪ ✉ ul. Naberežnaja/A. Bebelja 80/2, ROSSIJA-392000 Tambov • [7] 4752 718499, fax 759983, 751897, 486139 • admin@eparhia-tmb.ru • info@eparhia-tmb.ru • teu@tmb.ru • www.eparhia-tmb.ru

*26.1.1961 Tambov. N16.5. diak28.8.1987 ⊖12.7.1988. 10.12.1989 – 22.7.1990 Regensburg. 1990-1993 Department for External Church Relations Moskva. 1992 Symposion. archim1993. 1993-2002 head Mission Jerusalem ⊕21.4.2002 B Vetluga, vicar Nižnij Novgorod. 2002 B Tambov+Mičurinsk, 2012 M Tambov+Rasskazovo, Metr. Tambov. 11.6.2013 İstanbul.

Ignatij Georgij Rumjantsev ***Uvarovo***
T: B Uvarovo+Kirsanovo, Metr. Tambov ▪ ✉ Pervomajskij pereulok 17, ROSSIJA-393460 Uvarovo • [7] 47558 42885, fax 40450 • uvarovo.ep@ yandex.ru • admin@uvar-eparhia.ru • pressa@uvar-eparhia.ru • www.uvar-eparhia.ru
*7.8.1971 Čerkizovo Puškinsk Moskva. N? 1989-1994 stud forest-economy University Moskva. 1995 monastery Poščupovo Rjazan. mon20.4.1997 diak21.5.1997 ⊖10.12.1999. 2000-2009 stud Seminary Academy Moskva. archim2012 ⊕25.1. 2013 University Chapel Moskva, B Uvarovo+Kirsanovo, Metr. Tambov (Patr Kirill).

Germogen Vladimir Seryj ***Mičurinsk***
T: B Mičurinsk+Moršansk, Metr. Tambov ▪ ✉ ul. TsGL 10A, ROSSIJA-393770 Mičurinsk • [7] 4752 718499, fax 759983, 751897, 486139 • mich-eparhia@mail.ru • www.michurinsk-eparchia.ru
*22.2.1973 Pjatiletka Novosibirsk N? 1990-1995 Agricultural University Novosibirsk "agronom selektsioner", 1992 baptized Cathedral Novosibirsk. 1995-1997 Aspirantura genetika. 1995-1997 Theol Institute Novosibirsk. 1997-2001 Seminary Tobolsk. mon17.12.1999 "Germogen" (A Dimitrij Tobolsk) diak26.12.1999 ⊖26.11.2000. 2000-2002 sekretar eparchy, 2001 teacher patrologia Seminary Tobolsk. 2002 ekonom. 2002 dipl "Apologetičeskije trudy donikejskogo perioda", 2002-2013 first prorector Seminary Tobolsk. 2003-2007 Academy Moskva (correspondence course). Kandidat "History Theol. Education Tobolsk 1620-1937". 2005 namestnik Mon Abalak. archim2.8.2013 Abalak ⊕27.9.2013 St. Nicholas Pyžah Moskva, B Mičurinsk +Moršansk, Metr. Tambov (Patr Kirill).

Metropolia Tatarstan

Feofan Ivan Ašurkov ***Kazan***
T: M Kazan+Tatarstan, Metr. Tatarstan ▪ ✉ Karla Marksa 9/15, ROSSIJA-420111 Kazan • [7] 843 29201-45, -75, -84 • eparhia-tatarstan@mail.ru • www.kazan-mitropolia.ru • www.tatarstan-mitropolia.ru
*22.11.1947 Dmitrov Kursk, N24.10. Soviet Army. 1969-1970 hypodiakon B Gedeon Smolensk. 1970-1972 Seminary Moskva. 1972-1976 Academy Moskva, Kandidat "Dogmatic teaching of Basilios the Great". mon19.12.1973 Troice-Sergieva Lavra. diak1974 (Sergij Golubtsov) ⊖25.3.1976 Tula (M Iuvenaly). 1977-1982 Mission Jerusalem. 1979 igumen. 1982-1984 Lavra Zagorsk. 1984-1987 Secretary eparchy America. 1985 Orden Sergij Radonež, 1987-1989 Department External Church Relations. 1989-1993 exarch Alexandria, 1993-1999 Department External Church Relations. 1999-2000 exarch Antiochia. 2000 Orden pr. Daniil ⊕2000 B

Magadan+Sinaj. 2003 B, 2008 A Stavropol. 2005 Znak Slavy Respublika Severnaja Ossetija Alanija. 2011 A, 2012 M Čeljabinsk. 2015 M Kazan+Tatarstan.

Mefodij Dmitrij Zajtsev ***Almjetjevsk***

T: B Almjetjevsk+Bugulminsk, Metr. Tatarstan ▪ ✉ ul. Černyševskogo 22, ROSSIJA-423450 Almjetjevsk • [7] 553 30613-3, -4 • almet.eparhia@yandex.ru • www.almet-eparhia.ru

*25.10.1978 Kazan N24.5. 1993 altarnik Monastery Raifsk. 1997-2007 St. Tihkon University Moskva. diak10.8.1997 mon19.3.1998 ⊖2.5.1999. 2003 rector Kazan, teacher Church history Seminary Kazan. 14.5.2009 igumen. 2010 Aspirantura Uni Povolžsk. archim14.6.2012 ⊕11.7.2012 Almjetjevsk+Bugulminsk, Metr. Tatarstan.

Parmen Viktor Šipilev ***Čistopol***

T: B Čistopol+Nižnekamsk, Metr. Tatarstan ▪ ✉ ul. Karla Marksa 67, ROSSIJA-422980 Čistopol • [7] 4342 54260 • info@chistopol-eparhia.ru • www.chistopol-eparhia.ru

*1.5.1956 pos. Glubokij Rostov, baptized joungster, N10.8. 1973-1979 Seminary Odessa. 1980-2014 parishes Rostov. diak17.9.1980 ⊖21.9.1980. 1988 protoierej. 1995 Kandidat Moskva. mon21.11.2002. 2014-2015 skitonachalnik Starocherkassk. archim10.5.2015 ⊕18.5.2015 Moskva B Čistopol+Nižnekamsk, Metr. Tatarstan (Patr Kirill).

Metropolia Tobolsk

Dimitrij Aleksej Kapálin ***Tobolsk***

T: M Tobolsk+Tjumen, Metr. Tobolsk, rector Theol Seminary ▪ ✉ Krasnaja pl. Kreml, ROSSIJA-626152 Tobolsk • [7] 3456 222288, 222439, [7] 912 9968285, fax 222439 • tte_tds@mail.ru • tte_eu@mail.ru • www.tobolsk-eparhia.ru

*11.3.1952 Udolnoe Ramenskoe. N24.2. 1974 absolvent Institut Transport Moskva. 1984 absolvent Theol Seminary Moskva. mon31.1.1986 diak23.11.1986 ⊖7.4.1986. 1987 Kandidat Moskva. archim13.4.1987, ekonom Seminary Academy. 1989 Inspektor Seminary Moskva ⊕4.11.1990 Moskva. 1999 A. 2009 Dr. soc. 2013 M Metr. Tobolsk.

Tihon Viktor Bobov ***Išim***

T: B Išim+Aromashevo, Metr. Tobolsk ▪ ✉ ul. Leningradskaja 34, ROSSIJA-627750 Išim • [7] 982 9327922 • ishimeparhia@mail.ru • www.ishim-eparhia.cerkov.ru

*12.9.1954 Pervouralsk Sverdlovsk. N24.2. 1972 absolvent Gymnasium Matvejevke Kurgan. absolvent Technikum Tobolsk. 1981 absolvent Veterinary Academy, 1981-1992 teacher Moskva. 1989 Kandidat biology. mon1.8.1992 diak28.8.1992

⊖7.1.1993. 1993-1996 teacher Seminary Tobolsk. 21.2.1996 igumen namestnik monastery Tjumen. Archimandrit dean rajon Tjumen, rector Theol school Tjumen ⊕3.11.2013 Moskva, B Išim+Aromačevo, Metr. Tobolsk (Patr Kirill).

Metropolia Tomsk

Rostislav Sergej Devjatov ***Tomsk***

T: M Tomsk+Asino, Metr. Tomsk ▪ ✉ pr. Lenina 119, ROSSIJA- 634050 Tomsk • [7] 3822 511385, 511318-6, fax -5, 528123 • eparchy@pravoslavie.tomsk.ru • www.pravoslavie.tomsk.ru

*27.1.1963 Kimry Kalinin. N27.3. 1980-1981 Architect class Moskva. 1981-1984 sekretar eparchy Kalinin. 1981-1983 Soviet Army. 1984-1988 Seminary Moskva. mon9.3.1987 Lavra Sergiev Posad. diak28.3.1987 ⊖28.5.1987. 1988-1992 Academy Moskva. 1992 teacher Seminary Moskva ⊕28.11.1993 Moskva B Magadan+ Čukotska. 1998 B, 2013 M Tomsk, 2003 Orden Sergij Radonež (II), 2013 Orden St. Innokentij Moskva.

Siluan Aleksandr Vjurov ***Kolpaševo***

T: B Kolpaševo+Streševoj, Metr. Tomsk ▪ ✉ ul. Obskaja 50, ROSSIJA- 636460 Kolpaševo • [7] 38254 50670 • eparchia@mail.ru • www.svjatoynarym.ru

*20.2.1972 Kaliningrad. N? baptized 21.7.1989 Tver (Rostislav Devjatov). 1989-1994 Fakultet Filolog. University Immanuel Kant Kaliningrad "Russian language and literature". 1993-1994 hypodiakon B Panteleimon. mon24.8.1994 Magadan diak4.9.1994 ⊖23.10.1994. 1995-1998 rector Magadan. 6.2.1999 namestnik Tomsk. 1.11.1999 igumen. 1999-2013 teacher Seminary Tomsk. 2009 Academy Moskva. archim21.7.2012 ⊕31.3.2013 Kolpaševo+Streševoj, Metr. Tomsk.

Metropolia Tula

Alexij Andrej Kutjepov ***Tula***

T: M Tula+Jefremov, Metr. Tula ▪ ✉ ul. Žukovskogo 61, ROSSIJA- 300041Tula • [7] 4872 312460, 3639-95, -85, fax 361507, 360507 • o.agafangel@mail.ru • eparhia.new@yandex.ru • www.tulaeparhia.ru

*10.5.1953 Moskva. N18.10. 1970 Chimičeskij Fakultet. 1972-1975 Seminary Moskva. diak15.2.1975 ⊖22.6.1975. 1975 Irkutsk mon7.9.1975 archim20.11.1975. 1979 Kandidat Moskva. 1980 Vladimir. 27.4.1984 namestnik Troice-Sergieva Lavra. 1988 chairman Department Economics ⊕1.12.1988 B, 1989 A Zaraisk. 1990-2002 A Alma Ata+Kazakhstan = 1991 Alma-Ata+Semipalatinsk, 1994 Alma-Ata = Almaty. 1995-2002 chairman Intereparchial Commission Kazakhstan. 1999 Astana +Almaty. 2002 A Tula, in charge of the Chinese Autonomous Church in the Xinjiang Uygur region. 2012 M Tula+Jefremov, Metr. Tula.

Serafim Dimitrij Kuzminov ***Beljov***

T: B Beljov+Aleksin, Metr. Tula ▪ ✉ ul. Rabočaja 13 A, ROSSIJA-301530 Beljóv • [7] 48742 41958 • belev.info@yandex.ru • www.belev-eparhia.ru

*31.8.1977 Bogoroditska Tula. N? mon9.12.1997 Tula. diak10.12.1997 Bogoroditska ⊖5.4.1998 teacher history Tula. 2001-2004 Seminary Kaluga. 2004-2007 Academy Sankt-Peterburg. 2005 teacher Theology University Tula. 1.12.2007 igumen ⊕3.9.2011 B Kamensk+Alapajevsk. 2012 B Beljov+Aleksin, Metr. Tula.

Metropolia Tver

Viktor Vladimir Olejnik ***Tver***

T: M Tver+Kašin, Metr. Tver ▪ ✉ ul. Sovjetskaja 10, ROSSIJA-170100 Tver • [7] 4822 323557, Kancelaria 321208, 337268, 235312, dom 356620, fax 343738 • 343738@mail.ru • eparhia@tvcom.ru • tver@eparhia.ru • www.tver.eparhia.ru

*21.9.1940 Počajev Kremenets Ternopol. N13.2. 1958-1962 Seminary Leningrad, 1962-1966 Akademy Leningrad. 1966 Kandidat. mon2.1.1966 diak6.1.1966 ⊖22.10. 1967. 1968-1978 Ključar Krasnodar, 1969 igumen. archim1974. 1978-1982 Kalinin (=1990 Tver). 1982 sekretar eparchy Kalinin ⊕4.12.1988 B Kalinin, 1997 A, 2012 M Tver+Kašin, Metr. Tver.

Filaret Dimitrij Gavrin ***Bežetsk***

T: B Bežetsk+Vjesjegonsk, Metr. Tver ▪ ✉ ul. Nečajeva 45, ROSSIJA-171980 Bežetsk • [7] 48231 5-05-44, 20846 • bezheparhia@yandex.ru • www.bezheparhia.ru

*19.9.1973 Novozabidovskij Tver. N? 1992-1996 Mechanical-Technol. University Tver. 1996 Economical office Academy Moskva. 2001-2005 Seminary Moskva, 2005-2009 Academy Kiev, Kandidat "Orth Church in the Ukraina in the years of World War II." mon21.12.2008. 2008 teacher Seminary Kiev History. diak2.1.2009 ⊖8.1.2009. 13.12.2009 igumen Tver. archim1.8.2012 klirik Tver ⊕25.11.2012 B Bežetsk+Vjesjegonsk Metr. Tver.

Adrian Aleksandr Uljanov ***Ržev***

T: B Ržev+Toropets, Metr. Tver ▪ ✉ ul. Partizanskaja 35, ROSSIJA-172381 Ržev • [7] 48232 31582 • rjeveparhia@yandex.ru • www.rzheveparhia.ru

*30.1.1951 Moskva. N? 1969-1971 Soviet Army. 1972-1974 psalomščik Taranka. 1975-1979 Seminary Moskva. mon1981 Vilnius diak1981 ⊖1983. 1984-1990 blagočinnyj dean Kaunas. 1985-1989 (correspondence course) Academy Moskva. 1986 igumen. 1990-1993 Degunino Moskva. 1993 Tver. archim1994 ⊕21.9.2011 B Bežetsk, vicar Tver. 2011 B Ržev+Toropets, Metr. Tver.

Metropolia Udmurtija

Viktorin Viktor Kostenkov ***Izhev***

T: M Izhev+Udmurtija, Metr. Udmurtija ■ ✉ Udmurtskaja 220, ROSSIJA-426004 Iževsk • [7] 3412 780087, 785318, 741623 • pravsarapul@gmail.com • kadry@udmeparhia.ru • eparhiya@udm.net • www.eparhia-sarapul.ru • www.udmparhia.ru

*10.5.1953 Sarapul Udmurtia N? 1970 Pedagogical Institute Udmurtija. 1976 Kazan. diak7.1.1979. 1979 Seminary Moskva (correspondence course). 1980 Ioškar-Ola ⊖1983. 1993 mitra, rector Iževsk. 2005 absolvent Academy Kiev (correspondence course), military chaplain Kavkaz. mon15.9.2013, Orden Sergij Radonež, Serafim Sarov ⊕23.2.2014 B Sarapul+Možga. 2015 M Udmurtija.

Antonij Aleksij Prostihin ***Sarapul***

T: B Sarapul+Možga, Metr. Udmurtija ■ ✉ P.O.Box 6100, ROSSIJA-427960 Sarapul • [7] 3412 74-16-23 • pravsarapul@gmail.com • www.eparhia-sarapul.ru • http://vk.com/eparhiasarapul

*20.10.1976 Glazov Udmurtija, baptized youngster. 1984-1994 secondary school. 1994-1995 stud Theol school Volgograd. 1995-1996 novice Kremensky Monastery Volgograd. 1996-1998 Russian army. 1998-2002 altar boy Transfiguration Church Glazov. diak17.3.2002 Transfiguration Church of Glazov (A Izhevsk Nikolaj) ⊖6.5.2003 (A Izhevsk Nikolaj), Rector Protection Church Seva. 2009 dipl Seminary Moskva (correspondence course). mon14.4.2009 Holy Trinity Aleksandr Nevskij Lavra (M Vladimir). 2012 Fac jur of the Institute of Foreign Economic Relations, Economics and Law in St. Petersburg (correspondence course). 2015 dipl Academy St. Petersburg (correspondence course). Confessor of the Leningrad regional branch of the Brotherhood of Alexander Nevsky. archim25.12.2015 ⊕28.12.2015 B Sarapul+Možga, Metr. Udmurtija (Patr. Kirill).

Viktor Sergejev ***Glazov***

T: B Glazov+Igrinsk, Metr. Udmurtija ■ ✉ pl. Svobody 10 A, ROSSIJA-426019 Glazov • [7] 3412 741623 • glasoveparh@gmail.com • www.eparhia-glazov.ru

*22.12.1954 Kambarks, Udmurtia. 1970-1974 technicum Kambarsk. 1974-1979 stud Fac Mechano-Technology Izhevsk. 1979-1987 fabric Kambarsk. 1987-1992 kino-operator. 1991 dipl Cinematography University. 1993 parishes Udmurtia. diak21.7. 1993 ⊖8.8.1998. 2001 dipl (correspondence course) Seminary Moskva. 2002 Orden St. Sergij Radonež (III). mon11.4.2014 archim12.7.2014 ⊕31.8.2014 Cathedral Tambov B Glazov+Igrinsk (Patr Kirill).

Metropolia Vjatka

Mark Aleksej Tužikov ***Vjatka***

T: M Vjatka+Slobodskoj, Metr. Vjatka ▪ ✉ ul. Gorbačeva 4, ROSSIJA-610000 Kirov Vjatka • [7] 332 642547, 675-111, -497, 490229 622541, 629357, 629875 • kancelyaria@mail.ru • yurist@eparhia-vtk.ru • www.vjatskaja-eparhia.ru

*26.9.1961 Moskva. N17.1. 1978-1981 Konstruktor. 1981-1985 Hydrometcenter. 1985-1988 Intourist. 1988-1991 Seminary Moskva. 1991-1994 Academy Moskva. mon 1991 diak18.6.1992 ⊖1.11.1992. 1993-1995 namestnik Cathedral Astrahan ⊕3.9.1995 B, 2005 A Khabarovsk+Priamurje. 2011 A, 2012 M Vjatka+Slobodskoj, Metr. Vjatka.

Leonid Denis Tolmachev ***Uržum***

T: B Uržum+Omutninsk, Metr. Vjatka ▪ ✉ ul. Sovjetskaja 34, ROSSIJA-613530 Uržum • [7] 3363 22209 • kancelyaria@eparhiya-urzhum.ru • urzhum_eparhiya@mail.ru • www.eparhiya-urzhum.ru

*12.5.1975 Moskva. 1976 baptized youngster 1982-1992 school Odintsovo oblast Moskva. 1992-1997 stud Agriculture Academy K.A.Timirjazeva. 1997-2001 Theol school Perervinsk Moskva. 1.5.2002 Optina Pustyn. mon20.4.2003 diak4.5.2003. 2005 book: "Nikolo-Perervinskij monastyr" ⊖23.10.2006. 2007-2012 (correspondence course) Academy Moskva. 2013-2014 podvorje Optina Pust. Sankt-Peterburg. archim1.11.2014. ⊕14.12.2014 John the Baptist Monastery Moskva B Urzhum+Omutninsk, Metr. Vjatka (Patr Kirill).

Paisij Andrej Kuznetsov ***Jaransk***

T: B Jaransk+Luza, Metr. Vjatka ▪ ✉ ul. Karla Marksa 14, ROSSIJA-612260 Jaransk • [7] 3367 22318 kancelyaria@mail.ru • www.jaranaskajaeparhia.ru

*22.8.1975 Jaransk Kirov. school Škalanka Kirov. N? 1990-1994 stud pedagogics Oršanka Marij El. 1994-1996 altarnik, sunday school Jaransk. diak1.3.1996 ⊖24.3.1996 Kirov (A Hrisanf Vjatka). 1996-2001 priest Jaransk. 2001-2006 rector Matvinur. 2002-2011 (correspondence course) Seminary Academy Moskva, 2006-2012 rector Tuža. 2007 protoierej mon7.9.2012 blagočinnyj dean Vjatka. archim14.10.2012 ⊕6.12.2012 Jegorjev B Jaransk+Luza, Metr. Vjatka (Patr Kirill).

Metropolia Vladimir

Evlogij Jurij Smirnov ***Vladimir***

T: M Vladimir+Suzdal, Metr. Vladimir ▪ ✉ ul. Bolšaja Moskovskaja 68б, ROSSIJA-600000 Vladimir • [7] 4922 324054, 324781, fax 421216 • eparhia33@gmail.com • eparhia33@list.ru • www.eparh33.ru

*13.1.1937 Kemerovo. N18.3. 1955-1966 Seminary Academy Moskva. 1960-1963 Soviet Army. mon15.3.1965 diak21.5.1965. 1966 Kandidat. 1966-1972 teacher Seminary Moskva ⊖18.10.1967. 1970 igumen. 1972-1983 ekonom Troice-Sergieva Lavra, Prof liturgics Akademy. archim25.3.1973. 1977 MTh Moskva. 1983-1986 namestnik Danilovski Monastyr Moskva. 1986-1988 Prof. Pastoral Academy Moskva. 1988-1990 namestnik Optina Pustyn ⊕11.11.1990.1990-1995 President Synodal Commission Monasteries. 2012 Orden Sergij Radonež (I). 2013 M Metr. Vladimir.

Jevstafij Jevgenij Jevdokimov ***Aleksandrov***

T: A Aleksandrov+Jurjev-Pol, Metr. Vladimir ▪ ✉ per. Sovjetskij, dom 6, ROSSIJA-601650 Aleksandrov • [7] 49244 23711 • alex.eparh@mail.ru

*1.11.1951 Baškirija. N3.10. 1974-1981 Seminary Academy Kandidat Moskva. mon4.12.1980 Troice-Sergieva Lavra. diak4.1.1981 ⊖27.3.1982. 1984-1988 St. Daniel Monastery Moskva. 1988-1991 Monastery Tolgsk Jaroslavl. 1991 St. Dimitrij Monastery Rostov Velikij. archim24.4.1994 ⊕30.1.2000 B Čita+Zabajkalje. 2009 B, 2013 A Čita+Krasnokamensk. 2014 A Aleksandrov+Jurjev-Pol, Metr. Vladimir.

Nil Andrej Sičev ***Murom***

T: B Murom+Vjaznikov, Metr. Vladimir ▪ ✉ ul. Lakina 1A, ROSSIJA-602267 Murom • [7] 49234 22050 • muromeparh@rambler.ru • www.meparhia.ru

*19.4.1964 Gorkij. N? baptized youngster, 1982-1984 ponomar St. Nikolaj Lolatino. 1984-1986 Soviet Army. diak17.6.1986 Vladimir mon24.6.1986 A Serapion ⊖19.8.1986 Uspenskij Sobor Sergiev Posad rector Vladimir. 1988 igumen. archim8.9.1988 M Serapion. 1990-1991 sekretar Tambov. 1991-2012 ekonom Vladimir. 2001-2005 Seminary Vladimir (correspondence course). 2001-2005 University Vladimir Fac Psychology (correspondence course) ⊕2.5.2012 Pokrov Moskva. 2012-2013 B Murom, vicar Vladimir. 2013 B Murom+Vjaznikov, Metr. Vladimir.

Metropolia Volgograd

German Gennadij Timofejev ***Volgograd***
T: M Volgograd+Kamyšin, Metr. Volgograd ▪ ✉ Čapajeva 26, ROSSIJA-400012 Volgograd • [7] 442 368606, 327797, 449186, 447326, 447338, fax 327894, 327997 • volg.eparhia@mail.ru • www.volgeparhia.ru
*11.11.1937 Taškent. N11.7. mon19.12.1965 diak26.12.1965. 1966 Kandidat Leningrad ⊖29.5.1966 ⊕6.12.1968 B Tikhvin, vicar Leningrad, rector Theol Akademy 1970 B Wien. 1974 B Vilnjus. 1978 B. 1983 A Tula. 1986 A Berlin+Mitteleuropa (+Leipzig 1989-1991). 1991 A, 2000 M Metr. Volgograd. 2003 Orden M Makarij.

Elisej Aleksandr Fomkin ***Urjupinsk***
T: B Urjupinsk+Novoannin, Metr. Volgograd ▪ ✉ ul. Malaja Peschanaja 61, ROSSIJA-403114 Urjupinsk • [7] 4442 37254 • office@urp-eparhia.ru • www.urjupinskaja-eparhia.ru
*8.5.1963 Volgograd. N27.6. 1981-1983 Soviet Army. electrician. 1991-1992 Theol school Volgograd. diak2.8.1992 Volgograd A German ⊖9.8.1992 rector Volgograd, Volžk. 1994-2000 duhovnik Dubovka. mon19.4.1995. 1997-2001 Seminary Sankt-Peterburg (correspondence course). 2001-2005 Kandidat Sankt-Peterburg "Monastyri Volgogradskoj eparhii". 12.5.2004 igumen. archim18.3.2012 ⊕31.3.2012 B Urjupinsk+Novoannin, Metr. Volgograd.

Ioann Andrej Kovalenko ***Kalač***
T: B Kalač+Pallasovka, Metr. Volgograd ▪ ROSSIJA-404500 Kalač-na-Donu • [7] • www.kalach-eparx.ru
*1.2.1970 Karaganda. N? 1987 absolvent school Moskva. 1987-1992 Medical Academy Moskva. 14.4.1991 baptized and marriage. diak19.4.1992 Jaroslavl ⊖24.5.1992. 1992-1996 nastojatjel Mosejtsev. 1996 together with wife decided to be monk. mon1.1.1997. 1997-2001 Seminary Academy Moskva (correspondence course), Kandidat. 1999 igumen Jaroslavl. 2012 eparchy Rybinsk. archim5.10.2013 ⊕6.11.2013 B Kalač+Pallasov, Metr. Volgograd.

Metropolia Vologda

Ignatij Alexij Deputatov ***Vologda***
T: M Vologda+Kirillov, Metr. Vologda ▪ ✉ pl. Sobornaja 1 (ul. Sovjetskaja 74), ROSSIJA-346500 Vologda • [7] 8636 250985, 253682 • shahteparh@gmail.com • www.shahteparh.ru
*22.1.1977 Turoles Šatura Moskva. N? 1994-1996 theol učilišče Rjazan. 1996-1998 Seminary Samara. 1998-2002 Academy Sankt-Peterburg. mon27.10.2002 Rjazan teacher biblical history. diak31.10.2002 ⊖4.11.2002. 2004-2006 Aspirantura

Moskva. 2007 igumen. 2008 dipl jur University Rjazan. 2009 prorector Seminary Rjazan. 2010 Kandidat civil administration University Moskva ⊕21.8.2011 B Šahty+ Millerovo. 2014 M Vologda.

Flavian Maksim Mitrofanov ***Cherepovets***

T: B Cherepovets Belozersk, Metr. Vologda ▪ ✉ Makarinskaja roshcha 1, ROSSIJA-162600 Cherepovets • [7] 8202 232569, 262980 • consistorium@ya.ru • http://cherepovets-eparhia.ru

*17.11.1975 Saratov. 1994-1996 teacher Catechisme Saratov. diak31.12.1995. 1997 absolvent Fac History University Saratov, Seminary Saratov. 1997-2002 Kandidat Akad Moskva (correspondence course) "Genre hagiography Russian literature XIX century". 1997 teacher prorector Seminary Saratov ⊖13.4.1997. 1998 parishes Saratov. 2007-2014 London. 2014 eparchy Vologda, parishes Cherepovetsk. mon 19.8.2014 archim25.10.2014 ⊕23.11.2014 B Cherepovets Belozersk, Metr. Vologda.

Metropolia Voronež

Sergij Vitalij Fomin ***Voronež***

T: M Voronež+Liskinsk, Metr. Voronež ▪ ✉ Osvoboždenije truda 20, ROSSIJA-394000 Voronež • [7] 4732 5534-94, -35, 556285 • vle@vle.ru • ve553435@mail.ru • press@vob.ru • www.vob-eparhia.ru

*24.8.1949 Krasnozavodsk. N8.10. mon26.8.1973 diak21.9.1973 ⊖22.9.1973. 1978-1982 Prag. 1982-1996 Deputy Chairman Department External Affairs Moskva ⊕30.1.1983 B, 1988 A, 1999 M Solnečnogorsk. 1984-1991 Representative to the WCC Geneva. 1991 Caritas. 1996-2003 Chancellor Moscow Patriarchy. 1999-2010 chairman Department Humanitarian Aid, Social welfare. 2003 M Voronež+Borisoglebsk. 2013 M Voronež+Liskinsk, Metr. Voronež.

Andrej Tarasov ***Rossoš***

T: B Rossoš+Ostrogožsk, Metr. Voronež ▪ ✉ Oktabrskaja pl. 19 A, ROSSIJA-396659 Rossoš • [7] 47396 57895 • palross@yandex.ru • www.roseparhia.ru

*19.7.1975 Tomsk. N? 1992-1996 Seminary Moskva, 1995 Barnaul. diak18.10.1995 Barnaul ⊖30.10.1995 Barnaul mon7.3.1996 duhovnik Barnaul. 1998 igumen. 1999 prorector učilišče. 2000-2004 (correspondence course) Academy Moskva. 2003 ekonom Barnaul, sekretar Voronež. archim2005 member commissions oblast Voronež. 2009 Aspirantura Moskva, English language course Oxford ⊕18.9.2011 Ostrogožsk vicar Voronež. 2013 B Rossoš+Ostrogožsk, Metr. Voronež.

Sergij Viktor Kopylov

T: B Semiluki, vicar Voronež, Metr. Voronež ▪ ✉ ul. 40 let Oktojabrja 35 A, Rossija-397160 Borisoglebsk • [7] 47354 91124 • www.b-eparhia.ru

*21.8.1983 Grjazi, Lipetsk region. 1989-1998 school Grjazi. 1998-2003 pedagogical College Usman, Lipetsk region. 2003-2008 Theol Seminary Voronež. 2008-2014 teacher Seminary Voronež. mon28.3.2008 diak21.9.2008. 2009-2014 (correspondence course) Academy Moskva ⊖17.9.2009. 25.7.2014 elected B Borisoglebsk+Buturlinov Metr. Voronež. archim3.8.2014 ⊕19.12.2015 Moskva Krestovozdvizhenskij Jerusalim Monastery B Semiluki, vicar Voronež, Metr. Voronež (Patr Kirill).

Metropolia Zabajkal

Vladimir Mihail Samohin ***Chita***

T: M Chita+Petrov-Zabajkal, Metr. Zabajkal ▪ ✉ ul. 9 Januarja, dom 50, Rossija-672039 Chita • [7] 3022 325478, 353088 • eparh_chita@mail.ru • www.eparhiachita.ru

*18.11.1979 Skopin Rjazan. N? 1995 abitur Skopin. 1995-1997 Theol school Rjazan. 1997-1999 Seminary Kaluga. 1999-2003 Academy Sankt-Peterburg dipl "Obšestvo Iisusa (iezuity). Kontrareformatsionnyj aspekt dejatelnosti". 7.4.2000 čtets (A Konstantin Tihvin). 2003 teacher History Rjazan. 2003-2004 ekonom Seminary Rjazan. diak7.11.2004 Rjazan (A Pavel) ⊖15.2.2005. 2005-2011 prorector Seminary Rjazan, fioletova kamilavka. 5.4.2010 protoierej blagočinnyj dean Skopin. mon23.6. 2011 Rjazan (A Pavel) archim9.10.2011 ⊕25.11.2011 B Skopin+Šatsk. 2014 M Chita+Petrov-Zabajkal, Metr. Zabajkal.

Dimitrij Vitalij Eliseev ***Nerchinsk***

T: B Nerchinsk+Krasnokamensk, Metr. Zabajkal ▪ ✉ Rossija-673400 Nerchinsk

*1.11.1961 Szolnok Hungary in the family of a Russian soldier. 1983 military Tank Engineering School, Kiev. 1983-1997 officer Zabajkal military region. 1997 secretary eparchy Chita. 1998-2011 pastoral courses Chita, Seminary Moskva (correspondence course). diak8.3.1998 ⊖10.5.1998. 2000-2014 Military Chaplain, secretary eparchy, dean parishes Chita. mon6.12.2001 archim4.1.2015 ⊕22.2.2015 Moskva B Nerchinsk+Krasnokamensk, Metr. Zabajkal (Patr Kirill).

Autonomous Church Latvia

Aleksandr Aleksandrs Kudrjašovs ***Rīga***

T: M Rīga+Latvia, Autonomous Church Latvia ▪ ✉ Krišjana Barona 126, LATVIA-1012 Rīga • [371] 67294508, 67275743 • Sinod 67224345, 67225855 • sinod@pravoslavie.lv • www.pareizticiba.lv • www.orthodox.lv

*3.10.1939 Preiļi. N12.9. school teacher. stud Seminary Moskva. diak1982 ⊖1982. 1982-1985 rector Perm. 1985-1989 rector Rīga. mon10.7.1989 archim11.7.1989 ⊕23.7.1989 B Daugavpils vicar Rīga. 1990 B, 1994 A, 2002 M Rīga, Autonomous Church Latvia. 2004 Orden Sergij Radonež.

Ioann Vladimir Sichevskij

T: B Elgava, auxiliary Rīga+Latvia ▪ ✉ Krišjana Barona 126, LATVIA-1012 Rīga • [371] 67294508, 67275743 • Sinod 67224345, 67225855 • sinod@pravoslavie.lv • www.pareizticiba.lv

*12.7.1978 Valmiera Latvia, baptized. 1986-1996 school Limbazhi Latvia. 1996-2002 instruktor sportsmen. 2001 ponomar Limbazhi. 2002-2003 Olympic Center Limbazhi. 2002-2004 MPedagogics Fac Sport. 2002 starosta church of Transfiguration, Limbazhi. 2002-2008 Theol Seminary Rīga. 2006 secretary Synod Latvia. diak5.2.2006 ⊖26.3.2006 mon17.3.2007. 2010 doctoral studies Pedagogical Fac University Latvia. 19.6.2012 rector St. Simeon and Anna church in Elgava. 2013 chosen B Elgava, auxiliary Rīga Latvia, by Synod Latvian Orth. Church. 2014 the decision is confirmed by the Holy Synod of Russian Orthodox Church ⊕19.3.2014 B Elgava archim23.3.2014.

Aleksandr Sergej Matrenin ***Daugavpils***

T: B Daugavpils+Rēzekne, Autonomous Church Latvia ▪ ✉ Pils iela 14, LATVIA-1050 Rīga • [371] 67224345

*6.9.1973 Rīga citizen Latvia, speaking Latvian. N? 1988-1991 Railway Institut Rīga. 1996-2000 Theol Seminary Rīga. mon20.4.1997 Aleksandr Svirskij. diak22.3.1998 ⊖6.9.1998. 1999 igumen. 2005 sekretar church court. archim21.7.2006 ⊕19.8.2006 B Daugavpils vicar Rīga. 2013 B Daugavpils+Rēzekne, Autonomous Church Latvia.

Autonomous Church Estonia

Kornilij Vjačeslav Jakobs ***Tallinn***

T: M Tallinn+Estonia, Autonomous Church Estonia ▪ ✉ Pikk 64-4, ESTONIA-10133 Tallinn • [372] 641130-1, fax -2 • mpeok@orthodox.ee • www.orthodox.ee

*18.6.1924 Tallinn. N5.3. 1943 psalomščik Tallinn. diak19.8.1945 Tallinn (A Pavel Dmitrovskij) ⊖5.2.1948 Haapsalu, 1951 Vologda. 1957 prison "antisoviet agitation"

Mordovia (Dubralag), rehabil. 1960-1990 priest Tallinn. 1971 stud Leningrad. mon21.8.1990 archim6.9.1990 ⊕15.9.1990 B, 1996 A, 1999 Holy Synod asks to continue. 2000 M Tallinn+Estonia, Autonomous Church Estonia.

Lazar Aleksandr Gurkin ***Narva***
T: B Narva+Pričudsk, Autonomous Church Estonia ▪ ✉ Joala 56, ESTONIA-20103 Narva • [372] 3 561-234, fax -006 • info@narvaeparhia.ee • www.narvaeparhia.ee
*13.3.1969 Nikolajević, Mordovia. N30.10. 1989-1991 Military Service. mon27.3.1991 diak30.3.1991 ⊖4.4.1991. 1991-1992 Kelar ekonom Mon Sanaksar. 1992-1993 nastojatjel Staroje Drakino Mordovia. 1993-2000 blagočinnyj dean Romodanovsk. 2000-2009 namestnik Saransk. 2001 absolvent Seminary Saransk, 2005 Kandidat Academy Moskva "Monastyri Mordovskogo kraja XVII-XX vjekov" ⊕21.7.2009 B Narev, vicar Tallinn. 2011 B Narva+Pričudsk, Autonomous Church Estonia.

Eparchia Lietuva

Innokentij Valerij Vasiljev ***Vilnius***
T: A Vilnius, Lietuvos Respublikos Arkivyskupu ▪ ✉ Aušros Vartu 10, LITHUANIA-01303 Vilnius • [370] 52613641, p 52123747, 5217765, Kabinet 52626469, 52626459 • info@orthodoxy.lt • www.orthodoxy.lt
*9.10.1947 Staraja Russa Novgorod. N13.4. 1966-1969 Soviet Army. married. 1969-1974 Institute International Communication Moskva. 1974-1980 Sojuzzarubež, Gosteleradio USSR, Institute Scientific Information Academy Sc. USSR. 1980-1981 hypodiakon Kursk. 1981-1982 Železnogorsk. diak5.1981 ⊖8.1981. 1982-1985 sekretar eparchy Kursk. 1985-1990 Khabarovsk. 1990-1992 teacher bibliotekar Seminary Odessa ⊕26.1.1992 Moskva B Khabarovsk+Blagoveščensk, 1994 +Priamurje. 1995-1996 B Dmitrov, vicar Moskva, Deputy chairman Department External Church Relations. 1996-1999 B Čita+Zabajkalje, Republic Burjatia. 1999 B, 2002 A Korsun Paris. 2010 A Vilnius. 2012 Orden Serafim Sarov II.st.

Metropolitan Region Kazakhstan

Aleksandr Aleksandr Mogilëv ***Astana***
T: M Astana+Almaty, Metr. Kazakhstan ▪ ✉ ul. Gogola 40, Park 28-mi Gvardejtsev-Panfilovtsev, KAZAKHSTAN-050010 Alma-Ata • [7] 727 2737291, fax 2738495 • kazakhstan@mitropolia.kz • cross@orthodox.kz • mitropolia.kz@yandex.ru • www.mitropolia.kz • www.orthodox.kz
*18.5.1957 Kirov. N12.9. 1975-1976 Seminary, 1976-1979 Academy Leningrad. diak1.8.1983 ⊖2.8.1983. 1988-1989 Academy Moskva. mon21.9.1989 ⊕27.9.1989 B, 1994 A Kostroma+Galič. 1989-2010 Responsable Allrussian Orthodox Youth

Movement ASOYM. 1993 Administrator Jaroslavl. 26.11.1996 visit Regensburg. 1999 chairman Commission problems Jekaterinburg. 2010 A, 2011 M Astana, Metr. Kazakhstan.

Gennadij Mihael Gogolëv
T: B Kaskelen, vicar Astana, Metr. Kazakhstan, secretary Regional Synod ▪ ✉ mikrorajon "Dorožnik" 29, KASAKHSTAN-050014 Almaty • [7] 7272 98-9080, -9415 +fax, -9361, School 628485

*10.3.1967 Leningrad. N? 1984-1986 Institut Kryptographics Moskva. 1986 Soviet Army. 1987-1990 Seminary, 1989 psalomščik Tambov. 1990-1994 Academy Leningrad. diak21.9.1990 ⊖18.11.1990 (M Kirill). 1990-1994 priest Sankt-Peterburg, 1994 Kostroma mon1.1.1995. 1995-1996 rector Theol school Kostroma. 1996 igumen, rector Seminary Kostroma. archim1.9.1998. 2010 klirik Almaty ⊕10.10.2010 B Kaskelen, vicar Astana, Metr. Kazakhstan.

Nektarij Sergej Frolov
T: B B Taldykorgan, vicar Astana, Metr. Kazakhstan ▪ ✉ ul. Gogola 40, Park 28-mi Gvardejtsev-Panfilovtsev, KAZAKHSTAN-050010 Alma-Ata • [7] 727 273729

*17.7.1961 Lubotin Kharkiv, N22.11. 1976-1979 Technikum Kharkiv. 1979-1982 Soviet Army. 1981 Lavra Počajev. 1982-1989 dipl ingenieur-ekonom Kharkiv. 1984 Seminary Sankt-Peterburg. diak19.4.1984 ⊖21.4.1984. 1994-1998 Kursk. 1999 Kandidat Academy Kiev. 2000 rector Dubno. 2006 Dr. theol Užgorod. mon7.4.2008 ⊕12.11.2008 B Džankoj+Razdolninsk. 2009-2014 B Dubno, vicar Rovno. 2014 B Taldykorgan, vicar Astana.

Serapion Sergej Kolosnitsin ***Kokšetau***
T: B Kokšetau+Akmola, Metr. Kazakhstan ▪ ✉ ul. Bauržan-Momyšuly 117, KAZAKHSTAN-021400 Kokšetau • [7] 7162 251879 • www.pravest-kokshe.kz

*6.7.1964 Podgornij Džambul Kazahstan N12.9. 1982-1984 Soviet Army. 1985-1989 Seminary. mon3.7.1988 diak17.7.1988. 1989-1993 Academy Moskva ⊖10.10.1990. 1993-1997 kanonarh Lavra Sergiev Posad. 1997-2002 Abakan. 1999 igumen. 2005 eparchy Lipetsk. archim13.10.2013 Astana ⊕23.10.2013 B Kokšetau+Akmola, Metr. Kazakhstan.

Anatolij Vladimir Aksenov ***Kostanaj***
T: B Kostanaj+Rudnensk, Metr. Kazakhstan ▪ ✉ ul. Altynsarina 206, KAZAKHSTAN-110000 Kostanaj • [7] 77142 545593 • ksteparhiya@mail.ru • keparhia@gmail.com • www.keparhia.kz • www.kst-eparhiya.kz

*22.11.1958 Afonin Pereslavl. N? school Pereslavl. 1981-1989 Seminary Academy Moskva. mon1987 diak1987 ⊖1987. 1989 teacher, 1990-1994 vice-rector Seminary Academy Moskva. 1990 igumen. archim1994 namestnik Nikita Monastery Pereslavl Zalesskij ⊕15.2.1998 B Pereslavl-Zalesskij, vicar Jaroslavl. 1998-2000 B Magadan+ Čukotka. 2000-2001 B Jalutorov vicar Tobolsk. 2001-2010 na pokoj. 2010 B Kostanaj, Metr. Kazakhstan.

Varnava Vasilij Safonov ***Pavlodar***

T: B Pavlodar+Ekibastuz, Metr. Kazakhstan ▪ ✉ ul. Torajgyrova 1/1, KAZAKHSTAN-140005 Pavlodar • [7] 7182 537073 • pavlodar.eparhia@gmail.com • www.pavlodar-eparhia.ru

*21.2.1957 Urjupinsk Volgograd. N24.6. school Urjupinsk. 1975-1977 Soviet Army. 1977-1979 fishing fleet Primorskij. 1978-1981 Seminary, mon28.2.1980 diak20.7.1980. 1981-1985 Academy Moskva, Kandidat "Fenomen religioznogo sekuljarizma" ⊖14.3.1982. 4.4.1987 igumen. 1988-1991 Optina Pustina. archim10.1. 1990 ekonom Daniel Monastery Moskva. namestnik Saransk. 1997 Orden St. Vladimir, 2000 St. Sergij Rad., 2005 Serafim Sarov ⊕14.11.2010 B Pavlodar+Ust-Kamenogorsk. 2011 B Pavlodar+Ekibastuz, Metr. Kazakhstan. 2012 Orden Serafim Sarov (II).

Vladimir Viktor Mihejkin ***Petropavlovsk***

T: B Petropavlovsk+Bulaevsk, Metr. Kazakhstan ▪ ✉ ul. Jubilejnaja 55, KAZAKHSTAN-150013 Petropavlovsk • cathedral@pbe.kz • www.petr-pavel.kz • http://pbe.kz

*11.9.1968 in Petropavlovsk Kazakhstan. 1985 school Petropavlovsk.1991 dipl Pedagogical Institute (historian). diak1992 ⊖14.2.1993. 1996-2002 Tobolsk Seminary (correspondence course). 2002-2007 St. Tikhon's Orthodox University. 2002 archpriest mon5.6.2014 archim7.6.2014 ⊕8.6.2014 Sergiev Posad, B Petropavlovsk+ Bulaevsk, Metr. Kazakhstan (Patr. Kirill).

Gurij Jurij Šalimov

T: former B Petropavlovsk+Bulajev, Metr. Kazakhstan ▪ ✉ ul.Jubilejnaja 55, KAZAKHSTAN-150013 Petropavlovsk • [7] 7152 423608 • cathedral@pbe.kz • www.petr-pavel.kz

*17.9.1946 Lučinki Gorohovjets Vladimir. N17.10. 1969-1974 Technikum, Fac Interpreter Pedinstitut Gorkij, teacher English Français Gorkij. 1970-1972 Soviet Army. 1974-1975 Pedinstitut Moskva. 1976 Psalomščik Donetsk. 12.1976 hypodiakon Vladimir. diak24.7.1977 ⊖29.10.1977. 1977-1980 Seminary Moskva. 1980-1984 Academy Moskva. 1984-1986 Rabat. mon5.10.1985. 6.10.1985 igumen. 4.1986-2.1988 Moskva waiting for visa. 1988-1993 parish Zürich. archim29.4.1989

⊕14.1.1993 Moskva B Korsun, Chersonèse Paris. 1999 Moskva. 2003 B Magadan. 2011 B Petropavlovsk+Bulajev, Metr. Kazakhstan. Orden: 2006 Daniel Mosk., 2007 Sergij Radon 2011 Innokentij Mosk., Za zaslugi pered Pravoslav. Cerkovju Kazakhstana. 30.5.2015 retired, rector church council icon Kazan Kolomenskij Moskva.

Sebastian Aleksandr Osokin ***Karaganda***
T: B Karaganda+Šahtinsk, Metr. Kazakhstan ▪ ✉ ul. Gapjejeva 1[a], KAZAKHSTAN-100024 Karaganda • [7] 7217 742225 • www.eparhia.kz
*23.11.1961 Perm. N? 1979-1984 stud Polytechnikum Perm and Vladimir. grašdanskoe strojtelstvo. 1984-1985 Soviet Army Germany. 1986-1989 altarnik Alma-Ata. diak29.3.1989 ⊖7.4.1989 rector Alma-Ata, Karaganda. 1995-1997 stud Theol school Alma Ata, 1998-2009 Seminary Academy Moskva. mon4.1.2011 ("Sebastian" starets Karaganda) ⊕20.2.2011 B Karaganda, Metr. Kazakhstan. 2012 Orden St. Aleksij (III).

Elevferij Georgij Kozorez ***Čimkent***
T: A Čimkent+Taraz, Metr. Kazakhstan ▪ ✉ Ušakova 6, KAZAKHSTAN-160000 Šymkent • [7] 7252 549440, fax 432014 • shm_eparhia@mail.ru • www.eparhiya.kz
*17.9.1953 Obarove Roven Ukraina. N17.8. 1975-1979 Seminary Moskva, 1979-1984 Academy Moskva, Kandidat. diak13.4.1985 ⊖17.10.1985 klučar Alma Ata. 1986 blagočinnyj dean Čimkent. mon26.3.1987. 1988 igumen. archim14.2.1991 ⊕15.2.1991 B Čimkent+Celinograd, 1993 name eparchy Čimkent+Akmola (=Celinograd), 1995 Member Intereparchial Commission Kazakhstan. 2004 A. 2011 A Čimkent+Taraz, Metr. Kazakhstan. 2011 president Church Court Kazakhstan.

Antonij Vladimir Moskalenko ***Uralsk***
T: A Uralsk+Atyrau, Metr. Kazakhstan ▪ ✉ ul. Komsomolskaja 69, KAZAKHSTAN-090000 Uralsk • [7] 3112 503883, 503843, 504396, 509485, fax 504398 • ro-ue@mail.ru • www.uralsk-eparhiya.kz
*29.9.1940 Khabarovsk. N23.7. 1965-1969 Fac jur Krasnojarsk. diak27.9.1969 ⊖12.10.1969 mon13.4.1970. 19.7.1977 Kandidat Moskva ⊕13.10.1985 B Perejaslav Khmelnitskij vicar Kiev. 1987-1991 B Chernovtsy+Bukovina, 1991 B, 1997 A Uralsk+ Gurjev, 1999 A Uralsk+Atyrau, Metr. Kazakhstan. 1995 Member Intereparchial Commission Kazakhstan. 2005 Orden Družby.

Amfilohie Andrej Bondarenko ***Ust-Kamenogorsk***
T: B Ust-Kamenogorsk+Semipalatinsk, Metr. Kazakhstan ▪ ✉ Ušakova 6, KAZAKHSTAN-Ust-Kamenogorsk • [7] 7232 251030, 254029, 525593 • eustkamenogorsk@bk.ru • www.orthovko.kz

*1969 Kurčum Kazahstan. baptized youngster. N6.12. 1975 Dušanbe Tadžikistan. 1987-1989 Soviet Army Čekoslovakia. 1990 Kurgan, 1991 altarnik čtets Tekeli Taldy-Kurgan. 1993-2011 Theol school Alma-Ata, Seminary Tomsk. diak22.5.1994 ⊖25.5.1994 (A Aleksij) mon1998 Ust-Kamenogorsk Öskemen. 2007 Pavlodar. 2011 Academy Moskva (correspondence course). 2011 Alma-Ata, absolvent Institut Administration Moskva. archim1.1.2012 ⊕26.2.2012 B Ust-Kamenogorsk+Semipalatinsk, Metr. Kazakhstan.

Metropolitan Region Asia

Vikentij Viktor Morar ***Taškent***

T: M Taškent+Uzbekistan, Metr. Srednjaja Asia ▪ ✉ ul. Sadyk Azimov 3.tupik 22, UZBEKISTAN-700047 Taškent • [998] 71 2333321, fax [998] 72 2367939 • alakhtaev@list.ru • church@albatros.uz • www.pravoslavie.uz

*4.10.1953 Sculiani Moldova. N24.11. 1971-1973 Soviet Army. 1974-1982 Seminary Academy Moskva, Kandidat "Ignatij Brjančaninov o Molitve". mon1981 diak19.5. 1981 ⊖1.1.1982. 1982-1990 Lavra Sergiev Posad. 1985 igumen. archim28.8.1990 ⊕2.9.1990 B Bendery vicar Chişinău, rector Seminary. 1995 B, 1999 A Abakan+ Kyzyl, Republik Hakasija, Tuwa. 1999-2011 A Jekaterinburg. 2011 M Taškent+ Uzbekistan, M Srednjaja Asia.

Daniil Semen Kuznetsov ***Bishkek***

T: B Bishkek+Kyrgyzstan, Metr. Srednjaja Asia ▪ ✉ ul. Zhibek-Zholu 497, KYRGYZSTAN-720033 Biškek • [996] 700 583 444, [996] 312 69000-2, fax -3 • bishopbkmail@mail.ru • urzhum_eparhiya@mail.ru • www.eparchia.kg • www.eparhiya-urzhum.ru

*16.2.1980 Černaja Holunitsa Omutninsk. 1997-2001 Seminary Saratov. diak12.7. 2001 prorector Seminary Saratov ⊖2.8.2001. 2002 klirik eparchy Vjatka Omutninsk. mon20.4.2008. 2009 Academy Moskva. 26.3.2010 igumen. rector Theol school Vjatka. archim14.10.2010 ⊕23.12.2012 Kaliningrad B Uržum+Omutninsk (Patr Kirill). 25.7.2014 B Bishkek+Kyrgyzstan, Metr. Srednjaja Asia.

Pitirim Konstantin Tvorogov ***Dušanbe***

T: B Dušanbe+Tadžikistan, Metr. Srednjaja Asia ▪ ✉ pr. Družby narodov 58, TADZHIKISTAN-734024 Dušanbe • [992] 2220505 • www.eparhia.me • www.lifted.asia

*7.6.1967 Zagorsk (Sergiev Posad) N? 1987-1991 Pedagogical Institute Moskva. 2001-2007 Seminary Academy Moskva. 2004-2012 teacher Homiletics Academy Moskva. mon22.4.2005 diak11.9.2005 ⊖12.3.2006 archim29.7.2012 ⊕1.8.2012 Serafim Monastery B Dušanbe+Tadžikistan, Metr. Srednjaja Asia (Patr Kirill).

Moldavian Orthodox Church

Vladimir Nicolae Cantarian ***Chişinău***

T: M Chişinău+Moldova, BOMoldova ▪ ✉ str. Bucureşti 119, MOLDOVA-2004 Chişinău • [373] 22 235000, 232929, 233344, 237878, 203574, 232929, fax 235005, 265401 • vladimir@mitropolia.md • cheibas.vadim@gmail.com • sec@mitropolia.md • www.mitropolia.md

*18.8.1952 Kolenkovtsy Chernovtsy Ukraina. N28.7. 1970-1973 Black Sea Fleet Sov. Army. diak22.5.1974 ⊖22.5.1976. Theol school Moskva. 1981-1989 Secretary administration eparchy Chernovtsy. mon29.11.1987. 1988 igumen. archim1989. 1989 absolvent Academy Moskva ⊕21.7.1989 B, 1990 A, 1992 M Kišinjev, Chişinăului şi al întregii Moldove. BOMoldova. 7.2.2000 birthday Patr Teoctist Bucureşti.

Ioann Ivan Moshnegutzu

T: B Soroca, vicar Chişinău BOMoldova ▪ ✉ str. Bucureşti 119, MOLDOVA-2004 Chişinău • [373] 22 235000, 232929

*27.1.1979 Prazhila, region of Floreshty, Moldova. 1986-1994 school Prazhila, lyceum Floreshty. 1994-1996 Chisinau Seminary. 2000 Theol Academy Chisinau. diak5.3.2006 ⊖22.5.2006. 2007 Master Historical Fac of Moldova State University. mon12.4.2008 archim24.10.2010. 2011-2013 teacher dogmatics Seminary Ungensk. 2011 kurs povyshenija kvalifikatsii in Obshetserkovnaja Aspirantura i Doktorantura. 25.12.2014 chosen by Holy Synod B Soroca, vicar Chişinău. ⊕8.3.2015 B Soroca, vicar Chişinău.

Petru Valeriu Mustaţă ***Ungheni***

T: B Ungheni+Nisporeni, BOMoldova ▪ ✉ str. Mihai Eminescu 10, MOLDOVA-3606 Ungheni • [373] 263 24630, 25171, 29772, 22373 • episcopia-ungheni@yandex.ru • www.episcopia-ungheni.md • www.eph.md

*29.10.1967 Lupa-Recea Străşeni Pelenia Rişcani. N29.6. 1986-1988 Soviet Army. 1988-1992 Seminary Odessa. mon1992 diak12.7.1992 ⊖28.8.1992. 12.7.1993 igumen. 1994-1998 Academy Kiev (correspondence course). archim1995. 1996 Orden St. Vladimir (III).1997 member synod Moldavia. 1999 lawyer Fac Chişinău. 2000 Orden Gloria Muncii. 2002 Orden St. Nestor. 2004 chairman diocesan court ⊕13.11.2005 Chişinău. B Nisporeni vicar Chişinău (Patr Alexij). 2006 B Ungheni+ Nisporeni, BOMoldova, 2007-2010 B Hincu vicar Chişinău. 2011 B Ungheni+ Nisporeni, BOMoldova.

Savva Sergej Volkov *Tiraspol*

T: A Tiraspol+Dubossari, BOMoldova ▪ ✉ str. Şevcenco 25, MOLDOVA-3300 Tiraspol • [373] 533 95218, 95674, fax 80053 • diocese@idknet.com • tdeu@mail.ru • www.diocese-tiras.org

*27.9.1958 Šiton Mordvinija ASSR. N1.2. 1976-1980 Seminary Moskva. 1986 Kandidat, diak18.5.1986 mon27.12.1986 Sv. Danilov Monastyr Moskva ⊖6.1.1987. 1987 igumen. 1987-1989 ekonom Sv. Danilov Monastyr Moskva. archim17.3.1988. 1989 Aspirant Academy Moskva. 1989-1990 responsable for guests. 1990-1995 rector Transfiguration Serpuh. Moskva ⊕12.9.1995 B Krasnogorsk, vicar eparchy Moskva. 1995-2010 chairman Department Contacts with Armed Forces and Legal Protection Forces. 2010 B, 2013 A Tiraspol, BOMoldova.

Anatoli Gheorghe Botnar *Cahul*

T: B Cahul+Comrat, BOMoldova ▪ ✉ str. Mihai Hîncu 146, MOLDOVA-3401 Hînceşti • [373] 22 513921, [373] 671 52600 • anatolii_episcop@mail.ru • www.eparhiasud.md

*3.5.1950 Pituşcă Călăraş Moldova. N6.5. 1968-1970 Soviet Army. 1971-1974 Seminary Odessa. diak3.3.1974 Odessa (M Sergij Petrov) ⊖31.3.1974. 1974-1975 rector Lazov. 1975-1998 rector St. Michail Abakli. 1990 protoierej. 1994 mitra. mon28.8.1998 archim30.8.1998 ⊕12.9.1998 St. Daniel Monastery Moskva B Cahul+Căuşani. 1999 new name eparchy Cahul+Lapuşna, BOMoldova.

Nikodim Ioann Vulpe *Edineţ*

T: B Edineţ+Briceni, BOMoldova ▪ ✉ şos. Bucovinei 35/4, MOLDOVA-4601 Edineţ • [373] 246 21523, fax 23450, [373] 79543015 • episcopia_eb@moldova.ec • episcopia@yandex.ru • www.eparhia-edinet.md • www.teologia.net

*4.9.1956 Kiperčen Moldova. N? 1974-1976 Soviet Army. 1977-1980 Seminary Leningrad. 1980 Academy Leningrad. diak18.3.1981 Leningrad ⊖21.5.1981 Leningrad. 1981 eparchy Kišinjev. 1988 protoierej, mitra. 1999 blagočinnyj dean Orge. mon23.1.2009 archim7.4.2009 ⊕26.12.2010 Edineţ+Briceni, BOMoldova.

Marchel Nicolae Mihăiescu *Bălţi*

T: B Bălţi+Făleşti, BOMoldova ▪ ✉ str. Visarion Puiul, MOLDOVA-3100 Bălţi • [373] 231 35318, 33344, fax 32248, [373] 69113012

*18.8.1959 Pîrliţa Soroca Făleşti. 1981-1985 Seminary Odessa. diak16.9.1985 (A Ionafan) celibate. mon3.1.1988 Marchel (M Kišinjev Serapion) ⊖6.1.1988 (M Kišinjev Serapion). 1988-1990 Akademija Moskva (correspondence course). 15.4.1988 igumen (M Serapion) archim20.11.1988 (M Serapion). 1992-2007 secr eparchy Bălţi. 2000-2003 Academy Kiev ⊕11.3.2007 Christ the Saviour Moskva

B Belts BOMoldova (Patr Kirill). 2015-2016 member Holy Synod. 2016 member Synodal Commission Theology.

Ukrainian Orthodox Church

Onufrij Orest Berezovskij *Kiev*

T: His Beatitude Metropolitan Kiev and All Ukraina UOC ▪ ✉ vul. Lavrskaja 15, korp. 49, UKRAINA-01015 Kiev • [380] 44 25512-13, -89, -90, fax 254 5301 • presschurch@gmail.com • kmsekr@gmail.com • eparhia-cv@utel.net.ua • www. orthodox.org.ua • http://mitropolia.kiev.ua

*5.11.1944 Korytno Chernovtsy, N25.6. 1962-1964 Technikum Chernovtsy. 1966-1969 Fac Tech University Chernovtsy. 1969 Seminary Moskva. Kandidat Moskva. mon18.3.1971 diak20.4.1971 ⊖29.5.1972. 1980 igumen. 1984 namestnik Podvorie Peredelniko. palitsa, archim blagočinnyj dean Troice-Sergieva Lavra. 1988 namestnik Počajev ⊕9.12.1990 B, 1994 A, 2000 M Chernovtsy+Bukovina. 2005 Orden Knjaz Vladimir. 2014 M Kiev and All Ukraina UOC. 22.-28.1.2016 Synaxis of the primates of the Local Orthodox Churches Chambésy Switzerland.

Panteleimon Viktor Baščuk

T: A Buchan vicar Kiev UOC ✉ vul. Lavrskaja 15, korp. 49, UKRAINA-01015 Kiev • [380] 44 25512-13

*14.1.1961 Bilogorod Khmelnitskij. N9.8. 1980 absolvent Technikum Khmelnitskij. 1980-1982 military service. 1984 Lavra Sergiev Posad. mon5.1.1986 diak9.3.1986. 1988-1990 Mission Jerusalem ⊖28.7.1988. 1988-1991 Academy Moskva. 1990 Danilov Monastery Moskva. 29.3.1990 igumen. archim13.4.1996 Pečerska Lavra Kiev. 1996 namestnik Monastery Glinskaja Pustin ⊕24.12.2000 B Vasilkov, vicar Kiev, 2005 B Šargorod, vicar Vinnitsa. 2007 B Aleksandria+Svetlovodsk, 2008 B Uman, UOC. 29.1.2016 A Buchan.

Antonij Ivan Pakanič

T: M Borispol+Brovar UOC, Administrator UOC, rector Seminary Academy ▪ ✉ vul. Lavrska 25, korp 64, UKRAINA-01015 Kiev • [380] 44 2551207 • staff@kdais.kiev.ua • www.orthodox.org.ua • www.kdais.kiev.ua

*25.8.1967 Čumalevo Transkarpatia. N23.7. 1982-1992 Zagorsk. 1985-1987 Soviet Army. mon4.1.1994 diak18.2.1994 ⊖7.10.1994 igumen. 1999 chancellor Kiev ⊕26.11.2006 B, 2008 A Borispol. 14.10.2010 Sergiev Posad Moskva Theol Academy 325 years. 2010 president Theol-Jur commission. 19.1.2013 M Borispol+Brovar UOC.

Nikolaj Ivan Groh

T: A Bilohorodka, vicar Kiev UOC ▪ ✉ ul. Akad. Lebedeva 14, UKRAINA-01015 Kiev • [380] 97 6823569 • vladikamykolay@gmail.com • xram.com.ua

*5.9.1954 Halič Berežany Ternopil. N6./19.12. 1971 bacc. 1973-1975 Soviet Army ⊖14.6.1976. 1976-1979 Seminary Moskva. 1979-1986 rector Aleksentsy Ternopol, 1986-1990 Rybniki Ternopol. mon17.5.1990 (Ioann Bodnarčuk Ukrain autoc) ⊕19.5.1990 B Lutsk+Volynia (Ukrain autoc). 25.6.1992 to UOC ⊕16.7.1992 Pečerska Lavra Kiev B Kovel, vicar Volynia UOC. 29.7.1992 B, 2004 A Ivano-Frankovsk+Kolomyja UOC. 2004 Orden Sergij Radonež. 2007 A Bilohorodka, vicar Kiev UOC.

Pavel Petro Lebid

T: M Vyšgorod+Chornobyl, vicar Kiev UOC, Deputy of Pečerska Lavra Kiev UOC ▪ ✉ vul. Lavrska 25, korp 70, UKRAINA-01015 Kiev • [380] 44 2804627, 25511-11, -05, fax -76 • kpl.church.ua

*19.4.1961 Borbin Rovno. N12.7. 1978 bacc. 1978-1980 Technikum Lutsk. 1981-1983 Soviet Army. 1984-1988 Seminary Moskva. diak24.5.1987 ⊖7.1.1988. 1988-1994 rector Niskiniči Volyn. 1988-1996 Academy Kiev. mon1989 (A Varlaam Rovno) archim1992 (B Varfolomej Volyn). 1994 namestnik vicar Pečerska Lavra Kiev ⊕19.4.1997 B, 2003 A, 2011 M Vyšgorod+Chornobyl, vicar Kiev, UOC. 2011 Standing Member Holy Synod UOC.

Vladimir Viorel Moroz

T: M Počajev, vicar Kiev, UOC ▪ ✉ vul. Vozzednanija 8, UKRAINA-47025 Počajev • [380] 3546 61218, 61699, 61044 • pochaevlavra.curch.ua

*15.8.1959 Molodija Chernovtsy. N28.7. 1977-1979 Soviet Army. 1979-1980 eparchy Chernovtsy. 1981 Počajev. mon1983 diak1983 ⊖1984. 1988 absolvent Seminary Moskva. 1989 igumen. 1991 namestnik Chreščatik. archim7.7.1992. 1992 regent ekonom. 1996 namestnik Lavra Počajev ⊕3.12.2000 B, 2006 A, 2012 M Počajev, UOC.

Oleksandr Oleksandr Drabinko

T: M Perejaslav-Khmelnitskij+Vyshnevsky, vicar Kiev UOC ▪ ✉ vul. Lavrska 25, korp 70, UKRAINA-01015 Kiev • [380] 44 2904627, fax 2949243, 2545301 • drabinko77@mail.ru • http://mitropolia.kiev.ua

*18.3.1977 Korets Rovno. N12.9. 1994-1998 Seminary Kiev. 1998 referent hypodiakon mitropolit. 1998-2002 Academy Kiev, Kandidat "Pravoslavie v post-totalitarnoj Ukraine" diak20.5.2004 ⊖28.7.2006 mon26.8.2006 Mount Athos (M Volodymyr). 28.8.2006 igumen. archim24.9.2006 Seminary Moskva ⊕19.12.2007 B, 2010 A, 2013 M Perejaslav-Khmelnitskij+Višnevskij, UOC.

Serafim Vladimir Demjaniv
T: A Jagotin, vicar Kiev, UOC ▪ ✉ Svjato-Pantel.Monastyr, ul. Akad. Lebedeva 14, UKRAINA-03143 Kiev • [380] 44 2551202, fax 2804396 • info@mitropolia.kiev.ua • mitropolia.kiev.ua
*9.7.1953 Zozulintsi Ternopol. N19.7.1969 Technikum Ternopol. 1972-1974 Soviet Army. 1975 hypodiakon Černigov. diak4.7.1976 ⊖7.7.1976 rector Bahmač. mon15.1.1979. 1984-2007 rector Kiev. 1995-1999 Seminary Kiev, 1999-2000 Academy Kiev (correspondence course) ⊕16.11.2007. 2012 A Jagotin vicar Kiev, UOC.

Aleksandr Vasilij Nesterčuk
T: A Gorodnij, vicar Kiev UOC ▪ ✉ vul. Monastyrski 1, UKRAINA-03143 Gorodnica • [380] 4141 65352, 65130, [380] 503135530, [380] 671193181 • horodnica@i.ua • www.gorodnitsa-monchurch.ua
*11.11.1950 Ilimka Žitomir. N29.5.1958-1968 school Sorokolensk. 1968 Monastery Odessa. 1971-1975 Theol Seminary Odessa. diak27.9.1973 ⊖1.9.1974. 1974 rector Dokučajev. mon1976. 1977 rector Žitomir. 1981 igumen. archim1986 ⊕16.11.2008 B, 2012 A Gorodnij, vicar Kiev. UOC.

Ilarij Eduard Šiškovski
T: A Makariv, vicar Kiev UOC ▪ ✉ vul. Lavrska 25, korp 49, UKRAINA-01015 Kiev • [380] 44 2551202, fax 2804396 • info@mitropolia.kiev.ua • www.mitropolia.kiev.ua
*18.4.1969 Nikolajev. N7.9. 1980 school Lugansk. 1988-1990 Soviet Army. 1990-1997 Seminary Academy Kiev. 1999 Kandidat "... dosinodalnij period". 1999 teacher Moral Academy ⊖2000 2001 igumen. archim21.11.2003 member commission Ethics Ukrainian Government. 2005 sekretar, 2007 vize-rector Seminary Academy Kiev ⊕29.7.2007 B Severodonetsk+Starobjelsk. 14.12.2007 B Sumy. 11.11.2008 B Chersonnes. 17.11.2008 B, 2015 A Makariv, vicar Kiev, UOC. 2008-2011 chairman Synodal commission Education and Catechesis. 2010 chairman Synodal commission Ethics.

Kliment Oleg Večerja
T: B Irpin, vicar Kiev UOC ▪ ✉ vul.Lavrska 25, korp 49, UKRAINA-01015 Kiev • [380] 44 255125-7, fax -6 • info@mitropolia.kiev.ua • www.o.church.ua
*16.8.1977. 1999 dipl Fac Biology University Kiev. 2000-2007 Seminary Academy Kiev, Kandidat, diak2002 ⊖2003 mon2003. 2004 Head Information Department Holy Synod UOC-KP. archim2008. 2009 teacher Academy Kiev ⊕23.7.2012 B Irpin, vicar Kiev, UOC, chairman commission Education.

Feodosij Denis Snigirev

T: B Boyarka, vicar Kiev UOC ▪ ✉ vul. Lavrska 25, korp 70, UKRAINA-01015 Kiev • [380] 44 2551164, fax 2554396 • info@mitropolia.kiev.ua • mitropolia.kiev.ua

*31.8.1974 Kiev. N16.5. 1994 feldšer medicine school Nikolajev. 1994-1998 Seminary Kaluga. mon2.4.1998 diak21.4.1998 ⊖30.6.1998. 1999-2003 Academy Moskva, Academy Kiev. 2001 rector Kiev. 2002 redaktor Pravoslavnyj Pečersk. igumen ⊕6.1.2011 B Boyarka, vicar Kiev UOC.

Iona Maxin Čerepanov

T: B Obuhov, vicar Kiev UOC ▪ ✉ vul. Lavrska 25, korp 70, UKRAINA-01015 Kiev • [380] 44 2551164, fax 2804396 • chancellery.upc@gmail.com

*29.12.1971 Kiev. N22.1. 1979-1989 school Kiev. Seminary Academy Kiev. 1992 National Medical University NMU A.A.Bogomoltsa, Monastery Pechera. mon1995 diak1995 ⊖1995. 2010 chairman Synodal Youth Department ⊕10.9.2011 lav Pechera B Obuhov, vicar Kiev, UOC (M Vladimir).

Antonij Sergij Kripak

T: B Putivl, vicar Kiev UOC ▪ ✉ Sosnovka, UKRAINA-01015 Glukhiv • [380] 5444 67437 • glynskaya-pustyn.church.ua

*16.2.1977 Čovno-Fedorivka Poltava. N23.6. 1996 Deputy of the Glynskaya Pustyn Stavropigial Monastery. 1997 Theol school Tavrik. mon20.4.2002 diak12.5.2002 ⊖19.12.2002. 26.10.2003 igumen. archim6.4.2006. 23.12.2010 namestnik Glinska Pustina. 6.5.2012 second cross ⊕13.5.2012 B Borodianka, 2012 B Putivl, vicar Kiev, UOC.

Varsonofij Vasilij Stoljar

T: B Borodjanka, vicar Kiev UOC ▪ ✉ vul. Lavrska 25, korp 70, UKRAINA-01015 Kiev • [380] 44 2551164, fax2804396 • chancellery.upc@gmail.com

*1.9.1972 Ladižin Vinnitsa. 1987-1991 stud Metrologia Radiotechnics University Odessa. 1991-1993 military service Chernovtsy and Prikarpatia. 1993-1997 Seminary Kiev, 1997-2001 Academy Kiev. mon24.12.1998 Pečerska Lavra Kiev. diak17.1.1999 ⊖7.4.1999 Pečerska Lavra Kiev (M Volodimir) 7.4.2001 igumen. archim14.3.2004 ⊕28.8.2012 B Borodianka, vicar Kiev, UOC.

Damian Oleg Davydov

T: B Fastov, vicar Kiev UOC ▪ ✉ vul. Lavrska 25, korp 70, UKRAINA-01015 Kiev • [380] 44 2551164, fax 2804396 • info@mitropolia.kiev.ua • www.mitropolia.kiev.ua

*1.12.1959 Odessa N18.10. mon27.10.1988 monastery Uspenski Odessa. diak30.10.1988 ⊖13.11.1988. 1990 absolvent Seminary Odessa. 1992 Pečera Kiev. archim21.4.1997 ⊕30.8.2012 B Fastov, vicar Kiev UOC.

Nikolaj Aleksandr Počtovyj

T: B Vasilkov, vicar Kiev UOC ▪ ✉ vul. Lavrska 25, korp 70, UKRAINA-01015 Kiev • [380] 44 2551164, fax 2804396 • info@mitropolia.kiev.ua • www.mitropolia.kiev.ua

*13.3.1970 Kiev, father priest. N10.4. 1987-1995 Seminary Academy Kiev. diak1992 ⊖1992 mon1999 archim2009 ⊕17.3.2013 B Vasilkov, vicar Kiev UOC.

Bogolep Valerij Gončarenko ***Aleksandrija***

T: B Aleksandria+Svetlovodsk, UOC ▪ ✉ Kremenčugskaja, Pokrovskij sobor, UKRAINA-28000 Aleksandrija • [380] 5235 78033 • alexandria_eparh@mail.ru • bogolep78@mail.ru • shtank.62@mail.ru • www.alexandria-eparh.ortodox.ru

*4.12.1978 Svetlovodsk Kirovograd. N4.9. 1996-2001 Technical University Kirovograd. 2001-2004 inspektor administration. 2002-2005 Theol school Poltava, Seminary. diak8.8.2004. 2005-2006 (correspondence course) Seminary Kiev ⊖7.1.2005 Kirovograd (B Panteleimon). mon24.4.2005. 2005 blagočinnyj dean Kirovograd. 23.4.2006 igumen. archim21.6.2008. 2010 Pedagogical University Kirovograd ⊕23.12.2012 Lavra Kiev B Aleksandrija+Svetlov UOC (M Vladimir).

Jefrem Valentin Jarinko ***Berdjansk***

T: B Berdjansk+Primorje UOC ▪ ✉ ul. Uljanovyh 23, UKRAINA-71118 Berdjansk • [380] 6153 47256+fax • berd_eparhiya@mail.ru • www.berdyansk.church.ua

*11.12.1978 Kostilivka Zakarpatia. N10.2. Ephrem Syr. 1995-1999 Theol school Hust. mon23.3.1997 diak2.11.1997 ⊖4.11.1997 archim2.4.2006. 2011 Kandidat Theol Kiev, sekretar eparchy Hust ⊕5.8.2012 B Berdjansk+Primorje UOC. 6.11.2012 ORTHODOXIA send from Hildesheim.

Avgustin Adam Markevič ***Bila Cerkva***

T: M Bila Cerkva+Boguslav, UOC ▪ ✉ Sobornaja ploščad, vul. Gagarina 12, UKRAINA-09100 Bila Cerkva • [380] 4563 91549 • diocese@bel.com.ua • www.bc-eparchy.org.ua

*7.4.1952 Gluškoviči Gomel. N18.6. Seminary Academy Moskva. 1977-1978 rector Bililovka Žytómyr. 1978-1992 rector, 1989-1992 blagočinnyj dean Kórosten Žytómyr. widower ⊕20.9.1992 Pečerska Lavra Kiev B Lviv+Drogobyč. 1995 and 2011 chairman Synodal Commission Theology UOC. 1995 chairman Office Military Chaplains. 1998 B, 2001 A Lviv+Galicia, 2012 A, 2013 M Bela Cerkov UOC.

Sofronij Dmitrij Dmitruk ***Čerkasy***

T: M Čerkasy+Kaniv UOC ▪ ✉ Iljina 230, UKRAINA-18015 Čerkasy • [380] 472 637441, 635463, fax 636817 • admin@cherkasy-orthodox.com.ua • jsmeprav@gmail.com • www.cherkasy-orthodox.com.ua • www.cherkasy.church.ua

*15.2.1940 Mnišino Rovno. N12.4. 1957-1960 construction worker. 1960-1962 Soviet army. 1962-1970 Seminary Academy Moskva. diak24.11.1968. 1970-1972 prof. stipendiat Academy, teacher Seminary. mon12.4.1971 archim. 1972-1980 teacher Academy Moskva ⊖7.1.1973. 1980-1987 rector Čerkasy. 1987-1989 Gorodišče. 1989-1992 Borispol Kiev ⊕9.8.1992 sv. Panteleimon Kiev B, 2001 A, 2008 M Čerkasy+Kaniv, UOC. 1995 Deputy Chairman Comm Canonization.

Ioann Sergij Vahnjuk

T: B Zolotonoša, vicar Čerkasy, UOC ▪ ✉ Iljina 230, UKRAINA-18015 Čerkasy • [380] 472 637441, 635463, Bishop 636817, Borg 4495 52340 • admin@cherkasy-orthodox.com.ua • www.cherkasy.church.ua

*12.2.1968 Kiev. 23.6.1991 rector parish Irklijv Cherkassy. diak9.6.1991 ⊖16.6.1991. 1993 dipl Seminary Kiev. mon6.12.1994 archim1996. 3.4.2015 narechenje ⊕5.4.2015 B Zolotonoša, vicar Čerkasy UOC.

Amvrosij Andrej Polikopa ***Černigov***

T: M Černigov+Novgorod-Severski UOC ▪ ✉ ul. Tolstogo 92 e, UKRAINA-14014 Černigiv • [380] 462 774579, 48120 • ogorel.pidan@mail.ru • www.chernihiv.church.ua

*20.9.1943 Zalivanšina Vinnitsa Kalinovski. N23.10. Soviet Army, worker Odessa. 1967 Seminary Moskva. 1971 Academy Moskva. diak1972 (Patr Pimen) ⊖1973. 1974 Cathedral Charkov. 1987 wife and son died in automobile crash. mon1998 archim1998 ⊕28.6.1998 B Novgorod-Severski vicar Černigov. 2003 B, 2008 A, 2015 M Černigov+Novgorod-Severski UOC.

Meletij Valentin Jegorenko ***Chernovtsy***

T: A Chernovtsy+Bukovina, UOC ▪ ✉ Russkaja 33, UKRAINA-58003 Chernovcy • [380] 372 523351, 585918, fax 551524 • eparhia-cv@utel.net.ua • http://chernivtsi.church.ua

*17.7.1962 Dzhambul Kazakhstan, N6.6. 1963 Kropotkin Krasnodar. 1969-1979 school Kropotkin. 1980 chtets Kropotkin. 1981-1983 Soviet Army. 1983-1996 Seminary Academy Moskva. mon3.12.1986 diak19.12.1986. 1990 eparchy Chernovtsy ⊖6.1.1991 archim24.6.1992 ⊕30.7.2006 B, 2013 A Hotyn, vicar Chernovtsy. 2014 A Černovtsi UOC.

Longin Mihail Žar ***Bančeni***
T: B Bančeni, vicar Chernovtsy, UOC ▪ ✉ Russkaja 33, UKRAINA-58003 Bancheny • [380] 3740 21150, 33319, 22178 • bancheny-monchurch.ua
*1965 Petraševka Gertsajev Chernovtsy. N29.10. 1984 married with Lipia Solomia: Vladimir *1987, Mihail *1989, Maria *1990. diak, ⊖1997 mon, nastojatjel Monastery Bančeni 200 orphans. 2008 Geroj Ukrainy ⊕22.5.2012 B Bančeni, vicar Černovtsy, UOC.

Onufrij Oleg Legkij ***Kharkov***
T: M Kharkiv+Bohodukhiv, UOC ▪ ✉ Universitetskaja 8, UKRAINA-61002 Charkov • [380] 57 7313523, 73123-01, fax -87 • office@pravoslavie.kharkov.ua • www.eparchia.kharkov.ua
*27.3.1970 Chodorov Lvov. N1.6. 1987 eparchy Lvov. 1989-1993 Seminary Odessa. diak28.8.1990 ⊖4.10.1992. 1993-1998 Academy Kiev (correspondence course). 1993 rector Charkov. mon20.4.2000 archim21.4.2000 ⊕22.4.2000 B Izjum vicar Charkov. 2003 MTh Warszawa. 2012 A, 2013 M Kharkiv+Bohodukhiv, UOC.

Elisej Oleg Ivanov ***Izjum***
T: A Izjum+Kupjan UOC ▪ ✉ ul. Sobornaya 7, UKRAINA-64300 Izjum • [380] 5743 22257 • eparhiay-izyum@mail.ru • www.izum.church.ua
*19.6.1973 Šahtersk Donetsk. N27.6. 1991 Technikum. 1992 Cathedral Donetsk. diak3.6.1996 mon27.6.1996 ⊖4.8.1996. 1997-2001 Seminary Odessa. 1998 igumen. 2002-2006 Academy Kiev Kandidat "Psalms first prayer Old and New Testament". archim2004 ⊕21.3.2007 B Amvrosiiv, vicar Donetsk. 18.10.2007 B Berdjansk+ Primorje. 2012 A Izjum+Kupjan, UOC.

Filaret Jurij Zverev ***Nova Kakhovka***
T: B Nova Kakhovka+Genichessk UOC ▪ ✉ Ščorsa 14 a, UKRAINA-74900 Nova Kahovka • [380] 55 4990204 • ortho-kahovka@ukr.net • www.eparhiya.org.ua
*1971 Lugansk. N2.12. Master Medicine, reader hypodiakon Poltava. diak1995 ⊖1996. 1999 dipl Seminary Kiev, 2002 rector Poltava, press-sekretar. mon2007 chairman Synodal Commission Liturgia. 2008 dipl Academy Užgorod. archim2008 ⊕12.2.2011 B Novaja Kahovka+Genitsa, UOC.

Ioann Igor Siopko ***Kherson***
T: A Kherson+Tavričessk, UOC ▪ ✉ ul. Dekabristov 36, UKRAINA-73025 Kherson • [380] 552 262979 +fax, 229632, 262023 • info@pravoslavie.ks.ua • www.pravoslavie.ks.ua
*14.3.1964 Rovno. N9.10. 1981 absolvent school Rovno. diak19.8.1985 (A Damian Volyn) ⊖22.2.1987 (B Varlaam Volyn). 1991-1993 UAOC. 1992 absolvent Seminary

Lvov. mon31.12.1993 (Io Ev) Pečerska Lavra Kiev. 7.1.1994 igumen. archim2.8.1994. 1994 sekretar eparchy Kiev. 1996 absolvent Academy Kiev ⊕13.12.1996 B Perejaslav -Khmelnitskij, vicar Kiev. 2000 B Hust+Vinogradiv. 2006 A Kherson, UOC.

Antonij Vasilij Fialko ***Khmelnitskij***
T: M Khmelnitskij+Starokonstantinov, UOC ▪ ✉ Volodimirska 113, UKRAINA-29013 Khmelnitskij • [380] 382 650332,764338, fax 765511 • antony@fialko.org • www.khmelnytsky-sob.church.ua
*2.10.1946 Duditskoje Kiev. N23.7. absolvent Institut Construct Voroneš. 1975 Seminary Leningrad. 1975-1978 eparchy Kursk. diak24.4.1976 ⊖14.8.1977. 1978-1989 Vinnitsa. mon10.4.1979 1982 absolvent Academy Moskva. 7.4.1982 igumen. archim1985. 1989-1991 rector Cathedral Khmelnitskij, blagočinnyj dean, sekretar administration. 1991-1992 igumen Voznjesenije Zoločiv (UAOC) ⊕23.6.1991 Kiev B Kamjanets Podilskyj+Chmelnyckyj (Patr Mstyslav UAOC) ⊕27.7.1992 (Moskva: Pečerska Lavra Kiev) B Perejaslav Khmelnitskij vicar Kiev. 1993 B. 1999 A. 2001 M Khmelnitskij+Šepetovka (2007 +Starokonstantinov) UOC.

Dionisij Dimitrij Konstantinov
T: B former Šepetivka+Slavuta, UOC ▪ ✉ prospekt Miru 27, UKRAINA-30400 Šepetivka • [380] 3840 51405, 55154, 53590 • [380] 97 5601604 • shepeteparhia@gmail.com • www.shepetivka church.ua
*7.7.1960 Čadir Lunga Moldova.N16.10. stud Seminary Odessa, Academy Kiev. diak1995 mon1996. 1996-2003 kancelaria Kiev ⊖1997 archim2000. 2003 naselnik Pečerska Lavra Kiev ⊕18.6.2011 Pečerska Lavra Kiev. B Šepetivka+Slavutsk, UOC. 24.12.2014 retired.

Irinej Valentin Semko ***Nežin***
T: A Nežin+Priluki, UOC ▪ ✉ ul. Stefan Javorskij 2, UKRAINA-16600 Nežin • [380] 4631 25253 • nizhin.church.ua@gmail.com • www.nizhin.church.ua
*11.6.1963 Ropotuka Čerkasy, N5.9. 1980-1981 worker Kievtorgstroj. 1981-1983 institut ingenieur Kiev. 1983-1992 Seminary Akademija Moskva. mon26.2.1985 diak6.4.1985 ⊖30.11.1986 dean Pečerska Lavra Kiev. 1992 teacher Seminary Kiev. 2006 Kandidat Moskva "Monasteries Ukraina 20th century" ⊕10.6.2007 Kiev B, 2014 A Nežin+Priluki, UOC.

Vladimir Stanislav Oračev ***Dnjeprodzeržinsk***
T: B Dnjeprodzeržinsk+Caričansk, UOC ▪ ✉ ul. Kirov 1, UKRAINA-51900 Lugansk • [380] 5692 37279 dndz-ep@ukr.net • www.eparchia.at.ua
*8.3.1973 Lugansk Stanislav Nikolajević. 7.2. 1988-1992 art school. diak24.4.1992 mon15.9.1992. 1992-1996 Seminary Kiev ⊖7.1.1994. 1994 sekretar eparchy Lugansk.

21.5.1994 igumen. archim17.11.1996. 1996-2003 Academy Kiev. 2006 Kandidat. parish Lugansk ⊕12.11.2008 B Kremenčug. 2009-2010 B Rovenkov vicar Lugansk. 2011 B Dnjeprodzeržinsk+Caričansk UOC.

Irinej Ivan Serednij ***Dnjepropetrovsk***
T: M Dnjepropetrovsk+Pavlograd, UOC ▪ ✉ Červona Ploščad 7, UKRAINA-49070 Dnipropetróvsk • [380] 56 7444849, 452039, 453373, 447646, 223351 • mitropolitiriney@mail.ru • www.eparhia.dp.ua
*10.5.1939 Stolpin Rovno. N5.9. diak21.5.1968 ⊖22.5.1968. 1968 Kandidat Leningrad. 1968-1970 priest Lavra Zagorsk. mon1.9.1970. 1970-1971 Lektor, sekretar, vice-inspektor Seminary Academy Leningrad. 1971-1975 podvorije Tokio ⊕27.7. 1975 B Ufa. 1976 B Serpuhovsk USA Canada. 1982 A Alma Ata. 1984 A Charkov. 1989 A Lvov. 1990 A Rovno. 1993 A Dnjepropetrovsk+Kryvyj Rih, 1996 divided. 2002 M Dnjepropetrovsk+Pavlograd, UOC.

Evlogij Vasilij Patsan
T: B Novomoskovsk, vicar Dnjepropetrovsk, UOC ▪ ✉ Maydan Peremogy 1, UKRAINA- 49070 Novomoskovsk • [380] 569 380073 • www.novomoskovsk-sob.church.ua
*6.6.1970 Mala Moščanica, Rovno, Aleksejević. N7.3. 1977-1985 school. 1985-1988 cultural school Dubno. 1988-1990 military service. 1993 absolvent Seminary Kiev, 1993-1997 Academy Kiev. 1997 teacher Seminary. diak14.1.1998 mon27.3.1998 "Evlogij" ⊖14.6.1998. 28.8.1998 igumen. 2000 parish Plosk. archim9.11.2007. 2008 Dr. theol Kiev, professor Academy Kiev ⊕13.12.2009 Novomoskva, vicar Dnjepropetrovsk, UOC.

Ilarion Roman Šukalo ***Donetsk***
T: M Donetsk+Mariupol, UOC ▪ ✉ ul. Tušinska 7, UKRAINA-83062 Donetsk • [380] 62 313129-7, -8, fax 62 3850 885 • ortodox.donbass@gmail.com • eparhiadonetsk@yandex.ru • www.ortodox.donbass.com
*3.5.1951 Rudno Lvov. N3.11. 1968-1979 Agricultural Institute Lvov. diak15.2.1980 ⊖23.10.1980. 1980-1986 Seminary Odessa. 1986-1988 rector Rovno. 1988-1991 blagočynnyj Starobjelsk. 1989 protoierej ⊕29.9.1991 (Filaret Denisenko) B Ivano-Frankivsk (B Černovtsy+Bukovina). 1992 B Cherson+Tavria. 1995 A Cherson+Tavria. 1996 Donetsk+Mariupol (until 1995 D.+Slavjansk). 2000 M Donetsk+Mariupol, UOC 2010 second panagia. 2011 permanent member of the Sacred Synod UOC.

Arsenij Igor Jakovenko
T: M Svjatogorsk, vicar Donetsk, UOC ▪ ✉ Zarichnastr. 1, UKRAINA-84131 Svjatogorsk • [380] 62 6253024 • eparhiadonetsk@yandex.ru • www.svlavra.church.ua

*21.6.1968 Porosozero Karelia Igor Fjodorović, N21.5. 1985 Agricultural institute. 1986-1988 military service. 1988 čtets Voronež. 1989-1992 Seminary Moskva. diak1992 ⊖25.7.1992 mon21.8.1992. 1993 blagočinnyj dean monastery Svjatogorsk. 20.1.1995 igumen. archim1995 Orden Knjaz Volodymyr, second cross ⊕5.12.2005 B Svjatogorsk, vicar Gorlov. 2010 A Svjatogorsk, vicar Donetsk UOC. 17.3.2015 M Svjatogorsk UOC.

Varnava Vjačeslav Filatov
T: A Makeev, vicar Donetsk, UOC ▪ ✉ ul. Tušinska 7, UKRAINA-83062 Donetsk • [380] 62 3131298, 2613980, 3850-500 • eparhiadonetsk@yandex.ru • www.donetsk.church.ua
*21.4.1953 Ashgabadi Turkmenistan, N17.1. 1974 Suhumi Avkazia. painter of icons. diak22.4.1976 Suhumi (M Ilia). 1991 Makeev Donetsk. Seminary Kiev (correspondence course) ⊖2.5.1991 Lugansk (B Ioannikij) 1993 parish Makeev. 1995-2007 blagočinnyj dean Makeev. mon5.1.1995. 11.10.1996 igumen (A Ilarion). archim31.8.1997 Kiev (M Vladimir) ⊕11.2.2007 Makeev kathedral St. George. 18.10.2007 vicar Donetsk. 2013 Orden St. Serafim Sarov. Orden "Za zaslugi". 2014 A Makeev, vicar Donetsk, UOC.

Varsonofij Volodimir Vinničenko
T: B Novoazovsk, vicar Donetsk, UOC ▪ ✉ ul. Tušinska 7, UKRAINA-83062 Donetsk • [380] 62 3850-500 • eparhiadonetsk@yandex.ru • www.donetsk.church.ua
*19.3.1961 Donetsk, N1./14.4. 1981 absolvent Technikum Donetsk, constructeur Rostov-na-Donu, Maikop. 1993 absolvent Techn University Moskva. 1994 ekonom eparchy Maikop. diak7.1.1995 ⊖19.1.1995 Maikop (A Aleksandr), eparchy Donetsk. mon21.8.1996. 1998 blagočinnyj dean Novodonetsk eparchy Gorlov. 15.11.1998 igumen Donetsk. 2004-2007 Seminary Moskva. archim15.4.2004. 2008 teacher History University Donetsk. Donetsk ⊕30.3.2013 Mon Panteleimonov Feofanija B Novoazovsk, vicar Donetsk, UOC (M Vladimir).

Mitrofan Andrij Nikitin ***Gorlovka***
T: B Gorlovka+Slavjansk, UOC ▪ ✉ Vostruhina 2, UKRAINA-84634 Gorlovka • [380] 6242 93593. 43464, 46434, 46319 • Krasnij Liman [380] 6261 22827 • G.eparhia@gmail.com • www.gorlovka-eparhia.com.ua
*31.10.1976 Vorošilovgrad (Lugansk). N20.8. 1994 monastery Svjatogorsk. diak 21.11.1994 mon23.12.1994. 1996-2000 Seminary ⊖18.5.1997. 2001-2005 Academy Kiev. 2004 teacher New Testament University Donetsk ⊕28.1.2007 B Gorlovka+ Slavjansk, UOC.

Alipij Vasilij Pogrebnjak
T: A Krasnoliman vicar Gorlovka, UOC ▪ ✉ Kirova, 41, UKRAINA-84634 Gorlovka • [380] 6242 43464, 46319 • Krasnij Liman [380] 6261 22827 • nikolosa77@gmail.com • www.gorlovka-eparhia.com.ua
*21.6.1945 Malievka Charkov. N30.8. 1964-1966 Soviet Army. 1966-1974 Kandidat Moskva. mon1971 Troice-Sergieva Lavra ⊕6.10.1991 B Donetsk+Slavjansk (Filaret Denisenko) 1992-1994 retired. 1994-1997 B new eparchy Gorlovka+ Slavjansk, UOC. 1994-2014 retired. 2014 A Krasnoliman, vicar of Gorlovka.

Mark Nikolaj Petrovtsy ***Hust***
T: M Hust+Vinogradiv, UOC ▪ ✉ pl. Nezaležnosti 12, Eparhalnoje upravlenie, UKRAINA-90400 Hust • [380] 314 242132, fax 242079 • eparhia@orthodoxkhust.pravsvit.org • www.orthodoxkhust.pravsvit.org
*6.12.1951 Priboržavskoje Iršava Transkarpatia. N8.5. 1970-1972 Soviet Army. 1972-1973 Troice-Sergieva Lavra. 1973 Seminary Moskva (4. Kl.). 1973-1982 vicar igumen archimandrit Ieronym. mon6.3.1974 diak17.3.1974 ⊖7.4.1974. 1978 Kandidat Moskva. archim1982. 1985-1988 igumen Počajev ⊕28.7.1988 B Kremenec, vicar Lvov. 1989-1993 B Argentina. 1993-2005 B Kašira vicar Moskva, Administrator of Patriarchal Parishes of the Russian Orthodox Church in Canada. 2005 B Sumy, 2007 A, 2014 M Hust+Vinogradiv UOC. 2012 Orden St. Innokentij (II).

Antonij Oleksandr Borovik
T: B Ugolsky, vicar Hust UOC ▪ ✉ Lvivska, UKRAINA-90400 Hust • [380] 3142-52123, fax -51830 • eparhiahust@gmail.com • www.khust.church.ua • www.orthodoxhust.org.ua
*30.3.1968 Lubny Poltava. N23.7. 1986-1988 Soviet Army. 1989-1993 Seminary Odessa. diak10.12.1990 mon24.12.1990 ⊖29.8.1993 blagočinnyj dean Odessa. 1993-2001 Academy Kiev (correspondence course). 31.10.1995 igumen. archim7.1.2000. 2004 Kandidat ⊕18.5.2008 B Uman+Svenigorod. 2008-2012 B Aleksandrija+ Svetlovodsk. 2012 Počajev. 16.9.2014 B Ugolskij, vicar of Hust UOC.

Tihon Stepan Chizhevskij ***Ivano-Frankivsk***
T: B Ivano-Frankivsk+Kolomyja, UOC ▪ ✉ Vinogradna 10, UKRAINA-76493 Kryhivtsy • [380] 342 753108, 235059, kantsler 245176, cerkov 230584 • if.eparhia@gmail.com • boechko@inbox.ru • www.svt-vasiliy.if.ua • www.ivano-frankivsk.church.ua
*31.8.1947 Maljatintsy, district Kitsman, region Chernovtsy, N25.3. 1965-1966 music school Chernovtsy. 1966-1969 Soviet Army. 1969-1971 Technical school Chernovtsy. 1969-1971 Turner in Experiments Factory Chernovtsy. diak17.6.1973 Smolensk Cathedral (B Feodosij Protsjuk). 1977-1987 deacon Chernovtsy Cathedral,

(correspondence course) Seminaryy Moskva. 7.4.1979 protodeacon. 29.3.1987 kamilavka. 1987 St. Nicholas Cathedral New York (Moskva), 1990-1993 San Francisco. mon1.3.1990 Monastery St. Tikhon OCA (B Kliment Kapalin, Serpuhov). 1991 igumen St. Nicholas New York (A Makarij Svistun, Klin) ⊖7.7.1991. 1993-2001 Chernovtsy Cathedral (M Onufrij). archim30.4.1994. 2001-2010 UOC Canada, Patriarchate of Constantinople. 2010-2014 dean Chernovtsy (M Onufrij) ⊕28.12. 2014 Cathedral Lavra Kiev B Ivano-Frankivsk+Kolomyja, UOC (M Onufrij).

Evsevij Ivan Dudka ***Shepetivka***
T: B Shepetivka+Slavuta, UOC ▪ ✉ prospekt Mira 27, UKRAINA-304000 Šepetivka • [380] 3840 51405, 55154, 53590 • cerkva-sh@ukrpost.ua • if.eparhia@gmail.com • www.shepetivka-orthodox.org.ua
*4.4.1964 Balamutovka Ukraina. 1982-1984 military service. 1985 Seminary Moskva. mon18.11.1986 Troice-Sergieva Lavra diak1986 ⊖1988. 1992 Chernovtsy. archim1994. 2006 Theol Institute Chernovtsy ⊕28.9.2014 B Hotyn, vicar Chernovtsy. 29.1.2016 B Shepetivka+Slavuta.

Feodor Aleksej Gajun ***Kamenets Podolskij***
T: M Kamenets Podolskij+Gorodok,UOC ▪ ✉ vul. Frantsiskanska 8, UKRAINA-32300 Kamjanets Podilskij • [380] 3849 27034, 23985, 24581, 25985 • kp_eparhy@mail.ru • www.kamyanets-podilskiy.church.ua
*17.2.1958 Nemoviči Rovno Ukraina, N24.8. 1975-1976 ingenieur water technical Institute Rovno. 1977-1978 fabric worker. 1978-1984 Seminary Moskva. 1979-1981 Soviet Army. 1984-1987 Kandidat Moskva. mon24.12.1987 diak10.1.1988. 1988 medal, 2003 Orden St. Sergij Radonež, 2008 Orden St. Serafim Sarov, 2013 Orden St. Innokentij Moskva ⊖7.10.1990. 1991 teacher Theol school Pochajev ⊕5.8.1992 B Počajev, vicar Ternopol. 1992-1996 namestnik Lavra, igumen. 1997 B Počajev vicar Ternopol, namestnik Sv. Uspenska Počajevska Lavra, rector Theol school. 1997 B, 2008 A, 2014 M Kamenets Podolskij+Gorodok, UOC. 2014 head Ecclesiastical Court, standing member Holy Synod.

Ioasaf Pjotr Hubjen ***Kirovograd***
T: A Kirovograd+Novomirgorod, UOC ▪ ✉ Karla Marksa 74, UKRAINA-25001 Kirovograd • [380] 522 221662, 235124, 224848, 230225, 247641 • orthodox-kr@ukr.net • www.orthodox-kr.org.ua
*8.4.1961 Kuta Čerkasy. N4./17.9. 1976 Technikum Kiev, 1980-1990 worker Jugozapadtransstroj. 1980-1982 Soviet Army. 1990-1994 Seminary Kiev, 1994-2002 Academy Kiev. diak28.7.1995 mon27.3.1998 ⊖1999. 2002 teacher Canon Law Academy Kiev ⊕16.12.2007 B Nova Kahovka+Bereslav. 2012 A Kirovograd+ Novomirgorod, UOC.

Roman Kimovič *Konotop*
T: B Konotop+Gluchov, UOC ▪ ✉ vul. B. Chmelnitskogo 7, UKRAINA-41600 Konotop • [380] 5447 70921, [380] 5444 23083 • palomnik@eparhija.org.ua • www.eparhija-org.ua
*1971 Bukovina. Choir regent Počajev. mon Počajev ⊖2007 Gorodišče ⊕22.7.2012 B Konotop UOC.

Nikolaj Maxim Kapustin *Kremenčug*
T: B Kremenčuk+Lubny, UOC ▪ ✉ Respublikanskaja 107, UKRAINA-39621 Kremenčug • [380] 536 703018, 79088, 20598, 30399, [380] 5366 61109 • www.kremen-eparh.org
*6.9.1977 Sevastopol. 1997 Monastery St. Vladimir Krivoj Rog. mon1998 diak1998 ⊖1998 absolvent Seminary Academy Kiev. 2005 namestnik Mon St. Vladimir Krivoj Rog. archim2007 ⊕16.6.2011 Pečerska Lavra Kiev. B Kremenčuk+Lubny, UOC.

Jefrem Ivan Kitsai *Kryvyj Rih*
T: A Kryvyj Rih+Nikopol, UOC ▪ ✉ Kaliničenka 4, UKRAINA-50063 Kryvyj Rih • [380] 564 901953, 901861, 298771, 294732, 441348, fax 924810 • consistoria@meta.ua • www.eparhia.com.ua
*5.7.1966 Zaškoviči Lvov. N10.2. Bacc 1983 Zavidovits. 1983-1985 Nutrition school Lvov. 1985-1987 Soviet Army. 1987-1988 Psalomščik Novgorod. 1988-1992 Seminary Moskva. 1992-1996 Academy Kiev, Kandidat Kiev. mon25.9.1992 Pečerska Lavra Kiev. diak27.9.1992 ⊖10.10.1992. 1992-1996 blagočinnyj dean Lavra ⊕13.9.1996 B Kryvyj Rih+Nikopol, Dnjepropetrovsk+Kryvyj Rih divided. 2010 again divided, new eparchy: Dnjeprodzeržinsk+Caričansk, UOC.

Mitrofan Mihail Jurčuk *Lugansk*
T: M Lugansk+Alčevsk, UOC ▪ ✉ per. Krupskoj 29-b, UKRAINA-91002 Lugansk • [380] 642 932-722, -116, fax 642 2525085 • lg.eparh@mail.ru • www.lugansk.church.ua • www.eparhia.lg.ua
*19.11.1962 Bilogirja Khmelnitskij, N20.8. 1981-1983 Soviet army. 1984-1987 Seminary Odessa. 1987-1988 Academy Moskva. 1988-1993 MTh Warszawa, teacher Seminary Warszawa. mon21.8.1990 Sergiev Posad diak1.9.1990 ⊖16.9.1990. 1994-2012 prorector Theol schools Kiev. 1994 igumen. archim1995 ⊕30.7.2000 B Perejaslav-Khmelnitskij. 2000 vicar Kiev. 2007 A Bila Cerkva+Boguslav. 2012 A, 2014 M Lugansk+Alčevsk, UOC.

Nifont Vasilij Soloducha *Volyn*
T: M Volyn+Lutsk UOC ▪ ✉ Karaimska 11, UKRAINA-43016 Lutsk • [380] 332 725177, 724097, kantsler 332 728713 • orthodox.lutsk@gmail.com • www.orthvoldiocese.lutsk.ua • www.volyn.church.ua

*5.10.1948 Galyna Volja Volynia, N21.4. 1967-1969 Soviet Army. 1970-1974 Seminary, 1971 hypodiakon to Patr Pimen. 1974-1977 Academy Moskva, Kandidat. mon20.3.1974 diak15.4.1974 ⊖26.2.1977 rector Rudka Volynskoj obl. 1985 igumen. archim1988 ⊕31.3.1990 B Khmelnitskij+Kamenets Podolskij. 1996 Lutsk+ Berestečko, 1996 Lutsk+Volyn. 2001 M Volynia+Lutsk. 2012 Volyn+Lutsk UOC. 28.8.2014 second panagia.

Nafanail Pjotr Krikota
T: B Kamin-Kashyrskyj, vicar Volyn UOC ▪ ✉ Karaimska 11, UKRAINA-43016 Lutsk
*12.7.1959 Zapljutje Volynija, his brother Nikolaj protoierej, sister Vera married protoierej Leonid, brother Valentij (*1976) protoierej. 1985 dipl Academy Moskva "Articles on Liturgy in the Journal Mosk Patr 1943-1957". mon31.3.1986 (Archim. Aleksij) diak22.5.1986 Vladimir (A Serafim) ⊖7.12.1986 Vladimir (A Serafim). 8.11.1990 igumen. 1990-1997 teacher Theol Seminary Odessa. archim 6.1.1996. 1997-2016 rector Theol Seminary Pochajev ⊕5.8.2015 B Shumsk vicar Ternopol, UOC. 29.1.2016 B Kamin, vicar Volyn.

Filaret Kučerov *Lviv*
T: B Lviv+Galicia, UOC ▪ ✉ vul. Korolenka 3, UKRAINA-79008 Lviv • [380] 322 6017-45, fax -46 • st.georgiy@i.ua • www.upc.lviv.ua • www.lviv-sob.church.ua
* Kiev, N? stud med, stud theol Seminary Moskva, Academy Kiev, teacher Seminary Moskva, hypodiakon Patr Alexij. mon1996 Pečerska Lavra Kiev (St. Filaret Amfiteatrov, M Kiev). 2003 chairman Synodal Mission social help for children. 2008 rector St. Sergij Kiev ⊕2.1.2011 Pečerska Lavra Kiev B Drogobyć, vicar Lvov, Mission Youth (M Volodymyr). 2012 B Lviv+Galicia, UOC.

Fjodor Oleksandr Mamasujev *Mukačevo*
T: A Mukačevo+Užgorod, UOC ▪ ✉ ul. 8 Bereznja Marta 12, UKRAINA-89600 Mukačevo • [380] 3131 21515, kantsler 21461, 21298 • post-eparhia@mail.ru • www.m-eparchy.org.ua • www.mukacheve.church.ua
*4.11.1966 Sambor Lvov, N16.11. 1983-1985 agricultural Technikum. 1985-1987 Soviet Army. 1988-1992 Seminary Academy Moskva. mon31.12.1989 Sergiev Posad diak31.12.1989 (B Aleksandr). 1990 rector Mukačevo ⊖1.5.1990. 1994 igumen (A Evfimij Mukachevo). archim1996 (Metr Vladimir Kiev) ⊕23.12.2007 B, 2009 A Mukačevo+Užgorod, UOC. 2015-2016 member Holy Synod.

Pitirim Nikolaj Starinskij *Nikolajev*
T: M Nikolajev+Očakov, UOC ▪ ✉ Potemkinskaya 50, UKRAINA-54001 Nikolajev • [380] 512 3737-59, -52, -63 • eparhianik@gmail.com •

www.eparhia.mk.ua • www.mykolaiv.church.ua

*6.3.1944 Červoni Jary Kiev. N10.8. 1964-1972 Seminary Academy Moskva. mon1969 diak1969. 1972-1992 Monk Počajev ⊕26.8.1992 (Pečerska Lavra Kiev) B Khmelnitskij+Kamenets Podolskij. 23.2.1993 namestnik. 1993 B, 2000 A, 2009 M Nikolajev+Voznesensk = 2012 Nikolajev+Očakov, UOC. 2004 Orden Sergij Radonež (II).

Aleksij Oleksij Špakov ***Voznesensk***

T: B Voznesensk+Pervomaisk, UOC ▪ ✉ Korabelnaya str.46, UKRAINA-55220 Pervomaisk, Mykolaiv region • [380] 5161 35330 • ea.eparchy@live.ru • www.voznesensk.church.ua • www.voznesensk.orthodox.ru

*25.1.1975 Lvov.N25.2. 1993-1995 military service. 1995-2000 church Pokrov Zaporiže. 2000-2004 Seminary Kiev. 2004-2006 (correspondence course) Pedagogical Institute Chernovtsy. mon2008 Kiev diak2008 ⊖2008 klirik Berdjansk, press-sekretar, sekretar eparchy, Academy Kiev (correspondence course). 2009 ekonom Academy Kiev. archim26.8.2012 ⊕4.9.2012 B Voznesensk, UOC.

Agafangel Aleksij Savvin ***Odessa***

T: M Odessa+Ismail, UOC ▪ ✉ Puškinska 79, UKRAINA-65038 Odessa • [380] 48 7225365 (fax), 7224073 • od-eparhia@mail.ru • kancelyaria-oey@mail.ru • www.eparhia.od.ua

*2.9.1938 Burdino Lipetsk. N5.2. mon2.4.1965 diak18.4.1965 ⊖22.4.1965. 1966 Kandidat, 29.5.1967 rector Seminary Odessa ⊕16.11.1975 B, 1981 A, 1989 M Winnytsja. 1992 M Odessa+Ismail, divided 21.12.2012 "Balta" and "Odessa+Ismail", second panagia, Permanent Member of the Sacred Synod UOC.

Viktor Vladislav Bykov

T: B Artsiz, vicar Odessa ▪ ✉ Puškinska 79, UKRAINA-65038 Odessa • [380] 4873-85638, -85602 • od-eparchia@gmail.ru • iliya-monastery@mail.ru • www.iliya-monastery.org • www.ilynsky-monchurch.ua

*20.4.1983 Tambov. 2002 stud Seminary Odessa, Fac History University Kiev. diak8.1.2003 mon24.11.2003 ⊖30.11.2003. 2005 igumen. 2005-2008 chief redactor Pantelemonov Listok. archim2006. 24.1.2007 namestnik monastery Pokrov Odessa. 2007 commission canonisation Moskva ⊕29.9.2014 B Artsiz, vicar Odessa.

Sergij Aleksandr Mihajlenko

T: B Bolgrad, vicar Odessa UOC ▪ ✉ Puškinska 79, UKRAINA-65038 Odessa • [380] 48 7225365 (fax), 7224073 • kancelyaria-oey@mail.ru • od-eparhia@mail.ru • www.eparhia.od.ua

*29.7.1975 Donetsk. mon20.4.1997 diak29.4.1997 ⊖5.6.1997. 1997-2001 stud Academy Kiev. 20.4.1998 igumen. archim4.5.2000 Ismael, Monastery Konstantin-Helena ⊕15.11.2015 B Bolgrad, vicar Odessa (M Onufrij).

Arkadij Oleksandr Taranov
T: B Ovidiopol, vicar Odessa, UOC ▪ ✉ Puškinska 79, UKRAINA-65012 Odessa • [380] 48 7224073 • od-eparhia@mail.ru • www.eparhia.od.ua
*1957 Yasenerskiy Lugansk region,N19.3. 1978-1982 stud Seminary Odessa. mon8.3.1982 ⊖6.1.1983 archim1996 namestnik Odessa. 2002 Academy Kiev ⊕4.8.2012 B Ovidiopol, vicar Odessa, UOC.

Diodor Vitalij Vasilčuk
T: B Jušne, vicar Odessa, UOC ▪ ✉ Puškinska 79, UKRAINA-65012 Odessa • [380] 48 7224073 • od-eparhia@mail.ru • www.eparhia.od.ua
*22.6.1979, N12.5. 1996-2000 Seminary Odessa, mon9.12.1996, Odessa (M Agafangel) diak22.12.1996 (M Agafangel) ⊖27.2.2000 (M Agafangel) archim13.4.2004. 2010 MTh Užgorod, 2011 Academy Kiev ⊕29.9.2013 B Jušne, vicar Odessa, UOC (M Vladimir Kiev).

Aleksij Sergij Groha ***Balta***
T: A Balta+Ananjev, UOC ▪ ✉ Uvarova 106, UKRAINA-66100 Balta, Odessa region • [380] 505761148 • baltaeparchia@mail.ru • www.balta.church.ua
*27.9.1972 N25.2. 1992 dipl Medicine Feldšer Dnjepropetrovsk. stud economy. mon20.12.1992 diak3.1.1993 ⊖7.1.1993. 1993 igumen (Patr Alexandria). 1994 prorector, teacher Law Seminary Odessa. archim1995. 1997 blagočinnyj dean monasteries Odessa. 1998 rector Odessa. 1999 absolvent Academy Moskva. 1999 abbot Odessa. 2000 absolvent Fac jur Odessa ⊕19.8.2006. 2012 A Belgorod-Dnestr, vicar Odessa. 2013 A Balta UOC.

Vissarion Vasilij Stretovič ***Ovruč***
T: M Ovruč+Korosten, UOC ▪ ✉ Soborna (Karla Libknehta) 3, UKRAINA-11108 Ovruč • [380] 4148 22122 • www.ovruch.church.ua
*4.12.1953 Poljanka Korosten Žitomir. N19.6. 1971 bacc. 1972 Soviet Army. 1975-1983 Seminary Moskva, Academy Moskva. mon1.4.1983 Troice-Sergieva Lavra. 1983-1987 Cathedral Žitomir. 1987-1991 Ovruč. 1990 igumen ⊕24.8.1992 B Korosten, vicar Žitomir+Ovruč. 1993 B, 2000 A, 2010 M Ovruč+Korosten, UOC.

Filipp Roman Osadčenko ***Poltava***
T: M Poltava+Mirgorod, UOC ▪ ✉ Heroer Stalingrada 1b, UKRAINA-36039 Poltava • [380] 532 595991, 59576-1, -3, fax -2 • pravpoltava@ukr.net • www.pravoslavie.poltava.ua

*2.7.1956 Dnjipropetrovsk. N22.1. 1973-1979 Fac Biology University Charkov. diak11.9.1980 ⊖28.9.1980 rector Kursk. 1984-1988 Seminary Moskva. 1985 sekretar eparchy Irkutsk. 1986 Poltava. mon1993 archim1994. 1994-1999 Academy Kiev (correspondence course) ⊕30.12.2001 Kiev, B, 2006 A, 2012 M Poltava+Mirgorod UOC. 2008 Chairman Mission Department. 2011 Chairman Department Catechisis.

Veniamin Vladimir Pogrebnoj

T: B Novi Sanshari, vicar Poltava UOC ▪ ✉ Heroer Stalingrada 1b, UKRAINA-36039 Poltava • [380] 532 595991, 59576-1, -3, fax -2 • pravpoltava@ukr.net • www.pravoslavie.poltava.ua

*19.1.1979 Pervomajsk Lugansk Ukraina. 1996-2000 Seminary Poltava. 2000-2004 St. Tikhon Theol Institute Moskva ⊖22.5.2004. 2004-2008 Academy Kiev. mon14.3.2009. 2009-2010 University Karpatia. 2011 igumen. archim30.8.2011, pro-rector Seminary Poltava, teacher AT and NT. 2013 Dr. phil University Lugansk. 10.11.2015 narechenje Feofania (M Onufrij) ⊕6.12.2015 Pečerska Lavra Kiev B Novi Sanshari, vicar Poltava UOC (Metr Onufrij).

Iosif Aleksij Maslenikov ***Romny***

T: B Romny+Buryn, UOC ▪ ✉ Bazarna sg.15a, UKRAINA-42000 Romny • [380]6761 77540 • romnyeparchia@yandex.ru • www.romnyeparchia.org.ua • www.romny.church.ua

*3.11.1978 Slobodeja Moldova. N22.5. 1992 Ukraina. mon22.3.1996 diak24.3.1996 ⊖7.1.1997. 1997-2005 parishes Melitopol. 2001 igumen. 2004 absolvent Seminary Belgorod. 2005 rector Vitebsk. 2006 absolvent Academy Kiev, rector Zaporižžja. archim19.6.2008 ⊕18.11.2008 B Volnjan, vicar Zaporižžja, 2009 B Zaporižžja, 2010 B Konotop, 2012 B Yampil, vicar Konotop, 2013 B Romny+Buryn, UOC.

Panteleimon Vasilij Povoroznjuk ***Rovenky***

T: A Rovenky+Sverdlovsk, UOC ▪ ✉ Gagarina 25, UKRAINA-94707 Rovenky, Lugansk region • [380]6433-53570, -53802, fax -53430 • episkop@rovenky-ep.org.ua • www.rovenky-ep.org.ua

*24.8.1973 Bubnovka Vinnitsa. N9.8. 1991 psalomščik. 1991-1993 military service. 1994-1998 Seminary, 1998-2002 Academy Kiev, Kandidat "Cerkovno-obščestvennaja dejatelnost v XVIII stoletie". mon11.7.2002 diak12.7.2002 ⊖12.7.2003. 13.11.2004 igumen. archim28.8.2007 ⊕23.9.2008 B Vasilkov, vicar Kiev. 2011-2012 B Severodonetsk. 2013 B Rovenky+Sverdlovsk, UOC. 17.8.2015 A Rovenki+Sverdlovsk, UOC.

Varfolomej Viktor Vaščuk ***Rivne***

T: M Rivne+Ostrog, UOC ▪ ✉ Lermentova 3, UKRAINA-33028 Rivne • [380] 362 221562, 226929, 223009, M. 223466 • www.rivne-pravoslavne.org.ua

*1.3.1953 Gorodno Ljuboml Volynia. 1971-1973 Soviet Army. 1975 Seminary Odessa. 1983 Kandidat Moskva. 1983-1989 Staraja Vyževka. diak16.10.1983 ⊖18.10.1983 mon22.12.1989. 1989 sekr eparchy Volyn, protoierej. archim18.1.1990 ⊕24.2.1990 B Volynia+Lutsk. 1992-1993 B Nikolajev+Vosnesensk. 1993-1995 B Sumy+Ahtyrka. 1995 B, 1996 A, 2014 M Rovno, UOC 28.8.2014 M Rivne+Ostrog, UOC.

Anatolij Aleksej Hladkiý *Sarny*

T: M Sarny+Polessje, UOC ▪ ✉ vul. Železnodorožna 27, UKRAINA-34500 Sarny • [380] 3655 32287, 32973, fax 32264 • eo365532287@gmail.com • www.sarny.church.ua

*28.7.1957 Ladigi Khmelnitskij. N16.7. diak1982. 1984 absolvent Academy Leningrad. rector Obuchov. sekretar to M Volodimir Kiev ⊖1992 igumen Kiev ⊕28.10. 1993. 1993-1995 B Rovno+Ostrog. 1995-1999 B Gluchiv+Konotop, (1998 = Konotop+Gluchiv), 1999 B, 2004 A, 2013 M Sarny+Polessje, UOC.

Nikodim Baranovskij *Severodonetsk*

T: B Severodonetsk+Starobilsk, UOC ▪ ✉ pl. Sobornaja 1, UKRAINA-93411 Severodonetsk • [380] 6452 34070, [380] 98 3112288 • sever_eparhia@mail.ru • www.sed-eparhia.com • www.severodonetsk.church.ua

*15.5.1975 Gošev Ovruč Žitomir. N3rd Sunday after Pascha. 1992-2000 Seminary Academy Kiev. 1997-2007 teacher liturgics Seminary Kiev. mon11.4.2000 diak15.4. 2000 ⊖27.4.2000. 2001 Kandidat Liturgics Kiev. 2001 igumen Pascha. archim2003. 2007 sekretar eparchy Belaja Cerkva ⊕25.12.2010. 2010-2012 Rakitno, vicar Bila Cerkva. 2012-2013 B Roven, vicar Lugansk. 2013 B Severodonetsk+Starobilsk, UOC.

Lazar Rostislav Švets *Simferopol*

T: M Simferopol+Krim, UOC ▪ ✉ ul. Geroev Adžimuškaja 9/11, UKRAINA-95011 Simferopol • [380] 652-254511, -505603, -270059, fax -251470 • cr_eparx@sf.ukrtel.net • www.crimea.orthodoxy.su • www.simferopol.church.ua

*22.4.1939 Komarin Ternopol. N21.3. 1958-1961 military service. 1961-1964 Seminary Odessa. 1964-1968 Kandidat Academy Moskva. 1968-1971 teacher. diak 5.3.1972 ⊖12.3.1972. 1975 Argentina. 1978 protoierej. mon1.4.1980 archim7.4.1980 ⊕18.4.1980. 1980-1989 B A Argentina. (19.4.-20.9.1985 A Ivano-Frankivsk) 1989-1991 A Ternopol. 1991-1992 A Odessa. 1992 A, 2001 M Simferopol+Krim, UOC.

Platon Vladimir Udovenko *Feodosija*

T: M Feodosija+Kerch, UOC ▪ ✉ Doskogo,5, UKRAINA-98320 Kerch • [380]662466549, Cathedral 656192288 • mplaton@arnetbiz.com.ar • www.feodosiia.church.ua

*17.11.1940 Uspenka Lugansk (=Vorošilovgrad), N18.4. 1957 Odessa Monastery, 1958 Seminary Kiev, 1960 Seminary Odessa. 1961-1964 Soviet Army. 1965-1969 Akademy Leningrad. 1969-1972 Academy Moskva. mon14.4.1971 diak17.4.1971 ⊖12.9.1971 ⊕16.12.1973 B, 1977 A Argentina. 1980 A Sverdlovsk (Jekaterinburg). 1984 A Jaroslavl. 1993 A, 2001 M Argentina. 2012 M Feodosij+Kerč, UOC. 2004 Orden St. Innokentij, 2010 Orden St. Serafim Sarov.

Alipij Anatolij Kozolij ***Džankoj***
T: B Džankoj+Razdolninsk, UOC ▪ ✉ ul. Rosa Luksemburg, 33, UKRAINA-96100 Džankoj • [380] 6564 41636 • dzh.eparhia@mail.ru • www.dzhankoy-sob.church.ua • www.dzhankoy.church.ua

*27.10.1971 Kalinovka Kiev. N30.8. 1989-1991 Soviet Army. 1991-1994 Seminary Odessa, mon11.9.1993 diak26.9.1993 ⊖3.10.1993. 2002-2006 Kiev. 2006 igumen. 2007 teacher Seminary Tavrijsk, rector Gaspra Krim ⊕14.2.2010 B Džankoj+Razdolninsk, UOC.

Evlogi Evgen Gutčenko ***Sumy***
T: A Sumy+Ahtyrka, UOC ▪ ✉ ul. Soborna 31, UKRAINA-40000 Sumy • [380] 542-222453, -220560 fax -223371 • sumep@mail.ru • www.portal-pravoslavie.sumy.ua

*21.3.1967 Odessa Evgen Anatolević. N7.9. mon20.10.1991 diak27.10.1991. 1991 teacher Seminary Odessa, 1992 absolvent Seminary Odessa ⊖19.8.1992. 1992-2000 Academy Moskva. 22.10.1994 igumen. 1994-1998 blagočinnyj dean Odessa. 1995 Member commission canonization. archim13.12.1995. 1998 rector Seminary Odessa ⊕20.11.2007 B Kremenčug. 2008 Member of Church Court UOC. 2009 B Sumy, UOC. 9.7.2013 A Sumy+Ahtyrka, UOC.

Sergij Boris Gensitskij ***Ternopol***
T: M Ternopol+Kremenets, UOC ▪ ✉ ul. Konovaljtsa 1, UKRAINA-46020 Ternopil • [380] 352 -245057, -515029 • hramsofiya@inbox.ru • www.ternopil.church.ua

*4.12.1951 Dolinjanij Černovic. N8.10. 1970 absolvent Medical College Novoselica. 1970-1971 Hospital Draginec. 1971-1973 Soviet Army. diak15.7.1973, 1973-1975 Cathedral Smolensk. 1975-1985 sekretar eparchy Smolensk. 1983 absolvent Seminary Moskva. mon6.12.1985 Lavra Počajev. 1986 Archidiakon ⊖28.8.1990 (A Lazar) ⊕17.2.1991 B, 1998 A, 2011 M Ternopol+Kremenets UOC. 2012 Orden Serafim Sarov (III).

Serafim Vasilij Zaliznitskij
T: B Shumsk, vicar Ternopil UOC ▪ ✉ ul. Konovaljtsa 1, UKRAINA-4620 Ternopil

*16.1.1953 Losatin Ternopil. N1.8. 1968 absolvent school Losatin. 1973 absolvent Technikum Agriculture Kremenets. 1975-1979 Seminary Moskva. 1979-1983 Academy Moskva. diak24.2.1985 ⊖3.3.1985. 1985 rector Sv. Pokrov Glevaha Kiev. 1985-1994 blagočinnyj dean Bila Cerkva ⊕1.8.1994. 1994-2007 B Bila Cerkva+ Boguslav. 1995-2000 President Commission Humanitarian Aid Ukraina. 2007-2008 vicar Moskva. 29.1.2016 rector Theol Seminary Pochajev, B Shumsk, vicar Ternopil.

Ionafan Anatolij Jeletskih ***Tuljčin***
T: M Tuljčin+Bratslav, UOC ▪ ✉ Lenina 41, UKRAINA-23600 Tuljčin • [380] 4335-21804, fax -21264 • yeletskykh@mail.ru • tulchin-eparhiya@ukr.net • www.sobor.co.ua • www.vladyka-ionafan.ru
*30.1.1949 Shatalovka Voronesh Rossija (now Bjelgorod), N Sunday before Christmas, Sv. Praotets. 1966 absolvent school Kiev. 1966-1968 Medicine Department Kiev. 1968-1970 Military service. 1970-1972 Seminary Leningrad. 9.10.1971 čtec (M Nikodim). 1972-1976 Theol Academy Leningrad. hypodiakon to M Nikodim. absolvent Regentski Klass, Komponist. 1976-1986 teacher Church Music Seminary Leningrad. mon5.4.1977 (M Nikodim) diak16.4.1977 (M Nikodim) ⊖24.12.1978 (A Kyrill) igumen. 1980 Kandidat "Pastoral and Moral Doctrine of St. Theodor Studion". 1987-1988 St. Vladimir Kiev. 1988-1991 namestnik Pečerska Lavra Kiev ⊕23.4.1989 B Perejaslav-Khmelnitskij (M Filaret Denisenko). 1989-1991 sekretar to M Kiev. 1989-1991 vicar Kiev. 1992 B Bila Cerkva, vicar Kiev. 1993 Chancellor sekretar Synod UOC. 1993 B, 1994 A Gluchov+Konotop 1995-1999 A Sumy+Ahtyrka. 1999 Cross St. Antonij Feodosij. 1999 Cross St. Daniel (Patr Moskva). 1999-2006 A Cherson+Tavričessk. 2000 Official Director website UOC, chairman PIA Orth Information Agency. 2000 Member Synodal Commission Theology UOC. 2000 Jury International Festival Church Music Hainówka Poland. 2004 Orden Sergij Radonež. 2004 lecturer Fribourg Switzerland. 2006 A, 2014 M Tuljčin. 2009 1. Dekret Patriarch Kirill: Orden St. Vladimir (II) (56 bearers). 2009 Orden Družby, Dimitrij Medvedev for collaboration Ukraina Rossija. 2010 Patriarchal Commission Culture. 2014 Orden St. Andrews. 14.11.2014 Participation "50 years Institute for Ecumenical Studies Fribourg".

Panteleimon Mihailo Lugovoj ***Uman***
T: A Uman+Zvenigorod, UOC ▪ ✉ Sovietskaja 35/2, UKRAINA-20300 Uman • [380] 4744 -42330, fax -50550 • uman_eparhia@mail.ru • uman-eparhia@i.ua • www.eparhia-uman.org.ua
*11.5.1967 Kopanki Ivano-Frankovsk, N9.8. 1976-1984 school Kopanki. 1984-1990 Institut Paed. 1985-1987 military service. 1987-1996 Seminary Academy Kiev. 1996 Kandidat, teacher Academy, starčij pom. inspektora. diak21.3.1996 ⊖9.11.1996 mon20.3.1997. 1997-2004 sekretar Education Academy. 9.7.1997 igumen. 2000-

2005 teacher Church History University Kiev. archim11.4.2004 Pascha. 2005-2007 teacher Slavistik University Kiev ⊕19.10.2007 B, 2014 A Ivano-Frankivsk +Kolomyja. 24.12.2014 A Shepetivka+Slavutam, UOC. 29.1.2016 A Uman.

Simeon Vladimir Šostatskij *Vinnitsa*
T: M Vinnitsa+Bar, UOC ▪ ✉ vul. Peršotravneva 162, UKRAINA-21020 Vinnitsa • [380] 432 557801 fax 557802 • vineu@ukr.net • www.orthodox.vinnica.ua • www.vinnytsa.church.ua

*3.11.1962 Raihivtsi Hmelnitskij. N14.9. 1970-1980 school, 1980-1982 Soviet Army, 1983-1987 Medicine Institute Vinnitsa. 1987-1991 Seminary Moskva. mon6.12. 1990. 1990-1994 Daniel Monastery Moskva. diak14.1.1991 ⊖28.4.1991. 1994-1996 Pečerska Lavra Kiev. 1994 Fac theol Kiev. archim23.11.1995 ⊕4.5.1996 B, 2002 A Volodymyr Volynskij+Kovel. 2007 A, 2011 M Vinnitsa+Mogilev-Podolsk, 2013 M Vinnitsa+ Bar, UOC.

Agapit Ivan Bevtsik *Mogilev*
T: A Mogilev-Podolsk+Šargorod, UOC ▪ ✉ Soborna, 2/1, UKRAINA-24000 Mogilev • [380] 433-464295, fax -764295• mogilev.eparh@gmail.com • www.mogilivpodilskiy.church.ua

*6.3.1965 Davidivtsi Černovits. N14.6. 1979-1983 Music School Černovits. 1983-1985 Soviet Army. 1985-1988 monasteries Vilnius, Kiev. diak1988 ⊖1990. 1990-1994 Seminary Kiev. 1994 namestnik St. Jona Holy Trinity Monastery Kiev. 1994-1998 Academy Kiev, dipl theol ⊕22.11.1998. 1998-2000 B Hust+Vinogradiv. 2000 B Mukačevo+Užgorod. 2007 B, 2010 A Severodonetsk+Starobilsk. 2013 A Mogilev-Podolsk+Šargorod, UOC.

Volodymyr Kostjantin Melnik *Volodymyr*
T: A Volodymyr Volynskij+Kovel, UOC ▪ ✉ vul. Soborna 27, UKRAINA-44700 Volodymyr Volynskij • [380] 3342 21864 • eparhia_w@ukr.net • starsenij@yandex.ru • www.vv-orthodox.org • www.volodimirvolynskiy.church.ua

*26.2.1972 Nevir Volynia, N 7.2. 1976-1984 school Nevir. 1984-1988 Technikum Pinsk. 1988-1990 Soviet Army. 1990-1994 Seminary Volynia. 1994-2003 stud, teacher Academy Warszawa. mon1995 Pečerska Lavra Kiev diak14.12.1996 Volodymyr V. ⊖3.6.2001 Volodymyr V. 19.5.2002 igumen. archim24.9.2003 ⊕4.6. 2007 B Šepitovsk+Slavutsk. 2009 Academy Kiev. 2011 B, 2014 A Volodymyr Volynskij+Kovel, UOC.

Luka Andrij Kovalenko *Zaporižžja*
T: A Zaporižžja+Melitopol, UOC ▪ ✉ vul. Kijaško 26, UKRAINA-69015 Zaporižžja • [380] 61 224839-3, fax -5 • eparh.zp@ukr.net •

www.hram.zp.ua • www.zaporizhzhia.church.ua
*11.7.1971 Khartsitska Donetsk. N11.6. 1989-1991 Soviet Army. 1992-1998 Donetsk medical University 3. diak1998. 1998-2002 Seminary Kiev (correspondence course). 1999-2005 rector Donetsk. mon25.12.2003 archim5.2004 ⊕13.11.2005 B, A Vasilkov, vicar Kiev. 2005-2010 igumen Glinskaja pustinj. 2008-2010 A Konotop. 2010 A Zaporižžja, UOC. 2011 teacher bioethics. 30.6.2015 Doctor med. Zaporižžja State University.

Nikodim Viktor Gorenko ***Žitomir***
T: A Žitomir+Novograd Volynskij, UOC ▪ ✉ Podilska 19, UKRAINA-10003 Žitomir • [380] 412 470375 • kane@mail.ru •
www.zhytomyr-eparchy.org • www.zhytomyr-sob.church.ua
*26.2.1972 Zalessia Chernobyl. N3rd Sunday after Pascha. 1986 Kryvyj Rih. 1987-1991 Music school Kryvyj Rih. 1991-1993 military service. 1995 Pečerska Lavra Kiev. diak14.12.1996 Volodymyr Volynskij. 1998-2000 Seminary Kiev ⊖3.6.2001 Volodymyr V. mon2.3.2002 19.5.2002 igumen. archim24.9.2003. 2006 sekretar eparchy Volodymyr Volynskij ⊕4.6.2007 B Šepitovsk. 10.6.2007 B Volodymyr Volynskij+Kovel. 2009 Academy Kiev. 2011 B, 2012 A Žitomir+Novograd, UOC.

Belarussian Orthodox Church

Pavel Georgij Ponomarjov ***Minsk***
T: M Minsk+Zaslavsk, Metr. Minsk, Exarch Bjelorussia, Archimandrit Žirovitsi, Belarussian Orthodox Church ▪ ✉ Osvoboždenija 10, BELARUS-220004 Minsk • [375] 17 2064481, 2034601, 2037348 fax 2094299, 2032570 • orthobel@gin.by • minsk.eparchy@gmail.com • www.church.by
*19.2.1952 Karaganda, N12.7. 1971-1973 Soviet Army. absolvent Proftechnikum. 1973-1976 Seminary Moskva. 1976-1980 Academy Moskva. mon1.10.1977 diak1.3.1978 ⊖8.5.1978. 1979-1981 Referent Department External Church Relations Moskva. 1980 Kandidat Moskva. 1980-1981 Postgraduate course Academy Moskva, Aspirant. 1981-1988 Jerusalem. 1982 Deputy Head, 1983 igumen (Patr Diodoros). 1986 Head Russian Orthodox Mission Jerusalem. archim28.8.1986 (Patr Diodoros). 1988-1992 namestnik Monastyr Pskov ⊕22.3.1992-1999 (Moskva) B Zaraisk. Administrator of Patriarchal Parishes of the Russian Orthodox Church in the USA, 1992-1993 also in Canada. 2000-2011 B, 2003 A Wien. 9.5.2007 Bari. 25.2.2007 Orden Serafim Sarov (II), 2011 M Rjazan. 2012 Orden St. Innokentij (II). 2013 M Minsk+Slutsk.

Filaret Kirill Vahromejev
T: Honorary Exarch Belarus, Belarussian Orthodox Church ▪
✉ Osvoboždenija 10, BELARUS-220004 Minsk • [375] 296501368 •

orthobel@gin.by • www.church.by

*21.3.1935 Moskva. N14.12. Music school. 1953-1961 Seminary Academy Moskva, hypodiakon Patr. Alexij. mon3.4.1959 diak26.4.1959. 1961 Kandidat ⊖14.12.1961. 1961 teacher, 1963 inspektor Theol Akademy. 4.8.1963 igumen. archim8.10.1963 ⊕24.10.1965 B Tihvin, vicar Leningrad. 1966 B, 1971 A Dmitrov vicar Moskva, rector Theol Academy Moskva. 1973 A, 1975 M Berlin. 1978-2013 M Minsk, Archimandrit Žirovitsi. 1979 visit Paris Institut Cath recteur Paul Poupard. 1981-1989 chairman Department External Church Relations Moskva. 1984 Halle. 1986 Fac Jan Hus Prag, Prešov, Bratislava, 1992 Exarch Belorussia. 1993-2011 chairman Synodal Commission Theology. Dr. theol h.c.: 1995 Minsk, 2000 Professor, 2001 Grodno, 2002 St. Vladimir, 2002 Veteran University (with Prof Paško, Dovgallo), 2003 Institut St-Serge Paris, 2003 Honorary citizen Minsk, 2003 Orden Frantsisk Skorina. 2005 Orden Serafim Sarov, Družba Narodov (Belarus). 2006 Geroj Belarusi. 2013 Honorary Exarch Belarus. Belarussian Orthodox Church.

Antonij Denis Doronin ***Slutsk***

T: B Slutsk+Soligorsk, Metr. Minsk, Belarussian Orthodox Church ■ ✉ ul. Maxima Bogdanovicha 9, BELARUS-223610 Slutsk • [375] 17 95-22615, 95-57196 • info@sluck-eparchiya.by • http://sluck-eparchiya.by

*18.12.1980 Baku Azerbaidzhan. 1986 the family moved to Belarus. 1987-1998 school Dubovljansk. 1998-2005 Seminary Academy Minsk. 2005-2006 Orth Theol Institute Chambésy Geneva. 2006-2008 Kandidat Minsk "Belorusskie trebniki 17th-18th c." 2007-2010 hypodiakon to M Filaret. mon14.8.2009 diak28.8.2009 ⊖6.4.2010. 14.12.2010 igumen. 2010-2011 Aspirantura Moskva. 2011 teacher history Minsk. archim7.1.2012. 2012 teacher Liturgics Minsk Theol Academy. 24.11.2012 qualification "Pedagog-Psycholog" at Pedagogical University Minsk ⊕3.1.2015 Cremlin, Moskva B Slutsk+Soligorsk, Metr. Minsk, Belarussian Orthodox Church (Patr. Kirill).

Pavel Oleg Timofejenkov ***Maladechna***

T: B Maladechna+Stoubzy, Metr. Minsk, Belarussian Orthodox Church ■ ✉ Osvoboždenija 10, BELARUS-220004 Minsk • [375] 17 2064481 • www.molod-eparchy.by

*31.3.1963 Mogilov Belarus, N12.7. 1970-1978 school Mogilov. 1978-1981 Fac Architecture University Mogilov. 1982-1984 Soviet Army. 1988-1991 culture school Mogilov. 1994-1998 Seminary Minsk. 1996-2000 vice inspector Seminary Academy, teacher regentskij klass. mon4.7.1997 diak12.7.1997. 1998-2001 Kandidat Academy Minsk ⊖20.6.1999. 2005-2008 rector (correspondence course). 7.6.2006 igumen. 4.2.2008 inspector Seminary Academy, archim27.9.2012 ⊕2.12.2014 B Maladsechna +Stoubzy, Metr. Minsk, Belarussian Orthodox Church.

Veniamin Vitalij Tupjeko ***Borisov***

T: B Borisov+Marinogorsk, Metr. Minsk, Belarussian Orthodox Church ▪ ✉ ul. Lopatina 34, BELARUS-222514 Borisov • [375] 17 794-29-60 • postmaster@borisoveparhia.by • http://borisoveparhia.by

*16.9.1968 Lunints Brest. N13.8. 1987-1989 military service. 1992 dipl Fac Radio-Physik Minsk. 1992-1999 Seminary Academy Minsk, Kandidat "Protoierej Ioann Vostorgov". mon16.12.1994 Žirovitsi diak9.1.1995 (M Filaret) ⊖13.2.1995. 1996-1997 teacher Moral Seminary. 14.12.1999 igumen. 2005 blagočinnij Žirovitsi. archim20.5.2006. 2009 namestnik monastery Blagoveščensk Minsk. 2009 Orden Kirill Turov (I). ⊕21.3.2010 Moskva, B Borisov vicar Minsk (Patr Kirill) 2014 B Borisov+Marinogorsk, Metr. Minsk, Belarussian Orthodox Church.

Ioan Leo Choma ***Brest***

T: B Brest+Kobrin, Belarussian Orthodox Church ▪ ✉ Sovietskih Pograničnikov 35, BELARUS-224000 Brest • [375] 162 234450, 251459, 251359, 250045, 255625, fax 201359 • orthodox-brest@yandex.ru • www.brest.hram.by

*25.3.1963 Kolbaeviči Lviv. N17.12. 1982-1984 Soviet Army. 1986-1989 Seminary, 1989-1993 Akad Moskva. 1990 upravlenje eparchy Minsk. mon15.12.1992 (Damaskinos). 1992 teacher Liturgics Seminary. diak3.1.1993 ⊖20.6.1993. 1994 sekretar eparchy Minsk. 1995 Kandidat Moskva "Svatoj pravednyj Ioan Kronštadtskij i jego duhovnoe nasledie". 1995 igumen Pascha. 2001 teacher history Academy ⊕31.3.2002 B Borisov, vicar Minsk. 2002 B Brest, Belarussian Orthodox Church.

Porfirij Oleg Prednjuk ***Lida***

T: B Lida+Smorhon, Belarussian Orthodox Church ▪ BELARUS-231300 Lida • [375] 1545 50848

*25.3.1970 Kobrine, Brest region, Belarus. 1987-1994 Polytechnikum Brest "ingenieur mechanik". 1988-1990 military service. 1994-1998 ponomar reader Buhovichi, Kobrin. 1998-2002 Seminary Minsk Žirovitsi. 2002 brotherhood Dormition Monastery Žirovitsi. mon21.4.2005 diak4.5.2005 ⊖3.12.2006. 2007-2010 Stud Minsk Theol Academy. Kandidat Pastoral Theology. 2013 teacher Seminary Academy Minsk. 2014 zamestitel' namestnika Žirovitsi. archim28.12.2014 ⊕5.4.2015 B Lida+Smorhon, Belarussian Orthodox Church.

Stepan Anatolij Neščeret ***Gomel***

T: B Gomel+Žlobin, Belarussian Orthodox Church ▪ ✉ ul. Baumana 16, BELARUS-246050 Gomel • [375] 232 7409-94, -93, fax -78 • eparhia.gomel@mail.ru • www.eparhiya.by

*3.1.1966 Vertievka Nežin Černigov. N9.1. 1983-1985 Soviet Army. 1985-1988 Seminary Moskva. mon4.1.1987 (Diakon Stefan) diak14.1.1987 ⊖3.6.1987. 1987-1988 rector Sv. Nikolaj Rabotin Černigov. 1988-1990 Pečerska Lavra Kiev. 1990 rector Sv. Nikolaj Svaryčevka Černigov. 1990-2005 rector Karma monastery Gomel. 13.1.1994 igumen. archim14.10.1997. 1998 blagočinnyj dean. 2002 absolvent Academy Kiev ⊕30.1.2005 (Gomel). 2005-2012 B Turov Mozyr. 2007 Orden Sergij Radonež (II). 2012 B Gomel, chairman Commission Canonization, Belarussian Orthodox Church.

Gurij Nikolaj Apalko ***Novogrudok***
T: A Novogrudok+Slonim, namestnik, Belarussian Orthodox Church ▪
✉ Monastyr Uspenija, ul. Sobornaja 57, BELARUS-231822 Žirovitsi •
[375] 156 296391, 296590, fax 296460 • novogru.eparhia@mail.ru •
www.eparhia.by

*30.5.1956 Lnozavod Kollektivnaja Polotsk Vitebsk. N3.11. 1971-1975 Technikum Vitebsk. 1975-1979 frequenting churches, workman Polotsk. 1979-1982 Seminary Moskva. 1982-1986 Academy Moskva. mon20.7.1985 Troice-Sergieva Lavra diak1985 ⊖19.12.1985. 1986 Kandidat Moskva, absolvent ikonopisnaja. 1986 igumen Monastyr Uspenija Žirovitsi, teacher Bible History. 1989-1990 Inspektor Seminary Uspenija Žirovitsi. archim 4.3.1990 namestnik Monastyr Uspenija ⊕4.8.1996. 1996 B, 2007 A Novogrudok+Lida. 2014 A Novogrudok+Slonim, Belarussian Orthodox Church.

Pjotr Viktor Karpusiuk
T: B Djatlov, vicar Novogrudok, Belarussian Orthodox Church ▪
✉ Monastyr Uspenija, ul. Sobornaja 57, BELARUS-231822 Žirovitsi •
[375] 156 296391, 296590, fax 296460, Lida [375] 1545 50848 •
novogru.eparhia@mail.ru • www.eparhia.by

*5.1.1959 Brest. N12.7. 1977-1979 Soviet Army near Zagorsk. mon12.3.1982 diak22.3.1982. 1982-1986 Academy Moskva, hypodiakon Patriarch Pimen. 1986-1989 Referent Patriarchate ⊖15.8.1989. 1990-1991 ekonom Troice-Sergieva Lavra Zagorsk. 1991-1992 Kommendant Patriarchate (mirovarenie), Spiritual Director Stavropigial Convent Elevation Holy Cross Domodedovo ⊕24.7.1992 (Minsk). 1992-2004 B Turov. 2004-2005 B Bobrujsk+Byhov. 2005-2013 B Druts, vicar Vitebsk. 2013 B Smorgon, 2014 B Djatlov, vicar Novogrudok, Belarussian Orthodox Church.

Sofronij Stepan Juščuk ***Mogilëv***
T: B Mogilëv+Mstislavl, Belarussian Orthodox Church ▪
✉ ul. Pervomaiskaja 75, BELARUS-212030 Mogilëv •
[375] 222 221795, 220190, fax 220298 • meu@fromru.com

*11.4.1951 Kotelnja-Bojarska Brest. N30.7. 1958-1968 school. 1969-1971 Soviet Army. 1979-1982 Seminary Leningrad. 1982-1986 Academy Leningrad. mon9.4. 1987 diak21.4.1987⊖20.5.1987. 1990 igumen Žirovitsi. archim1994 namestnik Ljady Minsk ⊕4.2.2001 B Brest+K. 2002 B Mogilëv+Mstislavl, Belarussian Orthodox Church.

Serafim Aleksij Belonožko ***Bobrujsk***

T: B Bobrujsk+Byhov, Belarussian Orthodox Church ▪ ✉ Karbyševa 28, BELARUS-213800 Bobrujsk • [375] 225 580783, 473238, 550035, fax 585099 • bobruisk.hram@gmail.com e.s.@hram.by • www.bobruisk.hram.by

*5.9.1973 Sverdlovsk (Ekaterinburg). N30.7. father soldier, school Sverdlovsk and Bobrujsk. 1990-1994 Seminary Žirovitsi. 1994-1999 scholarship Patr Kon/pel Moni Vlatadon. 1.5.-31.7.1997 Ostkirchliches Institut Regensburg, Germany. 22.-29.6. 1997 2. European Ecumenical Assembly Graz. 30.9.1997 OKI meeting Thessaloniki. Regina Ott Hochzeitsessen Tübingen. 1999-2000 stud Exegese Ev. Landeskirche Baden-Württemberg. 2000 Prof Fac theol Minsk, Academy Žirovitsi. 4.2001 Roma. mon2003 diak2003 ⊖27.11.2003. 2005 Seminary Zwochau, Germany ⊕3.4.2007 B Bobrujsk+Byhov, Belarussian Orthodox Church.

Stefan Igor Korzun ***Pinsk***

T: A Pinsk+Luninets, Belarussian Orthodox Church ▪ ✉ ul. Pervomajskaja 15, BELARUS-226710 Pinsk • [375] 165 356686, 351700, fax 351842 • pinskeparh@yandex.ru

*25.3.1944 Korzuny Červen Minsk. N9.1. 1958-1962 Technikum Marnoj. 1962-1963 sovhos Rassvet. 1963-1966 Soviet Army. 1966-1968 director sovhos Tsvetoč. 1968-1972 Lektor agronom Institut Smilovič. 1972-1975 Seminary, 1975-1978 Academy Moskva, mon9.1.1978 Žirovitsi diak18.2.1978 ⊖6.11.1978. 1979 Kandidat Moskva. archim1981. 1987-1990 namestnik Dormition monastery. 1989-1990 rector Seminary Žirovitsi ⊕4.3.1990 B, 2000 A Pinsk, Belarussian Orthodox Church.

Dimitrij Nikolaj Drozdov ***Vitebsk***

T: A Vitebsk+Orša, Belarussian Orthodox Church ▪ ✉ ul. Čehova 19, BELARUS-210015 Vitebsk • [375] 212 373509, 373205, 374831, fax 362015 • vitebsk_eparhia@mail.ru • www.vitebsk.orthodoxy.ru

*22.1.1953 Bobrujsk. N4.10. 1972 dipl Forestry. 1974-1978 Seminary Moskva. mon1978 diak1978. 1982 Kandidat Moskva ⊖1984 igumen. 1986 confessor Troice-Sergieva Lavra ⊕23.7.1989 B Polotsk+Vitebsk. 1992 new eparchy Vitebsk+Orša. Belarussian Orthodox Church. 1999 A Vitebsk+Orša, Belarussian Orthodox Church.

Leonid Feodosij Fil ***Turov***
T: B Turov+Mozyr, Belarussian Orthodox Church ▪ ✉ Komsomolskaja 16, BELARUS-247760 Mozyr • [375] 236 324670, [375] 2351 21490, 23163, fax 24554 • turov.eparhia@mail.ru • www.turov-eparhia.hram.by
*2.9.1960 Njesterovtsi Dunavetsk Khmelnitskij. N30.7. 1978-1980 Soviet Army. 1981-1989 Seminary Academy Moskva. mon8.3.1987 diak20.3.1987 ⊖12.7.1987 archim1996. 1996 rector Seminary Minsk, 1997 Kandidat, 1997 rector Academy Minsk. 1999 Orden Daniel Mosk. 2000 teacher NT Minsk. 2000 Orden Sergij Radonež ⊕10.2.2008 B Rečitsa, vicar Gomel. 2012 B Turov+Mozyr, Belarussian Orthodox Church.

Feodosij Pavel Bilčenko ***Polotsk***
T: A Polotsk+Glubokoje, Belarussian Orthodox Church ▪ ✉ Evfrosinij Polotskoj 80, BELARUS-211413 Polotsk • [375] 214 418375, 481278 • polotsk_eparh@telegraf.by
*24.12.1943 Batumi. N16.5. 1960-1964 Electromechanical Institute Charkov. 1965-1970 Ingenieur Universität Kiev. 1969-1978 Seminary Academy Moskva. mon4.4.1977 diak19.5.1977 ⊖6.11.1977. 1983-1997 Prof. Academy Moskva. archim1993 ⊕10.8.1997 B, 2006 A Polotsk+Glubokoje, Belarussian Orthodox Church (M Filaret).

Artemij Aleksandr Kiščenko ***Grodno***
T: A Grodno+Volkovyssk, Belarussian Orthodox Church ▪ ✉ Ožeško 23, BELARUS-230023 Grodno • [375] 152 720193, p 444360 [375] 296773378 • eparh_gr@mail.ru • artemibishop@mail.ru • www.orthos.org
*25.4.1952 Minsk. N2.11. 1969-1972 Institute Mechanization Minsk. 1972-1976 Soviet Army. 1976-1979 Seminary Leningrad. 1979-1982 Academy Leningrad. diak21.2. 1982 (celibat) Aleksandr Nevskij Minsk ⊖24.3.1984. 1984-1996 rector Aleksandr Nevskij Minsk. 1993 protoierej. 1994 Prof Katechesis Minsk. mon3.1.1996 archim8.1.1996 ⊕4.2.1996 B, 2012 A Grodno+Volkovyssk, Belarussian Orthodox Church. Orden St. Innokentij, Sergij Radonež (II), Efrosoniie Polotsk, Daniel Moskva.

Bishops outside former USSR

Elisej Ilya Ganaba ***Surož***
T: A Surož ▪ ✉ 67 Ennismore Gardens, GREAT BRITAIN-London, SW7 1NH • [44] 20 7352 7108, 7603 5200, 7584 0096 Answerphone, fax 7584 9864, [44] 1223 335062 • office@sourozh.org • sourozh@mail.ru • surozh@mail.ru • www.sourozh.org

*1.8.1962 Leningrad. N27.6. 1971-1979 Penza, hypodiakon Cathedral. 1980-1986 Seminary Akademy Leningrad. 1982 akolit. mon1985 diak1985 ⊖1986. 1987 Danilov Monastery Moskva. 1988-1990 deputy head Mission Jerusalem. 1990-2000 chairman Interorthodox relations Department External Church Relations Moskva. archim1997. 1998 Theol Commission Synod. 1999-2000 rector Cathedral Tallinn. 2000-2002 representative Antiochia. 2002-2006 Head Mission Jerusalem ⊕7.10.2006 B Bogorodsk admin Surož. 2007 B, 2010 A Surož.

Anatolij Evgenij Kuznetsov
T: A Kerč ▪ ✉ 14 A Bloom Park Road, Fulham, GREAT BRITAIN-London, SW6 7BG • [44] 20 73867837

*28.5.1930 Irkutsk. N6.5. 1949-1951 Seminary Moskva. 1951-1954 Soviet Army. diak31.10.1954. 1954-1960 Academy Moskva ⊖1.7.1956 mon11.10.1960. 1960 Kandidat. 1960-1968 Lektor AT NT Seminary Moskva. 1963 igumen. archim1968. 1968-1972 teacher NT Academy Moskva ⊕3.9.1972 B Vilnius. 1974-1979 B Zvenigorod representant Antiochia. 1979-1990 B Ufa. 1993 A Kerč, vicar to A Anthony (Bloom, Sourož/London). 1994 Regensburg Germany Symposion "Sergij of Radonež". 27.12.2001 former, 17.7.2002 A Kerč. 2005 Orden M Innokentij.

Simon Vladimir Išunin ***Bruxelles***
T: A Bruxelles+Belgium, Admin. Netherlands ▪ ✉ 29, rue de Chevaliers, BELGIUM-1050 Bruxelles • [32] 2 513 3374 +fax • info@archiepiskopia.be • www.archiepiskopia.be

*7.12.1951 Leningrad. N29.1. mon17.1.1975 diak19.1.1975 ⊖13.6.1976. 1975-1978 personal secretary to M Nikodim. 1978-1981 vice-inspector Leningrad, 1979 absolvent Leningrad. 1981-1982 Finland. 1981 Kandidat Leningrad. archim1982 ⊕11.4.1987. 1988 Bruxelles. 1991 Admin. Netherlands. 1994 A Bruxelles, 2003 Orden St. Sergij Radonež (II).

Nestor Jevgenij Sirotenko ***Korsun***
T: B Korsun ▪ ✉ Metochie des Trois Docteurs, 26 rue Péclet, FRANCE-75015 Paris • [33] 1 4828 9990, fax 4828 7454 [33] 671 745922 • korsoun@orange.fr • korsoun@noos.fr • www.cerkov-ru.eu

*4.9.1974 Moskva. N? 1991-1995 stud informatics. 1995-1999 Seminary. mon28.3.1998 diak24.4.1998. 1999-2004 Academy Moskva. 1999-2004 Institut St-Serge Paris, recteur d'Asnières (Konst) ⊖29.11.1999. 2008 igumen. 2008 blagočinnyj dean Paris, prof Séminaire Epinay-sous-Sénart. archim28.8.2010 ⊕5.9.2010 Moskva B Kafa, vicar Korsun. 24.12.2010 B Korsun.

Theophan Oleg Galinskij ***Berlin***

T: A Berlin+Deutschland ▪ ✉ Wildensteiner Str.10, GERMANY-10318 Berlin • [49] 30 50379488, p 50379489, fax 5098153 • red.stimme@arcor.de • www.rokmp.de

*8.7.1954 Bjelaja Cerkov Kiev. Chemical Institute Dnjepropetrovsk. 6.12.1970 baptized. N24.10. 1972 Seminary Leningrad. mon4.1.1976 diak7.1.1976. 1977 Kandidat Leningrad "Geschichte ... der Altgläubigen" ⊖17.4.1977 Vyborg (B Kyrill). 1977-1979 Ostkirchliches Institut Regensburg OKI Germany. 1979 teacher Liturgik, 1985 Inspektor Academy Leningrad. archim14.2.1986. 1986-1988 Vice-President Department External Church Affairs Moskva ⊕11.1.1987 Minsk B Kašira. 1988-1991 Predstavitjel Russkoj Pravosl Crkve Karlovy Váry. 1991 Administrator Berlin. 1991 B Berlin+Leipzig. 23.12.1992 B, 1996 A Berlin+Deutschland. 1992-1997 Central Committee CEC. member Synodal group relations Church State. 1998 member Synodal Commission Theology. 1998 member "Faith and Order" Geneva. 2002 Orden St. Sergij Radonež (II), 2004 Orden St. Innokentij (II). 2007 Orden St. Serafim Sarov (II). 2011 Orden Daniel Moskva.

Tihon Aleksandr Zaitsev ***Wien***

T: B Wien ▪ ✉ Jauresgasse 2, AUSTRIA-1030 Wien • [43] 1 7138250

*13.4.1967 Moskva. N7.4. 1985-1987 Soviet Army. 1987-1995 Seminary Academy Kandidat Moskva. mon25.3.1993 diak7.4.1993 ⊖6.1.1996 Sergiev Posad Academy. 2004-2009 Russian Mission Jerusalem. 2009-2014 chairman finances commission ⊕26.4.2009 B Podolsk, vicar Moskva. 2011 Member Supreme Council Russian Orthodox Church, vicariat North-East. 2015 B Wien.

Leonid Leonid Gorbačev ***Argentina***

T: B Argentina+South America ▪ ✉ Bulnes 1743, ARGENTINA-1425 Buenos Aires • [54] 1 48236534 • secrdiocese@mail.ru • agipablo-an@mail.ru • www.rusmissionsouthamerica.com

*26.10.1968 Stavropol. N? 1970 Krasnodar. 1985-1986 laborant aerodynamika. 1986-1988 military service. 1988-1989 hypodiakon to A Isidor. 1989-1992 Seminary Sankt-Peterburg. diak8.4.1990 Krasnodar ⊖18.6.1990. 1990-1997 Ekaterinodar. 1997-2002 Moskva Synodal commission contacts military services. 2002 Department External Church Relations Moskva. 2003-2004 Jerusalem. 2004-2013 representative Alexandria with missions Ethiopia, Kenya, Tanzania, South Africa, Botswana, Greece ⊕17.6.2013 Danilov Monastery Moskva, B Argentina+South America (Patr Kirill).

Russian Orthodox Church outside Russia (ROCOR)

Hilarion Igor Kapral

T: M East America+New York, President Arhierejskij Synod, A Sydney, Australia, New Zealand, ROCOR ▪ ✉ 75 East 93rd Street, USA-New York, NY10128 • [1] 732 961 191-7, fax -6 7333773, [1] 212 534-1601, fax -1798, [1] 212 7226577 • synod@superlink.com • diocese@rocor.org.au • met.hilarion@gmail.com • www.rocor.org.au

*6.1.1948 Spirit River Canada, ukrainian. N3.11. 1967-1972 Seminary Jordanville. mon2.12.1974 diak 4.12.1975 ⊖1976. 1976 MA Slavistics Syracuse University ⊕10.12.1984 B Manhattan, 1984-1996 Vicar to the Primate, Deputy Secretary Holy Synod. 1995 B Washington. 1996 A Sydney, Australia, New Zealand. 2008 M East America+New York, President Archierejskij Synod, A Sydney, Australia, New Zealand, ROCOR.

Ionah James Paffhausen

T: M ROCOR ▪ ✉ Route 25 A, Oyster Bay Cove, P.O.Box 675, USA-Syosset, NY 11791-0675

*20.10.1959 Chicago, Episcopal Church, N15.6. 1978 Orthodox Church of America OCA, San Diego. 1985 MD, 1988 MTh St. Vladimir's Seminary. mon1989 Valaam Monastery Russia diak5.11.1994 OCA ⊖6.11.1994. 1995-2008 igumen Redding. archim 2008 OCA ⊕1.11.2008 B Fort-Worth OCA, diocesan chancellor. 2008-2012 A Washington, M All America and Canada OCA. 2015 from OCA to ROCOR.

George Paul Schaefer

T: B Canberra, vicar ROCOR ▪ AUSTRALIA-2600 Canberra • bpgeorges@gmail.com

*25.5.1950 Belleville Illinois N23.4./6.5. Catholic High school. 1968-1972 Southern Illinois University. 1974 received into Greek Orth Church Modesto CA. 1975-1980 ROCOR Holy Trinity Seminary Jordanville New York. 7.1.1976 novice (A Averky Taushev) working in the farm and cemetery. mon 1980 (Mitrophan of Voronež), subdeacon on Palm Sunday. 1981-1986 sent by A Laurus to Mount Athos, great schema (Nektarios Koutloumousiou) "George the Great Martyr". 1986-1998 Jordanville Printshop, Orthodox Life. diak8.11.1986 ⊖12.4.1987. 1998 abbot, 2007 Dean. archim6.5.2005. 2006 translated Optina Elders "Living without Hypokrisy" ⊕7.12.2008 B Mayfield, vicar East USA, ROCOR (B Gabriel of Montreal, B Peter of Cleveland, B John of Caracas). 17.4.2015 vicar Australia ROCOR Life-Giving Font Canberra, M Ilarion, B Irinej (Serb).

Jeronim John Robert Shaw

T: former B Manhattan, ROCOR ▪ ✉ 75 East 93rd St, USA-New York, NY10128-1390 • [1] 212 534-1601, fax -1798 • rshawl@wi.rr.com

*26.12.1946 New England USA anglican, 1963 orthodox. N28.6. stud University Pittsburgh Russian Linguistics, History East Europa. 1968 Seminary Jordanville. diak11.4.1976 ⊖25.4.1976. 1976-1991 Chicago. 1991-2008 Milwaukee. mon5.12. 2008 ⊕2008 vicar of the East, ROCOR, Deputy Secretary Synod. 2013 retired.

Nikolaj Nikolaj Olhovskij

T: B Manhattan ▪ ✉ 75 East 93rd Street, USA-New York, NY10128-1390 • [1] 212 534-1601, fax -1798 • NOlhovsky@aol.com • www.eadiocese.org

*17.12.1974 in Trenton, NJ, USA. 1991 graduated from St. Aleksandr Nevskij Russian Parish School in Lakewood, NJ. 1993 graduated from Hamilton West High School. 1998 graduated from Holy Trinity Seminary in Jordanville, NY, where he received a BTh Degree. 1999-2008 he served as cell attendant to Archbishop Laurus. 2000 graduated from the State University of New York Technology School, receiving a Bachelor's Degree in Information & Communications. diak12.6.2006. 2007 he participated in the celebration of the signing of the Act of Canonical Communion in Moscow, accompanying Metropolitan Laurus ⊖1.8.2012 mon4.4.2014 archim27.4.2014 ⊕29.6.2014 B Manhattan.

Alipy Nikolai Gamanovih

T: A Chicago+Mid-America, ROCOR ▪ ✉ POBox 1367, 1800 Lee St., USA-Des Plaines, IL 60018 • [1] 847 8246531, fax 7599836 • dcma.rocor@gmail.com • www.russian.chicagodiocese.org

*19.12.1926 Majačok Cherson. N17./30.8. 1941Germany. mon1948 USA diak1950 ⊖1954. stud Jordanville, 1966 igumen ⊕12.7.1974 B Cleveland, Vicar Chicago. 1989 B, 1990 A Chicago+Detroit, 2002 accident.

Peter Pavel Lukianoff

T: B Cleveland, admin. Chicago, ROCOR ▪ ✉ POBox 1367, USA-Des Plaines, IL 60017 • [1] 847 298538-3, fax -0 • bppeter@orthodoxws.com

*9.8.1948 San Francisco. N? 1971 Holy Trinity Seminary Jordanville. 1972 MA Norwich University Vermont. 1986 dipl theol Beograd. mon1988 diak1988 ⊖1989. 2002 administrator Chicago ⊕12.7.2003 B Cleveland.

Mark Michael Arndt

T: A Berlin+Deutschland, Great Britan, ROCOR ▪ ✉ Hofbauernstr. 26, GERMANY-81247 München • [49] 89 2031 9085, fax 886777, [49] 176 18348959 • hiobmon@googlemail.com • www.russian-church.de

*29.1.1941 Chemnitz Sachsen (prot.), N? 1962 Oberleutnant Bundeswehr, 1964 orth. N18.3. 1969 Dr. phil Heidelberg. mon1975 diak1975 ⊖1975. 1980 dipl theol Beograd ⊕30.11.1980 B München+Süddeutschland. 1982 B, 1990 A Berlin, Admin Great Britain. 1990 A First Deputy of the President of the Synod of Bishops. Supervisor of the Russian Ecclesiastical Mission in Jerusalem.

Agapit Alexander Goraček

T: B Stuttgart, Vicar Deutschland, ROCOR ▪ ✉ Hofbauernstr. 26, GERMANY-81247 München • [49] 89 2031 9085, fax 886777 • agapit@rocor.de • www.rocor.de

*25.9.1955 Frankfurt am Main Czech family. N3.3. stud Architecture Frankfurt. 1979 München. mon29.3.1983 diak25.12.1983 ⊖8.4.1991 ⊕1.5.2001 B Stuttgart.

Kyrill Boris Dimitriev

T: A San Francisco, West America, Secretary Holy Synod, ROCOR ▪ ✉ 109 6th Ave, USA-San Francisco, CA-94118 • [1] 415 3878757, fax 3875955, 2761935 • archbishopkyrill@pacbell.net • www.wadiocese.com

*24.11.1954 San Francisco. N27.2. mon1981 Jerusalem diak1981 ⊖1981 San Francisco ⊕7.6.1992 San Francisco B Seattle, vicar. 2004 A San Francisco, Delegation Moskva.

Feodosij Evgenij Ivaščenko

T: B Seattle, vicar San Francisco, ROCOR ▪ ✉ 598 15th Ave, USA-San Francisco, CA-94118 • [1] 415 4124047 • www.wadiocese.com/wad.php

*8.6.1964 Kiev, baptized Moskva. N? Technikum Kiev. 1989 Pečerska Lavra Kiev. 1989-1992 Seminary Kiev. 1992-1996 Russian Mission Jerusalem ⊕7.9.2008 San Francisco B Seattle, vicar San Francisco.

Gabriel George Chemodakov

T: A Montreal+Canada, ROCOR ▪ ✉ 8011 Champagneuer Ave, CANADA-Montréal, Quebec H3N2K4 • [1] 514 279-8350, fax -5404 • bp_gabriel@yahoo.com • synod@superlink.com • www.mcdiocese.com

*2.6.1961 Sydney. NNew Russian Martyrs. 1984 absolvent Seminary Jordanville. 1984-1989 teacher Jordanville. 1989-1996 hypodiakon Manhattan. mon1996 diak1996 5th Sunday lent ⊖1996 Palm Sunday ⊕7.7.1996 B Brisbane, assistant to A Sydney, Australia, New Zealand. 1997-2008 B Manhattan, secretary Holy Synod. 2011 A Montreal Canada, Orden Sergij Radonež.

Michail Simeon Donskov

T: A Genf, West Europa, ROCOR ▪ ✉ 18, rue de Beaumont, SUISSE-1206 Genève • [41] 22 3464709 +fax, [41] 78 8984411 • episkop.mikhail@gmail.com • www.diocesedegeneve.net

*29.3.1943 Paris family Don-Kosak. N29.11. Russian school Paris. 1959-1966 scout camp leader France, Austria. 1960 psalomščik, regent. 1965-1966 military service. 1969-1978 hospital reanimation. 1979 čtets. diak1981 ⊖1991 Paris. 1995 silver medal 25 years service in hospitals. mon1996 ⊕12.7.1996 B Toronto. 2001 B Boston. 2008 Orden Sergij Radonež. 2011 A Geneva and Western Europe.

Ioann Peteris Berzinš

T: B Caracas+South America, ROCOR ▪ ✉ Nuñez 3541, ARGENTINA-1430 Buenos Aires • [54] 11 4541 7691 • episkop.ioann@gmail.com • www.iglesiarusa.org

*16.3.1957 Cooma Australia (Lettonian background). N7.7. BA, BTh Australian National University. 1982-1985 Holy Trinity Seminary Jordanville. mon1985 diak12.4.1987 ⊖4.11.1987. 1992-1996 confessor Gethsemani Jerusalem. 2000 Mikhalovskaya Sloboda. 2001-2005 confessor Gethsemani Jerusalem. 2005 igumen, Chicago ROCOR (M Laurus) ⊕21.6.2008 Erie B Caracas (M Hilarion). 2012 Orden Serafim Sarov.

Retired Hierarchs:

Jeftihi Ivan Kuročkin

T: B Domodedovo, ROCOR ▪ ✉ ul. Rokossovskaja 41, ROSSIJA-627400 Išim • [7] 034551 23767, fax 92161 • sobor@ishim.ru

*6.3.1955 Išim Sibiria. N6.9. 1978-1982 Seminary Moskva. 1982-1984 Academy Moskva. diak25.7.1982 ⊖24.10.1982 Omsk mon1983. 1987 igumen. 1989 ROCOR blagočinnyj dean Južn. Sibiria. archim1994 ⊕24.7.1994 New York. 1994-2007 B Išim+Sibiria. 2007 B Domodedovo, vicar Patr Moskva. 2010 Orden Sergij Radonež. 2012 retired Išim.

Gavriil Jurij Stebljučenko

T: former A Ust-Kamenogorsk+Semipalatinsk ▪ ✉ Ušakova 6, ROSSIJA-675000 Blagoveščensk • [7] 4162 424496, 549440, fax 214854

*30.6.1940 Cherson. N25.7. 1958 Seminary Odessa, 1966 Kandidat Leningrad. mon15.6.1966 (M Nikodim) diak19.6.1966 Vyborg. 1967-1968 Jerusalem ⊖1968 rector Cathedral Vyborg, 1972 Pskov. archim7.4.1975 igumen Pskov ⊕23.7.1988 B Khabarovsk+Vladivostok. 1991 B Konevskij Sankt-Peterburg. 1994 B, 2003 A Blagoveščensk+Tynda. 2011 A Ust-Kamenogorsk+Semipalatinsk. 2011 retired.

Feodosij Igor Protsjuk

T: former M Omsk+Tara ▪

*7.1.1927 Topulno Volynia. N22.9. diak24.3.1945 ⊖1.4.1945. 1956 Kandidat Academy Leningrad. mon29.11.1962 ⊕2.12.1962 B Černigov. 1964 B Poltava. 1967

B Černovtsy. 1972 B, 1978 A Smolensk. 1984 A Berlin Exarch Central Europe, 1986 A. 1997-2011 M Omsk+Tjumen (=1990 Omsk+Tara), 25.2.2007 Orden Serafim Sarov (II).

Iov Dmitrij Tyvoniuk
T: former M Čeljabinsk+Zlatoust ▪
*6.11.1938 Počajev. N10.9. mon1968 diak1968. 1969 Kandidat Moskva ⊖1969 archim26.12.1974 ⊕3.1.1975 B Zaraisk Administr Canada. 1976-1989 Department External Affairs. 1982 A Zaraisk. 1988 A Kostroma. 1989-1994 A Žitomir+Ovruč. 1993 name eparchy: Žitomir+Novograd Volynia. 1994-1996 A Odincovo vicar Moskva. 1996-2000 A, 2000-2011 M Čeljabinsk+Zlatoust. 2005 Orden Serafim Sarov. 2011 retired.

Filaret Anatolij Karagodin
T: former A Penza+Kuznetsk ▪
*21.8.1946 Odessa. N14.12. 1962-1965 Elektriker, 1965-1968 Soviet Army, 1968-1971 Seminary Odessa. 1971-1975 Kandidat Academy Moskva. 1974 Regentskij Klass. mon4.4.1975 Troice-Sergieva Lavra. diak29.6.1975 ⊖30.5.1977. 1977 Sv. Uspenskij Monastyr Odessa, Prof Seminary, Dirigent Chor. archim1987 ⊕12.3.1990. 1990-1992 B Astrahan+Jenotajevka. 1992-1995 B Dmitrov, vicar Moskva, rector Theol Academy and Seminary. 1995-2001 A Majkop+Armavir. 2001-2010 A Penza.

Vasilij Boris Zlatolinskij
T: former A Zaporižžja+Melitopol, UOC ▪ ✉ vul. Kijaško 26, UKRAINA-69015 Zaporižžja • [380] 612 522039, 594659 • eparh.zp@ukr.net • www.hram.zp.ua • www.zaorizhzhia.church.ua
*12.11.1932 Taškent. N13.3. 1943-1954 school, Politechnikum, Institute for Seismography Taškent. 1954-1957 Academy Moskva. diak1956 (A Taškent Hermogen) ⊖1957. 1957-1960 rector Talas Kyrgyzstan. 1960-1961 rector Taškent. 1961-1970 rector Ašhabad. 1970-1972 rector Gulistan Uzbekistan. 1972-1975 rector Šahty Rostov. 1975-1979 rector Feodosia Krym. mon1979 (A Leonti Poltava). 1981-1984 rector Kirovo Donetsk. 1984-1985 rector Petrikovka Dnjepropetrovsk. 1985-1990 blagočinnyj dean Krim ⊕2.12.1990 B Simferopol+Krim. 1992-2009 A Zaporižžja+Melitopol, UOC.

Ieronim Igor Černišov
T: former B Orël+Livny, former Dean St. Gregory Moskva ▪
*12.7.1966 Anatolević, Voronež. N7.5. 1985-1987 Soviet Army nuclear missiles Kolomna. 1987-1989 stud history Voronež. 1989-1994 Nikolo-Ugreškij Monastery, Danilov Monastery. mon1990 diak1990 ⊖1990. 1994-2008 nastojatjel Moskva, chaplain Kreml Guard Regiment. 1996 igumen. archim2003. 2006 St. Daniel Order ⊕2.6.2008. 2008-2009 B Orël+Livny.

Melhisedek Vasilij Lebedev
T: former A Brjansk+Sevsk ▪ ✉ ul. Arsenalnaja 6, ROSSIJA-24100 Brjansk, Klimenovsk • [7] 495 5465922
*26.1.1927 Novo-Čerkasovo Moskva. NSunday before Christmas, Sv. Praotets 1950-1961 Molodi obl. Moskva ⊖21.7.1950 mon1963 ⊕17.6.1965 B Vologda, B Wien. 1967 B, 1970 A Penza. 1978-1984 A Berlin Exarch Mitteleuropa. 26.5.1980 Consecration Byzantine Chapel Ostkirchliches Institut Regensburg Germany. 1984-1994 A Sverdlovsk (Jekaterinburg). 1994-2002 A Brjansk+Sevsk.

Arkadij Aleksandr Afonin
T: former B Južnosachalinsk+Kurily ▪
*15.7.1943 Čekalino Kujbyšev. N8.2. 1968-1970 Seminary Moskva ⊕21.4.1991. 1991-1992 B Magadan. 1992-1997 B Južnosachalinsk+Kurily. 1992-1993 Administrator Magadan. 1997-1998 B Tomsk. 1998-1999 B Vetluga, vicar Nižnij Novgorod+ Arzamas. 2000-2001 B Južnosachalinsk+Kurily.

Ilian Gennadij Vostrjakov
T: former B Serpuhov ▪
*16.10.1945 Čeljábinsk. N8./22.3. 1969-1971 Seminary, 1971-1975 Academy Moskva. mon24.2.1974 diak27.2.1974 ⊖19.12.1974. 1975 Kandidat Moskva. 1975-1978 stud theol Roma. 1978-1979 Department of External Church Relations ⊕25.11.1979 B Solnečnogorsk, vicar Moskva. 1982-1990 B Kaluga. 1990-1991 B Tobolsk. 1991-1995 B Serpuhov, vicar Moskva. Zastupitel Ruské pravoslavné církve v českých zemích a slovensku Karlovy Vary. 1995 retired.

Nikandr Aleksej Kovalenko
T: former B Zvenigorod ▪
*22.9.1954 Ulan Bator. N7.10. 1971-1981 stud Physics Lomonossov University Moskva. 1981 Seminary Moskva, 1985 Akad Moskva. mon25.2.1985 diak17.3.1985 ⊖7.4.1986. 1988 Kandidat Moskva. archim5.8.1988 ⊕7.8.1988 B Zvenigorod Representant to Patr Antiochia in Damascus. 1996 retired.

Innokentij Vasilij Šestopalj
T: former B Konotop UOC ▪ ✉ Svjatogovskaja-Uspenskaja Lavra, Zarechnaja1, UKRAINA-Svjatogorsk • [380] 6262 53024 • www.svlavra.church.ua
*8.1.1945 Gorlov Donetsk. N6.10. 1972 absolvent Seminary Moskva. 1975-1977 Referent Otdela vnešnih cerkovnyh snošenij Moskva Department External Church relations, Aspirant Academy. 1976 absolvent Academy Moskva. 1977-1991 Lektor sekretar, 1992-1994 prorector Seminary Odessa ⊕5.10.1994. Tuljčin+Bratslav. 1999-2008 B Konotop.

Ippolit Aleksej Khiljko
T: former B Hust+Vinogradiv UOC ▪
*10.5.1955 Kramatorsk Donetsk. N12.2. 1984-1987 Lavra Sergiev Posad. 1988-1989 Russkaja Duhovnaja Missia Jerusalem. namestnik Danilov Monastyr Moskva ⊕16.8.1992 B Belocerkov vicar Kiev. 1992 B namestnik Pečerska Lavra Kiev. 1992-1996 B Donetsk+Slavjansk. 1994 new name eparchy Donetsk+Mariupol. 1996-1999 retired. 1999-2006 B Tuljčin+Bratslav. 2006-2007 B Hust, retired.

Diomid Sergej Ivanović Dzjuban
T: former B Anadyr+Čukotka ▪ diomid3@yandex.ru
*24.6.1961 Kadievka (Stakhanov) Lugansk. N29.8. 1978-1983 Charkov radio-electronic Institute. 1986-1988 Seminary Moskva. mon3.7.1987 diak18.7.1987. 1989-1993 Academy Moskva ⊖1.9.1991 to Magadan. 1992-2000 parish Jelizovo Kamčatka ⊕10.8.2000 B Anadyr+Čukotka. 2008 monk izverhen iz sana.

Chryzostomus Georgij Martyškin
T: former M Vilnius, Lietuvos Respublikos Arkivyskupu ▪ ✉ Aušros Vartu 8-I, LITHUANIA-01303 Vilnius • [370] 52613641
*3.5.1934 Kazinka Rjasan. N26.11. 1951-1992 Restaurator. diak12.9.1964 mon31.10. 1966 ⊖4.11.1966 ⊕23.4.1972 B Zaraisk vicar Moskva. 1974 B, 1977 A Kursk. 1984-1990 A Irkutsk. 1990 A, 2000-2010 M Vilnius. 2004 Orden Sv. Andrej Rubljov.

Panteleimon Pavlo Romanovskij
T: former B Kirovograd+Novomirgorod ▪
*21.5.1952 Kirovograd Ukraina. N9.8. 1980 Kandidat Moskva ⊖1981 ⊕21.7.1991 (ukrain) Mykolaiv+Cherson, 1992 (ukrain) B Vinnytsa+Kirovohrad ⊕25.7.1992 (Moskva) B Kicman vicar Černovtsy+Bukovina. 1993 (Moskva) B Gluchov+ Konotop. 1993 Čerkasy. 1994-1995 B Volnja, vicar Zaporižžja. 1995-1998 B Brusilov, vicar Ovruč. 1998 B Svetlovodsk, vicar Kirovograd. 1998-2011 B Kirovograd+ Alexandrija (2007 +Novomirgorod).

Gurij Sergej Kuzmenko
T: former A Žitomir+Novograd Volynskij ▪
*11.8.1964 Debalcevo Donetsk. N17.10. 1979 absolvent school Debalcevo. 1983 absolvent Railway Technical school. 1984-1987 Seminary Odessa. 1987-1991 Academy Moskva. 1990 Poslužnik St. Daniel monastery Moskva. mon2.7.1990 diak15.7.1990 (B Vladimir Podolsk) ⊖28.7.1990 (B Vladimir Taškent). 1991-1992 Mission Jerusalem. 1992 Pečerska Lavra Kiev. 1992 eparchy Donetsk. 1.1.1993 igumen. archim1.4.1993 sekretar eparchy Donetsk. 1994 Pečerska Lavra Kiev ⊕31.7.1994-2011 B, A Žitomir+Novograd Volynia. 1994-2010 Chairman Youth Mouvement. 2010-2011 Chairman Theol-Jur commission Holy Synod.

Ioannikij Ivan Kobzev
T: former M Lugansk+Alčevsk UOC ▪ ✉ per. Krupskoj 29-b, UKRAINA-51900 Lugansk • [380] 642-93722, -932116 fax -525085 • lg.eparh@mail.ru • www.eparhia.lg.ua • www.lugansk.church.ua
*7.2.1938 Novoselovko Bjelgorod. 1955-1958 railway ingenieur Prohorovka. Seminary. 1958-1960 Kiev, 1960-1962 Odessa. 1962-1966 Academy Moskva. mon16.11.1964 diak24.11.1964. Kandidat Moskva. 1966-1971 Patriarchate. 1971 teacher Odessa. 1971 igumen. 1975-1986 ekonom Seminary Odessa. archim1983. 1986-1988 Dekan Ismail, teacher Seminary ⊕13.12.1988 B Slavjansk, vicar Odessa. 1.2.1990 B Donetsk+Lugansk (=Vorošilovgrad). 1991 A Donetsk+Slavjansk. 2002-2012 M Lugansk+Starobjelsk (2007 +Ančevsk) UOC. 20.7.2012 former Lugansk+Alčevsk UOC.

Valentin Timofei Miščuk
T: former M Orenburg+Saraktaš, Metr. Orenburg ▪ ✉ pereulok Ševčenko 4, ROSSIJA-460000 Orenburg • [7] 3532 779718, [7] 922 547 1476 • kanc_eparh@mail.ru • www.oepress.ru
*14.10.1940 Brest. N7.5. mon30.3.1969 diak20.4.1969 ⊖18.7.1969. 1970 Kandidat Moskva ⊕25.7.1976 B Ufa, 1979 Representative at the Patriarchate of Antiochia, vicar Moskva. 19.4.1985 B Tambov. 1987 A Vladimir. 1990 A Korsun. 1992 A Grodno+Volkovsk. 1994 A Baku, Rector Seminary Stavropol. 1995 Moskva. 1999 A Orenburg 2004 M Metr. Orenburg. 2015 retired.

Orthodox Church of Poland

His Beatitude **Sawa**
Metropolitan of Warszawa and all Poland
Prawosławny Metropolita Warszawski i całej Polski

Sawa Michal Hrycuniak ***Warszawa***
T: M Warszawa and all Poland ▪ ✉ Al. Solidarności 52, POLAND-03402Warszawa • [48] 22 6190886, Seminarium Duchowne 6178348 • orthodox@orthodox.pl • www.orthodox.pl
*15.4.1938 Śniatycze. N12.1. 1957 absolvent Seminary. 1957-1961 MTh Warszawa. 1961 Lektor Seminary, 1962 also Academy Warszawa. diak27.9.1964. 1965-1966 Dr. theol Beograd. mon6.2.1966 Beograd (St. Sawa of Serbia) ⊖6.3.1966 archim1970 rector Monastery Jabłeczna, 1974 rector Seminary Jabłeczna ⊕25.11.1979 B Łódź, 2.12.1979 B, 1987 A Łódź+Poznań., 12.11.1990 Prof Theol 1993-1998 Ordinariat Militar, 1996 General. 1998-1999 Administrator Białystok+ Gdańsk. 5.5.1998 M. Dr.h.c.: 2000 St. Vladimir's Seminary New York. 2001 Uni Białystok. 2002 Uni Thessaloniki, Theol Academy Minsk. 2008 Kiew.

Jerzy Jerzy Pańkowski
T: B Siemiatycze, vicar Warszawa-Bielsk, Ordinary Polish Armed Forces ▪ ✉ ul. Banacha 2, POLAND-0090 Warszawa • [48] 22 6826 77-3, fax -4 • j.wiluk@wp.mil.pl • www.ordynariat.republika.pl
*4.8.1974 Białystok. N? 1993 absolvent Seminary Warszawa. mon17.12.1993. 1994-1999 stud Fac theol Athens. diak1.1.1995 (A Bialystok Sawa) ⊖15.10.1998 (Patr Bartholomeos). 1999 igumen Jabłeczna Monastery. 1999 MTh Academy Warszawa. archim3.4.2000. 2003 Dr. theol Warszawa. 2003 teacher Seminary Academy Warszawa. 2006-2012 Dekan Fac Practical Theol Academy ⊕28.1.2007. 2010 Ordinary Polish Armed Forces. 2012 Professor. 22.-28.1.2016 Synaxis of the primates of the Local Orthodox Churches Chambésy Switzerland.

Jakub Jakub Kostiuczuk ***Białystok***
T: A Białystok+Gdańsk ▪ ✉ ul. Św. Mikołaja 3, POLAND-15420 Białystok • [48] 85 7424088 +fax • bpjakub@orthodox.bialystok.pl • kancelaria@orthodox.bialystok.pl • www.orthodox.bialystok.pl
*22.10.1966 Narew. N? 1987 absolvent Seminary Moskva, Jabłeczna, 1987-1992 stud theol Moskwa. diak19.8.1987 (A Sawa) ⊖10.8.1989 (A Sawa) mon17.12.1993 Supraśl (A Sawa). 1994-1999 abbot Supraśl. 1994 igumen, assistant Academy Warszawa ⊕11.5.1998 B Supraśl. 1999 B, 2008 A Białystok+Gdańsk. 2011 Dr. theol.

Grzegorz Jerzy Charkiewicz
T: B Supraśl, vicar Białystok+Gdańsk ▪ ✉ ul. Klasztorna 1, POLAND-16030 Supraśl • [48] 85 7183780 +fax
*4.12.1964 Białystok. N? 1985 absolvent Seminary Jabłeczna, 1985-1992 stud theol Leningrad Sankt-Peterburg. diak28.8.1989 (A Sawa) mon7.4.1992 Supraśl (A Sawa) ⊖7.4.1992 (A Sawa). 1994 igumen, assistant Prof Academy Warszawa Ikonography ⊕12.5.1998 B Bielsk Podlaski, vicar Warszawa-Bielsk. 2008 vicar Białystok+Gdańsk.

Szymon Szymon Romańczuk ***Łódź***
T: A Łódź+Poznań ▪ ✉ skr. poczt.37, Narutowicza 46, POLAND-90135 Łódź • [48] 42 6334169, sekretarz 6308732
*12.8.1936 Guszczewina. N? 1955-1960 stud phil Minsk, 1965-1969 stud theol Warszawa, mon11.2.1970 diak15.2.1970 ⊖22.2.1970. 1970-1973 Inspektor Gymn Warszawa ⊕26.11.1979 B Lublin, Ass Metr. 1980-1983 Chairman External Church Relations. 1981 B, 1993 A Łódź+Poznań.

Adam Aleksander Dubec ***Przemyśl***
T: A Przemyśl+Nowy Sacz ▪ ✉ Zamkowa 16, POLAND-38500 Sanok • [48] 13 4630681, office dziekan 4641004 • www.eparchia.prv.pl • www.eparchia.prv.pl
*14.8.1926 Florynka Łemko. N? 1960 absolvent Seminary Warszawa, 1964 absolvent Akad ⊖1965. 1966 dekan Rzeszow. mon6.1.1983 archim19.1.1983 ⊕30.1.1983 B Lublin, Ass. Metr., 29.9.1983 B, 1996 A Przemyśl+Nowy Sacz.

Paisjusz Piotr Martyniuk
T: B Gorlice, vicar Przemyśl ▪ ✉ ul. Jana Brzechwy 2, POLAND-38300 Gorlice • [48] 18 3526989 • [48] 504 109548 • paisjusz@interia.pl
*7.7.1969 Szczecinek N? mon6.4.1989 diak7.4.1989 ⊖22.4.1989. 1989-1990 referent Lublin. 1990-1991 vicar Łosinka. 1992 absolvent Seminary Jabłeczna. 1992-1996 dziekan, 1996-1999 namestnik Jabłeczna. 1998 igumen. 1998 MTh Prešov. 2001 Dr. theol Prešov. 2001 prorector, Lektor Pastoral Spiritual Theol Orth Seminary Warszawa. archim2003 rector parish Warszawa ⊕13.4.2007 B Piotrków Trybunalski, vicar Łódź. 2009 B Gorlice, vicar Przemyśl.

Jeremiasz Jan Anchimiuk ***Wrocław***
T: A Wrocław+Szczecin ▪ ✉ ul. Św. Mikołaja 40, POLAND-50128 Wrocław • [48] 71 3441312, fax 3417558, p 6196995, hram 3446916, office 3427080, [48] 601 415572 • kancelaria.wroclaw@poczta.fm
*3.10.1943 Odrynki Białystok. N? 1957-1961 gymnasium Warszawa, 1961-1965 Seminary Warszawa. 1965-1966 stud theol Moskva, 1966-1968 stud theol Zürich. 1968 instructor Theol Seminary Warszawa. 1975 Central Committee WCC Geneva.

22.2.1977 Dr. theol Warszawa "Origenes and modern Exegesis". 1979 Lektor NT. 1980 Habil "Elemente von Anthropologie und Angeologie 1 Kor 6,3", Prof. diak2.2.1983 ⊖9.2.1983 ⊕13.3.1983 B, Bielsk, Ass Metr, 20.8.1983 B, 1997 A Wrocław+Szczecin.1983 Chairman External Church Relations. 1996-2002 Rector Theol Academy Warszawa. 1999 Commission Orthodox Collaboration WCC Geneva. 2001 President Ecum Council Poland. 2008-2012 Rector Theol Academy Warszawa.

Abel Andrzej Popławski ***Lublin***

T: A Lublin+Chełm ▪ ✉ ul. Ruska 20, POLAND-20126 Lublin • [48] 81 7473175, sekretarz 7477438 • lublin@cerkiew.pl • diecezjalubelska@wp.pl • www.lublin.cerkiew.pl

*8.4.1958 Narew. N? 1972-1978 gymnasium Warszawa, diak15.2.1979 ⊖30.11.1980 mon27.2.1981 archim7.1.1989. 27.2.1989 MTh ⊕25.3.1989. 2001 A Lublin.

PATRIARCHATE OF ROMANIA

His Beatitude **Daniel**
Patriarch of Romania

Metropolia Muntenia+Dobrogea

Daniel Dan Ilie Ciobotea ***Bucureşti***

T: Patriarh, M Muntenia+Dobrogea, A Bucureşti ▪ ✉ Aleea Dealul Mitropoliei 2, ROMANIA-040163 Bucureşti • [40] 21 40671-60, -61, fax -62 • cancelaria@dnt.ro • patriarhia.diaconia@dnt.ro • patriarhia@dnt.ro • www.patriarhia.ro • www.bor.ro • www.crestinism-ortodox.ro

*22.7.1951 Dobreşti Lugoj, N? 1970-1974 Inst Theol Sibiu. 1974-1976 Inst Theol Bucureşti (Prof. Dumitru Stăniloae). 1976-1978 Faculté de Théologie protestante Strasbourg, bourse du Gouvernement français. 1977-1980 Ostkirchliches Institut Regensburg, stud Freiburg i.Br. (Prof. Karl Lehmann). 1979 Dr theol Strasbourg "Réflexion et vie chrétienne aujourd'hui", 1980 Dr. theol Bucureşti. 1980-1988 Inst Oecoum Bossey. mon6.8.1987 Sihăstria diak14.8.1987 ⊖15.8.1987 ⊕4.3.1990 B Lugoj Vicar Timişoara. 1990 M Iaşi, Prof. Dogmatic Fac theol. 1992 Moskva, 1997 Presidium CEC Athens, 1998 Manila. 1998 Abt Emmanuel Heufelder Preis Abtei Niederaltaich Germany with B Gherghel, Prof. Suttner. 2000 Interorth Seminary Cooperation Churches İstanbul. 2003 Hon. citizen Botoşani. 2003 Dr. theol h.c.: 2003 Sacred Heart Fairfield Connecticut, George Enescu University, Lucian Blaga University. 2008 Andrei Şaguna University, Alba Iulia, Arad. 2009 Institut St-Serge Paris. 2010 Reşiţa, Oradea, Iaşi. 2011 Babeş Bolyai University Cluj 21 faculties. 12.9.2007 patriarch. 22.-28.1.2016 Synaxis of the primates of the Local Orthodox Churches Chambésy Switzerland.

Varlaam Merticariu

T: B Ploieşti, vicar patriarhal, Metr. Muntenia+Dobrogea ▪ ✉ str. Aleea Dealui Mitropoliei 25, ROMANIA-040162 Bucureşti • [40] 21 40671-61, fax -62

*28.10.1960 Ştiubeni jud. Botoşani. N? 1975-1977 liceu Săveni. 1977-1982 Seminary theol Neamţ. 1983-1987 Fac theol Bucureşti. 1991-1992 stud Bossey. 2003 Dr. theol. 2004 stud St. Steven's College England. 2008-2009 Louvain (Erasmus) ⊕20.12.2009 B Ploieşti vicar patriarhal.

Ieronim Creţu

T: B Sinaia, vicar patriarhal, Metr. Muntenia+Dobrogea ▪ ✉ str. Antim 29, ROMANIA-040162 Bucureşti • [40] 21 40671-69, fax -70

*21.11.1959 Brăeşti jud. Buzău. N? ⊖20.4.1988 Bistriţa Neamţ, bibliotecar patriarhal. 1992-1993 stud Bossey. 1994-2009 head mission Jerusalem. Crucea patriarcal: 1994 Romania, 1994 Ecum Patr, 1995 Patr Jerusalem, 1996 Patr Moskva. 20.12.2009 elected (Holy Synod) B Sinaia vicar patriarhal ⊕29.5. 2014 Cathedral Bucureşti B Sinaia vicar patriarhal (Patr Daniel).

Timotei Aioanei

T: B Prahova, vicar Bucureşti ▪ ✉ Întrarea Patriarhiei 21, ROMANIA-040162 Bucureşti • [40] 21 337-4957, -2776, -0908, fax -4356

*13.11.1966 Radaseni Falticeni. 1984-1993 Theol Seminary Manastirea Neamţ, Fac theol Iaşi. mon1.2.1989. 1995-1996 ellinika moderna Fac theol Athens. 2002 exarch cultural Bucureşti, eclesiarh Catedrala. archim24.3.2002 ⊖30.10.2002 ⊕30.10.2014 B Prahova, vicar Bucureşti.

Galaction Gheorghe Stângă ***Alexandria***

T: B Alexandria+Teleorman, Metr. Muntenia+Dobrogea ▪ ✉ C.P. 1-46, str. Carpaţi 15, ROMANIA-140059 Alexandria • [40] 247 322057, Office 326321, fax 326654, 316654

*17.5.1953 Constantin Brâncoveanu Ialomiţa. N? 1971-1976 Theol Seminary Bucureşti. mon6.11.1977 Crasna (Prahova). diak1977. 1977-1982 Lic Theol Institute Bucureşti ⊖2.11.1978. 1980 igumen onorific Crasna. 1983 protosinghel. 1985-1986 Bossey. 1990 exarch mânăstirilor arhiepiscopia Bucureşti. archim1994 ⊕1.9.1996 B Alexandria.

Ambrozie Valentin Meleacă ***Giurgiu***

T: B Giurgiu, Metr. Muntenia+Dobrogea ▪ ✉ str. Portului 13, ROMANIA-080015 Giurgiu • [40] 246 2140-79, -83, fax -81 • ep_ambrozie@yahoo.com • www.episcopiagiurgiului.ro

*20.4.1969 Scorţeni Prahova. N? school Urleta. 1983-1987 Liceul Câmpina. 1987-1989 military service. 1989-1990 picture school. mon19.4.1992 Crasna ⊖11.5.1992. 1992-1996 Lic Fac theol Bucureşti "Isihasmul românesc". 1996 Stareţ Darvari. 1998 protosinghel. 1998 stud Thessaloniki (Apostolos Glavinas) ⊕15.10.2000 B Sinaia. 2000-2006 vicar patriarhal. 2006 B Giurgiu.

Ciprian Cezar Spiridon ***Buzău***

T: A Buzău+Vrancea, Metr. Muntenia+Dobrogea ▪ ✉ Aleea Episcopiei 3, ROMANIA-120043 Buzău • [40] 238 710-714, fax 713608. 413608, 416714, cons. 411061, [40] 744 875310, [40] 744 470888 • contact@arhiepiscopiabzvn.ro • www.arhiepiscopiabzvn.ro

*19.4.1965 Ciocâlia de Jos. N? gimnaziul Ciocâlia de Jos, liceul Constanţa, 1988 Seminary Buzău. 1988-1992 Fac theol, Academy of Music Bucureşti. mon13.9.1992

Crasna. diak14.9.1992 (Nifon Ploieşti). 1992-1998 stud, 1997 Dr. theol Thessaloniki "Arhiereii greci care au păstorit Mitropoliile Ungro-Vlahiei şi Moldovei". 1998-1999 stud San Nicola Bari/Università Angelicum Roma. 1999 inspector Admin Patr. 2000 consilier patriarhal ⊖21.5.2000 Bucureşti (A Christodoulos Athen). 2000 protosinghel, archim7.4.2002 ⊕22.9.2002. 2002-2013 B Câmpina, vicar patriarhal. 2009 secretary Holy Synod.

Nifon Nicolae Mihăiţă ***Târgovişte***

T: M Târgovişte, Metr. Muntenia+Dobrogea ▪ ✉ str. Mihai Bravu 5, ROMANIA-130049 Târgovişte •

[40] 245 213713, fax 217606, [40] 744 56 11 11 • ipsnifon@yahoo.com

*5.1.1944 Creţeşti -Vidra, Giurgiu. N11.8. St. Niphon II Patriarch of Constantinople. 1968 Lic theol Bucureşti. 1969-1971 doctorat Old Testament and Hebrew Literature . 1971-1974 stud London, Oxford, Jerusalem. 1975-1977 teacher Seminary Bucureşti, 1977 India, 1977-1978 stud Geneva, Dr. theol Oradea. 1978-1980 director External Church Relations patriarcate. 1980 mon Cernică ⊖5.5.1980 Antim. archim1980. 1980-1982 Canada. 1982-1985 director External Church Relations patriarcate ⊕24.11.1985 B Ploieşti, vicar patriarhal. 1994 B, 1999 A. Slobozia+ Călăraşi. 1998 Dr. theol Bucureşti "Cartea profetului Mihea".1991-2002 Vice-president, President Aidrom, Central and Executive Committee WCC. 1999 Commission Orthodox Collaboration WCC Geneva. 2000 Dean Fac theol State University of Târgovişte. 2002-2007 President of the National Society Red Cross of Romania. 2008 M Târgovişte. 2008 Patriarchal Exarch for Relations with European Christian and Political Institutions. 16.12.2015 Athens Interorthodox committee preparation Panorthodox Synod. 22.-28.1.2016 Synaxis of the primates of the Local Orthodox Churches Chambésy Switzerland.

Vincenţiu Victor Grifoni ***Slobozia***

T: B Slobozia+Călăraşi, Metr. Muntenia+Dobrogea ▪ ✉ str. Episcopiei 2, ROMANIA-920023 Slobozia • [40] 243 231154, fax 231205, [40] 722 212085 • [40] 744 648245 patriarh@mail.itcnet.ro

*23.8.1954 Bucureşti. N? Lice "Matei Basarab" Bucureşti. 1974-1978 Theol Institute University Sibiu, Lic theol. 1978-1983 Editura Biblical Institute Bucureşti. mon1983 Mânăstirea Lainici, judeţ Gorj. diak1983 ⊖1983. 1983-1990 Redactor Editura Mitropolia Olteniei. 1990-1994 Superior Aşezăminte Româneşti Ierusalim şi Iordan ⊕12.1.1994 B Ploieşti Vicar Patriarhal. 2000-2009 secretary Holy Synod. 2009 B Slobozia.

Casian Constantin Crăciun ***Dunărea de Jos***
T: A Dunărea de Jos, Metr. Muntenia+Dobrogea ▪ ✉ str. Domnească 104, ROMANIA-800201 Galați • [40] 236 41-1580, -5065, 413837, 460197, fax 460014 • edj@rls.roknet.ro • www.edj.ro
*18.3.1955 Lopătari Buzău, N? Theol Seminary Buzău, Theol Institute București. mon20.12.1980 diak21.12.1980. 1980-1985 Prof Seminary Buzău. 1984 Dr. theol Strasbourg. 1985 Dr. theol București ⊖10.11.1985 Sibiu. 1985-1988 assistant Directeur Spir Sibiu. archim 1987. 1988-1989 assistant Theol Institute București, Patr Inspector of studies ⊕18.2.1990 B Galați, vicar, 1994 B, 2009 A Dunărea de Jos.

Teodosie Macedon Petrescu ***Tomis***
T: A Tomis, Decan Facultatea, Metr. Muntenia+Dobrogea ▪
✉ str. Constantin Brâncoveanu 1, ROMANIA-990732 Constanța •
[40] 241 614020, 614257 +fax • cabinet 614449, 611732 •
Fac theol 614576, 670900, fax 618372
*12.12.1955 Vatra Dornei 17th child. N? 1970-1975 Theol Seminary Monastery Neamț. 1976-1980 Theol Institute București. 1977 brother Sf. Mânăstirea Crasna, jud. Prahova. 1980 Examen of admission to doctorat, Lic theol stud bibl București. 1982-1986 cântăreț Antim. 1986-1994 assistant Fac theol București. mon6.12.1990 Crasna diak16.12.1990 ⊖3.3.1991 Sf. Ecaterina. 1.10.1992 -27.3.1993 stud English Birmingham ⊕22.3.1994 B Snagov vicar București. 2001 A Tomis.

Calinic Argatu ***Argeș***
T: A Argeș+Mușcel, Metr. Muntenia+Dobrogea ▪ ✉ Bulevardul Basarabilor 1, ROMANIA-115300 Curtea de Argeș • [40] 248 7224-00, -10, fax 210399. [40] 744 849371 • Facultatea 627000, fax 722401 • www.eparhiaargesului.ro
*6.6.1944 Crăcăoani Neamț N? 9 ⊖1964 celibatar. Lic theol Sibiu. mon1970 archim 1980 stareț Sinaia și Cernica ⊕17.11.1985 B Argeș, Vicar Râmnic. 1990 B, 2009 A Argeș.

Visarion Dumitru Bălțat ***Tulcea***
T: B Tulcea, Metr. Muntenia+Dobrogea ▪ ✉ str. Mircea Vodă 6 A, ROMANIA-820017 Tulcea • [40] 788053430, [40] 751509140
*19.10.1959 Tălmaciu, Sibiu. N? 1976-1981 Theol Seminary Cluj. 1982-1986 Theol Institute University Sibiu. 1986-1989 doctoral course ITUS. mon5.5.1989 Brâncoveanu Sâmbăta de Sus. diak15.8.1989. 1989-1996 secretary Mitropolie Sibiu. 1991-1997 assistant Prof ITUS class languages. 1994-1997 stud Fac phil Athens, 1995-1997 stud Fac theol Athens (Prof. Konstantin Skouteris). 1996-1997 Consilier Cultural Sibiu ⊖5.10.1997 ⊕12.10.1997. B Rășinari, vicar Sibiu. 2005 Dr. theol Sibiu

"Învăţătura mariologică a Sf. Nicolae Cabasila în spiritualitatea ortodoxă a sec. XIV". 15.-18.6.2007 OKI Regensburg. 2008 B Tulcea.

Metropolia Moldova+Bucovina

Teofan Savu ***Iaşi***

T: A Iaşi, M Moldova+Bucovina ▪ ✉ str. Ştefan cel Mare şi Sfânt 16, ROMANIA-700497 Iaşi • [40] 232 215584, p 214771, 21545-4 -6 -8, fax 212656, 215300 • mitropolia iasi@yahoo.com • iecum@mail.dntis.ro • www.mmb.ro

*19.9.1959 Corbi Argeş. N? Lic theol Bucureşti. mon1985 diak1985 ⊖1985. 1990 Dr. theol Paris ⊕15.9.1991 B Sinaia Vicar Patriarhal, External Relations. 1992 Central Committee CEC. 1994-2000 secretary Holy Synod. 2000-2008 M Craiova. 2008 M Iaşi.

Calinic Constantin Dumitriu

T: B Botoşani, Vicar Iaşi, Metr. Moldova+Bucovina ▪ ✉ Bd. Ştefan cel Mare 16, ROMANIA-700497 Iaşi • [40] 232 p 145987. cabinet 112483

*18.11.1957 Bucium Iaşi. N? 1970-1975 Lice Technologic Iaşi, mon4.3.1984 Putna, 1985-1989 Fac theol Sibiu. 1985-1990 Eclesiarh Ghid Putna. diak1.3.1985 ⊖15.8.1985. 1989 Lic theol Sibiu, Stareţ Râşca, protosinghel. archim22.1.1991 ⊕25.3.1991 B Botoşani Vicar Iaşi.

Pimen Zainea ***Suceava***

T: A Suceava+Rădăuţi, Metr. Moldova+Bucovina ▪ ✉ str. Vasile Bumbac 2, ROMANIA-720071 Suceava • [40] 230 215796, 221124, 521295, 5515551, fax 522020, [40] 744 142083 • candelasuceava@yahoo.com • www.arhiepiscopiasucevei.ro

*25.8.1929 Greabănu Buzău, N? mon10.3.1951 Neamţ, diak29.6.1951 ⊖29.6.1957. 1974-1978 Stareţ Suceava. Lic theol Bucureşti ⊕24.6.1982 B Suceava Vicar Iaşi. 1991 A Suceava in Suceava.

Ioachim Giosanu ***Roman***

T: A Roman+Bacau, Metr. Moldova+Bucovina ▪ ✉ str. Alexandru cel Bun 5, ROMANIA-611065 Roman • [40] 233 744254, fax 731683 • arhiep.romanuluibacaului@gmail.com • www.epr.ro

*29.3.1954 Stăniţa Neamţ, N? 1969 Monastery Sihăstria Neamţ. 1970-1975 Seminary Neamţ, serviciul militar, 1976-1980 stud theol Bucureşti. Lic "Sabatul la cultele neoprotestante şi poziţia ortodoxă". mon1980 Bistriţa Neamţ diak1985 Iaşi (M Teoctist), 1985-1990 arhidiacon catedrala Iaşi ⊖30.12.1990. 1991 protosinghel. 1991-1994 Institut St-Serge Paris, 1994 Dr. theol "La deification de l'homme d'apres

la pensée de Dumitru Stăniloae 1903-1993". 1994-2000 service pastoral Rosiers Paris. ⊕1.5.2000 Roman B Băcău, arhiereu-vicar Roman, 2009 Episcop vicar Roman. 4.1.2015 A Roman+Bacau.

Corneliu Onilă ***Huşi***

T: B Huşi, Metr. Moldova+Bucovina ▪ ✉ Mihail Kogălniceanu 19, ROMANIA-735100 Huşi • [40] 235 481132, fax 481822 • pscornel@servex.dntis.ro • www.episcopiahusilor.ro

*25.7.1966 Corni-Albeşti Vaslui. N? 1982-1987 Seminary Neamţ. 1988-1992 Fac theol Bucureşti. 1993-1996 stud (EKD) Exegese Marburg. 1996-1997 assistant Prof. Hans-Martin Barth Marburg. mon21.11.1997 Mân. Sf. Petru şi Pavel Huşi. diak21.11.1997 Huşi ⊖23.11.1997 Huşi. 1998-1999 teacher NT Greek language Seminary Huşi, protosinghel. archim1.6.1999, administrative vicar, Caritas, Ecumenical contacts ⊕21.11.1999 B Bârlad vicar Huşi. 2009 B Huşi.

Metropolia Ardeal

Laurenţiu Liviu Streza ***Sibiu***

T: A Sibiu, M Ardeal ▪ ✉ str. Mitropoliei 24, ROMANIA-550179 Sibiu • [40] 269 211584, 218154, 217863, fax 215905, p 215521 +fax, [40] 744 510266, fax 215905 • ipslaurentiu@yahoo.com • www.mitropolia-ardealului.ro

*12.10.1947 Sâmbăta de Sus. N? Lice "Radu Negru" Făgăraş. 1965-1969 Theol Institute Sibiu. diak18.12.1969 ⊖19.12.1969. 1969-1976 parish Lisa, Sibiu. 1970-1973 doctorat Theol Institute Bucureşti. 1976-1980 spiritual Sibiu. 1980-1985 assistant, 1982-1983 Bossey, Fac theol Fribourg. 1985-1996 prof Liturgics Theol Institute Sibiu. 1985 Dr. theol "Botezul în diferite rituri liturgice creştine". 1992 secretary ştiinţific Theol Institute Sibiu. 1992 Societas Liturgica. mon1996 Mânăstirea Sâmbăta ⊕15.8.1996 B Caransebeş, 2005 M Transilvania, 2006 M Ardeal. 4.2011 OKI Regensburg.

Ilarion Ioan Urs

T: B Fagaras, vicar Sibiu ▪ ✉ Mitropoliei 24, ROMANIA-550179 Sibiu • [40] 269 211584 • www.mitropolia-ardealului.ro

*4.3.1955 Recea Brasov. 1970-1973 car mechanics school. 1977-1981 Liceu Industrial Sibiu. 1983-2000 ekonom Sambata. mon12.8.1983 Sambata de Sus. diak7.11.1984 Sambata (Antonie Plamadeala). 1985-1989 Theol Institute Sibiu ⊖15.8.1987 archim15.8.1998. 2000 Abbot Sambata. 2002 Orden Merit President Iliescu. 2014 Orden Brancoveni (Patr Daniel), Exarch Monasteries ⊕7.6.2015 B Fagaras, vicar Sibiu.

Irineu Pop ***Alba Iulia***
T: A Alba Iulia, Metr. Ardeal ▪ ✉ str. Mihai Viteazul 16, ROMANIA-510010 Alba Iulia • [40] 258 811821, 811690, fax 812797 • Facultatea de Teologie Ortodoxă 811512, fax 812630 • www.reintregirea.ro
*2.7.1953 Băseşti Maramureş. N? stud USA ⊖1980. 1989-1990 Jerusalem. 1990 Dr. theol Bucureşti ⊕21.11.1990 B Bistriţa Vicar Cluj. 2011 B Alba Iulia.

Sofronie Radu-Ştefan Drincec ***Oradea***
T: B Oradea, Bihor, Metr. Ardeal ▪ ✉ str. Episcop Roman Ciorogariu 3, ROMANIA-410017 Oradea • [40] 259 13-7883, 43-7883, cabinet -3487, secr fax 132786 • www.eparhiaortodoxaoradea.ro
*3.11.1967 Arad. N11.3. 1986-1993 Fac medicine Timişoara, 1993-1997 Fac theol Pastoral Arad. 1994-1995 Orth. Monastery John Baptist Essex. mon11.8.1995 Hodoş Bodrog Arad. diak12.8.1995 (M Serafim Joantă) ⊖13.8.1995 (M Serafim Joantă). 1998 doctorat Athens, secretary to Patr Teoctist ⊕28.2.1999 B Gyula, 2003 Sant' Egidio Aachen. 2007 B Oradea.

Andrei Nicolae Moldovan ***Covasna***
T: B Covasna+Harghita, Metr. Ardeal ▪ ✉ Str. Patriarh Miron Cristea 5, ROMANIA-530112 Miercurea Ciuc • [40] 266 114453, 124453, p 171269, 124269
*22.11.1967 Chetani jud. Muresh. mon19.7.1990 Toplita (A Andrei Alba Iulia) diak20.7.1990 (A Antonie Plamadeala) ⊖21.7.1990 (A Andrei Alba Iulia). 1995 stareţ Monastery Fagetel. 1999 protosinghel. 2000 absolvent Fac theol Bucuresti. 2002-2005 stud theol Thessaloniki. archim29.8.2006 ⊕15.8.2008 B Fagaras vicar Sibiu. 2014 B Covasna+Harghita.

Gurie Georgiu ***Deva***
T: B Deva+Hunedoara, Metr. Ardeal ▪ ✉ str. Avram Iancu 2, ROMANIA-330087 Deva • [40] 254 211241 • www.episcopiadevei.ro
*31.12.1968 Huta Chineşti Cluj. N? mon1990 diak1990 ⊖1992. 1992-1996 Fac theol Craiova. 1997-2001 stud Missionary Pastoral Padova. archim2001 ⊕5.8.2001 B Strehaia, vicar Craiova. 2009 B Deva.

Metropolia Cluj Maramureş Sălaj

Andrei Ioan Andreicuţ ***Vad***
T: A Vad+Feleac+Cluj, M Cluj Maramureş Sălaj ▪ ✉ Piaţa Avram Iancu 18, ROMANIA-400117 Cluj-Napoca • [40] 264 43100-4, -6, fax 195184 • Fac theol Decan 431005, fax 111737 • Seminary 194396 • www.arhiepiscopia-ort-cluj.org • www.mitropolia-clujului.ro

*24.1.1949 Oarţa de Sus Maramureş. N? Railway engineer. 1976-1978 Theol Institute Sibiu, diak1978 ⊖27.8.1978. 1978-1985 parish Turda, 1985 Alba Iulia. 1985-1988 stud theol Bucureşti, mon1990 ⊕25.2.1990 B Mureş Vicar Alba Iulia. 1998-2011 A Alba Iulia. 1998 Dr. theol Bucureşti "Spovedanie şi comuniune" (Dumitru Popescu). 2000 Decan Conferenţiar Fac theol. 2011 M Cluj.

Vasile Fluieraş

T: B Someş, vicar Vad, Metr. Cluj Maramureş Sălaj ▪ ✉ str. Bisericii Ortodoxe 10, ROMANIA-400090 Cluj-Napoca • [40] 264 office 431004, 196566, [40] 722 408443

*1948 Mănăştur Cluj. N? Fac theol Sibiu ⊖1976 ⊕15.8.1998 B Someş, vicar Vad.

Iustinian Chira ***Maramureş***

T: A Maramureş+Satu Mare, Metr. Cluj Maramureş Sălaj ▪ ✉ str. Avram Iancu 5, ROMANIA-430134 Baia Mare • [40] 262 214614, 414674 fax, 414614 • Facultatea 413605, fax 426936

*28.5.1921 Plopiş Maramureş, N? mon2.3.1942 Lic theol Sibiu ⊖1.4.1943 ⊕9.9.1973 B Maramureş. 1973-1990 Vicar Vad. 1990 B, 2009 A Maramureş+Satu Mare.

Iustin Hodea

T: B Sighet, vicar Maramureş, Metr. Cluj Maramureş Sălaj ▪ ✉ Mânăstirea Rohia, ROMANIA-435612 Rohia • [40] 262 466241

*23.6.1961 Rozavlea Maramureş. N? 1978-1983 Theol Seminary Cluj-Napoca. diak1983 ⊖1984 mon1985. 1988-1992 Theol Institute Sibiu, Lic theol ⊕17.4.1994 B Sighet Vicar Maramureş.

Petroniu Petru Florea ***Sălaj***

T: B Sălaj, Metr. Cluj Maramureş Sălaj ▪ ✉ str. Avram Iancu 29A, ROMANIA-401430 Zalău • [40] 360 100321 • episcopiasalajului@yahoo.com • petroniuf@hotmail.com • www.episcopiasalajului.ro

*30.11.1965 Târgu-Mureş. N? 1983-1988 Theol Seminary Cluj. 1988-1989 militar Lugoj. 1989-1990 Sibiu. 1990-1993 Theol Institute Cluj Lic "Moise la interferenţa realităţii şi a reflecţiilor patristice". WCC Canberra. 1993-1994 stud Greek language, 1994-1998 stud theol Dr. theol Thessaloniki (Patristics), teacher Calcutta. 1998 "Opera exegetică a Sf. Maxim". 1999 preparator Fac theol Alba Iulia. diak10.4.1999 ⊖11.4.1999. 2000 ekonom stavrofor. mon27.6.2000 "Petroniu" protosinghel ⊕1.10.2000 B Sălaj, vicar Oradea. 2008 B Sălaj.

Metropolia Oltenia

Irineu Ioan Popa ***Craiova***

T: A Craiova, M Oltenia ▪ ✉ str. Mitropolitul Firmilian 3, ROMANIA-200381 Craiova • [40] 251 415054, fax 418369

*16.11.1957 Spinu Perişani Vâlcea. N? 1975-1980 frate Frăsinei. mon1983. 1985 absolvent Seminary Craiova. diak1986. 1986 Dr. theol Bucureşti "Politica religiosă a Împăratului Iustinian" (Dr. Stefan Alexe). 1986-1987 stud Grenoble ⊖1987. 1989-1990 stud English London. 1990-1991 Tantur Jerusalem. 1991 Dr. theol Institut St-Serge Paris "Théologie de St Basile le Grand" (Boris Bobrinskoj) ⊕6.10.1991. 1991-2008 B Slatina Vicar Râmnic. 1991-2008 Dr. iur. Prof Decan Craiova. 2003 secretary canonizarea Sfinţilor. 2005 Dr. iur civil Craiova. 2008 A Craiova.

Varsanufie Gogescu ***Ramnic***

T: A Ramnic, Metr. Oltenia ▪ ✉ Str. Episcopiei 1, ROMANIA-240175 Râmnic • [40] 250 73117-0, -2, fax 738820 • secretariat@episcopia-ramnicului.ro • patriarhia@dnt.ro • www.episcopia-ramnicului.ro

*21.1.1968 Bucureşti. 1990-1994 Fac theol Bucureşti. diak1998 mon protosinghel ⊖1998. 1999-2006 stareţ Radu Voda ⊕30.9.2001 B Prahova, vicar Bucureşti. 2013 Dr. theol. 2014 A Ramnic.

Emilian Nica

T: B Lovişte, vicar Râmnic, Metr. Oltenia ▪ ✉ Str. Episcopiei 1, ROMANIA-240175 Râmnic • [40] 250 73117-0, -2, fax 738820 • secretariat@episcopia-ramnicului.ro

*12.2.1972 Berezeni, jud. Vaslui. N? 1990-1995 Seminary Neamţ. 1996-2000 Fac theol Constanţa. 2000-2002 Master History of Old-Medieval Constanţa. 2001 English course Vilemov Cechia ⊖2002. 2003-2009 Dr. theol Iaşi "Metropolia Moldovei,1900-1948" (Emilian Popescu). 2005 English course Mirfield GB. 2009 exarch judeţul Iaşi ⊕14.11.2009 B Lovişte, vicar Râmnic.

Nicodim Nicolae Nicolăescu ***Severin***

T: B Severin şi Strehaia, Metr. Oltenia ▪ ✉ str. Gh. Bibescu 6, ROMANIA-220189 Drobeta Turnu Severin • [40] 252 3330-48, fax -39, [40] 788 258 896 • cancelaria@episcopiaseverinului.ro • www.episcopiaseverinului.ro

*6.4.1962 Godeanu jud. Mehedinţi. N? mon1983 Seminary Craiova. diak1983 ⊖1985. 1985-1994 parish Baloteşti. 1989-1993 Fac theol Bucureşti. 1990 protosinghel. 1990-1991 stareţ Topolniţa, 1991-2001 stareţ Vodiţa. 1997-2000 stud Athens. archim2000 cursuri doctorat ⊕19.8.2001 Gorj, vicar Craiova. 2004 B Severin.

Sebastian Sorin Petrică Paşcanu *Slatina*

T: B Slatina şi Romanaţilor, Metr. Oltenia ▪ ✉ str. Fraţii Buzeşti 15, ROMANIA-230150 Slatina • [40] 249 421 026, [40] 349 41686-1, -2, 3,-4 • episcopaslatinei@gmail.com • www.episcopaslatinei.ro

*5.11.1966 Moreni Dâmboviţa. N? Bruder von Nectaria Paşcanu. 1973-1981 school Minieri. 1981-1983 Ploieşti. 1983 Monastery Crasna Prahova. 1983-1988 Theol Seminary Neamţ. mon1988 Crasna diak1988 Crasna. 1988-1992 Fac theol Bucureşti. 1992-1997 Dr. theol Thessaloniki "Teologia liturgică românească în secolul X" ⊖1996. 1996-1999 stareţ Crasna. archim 2000 ⊕25.3.2001 B Ilfov vicar Bucureşti. 2008 B Slatina.

Metropolia Banat

Ioan Selejan ***Timişoara***

T: A Timişoara, M Banat ▪ ✉ B-dul. C.D. Loga 7, ROMANIA-300021Timişoara • [40] 256 490287, 493232, fax 491176 • mitropolia_banatului@yahoo.com • www.mitropolia_banatului.ro

*14.11.1951 Pietrani Bihor. 1976 ingenieur 1990 Lic theol Sibiu. diak6.8.1990 ⊖15.8.1990. 1991-1994 Biblical Institute Jerusalem ⊕20.7.1994 B Toplita. 25.9.1994 B, 2009 A Covasna+Harghita. 2014 A Timisoara, M Banat.

Paizie Ion Gheorghe

T: B Lugoj, vicar Timişoara, Metr. Banat ▪ ✉ B-dul. C.D. Loga 7, ROMANIA-300021Timişoara • [40] 256 295228, 490287, fax 491176 • paisieungurul@hotmail.com

*24.10.1971. N? 1986-1990 liceul Agroindustrial Timişoara. 1991-1997 Fac Veterinary Medicine Timişoara. 1992-1998 A.S.C.O.R. Timişoara. 1997-2001 Fac theol Timişoara. Lic "Aspecte ale creştinismului în primele trei secole". mon1999 Gyula. 1999-2006 protosinghel secretary eparchy of Ungaria. diak6.8.1999 Gyula ⊖7.8.1999 ⊕9.2.2006 B Lugoj vicar Timişoara.

Timotei Seviciu ***Arad***

T: A Arad, Ienepole+Hălmagiu, Metr. Banat ▪ ✉ str. Episcopiei 60, ROMANIA-310084 Arad • [40] 257 281-856, fax -904, cabinet -262, Fac 283088 285855, fax 280070

*4.6.1936 Timişoara, N? diak22.10.1961. 1967-1968 stud Bossey, Neuchâtel ⊖10.3.1968 mon1969 archim6.12.1970. 1971-1972 stud Fribourg Switzerland. 1972-1976 secretary Arad, Timişoara. 1973 Dr. theol Bucureşti ⊕8.2.1976 B Lugoj, assistant Banat. 1984 B, 2009 A Arad.

Lucian Micu ***Caransebeş***

T: B Caransebeş, Metr. Banat ▪ ✉ str. Episopiei 11, ROMANIA-325400 Caransebeş • [40] 255 516412, 229412, fax 516402, 229402, [40] 744 510266 • secretariat@episcopiacaransebesului.ro • episcop@cs.ro • www.episcopiacaransebesului.ro

*9.9.1965 Arad. N? 1977-1987 school Arad. 1988-1992 Seminary Caransebeş. mon1990 Hodoş Bodrog. diak1990 ⊖1.4.1990. 1990-1992 Hodoş Bodrog, Gai. 1992-1994 Cathedral Timişoara. 1994-2000 stareţ Monastery Izvorul Miron Româneşti. 1996 Lic Fac theol Arad "Limonariul lui Ioan Moshu". 1999 protosinghel. archim1.1.2000 exarch monasteries Timişoara ⊕1.10.2000 B Lugoj vicar Timişoara. 2006 B Caransebeş.

Metropolia Basarabia

Petru Păduraru ***Basarabia***

T: A Chişinău, M Basarabia ▪ ✉ str. 31 August nr. 161, MOLDOVA-2001 Chişinău • [373] 22 755722 +fax, 226043, 2247758, fax 244105 • www.mitropoliabasarabiei.ro

*14.10.1946 Selo Ţiganca Cantemirscin Zadon. N12.7. 1968-1972 Seminary Odessa. diak1971 ⊖23.2.1973. 1973-1986 rector Hust. 1987-1990 rector Cantemirscin Zadon ⊕1.9.1990 Bălţi B Belcy vicar Moldova (Moskva). 1992-1995 Locum tenens Metropolia Basarabia (rom). 1995 M Basarabia. 1999 official letter discharge Holy Synod Moskva.

Antonie Iosif Telembici

T: B Orhei, assistant Bessarabia ▪ ✉ str. 31 August nr. 161, MOLDOVA-2001 Chişinău • [373] 22 755722 • www.mitropoliabasarabiei.ro

*1963 Harbovat Anenii Noi Moldova. 1981-1987 Fac Medicine and Pharmaceutics University Chişinau. 1994 dipl theol University Iaşi ⊖1995. 1995-2014 secretary eparchy Chişinau ⊕24.5.2014 B Orhei, assistant Bessarabia.

Episcopia Dacia Felix

Daniil Stoenescu Nacu ***Vârşeţ***

T: B locţiitor al episcopiei Daciei Felix ▪ ✉ bulv. C.D. Loga 5, ROMANIA-300030 Timişoara • [40] 256 295228, fax 191176 • [40] 744 153122 • Zarko Zrenjanina 60, SERBIA-26300 Vršac • [381] 13 811071

*23.9.1957 Hăţăgejl Densuş Huneodara. N? 1972-1977 Seminary Caransebeş. 1977-1979 military service. 1982 absolvent Sibiu. 1982-1985 doctorat Bucureşti. mon25.3.1984 Hodoş-Bodrog. diak30.3.1984 ⊖1.4.1984 Hodoş-Bodrog. 1986-1996 duhovnic Prislop. 1993-1996 Dr. theol Thessaloniki "Învăţături dogmatice în

Apophtegmata Patron". 1996-2001 Densuş and Monastery Schimbarea la Faţa ⊕1.4.2001 B Partoşan, vicar Timişoara, administrator Vârşeţ. 8.4.2001 recognized "locţiitor" by Serbian Church.

Episcopia Ungaria

Siluan Mănuilă ***Gyula***

T: B Gyula, Magyarországi Román Ortodox Püspökség ▪ ✉ parcul Sf. Nicolae 2, Szent Miklós park, HUNGARY-5700 Gyula • [36] 66 361281, fax 463867 • www.ortodoxia.hu

*16.9.1971 Lipova Arad. N? 1994 Lic Fac theol Sibiu. 1994 stud French Aubazine, Terrason. mon11.8.1995 Hodoş Bodrog, igumen. 1997-2002 Master Athens. 6.4.2002 Hajdu Bihar. 2003-2007 consilier Gyula ⊕8.7.2007 B Gyula.

Metropolia Europa Centrala, Europa Nord

Serafim Romul Joantă ***Deutschland***

T: A Deutschland Österreich Luxemburg, M Germania, Europa Centrala, Europa Nord ▪ ✉ Fürther Straße 166, GERMANY-90429 Nürnberg • [49] 911 323691-3, -0, fax -2 • mitropolia@mitropolia-ro.de • serafim@mitropolia-ro.de • www.mitropolia-ro.de

*4.9.1948 Boholţ Braşov. N2.1. 1970-1974 Sibiu. diak10.11.1974 ⊖11.11.1974 celibatar, Făgăraş, Alba Iulia. 1982-1985 stud Institut St-Serge Paris. 1985 Dr. theol Paris "La tradition hésychaste et le renouveau monastique en Roumanie". 1986-1989 professeur St-Serge. 1989 director spiritual Sibiu. mon17.2.1990 ⊕11.3.1990 B Făgăraş. 1990-1993 Vicar Sibiu Hermannstadt. 1994 M Deutschland, 1994-1998 Locum tenens Romanian Diocese of Western Europe Paris. 1994-2001 Ostkirchliches Institut Regensburg. 28.-30.1.2000 COMECE Bucureşti. 2001 Nürnberg. 2009 Bayerische Verfassungsmedaille. 2012 The Star of Romania. 2013 Wilhelm Löhe Medaille.

Sofian Gheorghe Pătrunjel

T: B Braşov, vicar Deutschland ▪ ✉ Paul-Heyse-Straße 19, GERMANY-80336 München • [49] 89 54572059, 66060884 • [49] 176 61048133 • ep_sofian@cbrom.de episcopulsofian@yahoo.de • episcopulsofian@cbrom.de • www.cbrom.de

*22.7.1970 Băcel Covasna Transilvania. N? 1984-1988 liceul Sfântu Gheorghe, stenodactiligraf. 1989-1990 military service. mon27.2.1990 "Serafim" Brâncoveanu Sâmbata de Sus (p. Teofil Părăian). 1992-1996 Fac theol Sibiu. diak23.4.1993 ⊖30.5.1993. 1995-1998 stud Chur. 1997 Lic "Penticostarul şi spiritualitatea ortodoxă". 1998 stud Deutsch Würzburg, "Der Christliche Osten". 1999-2003 stud

theol Thessaloniki. elected vicar Deutschland. 19.5.2002 Nürnberg. 2.7.2002 Bucureşti ⊕11.5.2003 Nürnberg (Patr Teoctist). 2005 München. 2010 Dr. theol Thessaloniki "Pneumatiki patrótis katà tou M. Basilíou".

Macarie Marius-Dan Drăgoi ***Skandinavia***

T: B Scandinavia ▪ ✉ Hasslingbyvagen 7, SWEDEN-13691 Hanninge • [46] 853 035 60-0, fax -1 [46] 853 03560-0, fax -1 • mdandragoi@yahoo.com • www.episcopiascandinavia.se

*9.5.1977 Căianu-Mic Bistriţa. N? 1991-1996 Seminary Suceava. 1996-2000 Fac theol Cluj. 1997 langue française Aubazine. 1998-2003 secretary B Vad. 2002 English language York. mon23.6.2003 Alba Iulia. diak24.6.2003. 2004-2005 stud Leeds ⊖6.1.2004 preparator Fac theol Alba Iulia. 2005 Dr. theol Cluj "Ortodocşi şi grecocatolici în Transilvania". 2005 protosinghel Cluj ⊕2.5.2008 Cluj B Scandinavia.

Metropolia Europa Occidentala, Europa Meridionala

Iosif Ilie Pop ***Paris***

T: A Paris M Europe Occidentale et Méridionale, Directeur Représentation de l'Église de Roumanie auprès de l'Union Européenne ▪ ✉ Bd. du Général Leclerc, FRANCE-92470 Limours • [33] 1 6491-5924, fax -2683 • joseph_pop@hotmail.com • www.mitropolia.eu

*19.2.1966 Vişeu de Jos, Maramureş. N? Liceul Baia Mare. 1985-1986 Fac Politechnică. 1989-1993 Fac theol Sibiu, diak19.10.1993 ⊖26.10.1993. 1993 Prof. Seminary Alba Iulia, assistant Prof Fac theol Alba Iulia Section Social. mon17.4.1994. 1994-1997 Dr. theol Institut St-Serge Paris, (prof. Olivier Clement, prof. Boris Bobrinskoj), "Le mystère de la personne humaine chez St-Syméon le Nouveau Théologien". 30.11.1997 protosinghel ⊕15.3.1998 A Paris et Europe Occidentale et Méridionale (M Serafim). 28.-29.1.2000 COMECE Bucureşti. 2001 M. 2001-2002 Locum tenens USA. 2004 Mondo Migliore.

Marc Alric

T: B Paris, vicaire ▪ ✉ rue Mazarin 62, FRANCE-33000 Bordeaux • [33] 6 64493277

*11.5.1958 Paris. N? 1981 Fac Architecture Paris, Institut d'Urbanisme Paris. 1987 orth. 6.9.1992 Sihastria Moldova. diak9.9.1992 (M Daniel) ⊖20.8.1994 (M Daniel). 1995 Lic Fac theol Iaşi. 1996 paroisse Louvenciennes, 1997-2003 monastère St-Silouane St-Mars-de-Locquenay. 2003 Bordeaux. archim2004 ⊕7.5.2005.

Siluan Ciprian Şpan ***Italia***

T: B Italia ▪ ✉ via Ardeatina 1741, ITALIA-00134 Roma • [39] 0187 850343 cabinet • episcopia.italiei@mitropolia.eu • www.episcopia-italiei.it

*5.3.1970 Gura Râului jud. Sibiu. N? Liceul Sibiu. 1989-1993 Fac theol Sibiu. diak21.1.1994 (M Serafim) ⊖6.3.1994 (M Serafim). 1994-1998 doctorat Institut St-Serge Paris. 1994-2001 Monastère Bussy-en-Othe (F-Yonne). mon24.6.2001 ⊕21.10.2001 Bordeaux vicar F (sud) E P. 2004 in Italia, 2008 B Italia.

Timotei Felician Lauran ***España***

T: B España, Portugal ▪ ✉ calle Malaga 5, Zulema Villalbilla, SPAIN-21810 Madrid • [34] 91 8792324 • episcopia.spaniei.portugaliei@mitropolia.eu • www.episcopia.ro

*12.4.1975 Satu Mare. N? 1981-1989 Şcoala, 1989-1993 Liceul Teoretic Satu Mare. 1992 dipla cântăreţ bisericesc. 1993-1997 Lic theol Cluj "Validitatea hirotoniilor anglicane". 1998-1999 stud Fac Medicine Cluj. mon24.3.1998 Nicula diak25.3.1998 ⊖14.6.1998 Nicula. 1999-2001 duhovnic France, MTh Institut St-Serge Paris. 2000 protosinghel. 2001 Dr. theol Cluj "Ortodoxie şi erezie" (Vasile Leb). 2002-2004 duhovnic Ciucea, Radio Renaşterea. 2004-2005 Mon Malvialle, France. 2005-2008 exarch mânăstirilor ⊕8.3.2008.

Ignatie Trif

T: B Mureşan, vicar España, Portugal ▪ ✉ calle Malaga 5, Zulema Villalbilla, SPAIN-21810 Madrid • [34] 91 8792324 • ps.ignatie@mitropolia.eu

*7.7.1976 Bilbor jud. Harghita. N? 1991-1992 liceul Topliţa. 1992-1997 stud theol Seminary, 1997-2001 Fac theol Alba Iulia. 1998-2003 redactor "Credinţa străbună". 2001 cursurile doctorat Sibiu. diak6.8.2001 Mânăstirea Poşaga ⊖11.8.2001 Cathedral Alba Iulia. 2003-2008 stud Athens. 2004-2008 asistent, 2007 Bucureşti, 2008 protosinghel. mon24.2.2008. 2009-2011 Lektor Patrologia Fac theol Alba Iulia. 2011 Dr. theol Bucureşti (Prof. Ioan Caraza) "Sfântul Grigorie Palama şi doctrina despre energiile necreate." archim21.5.2011 ⊕11.12.2011 Paris B Mureşan, vicar España, Portugal with residence in England.

Arhiepiscopia America

Nicolae Condrea ***USA***

T: A Romanian Orthodox Missionary Archdiocese in USA and Canada ▪ ✉ 5410 N. Newland Avenue, USA-Chicago, IL60656-2026 • [1] 773 7741-677, fax -805 • romarch67@aol.com • ArchNicolae@gmail.com • www.romarch.org

*15.4.1967 Constanţa. N? 1981-1983 liceu Constanţa, 1983-1988 Bucureşti. 1988-1993 Lic theol "Andrei Şaguna" Sibiu. 1992-1994 prof religie Bucureşti. 1994-1995 stud Strasbourg (WCC Genève). 1996 parish Stuttgart. diak 9.3.1997 ⊖27.4.1997. 1999-2001 Dialogue Committee for European Integration CEC Bruxelles. 2001 Dr.

theol "Psychological Problems in Evagrios of Pontus". mon18.12.2001 Radu Vodă, Darvari. archim12.3.2002 ⊕27.7.2002 Montreal Quebec.

Ioan Casian Liviu-Ionel Tunaru

T: B Vicina, vicar USA and Canada ▪ ✉ 5410 N. Newland Avenue, USA-Chicago, IL60656-2026 • [1] 773 7741-677, fax -805 • tcasian@hotmail.com

*20.2.1969 Comăneşti Bacău. N? Liceul Comăneşti. 1988-1993 Lic theol Sibiu "Iconomia în Biserică Ortodoxă". 1993-1998 stud Institut Pontifical Flagellazione Jerusalem, St. Anselm Canterbury, Lic theol Orientale Roma "Conceptul de libertate în ... Maxim Marturisitorul". 1998-2001 secretary Metropolia Europa Occidentale. diak1.6.2001 ⊖2.6.2001 mon1.11.2001 Înălţarea Sf. Cruci Malvialle France. 2002-2003 parish Sf. Nicolae Bordeaux. archim12.3.2002. 2003 parish Sf. Nicolae New York ⊕2.3.2006.

Episcopia Australia

Mihail Maricel Filimon ***Australia***

T: B Australia, New Zealand ▪ ✉ 61 Queensberry St, Carlton 3053, AUSTRALIA-Melbourne • [61] 3 9701 8088 • office@roeanz.com.au • www.roeanz.com.au

*25.1.1964 Matca Galaţi. N? 1978-1982 gymnasium Tecuci. 1984 Cernica. mon7.1.1986. 1987-1991 Lic theol Sibiu "Preocupări privind canonizarea". diak18.4. 1987 ⊖11.9.1988. 1991 protosinghel. archim22.1.1995. 1998 Dr. theol Thessaloniki "Slujirea Catehetica". 2003-2008 stareţ Detroit. 2008 administrative vicar Bucureşti ⊕2.5.2008.

Serbian Orthodox Church

His Holiness **Irinej**
Archbishop of Peć
Metropolitan of Belgrade-Karlovci
Serbian Patriarch

Irinej Miroslav Gavrilović *Beograd*
T: A Peć, M Beograd -Karlovci, Patriarch Serbia ▪ ✉ Kralja Petra I br.5, SERBIA-11000 Beograd • [381] 11 186371, 32825938 • Kabinet 3283997, fax 3283997 • dekan@pbf.rs • sekretar@pbf.rs • biblioteka@pbf.rs • www.spc.rs
*28.8.1930 Vidova Čačak. N? gymnasium Čačak. Seminary Prizren, Fac theol Beograd. mon1959 Rakovica, teacher Prizren. diak24.10.1959 ⊖27.10.1959 stud Athens. 1969 director Seminary Ostrog, director Prizren ⊕14.7.1974 B Moravica Vicar patriarcal. 1975-2009 B Niš. 1992-1993 pastoral care Skoplje, Zletovo, Strumica, Ohrid, Bitolj. 2010 Patriarch, 2010-2011 admininstrator Niš. 2011 Orden Republika Srpska (President Milorad Dodik, Modrica). 22.-28.1.2016 Synaxis of the primates of the Local Orthodox Churches Chambésy Switzerland.

Arsenij Milomir Glavchić
T: B Toplitsa, vicar to Patriarch ▪ ✉ Kralja Petra I br.5, SERBIA-11000 Beograd • [381] 11 186371, 32825938 • Kabinet 3283997, fax 3283997
*10.3.1978 Vrsac. 1993-2005 Seminary St. Sava and Fac theol Beograd with the blessing of B Hrizostom Stolic of Banat. 2002-2005 treasurer diocese Banat. 2005-2006 secretary to B Hrizostom. 2006-2012 MTh Thessaloniki "Typicon of St. Nikodim". mon1.8.2007 Studenica (B Hrizostom). diak2.8.2007 feast Prophet Elia Studenica (B Hrizostom) ⊖15.8.2008. 2011 from Zica to Kraljevo with B Hrizostom. 2014 stud theol Thessaloniki ⊕31.7.2014 B Toplica, vicar to Patriarch Serbia.

Atanasije Cvetko Rakita
T: B Hvosno, vicar patriarha ▪ ✉ Kralja Petra I br.5, SERBIA-11000 Beograd • [381] 11 3282596, 3283997, 3025146
*7.11.1957 Babin Do, Janj, Bosnia. N? mon1977 diak1977 ⊖1977. 1977 absolvent Seminary Krka. 1977-1983 dipl theol St. Vladimir's New York. 1983-1994 teacher Seminary Prizren. 1991 protosynkellos. 1994 assistant Prof Patrology Fac theol Beograd, 1995-1999 redactor Pravoslavlje Press ⊕31.5.1999 B Hvosno.

Antonije Dragan Pantelić
T: B Moravitsa, vicar patriarha ▪ ✉ Petropavlovskij per. 4-6, ROSSIJA-109028 Moskva • [7] 495 9178036 • [7] 9265288774 •

antonije@rambler.ru • www.serbskoe-podvorie.ru

*23.7.1970 Valjevo. N? school Pričević. mon1988 Krka diak1989 ⊖1991. 1991 absolvent Seminary Krka. 1992-1996 Kandidat Moskva "Sovremennoe položenie Serbskoj Cerkvi". 1996-2000 ekonom namestnik, teacher Studenica. 2000-2002 teacher Latin History Liturgics University Foča. archim2001. 2002 Patriarchal Representative Moskva. 2003 teacher Liturgics Orth University St. John Moskva ⊕27.5.2006 B Moravica, vicar patr.

Jovan Culibrk

T: B Lipljan, vicar patriarha ▪ ✉ Kralja Petra I br.5, SERBIA-11000 Beograd • [381] 11 186371

*1965 Zenitsa. N? stud Literature Banjaluka, 1991 dipl Slavic languages Zagreb. stud theol Beograd, Foča, Yad Vashem Center Jerusalem. mon1993 Cetinje. 1993-2003 teacher Seminary Cetinje ⊖1997 Stanjevici. 1999 eparchy Peč. 2004 Jerusalem Orden "Golda Meir" ⊕4.9.2011 B Lipljan, vicar patr, Patriarchal Representative Peć, Synodal Commission Translation Old Testament, Synodal Commission Jasenovac, International Institutions Kosovo-Metohija.

Irinej Mirko Bulović ***Bačka***

T: B Bačka ▪ ✉ Bačka Eparhia, Vladičanski dvor, Gimnazijska 2, SERBIA-21000 Novi Sad • [381] 21 529437, fax 451830 • epbacka@eunet.rs • epbacka@nspoint.net

*11.2.1947 Stanišić Bačka. NSlava sv.Jovan 7./20.1. Slava sv. Gimnazija Sombor deutsch. 1965-1969 Fac theol Beograd, mon25.3.1968 (7.4. Justin Popović). diak11.11.1968 ⊖15.11.1968. 1969-1970 Monaška škola Ostrog. 1970-1980 stud theol Athens (Markus Ephesus), 1974-1975 Prof Seminary Prizren. 1981 Dr. theol Athens. 1981 Prof NT Fac theol Beograd ⊕29.5.1990 B Moravica. 13.12.1990 B Bačka. 1991 Comission Dialogue with the Roman Catholic Church. 1992 Central Committee CEC. 1999 Commission Orthodox Collaboration WCC Geneva. 2011 Admin B Wien. 16.12.2015 Athens Interorthodox committee preparation Panorthodox Synod. 22.-28.1.2016 Synaxis of the primates of the Local Orthodox Churches Chambésy Switzerland.

Jeronim Sinisha Mochevic

T: B Jegar, vicar Bachka ▪ ✉ Gimnazijska 2, SERBIA-21000 Novi Sad • [381] 21 529437

*26.9.1969 Sarajevo, elementary and secondary school. mon21.11.1990 Monastery Holy Archangels Kovilj. diak27.1.1991. 26.7.1999 archdeacon. 2002 graduated Fac theol Belgrad ⊖2003. 2003-2007 Master lit. science Pontificio Istituto Orientale Roma, CLA Besancon. archim2008 St. Philothea Smirna/Izmir, Turkey (M Jakovos of Mitilina). 2008-2014 spiritual father Monastery Prophet Elias Lesbos (M Theo-

lyptos), Uni Vienna, Dr. in the field of liturgical theology. Languages: Greek, Italian, French, Russian, German, English. ⊕28.9.2014 B Jegar, vicar Bachka (Patr Irinej).

Nikanor Veljko Bogunović ***Banat***
T: B Banat ■ ✉ Dvorska 20, SERBIA-26300 Vršac • [381] 13 80134-5, fax -6
*20.8.1952 Medveđa Dalmacia. NSlava 7./20.1. John Baptist. 1968-1973 Seminary Krka. mon27.8.1975 diak28.8.1975. 1975-1979 Zagorsk (Sergiev Posad) ⊖1.1.1978. 1979 Kandidat Moskva. 1981-1982 Deutschland ⊕11.8.1985 B Hvostan, Administrator Crna Gora. 1991-1999 B Gornji Karlovac. 1999-2003 B Australia+New Zealand. 2003 B Banat.

Jefrem Mile Milutinović ***Banjaluka***
T: B Banjaluka ■ ✉ Aleja Svetog Save 3, BOSNIA-51000 Banjaluka • [387] 51 305709, fax 316522 • spc-bl@inecco.net
*15.4.1944 Busovača Bosnia. NSlava? mon1967 diak1968 ⊖1970. 1975 Academy Moskva. 1975-1978 Prof. Krka ⊕17.9.1978 B Moravica, 1.6.1980 B Banjaluka.

Hrizostom Rajko Jević ***Bihać***
T: B Bihać+Petrovac ■ ✉ Marka Jokića 51, BOSNIA-77250 Bosanski • [387] 37 88333-4, -5, fax -3, [387] 61 396110 • eparhijaapb@gmail.com
*4.3.1952 Bočenica Bosanski Petrovac. NSlava sv. Georgije 23.4./6.5. 1968-1973 Seminary Krka. mon20.9.1971. 1980 dipl theol Thessaloniki. 1981-1991 Prof Krka ⊕12.7.1991 B Bihać+Petrovac. 13.7.2013 B Zvornik+Tuzla.

Ignatije Dobrivoje Midić ***Braničevo***
T: B Braničevo ■ ✉ Eparhia, Hajduk Veljkova 2, SERBIA-12000 Požarevac • [381] 12 223 832 +fax, 54063-5,-6,-7, 227 993, [381] 63 1111222 • spcbran@ptt.rs
*17.10.1954 Knez-Selo Niš. NSlava? 1974 Seminary Beograd. 1980 absolvent Fac theol Beograd. 1980-1987 Fac theol Athens. 1987 Dr. theol Athens Dogmatics St. Maxim Confessor. 1988-1994 teacher Moral Fac theol Beograd. 1991 stud Erlangen. mon1991 (B Atanasije Jevtić) diak1991 (M John Pergamon) ⊖29.12.1993 ⊕26.6.1994 B Braničevo. 1999 Commission Orthodox Collaboration WCC Geneva.

Joanikije Mićović ***Budimlje***
T: B Budimlje+Nikšić ■ ✉ Manastir Đurđevi Stupovi, MONTENEGRO-84300 Berane • [382] 51 24647-2, -4, fax -3, sekretar -3, [382] 69 548124 • ep.budimljanska@t-com.me • www.teofil.co.me
*20.4.1959 Velimlje Banjani. NSlava? gymnasium Nikšić. stud Fac phil Beograd. 1990 dipl theol Beograd. mon30.10.1990. 1991-1992 Mon. Savina. diak7.2.1991 ⊖2.1991. 1992 igumen rector Seminary Sv. Petra Cetinje. 1995 Sinđel ⊕3.6.1999. 1999 B Budimlje.

Amfilohije Risto Radović ***Crna Gora***
T: M Crna Gora+Primorje ▪ ✉ Crnogorsko-Primorska Mitropolia, MONTENEGRO-81250 Cetinje • [382] 41 231273, 232577, [382] 69 340631 • mitropolija@cg.me
*7.1.1938 Morača Crna Gora, NSlava sv. Mihail 8./21.11. 1958 Seminary Beograd. 1962 Fac theol Beograd. 1963 Christkath Fakultät Bern. 1964-1965 Roma ⊖1968. 15.6.1973 Dr. theol Athens. 1974-1975 teacher Institut St-Serge Paris, teacher Fac theol Beograd ⊕16.6.1985 Banat. 1990 M Crna Gora. 2006 Orden St. Andrew Moskva, Lomonossov University Moskva. 2006 Dr.h.c.: 2006 Moskva Theol Academy. 2015 St. Peterburg Theol Academy. 14.10.2010 Moskva Theol Academy 325 years . 2011 Admin B Buenos Aires. 22.-28.1.2016 Synaxis of the primates of the Local Orthodox Churches Chambésy Switzerland.

N.N. ***Dabar Bosna***
T: Administrator▪ ✉ ul. Zelenih Beretki 3, BOSNIA-71000 Sarajevo • [387] 33 269261, 201-469, fax -518 • www.mitropolijadabrosanska.org

Fotije Rade Sladojevic ***Dalmacija***
T: B Dalmacija ▪ ✉ Dalmat. Eparhia, Težačka 8, KROATIA-22000 Šibenik • [385] 22 216701, 214738, fax 200170 • eparhijadalmatinska@optinet.hr • eparhijski-upravni-obor@si.htnet.hr • www.eparhija-dalmatinska.hr
*1.2.1961 School Čurug, Novi Sad. NSlava? 1988 dipl theol Beograd. 1988-1990 stud NT Erlangen. mon8.11.1990 monastery Kovilj. diak21.11.1990 (B Irinej Bačka) ⊖27.1.1991. 1992-1993 Manastir Bođani. 1993 suplent nastavnik Seminary Sv. Arsenije Sremski Karlovci. 1998 MTh Fac theol Beograd ⊕30.5.1999 Novi Sad B Dalmacija.

Gerasim Zoran Popović ***Gornji Karlovac***
T: B Gornji Karlovac ▪ ✉ Slave Raškaj 14, PP 42, KROATIA-47000 Karlovac • [385] 47 64253-1, fax -2 • episkop@eparhija-gornjokarlovacka.hr • eparhija-gornjokarlovacka@htnet.hr • euo@eparhija-gornjokarlovacka.hr • www.eparhija-gornjokarlovacka.hr
*15.2.1972 Gornje Liplje. NSlava? Seminary Krka, Fac theol Moskva. diak21.11.1991 ⊖5.10.1998. 1998 igumen Krka. teacher Krka ⊕30.7.2004 B Gornjo-Karlovačka.

David Perović ***Kruševac***
T: B Kruševac ▪ ✉ Dositejeva 1, SERBIA-37000 Kruševac • [381] 37 350 1550 • [381] 66 8000177 • info@eparhijakrusevacka.com
*17.7.1953 Burakovtsi Metohia, eparchy Raško-Prizren. NSlava? Gymnasium Peč. 1972-1976 stud Academy Theatre Beograd. 1977-1983 stud theol Beograd. mon,

diak1983 Dečani. 1983-1989 teacher Krka and Prizren. 1989-1994 Dr. theol Athens (Prof. Stylianos Papadopoulos). 1995-2010 teacher Christian Ethics Fac theol Beograd, 1995-1999 teacher Dogmatics Foča, stud French language Paris ⊖2.6.2011 archim7.7.2011 ⊕24.7.2011 B Kruševać.

Filaret Jelenko Mičević
T: former B Maleševo ▪ ✉ Dušana Tomaševića Ćirka 66, SERBIA-31300 Prijepolje • [381] 33 23182, 710-071, fax -471, [381] 63 373823
*8.8.1947 Borci Konjic. NSlava? 1968-1969 Seminary Beograd. mon1.5.1969 diak11.9.1969 (Patr German) ⊖4.12.1969. 1969 Duhovnik Seminary Beograd. 1984 Sinđel, 1990 protosynkellos. archim9.12.1997 nastojatjel Monastery Sv. Arhangel Gavril Zemun ⊕23.5.1999 Sv. Mihail Beograd. 7.7.1999 B Maleševo. 12.3.2015 Holy Synod decided to finish B Filaret's mission in Maleševo.

Jovan Mladen Purić ***Niš***
T: B Niš ▪ ✉ Niška Eparhia ul. Dimitrijevića 3, SERBIA-18000 Niš • [381] 18 243799 • eparhija.nis@medianis.net
*6.6.1965 Mijači Valjevo. NSlava? 1985 absolvent Seminary Beograd. 1985 stud Fac theol Beograd, Kandidat Leningrad. mon17.6.1992 Tronoša (Atanasije Jevtić) diak18.6.1992 Ostrog (Atanasije Jevtić) ⊖14.5.1995 (Mileševa, Patr Pavle). 1999 protosynkellos. 2001 igumen Ostrog, teacher Cetinje ⊕4.7.2004 B Diokleia. 2004-2011 vicar Crna Gora, igumen Ostrog. 2011 B Niš.

Lukijan Jovan Vladulov ***Osijek***
T: B Osijek Polje+Baranja ▪ ✉ Osiječka Eparhia Patrijaršijski Dvor, ul. Zagrebačka 2 A, KROATIA-31226 Dalj • [385] 31 590020
*9.5.1933 Novi Kozarci (=Haifeld) Banat. NSlava 6./19.12. Nikolaus. Seminary Sremski Karlovci, Fac theol Beograd, mon21.11.1958 diak26.7.1959 ⊖15.8.1963 igumen Bođani Bačka. archim20.6.1989 ⊕14.7.1991 B Osijek+Polje+Baranja.

Teodosije Živko Šibali ***Raška-Prizren***
T: B Raška-Prizren ▪ ✉ Manastir Gračanica, KOSOVO-38405 Kosovska Gračanica • [381] 38 64939, 64203, 564634. 548739, [381] 63 402520 • Prizren [381] 29 24571, 25426 • Seminary 22030 • erpkim@kimradio.net • euerp@kosovo.com • erp_pz@eunet.yu
*1963 Čačak, NSlava? school Uziče, Fac theol Beograd (from Dečani), mon1989 Sv. Trojica Crna Reka Kosovo. 1992 igumen Dečani ⊕20.7.2004 B Lipljan, vicar Raška-Prizren. 2010 B Raška-Prizren.

Artemije Marko Radosavljević
T:

*15.1.1935 Lelić Valjevo, 1958 Seminary Beograd, mon21.11.1960 (Justin Popović) NSlava? diak1964. 1964 Fac theol Beograd, 1964-1968 Prof Krka. 1968-1976 stud Athens, 1976 Dr. theol Athens. 1976-1977 Ostkirchliches Institut Regensburg. 1977-1978 Prof Prizren. 1978-1991 igumen Sv. Trojica Crna Reka Kosovo ⊕23.6.1991. 1991-2010 B Raška-Prizren. 19.11.2010 monk, later lay person. 29.4.2015 "consecrates" vicar, Nikolaj.

Lavrentije Živko Trifunović ***Šabac***

T: B Šabac ▪ ✉ Šabačka Eparhia, Karađorđeva 3, SERBIA-15000 Šabac • [381] 15 351440, 354440, fax 344038, [381] 63 272707, 8807559 • eparhijasabacka@gmail.com

*27.1.1935 Bogoštica, NSlava 7./20.1. Johannes. gymnasium Krupanj, 1954-1958 Loznica. 1958 Seminary Beograd, mon12.8.1958 Krušedol (1690 Arsenije Kosovo) diak19.8.1958 ⊖21.9.1961. 1961 Ružica, 1962 Fac theol Beograd. 1962-1964 parish Kupres. 1964-1967 Suplent Prof Krka ⊕16.7.1967 B Moravica Vicar Patr. 30.3.1969 B Australia, 1973 B Westeuropa London, Hildesheim Germany. 1989-2006 B Šabac-Valjevo. 1991-1998 Central Committee WCC. 1995 Großes Goldenes Ehrenzeichen der Verdienste um die Republik Österreich für Völkerverständigung und Ökumene. 2006 B Šabac (eparchija divided).

Milutin Milutin Knežević ***Valjevo***

T: B Valjevo ▪ ✉ Vojvode Živojina Mišića 30, SERBIA-14000 Valjevo • [381] 14 2449-20, -30, 220-921, fax -597

*10.1.1949 Mijač Valjevo. NSlava 8./21.11.Arhangel Mihail. school Poćut. 1963 monastery Kaona. 1967-1969 Seminary Ostrog ⊖1.1.1969 stud Seminary Beograd, Fac theol Beograd, dipl theol St. Sava Libertyville USA. Starec Kaona, 2002 protosynkellos Šabac ⊕20.7.2003 Beograd B Australia+New Zealand. 2006 B Valjevo (divided from Šabac-Valjevo).

Sava Jurić ***Slavonia***

T: B Slavonia ▪ ✉ Kneza Branimira 2, P.P.20, KROATIA-34550 Pakrac • [385] 34 411-553, -638 • slavonskaeparhija@yahoo.com

*27.2.1942 Chicago. NSlava? gymnasium Chicago. St. TikhonTheol Academy South Canaan PA mon15.2.1964 diak16.2.1964 Monastery New Gračanica USA ⊖23.2.1964. 1980-1984 secretary Construction Committee Monastery New Gračanica. 1982 Synkellos, 1984 protosynkellos. 1984-1988 Abbot St. Mark Monastery Sheffield CA. 1988 Archimandrite St. Sava Monastery Libertyville. Archimandrit St. Sava Mon. Canberra Hall Australia. 1988 Deputy of bishop of Australia ⊕17.6.1994, Monastery New Gračanica (Patr Pavle). 1994 B Australia+ New Zealand New Gračanica Metropolia, full communion Serbian Church 15 February 1999. 1999 B Slavonija in Daruvar, 2005 in Jasenovac.

Vasilije Vaso Vadić *Srem*
T: B Srem ▪ ✉ Sremska Eparhia, Trg Branka Radičevića 8, SERBIA-21205 Sremski Karlovci • [381] 21 882640, 821729, 881-729, fax -640 • spcsrem@ptt.rs
*10.12.1945 Čelinac Bosnia, Slava 20.7./2.8. sv. Elija. mon19.12.1967 diak19.12. 1967. 1967 Seminary Krka ⊖28.6.1968. 1971 Bucureşti. 1971 Suplent Seminary Krka ⊕3.9.1978 B Australia. 14.9.1986 B Srem.

Jovan Jovan Mladenović *Šumadija*
T: B Šumadija ▪ ✉ Kralja Aleksandra I Karađorđevića 67, pf 54, SERBIA-34000 Kragujevac • [381] 34 302642, fax 300490 • vl.jovan@eunet.rs • episkop@eparhija-sumadijska.org.rs • kancelarija@eparhija-sumadijska.org.rs • www.eparhija-sumadijska.org.rs
*11.9.1950 Dobrača, Arilje. NSlava? Monastic School Ostrog, mon24.4.1971 diak25.4.1971. 1974 Seminary Beograd ⊖28.6.1976. 1980 Fac theol Beograd. 1981-1993 igumen Studenica ⊕25.7.1993 B Tetovo, Administrator 30.000 Serbs in Skoplje, Zletovo-Strumica, Ohrid-Bitolj. 1994-2002 B West USA. 2002 B Šumadija.

Hilarion Bojan Golubović *Timok*
T: B Timok ▪ ✉ Timočke bune 6, SERBIA-19000 Zaječar • [381] 19 421888, 32195 timocka@formanet.co.rs • www.eparhija-timocka.org
*26.5.1974 Zajechar.NSlava? 1992 dipl engineering High School Zajechar. Mon. Crna Reka. 1993 military service. 1994 Mon. Bukovo. mon1.1.1997 Bukovo diak1.5. 1997 ⊖19.12.1997. 1998 abbot Bukovo. 2002 protosynkellos. 2009 deputy of the bishop. 2009-2013 Fac theol Beograd ⊕10.8.2014 Zajechar B Timok (Patr Irinej).

Pahomije Tomislav Gačić *Vraje*
T: B Vranje ▪ ✉ Ivana Milutinovića 26, SERBIA-17500 Vranje • [381] 17 422695, 401017, [381] 63402814 • epvransska@ptt.rs • milvlada@ptt.rs
*17.10.1952 Čečava Bosnia. NSlava? mon1973. 1980 dipl theol Athens ⊖4.10.1980. 1985-1993 igumen Papraća Bosnia ⊕10.9.1992 B Vranje.

Porfirije Prvoslav Perić *Zagreb*
T: M Zagreb+Ljubljana ▪ ✉ Ilica 7/1, KROATIA-10000 Zagreb • [385] 4819506, fax 4877534 • mitropolija-zagrebacka@zg.htnet.hr
*22.7.1961 school Čurug, gimnazia Novi Sad. 21.4.1985 Dečani (Sunday Thomas). 1986 dipl theol Beograd. diak23.6.1986 Sv. Troica Prizren (monday Pentecost). 1986-1990 stud NT Athens. mon6.10.1990 Kovilj ⊖21.11.1990 Kovilj. 1990 rector. 1996 abbot Kovilj ⊕13.6.1999 B Jegar, vicar Bačka. 2004 PhD Athens "Possibility of knowing God in St. Paul's". 2005 therapeutic community "The Land of the Living" (drug-addicition). 2005 Prof Psych Fac theol Beograd. 19.9.2006 with Karan Dragan

Cath-Orth Commission in Beograd. 2008 president Republic Broadcasting Agency Serbia. 2011 Ordinary Armed Forces. 2014 M Zagreb+Ljubljana.

Grigorije Mladen Durić ***Zahum***

T: B Zahum+Hercegovina ▪ ✉ Svetosavska 2, BOSNIA-79300 Trebinje • [387] 59 260-075, -455, fax -688 • Monastir Tvrdoš 261003, fax 260455 • Crkvina, Hercegovačka Gračanica 261139, 260546

*17.12.1967 Vareš, Bosnia. N Slava? 1989-1995 Seminary Beograd. mon17.6.1992 diak17.7.1992 ⊖19.8.1992. 1995 Fac theol Beograd. 1996-1997 stud Athens. 1997-1999 igumen Monastery Tvrdoš ⊕5.6.1999 Trebinje B Hum vicar to B Atanasije. 3.10.1999 B Zahum+Hercegovina.

Atanasije Zoran Jevtić

T: former B Zahum+Hercegovina ▪ ✉ Monastir Tvrdoš, BOSNIA-79300 Trebinje • [387] 59 261003, fax 260455

*1938 Brdarica. NSlava? 1958 Seminary Beograd, diak1960 mon1960 (Justin Popović). 1963 Fac theol Beograd. 1967 Dr. theol Athens. 1968-1972 Prof St-Serge Paris. 1972 Prof Fac theol Beograd ⊕7.7.1991. B Banat. member Penclub Serbia. 1992-1999 B Zahum+Hercegovina, 2001-2002 Jerusalem. 2002-2003 zamenik Žiča. 2003 member Commission Dialogue Eastern Orthodox – Oriental Orthodox Churches. 2007 Dr.h.c. St. Vladimir's New York.

Justin Miroslav Stefanović ***Zica***

T: B Zica ▪ ✉ Trg Svetog Save 4, SERBIA-36000 Kraljevo • [381] 36 31708 -0, fax -1 euokraljevo@tron-inter.net • www.eparhija-zica.org

*26.5.1955 Čačak. NSlava? 1980 absolvent Fac Economy Beograd. mon1983 Crna Reka (B Pavle of Raska-Prizren, later Serbian Patriarch). diak1983 ⊖1983. 1987 absolvent Fac theol Beograd. woodcarving and woodcared crosses. 1987-1990 Fac theol Athens. 1991 abbot Monastery crna Reka ⊕1.7.1992 Monastery Sopocani B Hvosno assistant Timok (Patr Pavle). 1993 B Timok. 25.3.2014 MTh Beograd "Penitence according to the Apostolic Fathers". 3.8.2014 Kraljevo B Zica.

Vasilije Ljubomir Kačavenda

T: former B Zvornik+Tuzla ▪ ✉ Kralja Petra I br.5, SERBIA-11000 Beograd

*19.12.1938 Sarajevo, NSlava? mon15.9.1957 diak1.1.1960 ⊖7.1.1960 ⊕25.6.1978. 1978-2013 B Zvornik+Tuzla.

Lukijan Vojislav Pantelić ***Buda***

T: B Buda ▪ ✉ Patriarha utca 5, HUNGARY-2000 Szentendre • [36] 26 314 457, fax 500 457 • eparhijtemisvarska@yahoo.com

*19.8.1950 Mol Ada Bačka. NSlava 29.6./12.7. St. Peter. mon10.6.1979 Divostin (Sava Vuković) diak11.6.1979. 1979-1981 Ostkirchliches Institut Regensburg, 1980 stud iur. dipl theol Beograd. 1981 England ⊖22.9.1981 ⊕1.7.1984 B Moravica Vicar Patr. 1985-1999 B Slavonia. 1999-2002 B Szeged, 1999 Administrator Timişoara. 2002 B Buda.

Andrej Čilerdžić ***Austria***

T: B Austria+Switzerland ▪ ✉ Veithgassse 3/9, AUSTRIA-1030 Wien • [43] 1 7134765 • [43] 676 485 7944 • andreas@ikomline.net • eparhijabec@gmail.com • www.cilerdzic.com • www.crkva.at

*21.8.1961 Osnabrück. second son of protopresvyter stavrophor Dobrivoje and Mother Marianne. 1967-1971 Grundschule Düsseldorf. 1971-1980 Gymnasium Düsseldorf. 1980-1981 Mount Athos. 1981-1986 dipl theol Beograd. mon7.1.1987 Monastery Dečani (Irinej, later B Bachka). diak11.3.1987 Düsseldorf (B Lavrentije). 1987-1989 stud Greek language Thessaloniki, stud French Beausoleil, stud Italian. deacon Cathedral Thessaloniki. 1989-1993 teacher Seminary St. Kirill and Method Prizren Kosovo, dirigent choir ⊖21.11.1990 St. Sava Düsseldorf (B Irenej Moravitsa, Bachka). 1992 Monk St. Archangels Kovilj. 1993-2005 secretary International Relations Serbian Patriarchate Beograd. 26.7.1999 protosynkellos Novi Sad. archim19.8.2002 Novi Sad. 2005-2006 stud French Monte Carlo. 2008-2011 assistant, docent Orth Theol Institute München ⊕2011 Beograd B Remesiana (Bela Palanka), vicar patriarcal. 2014 B Austria Switzerland.

Sergije Zoran Karanović ***Mitteleuropa***

T: B Mitteleuropa ▪ ✉ Himmelsthür, Obere Dorfstraße 12, GERMANY-31137 Hildesheim • [49] 5121 6403-4, -5, fax 64136, [49] 89 6379962-2, -3, fax -4, [49] 171 5337367 • epsrednjoevropska@gmail.com • www.serbische-diozese.org

*4.7.1975 Backa Palanka. NSlava? 1990-1995 Seminary Krka Croatia. 1995-1996 stud theol Beograd. mon12.8.1995 Gomionica, brotherhood Monastery Rmanj, Martin Brod, expelled to Vojlovica Banat. diak31.10.1995. 1996-1998 eparchy Mitteleuropa Himmelsthür, Ostkirchliches Institut Regensburg. 1998-2002 brotherhood returns to Rmanj, with many of the Serbian profugies, teacher catechism Dvar, Martin Brod, Prekaja ⊖5.4.1998. 2001 dipl "catechist" Fac theol Beograd. 13.6.2002 Synkellos (Dvar, Ascension of Our Lord). archim7.4.2004 protosynkellos (Rmanj). 2005-2010 stud theol Aristoteles University Thessaloniki. 5.10.2008 abbot Rmanj ⊕27.7.2014 B Mitteleuropa.

Konstantin Krsto Đokić

T: former B Mitteleuropa ▪ ✉ Kralja Petra I br. 5, SERBIA-11000 Beograd • serbischediozese@t-online.de • serbische-diozese.org • kanzlei@serbische-diozese.org • sokdiakonia@aol.com • www.serbische-diozese.org

*26.9.1946 Gornje Crneljevo Bosnia. NSlava 23.4./6.5. St. Georg. 1967 Seminary Sremski Karlovci, Fac theol Beograd. mon28.3.1970 diak28.3.1970 ⊖29.3.1970. 1970-1978 eparchy Tuzla. 20.1.1977 Synkellos, 1978-1982 Prof Monastery Krka. 1982-1991 Prof Sremski Karlovci. 7.7.1985 protosynkellos. archim26.5.1991 ⊕21.7.1991 B Mitteleuropa Himmelsthür. 2014 retired.

Luka Brane Kovačević ***France***

T: B France et d'Europe occidentale ▪ ✉ rue du Simplon 23, B.P. 177-75864, FRANCE-75018 Paris • [33] 142 557768, 142 529990, 142 629929, 142 553 105, fax [33] 142582107, [33] 142 587466, [33] 620258276 • eglspc@club-internet.fr

*30.10.1950 Piskavica Banjaluka. NSlava? 1971 Krka, Fac theol Beograd, Fac jur Banjaluka. mon26.6.1976 diak27.6.1976 ⊖28.6.1976. 1976 Monastery Mount Mercer Elaine. 1976-1982 Institut St-Serge Paris. archim1991 ⊕17.8.1992 B Australia. 1997-1999 Administrator, 1999 B France.

Dositej Despot Motika ***Britannia***

T: B Britannia+Skandinavia ▪ ✉ Bögerstavägen 68, Eneskede SWEDEN-12047 Gård • [46] 8 7229930, fax 919737 • ep.dositej@stockholm.mail.telia.com

*14.10.1949 Zagoni Bijeljina Bosnia. NSlava? mon1970 diak8.11.1970. 1973-1984 Manastir Tavna. 1981 dipl theol Beograd. 1982-1983. Ostkirchliches Institut Regensburg. 1984 Bern, Ecumenical Institute Bossey. 1985-1988 Argentina. 1988-1990 secretary eparchy Canada ⊕31.5.1990 B Marča, vicar Westeuropa. 1.12.1990 B Britannia.

Mitrofan Radovan Kodić ***East USA***

T: B East USA ▪ ✉ 138 Carriage Hill Drive, USA-Mars, PA16046-2352 • [1] 724 77288-66, -12, fax -13 • eastern@zoominternet.net • krka@aol.com • www.easterndiocese.org

*4.8.1951 Ljupa. NSlava? diak1970 mon1970 ⊖6.1.1974. 1975 absolvent Beograd. 1975 Professor Krka. 1980 vize-rector Krka. 1987 rector Krka. archim1987 ⊕12.7.1987 B Toplica. 1987-1990 Administrator West USA. 1990-1991 Administrator Midwest. 1991 B East USA.

Maksim Milan Vasiljević ***West USA***

T: B West American Diocese ▪ ✉ 1621 West Garvey Ave, USA-Alhambra, CA 91803 • [1] 626 2899061, 284-6825, fax -1484 • westdiocese@earthlink.net smfa@smfa.com

*27.6.1968 Foča. NSlava? 1988 absolvent Seminary Beograd. 1993 absolvent Fac theol Beograd. 1996-1999 stud theol Athens, Dr. theol. mon18.8.1996 (B Atanasije Jevtić). diak19.8.1996 (B Atanasije Jevtić) ⊖9.8.2001 teacher Hagiology Beograd, Srbinje Foča. 2003-2004 stud Paris ⊕18.7.2004 Sarajevo. 2004-2006 B Hum, vicar Dabar Bosna. 2006 B West USA.

Georgije Djordje Đokić

T: former B Canada ▪ ✉ Holy Transfiguration Monastery, 7470 McNiven Rd, CANADA-Campbellville, ONT L0P 1B0 • [1] 905 878-3438, -0043, fax -1909. vladika@idirect.com vladika@istocnik.com • www.istocnik.com

*6.5.1949 Crnjelovo, NSlava 23.4./6.5. St. Georg. mon12.2.1971 diak12.2.1971 ⊖15.2.1971. 1981 dipl Fac theol Beograd. 1982-1984 England ⊕8.7.1984 B Canada. 1992-1994 B Budimlje, Administrator Canada. 1994-2015 B Canada. 20.5.2015 retired.

N.N. ***Buenos Aires***

T: B Buenos Aires ▪ ✉, ARGENTINA-1414 Buenos Aires

23.5.2011: South America, admin.

Longin Momir Krčo ***America***

T: B Midwestern Diocese of New Gračanica Metropolia ▪ ✉ 35240 North Grant Street, Third Lake, P.O.Box 371, USA-Grayslake, IL60030 • [1] 847 223-4300, -7185, fax -4312 • longinkrco@yahoo.com • eparhija@newgracanica.com

*29.9.1955 Kruščan. NSlava 6./19.12. St. Nicholas. 1970-1975 Krka. mon11.2.1975 diak12.2.1975 ⊖13.2.1975. 1975-1979 Akademy Moskva, Kandidat. 1980-1981 sekretar Zvornik. 1983-1985 Suplent Seminary Sv. Tri Jerarha Krka ⊕20.10.1985 B Moravica vicar Patr. 14.9.1986 B Australia. 1992 B Dalmacija. 1999 B America.

Irinej Mirko Dobrijević ***Australia***

T: B Australia+New Zealand ▪ ✉ 14 Renwick St, Box 512, AUSTRALIA-Alexandria, NSW 2015 • [61] 295179600, fax 295179700 • bishop@soc.org.au • irinej@earthlink.net • www.soc.org.au

*6.2.1955 Cleveland Ohio. NSlava? 1960-1973 High Distinction in Fine Arts. 1971-1975 stud Japanese painting. 1973-1975 stud Arts Cleveland, Byzantine Iconography. 1975-1979 stud St. Tikhon's Theol Seminary Pennsylvania. 1980-1982 MDiv St. Vladimir's New York "A 1921 Mission to America". 1982-1986 Diocesan

secretary Eastern America. 1984 Fellowship St. Alban and Sergius. CEC. 1986-1994 Director Religious Education Cathedral Chicago. 1992-2007 Senior Lecturer Loyola University Chicago, lecturer Fac theol Beograd. diak15.1.1994 Chicago (M Christopher) mon18.1.1995 Libertyville "Irinej of Lyon" ⊖27.1.1995 Washington. 2000 and 2003 Athens language course. 2004-2006 Consultant International and Interchurch Affairs Serbian Church, Coordinator Kosovo and Metohija Office Beograd. 2005 Orden Vuk Karađić Beograd ⊕15.7.2006 Beograd B Australia+New Zealand. 2007 International Heraldic Order Fleur de Lys. 2008 Major Feldman Award, Central Committee WCC, Board of Directors St. Vladimir's Seminary.

Jovan Zoran Vraniškovski
T: A Ohrid ▪ ✉ Kočanska 2/23, MACEDONIA-7000 Bitola •
[389] 47 293515, 222810, fax 203878 • arhiepohrid@t-home.mk
*28.2.1966 Bitola. NSlava? 1990 Fac Civil Engineering. 1990-1995 Fac theol Beograd. stud post-dipl. 1995-1996 Beograd, 1996-1997 Thessaloniki. 1997 preparing laurea Thessaloniki. 1998-2000 B Dremvica. mon7.2.1998 diak7.2.1998 ⊖8.2.1998 ⊕19.7.1998. 2000-2002 M Veles Povardarie. 2002 A Ohrid, M Skopje (Serbian Orthodox Church). 2011 Dr. theol Thessaloniki "Jedinstvo crkve i savremeni crkveni problemi" (Prof. Chrysostomos Stamulis).

Joakim Jakim Jovčevski
T: B Polog Kumanovo ▪ ✉ ul. 100, br. 31, MACEDONIA-1321 Kumanovo • [389] 31 444556
*7.11.1949 Lukovo Struga Makedonia. NSlava? 1992 absolvent theol. mon9.2.1996 Cetinje. diak1996 ⊖31.10.1996. 2001 igumen Rijeka Crnojeviča, teacher Cetinje ⊕30.11.2003 Beograd B Velički vicar. 2004 B Polog.

Marko Goran Kimev
T: B Breganica ▪ ✉ Sutjeska 12, MACEDONIA-2000 Štip •
[389] 32 388970 fax epmarko@poa-info.org • www.poa-info.org
*25.11.1977 Štip Makedonia. NSlava? 1997 Seminary Skopje. mon20.7.2002 diak2.8.2002 ⊖1.6.2003 ⊕7.12.2003. 2003 B Dremvica i mjestobljustitel bitolski, vicar. 2006 B Breganica.

David Janko Ninov
T: B Stoby ▪ ✉ Sava Kovačević 47 G/53, MACEDONIA-1000 Skopje • [389] 75 453648, fax [389] 2 748135 • epdavid@poa-info.org • www.poa-info.org
*27.7.1972 Skopje. NSlava? mon1996 diak1996 ⊖1997. 1999 igumen. 2004 Serbian Orthodox Church. 2004-2006 stud Thessaloniki ⊕17.6.2007.

The Russian Orthodox Old Believers' Church
Staryj obrjad

Kornilij Konstantin Ivanovič Titov *Moskva*
T: M Moskva and All Russia. The Russian Orthodox Old Believers' Church: Soglasie Belaja Krinica ▪ ✉ Rogožki Pasioluk 29, Rossija-109152 Moskva • [7] 495 361519-0, -1, Kancelaria -6, -2 • Redakcija 3610920, [7] 963 528 6776, besplatnij [7] 800 700 3900 • rpsc@rambler.ru • www.rpsc.ru

*1.8.1947 Orehovo-Zujevo. N? worked in a Foundry-Mechanical Factory, studied in Moscow Automotive Institute. diak1997 Orehovo-Zujevo (Alimpij Gusev) ⊖8.3. 2004 (Andrian Četvergov) mon14.3.2005 ⊕7.5.2005 B Kazan+Vjatka. 18.10.2005 M.

Zosima Zótik Jeremejev *Don*
T: B Don+Kavkas: Soglasie Belaja Krinica ▪ ✉ ul. Uljanovskaja 37, Rossija-344007 Rostov-na-Donu • [7] 8632 625431 • www.iz.drevle.ru

*1941 Sirkovo Moldavia N? ⊕21.10.1993 B Kišinjev, 2005 B Don.

Vikentij Valentin Novožilov *Jaroslavl*
T: B Jaroslavl+Kostroma: Soglasie Belaja Krinica ▪ ✉ ul. Volgarej 4, Rossija-156001 Kostroma • [7] 4942 514728 • dom Širokaja 13, 156001 Kostroma 668315, 535331

2004 Candidate for bishop's ordination, protoierej nastojatjel Durasovo. mon14.8. 2010 ⊕6.3.2011 B Jaroslavl+Kostroma.

Savvatij Stefan Kozko *Kiev*
T: A Kiev+Ukraina: Soglasie Belaja Krinica ▪ ✉ vul. Počajninska 26, Ukraina-04070 Kiev • [380] 44 4164228, 202 8748, [380] 50 334 7401 • agenvest@kiev.ua • www.starobryad.narod.ru

*11.4.1942 Kirovograd. N20.9. fashion designer. diak28.8.1987 ⊖30.8.1987 ⊕23.2.1993 B Kiev, 1996, 1998, 1999, 2002 Ostkirchliches Institut Regensburg. 1996 relics Metropolitan Amvrosij Trieste. 2012 A Kiev+Ukraina.

Jevmenij Jevgenij Mihejev *Kišinjev*
T: B Kišinjev+Moldova: Soglasie Belaja Krinica ▪ ✉ Mazaraki 3/5, Moldova-27700 Kišinjev • [373] 22 54-4839, -4733, -4788, -4439 • episkopia@mail.ru

*17.5.1942 Kandalakša Murmansk. N? 1954 Handicraft Institute Šuvoje Moskva. 1968-1999 married. diak1968 ⊖1968 Vereja Moskva. mon17.11.2004 Rogožk. kladbišče ⊕2.1.2005 B Kišinjev.

Silujan Simon Kilin ***Novosibirsk***
T: B Novosibirsk+Sibiria: Soglasie Belaja Krinica ▪ ✉ Starobrjad Hram, Bajdukova 1, ROSSIJA-630123 Novosibirsk • [7] 383 2002007, 2430623
*15.5.1939 Podojnikovo Altaj. N? Novonikolajevska Novosibirsk engineer. 1958-1961 Soviet Army Sachalin, Radiotechnik. 1961-1966 hypodiakon eparchy Kišinjev. Soglasie Belaja Krinica. 1962 marriage. diak25.12.1966 ⊖25.12.1966. 1966-1987 rector parish Kišinjev, 1987-1992 Minussinsk Chahasia Krasnojarsk. mon18.10.1992 Novonikolajevska Novosibirsk ⊕18.10.1992 B Novonikolajevska Novosibirsk. 1994 Ostkirchliches Institut Regensburg.

Viktor Kostromin ***Sankt-Peterburg***
T: B Sankt-Peterburg+Tver ▪ ✉ prospekt Aleksandrovskoj fermy 20, P.O.Box 38, ROSSIJA-192289-Sankt-Peterburg •
[7] 812 9258291 o. Gennadij Čunin
⊕18.10.2012 B Sankt-Peterburg+Tver.

Patermufie Pjotr Artemihin ***Irkutsk***
T: B Irkutsk-Amur+Far East ▪ ✉ ul. Iljiča 28, ROSSIJA-680018 Khabarovsk
*1952 Gorodišče Lugansk Ukraina N? ⊕28.4.2010 Moskva B Ussurijsk+Far East (M Kornilij).

Leontij Izot Lavrente ***Belacrinița***
T: Metropolit Belacrinița and All Oldorthodox Christians, Mitropolia Cultului Creştin de Rit Vechi ▪ ✉ str. Zidari 5/1, ROMANIA-810140 Brăila • [40] 239 611341, 645755 • kantsler 647023, fax 613915
*1964 N? ⊕1996 Brăila M "Biserica creştină de rit vechi (lipoveană)".

Nafanail Ikim ***Bukovina***
T: A Bukovina-Moldavia ▪ ✉ str. Zidari 5/1, ROMANIA-810140 Brăila • [40] 239 611341, 645755, kantsler 647023, fax 613915
⊕2001 B Roman Soglasie Belaja Krinica. 2012 A Bukovina-Moldavia.

Dionisie Alexandru ***Brăila***
T: B Brăila ▪ ✉ str. Zidari 5/1, ROMANIA-810140 Brăila •
[40] 239 647023, 645755
⊕23.11.2005 B Brăila.

Flavian ***Tulcea***
T: A Tulcea ▪ ✉ str. Zidari 5/1, ROMANIA-810140 Brăila • [40] 240 551633 [40] 744 499786 • vl_flavian@zappmobile.ro • vladflavian@psse.ro • vladflavian@yahoo.ca • www.psse.ro
⊕5.6.2000 B, 24.6.2000 A Slavsskij.

Antipa Dzhambul Skhulukhij
T: B former Zugdidi+Kolchida: Soglasie Belaja Krinica ▪
⊕23.11.2005 B Zugdidi Georgia. 22.10.2013 Holy Synod Braila decided: monk.

Sofronij Sergej Lipali *USA*
T: B USA, Canada, Australia ▪ ✉ 12971 Bethlehem Drive, 09 N.E., USA-Gervais, Oregon 97026 • [1] 503 981-1637, -1629, fax -5278
*1958 Carcaleo România. N? 1991 USA iconographer. diak14.10.1995 ⊖4.3.1996 ⊕5.3.1996 B USA, Canada, Australia.

Sergij Chalovskij *Öskemen*
T: B Ust-Kamenogorsk ▪ ✉ KAZAKHSTAN-070001Öskemen
⊖19.7.2010 hram Pokrovskj Ust-Kamenogorsk (B Siluan Novosibirsk). 2010-2014 parish Bobrovka East Kazahstan ⊕21.10.2014 B Ust-Kamenogorsk.

Evfimij Dubinov *Kazan*
T: B Kazan+Vjatka ▪ ✉ Ostrovskogo 81, ROSSIJA-420107 Kazan • [7] 8432 2388742 • www.kavera.ru
⊕9.8.2011 B Kazan+Vjatka.

Grigorij Gennadij Korobeinikov *Tomsk*
T: B Tomsk ▪ ✉ ul. Jakovleva 4, ROSSIJA-634003 Tomsk • [7] 2822 659862
*9.9.1948 Chernaja Rechka Ishevsk. 1949 family moved to Izhevsk to be near to staroobr. church St. Mary. school Izhevsk, Technikum Sarapul, Soviet Army. 1971 married to Anna Zadvornova ⊖22.5.1976 Saratov (A Nikodim Latyshev). 1976-1986 parish Saratov and parish Jekaterinburg. 1986 parish Tomsk, family (9 children) moved to Tomsk. 1993 protoierej (B Siluan, Novosibirsk). 25.12.2014 matushka Anna died (28 grandchildren). mon14.9.2015 (B Evfimij, Kazan) ⊕25.10.2015 Cathedral Rogozh Moskva B Pokrov (M Kornilij; A Flavian, Slavsk; B Siluan, Novosibirsk; B Zosima, Don+Kavkas; B Jevmenij, Moldova; B Patermufij, Irkutsk; B Vikentij, Jaroslavl; B Jevfimij, Kazan).

Sava Chalovskij
T: B ▪
23.10.2015 Holy Synod confirmed candidate for B.

Syrian Orthodox Church of Antioch

His Holiness, **Ignatius Cyril II.**
Syrian Orthodox Patriarch of Antiochia and all the East
Supreme Head of the Universal Syrian Orthodox Church

Ignatius Cyril Aphrem Karim
T: M Süryoye Patriarch of Antiochia and all the East ▪ ✉ Bab Touma P.O.Box 22260, SYRIA-Damas • [963] 11 5418100, 543240-1, fax -0, 5951870 • hasio@syrianorthodoxchurch.org • www.syrian-orthodox.com
*1965 Qamishly Syria. N? 1977-1982 stud St. Ephrem's Theol Seminary Atchane Lebanon. 1982-1984 Archdiocese Aleppo. 1984-1988 Coptic Theol Seminary Cairo B.D. mon1985 Cairo diak1985 Cairo ⊖1985 Qamishly. 1989-1994 St. Patrick's Maynooth with CCCC scholarship. 1994 Dr. theol ⊕28.1.1996 Qamishly Patriarchal Vicar Eastern USA (Mor Ignatius Zakka). 31.3.2014 Patriarch.

Maurice Yacoub Amsih
T: B assistant Patriarch ▪ ✉ P.O.Box 22260, SYRIA-Damas
⊕29.6.2015 B Director Department Public Relations and Protocol.

Gergess Kourieh Kourieh
T: B Director Seminary of Saint Ephrem Saydnaya ▪ ✉ Seminary of Saint Ephrem Ma'aret-Saydnaya, SYRIA-Damas • [963] 1 5951870
⊕29.6.2015 B Director Seminary of St. Ephrem Saydnaya.

Dionysius Jean Kawak *USA*
T: A Syriac Orthodox Archbishop of U.S.A. ▪ ✉ P.O. Box 22060, Bab Touma, SYRIA-Damas • [963] 96 303 424, [963] 11 595 18-70, fax -80 • jeankawak@hotmail.com
*27.5.1966 John Aziz. N? stud Economics Damascus University, stud theol St. Ephrem. 1984 Koroyo. 1988 subdeacon. mon1989 diak1990. 1990-1995 Istituto Orientale Roma ⊖10.7.1994. 1994 MTh ⊕21.3.2010 B for the Patriarchal curia Saidnaya (Mor Ignatius Zakka). 2015 Syriac Orthodox A of USA.

Eustathius Matta Roham *Jazirah*
T: M Jazirah+Euphrates ▪ ✉ P.O.Box 327, SYRIA-Hassake • [963] 52 312984, 320817, fax 312954 • tnener@aloola.sy • tnener@scs-net.org • matta.rohan@gmail.com
*24.11.1956 Qamishly Syria. N? diak1975. 1975-1983 in the patriarchate. 1982 BA Damascus University ⊖5.2.1984. 1984-1990 priest USA. 1987 MDiv General Theological Seminary New York. 1990 MA Catholic University of America

⊕1.7.1990 M Jazirah+Euphrates (Mor Ignatius Zakka). 1991 Dr. theol h.c. General Theol Seminary New York. 2006-2013 Member Central Committee WCC Geneva.

Timotheos Matta Al-Khoury ***Damascus***

T: Patriarchal vicar of Damascus ▪ ✉ B.O.Box 327, SYRIA-Hassake • [963] 53 312984 • malkhor4@hotmail.com

*1982 N? ⊕4.11.2012 Patriarchal Secretary (Mor Ignatius Zakka). 2015 M Jazirah. 11.3.2016 Patriarchal vicar of Damascus (Mor Ignatius Cyril II.).

Iwannis Boulos Al-Souqi

T: B, former Patriarchal vicar of Damascus ▪ ✉ P.O. Box 22260, Bab Touma, SYRIA-Damas • [963] 11 5418100, 5421150, fax 5443443, p 4456546

*14.2.1952 Homs Syria. N? married priest. Theology Course Atchane, Lebanon ⊕1.4.1990 (Mor Ignatius Zakka). 1990-2016 M Damascus, retired.

Gregorios Yohanna Ibrahim ***Aleppo***

T: M A Aleppo ▪ ✉ Mar Simon Al-Amoodi, Sulaimanieh 1 P.O.Box 4194, SYRIA-Aleppo • [963] 21 464030-4, p -5, 2210423, fax 4642260, 4655372, [963] 944 2466565 • margregorius79@yahoo.com • margregorius79@hotmail.com • morgregorius@gmail.com • www.alepposuryoye.com

*18.8.1948 Qamishly, Syria. N? mon26.7.1973. 1973-1976 Istituto Orientale Roma Scienze eccl., Diritto canonico. diak13.2.1976 ⊖15.2.1976. 1976-1977 Patr vicar Sweden. 1977-1979 rector Seminary Atchane Lebanon ⊕4.3.1979 A Aleppo (Mor Ignatius Yakoub III). 1980-1993 Member Central Committee WCC. 1980 Standing Committee Pro Oriente Wien. 1984 Standing Committee Syriac Dialogue. 1985 Board Faith and Order WCC Geneva. 1985-1987 Dr. artium Birmingham. 1988 Founder Al Raha Mardin Publishing House Aleppo. 1999 Commission Orthodox WCC Geneva. 1999-2003 Member Executive Committee Middle East Council of Churches MECC, Consultant "Uomini e Religione" Roma. 2013 kidnapped together with Antiochian M Aleppo.

Silvanos Petros Issa Al-nemeh ***Homs***

T: M Homs+Hama ▪ ✉ Patriarch Aphrem St., Boustan Eldiwan, SYRIA-Homs • [963] 31 2487346, fax 2482006, [963] 944479440 • selwanos@hotmail.com • www.zunoro.org

*4.9.1968 N? ⊕12.12.1999 Zakka M Homs (Mor Ignatius).

Daniel Climis Kourieh ***Beirut***

T: M Beirut rector Seminary ▪ ✉ Syrian Orth Seminary, Atchane, LEBANON-Bikfaiya • [961] 4 884446-7, -8 • Archbishopric Museitbeh, Beirut [961] 1 317275, fax 303373, [961] 3 275360

*27.8.1972 N? B.Th. Greece ⊕18.2.2007 Damas Mor Ignatius Zakka M Baden-Württemberg Bayern. Warburg. 1.9.2007 rector Seminary. 2009 M Beirut.

Chrysostomos Michael Shemoun
T: M Institutions ▪ ✉ Syrian Orth Institutions, Atchane, LEBANON-Bikfaiya • [961] 4 9836-73, -83, fax 984447 • mchmoun70@hotmail.com
*1970 Kamishli Syria. N? 2001 dipl theol Athens ⊕11.4.2011 (Mor Ignatius Zakka).

Philoxenos Mattai Shemoun
T: M ▪ ✉ Syrian Orth Seminary, Atchane, LEBANON-Bikfaiya • [961] 4 884446-7-8
*19.8.1930 Bartellah Iraq N? ⊖9.2.1958 ⊕25.11.1979. Mor Ignatius Yakoub III. 1979-2005 M rector Seminary. Wyrwoll in Atchane with M Theophilos, Kerala.

Timotheos Aphrem Aboodi
T: former M Canada ▪ ✉ Syrian Orth Seminary, Atchane, LEBANON-Bikfaiya
*1.1.1930 Mossul. N? mon16.2.1953 diak14.12.1954 ⊖25.3.1956 ⊕9.1.1972. (Mor Ignatius Yakoub III.) 1977 A Skandinavia+United Kingdom. 1986 Patriarchal vicar United Kingdom. 1991-1997 Patriarchal Vicar Australia. 1997-2008 M Canada.

Yustinos Paulos Safar ***Zahle***
T: M, Patriarchal vicar Zahle Bekaa ▪ ✉ St. George Church Al Midan, Boite 260, LEBANON-Zahle • [961] 8 820588, fax 810851, [961] 3 907222 • paolos50@hotmail.com
*18.3.1970 Qamishly. N? 1988-1993 stud med dent Aleppo. 1993 stud St. Ephrem Seminary. diak11.3.1995. 1995-1996 dipl theol Bari/Università Angelicum Roma. 1996-2000 PhD Canon Law Oriental Institut Roma ⊖23.3.1997 ⊕17.4.2005 (Mor Ignatius Zakka), 2011 jubilee of B Nifon, Antiochia with Wyrwoll and Netherlands ambassador Dirkse.

Theophilos Georges Saliba ***Mount Lebanon***
T: A Mount Lebanon ▪ ✉ P.O.Box 90420 Bouchrieh, Fardous St., LEBANON-Beirut • [961] 1 69031-2, -3, fax -4, p 68386-4, -5, [961] 3 780878 • bgsaliba@hotmail.com
*31.3.1945 Qamishly Syria. N? 1958-1962 Seminary Mossul. 1962-1967 teacher religion Syriac Qamishli. 1967-1977 principal Seminary Zahle ⊖23.3.1969. 1973 Patriarchal Vicar Lebanon ⊕8.2.1981. 14.9.2002 Mor Ignatius Zakka secretary Holy Synod. 2004 Mondo Migliore. 2011 International Joint Commission Theol Dialogue between Catholic and Oriental Orthodox Churches.

Severius Jamil Hawa ***Baghdad***
T: M Baghdad, Basra ▪ ✉ Syrian Orth Archbishopric, P.O.Box 843, IRAQ-Baghdad • [964] 1 7196320, 7181668, fax 7197583
*14.4.1931 Mossul. N? 1951-1953 secretary Patr Barsum Homs. 1953-1961 Seminary Mossul ⊖5.3.1955. 1961-1970 Vicar Patr Brazil ⊕18.10.1970 Damascus Vicar Patr. (Mor Ignatius Yakoub III.) 1977 Ostkirchliches Institut Regensburg. 22.10.1980 A Baghdad.

Nikodemos Dawood Sharaf ***Mossul***
T: M Mossul ▪ ✉ Syrian Orth Archbishopric, P.O.B. 11299, IRAQ-Mossul • [964] 60 817861, 815565, [964] 770122581, 774122581
*diak ⊖10.3.1976 N? ⊕27.11.2011 (Mor Ignatius Zakka).

Grigorios Saliba Shemoun
T: former M Mossul ▪ ✉ Syrian Orth Archbishopric, IRAQ-Mossul • [964] 60 817861, 815565, [964] 770122581, 774122581
*14.9.1932 Bartellah, Iraq. N? 1946-1953 stud Seminary Mossul. mon1954 diak1954. 1954-1960 teacher Seminary Mossul Syriac, English, Theology ⊖15.12.1958. 1960-1970 secretary to Patriarch Damas ⊕3.8.1969 (Mor Ignatius Yakoub III). 1969-2011 M Mossul, retired.

Timotheos Moussa Shamani ***Mor Matta***
T: A Mor Matta ▪ ✉ Syrian Orthodox, Bartellah Ninive, Hamdanieh, IRAQ-Mossul • [964] 60 313518, 313800
*1966 N? ⊕16.12.2005 (Mor Ignatius Zakka).

Severius Malki Murad ***Jerusalem***
T: M, Vicar Patriarchal Jerusalem Jordan ▪ ✉ St. Mark's Convent, P.O.Box 14069, ISRAEL-91140 Jerusalem •
[972] 2 62833-21, -04, fax 26277024, [972] 544 428030
*5.2.1965 Malkiyah Hassakeh Syria. N? 1977-1982 dipl St. Ephrem Orth Seminary Atchane Lebanon. 1982-1989 secretary to Patriarch Ignatius Zakka ⊖24.8.1986. 1989-1993 Principal St. Ephrem Seminary Damas. 1992 BA theol Coptic College Cairo. 1993-1996 Patriarchal Vicar Brazil ⊕15.9.1996 in St. Ephrem Monastery Maarrat Saidnayeh Vicar Jerusalem, Holy Land, Jordan (Mor Ignatius Zakka). 2009 represented by fr. Paulos delegation German bishops.

Bartholomew Nathanel Youssef ***Jerusalem***
T: M, Patriarchal Vicar of Arabian Golf and Emirates ▪ ✉ P.O.Box 81405 SHJ, EMIRATES-Sharjah • [971] 50 160 2259 • rabannathan@hotmail.com
*diak ⊖3.11.1975 ⊕26.10.2012 M Patriarchal Vicar of Arabian Golf and Emirates (Mor Ignatius Zakka).

Timotheos Samuel Aktaş ***Turabdin***
T: M Turabdin ▪ ✉ P.K. No 4, TURKEY-47510 Midyat • [90] 482 4621018, 213751-2, -3, fax -4
*1.1.1945 Bakisyan Alagöz Tur Abdin. N? 1961-1973 Monastery Mor Gabriel. diak1964 mon1964. 1967 Military Service. 1967-1969 director school Mor Gabriel ⊖1968. 1969 stud theol USA ⊕10.2.1985 (Mor Ignatius Zakka).

Filüksinos Yusuf Çetin ***İstanbul***
T: M, Patriarchal Vicar İstanbul+Ankara+İzmir ▪ ✉ Beyoğlu Tarlabaşı, Karakurum Sokak 10, TURKEY-34440 İstanbul • [90] 212 2501606, 2504059, 238547-0, -1, fax 2505827 • ist.suryaniortodoxmetropolitligi@mynet.com • www.syriankadim.org
*20.8.1954 Karburan Dargeçit Turabdin Turkey. N? School Dargeçit. 1969-1983 Monastery Mor Gabriel ⊖1977. 1984-1986 Director Mor Efrem Seminary Damas ⊕28.9.1986. (Mor Ignatius Zakka). 1986 Patriarchal Vicar İstanbul+Ankara+Izmir.

Philoxenus Saliba Özmen ***Mardin***
T: A Mardin ▪ ✉ Deyrulzafaran, P.K. No 6, TURKEY-47100 Mardın • [90] 482 219308-2, fax -5, [90] 533 656 3481 • salibazmen4@gmail.com
*1.1.1964 Marbobo. stud Monasteries Deyrulzafaran and Mor Gabriel, mon1985 diak1985 ⊖1993.1993-1998 teacher Mor Gabriel. 1998-2002 stud St. Anne's College Oxford, 2002 Master Syriac Studies. 2002 abbot Deyrulzafaran ⊕9.2.2003 Maarat Sednaya Mor Ephrem Seminary (Mor Ignatius Zakka) 8.7.2015 Tarlabaşı. 23.-30.11.2015 34th Ecumenical Meeting for Bishops, İstanbul.

Ğriğoriyos Melki Ürek ***Adıyaman***
T: M Adıyaman, Patriarchal vicar ▪ ✉ Süryani Kadim Mor Petrus Mor Pavlus Kilisesi, P.K. No.19, TURKEY-02030 Adıyaman • [90] 416 213 36 73, fax 216 55 36, [90] 533 375 55 81 • rabanmurek@hotmail.com • www.adiyamanmetropolitligi.org
*1.1.1959 Midin Turabdin. N? School Midin. 1972-1973 monastery Deyrulzafaran. 1973 Koruyo. 1973-1976 İstanbul Electro-technician. 1976-1978 Stuttgart. 1978-1979 Deyrulzafaran Turabdin. mon1979 (Mor Ivennis Efrem Bilgiç). 1979-1981 military service Samsun, İstanbul. 1981 Deyrulzafaran Turabdin. 1981-1993 stud Mor Gabriel. diak1984 Çankaya (Mor Filuksinos Ilyas) ⊖5.8.1985 (Mor Themoteos Saumi). 1993 Linz. 1993-1994 Regensburg (Ignatius Zakka Iwas). 1994-1996 Losser Glane Netherlands. 1996-1998 opened monastery Warburg. 2001 Maara Saidnaja cross Efitrufo (Epitropos) ⊕10.12.2006 Deyrulzafaran M Adıyaman (Mor Ignatius Zakka).

Dionysius Isa Gürbüz ***Helvetia***
T: M Helvetia Austria, Patriarchal Vicar ▪ ✉ St. Augin Klosterstraße 10, SUISSE-6415 Arth • [41] 41 855-1270, fax -3007
*1.1.1963 Keferze Tur Abdin (Altıntaş Köyü). N? 1984-1985 stud Monastery Mar Gabriel mon1985. 1985-1986 England. 1986-1991 teacher Syriac Mor Ephrem Seminary Damas ⊖1991 (Ignatius Zakka Iwas). 1991-1993 parish Egypt. 1993-1996 spiritual director Mor Ephrem Seminary Damas ⊕15.9.1996 Damas (Mor Ignatius Zakka) 1996-1997 Synkellos, Patriarchal vicar Bab Touma. 1997-2006 Patriarchal vicar Germany, 2006 M Helvetia.

Philoxenus Mattias Nayis ***Deutschland***
T: B Deutschland ▪ ✉ Klosterstraße 10, GERMANY-34414 Warburg • [49] 5641 740564, fax 741868, [49] 171 5388588 • mattiasnayis@hotmail.com • mattiasnayis@yahoo.com
*24.1.1977 Stockholm. N? 1991 Koroyo. mon7.1.1994 diak6.6.1998 ⊖20.2.2000. 2000 vice-principal, 2004 principal Mor Ephrem Seminary Saydnaya. 2006 English course Cambridge ⊕7.1.2007 Damas B assistant to the Patriarch, principal (Mor Ignatius Zakka) 2012 B Deutschland.

Julius Hanna Aydın
T: A, Patriarcal vicar ▪ ✉ Elsfletherstraße 2, GERMANY-27751 Delmenhorst • [49] 4221 16591, [49] 176 68809898 • abt_aydin@web.de
*1.4.1947 Mzizah Midyat. N? Turkish school Mzizah. 1959-1962 Church school Mzizah. 1962-1968 cutler Mzizah. 1968-1969 military service, chauffeur, music. 1969-1973 St. George's Austrian School Lazarists İstanbul. Technical dipl. 1973-1974 stud Atchane Lebanon. 1974-1975 stud Ostkirchliches Institut Regensburg. 1975-1978 stud phil theol OFM Schwaz Tirol, 1978-1982 stud Eichstätt. diak7.5.1978 Hengelo. 1982 dipl theol Eichstätt "Mönche im Tur Abdin". 1985 assistant Prof. Hübner Eichstätt ⊖28.5.1993 Losser. 1993-1995 stud Münster and Bochum (Prof. Peter Bruns, Geerling). mon1997 Warburg. 2002 PhD Cath Malankara Institute Kottayam ⊕18.2.2007 Damas. B Deutschland (Mor Ignatius Zakka) 2012 Vicar for the political and ecclesiastical affairs in Germany.

Severios Hazael Saome ***Belgium***
T: M Belgium France Luxemburg, Patriarchal Vicar ▪
✉ Av. Franz Guillaume 80, BELGIUM-1140 Evere •
[32] 476 991414, fax [1] 209 2548388 • hazail@hotmail.com
*5.11.1965 N? ⊕12.2.2007.

Polycarpus Augin Aydin ***Netherlands***

T: B Netherlands, Patriarchal Vicar ▪ ✉ St. Ephrem der Syrier Klooster, Glanerbrugstraat 33, NETHERLANDS-7585 PK Glane • [31] 53 461-4764, fax -5879, [31] 6 4602 1353 • monastery@morephrem.com • info@morephrem.com • polycarpus@me.com • www.morephrem.com

*10.6.1971 Gundukşikro Gundukke d-'Ito Nisibis. N? 1982-1988 Mor Gabriel Seminary Tur'Abdın. 1992-1995 BDiv Heythrop College London. 1996-1997 Oxford Oriental Syriac Studies. 1997-2000 MDiv St. Vladimir's New York. 2001 Ecumenical Institute Bossey. mon7.10.2001 St. Ephrem Damas (Mor Ignatius Zakka) ⊖4.8.2002 Mor Gabriel Tur'Abdın (A Samuel Aktaş) 2002 Dr. theol Princeton Theol Seminary ⊕15.4.2007 Damas, B Netherlands (Mor Ignatius Zakka).

Athanasius Toma Dawod Dakama ***England***

T: A England, Patriarchal Vicar ▪ ✉ St. Thomas Cathedral, 7-11 Armstrong Rd, GREAT BRITAIN-London,W3 7JL • [44] 20 8749 5834 • [44] 20 8654 7531, [44] 776 4432218 • athanasiustoma@yahoo.co.uk

*1965 Mossul N? ⊕3.12.2006 Damas (Mor Ignatius Zakka) 2012 England.

Julius Abdullahad Shabo ***Skandinavia***

T: M Sweden+Skandinavia ▪ ✉ Syr -Orth Archdiocese, Förvaltar Vägen 38, SWEDEN-15147 Södertälje • [46] 8 550-656 44, 55086086, fax 550 868 83

*8.3.1951 Qamishly Syria. N? 1962-1968 Seminary Mar Ephrem Zahle. 1968-1971 Seminary Mar Ephrem Atchane, dipl English, Arabic, Syriac. 1968-1975 teacher Seminary Atchane. mon12.11.1972 St. Peter and Paul Beirut (Mor Ignatius Jakoub III.) diak2.12.1973 Beirut (Mor Ignatius Jakoub III.) ⊖6.3.1977 Damascus (Mor Ignatius Jakoub III.). 1977-1980 head Eccl Court Damascus. 1980-1981 secretary to Patr Ignatius Zakka Iwas. 1981-1982 Selly Oak Colleges Birmingham, dipl Islam. 1982-1984 University Birmingham, MA Christian Muslim Relations, MA Biblical Studies, 1984 University Durham PhD Oriental Studies. 1984-1986 Representative to Anglican Church and British Council of Churches. 1986-1987 principal Seminary Atchane ⊕3.5.1987 A Sweden and Skandinavia (Mor Ignatius Zakka).

Dioskoros Beniamin Ataş

T: M Patriarchal Vicar Sweden ▪ ✉ Syrian Orth Archdiocese St. Ephrem, Klockarvägen 110, SWEDEN-15161 Södertälje • [46] 8 550-61170, -61176, -84140 fax -84300, [46] 707741607

*3.1.1964 Turkey. N? 1983-1986 Polhem Gymn. Stockholm. diak1984. 1986-1990 stud theol St. Ephrem Losser. mon1988 ⊖1989. 1991-1994 stud rel Felician College New Jersey ⊕13.2.1996 (Mor Ignatius Zakka).

Malatios Malki Lahdo *Australia*

T: M Australia, Patriarchal Vicar ▪ ✉ P.O.Box 257, 82 Joseph Street, AUSTRALIA-Lidcombe, NSW2141 • [61] 2 9749-5035, -4608 fax -2442, -2826 • mor_malatios@hotmail.com • mormalatios@gmail.com

*3.1.1971 Guerke Shamo Syria at the border with Turkey. N? Syrian Orth elementary school Qamishly. 1984-1989 Mor Ephraim Seminary Damascus. mon24.12.1989 (Mor Ignatius Zakka). 1991-1994 teacher Syriac Malankara Seminary Kerala. 1994 dipl theol. 1994-1996 patriarchal secretary Damascus ⊖1996. 1996-2001 BDiv Athens. 2001-2003 Södertälje Sweden ⊕7.9.2003 Damas Patriarchal Vicar M Australia (Mor Ignatius Zakka) 2003 MDiv Athens.

Athanasius Elia Bahi *Canada*

T: M Patriarchal Vicar Canada ▪ ✉ 4375 Henri Bourassa West, CANADA-St. Laurent, Que H4L1A5 • [1] 514 334-6993, fax -8233, [1] 514 2997474 • eliabahi@hotmail.com • www.syrianorthodoxcurch.com

⊕9.2.2003 Maarat Sednaya Mor Ephrem Seminary (Mor Ignatius Zakka) 2003 assistant to the Patriarch. 2008 Canada.

Climis Eugene Kaplan *West USA*

T: M Patriarchal Vicar Western USA ▪ ✉ 900 N. Glenoaks Blvd., USA-Burbank, CA51501 • [1] 818 8455089, 9537107, fax 818 4952440, E-fax [1] 206 2033813 • morclemis@hotmail.com • www.soc-wus.org

*1.1.1955 Qamishly Syria. N? mon27.6.1971. 1982-1991 Principal of Mor Gabriel Theol Seminary Turkey ⊖4.12.1983 ⊕12.4.1991. M Patriarchal assistant Damascus (Mor Ignatius Zakka) 1996 M Patriarchal vicar of the Western Archdiocese of the USA.

Yacoub Eduardo Aguirre Oestmann *Guatemala*

T: A Central America ▪ ✉ Syrian Orthodox, La Torre km 27.5, GUATEMALA-03008 San Lucas Sacatepéquez • [502] 78303512, 57091024 • icergua@gmail.com • eaguirrecesme@yahoo.com • www.icergua.org

⊕6.3.2013 A Central America, Iglesia Catolica Ecumenica renovada ICERGUA (Mor Ignatius Zakka).

Chrysostomos Yuhana Ghassali *Argentina*

T: M Patriarchal Vicar Argentina ▪ ✉ Patriarchal-Vicariate of Argentina, Calle 46 No.680 Piso 9 Dto 3, ARGENTINA-La Plata • [54] 221 5371744 [54] 9221 548 6826 • morchrysostom@yahoo.com

*19.9.1971 Syria. N? 1996 Civil Engineer University Aleppo. 1996-1999 dipl theol St. Ephrem monastery. mon20.7.1999 St. Ephrem. diak17.8.1999. 2000-2011 Patriarchal Representative and chaplain of the Syrian Church Greece ⊖5.8.2001.

archim6.9.2005. 2008 MTh University Athens "The christological teaching of St. Cyril of Alexandria in his two letters to the Queens". 2011-2013 teacher St. Ephrem Seminary ⊕28.2.2013, (all ordinations by His Holiness Ignatius Zakka) 2013 vicar Argentina.

Nicolaos Matti Abd Alahad

T: M▪ ✉ P.O.Box 22260, Bab Touma, SYRIA-Damas • rabanm10@hotmail.com • rabanm10@yahoo.com

*6.4.1970. N? Director St. Ephrem Seminary Mossul ⊕17.4.2005 (Mor Ignatius Zakka) 2005-2013 vicar Argentina.

Theethose Paulose Jorge Hanna ***Brazil***

T: B Brazil ▪ ✉ rua 14 de Julho, BRAZIL-79004 Campo Grande MS • [55] 67 3841515, 3247937, QN.208 Conjunto A Lt. o3, BRAZIL-72316 Sanambaia MS • [55] 61 3357 0720 • [55] 61 8582 8217 • blestuza@hotmail.com • blestuza@yahoo.com

*1.5.1961 ⊕19.2.2012 B Brazil (Mor Ignatius Zakka).

Malankara Jacobite Syrian Orthodox Church

Baselios Thomas I. ***Ankamaly***

T: His Beatitude, Mor Divannasios Thomas, Catholicos of the East ▪ ✉ Mount Sinai, INDIA-686691 Kothamangalam Kerala • [91] 484 -2732804, fax -2732624, [91] 485-2822197, 2822101, 2822485 • patriarchalcentre@yahoo.com • www.syrianchurch.org

*22.7.1929 Vadayampady. N? school Puthencruz. 1956-1957 Seminary Malelcruz ⊖21.9.1958. 1958-1966 parishes outside Kerala. 1966-1974 organizing secretary Hospital Kothamangalam ⊕24.2.1974 Damas M Ankamaly (Mor Ignatius Zakka). 6.-22.11.1995 OKI Regensburg and Trient focolare. 16.- 21.11.1996 London 15th Ecumenical meeting for Bishops with deacon Saji. 27.11.1996 OKI. 2002 Catholicos. 21.-23.11.2004 OKI İstanbul 23rd Ecumenical meeting with Dr. Adai und Theophilos (Saji). 2012 Germany.

Severios Abraham

T: M assistant Ankamaly, M of Mor Gabriyel Brotherhood ▪ ✉ Vengola P.O., INDIA-683548 Perumbavoor Kerala • [91] 484 2525937, 944 7465350

*12.4.1941 Peechanikadu Kerala N? ⊖1963. 1971-1973 Academy Leningrad, 1973-1974 Oxford. PhD Pacific Western University ⊕6.3.1982 assistant M Ankamaly, D.D. 1994 Perumbavoor. 1999-2005 "India".

Julios Elias
T: B assistant to the Katholikos ▪ ✉ St. Thomas Collector Nagar, Syrian Church Road 9, INDIA-600101 Chennai • [91] 9605796231
⊕2.1.2012 B assistant.

Alexandros Thomas
T: B assistant to the Katholikos ▪ ✉ St. Thomas Collector Nagar, Syrian Church Road 9, INDIA-600101 Chennai • [91] 9605796231
⊕2.1.2012 B assistant.

Polycarpus Zacharias
T: B assistant to the Katholikos ▪ ✉ St. Thomas Collector Nagar, Syrian Church Road 9, SYRIA-600101 Chennai • [91] 9605796231
⊕2.1.2012 assistant.

Themotheos Thomas ***Kottayam***
T: M Kottayam ▪ ✉ St. Joseph's Cathedral, L.B. Sastri Road, INDIA-686001 Kottayam Kerala • [91] 481 2304646, [91] 944 7114646 • tmstheos@sancharnet.in
*22.5.1950 Muriankal. N? diak1964. 1967-1970 Kottayam BA, 1973 MA Kerala, BEducation Pandalam. 1973-1975 Mar Ignatius Dayara Manjinikkara ⊖21.5.1975. 1976-1984 MTh Bangalore. 1980 BDiv Bangalore. 1987-1990 stud theol Göttingen ⊕3.1.1991 M Outside Kerala Diocese. 1991-2002 President Seminary. 1999-2002 President Holy Synod. 2000 also Kottayam.

Gregorios Joseph ***Kochi***
T: M Kochi, assistant Kotthamangalam Region ▪ ✉ Kyomtha Seminary, INDIA-682305 Thiruvamkulam Kerala • [91] 484 2777400, fax 2780540 • [91] 984 7037644 • hasiojoseph@gmail.com • josephmorgregorios@yahoo.com • mail@gregorianpublicschool.org • www.syrianorthodoxchurch-india.org • www.gregorianpublicschool.org
*10.11.1960 Mulanthuruthy Kerala. N? diak25.3.1974 ⊖25.3.1984. 1984-1988 Bangalore. 1988-1992 stud Trinity College Dublin Ireland with scholarship CCCC: BA, BDiv, MPhil. parish ministry. 1988-1992 London, 1993-1994 New York ⊕16.1.1994 M Kochi. 7.-10.11.1996 OKI Regensburg. 16.-21.11.1996 OKI London 15th Ecumenical meeting for Bishops.

Geevarghese Divannasios
T: M, of the Simhasana Churches and Institutions of the Holy Apostolic See in India ▪ ✉ Mar Ignatius Dayara, INDIA-689657 Mathoor Pathanamthitta Kerala • [91] 473 232392, 2353392, 2353192, [91] 468 2353392, [91] 944 7287953 • deevannasios@yahoo.com

*5.5.1948 Vattamalakkunnel-Karimbil family Pampady. N? M.G.M. school Pampady, Baselios college Kottayam. stud theol Manjanikkara Dayro. diak(Aprem Aboodi) ⊖1.1.1974. Syriac scholar "Masbolono Thoba" ⊕8.12.2002 Damas M Ankamaly (Patr Ignatius) 2004 M Simhasana.

Ivanios Mathews ***Kandanadu***

T: M Kandanadu ▪ ✉ Mor Baselius II. Catholicose Centre, Kadakkanad, INDIA-682311 Kolenchery Kerala • [91] 484 2768925, [91] 944 7510135

*29.4.1955 Kandanadu, Joy. N? MA B. theol Papal Seminary Pune ⊖1976. 1997-2001 Admin Kandanadu ⊕14.1.2001 Damascus Kandanadu and Thrissur, 2006 Kandanadu.

Yuhannon Militios ***Thumpamon***

T: M Thumpamon, Dubai, Abu Dhabi ▪ ✉ Michael Mor Dayro, Vadake Dathkav P.O., INDIA-691529 Adoor Kerala • [91] 4734 229192, [91] 944 7009192

*25.4.1957 Elavinamannil family Omallor. N? MA History. B Christian Studies Serampore and Manjannikkara Dayro. diak14.8.1976 ⊖5.12.1982 ⊕8.12.2002 Damas M Kollam (Patr Ignatius). President Sunday School Association. 2006 M Thumpanon. 2008 also M Dubai.

Dioskoros Kuriakose

T: M Bangalore Region, of the Simhasana Churches and Institutions of the Holy Apostolic See in India ▪ ✉ Malecruz Dayro, Vadayampady P.O., INDIA-682308 Choondy • [91] 484 2762661, 2761661, [91] 944 7161661 • malecuriz@yahoo.com

*11.5.1957 Ponnankuzhu family Arakunnam, N? BA, BDiv (MTh) stud St. James Seminary Perumpally, United Theol College Bangalore. diak16.3.1974 ⊖6.5.1988 mon22.12.1996 ⊕8.12.2002 Damas (Patr Ignatius) M Simhasana. 2008 also M Ireland.

Athanasios Geevarghese

T: M assistant of the Simhasana Churches and Institutions of the Holy Apostolic See in India ▪ ✉ Mar Ignatius Dayara, INDIA-689657 Mathoor Pathanamthitta Kerala • [91] 473 232392, 2353392, 2353192, [91] 468 2353392 • geevargiseraly@yahoo.com

*12.12.1957 Eralil family Ayyampilly Ernakulam. N? Chartered Accountant. diak15.10.1990 ⊖9.1.1993 mon15.8.1997 ⊕8.12.2002 Damas M Thrissur (Patr Ignatius) 2004 secretary to the Patriarch. 2008 M assistant of the Simhasana. 2008-2010 also M Bahrain and Doha.

Chrysostomos Michael Shimon
T: M, assistant of the Simhasana Churches and Institutions of the Holy Apostolic See in India ▪ ✉ Mar Ignatius Dayara, INDIA-689657 Mathoor Pathanamthitta Kerala • [91] 473 232392
⊕11.4.2011 Damas M assistant of the Simhasana (Patr Ignatius).

Theophilos Saji Kuriakose ***Europe***
T: M Resident Metropolitan ▪ ✉ Udayagiri Vettikal P.O., INDIA-682314 Mulanthuruthy • [91] 484 27480-72, -61, fax -79. [91] 944 7475105 • [49] 160 98143198 • theophilosethirumeni@yahoo.co.uk • bptheophilose@gmail.com • www.theophilosekuriakose.com
*1.2.1966 Ooramana Ramamangalam, name: Kodikuthiyil Saji Varkey. N15.7. School Ooramana. 1981-1986 St. Peter's College Kollenchery. 1986-1989 Malankara Syrian Orthodox Theol Seminary Malailcruz. 1989 secretary to B Thomas Mar Dionisius. diak 5.1.1989 (Catholicos Baselios Paulus II., B Gevarghese Mor Grigorios). 1989-1993 United Theol College Bangalore, B.D. 1993 Member, co-chairman Commission for Dialogue between the Roman Catholic Church and the Malankara Syrian Orthodox Church. 1993-1994 Teacher Theology Malankara Syrian Orthodox Theol Seminary Vettickal. 1994-2001 Ostkirchliches Institut Regensburg. 1994 Mariapoli Aschaffenburg. Priests meeting Focolare Roma. 1995 Ecumenical meeting Loppiano Genfest Roma. 1996 Ostkirchliches Institut Regensburg 15th Ecumenical meeting for Bishops. 2.8.1996 dipl India recognized by German Catholic Bishops Conference: necessary only course of Latin, three seminars, Rigorosum. 1997 Dialogo della vita, Roma. 1998 Symposion Novgorod. 1999 Fribourg, Arth Goldau. 2000 research material United Theol College Bangalore. 2002 Dr. theol Regensburg (Hubert Ritt) "Arme im Evangelium nach Lukas" ⊖12.11.2002. (His Beatitude Basilus Thomas) 2002 Prof NT Malankara Syrian Orthodox Seminary M.S.O.T. mon28.9.2003 ⊕29.9.2003. (His Beatitude Basilus Thomas). 2004-2008 Metropolitan Patriarchal Vicar Europe and United Arabic Emirates. 2005 President Ecumenical Secretariate Malankara Jacobite Syrian Church. 2005 International Joint Commission Theological Dialogue between the Catholic Church and the Oriental Orthodox Churches, member drafting committee. 28.1.-2.2.2006 Dialogue non-chalcedonian Churches Erivan. 2008 Patriarchal vicar of the Malankara Syrian Orthodox parishes in Europe except UK and Ireland, residing at Ostkirchliches Institut Regensburg, since 2013 Priesterseminar Regensburg. 2010 permanent visa Schengen. 23.11.-1.12.2015 OKI Istanbul: 34th Ecumenical Meeting for Bishops, İstanbul; participated in all meetings since 1996. 2015 member Faith and Order Commission Geneva. 2015 member Program Committee Christian Conference of Asia.

Theodosios Matthews ***Kollam***

T: M Kollam, Kuwait ▪ ✉ Michael Mor Dayro, Vadake Dathkav P.O., INDIA-691529 Adoor Kerala • [91] 4734 229192, [91] 944 7406625

*4.5.1959 Nedumoncadu. N? M.Com. diak18.1.1981 ⊖1.11.1988. 1998-2003 St. Peter's church Trivandrum. mon2.7.2006 ⊕3.7.2006 Kerala (Mor Baselios). 2006 diocese Kollam Thumpanon Niranam divided: M Kollam. 2008 also M Kuwait.

Chrysostomos Markos

T: B assistant of Evangelical Association of the East ▪ ✉ EAE Headquarters, Iringole P.O., INDIA-683548 Perumbavoor Kerala • [91] 485 2522626, p 2527226, [91] 944 7826999

*26.9.1966 Thattekkad Angamali. N? MA Sociology, dipl theol. diak25.2.1995 ⊖9.1.1997 mon12.7.2006 ⊕14.7.2006 Damascus.

Koorilose Geevarghese ***Niranam***

T: M Niranam, United Kingdom ▪ ✉ Theeram Bishop's House, INDIA-691529 Mezhuvangadu Thiruvalla • [91] 944 7840800 • nccigeorge@rediffmail.com

*14.11.1965 Nalunnakkal. N? 1992 MTh Ecological Theology Canterbury. diak2001. 2001 moderator Commission World Mission WCC Geneva Pro Oriente Syrian-Anglican commission. 2001 teacher United Theol College Bangalore ⊖2002 mon2.7.2006 ⊕3.7.2006 (Mor Baselios). 2006 diocese Kollam Thumpanon Niranam divided: M Niranam, 2008 also M United Kingdom.

Barnabas Geevargheese

T: B assistant Niranam, Spiritual Movements ▪ ✉ Theeram Bishop's House, INDIA-691529 Mezhuvangadu Thiruvalla • [91] 944 7840800 • nccigeorge@rediffmail.com

*23.5.1953 Karikulam. N? diak1979 ⊖1982 mon2005 ⊕1.2.2010 assistant Niranam, Spiritual Movements.

Ostathios Patrus

T: B Singapore, Bahrain ▪ ✉ Mount Sinai, INDIA-686691 Kothamangalam Kerala • [91] 931 2037842 • bishoposthatheos@rediffmail.com

*3.11.1963 Pengamuck. N? BA Madras, BDiv Serampur. MTh Bangalore. diak19.12.1993 ⊖6.8.1995. 2004 St. Peter's Cathedral New Delhi. mon2.7.2006 ⊕3.7.2006 Kerala, assistant New Delhi. 2010 B Singapore, Bahrain.

Eusebios Kuriakose ***Thrissur***

T: M Thrissur, Mumbay Region, Muscat ▪ ✉ Bishops' House, Poovanchira, INDIA-682311 Chuvannamannu Trichur • [91] 484 2768925, [91] 944 6300600

*26.3.1970 Pazhatthotam. N? BA Kottayam. MTh Papal Seminary Pune. diak1992 ⊖2000 mon2.7.2006 ⊕3.7.2006 Kerala M Thrissur (Mor Baselios) 2008 also M Muscat.

Athanasios Elias

T: B assistant Thrissur ▪ ✉ Bishops' House, Poovanchira, INDIA-682311 Chuvannamannu Trichur • [91] 484 2768925, [91] 944 6300600

*11.2.1964 Angamaly. N? diak22.7.1988 ⊖15.8.1995 (Catholicos) mon2.11.2002 ⊕1.1.2007 (Catholicos).

Aphrem Mathews

T: M Sharjah ▪ ✉ Mount Sehion, INDIA-685561 Adimaly Kerala • [91] 486 4223826 • [91] 949 5468864 • aphrem_thirumeni@yahoo.com

*15.5.1968 Panamaram. N? BA Kalikut. MA University Kottayam. MTh Bangalore ⊖27.5.1994 Prof Dogmatic Hebrew Syriac music Seminary. mon2.7.2006 ⊕3.7.2006 Kerala B assistant Highrange (Mor Baselios) 2008 M Sharjah.

Kuriakose Klimis *Idukki*

T: M Idukki ▪ ✉ Mount Thabore, S.N. Junction, INDIA-685508 Kattappana • [91] 944 7987090, [91] 938 861 9868

*10.8.1967 "Kuriakose T. Abraham" Mulanthuruthy. N? BA Physic St. Albert's College Ernakulam. Dr. Social Psychology. stud theol M.S.O.T. Seminary Mulanthuruthy. mon11.8.2008 ⊕24.8.2008 B Prayer fellowshops in India.

Irenios Paulos *Kozhikodu*

T: M Kozhikode Calicut, Australia, Patriarcal Centre ▪ INDIA-682308 Puthencruz • [91] 484 273-2624, -2804, -2603, -3200

*24.8.1972 Wayanad (Paul Ullas Varkey). N? BA Sociology Mysore University. diak27.5.1990 ⊖15.5.1998 parishes Karnataka, New Delhi. mon11.8.2008 "Semavun" ⊕24.8.2008 M Kozhikodu (Calicut), 2009 also Australia.

Zacharias Phelexinos *Malabar*

T: M Malabar ▪ ✉ Bishop's House, Christ Nagar, INDIA-673592 Meenangadi P.O. Wayanad Kerala • [91] 4936 247305, 246800, [91] 9495874313 • fr.therampil@gmai.com

*5.5.1972 name: Afroth. N? stud theol M.S.O.T. Vettickal, BDiv Serampore University. MA Sociology Kamarj University diak22.2.1998 ⊖3.7.2000 ⊕4.1.2010.

Anthonios Yaqub

T: M auxiliary Mangalore, Honovar Mission, assistant of Evangelical Association of the East ▪ ✉ St. Antony's Church, Lindbridge Jeppu, INDIA-575002 Mangalore Karnataka • [91] 824 2415263, [91] 944 7826999 • www.syrianchurch.org

*12.7.1952 Kalamboor Ernakulam Kerala. N? 1959 Karnataka. Primary school Honovar Mission. 1975-1979 Seminary Malecruz Dyro Puthencruz. diak3.2.1977 ⊖11.5.1979 MA Sociology Mysore University. 1996-1999 Manager St. Antony's mission. 18.2.2003 Chori-Episcopus. mon20.8.2009 ⊕23.8.2009 Damascus.

Isaac Osthathious ***Mylapore***

T: M Mylapore, assistant New Delhi ▪ ✉ St. Thomas Collector Nagar, Syrian Church Road 9, INDIA-600101 Chennai • [91] 9605796231 • deaconsaji@gmail.com

*17.1.1976 name: Saji. N? BDiv, MTh Holy Cross Seminary Boston USA. dipl Syriac language and liturgy diak13.5.1993 ⊖12.11.2006 ⊕4.1.2010.

Antimos Jomy Mathews ***Aluva***

T: M Aluva, assistant to the Katholikos ▪ ✉ St. Thomas Collector Nagar, Syrian Church Road 9, INDIA-600101 Chennai • [91] 9605796231 • matthewsjomy@yahoo.com

*3.11.1974 Aluva Kerala. N? 1992 BA Economics Aluva. BDiv 2000-2004 United Theol College Bangalore. 2.1.2004 Cross Seminary Boston USA. dipl Syriac language and liturgy. diak2.1.2004 ⊖26.9.2005. 2005-2006 Regensburg, 10.-11.2.2006 Ecclesiological Symposion Würzburg. 17.-25.4.2006 Florenz Rom Bari. 2006-2010 stud Pro Oriente Kolleg St. Benedikt Salzburg. 22.12.2010 Dr. theol ⊕15.1.2012 Damascus (Patriarch and Katholikos).

Severius Kuriakose ***Knaaya***

T: A Knanaya ▪ ✉ Mor Aprem Seminary, INDIA-686531 Chingavanam Kerala • [91] 481 2430327, p 2432544, [91] 944 7264441 • knanayasamudayam@sancharnet.in

*21.5.1959 N? ⊕15.1.2004 M Chingavanam. 2008 A.

Gregorios Kuriakose

T: B, assistant Knanaya, Kallisery region ▪ ✉ Mor Aprem Seminary, INDIA-686531 Chingavanam Kerala • [91] 481 2430327, p 2432544, [91] 944 7264441 • gregorioskuriakose@yahoo.com

*16.1.1954 Mannar. N? dipl Economics Indore. MTh Vadavathoor, Trinity College Maynooth Ireland. diak28.1.1975 ⊖28.8.1980. mon21.1.2007 ⊕2.2.2007 Damas B assistant Knanaya for Kallissery region (Ignatius Zakka).

Kuriakose Ivanios

T: B, auxiliary Knanaya, Ranni division ▪ ✉ Mor Aprem Seminary, INDIA 686531 Chingavanam Kerala • [91] 481 2430327, p 2432544

*9.6.1964 N? Pathikal Kolath family Perumbavoor. Post Graduation History English CMS college Kottayam, S.B. college Changanacherry. Degree theol Maynooth Ireland. Post-Graduation Pourasthya Vidya Peeth Vadavathoor. diak28.10.1982 ⊖26.9.1999 ⊕11.6.2008 Damas B auxiliary Knanaya, Ranni division.

Silvanos Ayoub

T: B auxiliary Knanaya, USA+EU ▪ ✉ Mor Aprem Seminary, INDIA-686531 Chingavanam Kerala •
[91] 481 2430327, p 2432544, [91] 944 7264441

*18.4.1972 Thottathil family. N? B.Th. UTC Bangalore. stud Syriac Mor Aphrem Theol Seminary Damas. MTh. Vicar of Knanaya St. Peter's and St. Paul Church UK ⊕11.6.2008 Damas.

Tithus Yeldho ***America***

T: M Archdiocese of North America ▪ ✉ 611 Roosevelt Ave., USA-Carteret, NJ 07008 • [1] 173-29690085 • thirumeni@gmail.com • www.malankara.com

*22.5.1970 Edavazhikkal family Kottayam. N? Postgradute Mathematics U.C. College Alwaye, BEducation Mahatma Gandhi University Kottayam. stud theol Damas. diak1.1.1971 ⊖4.2.1990 stud theol USA ⊕15.1.2004 Damas (Ignatius Zakka). 2013 assistant Thrissur. 2016 America.

Ukraina

Bishops in Ukraina see "Konst" and "Moskva".
More bishops below, often changing jurisdiction and title

Andrij Stepan Abramčuk
T: M Ivano-Frankivsk UAOC ▪ ✉ vul. Virmenska 5, Ukraine-76016 Ivano-Frankivsk • [380] 3422 30447, 22711, p Tismenica [380] 3436 23602
*21.1.1949 Tismenitsja Ivano-Frankivsk. N? 1970-1974 Seminary Odessa ⊖1974 Odessa. 1974-1976 USA ⊕7.4.1990. 1992 M (Filaret Denisenko), 1995 from Filaret to Dimitri Jarema.

Roman Mykola Balaščuk
T: M Vinnitsa+Bratslav, UAOC ▪ ✉ vul. Anastasij Medvid 2, Ukraine-21036 Vinnitsa • [380] 3622 23009, 4322 351525, 967195539
*24.3.1953 Bljudnyky Halič. N? diak10.12.1977 Leningrad (A Kirill) ⊖16.4.1978 Leningrad (M Nikodim). 1978 dipl theol Leningrad ⊕22.5.1990 B Chernigov+Sumy. 1996 A, 2005 M Vinnitsa+Bratslav UAOC. 2007 dipl theol Ternopol.

Ihor Jurij Isičenko
T: A Kharkiv+Poltava, UAOC ▪ ✉ Poltavskyj Šljah 44, Kharkiv • [380] 57 7121171 • Tryokhsvyatytelska 8a, Ukraina-01001 Kiev • [380] 44 2293218, 2286198, fax 2290278 • uaoc@uaoc.net • archbishop.ihor@gmail.com
*28.1.1956 Baškiria. N? 1974-1979 stud Kharkiv State University Ukrainian philology. 1981-1999 Lecturer Kharkiv State University history Ukrainian literature. 1987 Dr phil. Taras Ševčenko Institute Kiev. 1990 St. Andrew Brotherhood: Head Kharkiv, 1991-1992 Head All Ukraine. mon12.3.1992 ⊖4.1.1993 ⊕12.7.1993 B Kharkiv+Poltava (Lviv: A Petro Petruš, B Mihail Dutkevyč, B Teoktist Peresada). 1993-1998 stud theol Patriarch Mstyslav College Kharkiv. 1996 Administrator UAOC. 1997 A, Kharkiv+Poltava, UAOC. 1997-2002 Presidium Bible Society.

Ioann Jan Modzalewski
T: A Chersonnes+Krimea, UAOC ▪ ✉ vul. Enerhetykiv 11-26, Ukraina-98000 Sudak AR Krimea • uaoc_crimea@ukr.net
*7.1.1970 Moskva. N? 1991-1994 Holy Trinity Seminary Jordanville. 1991 Russian Truly Orthodox Church. diak25.12.1995 ⊖20.1.1996 ⊕17.6.1996. 1996 A. 1997 UAOC (Dimitri Jarema). 1997 A Uman. 1999 A Kremenets, 2002 A Chersonnes+Krimea, UAOC.

Makarij Mykola Maletyč
T: M Kiev and all Ukraina UAOC ▪ ✉ vul. Fedorova 11, UKRAINA-79008 Lviv • [380] 32 235-44-99, 235-48-48 • lvivkonsustorija@ukr.net • lvivuaoc@gmail.com
*1.10.1944 Krasna Turkiv Lviv. 1958-1975 worker in Sovchos, married. 1975 Seminary Odessa, expelled by Office for Religions. diak18.1.1975 St. Michael Gorlovka Donetsk (M Sergij, Odessa) ⊖10.8.1975 (Patr Moskva), priest in Dometsk, Lugansk, Rostov, Lviv. 1982 dipl Seminary Moskva (correspondence course). 1993 widower. passed from Moskva patriarchate to Ukrainian Autokephalous Orthodox Church UAOC ⊕3.11.1996 B Lviv (Dimitri Jarema, Igor Isichenko, Mefodij Kudrjakov). 2000 A Lviv UAOC. 2011 M Lviv UAOC. 4.6.2015 elected in Ternopil president UAOC.

Julian Hatala
T: B Horodok, vicar Lviv UAOC ▪ ✉ vul. Lyčakiwska 91, UKRAINA-79000 Lviv • [380] 322 755993, 7693-44, -60
*1.10.1944 N? ⊖10.8.1975 (Patr Moskva) ⊕19.2.2012 B Horodok vicar Lviv, UAOC.

Volodimir Šlapak
T: A Žitomir, UAOC ▪ ✉ vul. Kievska 53, UKRAINE-10014 Žitomir • [380] 67 928 19 88, 66 781 65 52, 93 149 77 80 • uaoc@uaoc.net • shlapak.vasil@mail.ru
*3.8.1979 Chernjakhiv Shitomir, N? diak28.11.1996 ⊖29.12.1996. 1997-2001 Seminary Kiev. 2001-2006 Fac theol Chernigov 2009 Dr. theol Preslav Slovakia. mon11.2.2009 ⊕21.6.2009 B, 2011 A Žitomir, UAOC.

Volodimir Volodimir Čerpak
T: B Višegorod, vicar Kiew UAOC ▪ ✉ ul. Prokovskaja 7, UKRAINA-04070 Kiev • [380] 44 425-33-22, [380] 96-704-61-35 • bishopvcherpak@gmail.ru
*1.7.1952 Bezugljaki Kiev, N? 1975 dipl jur University Odessa. 1989 dipl Seminary Leningrad. diak20.6.1990 Leningrad (B Arsenij) ⊖22.6.1990 Sablino (B Arsenij). mon15.11.2010 ⊕16.11.2010 Kiev (M Mefodij).

Afanasij Volodimir Škurupij
T: A Kharkiv, UAOC ▪ ✉ vul. Kievskij Chaussee 33, UKRAINA-36008 Poltava • [380] 97 8320774 • uaockhp@i.ua
*20.8.1954 Poltava, N? 1981 dipl pedagogics Cherkassij. 2005 dipl Seminary Zhitomir Ukrainian Orthodox Church Kiev Patriarchate UOC-KP. mon12.10.2005 diak13.10.2005 ⊖14.10.2005 UOC-KP ⊕15.11.2009 B, 2015 A Kharkiv.

Adrian Kulik

T: B Chmelnitski, UAOC ▪ ✉ vul. Proskurivskogo pidpilla 165 a, UKRAINE-29013 Khmelnitskij

*25.3.1972 N? diak3.5.1992⊖6.1.1995 mon16.2.2011 ⊕16.2.2011 Chmelnitski, UAOC.

German Pavlo Semančuk

T: B Černovtsi, UAOC ▪ ✉ Bulv. Geroiv Stalingradu 5/180, UKRAINA-58000 Černivtsi • [380] 3722) 71873, [380] 50 5278969 • bpgerman1973@yandex.ua

*27.10.1974 Ispas Chernigov, N? diak 9.3.1997 UOC-KP ⊖19.4.1997 UOC-KP. mo9.8.1997. 2000 dipl Seminary Lviv UOC-KP. 2009 MTh University Chernigov ⊕16.11.2009 B, 2015 A Černovtsi, UAOC.

Ioan Modzalevskij

T: A ▪ ✉ Novodevičij pereulok 2/44, ROSSIJA-119435 Moskva

*7.1.1970 N? mon25.3.1991 diak25.12.1995 ⊖archim20.1.1996 ⊕17.6.1996 B Uman, vicar Kiev. 24.1.2015 expelled from Patriarchate Kiev.

Ioan Švets

T: B Sambir, UAOC ▪ ✉ ul. Okružna 14, UKRAINA-81400 Sambirrnopol

*22.11.1955 N? diak 7.6.1979 ⊖17.6.1979 archim? mon30.10.2010 ⊕31.10.2010 Sambir, UAOC.

Mstislav Rostislav Guk

T: B Ternopil+Červonogorod, UAOC ▪ ✉ ul. Ruska 22, UKRAINE-46020 Ternopol • [380] 352 52 21 59, 52 23 46 • mstyslav_guk@ukr.net

*14.6.1978 Podorozhne Lviv, N? diak14.10.1999. 2000 dipl Seminary Lviv UOC-KP ⊖31.12.2000 archim? 2007 dipl Academy Ternopol. mon2.8.2009 ⊕28.12.2010 B, 2015 A Ternopil+Červonogorod, UAOC.

Filaret Mihail Denisenko

T: former (Moskwa) M Kiev, Patriarch of Kyiv and All Rus-Ukraina ▪ ✉ ul. Puškinska 36, UKRAINA-01004 Kiev •
[380] 44 2343055, 2241096, 2249000, fax 2354177 • www.cerkva.info

*28.1.1929 Blagodatnoje Donetsk. N14.12. mon1.1.1950 diak15.1.1950 ⊖8.6.1951 ⊕4.2.1962 B Luga assistant Leningrad. 1962-1964 B Wien. 1964-1966 B Dmitrov, rector Academy Moskva. 14.5.1966 A Kiev. 1968-1992 M Kiev. Dr. theol h.c. 1980 Prešov, 1984 Prag. 1992 UOC-KP. 21.10.1995 Patriarch UOC-KP. 20.2.1997 excommunication Sabor Moskva.

Aleksandr Tabinka

T: B Gorodnij, vicar Kiev ▪

⊕19.12.2007 Gorodnij, vicar Kiev.

Onufrij Jaroslav Chavruk
T: B Vinnitsa+Bratslav ▪ ✉ projisd Stanislavskogo 3, UKRAINA-21022 Vinnitsa • [380] 67 3028307, [380] 97 4528354
*25.6.1966 Derman Rovno. N25.6. diak10.3.1991 ⊖3.6.1992. 1993 absolvent Seminary Kiev (Moskva) ⊕30.10.2005 Vinnitsa.

Fedir Valentin Bubnjuk
T: B vicar Kiev, Youth department ▪ ✉ vul. Triohsvjatitelcka 6a, UKRAINA-01601 Kiev • [380] 44 5924086
*21.7.1978 Lipno Volyn. N? diak6.5.1999 ⊖23.5.1999 ⊕12.11.2006. 2010 chairman Youth department.

Danilo Mihajlo Kovalčuk
T: M Černivtsi+Bukowina ▪ ✉ vul. Zankovetska 22, UKRAINA-58002 Černivtsi • [380] 372 2523898, 2526572, 254501 • bishop@sacura.net
*15.5.1949 Golyn Ivano-Frankivsk. N30.12. 1970-1973 Seminary Moskva. diak12.9.1973 ⊖21.9.1973 ⊕27.4.1990 ?? ⊕16.12.1992 B, 1993 A, 1994 M Černivci+ Bukowina.

Volodymyr Myroslav Ladyka
T: A Mykolaïv+Bogojavlensk ▪ ✉ vul. Sadowa 12, UKRAINA-54000 Mykolajev • [380] 512 36136-8,-9, fax 460427, 460242
*5.1.1956 Vivna Stry, Lviv. N28.7 ⊕13.3.1993 (Filaret Denisenko) B Vinnitsa, 1997 B Mykolaïv+Bogojavlensk.

Mihail Timofei Zinkević
T: A Lutsk+Volynia ▪ ✉ Gradnij uzvuz 1, UKRAINA-43000 Lutsk • [380] 3322 24097 • kantsler 24182, 25363 • Plechanova 1: [380] 3322 725177
*9.5.1966. diak9.10.1997 mon10.10.1997 ⊖12.10.1997 ⊕22.10.2000 (Filaret Denisenko) B Sumy, 2002 B Černigov, 2005 B, 2009 A Lutsk.

Oleksandr Oleksandr Rešetnjak
T: A Bilocerkiv, vicar Kiev ▪ ✉ Kontraktova plošča 1, UKRAINA-01004 Kiev • [380] 44 4254842
*25.12.1954 Čmirovtsy Lugansk. N6.12. 1976-1979 Seminary Odessa. 1979-1983 Academy Moskva ⊖14.9.1983. 1989-1993 parishes Pravoslavná Církev v Čechách. mon15.1.1994 ⊕16.1.1994 B. 2010 A Bila Cerkva.

Dimitrij Vadim Rudjuk
T: M Perejaslav Khmelnitskij ▪ ✉ vul. Triohsvjatitelska 6 a, UKRAINA-01601 Kiev • [380] 44 2788044, fax 2788620 • rector@vidomosti.org.ua

*14.11.1971 Krivorudka Khmelnitskij. N4.10. 1989 absolvent gymnasium. 1989-1994 Fac History Kiev. diak19.6.1994 ⊖22.1.1995 rector sobor Kiev. mon4.10.1995 St. Michael Kiev. 1996 igumen Pascha. 1997 Kandidat Kiev. archim1997 Pascha. 1998 redaktor "Pravosl. Visnik" ⊕16.7.2000. 2010 M Perejaslav Khmelnitskij.

Efstratij Ioann Zora
T: B Vasilkiv, vicar Kiev ▪ ✉ Puškinska 36, UKRAINA-01004 Kiev • [380] 44 2352238
*21.10.1977 Čerkasy. N10.4. 1992-1966 hypodiakon. mon12.4.1998. 28.4.2003 igumen. archim4.2.2007 ⊕25.5.2008. 2010 Redakcija Pravoslavnij Visnik.

Adrian Valentyn Starina
T: M Dnjepropetrovsk+Kryvyj Rih ▪ ✉ Prospekt Svobodi 89, UKRAINA-49019 Dnipropetróvsk • [380] 56 7703-333, -610, fax 7202524
*13.12.1943 Dnjepropetrovsk. N8.9. 1973 Institut Pedagogics Kiev. 1982 Academy Leningrad. 1989 rector parish Epiphania Noginsk. archim1990 ⊕6.2.1993 (Filaret Denisenko). 1993-1995 B Sičeslav=Dnjepropetrovsk+Bogorodsk. 1995 A, 2002 M Dnipropetrovsk+Kryvyj Rih. 2008 M Bogorodsk. 2010 Dnjepropetrovsk.

Izjaslav Jurij Karga
T: A Žytomir+Ovruč ▪ ✉ vul. Pionerskij 5, UKRAINA-10006 Žytomir • [380] 412 420740, 241654 • [380] 50 4630160
*13.12.1949 Kijiv. Nvsih sv. zemli Ukr. mon1989 ⊖1992. 1993 teacher Seminary Kiev, 1994 igumen Monastir Sv. Feodosij. 1. Kurs Academy Kiev ⊕11.9.1994 (Filaret Denisenko). 1994-1996 B Zaporože+Nikopolsk. 1996 B Donetsk+Lugansk. 2002 A Žytomir+Ovruč.

Kirilo Mihajlo Mihajljuk
T: B Uzhgorod+Zakarpat ▪ ✉ vul. Zapiznichia 22, UKRAINA-88005 Užgorod • [380] 97 919 93 17 • orthodxkarpatdiocez@ukr.net
*5.12.1963 Šejkiv Ternopil. N22.6. 1985 Seminary Moskva. diak26.4.1988 ⊖19.7.1988 rector parishes UA. 24.11.1988 UAOC Mstyslav. 1993 protoierej. 1999-2003 Academy Kiev. mon22.6.2003 (Filaret) ⊕2003-2015 B Uzhgorod Patriarchate Kiev. 24.1.2015 expelled from Patriarchate Kiev 25.12.2014 B Uzhgorod+Zakarpat.

Ioasaph Valentin Šibajev
T: A Bilgorod+Obojan, member Holy Synod ▪ ✉ ul. Gagarina 6, ROSSIJA-309276 Maslova Pristan • [7] 7248 55505
*2.1.1954 Pristan Belgorod. N17.9 ⊖1977. mon1.8.1978. 1983 Theol Seminary Moskva ⊕19.2.1995 (P Vladimir Romanjuk). 1995 B Bielgorod+Obojan.

Iov Vasil Pavlyšyn
T: B Ternopil+Kremenets ▪ ✉ vul. Kniazia Ostrozkoho 19, bk.17, UKRAINE-46001 Ternopil • [380] 3522 255985, 255478, fax 430898
*5.6.1956 Ternopol. N10.9. 1983 Academy Leningrad ⊖1983 mon1995 ⊕11.5.1995 (Filaret Denisenko) B Kremenets+Zbarag, 1998 Ternopil+Kremenets.

Grigorij Jaroslav Kačan
T: A Zaporižžja+Melitopol ▪ ✉ vul. Kalinina 101 a, UKRAINA-69015 Zaporižžja • [380] 612 951681
*11.9.1939 Zastavcy Ternopil. N11.9. 1960 Institut Medicin Charkov ⊖1985. 1989 Seminary Moskva. 1992 blagočinnyj dean Gorohov Volynia ⊕10.10.1995 (Filaret Denisenko) B Melitopol vicar Dnjipopetrovsk. 2002 A Zaporižžja+Melitopol.

Sergij Horobtsov
T: B Slovjan, vicar Donetsk ▪ ✉ vul. Kujbyševa 105, UKRAINA-83096 Donetsk • [380] 6279 26216
*27.7.1972 Jenakiev oblast Donetsk. N20.10. diak1993 ⊖4.12.1993 Seminary Kiev. archim2001 blagočinnyj dean Telmaniv ⊕19.10.2005 B Slovjan, vicar Donetsk.

Baruch Volodymyr Tiščenkov
T: B Tobolsk+Jenisejsk ▪ ✉ vul. Černjahovskogo 164 P/Ja 1431, ROSSIJA-640014 Kurgan • [7] 35222 22764
*19.5.1956. N11.10. 1975 Poslužnik Voznesenia Novonikolajevska Novosibirsk. 1976 Istinnaja Pravoslavnaja Cerkov "Tihonovtsy". mon1976 ⊖1976. 1983-1990 prison. archim1992 ⊕14.12.1993. 23.2.1995 B Tobolsk+Jenisejsk. 2006 with Filaret.

Antonij Vladyslav Machota
T: B Khmelnitskij+Kamyanets-Podilski ▪ ✉ vul. Kozača 69, UKRAINA-29000 Khmelnitskij • [380] 382 720830
*8.11.1966 Slatino Kharkiv. N23.7 ⊖29.5.1991 ⊕21.7.1996 (Filaret Denisenko) B Simferopol+Krim, 1999 Khmelnitskij Kamyanets-Podilski.

Ioann Vassilij Bojčuk
T: B Kolomyja+Kosiv ▪ ✉ Iv. Franka 42, UKRAINA-78200 Kolomyja • [380] 3433 24416
*6.3.1953 Bytkov Ivano Frankovsk. N7.7 ⊖1987 ⊕7.7.1996 B Rowno UAOK. 1996 director office of Patr Jarema, 1997 office of Filaret Denisenko, B Kolomyja+Kosiv.

Kliment Pavlo Kušč
T: B Simferopol+Krimea ▪ ✉ vul. Sevastopolska 17a, UKRAINA-05000 Simferopol • [380] 652 21227, 480118

*9.4.1969 Simferopol N8.11. 1976-1986 school Simferopol. 1986-1992 Fac Dramaturg Kharkiv. 1987-1989 Soviet Army. 1992-1996 Theatre Krim. 1.3.1996 eparchy Simferopol. diak8.11.1996. 1997 Christmas kamilaf ⊖28.2.1997. 1997-2000 Seminary Kiev. mon4.7.2000 St. Michael Kiev ⊕23.7.2000 B Simferopol+Krimea.

Lavrentij Mihail Migović
T: B Kharkiv+Bohodukhiv ▪ ✉ vul. Volodarskoho 4, UKRAINA-61093 Kharkiv • [380] 572 72 88 56
*14.12.1959 Keretski, Transkarpatia. N? 1980-1983 Seminary, 1983-1986 Academy Moskva (correspondence course). diak1.3.1983 ⊖1989 archim1993. 1996-2000 Latvia (Moskva). 2000-2002 Mozyr (Moskva) ⊕13.12.2004 B Poltava (UAOC). 2005 to Filaret B Kharkiv+Bohodukhiv.

Jakiv Jaroslav Makarčuk
T: B Odessa+Balt ▪ ✉ vul. Pastera 7, UKRAINA-65000 Odessa • [380] 482 238225, 236196, 355148, fax 235967
*2.6.1952 Lviv. N5.11. Technikum, Nautic School Tallinn, 1987-1990 Seminary Leningrad ⊖18.5.1989 (Patr Moskva). 1989-1998 rector Preobraženskij Lvov ⊕8.11. 1998 B Čerkasy (Dimitri Jarema). 1998-2004 B Čerkasy UAOC. 2004 B Odessa.

Ioasaph Ivan Wasilikyv
T: A Ivano-Frankivsk+Halyč ▪ ✉ vul. Grjunwaldska 3, UKRAINA-76000 Ivano-Frankivsk • [380] 3422 23451, 97136
*7.2.1955 Hrušiv Drohobyć. N17.3. igumen ⊕6.4.1997 (Filaret Denisenko) B Donetsk+Luhansk, 1999 B, 2002 A Ivano-Frankivsk+Halyčyna.

Damian Pjotr Zamarajev
T: A Kherson+Tavrija ▪ ✉ vul. Engelsa 45, UKRAINA-73000 Cherson • [380] 552 380113, 436648, fax 436653
*29.1.1931 Vassilievka Voronež. N5./18.10. 1947 absolvent school Vassiljevka, 1950 Specialisation. 1953 Pilote Technik-Institut Saransk. 1959 absolvent Theol Seminary Odessa. diak5.4.1959 (Moskva) ⊖7.4.1959 (Moskva). 1959 rector Pokrov Cherson. Spiritual director eparchy Cherson (Moskva). 1997 from Patr Moskva to Kiev ⊕19.10.1997 (Filaret Denisenko) B, 2004 A Kherson+Tavrija.

Chrysostomos Georgios Bakomitros
T: B Cherson ▪ ✉ Admiton 52, UKRAINA-10440 Plateia Attikis • [30] 2108670888, 2104631281, 2104323034, 6947449660, 6936742623
*24.4.1950 Aigina. N? ⊕14.5.2005 Kiev.

Mefodij Mykola Sribnjak
T: B Sumy+Ahtyrka ▪ ✉ vul. Holodnogorska 6, UKRAINA-40030 Sumy • [380] 542 280126, 273297

*8.6.1957 Grabivka Kauzkogo Ivanov-Frankivsk. N24.5. 1979-1986 forest engineer. 1985 absolvent Sibirskij Technik-Institut. 1986-1992 stud Medicine Center Irkutsk. 1992-1994 director Ukrainian community Irkutsk. diak1995 ⊖1995. 1996-2004 sekretar eparchy Dnjepropetrovsk ⊕6.6.2004 B Sumy+Ahtyrka.

Afanasij Boris Javorski
T: B Lugansk+Starobilsk ▪ ✉ Uritskogo 80-g, UKRAINA-91022 Lugansk • [380] 642 327132

*8.8.1976 Orihovets Ternopol. N? Music school Ternopol. 1995 Seminary Kiev. 15.9.1998 diak 1998-2000 diakon Ternopol ⊖12.7.2000. 2001 eparchy Sumy. mon 24.2.2002. 2003 blagočinnyj dean Sumy. 2008 press-sekretar eparchy. 2010-2011 MTh Institute Ivano-Frankivsk ⊕21.8.2011. 2011-2013 B Konotop vicar Sumy. 2013 B Lugansk+Starobilsk.

Nestor Andrij Pysyk
T: B Ternopil ▪ ✉ vul. Klima Savuri, UKRAINA-46000 Ternopil • [380] 352 431622

*22.5.1979 Pilvovočisk Ternopol. N9.11. 1986-1996 school Pilvovočisk. 1996-1999 stud Seminary Kiev. mon26.10.2000 ⊖28.5.2001. 2003 absolvent Academy Kiev. 2003 sekretar to the patriarch ⊕5.3.2006 Ternopil.

Matfej Volodymyr Ševčuk
T: B Drogobyč+Sambir ▪ ✉ vul. Stebnitska bud.104, of.160, UKRAINA-82200 Truskavets • [380] 3244 410081

*6.9.1973 Sokal Lviv. N29.11. 1992 stud Seminary Kiev. diak13.12.1992 ⊖9.2.1993. 1994 rector Vjerba. 2006 sekretar to the patriarch ⊕17.12.2006 B Drogobyč.

Ioann Oleg Jaremenko
T: B Čerkasy+Čigirin ▪ ✉ Puškinska 36, UKRAINA-01004 Kiev • [380] 44 2284150, 2243055, 2241096, 2249000, fax 2354177

*12.3.1967 Žitomir. N? 1984-1992 Politechnikum Kiev. 1986-1988 Soviet Army. 1994-1997 Seminary Kiev. mon10.4.1997 diak13.4.1997. 1997-2001 Kandidat Academy Kiev ⊖1998. 1998-2003 Ekonom Monastery St. Michael Kiev. 5.7.2002 igumen ⊕29.3.2003 Kiev (Filaret, Joasaph, Dimitri).

Vsevolod Volodymyr Matvievskij
T: B Lugansk+Stavropol ▪ ✉ Uritskogo 80-g, UKRAINA-91022 Lugansk • [380] 642 327132

*28.7.1942 Novo-Fastiv Vinnitsa. N24.2. 1959-1975 Politechnikum Donetsk. 1962-1964 Soviet Army. 1965-1995 mines. 1995-1991 Seminary Kiev. diak199 ⊖1995. 1996-2002 sekretar eparchy Donetsk. 2002-2003 sekretar eparchy Lugansk. mon5.2.2003 ⊕28.3.2003 Kiev.

Epiphanios Dimitriou
T: B ▪ ✉ vul. Kujbyševa 105, UKRAINE-83096 Donetsk • [380] 622 598122, 532029

Pankratij Tarnavskij
T: former B Vinnytsya+Bratslav ▪
⊕27.7.1997 (Filaret Denisenko). 1997 na štat.

Volodymyr Poliščuk
T: former B Ivano-Frankivsk+Kolomyja, na štat ▪
⊕23.2.1997 (Filaret Denisenko) B Ivano-Frankivsk+Kolomyja. 4.1997 Ivano-Frankivsk+Halyčyna. 1999 B Donetsk+Luhansk.

Ioann Zinovjev
T: former B Donetsk+Lugan ▪
⊕18.7.1996 (Filaret Denisenko) B Čerkasy+Čygirin. 2.1997 B Poltava+Kremenec. 1999 B Boguslav. 1999 B Odessa+Balta.

Varsonofij Mazurak
T: former B Ivano-Frankivsk ▪
⊕8.6.1992 (Filaret Denisenko).

Myhail Bondarčuk
T: B Poltava+Kremenčug ▪
✉ ul. Roza Luksemburg 62 a, UKRAINA-36024 Poltava
⊕1.1.2006 Poltava+Kremenčug, (Filaret Denisenko), but 2006 to UAOC?

Filaret Teodor Pancu
T: B Faleşti+Moldova ▪ ✉ str. Unirii 62, MOLDOVA-3701 Straseni • [373] 22 797618, 79021622
*1.3.1965 Ţigira Ungheni. N14.12. 1983-1985 military service. mon1988 diak1988 ⊖1993 rector Monastery Sf. Nicolae Chişinău. 1995 dipl phil psych University Chişinău. 1996 dipl Seminary Chiţcani. 2000 dipl theol Academy Chişinău ⊕31.7.2005 (Filaret Denisenko).

Ilarion Dmitri Protsik
T: B Černigov+Nižni ▪ ✉ vul. Kotsjubinskogo 37, UKRAINA-14000 Černigiv • [380] 462 677711
⊕14.5.2008 Černigov+Nižni.

Epifanij Sergij Dumetsko
T: B Višgorod ▪ ✉ ul. Puškinska 36, UKRAINA-01004 Kiev

*3.2.1979 Volkov Odessa. N? 1996-1999 Seminary Kiev, 1999-2003 Academy Kiev. 2003 Kandidat Formuvannja cerkovnogo prava. 2003-2006 teacher Seminary Rovno. 2006-2007 stud phil Athens. 2007 teacher Academy Kiev. mon21.12.2007 diak6.1.2008 ⊖20.1.2008 sekretar eparchy Kiev. archim16.3.2008 Orden Volodimir, Orden za zaslugi ⊕15.11.2009 Kiev.

Simeon Oleg Zinkević
T: B Dnipropetrovsk+Pavlograd ▪
*5.5.1979 Leningrad. N? 1986-1997 school Leningrad. 1997-2001 Seminary Volyn. 2001-2004 Academy Kiev. diak2004. 2004-2007 Detroit USA ⊖2006 Detroit. mon2007 Lutsk. 2008 Ternopil. 2009 sekretar eparchy Kiew ⊕21.11.2009 Kiev.

Tihon Taras Petranjuk
T: B Starobilsk ▪
*19.10.1976 Kolomija Ivano-Frankivsk. N? 1983-1994 school Kolomija. 1994-2000 stud phil theol University Černovtsi, Academy Kiev. diak11.3.1999 Černovtsi ⊖14.10.1999 Lvov. 1999 rector sv. Barbara Lopušna, 2004 Černovtsi. 2004 protoierej. 2004 Kandidat Pnevmatologija Novogo Zavity. 2004 teacher University. mon25.8.2009 Kiev ⊕22.11.2009 Kiev.

Mark Vasil Grinčevskij
T: B Černigiv+Kitsman ▪
*18.1.1978 Demanskivtsi Dunaevets. N? 1996-2000 Seminary Volyn. 1999 marriage, Irina *2000. diak10.3.1999 ⊖21.3.1999. 2007-2008 magistratura Lviv. mon19.3.2008 ⊕17.3.2010 Kiev.

Varsonofij Volodimir Rudnik
T: B Uzhgorod+Zakarpatia ▪
✉ vul. Zalizničrna 22, Ukraina-88000 Užgorod
*20.7.1984 Pochaiv Ternopol. 2001-2005 Theol Institute Černovtsi. 2006-2012 dipl Economist Kiev. diak18.10.2012. 2012-2014 MTh Fac theol Lviv. 2013 igumen Virlja ⊖6.1.2013 mon7.6.2013 ⊕25.1.2015 B Uzhgorod+Zakarpatia.

Viktor Bed
T: B Mukachevo+Karpatij UAOC ▪ Ukraina-Užgorod
*5.5.1964 Tjachiv Zakarpatia. 1981-1982 worker Zakarpatlis. 1982-1983 Technikum Kiev. 1983-1988 stud jur Lviv. 1988-1994 advokat Zakarpatia. 1990 member parlament Ukraina. 1991 Prof Informatik Uzhgorod. 1992 created newspaper national democratic "Sribna Zemlja". 1998 Dr. phil, 2010 Dr. theol, 2011 Dr. iur 2002 rector Theol Academy Uzhgorod (blessing M Vladimir Sabodan). diak2.10.2004 (B Agapit, B Mukačevo+Užgorod. blessing M Vladimir Sabodan) ⊖8.10.2006 (B Agapit, B Mukačevo+Užgorod. blessing M Vladimir Sabodan).

24.5.2007 protoierej. 2010 Orden/medals Russian Orth Church, Ukrainian Orth Church, Greek Orth Church, Lawyers Ukraina. mon archim26.3.2010 Thessaloniki (M Anthim, blessing M Vladimir Sabodan). 2012 president International Theol Academy (blessing M Vladimir Sabodan) ⊕14.8.2015 B Mukachevo+Karpatij UAOC. 2015 eparchy Mukachevo+Karpatij UAOC created June. 2015 B founder and rector Theol Academy Uzhgorod Moscow Patriarchate, then during conflict with M Makarij member of Greek Church.

Boris Volodimir Kharko
T: B Kherson UAOC ▪ ✉ vul. Suvorova, UKRAINA-Cherson • [380] 0552-26, -29, -13 • tavria-epar_uaoc@ukr.net

*4.4.1979 Busk Lviv. 2000 dipl Economy Ternopil. 2013 Dr. jur University Lviv. diak19.7.2015 Sloviti Lviv (M Makarij) ⊖9.8.2015 Lviv (M Makarij) ⊕23.8.2015 B Chishki Pustomitiv Lviv B Kherson+Mykolajev (M Makarij, B Mstislav, B Viktor).

Gerontij Vasil Oljanski
T: B Drogobin vicar Kiev UAOC ▪ UKRAINA-Kiev • [380] 671246235 • vasul.t.1551@gmail.com

*14.3.1979 Voznesensk Minsk. diak5.8.2005 Monastery Chinadijiv (B Kirilo) ⊖27.9.2005 skit Khrestovozdvizhen (B Iosaf Kiev Patriarchate). 2007 dipl Academy Kiev. 2012 dipl Fac jur Kiev ⊕14.9.2014 B Drogobin, vicar Kiev (A Volodomir Zhitomir, B Afanasij, B German, B Mstislav).

Index of NAMES

Search for bishop's name or family name (followed by a comma)
As most of the names are transcriptions, look for other versions, if necessary: Vasilios=Basilios, Jeletskikh=Yeletskikh etc.

Index of PLACES

Country (capitals), City, Eparchy (*E), Metropolia (*M), Episkopia (*Ep), Metropolitan Region (*MR)